Jan Kodes

A Journey to Glory from behind the Iron Curtain

Petr Kolar

Dedicated to my parents

To my mother, father, two sisters and
also to Martina and my three children
who know just a little bit about my past.
Dedicated also to all my coaches for their
support and patience.

europrint

Copyright: © Jan Kodes, Petr Kolar, 2010.
ISBN 978-09-422-5768-7

If one looks back at his record, Kodes was probably the most underrated player of his era.

Richard Evans, The Times 1973

CONTENTS

Acknowledgements to:

Europrint, H&Hotels, Chemoprojekt, K-Triumf, Mart, Sport-Technik Bohemia, Technoexport.

FOREWORD

Jan Kodes appeared in the tennis world in an era when this sport was mainly an Anglo-Saxon affair. We were still under the enchantment of the great Australian players as Rosewall, Emerson, Laver, who were winning all the major international events.

In the late sixties and early seventies, besides players like Gulyas, Tiriac and Pilic, other players from Eastern European countries – Metreveli, Nastase, Franulovic – were making headlines at major championships like Roland Garros, Wimbledon and the US Open. Among them was a young Czech named Jan Kodes. I remember discovering him as a junior, and later watching him as he won two French titles, one Wimbledon championship and playing all the other great events, including the Davis Cup final against Sweden in Stockholm.

I was always impressed by his determination and his willpower as he was fighting every point in every match from the first to the last point. This young fellow never gave up, never made any concession to fatigue or lack of concentration. On the court, he had a tremendous attitude and he never used tricks like some of his opponents in order to disrupt his rivals. But he also never induced in any familiarity with spectators or press. He was, as the English say, "all business." Modest in his behaviour, Jan never received enough praise for his achievements.

Having witness all of his efforts, I can testify that he was one of the great champions of the early seventies, one who really deserved the titles he had won due to his talent and very hard work. In later years I was also present at the 1986 Federation Cup final and ATP Tour tournaments organized in Prague during his stint as the tournament director in the new stadium built under his leadership.

Truly dedicated to his sport, Jan Kodes is one of the leading figures in the history of our game.

Judith Elian
L'Équipe, France

INTRODUCTION

Motto:
"Love thy country even in the most trying of times!"

Dear Readers!

In tennis history Czechoslovakia has always produced players who made headlines around the world. Ladislav Zemla, brothers Karel and Jan Kozeluh, Roderich Menzel, Ladislav Hecht, Frantisek Cejnar, Jaroslav Drobny. We experienced dark-times after the WWII and our tennis recuperated from that only very slowly and with difficulties. Nobody ever paid attention to those struggles and complicated, arduously unpleasant, situations that gave rise to tennis stars that were later recruited from "behind the Iron Curtain".

It was a politically charged and immensely tense era but, gradually, a string of Grand Slam champions followed me – Martina Navratilova, Ivan Lendl, Hana Mandlikova, Jana Novotna, Petr Korda, Helena Sukova and several others who succeeded predominantly in doubles. They all experienced similar troubles and problems to the ones I had gone through, though situation became slowly more tolerant and conducive to better conditions. Two of the players, Martina Navratilova and Ivan Lendl, aided their country of origin in Federation and Davis Cup victories but they finished their careers as citizens of the United States of America and as such they were inducted into the International Tennis Hall of Fame in Newport.

Their stories are well known; I decided to write this book in order to describe my less celebrated journey into the World tennis that preceded theirs. I wanted to demonstrate the ongoing struggle in order to attain better conditions for my successors. I also wanted to illustrate events as they happened and help the World grasp the depth of my journey full of thorns...

Everybody, who is featured in this book, has crossed the path of my life in some fashion. As I gathered the documents and photographs for the book I re-lived many of the events, the good as well as the grisly. Much is difficult to forget even in spite of my more mature perspective and time that has since lapsed.

I have accepted development of Czech tennis as my life mission and I dedicated my life and soul to it so much so that it affected my personal life. I anticipated that upon retiring I would look back at my allegiance to our tennis as nothing more than mere sacrifice. I resolved to endure that mission; it was my own choice to do so and I have no regrets!

The seventies and the eighties of the previous century shall always be viewed as the "Golden" era in Czechoslovak, later Czech tennis, an era of the biggest accomplishments, an era that will hardly ever be possible to surpass. I figured in that time period in a position of a player as well as in the capacity of other functions; historians, witnesses and observers will soon be able to judge my efforts that always bore tennis' best interests in mind and the fact that tennis epitomized my life. The intensity of that fervor is only now fading.

I have tried to include some photos and available information from the history of Prague clubs that had reached beyond my time frame. I wanted to recall part of our tennis history that recognized some players that I, myself, admired and who had merit in tennis development in our country. These same players' performances later contributed to promotion of our country world wide; some of their paths crossed mine and finished in the Tennis Hall of Fame in Newport. I could not include everything and it troubled me that some accomplishments would be forgotten forever. I hope that this book assists in recognition of all our Grand Slam champions and draws respect for them. And not just for them; there have been numerous players who did not win Grand Slam titles but represented Czech tennis successfully in Davis and Federation Cups earning good name and respect; they too deserve honorable recognition.

My tale will amuse and delight some and it will upset others. It is construed to give a picture of Czech tennis during two political regimes, in times when our "white" sport played its role not only in the tennis arena but also on public and political platform. I am pleased to know that I was fully there during all those most successful years, be it as a player, Davis Cup captain, Tournament Director, Board member or President of the Association.

From my point of view Czech tennis has become mediocre by today and I hope it is only temporary. I wish all our players as well everybody in decision making positions a more propitious handling of issues and much success in the years ahead.

I foresee that history will ask about tennis after the year 2000 – tennis in the twenty-first century - and I wish that my grand era of accomplishments returns!

Jan Kodes,
Prague, March 1, 2010

WITH A RACKET

FAMILY BACKGROUND

It is the year 1946; the world is recuperating from the horrors of the Second World War. At this time, in still democratic Czechoslovakia, rudiments of a new system begin to bud, a system that two years later comes to power with definite might and that severs the course of normal development of that nation for forty years to come. Right at the beginning of the year, exactly on March 1, a youngster heralds his arrival in Kralovske (Royal) Vinohrady maternity clinic. Fairy Godmothers predict for him a love of sports, especially of a white and later yellow round little nonsense called a tennis ball, and they forecast for him an unbelievable fighting spirit that should help him conquer even the most difficult of obstacles.

A couple of days later his dad, Jan, and mom, Vlasta Kodes, took their third child, Jan junior, home to Karlin. He was baptized on March 6 at St. Ludmila Archdiocese in Royal Vinohrady and Christened Jan Jaromir upon his father's wishes, reportedly because "jaro" means spring and "mir" translates into "peace". In 1946 it was the first truly peaceful spring in six years, full of beautiful blossoms. Most likely, dad did not even dream then that the little bundle he was holding in his arms was going to turn into a future Wimbledon champion.

It is hard to tell if anyone ever contemplated of how Jan would have ended up if he grew up in an advanced capitalistic democratic country that Czechoslovakia undoubtedly was between the wars. Would he have ever devoted himself to sports? He could have been an excellent lawyer if he chose to follow in his father's footsteps. Possibly, he would have never even touched a tennis racket and, instead, would grow to become a superb soccer left wing. Most likely, with his outspanding training willpower he would have made it to the national soccer team.

Maybe he would have played tennis but under totally different conditions? He would have been able to travel the world without any restrictions; he would not have had to doggedly prove how much of the "union" money he spent on plane tickets. He would not have had to hand over a substantial portion of his prize money to the coffers of CUPES (Czechoslovak Union of Physical Education and Sports), later of Pragosport. It is for certain that the situation of traveling abroad with hardly any money in his pockets, which happened to Martina Navratilova when union officials sent her to tournaments in the USA with five dollars per day, would not have occured.

He would have been able to afford himself a several weeks long training camp in the United States of America where he could work out with the best players of the world. Under such circumstances, he might have personified a Wimbledon champion several times over and, perhaps, Czechoslovakia would have captured the Davis Cup trophy a few years earlier than 1980 and the name of our country would have been carved more times into the stand of this legendary silver cup. And, perhaps, Jan Kodes would have added the Australian Open title into his collection of Grand Slam titles. He regularly skipped the last Grand Slam tournament of the year because flying to Australia was way too far and the plane ticket thus excessively expensive in the eyes of the Czechoslovak officials.

Today we can only speculate but, possibly, things could have turned out very differently.

HOUSE IN KARLIN

House no.40 located in Sokolovska Street, at one time called the Royal Avenue, in Prague's Karlin, stands there till today. And today, once more after four decades, it is owned by Kodes' family.

I remember the building really well; there is two shops on the ground floor and apartments above shared by us and other tenants. At the street corner, in no. 32 there was my grandfather's famous patisserie.

My father was a lawyer but at the start of the nineteen fifties he like many others, was made to join the workforce for reasons of "too many lawyers". JUDr. Kodes "closed" his law office in 1951 and entered the ranks of proletariat of CKD (Czechoslovak Kolben-Danek) Dukla in Karlin. Every day therafter he punched in at six in the morning and all day long he welded caldron flanges. In order to deserve his spot at this new "profession" he had to pass welding tests. Jan's mother, by maiden name Richterova, was a homemaker.

Dad always secured the family's financial course; he wanted his wife to spend her entire time and energy running their household and bringing up their three children – little Jan and two older daughters Anna and Vlasta. However, it was not easy to maintain a five-member family. When JUDr.Kodes entered the CKD workforce his Karlín apartment house remained in his ownership but, soon after, he was forced to let go of the housekeeper Mr.Hervert. He was not allowed to employ anybody or he would loose the privilege to obtain food stamps. He was threatened to be labeled an "exploiter".

The above mentioned Mr.Hervert turned to Housekeepers Union for help and gave an untrue and incriminating statement regarding Kodes parents as childless and occupying too much footage while he, with three children, had nowhere to live. Mr. Kodes was summoned to the people's committee where they tried to make him regret his conduct and refused to understand that the situation was, in truth, exactly reverse.

I was five at the time and hardly understood what was going on but I felt the tension. Dad constantly quarreled with the housekeeper, mom wept, and I sensed that something very unpleasant was taking place. Mom dropped a hint that we needed new curtains but dad disputed it saying: "We shell not buy any new curtains; we can't give them any reason to think that we can't afford it!" The building was still in dad's ownership but somebody else had an

With my sisters, Vlasta (left) and Anna.

eye on our apartment and, one day, my father received a notice that we must move out to borderland called Přísečnice in Krušné Mountains. The entire family! Accused of being politically untrustworthy we were ordered to move to an objectionable house by any health standards. Dreadful situation! Mom wept again, I felt the strained atmosphere.

JUDr.Kodes appealed the decision. The family was threatened by enforcement, only two weeks were left. In the end, the eviction intimidation was warded off by Grandma and Grandpa, who offered the State their own apartment in Opletalova Street no.30. It was a gorgeous sunny two bedroom apartment on the third floor, with an elevator. The grandparents moved in with the Kodes' and thus saved them from eviction.

That same year the Kodes children spent their last summer vacation in Karaný. The People's Committee took over their real estate and put in a tenant who paid an equivalent of 10 cents a month.

From that time on we spent summers in Prague or in summer camps.

My mom was a lefthander. She loved to play.

After all that my father consented to take on the housekeeper's responsibilities; he took care of the building with the intention that when the time comes and the comrades claim their rights to the building he would "donate" it to the State. In addition, he accepted a custodial job in used-to-be Cechie Karlín Tennis Club, presently Spartak Karlin Dukla, in order to earn enough money to cover his family's expenses.

CHILDHOOD

Primary school in Pernerova Street. For nine years Jan headed there day after day. His mom woke him up at seven and prepared breakfast for him and his sister Vlasta. They drank tea or cocoa with milk and ate rolls; for midmorning snack he carried with him another roll with butter wrapped up in a napkin. Walking to school they turned to Vítkova Street at the corner of Kralovska Trida (Royal Avenue), and then they trotted along Krizikova Street to the corner of Peckova. At this point, where the church of Cyril and Methodius stood, Honza joined his friends with whom he walked the rest of the distance.

He did well in school, enjoyed history and geography, but struggled with math, later also with Russian language and chemistry. The first "Cs" came in the sixth and seventh grades in Russian and Czech languages. His report card, however, showed only one C and the rest was so good that he earned one of the top five spots in the class. At the end of nineth grade he even made the principal's list. Dad always lectured him on the importance of good grades for he wanted Jan to continue on to the secondary school and he knew that the communist criteria for school entrance considered political background of the parents before the youngster's grades; he had to make up in grades for the parents' "failure" as bourgeois elements.

In the winter Jan walked dutifully home after school. But, in spring and autumn...? As soon

Pupils soccer team Dukla Karlin at Prague – I am in the first row at the left end.

as the end of the last period bell rang he dashed out with friends to the Cyril and Methodius Square. Their satchels were thrown around the imaginary lines of the field and the game was on! Soccer was played right by the church. Satchels created the goals; a rubber ball was the object to kick around. Tens, hundreds of soccer groans were heard! Jan kicked with his left which proved advantageous when he was selected to join Dukla Karlin team. He was a catch to find to fill the position of a small quick left wing. He did not have a soccer idol he just enjoyed playing the game.

I did not look up to a specific football/soccer player but I constantly heard names like Pla-nicka, Puc, Nejedly, Bican a Pesek at home, and ice-hockey stars' names like Malecek, Tozic-ka, Drobny, Kobranov, Rozinak, Bubnik, or Zabrodsky. Our family were all sports enthusiasts and legends were told about each one of those champs. As soon as somebody visited us and started chatting with my dad about sports I was all ears!

Maniny. Uncanny nooks, old dilapidated houses. Adventure expeditions, juvenile skirmishes. Climbing fences was a question of momentary actions, sometimes a broken window resulted from our "missions impossible" and reproving sessions followed. The river Vltava (Moldav), the spot where tennis stadium Stvanice is located today. Older boys rode tractor innertubes all the way to the weir.

I did not know how to swim but I rode with them. If I turned over I paddled like crazy with my arms. I was about ten then. Thank God my mom had no idea about it!

After school Jan often picked up his dad in front of his plant. At 2:05 P.M. dad walked out, sometimes still in his overalls, and they strolled across Invalidovna to the tennis club. Along the way they walked by a military training field and they often watched the soldiers running the obstacle course. It was only a short distance from there to the tennis courts. There were five courts and an old clubhouse. Directly next to the courts was a soccer stadium.

Although I came to play tennis dad signed me up for soccer as well. I often helped him with his custodial chores. As soon as we arrived we started getting the courts ready for play. He watered the courts; I netted or brushed them. People started coming around four but by then I had climbed over to the soccer field to play various games with my friends. I was about eight and very small but I longed to play on a team.

The coach, Jan Civin, always claimed "next year we'll take you on; how old are you?" My dad bugged him continuously to put me on a team until, one day, Mr. Civin said victoriously: "come with me to the club house!"

They signed me in and announced that I would play on the "B" team of my age group. I got my uniform. Absolute ecstasy! I was ten, the smallest on the team, and because I kicked with my left foot they placed me as the left wing.

I remember the first game as if it were today. There was nobody in the stands, only my dad was watching me. And then he told me:" You know, you must play smart; pass the ball so that they don't hurt you. As soon as you get the ball, look where the nearest teammate is positioned, and when your opponent charges you, pass the ball.

SOCCER

As the years went by I started playing more tennis than soccer. My father did not push me into the "white sport" in a systematic way until one day, when he simply shook the racket. It was in 1955 and 9-year old Jan was playing simultaneously two sports. He was not crazy about tennis at the start.

My sister, two years my senior, was a better player and it really bugged me that she beat me. We worked out together most of the time on one of the back courts; court No: 5 was reserved for kids. I remember Jiri Süssland, brothers Pospichal, Mandera... from time to time we climbed up to Hajnovka where TJ Lokomotiva club was located and where Standa Chvatal and Milan Hostinsky played, Foltyn, Vinkler... We all hit the ball any which way, I usually banged it against the wall; I did not have a coach nor did I have anybody who would play with me.

His parents did not contribute to his tennis much at the beginning stages. Although his mother participated in a workshop for tennis empires she and the father played only the third level of the city league and their expertise was far from what it took to bring up a seasoned player.

I only remember one man–regrettably I fail to recall his name but I have a feeling it was maybe Mr. Lausman. One day he watched me hitting the ball against the wall and all of a sudden he said: "You are holding the racket incorrectly. You have to grip it like this" – and he showed me continental grip!.

The league matches were played on Saturdays and Sundays. Jan wasn't crazy about that. He had to get up early on Sunday since matches started at nine. But when they reached the courts the first thing Jan was interested in doing was climb the fence and watch the soccer league next door along with the other fans, rooting for Dukla Karlin.

We horse-played with other kids, climbed trees and played soldiers. Once I was climbing over a fence and my supporting foot slipped. I slid down but – there was a nail that was sticking out and I ripped open the palm of my left hand.

I screamed and ran to the courts. My mom was playing mixed-doubles on court no: 2 with Dr. Rybin from Central Military Hospital. He was an avid tennis player and later figured in our Tennis Federation committee and even became the Davis Cup team's physician.

I screamed in pain simultaneously dripping blood all over the place. They dropped their rackets at once and hurried to me. Rybin looked at it and yelled: "Do this! Move your fingers!"

I moved my fingers: "That's good! Let's go inside the clubhouse and somebody bring a washbowl!"

He poured some disinfection in it, took my hand and submerged it in the solution. I thought I would go mad! He then covered the wound with sterile gauze and ordered: "Take him to

Bulovka Hospital!" After that he turned to Jan's mom with "Vlasta, he'll be all right!" and headed back to the court.

Dad took me to the hospital. Two shots anesthetized my hand. It took about an hour for the doctor to sew up the cut. Ten stitches. He did a good job but I have a scar till this day.

In 1956 Jan played for a 12 and under junior age-group team for the first time. A year later his parents entered him in Prague Regional Championships. He did not feel like playing it but he advanced all the way to the semi-finals where he lost to Stepan Koudelka from Slavia VS.

I was crushed twice 6:1 but Stepan was considered a great talent with promising potential. He played alongside me all through the age-group and junior years; a few years later we met even at Roland Garros.

Jan received a Certificate of Award and that made him feel pretty good. It brought him closer to tennis.

His dad declared: "Look at that! You finished third!"

Although soccer remained his sport number one he automatically qualified for his first Tennis Nationals in Pelhrimov thanks to his third place in the Regionals.

They traveled by second class train to Pelhrimov. It took all morning to get there with several transfers along the way. Dad accompanied Jan but they could not sleep together. Kodes senior found accommodations in a hotel on the Main Square while Jan stayed in a dormitory arrangement with eight boys to a room. There was one adult with them in the dorm, Milos Solc, an excellent international tennis player.

Milos Solc was introduced to tennis at the age of fourteen and in 1925 he left for abroad where he earned his living teaching noblemen and spa visitors how to play the game of tennis. From 1931 he played regularly the World Professional Championships for the first time on the French Riviera and later in Berlin. Solc was the second best Czechoslovak professional tennis player besides Karel Kozeluh from 1932 till 1938.

Prague – Klamovka 1947. Before the match with Hungary. From left: Karel Kozeluh, Jaroslav Drobny, Milos Solc and Ferdinand Vrba.

In 1947 he represented Czechoslovakia together with Karel Kozeluh in an International match versus Hungary. In 1940 his amateur status was re-established and for the next ten years he represented Czechoslovakia alongside players like Cejnar, Caska, Siba, Drobny and Cernik. However, because of his prior professional career he was not allowed to play many important international tournaments, nor was he able to play in Davis Cup competition. For that reason he participated mainly in exhibition challenges.

In 1948 he became a Davis Cup coach of the team of Yugoslavia, and two years later he started to study theology. In the seventies he played many veteran tournaments where he was unconquerable.

His two sons and one of his daughters were the country's leading juniors in the 1950s and at the beginning of the 1960s. His son Josef was ranked as number one in 1961.

Both boys were playing in 14 and under category in Pelhrimov, and Milos' daughter was there as well. Since he was a pastor he knelt every night before going to bed and we all had to do the same! He recited the Lord's Prayer – it was, sort of, uncanny!

I have no idea how many of us were believers. I was baptized catholic and my dad supported a reasonable dose of religious teaching; for that reason I can say that I am a "believer". We had catechism classes in school for two years through which we received pictures of Saints and some stamps. However, the communists later suppressed all forms of religion and instead of following religious images to Church we followed lantern processions celebrating the Great Russian Revolution.

Jan played the Pelhrimov Age-Group Nationals four times. In 1957 he lost in the first round but the following year it looked like he could win the whole thing! However, after winning the first round he injured his right hand and had to default from the quarter-finals.

When our matches were over we had fun running around the park and chasing girls; we were ten or eleven and hormones started to mess with our heads. I climbed over some wire fence and tore open my hand but four stitches fixed it. The main thing was that my dad did not get angry with me! "Oh well, so you'll default; there is not much else we can do," he consoled me.

He treated me like any other regular kid and I am for ever grateful to him. He never scolded me for losing a match or for missing a clear chance to score in soccer or missing a penalty.

After a tournament in Chrudim in 1957 Kodes senior came up to his son and said: "You should have a coach and we should transfer to Stvanice. Let's go and check it out there; they'll look at you and, perhaps, they'll accept you."

We won't find out today who it was from the many tennis experts around the white sport establishments that recommended to Kodes senior: "Your son has a potential and should get some coaching. It would be a dire pity to squander his talent." It might have been Jan Civin or somebody entirely different...

Kodes family resolved to move from Dukla Karlin to TJ Motorlet at Stvanice that Fall. The fact that Jan won the Prague Youth Sport Games that May was the final impetus for the transfer. He was the Prague Schools' 12 and under Champion. Some seven hundred boys sifted through the district rounds. In the finals at Stvanice he represented Pernerova Grade School. Several tennis fans noticed Jan's talent in the finals and asked his dad: "Wouldn't you like to bring your boy here, to Stvanice? Such transfer should not be a problem since Karlin is only a provincial club." This was the final force that persuaded father and son to change the tennis training venue.

Kodes senior stopped playing for Dukla Karlin and, instead, became a leader and guide of a Motorlet Club junior team. Over the weekends he chaperoned young tennis hopefuls to tennis matches and he concerned himself with the junior team's progress with utter devotion that was inherent of his character. At that time there was another personality at Stvanice who endorsed the decisive role in tennis development of Jan Kodes junior. It was the professional Karel Semerad, who ran and taught the club's tennis school.

KAREL SEMERAD

"Well, son, tennis is not just playing on the court; you must also practice against the wall. That will help you strengthen your hand, particularly your wrist, and you will develop feeling for the ball that is crucial for volleys. Even the best of the professional players started out practicing against the wall! Kozeluh, Tilden... The best of world tennis players grew out of Tilden's school of tennis! You must fondle the strokes, follow through with them, and most of all you must contact the ball with proper timing and in front of your body," – advised the coach.

Jan Kodes heard those names and words daily. Karel Semerad repeated them over and over even till it became tedious.

At Stvanice they taught kids from the book "Tennis from A to Z" written by none other than the famous Bill Tilden himself. It was translated by an accomplished coach and tennis teacher Frantisek Burianek.

I received all pages typewritten. God knows what multiple of carbon copy it was?! I later had it bound into a book form and I boost of having it still!

Bill Tilden.

In the introduction, among other things, Bill Tilden says: "...With regard to contemporary tennis its level is inferior to the days of glory and shine before the war. However, I believe that we are at the cradle of a new grand era, when tennis will return to mean again all that it once meant in the past.... Most players of today enter the court with trepidation, or they drag their feet while they behave conceitedly; what they are showing is more likely arrogance than confidence. Present-day modern methods show much power, attack, and ball pounding and little strategy. It appears as if players no longer draw any enjoyment from the game of tennis. However, should the color and shine return to the game of tennis then tennis must bring joy and pleasure to the players...!"

Karel Semerad repeated the following lines to all his pupils many times over: "The key of a successful game is thinking, strategy and stroke precision! A pounded shot that is not placed well is waste of your energy and your opponent uses the power of your shot to his advantage. Preserve your arm, especially your wrist and elbow."

Jan Kodes won 12 and under Regional Championships in 1959 and thanks to that achievement he was selected and placed in, so called, tennis training base at Klamovka. In the fifties it was a predecessor of future junior training centers that were later envied to Czechoslovakia by the rest of the world.

I received one hour of practice on a half court in the indoor facility! It was with Eva Matejkova on Sunday morning from eight to nine! Stepan Koudelka, who had defeated Jan two years previously, practiced three times a week for two hours on a full court!

Sunday, six in the morning. Jan was getting up earlier than for school. He had a quick breakfast, grabbed his racket and hurried off to Karlin viaduct to catch a street car to Klamovka.

We played for an hour at Klamovka and went back again by street car. We got off at Wenceslas Square for our weekly

Karel Semerad with his kids.

treat of a strawberry smoothie at Koruna Bar. This became a ritual inherently typical of every winter Sunday morning. It became a bit monotonous tennis life – Stvanice, Klamovka, Stvanice.... But there was no other way.

Winter was a very important training season, especially during the age-group years. It is no longer true today since tennis competition goes on for eleven months of the year. Things were different then. Indoor facilities did not exist. Club tennis courts were closed and waited for the spring to reopen.

Stvanice was an exception to the rule. Lockers were transferred to one side of the locker room and that created a rather large space. The walls had small circle targets painted on them and Karel Semerad invited us, kids, to practice against the wall. "It is ok that you received only an hour at Klamovka. You'll make up for it in the summer. It is all the same whether you are on the court now or practice here against the wall. Let's get to it!"

Twenty volleys.

"You must hit the ball in the sweet spot. Concentrate!" he prompted.

"First forehand, then backhand, and after that alternate the two." My arm was falling off already after the first twenty hits. But Karel Semerad made no compromises: "Last time you hit twenty, so today you do twenty five." He raised the number of repetitions gradually. I ended up at a hundred! "Son, if you want to be a tennis champ you must be able to hit a great

With Vlasta and Karel Semerad in 1958. Behind us is the old Maternity building.

Even then, my backhand was not too bad.

number of strokes without your arm getting hurt. You are not doing it only to hit a target but also to strengthen your wrist."

Jan's parents usually came along with him and the coach kept stressing to them: "His wrist is terribly floppy; he needs to strengthen and firm it up."

His mom asked what they should do.

"He must reel up."

He fabricated a pole to which he attached a weight on a string and Jan had to reel up and reel out this concoction. "This you will do every day in the morning before you go to school, and every evening before going to bed. In addition you must drink a glass of milk." Jan hated drinking the milk but his mom always said: "You know what Mr. Semerad said! There is no way around it!"

He drank at least half a glass.

Tennis is not just basic stroke technical perfection, polished volleys, serve returns and serves but also quick feet. The ideal tool for footwork is jump rope. One foot, the other foot, both together. Ten times, twenty times, fifty times, in varied intervals.

It was unreal how much I disliked doing it; it seemed to me too "girlish". I also remember short sprints and quick starts to bases – a drill called the "compass"; jumps with feet together over benches, frog jumps that I literally could not stand or volley-squat drill, possibly volley-squat-jump up-smash and back to squat drill.

When I later befriended some American players they claimed that dancing rock-n'roll helped their footwork. My footwork foundation was in soccer. Quick sprints, sudden directional changes, endurance. Basketball, winter skating and hockey also helped me.

Karel Semerad did not stress the importance of footwork right from the start, only later, as soon as his pupils started practicing against the wall. He wanted them to move on light feline-like feet.

That means going over the balls of the feet down to the heels in a slightly forward-leaning position and with tiny steps. Top players of the past like Laver, Rosewall, Connors, Nastase, Borg, Wilander, Agassi were perfect examples of such footwork. Nowadays it is Rafael Nadal who demonstrates ideal foot movement on the court.

The coach taught us to shorten the steps through sort of a little dance and then he said: "It is always better to take one more step than be short of a step. You must fondle each ball a little rather than just get rid of it!" Those were the words he kept pounding into our heads.

Pupil and volleys. Would that be possible today?

Czechoslovak Nationals at Pelhrimov in 1959 In the finals:„Golias and David" (Vopicka – Kodes).

It is not easy to recognize the optimal point of contact, and to do it consistently is close to impossible. No player in the world hits the ball at an optimal point but the top player hits it there more often than a regular player. It is true that one can play many balls from an incorrect position – often your opponent makes you do so – and then force the hit just with your arm. But beware! Poor footwork brings on more mistakes, it wears one out sooner, and later it causes frequent injuries. In prolonged matches and in stressful situations footwork may be the critical factor. Poor footwork in that case may backfire.

Good footwork was one of Jan Kodes' precedence. However, he had a different sort of a handicap. From the time he was selected into the tennis center at Klamovka in 1959 he was the smallest one there.

Even girls my age were bigger than I however, I was the one winning trophies. In spite of everything I had to undergo special medical tests in the Sport Medicine Center in Salmovska Street. They prescribed for me to supplement my diet with fish oil. Regretfully, they also disco-vered heart murmur and according to one doctor that meant the end of my competitive athle-tics! My mom was devastated. Together with my dad they started consulting other doctors and found out that heart murmur was a defect but one should still be able to continue with sports. I do not know how my parents did it but they managed to obtain a passing approval stamp of my physical test that had to be placed in my registration card before I could compete again.

It took a long time for Jan to get rid of his small frame handicap.

"He is so scrawny, weak, no endurance" I heard people around me saying.

My endurance was ok but I lacked power that most other peers had plenty of. That was why I could not put away a ball with a hard bullet like shot. My opponents overpowered me. But, gradually, the difference lessened, and slowly the powers among us equalized.

In 1960 Jan Kodes became the 14 and under National Champion in Pelhrimov when he defeated Jaroslav Kurz 5:6, 6:5, and 6:2 in the finals. The competition was very strong. There were altogether 152 participants, 48 in 14 and under category. Jan had to win five matches to reach the championship title that he longed for so much.

It was a rule then that the 14 and under national finalists automatically received wild cards into the junior championships under 18 in Pardubice. In the past that tournament was consi-dered the gate into the international tennis arena. Kodes got to play in that tournament twice while he was still an under 14 age-group player. The first time in 1959 he came as a defeated finalist, and the following year already as the National Champion.

Both times he was lucky to meet players who later became outstanding ice hockey players. His doubles partner in 1959 was Pavel Wohl, the future prominent goalie. They lost in the third round. The following year brought another excellent future NHL hockey player in his way. He lost to Vaclav Nedomansky in the first round 8:6, 3:6, and 5:7. In spite of the defeat Jan was ecstatic. In those times players had to pass physical fitness tests immediately before the championships – one kilometer run, long jump, etc. Nedomansky was absolutely phenomenal in Jan's category, yet Jan put up a splendid fight and the match was pretty even-leveled.

In 1961 Kodes passed into the 18 and under junior category and began to challenge players like Stepan Koudelka. He defeated Stepan in the Regionals and lost in the finals 7:5, 8:6 to Miroslav Vyskocil, who was the Czech tennis hopeful at the time.

Jan still wasn't taken seriously as a player of potential significance because of his see-mingly poor physical frame. Only just before he passed from the age-groups to juniors many experts started to pay better attention to him.

At the national training camp in Sumperk his dedication to soccer was threatened for the first time! Many people started to persuade him to turn away from soccer: "Just drop it!" They meant well, advising Jan to put all his energy into tennis if he really wanted to achieve higher levels.

But, Jan obstinately refused to do so: "No! I want to go on with soccer."

Jan felt like between two millstones. The tennis buffs frightened him with: "You'll get hurt!" Soccer team wanted him to practice twice a week and play games on Saturdays. But, tennis was taking up more and more of his time. He was no longer so sure that soccer was first – he wanted to practice just once a week and if they found a sub for him he would stop altogether... But there was one prerogative about him – he was a leftie, and there weren't many of those in soccer. The coaches excused him from one weekly practice. Jan stayed with soccer for three more years until the 1964 Junior Nationals in Pardubice.

The days after Jan transferred to Stvanice were as similar as egg to an egg. He came home from school, changed bags, left for the tennis courts where he practiced from two to four. After four the club filled up with adults but the kids did not want to go home. They played hide and seek, or tag between the courts, they climbed the bleachers and horsed around.

They were capable of playing till the sun-down, when suddenly the custodian, Mr. Soucek, appeared from nowhere and yelled: "Boys, time to go home! Kodes, your dad is looking for you!"

It was usually dark by the time Jan returned home.

Ten to fifteen year old tennis players lived off not just playing tennis and fooling around but also by ball picking during adult matches. During that time period there was a terrifically coordinated elite group of ballboys. They took turns who would be at the net and who behind the baseline; they worked during all Davis Cup matches that took place in Prague.

Cyril Suk won the National junior title in 1960. As the winner of the under 14's category I was also invited to enter. Later Suk served as President of the Czechoslovak Tennis Federation.

This was my mega tennis school since I had a chance to absorb it all at the net – for instance, I witnessed a backhand smash by Roy Emerson. I got to appreciate the best world players' precise crosscourt and down-the-line shots – Laver's, Emerson's, Fraser's, Stolle's, Nielsen's, and also Javorsky' drop shots. I later learned those shots myself. As soon as the matches were over we ran to pick up our rackets from the locker room and attempted the "hot-dog" shots.

I also observed unimaginable match turning-points when the game development was pointing clearly in favor of a player but by the match end it was the other player who won. For instance, Pavel Korda lost to the German Bungert 4:6 in the fifth after his victory had been visibly within reach.

Another instance was the match between Javorsky and Kuhnke. Our player was 2:0 ahead in sets and lost in spite of such a lead! Javorsky was playing out of his mind in the first two sets and then, all of a sudden, was unable to execute passing shots. His slight weakness was his backhand but it seemed to be successful in this particular match. It was so until 4:4 in the fifth, when his confidence was shaken with finality and he lost the match.

All this was tremendously important for Jan's further tennis development because he was able to recognize those turning and breaking points in his matches.

I realized then that tennis was not only about the individual stroke perfection. It was possible that a situation would crop up when a player's strokes simply "disappeared". It is comparable to a similar situation of a singer who walks up to a micropho-

Vaclav Nedomansky, later the hockey star played NHL for Detroit, New York and Los Angeles.

Davis Cup, Prague, May 4-6, 1961. Czechoslovakia vs. West Germany 2:3. From left: capt. Jiri Rössler, Richard Schönborn, Jiri Javorsky, Pavel Korda and Jiri Parma. All players from the team became successful coaches.

ne and is unable to produce a sound in front of a panel of judges. Even in tennis it is known that everybody plays great in practice but only a half of those players manage matches that count with control! Only they engage in matches the same strokes they are capable of playing in practice. The players, who execute strokes with faults in practice, even if those faults are minuscule, show more profound failure under match pressure.

Nothing could ever replace the years spent at Stvanice for Jan because that opened a gate for him into the international tennis arena.

The only venue for international tennis events in Czechoslovakia at that time was Stvanice. By the time Jan transferred to Sparta Prague in the Fall of 1966 he was practically a seasoned player. He played international tournaments and did not need the close observation of foreign players playing in his backyard. He had ample opportunity to survey players while abroad.

School, practice, matches, tournaments, in-country travel. Jan was getting used to the endless tennis merry-go-round that followed him for the rest of his career. He won the 14 and under Nationals in 1960 and that fall he entered 9th grade. In spring 1961 Jan advanced to junior category and at this point he had to decide which direction he would choose to determine his future.

He was the third best student in his class and showed five "Bs" on his last report card. His decision about further studies was simple – he would enter the Secondary School! However, the reality was not so simple. It so happened that he was the only student in class who had not joined Pioneer, the Communist Youth Organization. His father resolutely refused to let Jan join the group. It was his way of protest against the regime.

In time Jan's mother tried to persuade the father: "For God's sake, let him join the Pioneers! Let him have some peace." Jan sensed the tension relating to this issue but he did not give it much importance. However, his application to the Secondary School was rejected. The school Principal wrote in his personal file: "Son of an independent businessman – reject application to Secondary education!"

I learned and understood all this with time. However, it affected my father terribly. He had no idea what to do with me; he wondered how I would be able to secure my future. It became a constant topic of discussion in our house.

At that time the Stvanice club Chairman was Bedrich Syrinek. He worked in Jinonice as a personnel officer of Jan Sverma Works that manufactured airplane motors.

"This is no problem. Why should you push him into further education while we can take him as an apprentice here? I'll take care of it," he told Kodes senior and arranged everything in no time.

Jan Kodes junior was thus going to earn his certificate as a miller. That meant that he had to get up at half past four every morning, take a street car and transfer at Wenceslas Square to a trolley bus that dropped him off at Smichov. Jan had to transfer again to another bus there and take it to the end station in Jinonice. At ten to six he was entering the plant and finished there at three in the afternoon. He did not get to Stvanice any sooner than 4:30 pm and there he just collapsed on a bench and did not practice. He couldn't. He did not have enough sleep and he was tired.

After about ten days I did not think I could do it. That was the end of my tennis! My dad grunted about the hopelessness of the situation but everybody put him off with: "Give me a break! Jiri Javorsky also works in Josef Sverma plant and so does Vera Puzejova."

However, they were already representing the country internationally! They finished at midday in order to train and prepare for tennis competition. That plant simply paid their wages and they were not expected to work much in return. Their responsibility was to do well in tennis competition.

Luckily, at the end of September, Kodes senior met Liliana Papikova, who was a Secondary School teacher in Liben. Her husband was on Sparta's tennis league team. After she heard the whole story of Jan's predicament she said: "I can't promise anything but I'll enquire and find out if my school would accept Jan even belatedly." She called back in ten days: "Our principal knows your little Jan; she says that he has a sharp mind, quick wit and demonstrates good grades; we are willing to accept him."

With that the "Motorlet apprenticeship" experiment came to an end. A few days later Jan directed himself to Liben Secondary School. About a month after the transformation from an apprentice to a secondary school student the classroom door opened in the middle of instruction and the Principal Dolanska entered with a regional school superintendent behind her: "Student Kodes! Your application has been reviewed and you can go back to Karlin Secondary School if you so choose. It is up to you now!"

As Jan was standing in the middle of his class and looked around reading his classmates' faces he uttered his historic sentence: "Comrade Principal Dolanska, I do not wish to return to Karlin!"

Everybody froze!

Mr. Kodes' accidental meeting Liliana Papikova signified not only that Jan was able to receive secondary education and matriculate but it also gave an impulse to the direction of his tennis training. Up to this point Jan represented Motorlet but whenever he bumped into Mrs. Papikova's husband at tournaments he almost always mentioned: "You should transfer to our Sparta club. Do not expect much felicity to bloom for you at Stvanice!"

Those beautiful college years! For some it is close to worry-less period of time, for others it represents a mound of responsibilities. It was clear to Jan Kodes that from campus he headed for the courts and the courts were replaced by studies. The three secondary school years passed like water under a bridge and matriculation exams were coming near. Jan was a good student though not a geek. He earned mostly the As and Bs, only in math he struggled a bit and earning a "C" was common.

In 1964 he traveled to the West for the first time: He represented the country in Galea Cup, the international junior team competition the final of which took place in Vichy, France, and he entered the junior French Open and Wimbledon.

It was in Paris that he experienced an incident that ushered Jan into a situation that repeated itself several times over in the following years. He confronted envy for the first time in his life.

The departure date to Paris was fast approaching and with it also the final grading period. His math standing was between a "C" and "D" and he had one last chance to better the grade. "Next time I'll call on those students whose grade is yet unclear so that you can improve it," announced the teacher. Jan Kodes was among the students who desired to be tested.

"Great, I have another chance to be tested and improve the grade" Jan calmed himself.

On Friday we had the last math class, on Saturday I was to fly to Paris. I raised my hand at once at the beginning of the class for the teacher to know that I desired to improve my grade. The teacher nodded but kept calling other students to the board. The class-time was advancing. It was five minutes before the end of the class and she still paid no attention to me. I raised my hand again.

Junior Nationals under „18" at Pardubice. Centercourt view with the old clubhouse in the back, built by Adolf Korda, the grandfather of Peter Korda in early 30s – later in October 1984 destroyed by fire. Pic. Kodes - Koudelka beat Laudin and Kurz in the doubles finals at 1963.

"Well, I'll call on you next time" she responded.

"But I have an excused release from school next week because I'll be representing the country as a junior in Paris; I'll be absent from school next week," I tried to explain to her.

"Well, friend, you have to make a choice! "C" in math or Paris?"

Dejectedly I returned home and told my dad all about it. "What shall I do?" I asked. "Do you know what? Just go to Paris! She won't give you the "D"; she won't dare!"

I left and proceeded all the way to the semi-finals.

Upon my return I looked at the report card and found out that she did dupe me with a "D". The first "D" on a report card in my life! It was altogether worrisome since the panel looked at the last report card during the Matriculation Exams. The result was to be expected – three "Bs" and a "D"! I had a strange feeling based on the behavior of several of my teachers once I started to travel to the West. As soon as they heard Paris or London one could read in their faces like in a book: "Oh well, he is on the road all the time...!"

It was at the time when most people had no chance to travel out of the country. The regime steadfastly tried to prevent people from finding for themselves what life was like in the West. Top athletics became one of the exceptions to the rule. In most cases our athletes represented the country with flying colors. Tennis players belonged to that group of athletes. Jealousy was a terrible phenomenon! It created resentment...

Jan Kodes and Marian Laudin.

In August 1964, two months after matriculation, Kodes won the Nationals in Pardubice at last. He defeated Marian Laudin in the finals 6:3, 6:2. A few days after conquering that title he and his dad sat down and started thinking about what to do next.

"You must enter the university! Though you are a tennis champion you also need some education and a degree! What would happen if you got hurt?"

"There is no way that they would accept me with a "D" in math" - argued Jan but sent the application form to the School of Economics in Prague anyway, and he also reported to the admissions interview. They asked him a few questions that he answered with ease. It was all about civics, general knowledge and, fortunately, nothing touched upon math.

He was accepted but battled with math right from the beginning. Integrals, derivations, statistics, all were problematic issues. Jan was lucky to have come across professor Smakal, who lectured the math course. He alone suggested to Jan to come for tutorials.

College years proved to be ideal for Jan Kodes. Patience he inherited from his father and his honest approach to tennis practice became evident also in his studies. He made a good name for himself at school during the first two years though he took exams at different times than other students since tennis took so much of his time: "Kodes? He passes exams with delay but he passes. We agree on a time-line and he sticks to it," relished his professors.

It was convenient for Jan that he did not have any morning classes; that gave him certain freedom and he was able to devote time to tennis. However, from junior year on it was close to impossible to juggle peak tennis and university studies at the level he had been able to do till then. He requested an individual study plan, he scheduled exams and semester courses in such a way that both, his junior and senior years, spread over two years to complete, and most of the course work was concentrated into the winter months. He studied at night, generally from ten to two, slept in a little the next morning and then went to practice. He hauled his textbooks and lecture notes along to Davis Cup matches and tournaments.

For instance, we played in Turin. We were down 1:2 against Italy, Jan Kukal was on the court sweating almost blood while I was stuck in the locker room studying. At the same time I was scared that he might win and I would have to battle for the third point. In a way, however, studying suppressed the jitterbugs before such an important match.

He studied domestic trade, commodities, and the exams were sometimes dreadful. He had to read through and study some twelve hundred pages for one exam! But he was lucky to have an older sister Anna who taught at the continuing education school of economy.

My sister helped me tremendously! Soon after I returned from abroad I had to go and take an exam. I brought home a pile of textbooks and she looked through them and pointed out: "Don't read those or those but study this from page twenty to fifty." Suddenly, there were only 400 pages to read instead of 1200 and seventy to eighty percent of the questions I had to answer during the exam included the material from those four hundred pages. There were instances when I failed at the exam but most of the time my big sis zeroed on the most important subject matter and I passed.

The end of my university studies was very demanding especially the end of the junior and beginning of my senior years. By then I had won Roland Garros, reached the US Open and Italian Open finals. I felt like throwing in the towel but my dad kept wheedling: "If you finish the junior year you'll manage to get it done all the way!"

He defended his dissertation in 1972. While his classmates were lining up in cap and gowns in the Municipal Hall for graduation Jan was traveling around the world tennis tournaments. In the end, it took another year before he was able to be present at his graduation and received his diploma with the title "Ing." before his name.

Since I was always away the university president Stanislav Hradecky wrote me a letter that he organized a private graduation ceremony on campus for me. Only a few people took part in the ceremony but it was jubilant especially since it took place right after I won Wimbledon in 1973.

My dad was immensely happy. Just like many years before around the Pioneer membership humiliation I sensed his persisting aversion towards the communist regime. I realized that my successful university entrance and completion brought him a huge satisfaction and inner compensation.

JUNIOR YEARS

Pardubice Junior Nationals! In the totalitarian regime this tournament held special significance. You wanted to make sure to participate here once you reached the junior category under 16 or under 18. Those who advanced to the last rounds in Pardubice usually made the later selection for international competition and participation in tournaments abroad.

Tennis "crème de la crème" of officials, coaches, trainers, and enthusiasts assembled for the final three days on the courts of LTC Pardubice. It was their duty to observe the budding talents. Little Jan caught their attention in Pardubice at even younger age than most other talented youngsters. He played here as a finalist and later champion of 14 and under National Junior Championship in Pelhrimov in 1959 and 1960.

Generally, observers of Pardubice Junior Championship concentrated on the eighteen-year-olds. However, Jan Kodes reached the finals already as a sixteen year old! When a player two or three years junior of eighteen reached that far it gave evidence of something clearly special. However, the 1961 Pardubice Junior Championship was Jan's first true touchstone. He lost 6:2, 2:6, 3:6 in the second round to Stepan Koudelka and the newspapers wrote: "Kodes demonstrated great fighting spirit and the ability to run favored Koudelka all over the court."

Pardubice visited that year yet another man who soon fell in the line of coaches who profoundly affected Kodes' tennis development. It was Ing. Frantisek Cejnar, a Wimbledon quarterfinalist from 1938, who lost to the two times Wimbledon Champion and Grand Slam winner, the American Donald Budge. He entered Jan's tennis life fulltime at Stvanice during the 1962 training camp of the most prospective young Czechoslovak players, when Cejnar was one of the two coaches.

I was extremely honored to have been selected and invited to this camp. It was a national selection and I was the youngest one. We played also practice matches. My club coach Karel Semerad, who was around the courts all those days, kept telling me: "Listen to that coach Cejnar; he was an amazing player!"

He was right. All of a sudden I was hearing things in slightly different terms from others; it was obvious that he understood tennis well. He always pointed out a convincing observation and reinforced it with an example exemplified often by Jaroslav Drobny: "Of course, Jaroslav! He had an amazing hand swing and great touch."

At that time I was not yet that familiar or impressed by the name Drobny...

At the close of that training camp Frantisek Cejnar wrote in the report: "Kodes proved his talent and strong will. Prerequisite for his further progress is improvement of his physical strength!"

The 1962 Pardubice Junior Championship experienced a shock. Jan Kodes fought his way into the finals at the young age of only sixteen! He won the Regionals prior to the Championships when he defeated Frantisek Pala, two years his senior, 8:6, 2:6, 6:3, and 7:5 in the finals and beat him here again 2:6, 6:3, 7:5 to reach the semis. In the semifinals he broke through the series of defeats by Stepan Koudelka! According to some experts Kodes' victory 7:5,

The under "18" Junior Championships at Pardubice. As a sixteen year old, I reached the finals but lost. Josef Vopicka, two years older, was still too strong.

International junior tournament in Tallin, Estonia.
From left: Terenau, Moczar, Kodes, Nastase and Laudin.

6:2 was almost painful. Stepan was their favorite mainly for his elegant style; he was perceived as the next prospective great player.

Jan lost in the finals to Josef Vopicka 6:3, 2:6, 2:6 in spite of his leading in the third set 2:1
and 40:15 on his serve. Still, it was a tremendous triumph for the sixteen year old Kodes. In
addition, he reached the finals with Milena Startlova in mixed doubles.

Jan's personal secret came true in 1963 when he was sent to play abroad three times! His
previous achievements must have ratified his selection. The first trip took him to the East
– where else – to the Soviet Union. He took part in the International Junior Championships
in Tallinn and then in Leningrad. In Tallinn he lost in the first round but won the consolation
event.

*The most interesting thing was meeting a player there for the first time who I later per-
formed many thrilling and important matches with during the peak of my career. It was the
Romanian Illie Nastase! In those days we had no idea yet that one day we would face off in
Roland Garros finals!*

After the Czechoslovak International Championships at Stvanice he was nominated to
play an international tournament in a spa town Zinnowitz in East Germany.

On the way there the Czechoslovaks took part in a friendly encounter in Halle. Kodes lost
to Luttropp 6:3, 5:7, and 4:6 there but he remembers an episode that he likes to laugh about
till today.

*I had a match-point in the second set at 5:2. Before the match-point my opponent's strings
broke. He proceeded to the net and extended his hand for an end-of-the-match handshake saying
that he had no other racket. He had two rackets but strings in the first burst right at the start.*

"Don't be silly," I told him, "here is my racket, let's finish the match."

*And that is what happened – I lost that match! I never again did anything similar to that.
I was young, honest, and fair. With time I learned that nobody gives anything gratis. It was yet
another lesson.*

GALEA CUP

Jan Kodes' success in reaching semifinals in the Baltic coast men's tournament opened a door for him into the junior team selection for Galea Cup 1963. (European team competition for juniors under 20, similar to Davis Cup) Final decision was made after a qualifying tournament in Olomouc.

At the close of the qualifying tournament the non-playing captain of the team, Frantisek Cejnar, called all the players and announced: "The coaches' council nominated the following players to represent the junior team..."

He cited three names that everybody expected – Holecek, Koudelka, Tajcnar. There were many candidates for the fourth spot: Pala, Vopicka, Brejcha, and Kodes, who was the youngest...

"And the fourth player" Cejnar continued, "is Jan Kodes!"

Since there where about 16 countries competing in four groups we had to play a qualifying round in Pilsen, where the road to the first Czechoslovak Galea Cup victory started. Jan Kodes got his earliest chance to perform in the initial match against Monaco in which the home team won easily 5:0. Jan defeated Landau 6:1, 6:2 at team score 3:0.

The following match against France, the favorite of the entire competition, was a hard fought battle. Koudelka and Tajcnar lost the opening matches but the doubles brought a turn around, when Holecek – Koudelka heroically conquered Patrice Beust and Daniel Contet 8:6 in the fifth set! Only doubles was played best of five sets. Koudelka as well as Holecek won their final day singles!

I remember particularly Milan Holecek's outstanding performance that third day; he had a lion's share in the team's advance to the finals in a French luxury spa Vichy.

Vichy is located in the heart of France. The first battles of the best European junior teams took place on these fourteen courts in 1950. It has been not only an athletic event but also a social affair. The pleasant spa township with charming hotels and pensions, the inevitable casino and beautifully equipped tennis club grew to Jan Kodes' heart. With his superb performance and gentlemanlike composure on and off the court Jan captured the fancy of local tennis enthusiasts and with that he practically opened the door to France's heart attracting admirers who, in later years of his most significant achievements at Roland Garros, loved him so much.

He did not get his chance during his first participation in 1963. He sat on the bench through the nerve-wrecking semifinal match with the Soviets as well as the subsequent final battle

Sporting Club de Vichy.

with Italy. Though he was entrusted with one fourth of the team responsibility for the final success he was left with nothing else but keeping his fingers crossed while his team-mates battled on the court. He took that with such emotional responsibility that the excitement and the resulting triumphant ecstasy made him ill!

The first-time involvement in Vichy had another key importance for Jan Kodes. He met there face to face his fateful Wimbledon counterpart Alexander Metreveli, two years his senior.

The next Junior Championships in Pardubice took place right after the

Returning from France. capt. F.Cejnar, M.Holecek, S.Koudelka and J.Kodes. (from bottom).

victorious return from Vichy. As in the previous year Jan advanced all the way to the finals, where he lost again. This time, however, to Stepan Koudelka.

What he said about Jan Kodes
Frantisek Cejnar

The packed crowd was drawn out of their seats numerous times during the dramatic final match of the boys. Stepan Koudelka deserved to win but it could not have been any closer... Kodes' game does not suit Koudelka and he had a very hard time prevailing. He was down 0:4 and 3:5 in the first set, and 2:4 in the second. Though he did not display his best game it is very important to value his effort; he literally scraped out the victory thanks to his constant attack. Kodes played a smart game and with prudence. He can still strive for the championship victory next year.

This was the first public praise of my performance. As a seventeen year old I occupied the 8th rank nationally among the adults.

Jan Kodes flew to Vichy again in 1964 this time no longer as a substitute. In the finals Czechoslovakia confronted the Soviet Union that was ready to take revenge. All matches were played the best of five sets.

"Kodes possesses a heart of a warrior," proclaimed the French newspaper headlines.

His opening match with Metreveli caused peoples' hearts to throb: 3:6, 3:6, 6:4, and 15:17! It took three hours to finish! Koudelka then defeated Ivanov in four but teamed up with Pala for doubles and they lost. However, Kodes overwhelmed Alexander Ivanov in a five set battle 5:7, 4:6, 10:8, 8:6, and 6:3 and thus evened out the team score to 2:2.

In the fourth set I was already losing 1:5 but I forced back four match points; one at that score, and the other three at 4:5. The match took three and a half hours. In the course of the match the Soviet captain was popping anti-stress pills in his mouth.

**Vichy, France in 1964: capt. Frantisek Cejnar, Stepan Koudelka,
Jan Kodes, Frantisek Pala, Marian Laudin.**

In the decisive match Stepan Koudelka came short against ever improving Metreveli and lost 1:6, 4:6, 1:6.

Kodes remembers:

We heard many impressions from Koudelka, Kodes, Pala, as well as Laudin. Jan remembers: When Ivanov and I shook hands at the end of the match I was so tired that I could barely stand. Cejnar picked me up like a small child and carried me off the court. I was overjoyed and it was memorable how everybody patted my back and shouted with glee. I collapsed in the locker room and did not even see Stepan's showdown match with Metreveli. I believe we became quite popular there."

Ceskoslovensky sport – Czechoslovak press

By stature he looks like little David. However, the day will come when he defeats even Goliath. He has not yet become a lion that symbolizes power in his country's Coat of arms. He is still a cub but with very sharp claws. What a unique and remarkable talent. I am sure we'll hear much about him in the future…

Judith Elian, L´Equipe

Jan Kodes' performance in the 1964 Galea Cup finals in Vichy was the best he exhibited on tennis courts that year. However, there were three events that preceded Vichy finals that should not be left out of mentioning in relationship to his quest to reach the world peak.

To begin with, it is necessary to accentuate that 1964 achievements qualified Jan for the Davis Cup team selection. He sustained his presence in this most prestigious team tennis competition for seventeen years and finished it in 1980 with a culminating victory in Prague, when he was able to hold the famous "salad bowl" at last after the final match with Italy.

TENNIS

7. JAHRGANG   HEFT **4**   JULI/AUGUST 1963   PREIS 1,– DM

MITTEILUNGSBLATT DES DEUTSCHEN TENNIS-VERBANDES IM DTSB

German tennis magazine – first time on the front page in 1963
with our leader Jindrich Höhm (sitting).

JUNIOR YEARS

Jan Kodes with Cliff Richey.

He gathered experience in the first year on the bench as a substitute. The Czechoslovak leadership did not nominate Jiri Javorsky that year. Supposedly, his performance was no longer sufficient. However, it proved to be an erroneous judgment. The Czechoslovak team was then named "the youngest European Davis Cup team". And Jiri Javorsky was hurt feeling that he was excluded prematurely.

I sympathized with him. The team rejuvenation was a little hasty. Koudelka and Holecek played all of the matches against Sweden and we lost 0:5. In the following year Javorsky was reinstated.

That year Kodes traveled to Paris and to Wimbledon to take part in Junior Championships for the first time. He advanced to the semis in both. In Paris he lost to the American Cliff Richey and in London to the Egyptian Ismail El Shafei.

In London I received my first grass-court lesson. El Shafei was a left-hander thus he served with reverse rotation. Not only that I had trouble dealing with movement on the grass surface and the fast bounce of the ball I also needed to adjust to his serve that curved to the opposite side; from the forehand side it jammed my body.

On the home turf he defeated Petr Strobl at Prague Open in Stvanice, which was a very respectable accomplishment but he lost in the following quarterfinal round to the American Perry in four sets. In the Nationals in Ostrava he reached again just quarter-finals. He received a lumping lesson from Javorsky: 3:6, 0:6, 2:6.

Opening ceremony of 1964 Soviet Union International championships in Moscow. From right: Koudelka, Kodes and Metreveli. I never dreamt then that I would meet Alex at the Wimbledon finals, nine years later.

The 1964 Pardubice Junior Championships confirmed its great significance in Kodes' tennis career. He achieved two titles there.

Newspaper headlines read: "Kodes unchallenged!" He ousted Laudin in the singles finals 6:3, 6:2, and with Lenka Rösslerova they defeated Marian Laudin – Helena Novakova from Pilsen 6:4, 6:3.

I won the Nationals at last and in no time I decided to quit soccer. It was at the moment when I was supposed to switch into the adult soccer league; I even made the cut and was invited to a camp of the selected Czech players, but I turned it down. I announced that I would definitely stick to tennis only!

FROM RIVIERA TO VICHY

The year 1965 did not begin as usual. A team of Holecek, Koudelka, Pala and Kodes traveled to a series of tournaments in the Italian Riviera under Frantisek Cejnar's guidance.

In tennis terms we gained enormously through this experience. At the same time we cut our dreary long winter shorter. We left Prague in February taking the train all the way to Sicily! We played in Salerno, Catania, and later in Sassari and Alghero in Sardinia, and we came across such tennis champs like Nicola Pilic and Martin Mulligan. We did not return home until the end of March or beginning of April. All this came about thanks to our success in Galea Cup competition two years previously. Had we not won in 1963 we would never have had these extra opportunities offered to us.

Jan Kodes was grateful to have Frantisek Cejnar as the team leader and mentor.

Though he was strict, he was also forthcoming. Unfortunately, he was not blessed to see our great achievements in the early 1970s. Only a few weeks after our return from Italy, on May 4, 1965, he succumbed to kidney ailment. He passed away at a young age of forty eight!

Jiri Javorsky returned to the Davis Cup team in 1965. Petr Strobl dropped out so our team roster was: Javorsky, Holecek, Koudelka, Kodes. Javorsky and Holecek played everything; Jan always played an exhibition against the opponents' fourth player after the conclusion of the doubles as a complementary addition to the program. And he always won....

At the Pilsen Nationals Jan lost to the later champion Milan Holecek in the semis. He reserved his best form for the Galea Cup. By then he was clearly in the number one position on the team, and the other team-mates were Laudin and Petr Stoces.

In the semifinal group in Athens we were first confronted by a Polish team. We upstaged them easily 4:1 and came across the host country's Greek team he-

Italian Riviera, Salerno. From left: Marco Girardelli, Vittorio Crotta, Frantisek Pala and Jan Kodes. In 1980 Czechoslovakia won the Davis Cup finals over Italy 4:1 in Prague and Crotta was the captain of the Italian team.

Prague, June 11-13, 1965 - Davis Cup Czechoslovakia vs. Italy 3:2.
From left: capt. Vasco Valerio, Beppe Merlo, Giordano Maioli,
Nicola Pietrangeli, Sergio Tacchini and M.D. Giorgio Santilli.

aded by the biggest star Nick Kalogeropoulos, the 1963 Wimbledon Junior Champion, and definitely one of the best European juniors. Their team was favored by all to win the Cup.

There was an odd omen that preceded the trip to Athens; something I did not pay any attention to at the time but when we brought the match under the hot Greek sun to the victorious finish and advanced to the finals in Vichy for the third time I recognized that as a sign of fate.

Before our departure I rode in a tramcar with my mom from Karlin to Namesti Republiky (National Square); just two stops from home. I carried a crystal vase in my bag as a souvenir for our opponents that all of us always brought along. As we were getting off the tram the vase mysteriously fell out and broke into pieces.

Mom promptly exclaimed: "That's for good luck! It is for sure that you'll advance to Vichy!"

And she was right! I saved one of the pieces and have it in my trophy case till this day!

The Czechoslovak tennis group deposited their suitcases in a hotel and hurried to see the courts. It was a dismal sight! Nine rectangles next to each other, no trees, no shade - only under the Umpire's Chair... The courts could have been placed in Prague on Letna with the addition of severe sun shining from above ....

The encounter reached the score 2:2. The last match was going to decide who would advance to the finals in Vichy. That fifth match was between Kodes and Kalogeropoulos; Jan received a "bagel" in the first set!

I was so freaking hot that I poured cold water over me. It was the first time I played in almost 40 degree Celsius heat (104 degrees Fahrenheit). I also played with a hat on for the first time which felt odd because I wasn't used to it.

Things turned around in the second set. The opponent slacked a bit and I started to play more aggressively thinking that there was nothing I should be afraid of at that point – there was not much I could lose; I evened the score to 1:1. In the decisive set the Greek was leading 5:3 and needed only two points to win the match.

Jan would never give anything without putting up a fight and he battled until the last point; that attitude stuck with him everywhere he played all over the world. He took a risk, attacked, approached the net and tied the

Beppe Merlo lost both his singles against
Milan Holecek and Jiri Javorsky.

Closing reception with the officials after our second victory in Vichy –1965.
From left: Kodes, capt. Tyra, G. Delort, President T.C. Vichy Chauchat, President FFT, R.Soisbault,
G.Pichard, Stoces and Laudin. On the trophy table is a picture of Mrs.Edmonde de Galea.

score! The Greek tensed up. During their change-over Jan came close to the bench, where his team-mates and team captain Dr. Tyra sat in a nervous stupor and through clenched teeth he uttered: "He is a goner now!"

I don't know what prompted me to say it. Maybe I needed to boost my own confidence and courage to approach the net. All of a sudden Kalogeropuolos seemed to have tensed up. He hit the balls late, his passing shots landed outside. It was evident that he lost steam in that heat. I won 7:5!

The fact that the team advanced into the Vichy final for the third time was an amazing triumph in itself. The Czechoslovak juniors first defeated the Hungarians and in the finals they faced the Soviets - again. Once more Jan Kodes came across Ivanov, who he defeated the year before. This time, however, he lost in a five set battle 5:7, 6:3, 6:3, 2:6, and 1:6, which was unexpected! He was cramping in his legs all through the last two sets.

However, Laudin defeated Vladimir Korotkov surprisingly 6:2, 6:0, and 9:7, and the following day the doubles team Kodes - Stoces overpowered Ivanov – Korotkov 6:3, 6:3, and 6:1, which created a situation for the third day when remaining singles matches would decide the overall winner. The first Sunday singles match decided the third crucial point: Kodes defeated Korotkov 6:3, 5:7, 7:5, 6:1. Czechoslovakia was thus leading 3:1 and Laudin's defeat 8:10, 2:6, 2:6 by Ivanov in the closing match did not alter the team's triumph.

At the end of 1965 tennis experts put together the European ranking of the best juniors and Jan Kodes' name appeared on

Score is: 2:2 – Kodes vs. Orantes. The result will decide who flys to Vichy for the finals.

Czechoslovak Nationals in Ostrava 1965. My volley in the air looks pretty good.

the third rung, after Kalogeropoulos and the Dutch Tom Okker. The Soviet Union's "Sport" placed him ninth among men, where the first spot was occupied by the Spaniard Manuel Santana, followed by the Swede Lundquist, the French Darmon and then Okker.

Since the maximum age for participation in Galea Cup was the age of twenty, Jan Kodes could have played it again in 1966. In the qualifying round in Pilsen the team confronted an immensely difficult opponent – Spain. The team was made up of Kodes, Laudin, and Medonos; the score was 1:1 after the first day singles. The key five set match was the Saturday doubles played by Kodes – Medonos. At set score 2:1 (3:6, 6:2, 6:3) play was suspended for darkness and resumed the next day. The conclusion was hugely dramatic and our team prevailed: 3:6, 7:5. Jan Kodes made the decisive third point when he defeated the outstanding Manuel Orantes 6:4, 3:6, 6:2, and Laudin beat Gustavo Guerrero 6:2, 5:7, 6:4 in the last singles match.

"Advancement over Spaniards hung mainly on one player and that was Jan Kodes", declared newspapers a day after the Czechoslovak team advanced into Vichy finals for the fourth time. After defeating England 4:1 the team encountered their biggest rival of the era – the USSR. That team was, however, short of Metreveli and so the match was clearly won by our juniors.

Reached the Galea Cup for the third time in 1966. From left: Jiri Medonos, Jan Kodes, capt. Ladislav Tyra and Marian Laudin.

I remember Vichy ever so fondly! I participated there four times and those were four amazing years. The local population almost considered me their good old friend. As soon as we arrived at the hotel I heard: "Well hello, monsieur Kodes, welcome back!" Naturally, it made me feel good, I felt a bit like on home turf.

Vichy was a beautiful spa town that reminded me of our Central Bohemian spa called Podebrady... in comparison, however, everything there was delightfully clean, manicured and looked after, the bushes were clipped and visitors found accommodation in an elegant De la Cloche hotel. Generally, when we traveled abroad, we ate in all kinds of Bistros, whereas here we ate in the hotel at a table that was designated just for us and our flag on top of it kept it reserved only for our group.

Our captain and leader of the team, Dr. Tyra, stressed on every occasion: "Do not dare come down to eat dressed in your sweat-suits and with flip-flops on. Always change and look decent!"

I remember him fondly; he spoke French flawlessly and he educated us in manners suitable to high society. When we won and attended the Champions' Dinner and celebration we had to wear a suit. It was the first time in my life that I had to dress up in the scope of an athletic endeavor so I brought along my black togs that I had used for ballroom dancing

Henri Cochet, five times Roland Garros champion.

L'artiste Kodes travaille une volée basse de coup droit.

KODES, L'ENCHAN-TEMENT DE VICHY

*D*ECIDEMENT, c'est aux jeunes de Tchécoslovaquie qu'il appartient de nous faire oublier à Vichy les absences de l'équipe française pendant les finales de la Coupe Galéa.

En 1963, Kléber Haedens s'était déclaré ici même enchanté par le talent de deux jeunes joueurs appelés Holecek et Koudelka. Les deux compères avaient enlevé la Coupe.

Cette année, c'est à un grand garçon blond et longiligne nommé Kodes, et dans une certaine mesure à son partenaire Laudin, que nous devons les meilleurs moments passés au début d'août sous les ombrages du Sporting Club de Vichy.

Kodes joua le dernier jour contre le Russe Korotkov, vainqueur de notre Goven en finale du tournoi juniors de Wimbledon, le match décisif de la finale Tchécoslovaquie-U.R.S.S. qui apporta aux Tchèques leur seconde victoire en trois ans dans la Coupe Galéa. A la puissance souvent désordonnée du petit bouledogue russe, Kodes opposa tout au long des quatre sets une finesse de toucher et une intelligence qui rappelaient le grand Hongrois Josef Asboth.

Kodes, impassible mais d'excellente humeur, trouvait aussi bien pour ses attaques que pour ses passing-shots des angles merveilleux qui finirent par mettre Korotkov à genoux au quatrième set. Le jeune Tchèque, s'il ne se laisse pas emporter par le tourbillon des voyages rémunérés et des faux succès, est capable de fournir au tennis international une personnalité qui sera fort bien venue au milieu des mécaniques australiennes.

Quant à Laudin, lui aussi vainqueur de Korotkov le premier jour, il est impossible de prévoir le joueur qu'il deviendra, tant son jeu est encore indiscipliné. Mais l'entrain de ce garçon filiforme, la manière féroce, pleine de toutes les audaces qu'il a d'attaquer toutes les balles, le plaisir évident qu'il prend à jouer au tennis en font un personnage intéressant et sympathique.

Korotkov, le plus doué des Russes, a paru bien souvent surpris devant Kodes par un jeu plus nuancé que le sien. Mais il faudra le suivre aussi attentivement.

Les Italiens Di Maso et Palmieri, eux, ont déçu et il ne faut sans doute pas en attendre plus que des jeunes Français, leurs victimes de Pedavena. Goven en tout cas pourra certainement prendre de jolies revanches.

Souhaitons-le à M. René Chauchat, l'excellent directeur du Sporting Club de Vichy et organisateur parfait de ces rencontres. Les Français qui ont déjà gagné cinq fois l'épreuve lui doivent de revenir au plus vite à Vichy.

— Philippe CHATRIER.

lessons in high school. There was no way I could come to Vichy without it.

When closing ceremony came about in the Casino ballroom we received a silver plaque designed by a famous French designer Boucheron and pictures were taken with the challenge trophy. What a difference it was in comparison to Russia or Tallinn. It was so evident here that tennis was a respected sport; in Russia it was considered little more than physical exercise. All of a sudden I realized that I was involved in a sport of value, sport that was ranked among top five most significant sports in the world. I also realized that it was a sport of the wealthy which gave it inherently a dash of snobbish and mighty breath.

Only years later I realized that, even at home, not everything was the way it ought to have been. The team coach, Jiri Parma, was left behind in Pilsen; he did not go along with us to Vichy. The organizers covered expenses of only four individuals – the captain and three players – our Tennis Federation could not, or would not, come up with money for the coach...

When Milan Holecek won the Czechoslovak Nationals in Pilsen in 1965 he said: "I am happy not only for my own triumph but also for the great achievements of the other younger players, namely Kodes and Laudin. I predict that they'll return from Vichy with the Galea Cup trophy." And he was right.

Jan Kodes holding the Galea Cup
for third time.

DAVIS CUP DEBUT

The years 1966 and 1967 represent a vital turning point in Jan Kodes' career. The former corresponded to Jan's reaching his premiere Czechoslovak tennis champion title, first time playing to represent the country in Davis Cup competition, the start of competing in men's Grand Slam tournaments, and first time conquering the doubles title in Bratislava together with Jiri Javorsky; he also transferred to Sparta Prague that year. In the latter he reached victories in several significant tournaments that assured him of entry onto the world major tennis scene.

During Christmas of 1965 he entered a junior tournament for players 20 years or younger called Coupe Michel Bivort in Paris for the first time. It was played on a very fast wooden surface and he defeated Patrick Hombergen from Belgium in the semifinals 6:4, 8:6, 16:18, 3:6, and 10:8. In the following year he succeeded in entering tournaments in which he confronted adult players of world significance. In the late sixties he reached the semifinals of the Swedish King's Cup team competition with his team-mates practically every year. His opponents were the likes of Jan Eric Lundquist from Sweden, the winner of the 1964 Italian Championships, Jan Leschly from Denmark the Wimbledon quarterfinalist, Jörgen Ulrich and others. In 1967 he even defeated the 1966 Wimbledon champion Manuel Santana!

The azure shoreline! Nice, Cannes, Monte Carlo, Aix en Provence. Formule One tunnel, swimming pools, casinos, Café de Paris, yachts docked in marinas. These were places that one was able to see only in movies with Brigitte Bardot, Sophia Loren, Alain Delon or Gérard Philipe. However, Jan took part in tournaments here many times during his career. He won in Nice and Monte Carlo the first time he came there to take part in tournaments of players under the age of twenty three. In the finals he defeated the Italian Giordano Maioli, several years his senior, with a fifth set "bagel"! He always loved that spectacular French nook. Most of all he loved Monte Carlo, the pearl of the Mediterranean coast and the host of one of the first annual clay-court tournaments in Europe. On the way to the finals he came across the Austrian Ernest Blanke. He beat him easily

1967 – King's Cup. Jan Kodes - Manuel Santana.

Czechoslovakia vs. Denmark 1966.
From left: Jan Kukal, Milan Holecek, František Pala, Jan Kodes, Jiri Rössler.

My 1966 debut with Austria in Bratislava. I found out that competing in the Davis Cup is very different from the other regular tournaments.

6:3, 6:0. At that point Jan had no idea that tennis fate was going to bring Ernest back his way a few weeks later under very different circumstances.

After his return home from Aix en Provence Jan found an envelope on the table from the Czechoslovak Union of Physical Education and Sport (CUPES). They informed him for the third time of the Davis Cup selection for the encounter against Austria in Bratislava! Somebody had kicked Milan Holecek during a soccer scrimmage and his Achilles tendon got partially torn. The non-playing team captain, Jiri Rössler, had no other choice but select a twenty-year-old Kodes beside Jiri Javorsky! The toss decided that Jan was going to play his premiere Davis Cup match as an opening match of the encounter. And it was, precisely, against Blanke!

Kodes abounded with optimism: "I'll take care of him three times 6:2! He had no chance against me in Monte Carlo." He did not yet know that a Davis Cup match felt differently from a regular tournament match. He was still immature and had no idea how much the responsibility of such an encounter immobilized one's hands and feet. He lost the first two sets 4:6, 3:6 and was down 1:3 in the third! It was very windy that day and Blanke dealt with it better than Davis Cup apprentice Kodes. In his mind Kodes insisted: "For God's sake, he can't go on like this for much longer; I must break him." He stopped messing up approach shots, calmed down, turned the match around and won. His amazing willpower and fighting spirit came to light already in that first Davis Cup match appearance.

Czechoslovakia defeated Austria 5:0, and subsequently they beat Israel in Prague with the same score. By then Antonin Bolardt replaced ailing Rössler as a non-playing captain.

Jan flew from Bratislava directly to Rome to take part in the Italian Championships. It was his first opportunity to measure his prowess against the World's best players. He defeated Francois Jauffret from France and Juan Gisbert from Spain, and then he came across Roy Emerson from Australia, the world number one amateur!

He had been my idol; I was a ball-boy at his court-side a few years before during an exhibition at Stvanice. On the Centre Court in Rome he made me realize that I might be a promising junior but, presently, I had much to learn to enter the men's world competition. He gave me a true lesson: 6:2, 6:4, 6:0! He rolled over me in all aspects. His shots were more penetrating, his strokes precise; I was under constant pressure that did not ease even for a moment. He

With Frantisek Pala in Vatican City.

kept on attacking, his net play was excellent. He showed me what to expect at world level of tennis. That defeat illuminated me; I began to apply myself in practice much more!

More matches against the tennis "giants" followed. In the semifinals of Czechoslovak International Championships in Prague Jan opposed the future champion, Tony Roche, in the semifinals. He lost in four sets. At Roland Garros in Paris he played two five-set matches; one against the Yugoslavian Zeljko Franulovic, the second against Ilie Nastase from Romania.

Besides his premiere Davis Cup match in 1966 Kodes participated also in his first main draw of Wimbledon. The draw was not kind to him as he came across seeded Cliff Drysdale from South Africa in the first round. Cliff later reached the semifinals there.

In the third round of Davis Cup competition we received a real treat – we played very favored France in Paris! The home team had a very strong team of Pierre Darmon and Francois Jauffret, who were among the European tennis elite. They did not doubt their victory even for a second. Javorsky and Kodes stood on the opposite side, Holecek was still recuperating from his Achilles tendon injury. Frantisek Pala was nominated

After two victories on Foro Italico I received a lesson from the best player in the world, Roy Emerson.

Davis Cup vs. France in Paris 1966. Francois Jauffret beat me from two sets down. This match started my career at Roland Garros.

to take the third position on the team. The local press disclosed that the French were definitely the favorites but should watch out for young Kodes!

Javorsky was even with Jauffret at 1:1 in sets but the Frenchman dominated the court to win the next two sets and the match. Kodes played a very good match with Darmon but lost in four sets. After the first day the score was 0:2 and the French expected a sure victory that should be sealed by the doubles on Saturday.

The team Patrice Beust – Daniel Contet were among the European top doubles players. In today's terminology we would say that they were doubles specialists. They won the first two sets against me and Javorsky 10:8, 7:5. However, they underestimated the further development of the match and after four hours and another three sets they left the court with their heads bowed. We won the last three sets 6:3, 6:4, and 6:2 and that was a real shock for them! They did not expect that at all!

On the third day animated Kodes was the first one to take the court against Jauffret.

"We are going to win! You'll see that we'll win. I'll knock out Jauffret; after all, I beat him in Rome. Then Jiri will finish off Darmon" hollered Jan in the changing room after their doubles victory. However, Jauffret was a very smart player. He was a difficult-to-conquer champion, particularly on clay and at home. A few days before the Davis Cup started he defeated Roy Emerson at Roland Garros and advanced all the way to the semifinals!

Kodes entered the court like a hurricane and whatever he touched reaped him points. He was demolishing his opponent with precisely placed drives that landed deep in the court and imposed pressure. He won the first two sets 6:3, 6:1! But, the game is not over until the Umpire calls "game-set-match, Kodes!" There is no wonder that after a few controversial line-calls the match with Jauffret turned out differently than what Kodes had imagined.

I was quickly in 3:0 lead in the third set and, theoretically, I needed only three more games to win the match. However, I suddenly felt weary. Something went haywire and I was getting to the balls late. The heat was intense and I sensed I couldn't take it any longer. Jauffret was like a rebounding wall; he sent me from one side of the court to the other. I had a game-point at 3:0 to be ahead 4:0. I knew I needed that game or I would be in trouble! My put-away shot landed four inches inside the court but was called out! Instead of a game in my favor the game was at deuce!

I protested. The crowd whistled – they were on my side! I felt like crying, and the Chief Umpire, Willy Baumeister from Switzerland, called "repeat", first serve! In those times the rules suggested playing the point over when a line-call was disputed. I was still rattled since my shot had been so clearly in and I lost the next two points and then the third set.

The game turned around. Kodes fought; he was not willing to give up, but his shots were losing power. In the tenth game of the fifth set the Frenchman was ahead 5:4. Kodes served three excellent serves and had an "ad" to tie the score at 5:5. However, the previous unsettling situation as if repeated itself. Kodes' good put away volley was called out. The umpire rose from the chair as if he wanted to see better the imprint in the battered surface; he did not find it and let the call stick. The game was back to deuce...

At that I started to cry by the net-post, I fumed and I felt totally helpless. It was all futile! I lost the next two points and the match was over. The umpire announced "Game, set, match – Jauffret 3:6, 1:6, 6:3, 6:4, 6:4,".

I was crying inconsolably when approaching to shake hands with my opponent. Jiri Javorsky ran onto the court to console me: "Don't worry, Jan; I would not be able to beat Darmon at 2:2, so we have no chance of winning anyway." So, that is how my first great Davis Cup encounter finished.

A crowd of ten thousand fans, a tremendous match, disgruntled scenes with umpires. Entrance onto the world tennis scene with everything included! Kodes, the "hero" of the day, was lying on the massage table, humbled and mentally spent. The crowd applause and the sound of chant "Kodes, Kodes" were fading away. On the other hand, jeer for the home player leaving the court was a weak consolation...

I realized that my performance in Paris that year was not great. Nastase beat me in the second round of the French Championships and during the Davis cup match I was the center of controversy related to line-calls. It did not occur to me then that I would return to the city upon Seine with such pleasure many times over.

The impressive face-off between Jauffret and Kodes will be discussed for a long time... Roland Garros witnessed a tense but exciting battle between two players who surpassed each other in courage, prowess, and immense heart. It could not have been easy for young Jan Kodes to play an important match on a court in foreign atmosphere. He was ahead 2:0 in sets delivering an impressive performance but lost, eventually, after a faulty call at 4:5 in the fifth set. It was a display of willpower and responsibility to the team that Roland Garros never before experienced. Undoubtedly, Paris has discovered a great future player in this twenty-year-old youngster from Prague. Bravo, Kodes, for the valor you exhibited in the match! We mustn't forget that the result is not just an athletic expression but also a proof of courage, will, and work ethics that he demonstrated for three hours in the "hot furnace"; those are the traits that define one's character in life... In the minds of the Parisians the visitors' team won but did not advance...

Judith Elian, L'Equipe

L'arbitre du K.O...DES
(Dessin de Luc Vincent.)

**French press joked
with their umpires.**

My first experience at Wimbledon in 1966: Court No: 2 - seeded Cliff Drysdale gave me a lesson in the opening round and went on to reach the semifinals.

At the Nationals in Ostrava he confirmed his position as a probable best European Junior, even when playing adult tournaments. In the finals he defeated a local player, Milan Necas, and with that he commenced his twelve-year long domination in Czechoslovak tennis. Only in 1978 he was "de-throned" by then eighteen-year-old Ivan Lendl, the world's best junior.

In August of 1966 Kodes competed successfully the fourth and the last time in Galea Cup. At the end of that year he won easily the Coupe Michele Bivort in Paris whipping the great French up-and-comer Chanfreau in the finals. His prestige and popularity in the land of Gallic rooster intensified. After the Ostrava Nationals a long time anticipated event took place – Jan Kodes transferred from Stvanice to Sparta Prague!

After winning our Nationals in Ostrava over Milan Necas 0:6, 6:3, 6:2, 6:3.

I. CLTK appealed the transfer and fought for me to stay but there were several outside reasons for this move. Besides the fact that Sparta helped me get admitted to a Secondary School and then to the University there was another very strong reason why I agreed to the transfer - my father.

Sparta officials "hit on" Jan Kodes at the right moment: "We'll give you an apartment!" He later received only a little money from them and had to look for and buy an apartment himself!

I vacillated for a long time but, in the end, I said to them: "Ok; I'll transfer to your club but you must arrange for my dad to return to administration and law practice the way he had always done!" It took time but they did take care of it. At last my dad left laboring in the CKD Dukla factory and commenced working in the law department of Sparta at Letna. It was an unbelievable victory for me, for I had felt immense debt toward my dad. This eased the guilt.

After winning Czechoslovak Nationals title in 1966 Jan Kodes held the number one position in his country for twelve years till 1977. His crown was taken by Ivan Lendl in 1978 at Ostrava.

A.C. Sparta Prague – in front of the old soccer stand at Letna, the tennis section founders!

SPARTA

Tennis Club Sparta was founded in 1905 as the third tennis club in Prague, after I. CLTK (1893) and LTC Prague (1904). Just like in the preceding two clubs tennis in Sparta came along as the third sport after soccer and ice hockey. The courts were located at Letna; they were part of the same premises as the soccer stadium next door. After the 1st World War tennis hardly survived in the Czech Lands. It boomed again after 1920 when famous Karel Kozeluh entered the scene. He reached the biggest achievements after 1926 when he won Bristol Cup, the Professional Championships that he won six times by 1932. In that same year he played a memorable exhibition with Bill Tilden on the AC Sparta soccer field at Letna. Kozeluh lost in

At Karel Kozeluh invitation, the legendary William "Bill" Tilden appeared at Letna Sparta soccker field in 1932.

front of fifteen thousand spectators 6:4, 2:6, 2:6, 3:6. His celebrity status lasted till 1935.

After the second World War tennis in Sparta did not rebound until 1950, when the club moved to Prague's Stromovka, where it is located till this day. In 1951 the tennis club Meteor 8 – Lodenice merged with Sparta and that brought in several excellent players. That year Sparta won the championship title under the name Spartak Prague Sokolovo. Simultaneously, Vladimir Zabrodsky and Vlasta Holeckova, Milan Holecek's mother, reached the championship titles in singles. The best player in Sparta in that time period was Richard Schonborn, who won the Czechoslovak National Championship title in 1959. The dominant female players were Jitka Horcickova-Volavkova, the world collegiate champion in 1961 and 1963 and three-time the National singles Champion in 1964-96, and Jana Dvorackova-Volkova.

In the course of decades many outstanding players passed through Sparta Club as members; several of these players entered the

Karel Kozeluh (center) as a Davis Cup coach with Jaroslav Drobny (left) and Vladimir Zabrodsky at Stvanice in 1948.

Czechoslovak as well as the world tennis history. Besides Jan Kodes, who was loyal to Sparta's colors for thirteen years, it was particularly Frantisek Pala, Martina Navratilova, Renata Tomanova and also Hana Mandlikova, Helena Sukova, and others. During that time the ex-Davis Cup player Josef Caska worked there as a coach.

In the exceptionally important year of 1967 Jan reached many victories but faced also some defeats. At the start of the season he won an indoor tournament in Lyon on very fast wooden surface. In Aix en Provence he lost in the finals to Alex Metreveli quite easily in four sets 6:4 4:6, 2:6, and 2:6.

I received a trophy that I never really liked. The most likely reason was remembering the defeat in the final. Six years later, when I returned from Wimbledon 1973 with my Championship title, there was a junior tournament in Sparta and the organizers asked me if I could donate something for the winner. During the closing and award ceremony I presented thirteen-year old Ivan Lendl with that silver cup.

The following week he swept the Romanian Nastase off the court 6:0, 6:1 in Cannes! But then he endured a defeat at home in Davis Cup against Chile. Dr. Jiri Rössler returned into the position of a non-playing captain and Milan Holecek was back in good health. The team consisted of Holecek, Kukal, Koudelka, Kodes.

Holecek lost to Jaime Pinto Bravo 3:6, 2:6,

Richard Schonborn won the Czechoslovak Nationals in 1959. Become succesful coach for German Federation (DTB), working as lector with ITF.

French Riviera: Finals at Cannes: Nastase – Kodes.

Roland Garros 1967. After I lost in the fourth round to number one seed Tony Roche in five sets, Henri Cochet predicted a great future for me.

1:6 and Kodes to Pato Rodriguez in five sets. At 0:2 we won doubles 6:1, 6:4, 6:3 and then Kodes evened the score to 2:2 defeating Pinto Bravo 6:2, 6:2, 6:3. Milan Holecek had two match-points against Rodriguez at 6:5 and 40:15 in the fifth! Unfortunately, he did not turn any into a match won and we lost 2:3. For a long time, exactly for nineteen years, this was the last Davis Cup defeat we suffered at home... the next one came in October 1986 when the Swedes defeated us in Prague at the new Stvanice Center 4:1.

After the encounter with Chile Kodes traveled to Sardinia, where he defeated Niki Pilic from Yugoslavia for the first time but lost badly to Martin Mulligan from Australia. After two successful rounds in Rome the following week he lost again to an Australian; this time it was to Bob Hewitt.

The year 1967 was kind of strange; it was an important year for me since I transferred from junior competition to men's. I did not expect much and for that reason my realization that I had the arsenal to play against the best players in the world was that much more surprising. However, my physical condition was not up to par yet; some matches were physically much too challenging.

In order to reach the sixteens in my second Roland Garros show-down I had to win three matches. I defeated Ingo Buding from Germany, then Robert Maud from South Africa, and in the third round I avenged my loss to Ilie Nastase from the previous year. I lost only to the second seed, Tony Roche, in front of a packed Centre Court after a physically intensive battle 4:6, 2:6, 10:8, 6:2, and 4:6!

It was here, where I experienced the Grand Slam atmosphere to the fullest for the first time. I realized that there was something special about it. It lasted for two weeks, each match was best of five sets – the results carried more significance than from the other tournaments!

One of the most famous French tennis players of all times, Henri Cochet, who was considered one of the tennis musketeers, approached Kodes after the five-set defeat by Tony Roche at Roland Garros and said: "My friend, you made me very happy. Your game is complete and resolute. You will reach the group of the best players in the world. You just need to learn to play more economically in the matches here, at Roland Garros and make more frequent use of your underspin backhand. Otherwise it will be difficult to withstand it physically.

Ceskoslovensky sport – Czechoslovak press

Philippe Chatrier also completed a very significant tennis chapter that year. He became the French Tennis Association president

I lost to Alex Metreveli in the finals and received the Cup from the TC President Aix en Provence Miguel Guérin. President FFT Roger Cirotteau (right).

We had to treat each other according to the rules. Not like today!

Six years later, thirteen year old, Ivan Lendl won my Cup from Aix en Provence. . Picture: Jan Kodes giving the Cup to Ivan Lendl in July 1973.

and right from the start he intended to inscribe himself into the world tennis awareness. He organized a tennis gathering and a work-out camp of sorts of several of the world's best players. This took place outside of Paris on the grass courts of Chantilly Club du Lis between the Roland Garros and Wimbledon championships. Naturally, the top French players Jauffret and Darmon were among the invited players in addition to Emerson, Pietrangeli, Pasarell, Pilic, Ulrich, Mukerjea, and from the "Eastern bloc" Nastase and Kodes!

The week full of conditioning and scrimmage matches was fantastic! For me, a twenty-one year old youngster, it was a dream come true to play and practice with the world top players. An amazing school! Philippe Chatrier knew well why he invited me and Nastase. We also played doubles together. He was sharp and had a foresight that our presence could bring him votes from the "Eastern Bloc" countries in the future, when he climbed the ladder in international tennis. At the time of the Iron Curtain separating the East and West this was an incredibly smart move. And, it paid off: a few years later he became the President of the International Tennis Federation known as the ITF.

In spite of good preparation on grass Kodes still lost the first day of the traditional Wimbledon Championship on court number one to the fourth seeded, Tony Roche, 6:4, 1:6, 2:6, and 6:8.

However, he avenged his previous year loss to Ion Tiriac from Romania at the International Championships in Bratislava and was delighted to win in four 1:6, 13:11, 6:1, and 6:2. Without losing a set he won the Nationals in Pilsen defeating Milan Holecek in the finals and, in addition, also winning the mixed doubles together with his sister Vlasta!

From a developmental perspective 1967 was, most definitely, Jan Kodes' break-through year. In the close of the year he won singles as well as doubles in a prestigious junior tournament under twenty, Trofeo Bonfiglio in Milan, defeating Robert Maud from South Africa in the finals. After his victory in Luxemburg he also played Coupe Porée that was a very prestigious French Club men's tournament. It took place in the famous Racing Club de France in the Parisian park Bolognese. However, he got whipped in the finals by Darmon who played with a new metal Lacoste racket!

Considering his young age Jan had gathered quite a few accomplishments by this date. They were not Grand Slam tournament titles but there have been a few titles of high significance. At the level of the tenth place in Europe, where he was ranked by tennis journalists, he carried out one feat more that year. He got married in December of 1967. His tennis and mixed-doubles partner, Lenka Rösslerova, became his wife.

René Lacoste – "the crocodile" was one of: "all time greats".

Coupe Porée. Pierre Darmon and his Lacoste "steel racket".

"Spaghetti" stringing racket was abolished by ITF.

My first international victory at Lyon. Cozon Cup was played on a very fast wooden surface and I surprisingly won over Jan Kukal 4:6, 6:1, 8:6. President TC Lyon, Mr.M.Frachon with his wife.

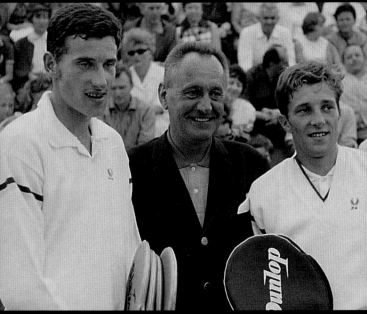

Pilsen 1967- I won my second Nationals over Milan Holecek (left). With my coach Josef Caska, who also played at Wimbledon in 1935-36 and represented Czechoslovakia in Davis Cup several times during period of 1935-1946.

My sister Vlasta won all three 1967 National titles – singles, doubles and mixed doubles! We only ever played „mixed"together once and won over Milan Necas – Olga Lendlova in the finals.

OVER THE ATLANTIC

Till 1968 Jan Kodes' tennis endeavors took place exclusively within Europe and especially in countries of the Eastern Bloc. Within the Czechoslovak tennis community professionals began to speak up about the importance of winter preparation and the prospect of playing in warm climates.

Our winter conditions were disastrous. There was only one indoor hall at Klamovka in Prague to satisfy almost the entire country; we had to fight to be allotted practice hours; to play two times a day was out of the question. I was assigned two hours daily and that was it. In addition I did conditioning, took long distance runs, and played little soccer, all of it outdoors in the snow and in freezing temperatures.

In those times one could not travel westwards out of the country without an invitation from the host country. The Tennis Federation was able to cover a certain number of trips that would be financed by the CUPES (Czechoslovak Union of Physical Education and Sport). Each sport had foreign currency allowance and it was difficult to add extra tournaments to the program that would cause the budget go beyond its limits.

Obviously, there was no problem adding tournaments in the East. That did not require hard currency spending because we used so called reciprocity system. Things were far more complicated when we wanted to travel to the West. Jan Kukal took initiative into his hands. He kept stressing that we had to think up a way to get out and play in the West. Ultimately we sent out personal letters to several tennis associations around the world asking them to send us an invitation via our Tennis Federation.

One of the first invitations came from India.

We found out about that possibility from the Russians during a tournament in Moscow. Metreveli played in India regularly, and besides that he also traveled to Australia annually where he played four tournaments. Upon our return home we broached the topic of possible entry in those tournaments....

"Australia? Forget that! We don't have money for the plane tickets; impossible!"

How come that it was possible in Russia? Metreveli entered the Australian tournaments already two or three years in a row!

In a long last we also succeeded in doing just that. Thanks to Kukal's initiative we found ourselves on board of a plane heading to India on January 7, 1968 ...

In the course of a month the Indians, Russians, Romanians, and Czechs played three tournaments – in New Delhi, Bombay and Bangalore. The team of India frequently reached advanced rounds in Davis Cup throughout those years.

Wimbledon semi-finalist Ramanhatan Krishnan was part of the Indian's team. We battled each other over and over again but it

Our dream was to play and practice in hot weather during our heavy winter at home. Kodes-Kukal (front).

was a fantastic experience especially since we played on different surfaces. We did not come across the European red clay at all but we had the benefit to "enjoy" plenty of hardpacked clay or grass surface with bad bounces.

Only in New Delhi the grass courts were superb and the lawn was cut evenly looking like a large tabletop. I lost to Lall there 3:6, 1:6, 8:10. In Bombay we practiced on a court that reminded us of red clay as long as it was watered, which did not last long. The searing sun dried the court in minutes causing the surface turn parched; at that point smoke started to rise emitting horrible smell.

After that practice I found out that the surface was a mixture of sand, cement and – cow dung! They mixed it all together and rolled it hard. Nice firm surface! However, as it dried up it not only released that ghastly smell but also became terribly slippery. In a matter of a few minutes the ball started to bounce totally differently.

After two wins in Bombay I lost to Alex Metreveli 4:6, 6:3, 1:6.

Everything was different in Bangalore that was situated in higher altitude. The courts were softer and resembled clay the most; however they got mangled up during long-lasting matches. And so it happened that on my set-point a ball landed in front of me but it did not bounce up! It got buried in that muddle. I was beside myself, I swore and I declared that it was impossible to play on such a court. It was an amazing stress on my nerves but an invaluable preparation for the future. What a lesson to learn in overcoming adverse and uncontrollable circumstances, bad luck, or some "player's misfortune", that lurked at me on the courts. And what awaited us away from the courts? - Very strong sun and horrific heat that was only some-times softened by breeze. What else could have befallen us?

I played two five setters in Bangalore beating Premjit Lall 3:6, 6:1, 8:6, 2:6, 6:3 and losing to Tiriac 6:3, 4:6, 0:6, 6:4, and 1:6 in the quarters.

CARIBBEAN CIRCUIT

There were two local television reporters in the arrival hall of the Salisbury airport. They came to meet two tennis ambassadors from a Central European country – Jan Kodes and Jan Kukal. "We want to introduce you to our public as representatives of a country that will parti-cipate in the United States Indoor Championships for the first time" they explained.

It was February 1968 and freezing cold outside.

At the same time, Josef Rehak, who also turned out to be a chairman of the tennis associa-tion for a brief period of time, was taking a seat as a new Minister of Education and Culture in Prague. And it was he who inspired positive atmosphere and tendencies in Czech tennis.

"We must send our chaps somewhere outside the country!" Though the association had a limited budget he announced resolutely "I'll pay for plane tickets to the United States for two players and take it from the funds of the Ministry!"

Soon after their return from India the twosome Kodes – Kukal were allowed to fly in the opposite direction, to the United States and the so called Caribbean Circuit.

At its origin was the promoter Bill Riordan who organized several indoor tournaments on the East Coast of the United States and negotiated a follow-up with the countries of the Carib-bean region.

It was Jan Kukal who had his hand in the fact that we got invited. He had written to Rior-dan that three of us would like to come. The two of us as the top two players of the country, plus Milan Holecek. Riordan answered that he could take on two and would be able to give us no more than $100 pocket money per week. Room and board would be taken care of.

Salisbury, where the US Indoor Championship took place, was a small town in Maryland. The indoor facility of the university's athletic complex was able to house four thousand spectators; the entries represented the best European and American players. The surface? Canvas top! By this time Jan had played on just about any surface there was but on canvas top?

"Who has never played on this will not fare well" forecasted an experienced Hungarian Istvan Gulyas, who was obviously amused when he watched the two of us stare in disbelief at the surface.

The curtain that is customarily hung on the fence behind the court was laid down on the court; there were small eye-loops on the sides through which they stretched out ropes and tied them to brackets. That secured the full tension; there was wooden floor underneath - in later years I came to witness even concrete covered by the canvas top. At any rate, it was an awfully fast surface.

However, we had had a good preparation from Europe. Within the scope of the Swedish King's Cup we had played on wood many times! The only difference was in the fact that on wood or parquet the foot somewhat gave way a little and was able to slide, whereas here it tucked. The shoe did not budge; we had to tread out softly each ball, run it out with tiny steps because we could not slide into it like on clay. And that we were not accustomed to.

It did not occur to Kodes then that he would use this experience in his favor a couple of years later on grass during the biggest and most important matches of his career at Forest Hills and Wimbledon.

Jan Kukal got to play against the top US player, of the time it was Charlie Pasarell from Puerto Rico. Kukal's serve was ferocious; Pasarell did not know him and since returning serves on this surface was tricky he experienced great difficulties. In the end Pasarell defeated Kukal, I think the final score was 6:4 in the third set, but it was an absolutely even-leveled match.

Luck of the draw put me to play Tom Edlefsen, the sixth top US player. I lost 5:7. 2:6; I played abominably.

As I was packing my stuff after the match and was about to depart from the court a fellow approached me and said: "Kodes and Kukal you are to go to Bill Riordan's office at once!"

What does he want?

We sat down; Bill was looking at us meaningfully before he said: "I watched your games; you played fantastic. I had no idea that you would play this well! So, I raise your pocket money to two hundred and fifty! And, in Central America, you'll get three hundred dollars a week!"

He was totally ecstatic while I felt I played under the weather! Most likely he had imagined that since we were Czech we did not know much. It was true that the Americans did not yet know the level of quality of European players. One of the invited European players was Mike Hickey from Ireland who lost double 6:0 and they must have deduced from that that all Europeans play at such level.

But, Riordan was a clever man. For one, he wanted to have players from all European countries playing the circuit, and secondly, he always tried to invite the best players. However, he had no experience with players from behind the "Iron Curtain". Jan Kukal knew well why he had written "first and second players of Czechoslovakia"...

Life on a tennis circuit is a nomadic life. Each week players are somewhere else. Macon in Georgia, Kingston in Jamaica, Barranquilla in Columbia, and then Caracas, heading for the Dutch Antilles and Curacao, a city that Kodes and Kukal recognized only from the well-known liqueur labels, if that.

Constantly on the move – unpack, get your tennis gear ready, go running, stretch, on-court practice, laundry, pack up and go on.

Bill Riordan arranged our living with local families, thus we always headed from the plane directly to the airport hall and there we found a flyer that told us where and with whom we were going to be put up. We were then escorted to the respective homes. After a few days we came to an understanding why Riordan arranged it this way. First of all, it was more economical since he did not have to pay for hotels but, above all, the Americans were very interested in housing "somebody" from the Eastern countries.

Arriving in Kingston, Jamaica. Mark Cox, Jan Kukal, Jan Kodes, Istvan Gulyas, Mike Sangster, Zeljko Franulovic, Boro Jovanovic, Manuel Orantes, Ingo Buding and Jose-Luis Arilla.

For them we were "exotic" and they tried to exceed each other in who had who. Some preferred housing exclusively the Czechs, others the Russians or the Hungarians. They enjoyed the "contest"; we felt a bit uncomfortable. We had no privacy and little time to rest since our hosts liked chatting with us and constantly asked about everything from "behind the Iron Curtain".

At the same time, it also offered something positive - we were getting to know the life in America. We realized how much time kids spent in front of their television sets, ate hotdogs and hamburgers, and stuffed themselves with popcorn drinking lots of Coca-Cola. We noticed that parents did not pass much time parenting, they had babysitters to do that who did not attend to the kids the way we were used to in our country.

Jan Kodes played the tournament series in the United States and the Caribbean Circuit three times in the years 1968-1970. The first year was somewhat difficult; in spite of it he delivered surprises when he defeated the second British top player R. K. Wilson and, in Caracas, the second seeded Australian Bill Bowrey. Later they won also doubles with Jan Kukal.

By that time we were well seasoned players and organizers were really interested in us. The Caribbean Circuit was very beneficial for us particularly thanks to the weather. We played tennis and at the same time we worked on our overall physical condition. We swam and went running.

Jan Kukal bossed me about and pestered me to work out even when we came against each other. He pressured me to constantly train and improve and thus prepare for the main European season. We also befriended many other players. Though we were rivals on court and exuded some very prestigious battles, when the games were over we often loosened up together with a light jog or swim in the hotel pool. And we always traveled together because even those who lost in the first rounds stayed around till the end of a tournament and practiced.

The entire circuit – the indoor tournaments in the USA followed by the Caribbean Circuit – was very demanding. It required a very strong physical constitution and it also demanded the ability to adjust quickly to varying climatic conditions.

From the airport hall we were transported to the open courts; from pleasant 20 degrees centigrade we switched almost to 40 in a period of forty-eight hours. Humidity was 80 percent. When you disembark from a plane in Caracas, for instance, you are drenched in sweat in no time. You feel like you are in a green house but you have to play tennis in it! However, it offered one great advantage in the following years; if I played the prestigious tournament in Rome after a month or a month and a half in the Caribbean region the temperature of "only" 30 degrees did not bother me.

The other difficult things to get used to were the ever changing types of surfaces.

Besides the tarp I had to get used to other types of surfaces during the two-months stay on the other side of the "Big Puddle" (the Atlantic); I had to adjust to carpet, rubber, concrete, grass and from time to time also to clay, meaning the American green-grey sandy clay. The classical red clay we found only in Columbia.

Usually it was very difficult to find an opportunity to practice on the new surface. We simply arrived one day and played the next. The day before yesterday I finished playing on clay that I was, fortunately, used to from home; today I play on a carpet, from which the balls bounce up so fast that I barely manage to raise my racket in time. On such surface a player must change the game style. One has to shorten the backswing in order to strike the ball in front of the body. It is not advisable to play from the base line to prepare the ball to attack and approach the net the way one would do on clay; here it is necessary to attack at once and do so always: serve, approach, volley and put away! Without a well placed serve a player has no chance to succeed on fast surface.

With time Jan Kodes managed to adapt to all surfaces. He also learned how to anticipate the line of the flight of a ball in windy conditions, a situation that he never favored and which players even of today dislike. Kodes utilized his experiences of playing on these fast surfaces like concrete and grass and turned them into a habit that proved essential for his later success in the most important tournaments of his career.

Fast surfaces make a player move faster; he must meet the ball in time! I gained this skill on American courts and every time I returned home I felt like a different player. I ran faster and with more ease, and I arrived at the balls in time without getting much tired.

The duo Kodes-Kukal made a good name for them right away as they played the circuit for the first time in 1968, mainly by reaching the finals in doubles in Curacao.

The match finished after mid-night, we lost to Okker - Riessen 3:6, 8:10 and at four in the morning we packed up and hurried to the airport. I was exhausted but the plane for New York was not going to wait for me. On board of the plane there was just about everybody we had met for the first time in Salisbury five weeks earlier. We were all tired...

After seven hours on the plane we switched from tropical heat and clean air to freezing temperatures and smog-filled metropolis. And from the airport we drove directly to Madison Square Garden! No official ever wanted to entertain an idea of postponing the matches. Only two hours after landing at Kennedy Airport Kodes was standing again on a tennis court. Less than seventeen hours since the last match and after three hours of restless sleep he was met by one of his idols, the Australian Roy Emerson.

It was my first appearance at Madison Square Garden and I received a lesson number two there from Roy: 1:6, 2:6. This time it was indoors.

Following the first round defeat Jan Kodes took advantage of the free time to rest and to do some serious sightseeing, and after a few days he flew to San Juan, Puerto Rico, along with Jan Kukal.

That was a nice tournament where I managed to reach the semifinals. But the event that was even more important was the fact that we met our best chess Czech player Ludek Pach-man there. We chatted with him for the longest time and he asked many questions about all kinds of things including our opportunities to compete abroad, the size of our pocket money, and we told him everything...

In those times people in the developed countries started discussing candidly the issue of "open" tennis. The fundamental problem lied in the fact that besides the group of amateurs like Kodes, Kukal and other Czechoslovak players, and, coincidentally, also Roy Emerson

Arthur Ashe remains the only African American ever to attain the No. 1 ranking on the men´s tour. With a powerful serve-and-volley game he won three GS singles titles: US Open in 1968, Australian Open in 1970 and Wimbledon in 1975.

Kodes, Cox Gain Semis

By JIM DOUGLAS
STAR Sports Editor

Vicky Rogers and Tom Edlefsen of the United States, who posted notable upsets over Australian seeds in the second round, were themselves beaten in the quarter finals of the 16th Caribe Hilton Internatiinal Tennis Tournament Thursday.

With the battle lines for the semifinals just about set, Valerie Ziegenfuss, No. 11 in the U.S. knocked off Miss Rogers, No 10, 6-3, 7-5.

Mark Cox, No. 1 in England, surprised Edlefsen, 6-3, 6-4, to be the first to reach the men's semifinals. He was followed by Jan Kodes, No. 1 in Czechoslovakia, who defeated Hungary's Istvan Gulyas, ninth in the world, 6-4, 6-3.

TODAY'S MATCHES

Today's matches are:

1:30 p.m.—Richey vs. Niessen, quarter final.
2:30—Harter vs. Ziegenfuss, semifinal.
3:30—Holmberg vs. McManus, quarter final.
4:30—Fox vs. Franulovic, quarter final.
5:30—Edlefsen-Gulyas vs. Sangster-Cox, quarter final.
6:30—Tegart-Bowery vs. Bartkowicz-Tuero, semifinals.
7:30—Bowery-Ruffels vs. Belkin-Budding, semifinal.
8:30—Franulovic-Jovanovic vs. Kukal-Kodes, quarter final.
9:30—Richey-Ziegenfuss vs. Harter-De Fina, semifinal.

Earlier Miss Rogers had upset second-seeded Lesley Turner Bowery while Edlefsen had ousted top-seeded Bill Bowrey.

Miss Ziegenfuss, who played beautiful tennis to eliminate the left-handed Miss Rogers was joined by Kathy Harter, No. 9 in the U.S. and third-seeded Judy Tegart of Australia in the semifinals.

Miss Harter, who will now meet Miss Ziegnfuss, upset a slow Peaches Bartowicz, fifth seed from the U.S., 6-2, 6-2. Miss Tegart defeated 17-year-old Linda Tuero of the U.S... 6-3, 6-4.

The final seminal encounter will pit Miss Tegart against the winner of the match today between top-seeded Nancy Richey of the U.S. and unseeded Helga Niessen of Germany.

Thursday Miss Richey defeated Sweden's Christina Sandberg, 6-0, 6-1, while Miss Niessen beat Stephanie De Fina of the U.S., 8-6, 6-1.

The men's singles finals shape up thusly:

Kodes vs. winner of fourth-seeded Alan Fox, U.S., and sixth-seeded Zeljko Franulovic Yugoslavia, and Cox vs. the winner third-seeded Ron Holmberg and unseeded Jim McManus both of the U.S.

McManus Thursday completed the quarter finals with a 6-2, 6-3 triumph over Jan Kukal of Czechoslovakia.

In women's doubles quarter finals, top-seeded Tegart-Bowery def. Puerto Rico's Shoengold-Bertran, 6-0, 6-0.

(See TENNIS, Page 54)

the San Juan Star

San Juan, Puerto Rico, Friday, April 5, 1968.

for whom the New York tournament was his farewell to amateur tennis, there also existed a group of professionals led by Jack Kramer.

The first open tournament that was entered by both, amateurs and professionals, was played in English Bournemouth in 1968; afterwards the best players entered the international championships in Paris and at Wimbledon.

At the start there were many contradicting opinions relating to this issue. It was mainly the Brits and the French who encouraged open tennis, the Americans were opposed to it. For a long time representatives of individual countries did not have a clear picture of what was going on or how things should operate.

The situation became rather absurd. Athur Ashe won the 1968 US Open at Forest Hills when he defeated the Dutch Tom Okker in a five set battle. At that time Ashe was a university student and could not accept prize money for his victory or he would have gotten expelled from the university. However, he was given the prize on the side deposited into a special account with an understanding that he would not cash the money before he finished the university.

The first prize went to Tom Okker as a defeated finalist!

So, it was not yet pure professionalism but the first steps have been taken toward opening the field to all. The entire situation was helped by the surprising victory of Mark Cox, a British Davis Cup player, over Pancho Gonzales, a member of Jack Kramer's professional group in the "Premier of the Open" in Bournemouth. A few weeks before that Emerson, an amateur, had defeated Laver, a professional! Until that time everybody believed that the professional players were superior to the amateurs and, suddenly, reality proved that such differences might not be there and it would be a good idea to let the players play it out.

This controversy was further stimulated up by an article by Ludek Pachman, based on his meeting with Kodes and Kukal in San Juan.

Obviously, he has written the article for our benefit and it resulted in opening up a debate around the issue of amateurism vs. professionalism. Besides that an article about Jaroslav Drobny came out and that stirred up the flame even more.

As soon as we returned to Prague, they plunged at us: "You let your big mouths go too far! Instead of being happy that we let you out you told Pachman that somebody here ill-treats you!"

Although traveling to the capitalistic countries was no longer that special in the second half of the 1960s when the political ambiance was easing up in Czechoslovakia and was heading towards Prague's Spring of 1968, the exotic time I and Jan Kukal experienced that winter in the Caribbean region was still just a dream for most!

As long as the players traveled within Europe there was always an official from the tennis association or a representative of the Central Committee of Czechoslovak Union of Physical Education and Sports accompanying them as their escort. Naturally, there was much interest for these posts among the officials particularly when the players headed to tournaments in the Western part of the Continent. In the case of the American and Caribbean Circuits the situation was different since there was not enough money for the additional plane tickets. And so, based on the mentioned initiative of Josef Rehak, then the chairman of our tennis association, only two were given the chance to "travel out into the world", and it was the two Jans – Kukal and Kodes.

When it was decided that would travel alone without any official escort, Jan Kukal was dubbed into the role of a leader. He was older, had more experience and spoke better English. He was supposed to take care of me, of all tournament paperwork, and upon return he had to write a report about the entire trip. There were moments when he moaned about it but a few weeks after our return he was almost glad he had taken it upon himself. The development of our Davis Cup match with Brazil showed clearly how good it was for us to have had the winter tournament experience first in India and then in America, where we accomplished playing in thirteen tournaments in a row!

Thank God that Josef Rehak had his way....

DAVIS CUP 1968

A Pan American aircraft headed from New York to Prague. Among the passengers were two Czech tennis ambassadors on the plane who were returning at last after seven "whirlwind" weeks. They were coming home enriched by many experiences and newly acquired knowledge but tired from the exhausting merry-go-round of tournaments and travel from one location to another. They had an opportunity to undergo winter training and proper tennis preparation for the first time in their lives: they practiced in warm temperate climate and succeeded in playing a string of practice matches against all kinds of opponents.

They were returning full of positive expectations resulting from such intense preparation. Perhaps, they also entertained a little trepidation over what might happen a few weeks later at Stvanice.

All of a sudden, somewhere above the Atlantic at thirty thousand feet altitude, Jan Kodes turned to Kukal: "Jan, do you really believe what Koch told us about Davis Cup? ... that they are afraid of us? I don't buy it; the Brazilians are too shrewd."

Brazil was a very formidable opponent. Their team included an excellent twosome Thomaz Koch and Edson Mandarino. In 1966 Inter-Zonal finals Brazil defeated even the United States! A year later they advanced into the Inter-Zonal finals again.

The toss up took place in Prague's Belveder Hotel lounge. The actress Pavlina Filipovska drew the ballots with names of the first singles match: Kodes – Koch.

From left: Edson Mandarino, Thomaz Koch, Milan Holecek, Jan Kodes.

Jan Kodes's anxiety of a wakeful night disappeared only with the approaching dawn. He got up and at once felt energized to play. And he played superbly! In the fourth set he knocked-out the long-haired Brazilian with unbelievably risky return winners. Koch shook his head in disbelief: 6:2, 6:3, 3:6, and 7:5.

Jan Kukal's match with Mandarino followed but was suspended for darkness at 3:6, 6:4, 2:6 and it was finished on Saturday with the final fourth set: 1:6.

That afternoon the packed Stvanice experienced a bombshell: Kodes – Holecek won their doubles! The entire responsibility then hung on Kodes on Sunday after Kukal lost his second singles 4:6, 2:6, 4:6.

I felt my heart pounding in my throat; Mandarino was an immensely difficult adversary.

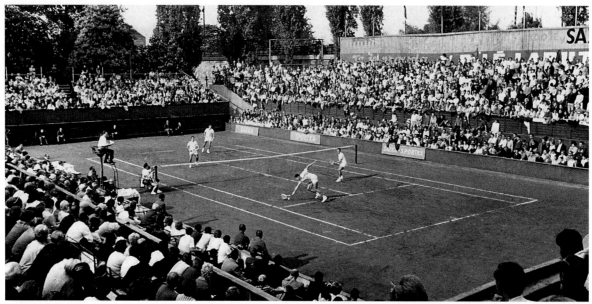

Stvanice 1968. Even for doubles was sold out...

He played many drop-shots and did not give out any unforced freebies.

In the third set the Brazilian player led by two games. During a change over Kodes almost collapsed.

"Doctor," he addressed the non-playing team captain Jiri Rössler, "I am exhausted. I'll let the set slip or I'll crumple..."

"No, no. You must win this set!"

The strength he compounded in Central America and in the United States got mustered up at the right moment! As if somebody poured energy into Kodes' arteries. He added point by point and slowly he eliminated his opponent's lead. After two hours and thirteen minutes he won 8:6 in the third!

Defeatist mood was soon gone. Only late that night, when he could not fall asleep and the most important points of the match replayed in his head over and over again he realized that the damaged reputation of Czechoslovak tennis since the defeat in Chile in 1967 was restored thanks to conquering the favored Brazilian team this time around.

Soon after the Davis Cup encounter with Brazil Jan Kodes headed for Rome to take part in the Italian Open Championships. That was a tournament of great

Prague 1968. For the first time I played Davis Cup at 2:2 and won over Mandarino.

world significance. He departed knowing that he should soon break into the world tennis scene.

In the third round he came across the Chilean Pato Rodriguez, who was one of the main players that eliminated Czechoslovakia in the first round of Davis Cup competition the year before. Kodes' anguish in the burning hot furnace of a court took more than three hours. In the forth set the Chilean led 5:4 but the Czech player's thoughts at that moment were: How am I ever going to defeat even better players if I now lose to him?

In the sweat running down his face Kodes' victory 6:0 in the fifth set was incubated. However, during one of the next shots he sprained his right ankle. It looked innocent at first but it swelled up over night and by the next morning his ankle looked like a pom-pom. In spite of it he showed up for another five set match but lost to the Australian Bob Hewitt.

At that point he still had no idea how much his injury was going to complicate the rest of his season. The only consolation for him was an article that came out in a Slovak magazine "Start", where the author quoted, besides others, also an excellent French player and Roland Garros 1946 Champion, Marcel Bernard:

"Kodes displays a game of amazing concentration; he strikes each and every ball with utmost attention. His best stroke is his topspin backhand return; his entire game shows characteristics of a well seasoned player. Kodes' footwork is swift; he has quick reaction and excellent judgment that stays with him even in the tightest of moments. Briefly: He personifies a future champion.

For the first time I become a native hero by winning the last match at 2:2... Captain Jiri Rössler did a lot for Czech tennis during the 50s and 60s, passed away in October 28, 1977.

For the next round of Davis Cup his ankle was so-so. Despite that a headline appeared in the newspaper: Limping against Belgium?

Kodes won the opening match in five sets with a careful play against Eric Drossart as if he wanted to persuade all those skeptics that nothing breaks him easily. Holecek then lost to

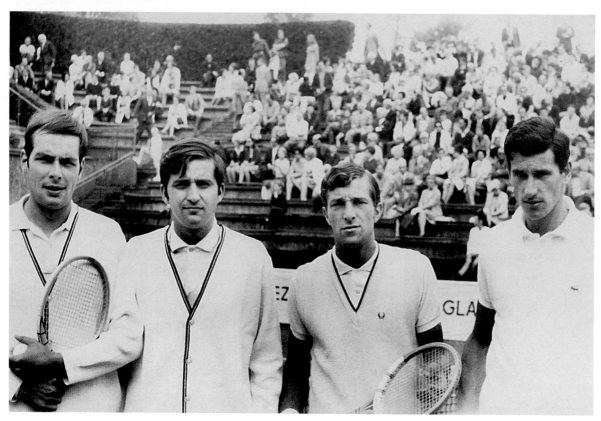

Davis Cup vs. Belgium at Brussels. Claude de Gronkel, Eric Drossart, Jan Kodes and Milan Holecek (from left).

Patrick Hombergen 1:3 but they won doubles easily on Saturday 6:3, 6:1, 6:2. On the third day Kodes faced Hombergen in good spirit and very confident since he had played the Belgian four times and always won. He took the first set in eighteen minutes 6:3, then second 6:2, and was leading 2:0 in the third, when....

There had been torrential rain in Brussels before the encounter. The courts of the King Leopold transformed into a lake. Luckily, the weather cleared and the organizers managed to prepare the Centre Court in time for this Davis Cup competition. However, wet clay is heavy and tricky...

"I am sure he'll smash that ball" thought Kodes in his mind.

As he started off towards the ball his right foot slipped on the unsteady clay. Ghastly pain shot through his not-yet-fully-healed ankle.

Damn! This is the end! I felt the ankle swelling up to mammoth proportions. It almost surprised me that my tennis shoe did not burst! I limped through the rest of the third set, which

I lost 4:6, pining for a 15 minute break in the locker room.

"Can I get back?" Not even the next injection helped much.

"Let me try! I must...,"I said and returned to the court only to lose 2:6, 2:6. Till this very day I have no idea how I ever finished that match. I sensed that I would suffer consequences. The following day I was wheeled from the airport lounge in Ruzyne directly to the hospital.

A West German player Ingo Buding was present at the match. He came to Brussels to observe his future opponents.

He would have been happier to see the Belgians win. I even heard him give advice to Hombergen on how to beat me while I was on the bench being treated. I did not think that was terribly fair....

The match that was supposed to bring a clear and decisive winning point eventually turned around and the host team's player won. Nevertheless, Buding still did not get his wish granted.

At 2:2 Milan Holecek avenged me! He overpowered Drossart 6:3, 6:1, 3:6, 5:7, and 6:2 displaying amazing play and effort. Thus we were ready to switch our concentration to Munich! That is to say – my team-mates were. My fate was in the air....

Physicians' finding could meet no concessions: profound ankle distortion and torn ligaments of the joint. Leg had to be set in cast for two weeks at least! This was heartbreaking for me for another reason – the following week my parents were getting ready to travel to Roland Garros for the first time to see me play in the French Open. Fortunately, my sister Vlasta played in Paris too and so they went anyway. The last time my dad was in Paris was some time before the World War II. It was the only Roland Garros Championship that I did not take part in during those years. It was upsetting since my mom looked forward to it so much.

Though the cast came off, Jan's ankle revealed all kinds of bright reddish to purple colors and it was still out of the question for him to start playing. Things became even more complicated when Jan Kukal fell ill not even a week before the match against Germany. The physician did not recommend Kodes to play but he did not say not to play either. Davis Cup leadership decided to have Petr Strobl replace Kukal for singles, and Kodes would play only doubles with Holecek. However, just before the official draw, Petr announced that he did not feel strong enough to play singles. "Jan is injured and still beats me in practice. Let him play!" Kodes vacillated; his ankle was not yet cured and the German team was strong: Wilhelm Bungert – Wimbledon finalist, Christian Kuhnke – Wimbledon quarterfinalist, and Ingo Buding. Excited debate about the lineup had no end to it.

Only a few minutes before the draw the leadership called me: "Jan, make the decision yourself."

I felt I could not refuse to play. How could one negate playing in such a situation?"

There were five minutes left till the toss up when the referee received a ticket with Jan Kodes' name. The Germans nominated Buding instead of Kuhnke.

Due to my right ankle I still was not quite ready for the best German Wilhelm Bungert (right) and lost openning match in straight sets.

Czechoslovakia has been out of luck against Germany in Davis Cup. They played each other five times since 1929 and Czechoslovakia always lost. 1968 was no exception.

Subconsciously I played carefully, not at full intensity. Though I did not mean to I delivered only what I had an alibi for. After the match I realized that I should not have played that game. But it was too late to take it back. I lost both singles. Yet, our performance in Munich was nothing to be ashamed of. Milan Holecek defeated Buding on the opening day in singles and we lost the doubles only after putting up a real fight. Both Milan and I played well and the opponent got the better of us 12:10 in the fifth in an impressive and dramatic show down! Overall we lost 1:4. It was a pity that Jan Kukal had fallen ill, for he might have been able to overcome Buding...

A series of articles on the topic of Czechoslovak Tennis came out in the newspapers after we were knocked out of Davis Cup. In those times tennis players reached almost "exotic" popularity to be written about and journalists enjoyed delivering news about us to the public quite frequently. When Jan Kukal and I played the Caribbean Circuit we mailed contributions to the press agencies of Czechoslovak Sport and Mlada fronta on regular basis.

On the other hand, new controversial topics popped up: "How much does top tennis cost?" or "A word from Tennis Federation Vice-Chairman Stanislav Chvatal." We had no idea who stirred up the aggression but it gained intensity after the Munich defeat.

Jan Kodes himself added a little fuel into the fire as he considered going to Wimbledon. His ankle was not yet completely healed yet he decided to go anyway. He lost in the first round, this time to an American Marty Riessen. Marty was an excellent grass-court player and Jan simply did not have enough arsenal against him.

In no time the press attacked Kodes in the newspapers: "Not yet well Kodes is in Wimbledon again! Who takes responsibility for that?"

AUGUST 21, 1968

The year 1968. It is often considered to be the year that separated significant periods of the second half of the 20th century. The year of contradictions, oppression and of cry for freedom. War in Vietnam, assassinations of Martin Luther King and Robert F. Kennedy, culmination of Hippie subculture's flower movement in California, war in Biafra, student protests in Paris. President of the United States Lyndon Johnson celebrated his sixtieth birthday, Sergio Leone made a classical Western film and Stanley Kubrick directed the Odyssey based on a story written by Arthur C. Clark. The legendary Manchester United soccer player George Best received the Golden Ball as the best European Footballer/Soccer Player of the Year, the Beatles recorded the famous White twin-album that included the song "Back to the USSR", and Vera Caslavska and Josef Odlozil gave their marriage wows and celebrated their wedding in Mexico City during the Olympic Games....

It was a milestone of a year for Czechoslovakia too. We got invaded by the "well-known" Red Army aided by other four Warsaw Pact armies in order to stop the country's revival and shift toward capitalism. In 1968 our homeland underwent the most cataclysmic political chapter since 1948, the year that transformed Czechoslovakia practically into a Soviet satellite. Our country strained to gain more freedom, people wanted to govern their own land. In January 1968 Antonin Novotny was recalled from his post of the Communist party secretary and Alexander Dubcek was appointed to take over that position. A month later the entire world watched our hockey team defeat the Soviets 5:4 in a memorable Olympic game in Grenoble. The team captain Jozo Golonka lay on his front on the ice laughing uncontrollably with glee

After my victory over Mandarino I received congratulations from Prime Minister Oldrich Cernik.

and simultaneously banging his stick against the ice. Those who witnessed these scenes will never forget them. Vaclav Nedomansky frantically jerked the Soviet goal-keeper's goal-cage after one of his successful goals. The same Vaclav Nedomansky, who defeated Kodes in Junior Nationals in Pardubice ten years earlier ... In spite of bitter February frost people marched out into the streets and celebrated the victory. Signs with "5:4" were visible everywhere...

After a long period of apathy the nation gained energy at last; the same kind of energy it exuberated before the WW II and during some three years after its end. The spring air sparked with excitement, meetings took place in city squares, people promised to work honestly in order to resurrect the damaged country. That was what Prague Spring 1968 stood for Dubcek, Cernik, Smrkovsky, Cisar, Svoboda... The elated atmosphere was evident even during athletic encounters and many of the members of the government took part in the audiences.

On June 27, 1968 the newspapers published a Petition of 2000 Words that was conceived and written by Ludvik Vaculik; seventy well-known and influential Czechoslovak personalities signed it right at its birth. This historic document asked for non-violent positive changes. It appeared that the time was right to take power away from the Communist party and let real democracy lead the country. However, the Soviets and a few Czechoslovak orthodox communist representatives evaluated the document as an anti-socialist pamphlet and several months later used it against all who had signed it. It had catastrophic consequences for many.

As in 1948 many lawyers ended up either with a shovel digging trenches, or as factory workers, or in boiler-rooms, and teachers found themselves mucking out. Familiar faces of popular television announcers disappeared, and officials tried to erase the memory of our singer Marta Kubisova from people's minds.

Jan Kodes missed many of those events because he spent a large portion of the first half of 1968 abroad. Initially he went to India, and then he played the Caribbean Circuit, the Italian Open in Rome, Davis Cup matches, at home against Brazil, then in Belgium and in Munich,

Wimbledon... He was spending a few days at home only towards the end of the summer, when he was still nursing and rehabilitating his ankle injury, and that was when the events in the country ended with the tragic August 21 invasion.

At the same time, the international tennis scene was undergoing changes that were instrumental in his further tennis career.

Rapprochement of amateur and professional tennis that was initiated at Bournemouth in spring of 1968 and continued at Roland Garros and Wimbledon was not a favored volition of many representatives from socialist countries. Only with great reluctance did athletic authorities come to terms with the fact that Czechoslovak players were going to be earning money. However, they could not stop the time-clock.

In early August the ITF sent out letters to all tennis federations informing them of their duty to report respective status of their players by the end of October. If they did not comply then the ITF reserved its right to consider those players as "semi-professionals at large" and base the tournament entry fees on that.

By taking this step the world tennis leadership officially allowed players to accept money for tournament entry and individual federations had to divide players according to their status - players who could accept money and players who would remain amateurs. The way the ITF formulated the rule was like putting a knife to the throat of national federations who had to make the division of players into those who could receive money and those who could not because of their amateur status. The intent was obvious – professionalize tennis all the way. This report caused uproar in Prague tennis circles. The Tennis Coach Council Chairman Antonin Bolardt reacted with the following words: "We know that the Brazilian players Koch and Mandarino pay their federation $25 each for a weeklong tournament that they alone had arranged to enter. We have not yet talked about the amount required from our players but it will be a lesser amount that corresponds to their present marketability."

There is no player in the world who would play the top tennis game for 29 years the way Ken Rosewall did!! Ken played his first Grand Slam event in 1951 and the last in 1978 (incl. 11 years as a "PRO" between 1957-1967).

Hilversum 1968. Mixed Doubles quarter-finals: Tom Okker, Margaret Smith-Court and Lenka and Jan Kodes (from left).

In no time an article came out in the "Reporter" magazine with a headline: "Semi-professionalism even with sticks thrown under the feet?" In the article Milos Konrad, Petr Strobl, Jan Kukal, Jiri Rössler and Jan Kodes expressed their opinion concerning the above dilemma.

It is embarrassing that our official for international affairs, Josef Brabenec, an experienced and, in his position, well versed person published several times over his opinion that our participation in Wimbledon was largely a social affair and our chances for success there were nil. On the contrary, our results on wooden and other fast surfaces in the Americas showed that we could do well even in Wimbledon provided that our Federation allowed us proper and longer preparation during the next season.

Our Federation leadership steadfastly believed: "Our players have been nursed on clay, they can never do well on grass, and they do not need to play on hard surfaces." Everybody zeroed down their attention to Davis Cup and clay-court tournaments.

This character of debate evolved at the beginning of August. National league matches took place on the weekend of August 17-18 and they exemplified very prestigious competition: Kukal played for Ostrava, Holecek for Ruda hvezda, Kodes for Sparta.

Jan Kodes found no competition. He defeated Holecek in the most magnetic match of the weekend, followed by a total knock out of Jan Kukal 6:1, 6:0 who did not deal well with the defeat.

Jan (Kukal) did not play well and he constantly argued with the umpires. On Monday the newspapers wrote that "Kukal forgot not only his tennis prowess in the locker room but also his sportsmanship etiquette". In addition, editorials targeted again our travels abroad and the possibility of turning professional. Envy transpired through and through and I thought to myself that newspapers were now interested in us too much. However, a few days later the nation faced altogether a different dilemma.

The night from Tuesday August 20 to Wednesday August 21. The phone rang at 4 am and Lenka answered it.

"What's up? I am playing tomorrow!" I grunted snuggled up in our bed.

But then I heard: "You must be kidding! That's impossible! After she put the receiver down she turned to me and said: "Get up! The Russian-

Bolsheviks are here!"

We lived by the Bubenec embankment close to Hlavkuv Bridge and we could see the Transit Company building from our window. The building is no longer there but instead of present day crossing there used to be a huge parking lot. When we looked out of our window that parking lot was full of tanks!!!

Rapid succession of events followed. The government prompted people to stay calm, they appealed to the Nation to stay away from impetuous actions. However, tempers escalated to the point of explosion. A huge crowd gathered in front of the Czechoslovak Broadcasting Station and demanded explanations. Tanks rolled, shooting rampaged, cars were set on fire, there was blood and the first victims fell.

Alexander Dubcek urged people not to act, and the president of the country, Ludvik Svoboda, ordered the armies to hold fire and leave us alone. The flash of hope for better tomorrow disappeared under the tracks of rolling Russian tanks. After thirty years people were reminded again of what it felt like to be occupied...

All athletic events between August 21 and September 6 were called off. Milan Holecek telephoned us all to play at least a little soccer since we could not play tennis. We gathered at Sparta, all of us miserable and distressed, nobody could even talk much. We had no idea what would happen next. Strobl and Hutka did not show up and we had no idea what happened to them. We later found out that they participated that day in the rally at the Broadcasting Station. When all hell broke loose and shots were fired they hid under some cars!

At the end of September Kodes received an invitation to play in the traditional Coupe Poreé in famous Racing Club de France, Paris.

He travelled out with Milan Holecek who he defeated there and thus avenged the semifinal loss to him at the Nationals in Ostrava. He beat Milan in the finals 8:6, 6:3, 6:2.

I admit that, for a while, I lost sight of the tragic situation at home. We left without strains; nobody made any problems for us. I fooled myself believing that as quickly as they came the Russians would also leave in a few weeks time. It did not occur to me to think that they would stay and would want to stay forever. Ultimately they remained for twenty one years...

Upon our return from France we found the situation at home calmer. Athletic events and competition got under way again. And so did the controversy around the issue of "professional tennis: yes or no?" At that time an article by Jiri Fabinger came out in the press: "Will a Czech Tennis Pro Emerge?" with a subtitle that asked: "Amateur, Semi-professional, or Professional?" The author himself answered: "A professional is under contract with the promoter and that is Pragosport in CSSR; under no circumstances the player would fall within tennis federation cognizance."

Jan Kodes was at odds with such stance and the discussion about the players' future accelerated:

"Those interested in turning professional or semi-professional must turn in applications via their clubs to the Central Office of Tennis Federation by 4 pm September 25, 1968. Otherwise players will be considered amateur throughout 1969."

Feeling the throb – Kodes, Kukal, Holecek and Palmeova were set to sign semi-professional contracts. Everything lay in the International Tennis Federation's intent; result would rest upon the craft of the professionals.

What is the difference between a professional and a semi-professional?

Jan Kodes: A professional lives merely off tennis, whereas a semi-professional has another job, in my case it would be my studies.

Aren't you afraid that you'll lose the joy you presently draw from playing the game if tennis becomes your job?

Jan Kodes: I would not face that; I enjoy the game and if professionalism does not fulfill my expectations I can always return to amateurism. After all, I do not see any difference between the load pressure of our top amateur and the professional. It all seems to be the same.

Jan Kodes' archives

Affiliation with Pragosport came about only a little later. Initially we signed contracts with the Tennis Federation and based on that we surrendered our monies to the Federation.

The Chairman of the coaches' council Antonin Bolardt and the secretary of the international affairs Josef Brabenec prepared the wording of the contracts. They asserted: "All is ready for a smooth motion ahead. Players had some technical queries that we intend to deliberate on. Those were mainly concerned with the Federation's requirement that the players play sixteen weeks a year on behalf of the Federation. Players expostulated that to be too many. Yet, it included representing the country in Davis Cup competition, the National Championships, and two or three tournaments of significance. Sixteen weeks is the absolute maximum and it could turn out to be less, depending on the circumstances. The International Tennis Federation (ITF) charter mandates that each player must be available to his/her National Federation at least twelve weeks."

In the end a group of players was selected with whom the Czechoslovak Tennis Federation drew up contracts – Jan Kodes, Jan Kukal, and Milan Holecek who were later appended by Frantisek Pala, Vladimir Zednik and Vlasta Vopickova.

Czechoslovak Tennis Federation avows Jan Kodes his status of a "player" by course of the rule # 32 of ITF charter valid since January 1, 1970, with all its incumbent rights and duties. Jan Kodes declares to be familiar with the obligations that ITF charter requires of him and he pledges to fulfill them duly to the full extent of his capability.

The ITF Article II of the agreement emphasized that the player must be available to the Czechoslovak Tennis Federation for 12 weeks; however, the Federation enforced the players to be at their command sixteen weeks a year.

They worked into the obligatory quota world tournaments like the Italian Open or Hamburg besides the Grand-Slams and with that we had a chance to play more in the West. Somehow the stingy CUPES (Czechoslovak Union of Physical Education and Sport) always found funds for Tennis Federation's events. According to the Union's rules an official had to accompany the players as the main spokesperson at all times.

It was at that point that Jan Kodes came to realization of two things. All tournament invitations that arrived from abroad came for Kodes, Holecek, Kukal. The world was interested mainly in these three players and above all in Kodes. And that put immense stress on Kodes.

I began to feel terrible pressure because everybody wanted me somewhere. All of a sudden they all yearned for travel. Sparta Club sent out letters to foreign clubs: "Kodes is playing for us; would you like to arrange a team challenge?" And they asked me to travel with them and play the club matches.

At the same time the Federation was sending me somewhere else. In addition I played the Davis Cup matches, the Czech Championship in Litvinov, the Nationals in Ostrava, the National League, the International tournaments in Bratislava, Centropa Cup team competition, the Royal Cup...

I finished one event and started the next without any rest. The other players often lost in early rounds and had days to recuperate. I usually reached the semis or finals, or even doubles competition finals. I tried to persuade the Federation to ease up on requiring me to play the Czech Championship in Litvinov, and I was happy when I was allowed to skip over some club matches.

Most of the time Kodes' requests did not receive any response. He had to play. And that much more it hurt him when newspapers aggravated the controversy regarding the transfer to professionalism. It did not help his peace of mind and proper match preparation when articles like "Over a pile of stones towards the heap of money" appeared.

Newspapers discussed the issue continuously. It was embarrassing. One of the reasons might have been that people involved in other sports envied us. The International Tennis Federation was the first one that unanimously declared: We shall fully open the door to professionalism and tennis players will be earning money! Tennis had one important advantage in comparison to other sports – tennis was not an Olympic sport and thus did not have to honor the Olympic charter.

**Great Lewis Hoad came within one match of winning the „Grand Slam"!
In 1956 he won first three GS events and then was beaten
by Ken Rosewall in the U.S. Championship final! Picture from Prague, Stvanice.**

SOUTH AMERICA

"Argentina is over the other side of the river" says the book title of Czech travelers Hanzelka and Zikmund's. However, the capital of that South-American country, Buenos Aires, is not located over the river but rather far over the Ocean. It is so far that if you board a plane in Prague you'll de-board it totally disheveled and bushed some twenty four hours later in Buenos Aires. At least that was the case in the Fall of 1968 after an invitation was extended from South America to the Czechoslovak Tennis Federation; it was only for Jan Kodes alone....

In those times it was not like today boarding a plane and flying maximum with one transfer all the way to Buenos Aires. I flew from Prague with Czechoslovak OK Airlines to Dakar in order to save the hard currency drain. I had to spend a night there before I caught the next leg with Air France and trudged along to Rio de Janeiro, San Paolo, and then Buenos Aires.... What a dreadful trip!

It was Kodes' friend Pato Rodriguez from Chile who had arranged for Jan's invitation.

I no longer remember where it was, perhaps in Rome, where Pato turned to me and said: "Jan, I have arranged for an invitation to be extended to you to play a tournament in Chile!" He furthermore promised to take care of me and play doubles together with me. That was a blockbuster!

Oscar Furlong, the Argentine Tennis Federation Secretary of their International section, organized a chain of South-American tournaments. And it was he, who invited me to Argentina. He promised to pay my room and board, and $600 pocket money to cover also my air travel! That I considered an amazing recognition!

According to the contract with our Federation we had to pay them flat amount of $25 for each tournament that we arranged ourselves. If we played tournaments that the Federation arranged for us then all monies went back to them and they covered everything. Each player

South American Championships at Buenos Aires. Doubles semifinals –
Pato Rodriguez, Jan Kodes, Roy Emerson and Rod Laver.

had his given value according to which he received pocket money amount.

It was enough to live off but compared to what players receive today it was a laughable figure. This figure increased as soon as prize money was awarded for each round that a player won. The better the performance the more money a player received.

In Argentina Kodes advanced all the way to the quarter-finals.

But I received a lesson number three from Roy Emerson in that match losing to him after a three-and-a-half-hour battle: 9:11, 11:9, 4:6, and 3:6. Roy then proceeded to win the tournament defeating Laver in the finals...

There were a few days off in between the tournaments in Argentina and Chile and Pato Rodriguez invited his Czech buddy to his brother Pedro's ranch.

Pedro lent his horse to Jan.

What splendor! It was the first time that I sat on a horse, and the first time that I held a rifle in my hands. They gave me bullets and I shot into a can. I went horseback riding and took a trip to the Andes.

Kodes played two tournaments in Chile and reached finals in both against Pato Cornejo, the Chilean player number one, succumbing to him in Santiago but defeating him in Viña del Mar 7:5, 7:5, 6:1.

On the farm: Pedro Rodriguez with his wife, Michele and Pato Rodriguez, J.Kodes and Herb Fitzgibbon with wife.

During my stay in the pleasant the seaside resort I realized that our Czechoslovak soccer team resided there throughout the World Cup six years previously. I asked about them but nobody remembered them. However, a year later, in Sao Paolo, everybody vividly remembered the final between Czechoslovakia and Brazil!

There was an interesting prelude to my trip to South America. Leaving socialist countries aside the Czechoslovak players always needed visas to all other countries of Europe. In case of events organized by the Federation the officials arranged for the visas and all that the players necessitated to travel; otherwise the players had to do the leg work themselves.

I looked up the address of the Chilean Embassy in the telephone book and found it in Prague 5 - Kosire. When I got there and applied for a visa presenting a letter of invitation to Argentina and Chile, the guy behind a desk looked at me and said: "You do not need a visa to go to Chile! You are our friends. There is friendly cooperation between our two nations."

I had a hard time believing the man! I was required to have visa to our neighboring Austria, Germany, France, and not to Chile? I could not believe it and kept asking over and over again if, indeed, I needed no visa to Chile? In the end I accepted that I would have, at least, a visa to Argentina in my passport and hoped that the Chileans would let me in without one.

I found out soon after landing in Buenos Aires how South America operated. I got off the plane and taking my passport out I headed towards the passport control.

A passport officer looked into my passport and sternly ordered: "Come along!" And he took me aside. All other travelers were long gone but I was being fingerprinted! All ten fingers! And they took my passport away for the duration of my stay in Argentina and gave me some identification card instead.

I was without a passport for a whole week and had to identify myself via that substitute ID card. And even with the fingerprints! The reason? I came from a communist country.

It was altogether different in Chile.

Upon arrival I showed my passport and that was it! As I looked around I observed that residence by residence was adorned by sickle and hammer – communist symbols!

I felt really content throughout my stay in Chile and enjoyed playing doubles with Rodriguez that much more. I believe that everybody treated me so well thanks to my connection to Rodriguez. There, so far away from home I realized, to my great surprise, how politics interfered even in sports. And I always remembered Chile whenever political squabbles of the mighty world powers affected athletic events.

SECOND CARIBBEAN

It was 1969 and the selected Czechoslovak tennis players were able to test their competence against Lamar Hunt's professional group. The Texas multimillionaire came to the realization early that spring that players of his group were not unconquerable. He soon calculated that he was losing money on his elite tennis players and he staged a counter-attack. He targeted Nastase, Ashe, Smith, Kodes and several others without much luck. Everything was in beginning bargaining stages and mutual discussion via Lamar Hunt's right-hand man, George McCall.

Kodes and Kukal spent the winter 1969 again in temperate climate. They did not travel to India this time but headed for indoor tournaments in the US and the subsequent Caribbean Circuit. They chose the series after the previous year's excellent experience.

The first tournament was in Omaha, Nebraska. The two Jans did not travel together.

I was held in New York due to a snow storm; we were delayed for two hours and because of it I missed my connection in Chicago. I was supposed to arrive in Omaha at 6 pm but arrived at four the next morning instead. I had no idea where the tennis hall was and I did not surmise where I should spend the rest of the night. I had no money, only about $50 of my travel allowance. One fellow traveler told me where the basketball hall was in Omaha and I just hitched a taxi there. There I found out where our accommodations were and at five in the morning I woke up the maid by phone. "Who is there?"

"This is Kodes, a tennis player from Czecholovakia!"

She started shrieking at the top of her lungs. I understood just about every third of her words but gathered that she was asking me if I was ok. I tried to explain to her why I was calling at such dreadful hour, that my plane had been delayed and I was standing in the lounge of the basketball hall. Half an hour later a car picked me up, I had a bite to eat and I jumped in bed. I slept like a log.

A phone call woke me up at eleven: "You play Torben Ulrich in the first round!"

Nobody stopped to consider my early morning arrival and the fact that I had not slept much. "Other players have not arrived yet. The tournament starts at 4 pm and you play the second match!"

The left-hander Torben wiped me off the court 4:6, 2:6! Kukal was nowhere to be seen and so I was left to myself to bitch. I arrived among the first players and I paid for it!

Kukal also lost in the first round. Together we lost doubles to the American team of Richey – Edlefsen 3:6, 6:3, and 2:6 but we were not too concerned with our demise. The first tournament after a trip over the Atlantic was always tricky. One was happy to be adjusting to the time-change.

After Omaha we played a small tournament of "8" in Pittsburgh which I won and then we transferred to Philadelphia for a significant US Pro Indoor in the Spectrum, the home of ice-hockey team Philadelphia Flyers. I glanced at the draw and saw my first round opponent

Pittsburgh 1969. Eight man event. Mark Cox, Ismail El Shafei, Ron Holmberg, Zeljko Franulovic (from left). Front row: Jan Kukal, Herb Fitzgibbon, Jan Kodes and Istvan Gulyas(from left). Kodes beat Gulyas 6:8, 6:3, 6:4, Cox 3:6, 6:4, 7:5 and Fitzgibbon 8:6, 6:1 in the finals.

ACE—Jan Kodes cranks up a big serve to Arthur Ashe (background) at the Spectrum last night. Kodes, an unranked Czechoslovakian amateur, upset Ashe, ranked second in the world.

Photo by Ray Stubblebine, of The Bulletin

Upset by Unseeded Jan Kodes

By RED HAMER

Arthur Ashe topped off a marathon session of tennis antics and upsets at the world's first indoor open with the wry suggestion that he needs a psychiatrist.

The comment came on the heels of his shocking 6-4, 4-6, 6-2 loss to Czech champion Jan Kodes last night in the opening round of the Philadelphia International Indoor Open at The Spectrum.

The second-seeded U. S. Open champion — and only amateur among the seeds—was joined on the sidelines by eighth-seeded Roy Emerson of Australia, and Dennis Ralston of Bakersfield, Calif., both pro. But the highly-regarded company was little consolation to Ashe.

"In 17 days I will be out of the Army," declared the lieutenant, "and then I go see a psychiatrist. I'm going nuts. I haven't won a tournament since Brisbane (second week in December)."

HAPPY FOR CZECHS

Kodes, whose best surface is clay, was jubilant. "The people of Czechoslovakia need something to be happy about," he said.

The former ice hockey player —he was a center on a Junior team—didn't even get an invitation to Forest Hills last year and was eliminated by Emerson in the first round of the Madison Square Garden Invitational.

He is a registered player, but chose not to play for money here because of the strength of the 32-man field. Kodes will accept expenses and merchandise instead.

Ashe claimed his elbow was more of a pyschological problem.

BLAMES HIS TIMING

"It might have been responsible for the (3) double faults," he said, then later added, "when you compensate for something, it messes up your rhythm.

"I couldn't keep the ball on the court; I had no timing. I had him going so many times and couldn't put the ball away. I hit everything too soon. Anybody with long strokes like me will have a problem on this court."

Ashe and Kodes exchanged service breaks to open the third set. In the sixth game, Kodes failed when he had an advantage on Ashe, but rallied to deuce and took a 4-2 lead when Ashe netted an overhead.

Kodes triumphed on a serve by Ashe that was a fault by at least a foot. The Czech played the ball anyway and drilled a forehand placement to Ashe's left that caught him charging the net.

Pleased with Crowd

Kodes was slightly surprised by his moment of glory. "I thought, If I play well I can win one set," said the University of Prague student.

Although Ashe's departure from the singles was a blow to the tournament, other top attractions such as the fiery Pancho Gonzales, Ken 'Muscles' Rosewall and the world's No. 1 Rod Laver, all advanced to tonight's Round of 16.

– Arthur Ashe! I could not have asked for a stronger adversary for the opening match of that tournament.

Oh well, if I lose I'll have time for a nice rest – I contemplated. However, everything turned out differently; Kodes won 6:4, 4:6, 6:2! And in the second round he defeated Stan Smith 6:2, 2:6, and 6:2! That had an effect of a bombshell among the home fans!

We played on supreme surface that was slower than the canvas cover over concrete. I did not lose until the semifinals against Tom Okker. In spite of that loss I returned to the hotel content, I made myself comfortable in my room when, suddenly, a phone rang.

"Hello Mr. Kodes. I am Mr. Kocourek from Radio Voice of America. Would you let us interview you?"

"I gulped, and he continued: "There is no need to be worried; we are not like Radio Free Europe, we are Voice of America! You should not have any problems, really; we'll just discuss sports and nothing about politics."

I agreed, he recorded the interview, and if I am not mistaken, they aired it right after. The next day the phone rang again at eight in the morning but this time there was somebody from Washington at the other end of the line: "Mr. Kodes, congratulations on your spectacular achievement; we read about you in the newspapers – it is amazing what you accomplished. But we also heard your interview on Voice of America!"

I started to equivocate and asserted that I knew where the reporter was from but we agreed on discussing only sports and no politics. "I believe I said nothing damaging."

"No, on the contrary, we liked it very much but in spite of it we must warn you to beware of Voice of America. Their questions can be very cunning."

Czechs admireing the Davis Cup trophy for the first time at Salisbury, Maryland in 1969. From left: Milan Holecek, Josef Brabenec (official), Jan Kodes and Jan Kukal.

I babbled acknowledging that I was aware of that. However, Mr. Kocourek called two more times and since he always did just what we agreed upon I gave him two more interviews. Admittedly, after the first "warning" call from Washington I did not face any fundamental problems. On the contrary, I arrived at a conclusion that very little was known about Czechoslovakia in the United States and since our athletes had not yet reached any accomplishments our compatriots were tickled and grateful to read about my success.

In Salisbury Jan Kodes lost to Ove Bengston from Sweden in the opening round and in Macon he succumbed to Nastase in three sets. After the indoor tournaments on the East Coast of the United States the Caribbean Circuit got on the way – Caracas, Curacao, Barranquilla.

In Caracas Kodes avenged himself beating Nastase 6:3, 7:5 but lost the next match to Koch. Playing this series of tournaments the second time around Kodes carried himself like a seasoned player. Teamed up with Kukal they won doubles in Macon and Caracas.

His wife Lenka joined Jan in Curacao in the Dutch Antilles and together they traveled to Baranquilla to take part in the Columbian International Championships. He advanced all the way to the finals where he met Nastase for the third time in three weeks. He lost after an exhausting battle that lasted four hours and twelve minutes: 4:6, 4:6, 10:8, 6:2, and 3:6!

The tournament in Baranquilla was superbly organized. We stayed in the hotel El Prado and after practices or matches we were able to swim in the local swimming pool. The tennis Center was about a mile away and we used a shuttle to go to the courts in the morning and return to the hotel in the evening. If we did not want to walk back to the hotel we had to stay at the courts all day long.

Gulyás from Hungary solved it his way. He came to the shuttle in the morning but said: "I am not taking the shuttle, I'll walk!"

"Why won't you take the shuttle?"

His response was that he wanted to stay in shape. He was capable of running a mile to the courts just about an hour before his match in scorching heat and doing the same after the match when returning to the hotel.

Stanislav Chvatal was the President of the Czechoslovak tennis Federation between 1969-1975, the time when our profi-status was discussed. After Martina Navratilova defected he had to resign!

I love to remember Pato Alvarez. He was a clever clay-court player, great runner and, at the same time, a showman. They called him the "Columbian Wizard" as he entertained people on and off the court. After he concluded his own tennis career he became Clerc's, Sanchez brothers' and Casal's coach. I would not be surprised to meet him at world championships even today.

After my finals with Nastase Pato approached me and said: "You have a week off before you fly to New York; how about playing three exhibitions – in Cali, Medellin, and in Bogota?"

He had it all worked out, and the crowds were huge. The finals with Nastase had inspired much interest. In Medellin, for instance, we played in the main Plaza; bleachers were erected on all four sides of the court and they were full to capacity, almost bursting in seams. We had a hard time making it through the crowd to the court. I was almost afraid that something would get snatched from me.

But nothing happened, and when we got to the court at last I asked him: "What kind of balls have you got?"

Pato responded that he had Dunlops and Tretorns: "Which do you prefer?" – he asked. I suggested playing with the Dunlops.

"You prefer the Dunlops? – In that case, I am taking the Tretorns!"

Rather than arguing I agreed to suffer through three sets with Tretorns. He had no chance of beating me anyway but the match lasted longer.

The last exhibition took place on Friday and Saturday in Bogota, and one of our Embassy officials came to watch me. I believe his name was Hroch. He might have even been a consul and he was definitely a very pleasant man. After the Friday match he took me and my wife sightseeing; we visited the Museum that was full of treasures and relics of the indigenous South American Indians.

As he was taking leave he gave me his business card and said: "Unfortunately, I won't see you playing tomorrow because I have a business engagement. But you are not leaving until Sunday, right? Should anything happen and you need my help, do not hesitate to call me."

The next tournament was going to start on Monday in New York's Madison Square Garden but I was not playing until Tuesday. When Lenka and I arrived at the airport there were people everywhere. We checked through our baggage and headed for the departure gate. The Colombian carrier Avianca operated the only direct flight from Bogota to New York twice a week. They had a special exit, it was almost ceremonial.

Twenty minutes before the flight departure we went through passport control right next to the departure gate. I extended the official both of our passports, he looked up the respective pages and raised his eyes to me; at that moment I knew that something was wrong.

"You are not flying anywhere! Though you have Colombian visa it is an emigrant visa. Most likely an error was committed but we cannot let you leave the country. On Monday you can go to the police in Bogota and they'll have to convert the visa for you."

I broke out in sweat in no time. Our bags were already on the plane and would arrive in New York in a few hours while we were stuck in Bogota. The next plane was flying out in two days, which meant that I would miss the biggest professional tournament at Madison Square Garden!

Thank God that Lenka retained a cool head: "You have a business card of that Embassy official Hroch; call him, perhaps he'll be able to help us!" The phone rang and rang but at long last somebody answered. It was him!

"Mr. Hroch, we are in trouble!"

"What happened?"

"We are ten minutes before the plane is supposed to depart and it seems that the visa in our passports is, allegedly, the kind that does not allow us to leave Colombia. The next connection to New York is in two days but I am expected to start a professional tournament with Laver and Emerson there tomorrow!" I almost wept into the phone.

"Hurry to the departure gate, wait there, and in the meantime I'll try to do something. Hopefully it'll work. If it does not work out call me again and I'll pick you up."

We went back to the gate; the stewardess was just making the last call to the delayed passengers to board immediately because the airplane door was going to be shut. And we just stood there totally immobile. Even the airport security wondered why we were not boarding.

I started to say that we were not permitted to board, when the phone on the counter rang. The guy who did not want to let us pass a few moments before reached below the counter and pulled our some red device"; all I heard then was: "Si, si señor, si!

He replaced the receiver, looked at us and said: "Go ahead!"

We slipped into the plane and the doors shut behind us. We did not even get the passports stamped! How Mr. Hroch achieved it is a mystery to me till this day. I never saw him again.

The flight to New York was uneventful. They landed on time, the bags did not get lost, and they were put up in a luxury hotel so Jan Kodes was content. The only thing he did not know was the name of his first round opponent.

He left the hotel for practice and as he was entering the Madison Square Garden he remembered the crushing loss to Roy Emerson there a year before.

That won't happen again, he thought, as he was taking the elevator to the locker room. However, as soon as he glanced at the draw he broke into sweat. First round: Kodes – Gonzales!

Oh damn! Pancho! Other players in the locker room started to taunt me: "Wait and see what his serve does to you! You'll shit in your pants!"

I worked out and when I returned to the locker room a fellow with a towel around his neck appeared and asked: "So, which one of you is Kodes?"

Pancho Gonzales during the match with Jan Kodes.

Sitting in the corner I shyly bleeped: "It's me!" He greeted me and everybody around laughed like crazy; they thought it was funny.

The next day I started off boldly, regardless of who was on the other side of the net. In no time I was ahead 3:0, and I had a game-point for 4:0! Unfortunately, I did not win that point and eventually lost the match in two sets 3:6, 5:7.

Hats off to him; he was an amazing server. Serve, approach, volley and the put-away! Hardly anybody had a chance against him on the fast indoor surface. I stretched him out with my returns to the point that it surprised him. Though I lost I played an even-leveled match with him.

Years later, when Pete Sampras appeared on the tennis scene, I thought of

With my aunt, Mary Kodes at the Empire State Building.

Pancho Gonzales whenever I watched Pete. He was a similar type of a player; well-built, with lean fast legs. They had very similar strokes and serve motion, and the same game style. Pete resembled Pancho so much that he could be his son as far as I saw it.

Since Kodes lost in the first round he had three free days before flying to Puerto Rico. There was no doubles so he used the time for New York sightseeing. With Lenka they walked the streets of Manhattan, they went up the Empire State Building, then the highest building in the world, and they strolled in Central Park.

Lenka was not his only female escort...

Before Jan's departure to the States his father stressed several times: "If somebody by the name of Kodes contacts you, it is my cousin Fred! We used to play together but he left for New York soon after the WWI, when he was only sixteen. He arrived in the US on December 2, 1919 and had pre-arranged accommodation with a relative on Long Island. He immediately applied for the U.S. Citizenship and much later settled with his wife in Cleveland."

He visited Prague after fifty years in 1969! In 1976 he retired and moved to Florida. After a bout with colon cancer he passed away in St. Petersburg on May 17, 1979.

It was this distant aunt who suddenly appeared in Madison Square Garden! She introduced herself as Mary Kodes from Cleveland, where her husband Fred owned a Gas Station. This was wonderful news for me. At last I had somebody in the United States who I could always contact! At least one kindred soul that could help in case of need or in case that something should happen to me.

Kodes arrived in San Juan feeling like a confident pro, who shouldn't suffer any harm. By then he had defeated Arthur Ashe as well as Stan Smith!

I went through all the practice balls in the hopper before working out but found none that was any good. Fortunately, the Americans came to practice with Clark Graebner and they had balls.

We played and I complained about the balls through most of that time. The next day the tournament director, Welby van Horn, approached us: "Who was the player complaining so much about the balls?"

"That was me; my name is Jan Kodes."

He also introduced himself and said: "I've heard about you; they say you defeated Arthur Ashe."

"Yes; I did!"

"Well, that is quite some accomplishment for a Czech."

During the 1969 season
I switched the rackets from
Dunlop to Spalding.

As we were returning to the locker rooms I asked Graebner: "Listen, does van Horn know much about tennis?"

"He reached the US Open finals twice, and played Davis Cup for the US for five years!"

That brought me back to humble reality. In the third round I lost to Jaime Fillol from Chile in three sets.

Kodes' enthusiasm got revived in the next tournament in Charlotte, North Carolina, where he received much praise from the respected US Davis Cup star Clark Graebner after beating him 6:2, 6:3 and where he succumbed only in the finals to Mark Cox from England 9:11, 2:6.

Jan Kodes returned to Prague considerably richer of tennis experiences and adventures. Naturally, the press did not miss his overseas accomplishments: "Kodes participated in eleven Caribbean tournaments" reported the headlines that often gave Jan the attribute of a "tennis traveler". "Jan Kodes returned home after three months of traveling from one US or Caribbean tournament to another. Participation in eleven tournaments embodied not only tennis accomplishments but also hundreds of travel miles and a wealth of adventures and experiences…"

At that point, however, his mind was somewhere else. A few days later he was to fly to the first significant clay-court tournament of the season – the Italian Open in Rome. The fatigue from long travel was quickly gone and all that remained was memory of the most successful matches and recollection of effective moments against the best players in the world.

Thanks to those triumphs he was gaining assurance that he was on the right track. He realized that he could be serious in his aspiration to enter the group of world tennis elite. There was one more phenomenon that he retained from the difficult US and Caribbean circuits and that he never forgot about.

Rod Laver once proclaimed about those circuits: "It is the best training school that a tennis player can ask for. If I had not played it I would not have accomplished what I am so proud of."

I would sign my name under that statement.

FORO ITALICO

Jan Kodes headed from the Caribbean Circuit 1969 almost directly to Rome. The tennis center, Foro Italico, was not large. There were six courts and a concrete spectator stand built conveniently in such a way that one could watch play on several courts at once.

Centre Court was unique: all marble! The auditorium housed ten thousand spectators; the court was set below the level of the ground, the outskirts were perfectly equipped. There was a swimming pool near by and an Olympic Stadium – these comprised a part of an athletic complex that was built practically in the midst of antique Roman sights for the 1960 Olympic Games. In that era tennis was not part of the most celebrated athletic gathering from around the world and had to wait to be included in the Olympic family of sports for another twenty some years. However, it must have been the remnants of the Olympic spirit and atmosphere that even nine years later elevated and inspired Jan Kodes to his peak performances.

He defeated Taylor from England in the first round, and he overwhelmed a home-national, Nicola Pietrangeli, in a languishing and exhausting four-hour long battle in the second 4:6, 4:6, 6:3, 7:5, and 6:2.

The next opponent was Arthur Ashe, who had secured a string of thirty consecutive victories between July and September 1968 and who had reached the Wimbledon semi-finals and won the US Open at Forest Hills. He was a complete player with a rich arsenal of strokes, hard serves, excellent volleys and very economical yet effective game-play.

It was in vain trying to figure out a weakness in his game and at last I told myself: Don't be afraid of him; you already beat him in the US during the winter season!

I countered his feared serves with punishing returns and Arthur visibly lost his confidence, when his biggest weapon proved ineffective. I tried to keep him away from the net, and if he approached I passed him down-the-line. After ninety minutes of scuffle I executed a beautiful backhand into his countermovement and that ended the unreal match.

Arthur looked bewildered; as if he did not understand what had just happened. But I knew

Foro Italico 1969. My victory over Arthur Ashe.

very well what had happened. I succeeded in overcoming the best amateur of the world! And decisively: 6:4, 6:3, 6:3.

In its time, the Italian Open occupied the same level of importance as the four most important Grand Slam tournaments. The one who wanted to achieve the Grand Slam title had to win the Australian Open, the French Open, Wimbledon, and the US Open in the same year. In the history of world tennis only two men succeeded in accomplishing such huge success. The first one was Donald Budge from the United States; the second was Rod Laver from Australia who carried it out twice – in 1962 and 1969. Laver was absent from the Italian Open in 1969 but John Newcombe substituted for him very well.

I sweated and battled in extreme Roman heat for five sets. We each tried to sway the match to our advantage. But John was the luckier one in the end and I helped him with a few totally silly serving faults. I lost to Newcombe in the semi-finals 3:6, 6:4, 1:6, 9:7, and 3:6, nevertheless, I considered the whole tournament performance a success.

Before leaving for Copenhagen to play Davis Cup against Denmark there was a nasty incident within the leadership of Czechoslovak tennis. A change of a Davis Cup captain was demanded and it struck like a lightning from a clear sky.

"Dr. Rössler is too old for the position and, in addition, he is ill," sounded the arguments of the change protagonists. They urged to appoint Antonin Bolardt.

There was a face off right away when Milan Holecek declared that he would not play under Bolardt's captainship: "I know him from ice hockey; he is a communist! Spineless!"

It culminated with a brawl at Tennis Federation, when Stanislav Chvatal was then the Chairman, and Ivan Lichner from Bratislava was the Federation captain. They called for a meeting at Sparta and asked everybody's stance with regard to the incurred situation.

I did not feel like expressing my mind one way or the other; I was the youngest one and it was all the same to me. I urged Holecek and Kukal to articulate their feelings. The committee talked to us, players, individually and in the end they decided that Bolardt would go with us to Copenhagen as a non-playing Davis Cup captain and Milos Konrad as a team coach.

I won both singles and along with Kukal we won doubles as well. Holecek lost both of his matches so the final score was 3:2 and we advanced to the next round against Monaco.

I have a feeling that it was then when Bolardt's campaign against Holecek started in order to push him out of the Davis Cup team. Milan, who did not agree with Bolardt's captainship in the first place, did not succeed in Copenhagen, and that gave Bolardt an easy reason not to nominate Milan for the match in Monaco. Only I, Kukal, and Zednik flew there.

"It is a weak opponent so we'll save some money," proclaimed Bolardt and left even Frantisek Pala at home.

Czechoslovakia won easily 5:0 in Monaco but then came a snag. The next opponent was going to be South Africa.

Still, before that Davis Cup round Kodes headed from Monaco to Paris to take part in the second Grand Slam event of the season. He did not know yet that in the Metropolis on Seine he was definitely going to start producing the big chapters of his tennis life! He won three rounds at Roland Garros and in the forth he faced John Newcombe again!

"Jan, isn't there even a bit of fairness in the world?" he lamented to Jan Kukal on the Eve of his next match.

"What do you mean?"

"Why do I have to play Newcombe again?" he said in despair and then added: "But, after all, it should not be so bad playing him on clay. I know his game by now."

The Australian with a face of a poker player started out the match like a hurricane. It was obvious that he was a bit worried and entered the match with full force from the beginning. In no time the Czech player was two sets behind 1:6, 4:6.

During the endlessly long flights around the world I often pondered over the game of tennis and tennis players. It occurred to me once that tennis was really like a poker game. The banker passed out all the cards and did not keep any trump card. So the trump card could then come even to the person who had been loosing all along.

That is how my match with Newcombe played out - like a Poker game on clay when the winning card started coming in my favor. I took more risks, John's concentration relaxed, most likely as a result of his 2:0 set lead. He began to make unforced errors and, all of a sudden, I was ahead 4:0 in the third. He let the set go 6:0 and then the real battle developed. I grabbed the forth set 10:8.

In the fifth set and the decisive game I was in trance-like state of mind. I did not notice anything or anybody but my opponent and the ball.

John played a great game again and made no mistakes. I felt the fatigue coming on, even cramps. Each point cost me much energy. Still, I gained 4:1 advantage, and then 5:2, but I slowed down a little and became less aggressive. And that was a big mistake! Newcombe gradually tied the score at 5:5 and that tied score carried on till 9:9.

Roland Garros 1969: My sister Vlasta(left) lost to Billie Jean King 3:6, 6:3, 5:7. B.J.King was already a triple winner at Wimbledon 1966-1968.

**On the way to play more than four hours...
Kodes-Newcombe.**

I was two points away from the match four times but it was gruesomely difficult to make that final step and John was not willing to help me.

11:9! After four hours John Newcombe raised his arms over his head in victory.

"Jesus Christ, what kind of a loser am I!" lamented Kodes in the locker room when many other players ran to congratulate him on a match tremendously played. "I was leading 4:1 and still managed to botch it!" However, there was no shame in losing to one of the world's best players, especially after such a battle!

All anger was gone the next morning and when Jan opened the French L'Equipe during breakfast there was a headline across the entire page: "Newcombe snatched victory away from Kodes!" The author of the article also wrote:"Jan Kodes struck a battle we have never seen at Roland Garros before..."

After a practice for the next Davis Cup encounter with South Africa Antonin Bolardt walked into the locker-room and fixed us dead saying: Well, gentlemen, we shall have to default; there will be no match!"

"Why?"

"Well, there circulates an opinion at the Czechoslovak Union of Physical Education and Sport that we cannot play for political reasons.

The International Olympic Games leadership is striving to boycott South Africa and have it banned from the Olympics because of its apartheid. That is what Frantisek Kroutil, the chief of the International department, told me."

"Look Antonin" started off Kukal, "what kind of nonsense is connecting tennis Davis Cup competititon and Olympic Games? Tennis is not an Olympic sport. Don't tell me that we'll default! We must do something about it! Let's write a letter to the Central Committee Chairman!"

They did not listen to us and we did not go to Africa! Consequently they played the finals against India!

It did not make me feel good. I have gone around the world and wherever I touched down they knew much about Czechoslovakia, they wrote and talked about us nicely. We represen-

**Fans start to leave centercourt to see our battle on court „A".
I was struggling with cramps at 9:9 in the fifth set.**

ted our country well, and I am confident that we would have done so again in the Southern tip of Africa. I considered this decision of our leadership totally unnecessary. It was the Olympic sports that backed the boycott of South Africa, supported by the Olympic Charter. Our argument was the fact that tennis was not an Olympic sport.

I was truly bothered especially after all the dreadfully hard work I delivered in Copenhagen. I asked Bolardt: "Why didn't we throw in the towel then?"

"Well, we could not have done that because the South Africans had a chance to lose in that round!"

"Only if God willed it, I thought to myself. They had a very strong team – Cliff Drysdale, Bob Hewitt, Frew McMillan and Robert Maud...

One cannot live off laurels based on one successful match. That is doubly true in tennis, where matches come one after another. A player can reach the pinnacle in one tournament and plunge out of the next one early on.

In Wimbledon Jan Kodes passed the first round defeating the Chilean Cornejo in five sets. In the next round, however, he lost in five to the American Bob Lutz. Though he reached three finals; won all of them at the Nationals in Ostrava his promising form evident in the first half of the season started to fade away. Perhaps it was caused by fatigue from too many matches.

In Ostrava I played about six to seven matches in each category. Altogether I played sixteen matches in six days. Each day was like the day before. Breakfast in the morning, a singles match, snack of a hot dog, doubles match, and another hot dog. In the evening a mixed-doubles match! All clubs wanted to grab as many titles as possible because the amount of their subsidy from firms depended on that. They made us play till exhaustion, and we had no other choice but comply.

In the years 1967 to 1969 I felt like I was wanted and obliged to play everywhere. I was under pressure to play everything because somebody else requested that of me. I was not yet mature or experienced, I did not know how to say "no". I was a little over twenty but my body was getting overworked. There were moments when my ankles and back felt the strain and that came back to haunt me later.

Nationals at Ostrava 1969. I won
all three titles! Singles over
J.Kukal 6:2, 6:3, 6:3, in doubles
with J.Kukal over M.Holecek
- V. Zednik and mixed doubles
(picture) with my wife Lenka
against sister Vlasta who
teamed with F.Pala.

Champions Cup – „4 Player
Special Event" at Baastad,
Sweden 1969. Martin Mulligan,
Wilhelm Bungert, Ove Bengtson
and Jan Kodes. King Gustav
from Sweden making a speech
at the Finals Ceremony.

TO THE CHICKEN COUP FOR MONEY

At Wimbledon Jan Kodes met a man who brought about an event that hardly any tennis player ever experienced.

I was constantly followed by a man, who turned out to be Turkish, and even a tennis player who had won his country's Nationals a few years earlier! His name was Ulug, a comical sort of a guy. He kept telling me that I had to come and play a great tournament in Istanbul. And he wanted me to play doubles with Kukal. He kept after me until I agreed and Jan Kukal and I decided to go there.

After my first match in Istanbul I returned to the hotel and quickly took a swim in the pool to soothe my tired muscles. At one moment I came to the curb and looked around. There were a few bungalows in some distance and, all of a sudden, I could not believe my eyes - there stood Charles Bronson between those cottages!

I thought to myself "this must be a dream!" I ducked under the water, came up - it was him and he was still there! He was shooting a film in Istanbul and was staying with his family in a bungalow by the pool. I saw him several more times during that week and I wondered, how could he be making Westerns when he was so small? But I was too timid to ask him.

I played several good matches there and together with Kukal we won doubles beating Hewitt-Maud in a five-set final 8:10, 6:4, 5:7, 7:5, and 9:7. Friday, prior to the final, approached quickly and we still received no pocket money.

Tournament Director from Istanbul Mr. Ulug kept his promises...

Hewitt Turns Back Maude In Istanbul Tennis Final

ISTANBUL, Turkey, Aug. 25 (AP)—Bob Hewitt of South Africa defeated Bob Maude, 6-3, 8-6, 6-1, to capture the singles title at the 24th Istanbul tennis tournament today.

Hewitt and Maude, also of South Africa, were beaten in a 4-hour-8-minute doubles final by J. Kodas and J. Kukal of Czechoslovakia, 8-10, 6-4, 5-7, 7-5, 9-7.

"Jan, I am worried and wonder if we'll see any money at all. We have been playing all these five-setters and I am concerned that they won't give us any money?" I expressed uneasily.

"Then you must approach Ulug and ask him for some down-payment, at least."

I did just that right away: "Mr. Ulug, it is almost Saturday; tomorrow we play the doubles final and we have received no money yet!"

He responded: "Calm down, Mr. Kodes. Go to the end of the complex; all the way in the back of it there is a hole in the chain link fence – go through it and turn left; there you'll find a wooden hut. Mr. Akef will wait for you there and will give you your money."

"Oh shit" slipped out of my mouth, and then I said: "Let's go, Jan." There was a fence, and then a field covered with brush like in the African bush. We passed through that hole and there, on the left, there was really a wooden hut. But what kind?! A chicken coup on stilts! Just like out of a fairy tale, the one where witches should live. There was a ladder leading up, and then a small gate.

I thought to myself: Where have we been sent to? I hope nobody just cuts our throats here!

Suddenly Jan said: "Look, there is somebody waving at us. Go first!" I stepped on the ladder and carefully climbed up till I reached the coup. There was hay inside and a round table with a few tree stumps around it to sit on. A man was sitting on one of them, a typical Turk: "Mr. Kodes, I am Akef; please, sit down."

He pulled out a suitcase from God-knows-where, opened it and it was full of US dollars! He counted off seven hundred dollars and placed them in an envelope. Then he pondered and said: "You are still in the doubles finals, right? So here you receive two hundred dollars more for the doubles."

I asked if he wanted me to sign something but he waved his arms vehemently: "No, no, nothing like that."

So, I picked up what I received, made my way down the ladder, and sent Kukal to get his share; all was well now.

We laughed about that episode for a long time and no matter to whom I told the story they had a hard time believing it. The culprit of the predicament was the fact that the official tennis currency was the US dollar. The organizers would not have been able to organize a tournament in Istanbul if they did not have enough US dollars. Their local currency was impossible to exchange into hard currency in those times so one can imagine what might have happened if they paid us with Turkish Liras. Beyond the borders of Turkey we would have been holding worthless banknotes. Not even this comical episode helped bringing back Jan's good form from the first half of the year. He received the news of his nomination for the US Open 128-draw at Forest Hills with mixed feelings.

His foreboding came true in the second round, when he lost to the Wimbledon quarter-finalist from the previous year and the past "Pro", the American Butch Buchholz, in five sets 2:6, 6:3, 3:6, 6:4, and 2:6. *I still felt unsteady on grass. I made errors when volleying, my feet faltered. I was in the process of learning how to move on grass surface.*

However, a curious thing happened on those grass courts at Forest Hills that year; something that has never repeated again. The final duel was between then thirty one years old Rod Laver from Australia and his seven years junior Tony Roche. Tennis experts alleged that it was going to be Tony who would succeed Laver at the top.

When Laver was entering the court his expression gave signs of evident fatigue and worry about what he would be facing in the next minutes. He was certainly aware of what he could gain but also lose in the upcoming match. If he won he would be the first player ever to accomplish winning the Grand Slam title, the dream of all tennis players, for the second time! In 1962 he won the Australian Open, the French Open, Wimbledon, and the US Open at Forest Hills for the first time. Now, seven years later, he had a chance to repeat that unprecedented triumph. He needed just that last step – win the 1969 US Open finals!

I have never seen Rod play as badly as he did in the first set. And my admiration and hats off went to him that much more because it was no easy task to overcome such a slump, wake up from it and deliver an amazing performance. In the following sets he ruled the court and Tony had no more chances. The Forest Hills stadium filled out to its capacity applauded the giant! He has been the only player so far to achieve that triumph the second time...

American Butch Buchholz was ranked fifth in the world in 1960 and turned professional. In 1962 he won the U.S. Pro Championships. Reached two quaterfinals at Wimbledon in 1960 and 1968.

Jan Kodes 1970. To win French Open is a dream
for many Australian and U.S. players. And not
only for them...

ROLAND GARROS

In the fall of 1969 Kukal and Zednik captured the first Swedish King´s Cup title for Czechoslovakia. Jan Kodes wasn't there since he had left for South America for the second time.

I traveled there with only one goal in mind: to adapt my organism to the highest physical stress for the period of, at least, ten months. In addition, it allowed me to prolong the playing season out of doors. The South American Championships took place in Buenos Aires at the beginning of November. Though competition was very strong there I was quite upset by my unexpected loss to Jauffret from France 5:7, 0:6, 10:12.

I met him again a week later, as if on purpose, in the semi-finals of the Chilean Championships. By then I was fully acclimatized and played considerably better winning the entire tournament! After two tough victories over the host country players Lito Alvarez 6:4, 6:4, 7:5 and Rodriguez 6:0, 3:6, 6:4, 6:8, 6:4 I also swept the French champ Jauffret off the court 6:4, 6:4, 6:3 and the following day I raised the trophy of the Champion of Chile above my head after defeating Milan Holecek in five sets 4:6, 6:3, 1:6, 6:1, and 6:2. That was the first trophy I conquered beyond my homeland! With Milan Holecek we defeated the Chilean Davis Cup doubles team Fillol – Cornejo in the doubles finals 4:6, 6:2, 6:0, 6:2, which was a sweet revenge for their victory over us in the semi-finals in Buenos Aires.

The South-American climate suited Kodes well. From Santiago he moved to Sao Paolo where he pulled off another victory and this time he became the International Champion of Brazil. In sequence he defeated the Brazilian Cunha, the Argentine Vilas, the German Buding and Milan Holecek in the finals, again in five sets. Milan played very well in this tournament and staged great surprises by defeating Mandarino from Brazil, the French Jauffret, and Cornejo from Chile.

Our entrepreneur Prokopio had bad luck during the tournament. There was a fire in the athletic equipment storage and in the course of those two weeks he never made an appearance around the tennis center. We wondered what had happened because in all previous tournaments we received money on Friday or Saturday before the tournament's closure. We asked Mandarino what was going on. "Prokopio has his head spinning due to some problems but he'll be here on Saturday for the semis." When he found out that two Czechs advanced all the way to the finals he informed us that he would hold the money until after the outcome of the finals. Did he worry that we would "fix" the match in some fashion? – Milan steadfastly proclaimed: "If we do not receive the money before the match we won't play the finals!" Prokopio squirmed and claimed that he couldn't get us the money since banks were closed during weekends. The next day Mandarino came to see us in the locker room and urged us to be calm. Prokopio gave him the money but asked him to hand the money over to the players only after the match. We trusted Edson Mandarino, went onto the court and "rewarded" him and the audience with another amazing five-setter. Just like in Chile, I won 4:6, 6:3, 1:6, 6:4, and 6:3. Everything turned out well!

After two winter months at home and passing successfully a few college exams Jan Kodes flew out of the country for the third time to the United States and subsequently to play the 1970 Caribbean Circuit. He started off in Philadelphia, where he lost badly in the first round to Tom Gorman 2:6, 7:6, 0:6! However, teamed up with the Mexican Loyo-Mayo they defeated Newcombe – Roche, but lost then to Santana – Gimeno.

The tournament in Salisbury was next on our schedule. Here I have to mention that soon after his arrival from Australia Milan Holecek told us that he was going to defect. That was quite a blow to me.

He dashed into the locker room and asked me and Jan Kukal to follow him to the next room and there he said: "Friends, I am not returning home. It is all clear to me that Bolardt is after

Kodes clan in the United States in 1969. Front left: Fred and Mary Kodes, Norma and Bill Sprague. Far left: Opel and Fred Kodes with both families' children.

me. He will put a stop to my Davis Cup play; he won't give me a chance any more. He started to eliminate me already last year when he did not put me in the line up against Monaco claiming that I needed rest....

I tried to talk him out of it: "Come on Milan; don't forget what invaluable doubles we play together! You can't just give that up!

But he insisted that his mind was definitely made up. And so, he was the second player to defect; Petr Strobl emigrated in 1969 and remained in Munich. However he was older and by the time he defected he was just coaching.

Milan was still a great competitive player. He returned home from the United States but left for good in spring 1971 to play the West German Bundes-league in Amberg and later moved to Kempten. By then his emigration status was definite.

In Salisbury, during the match with Jim McManus, I suffered a terrible left ankle sprain at 10:8, 3:4, and I had to default. The sprain occurred on the other leg than the year before when I hurt my ankle in Brussels during our Davis Cup match. The puffed-up left leg had to be set in cast. Since I had a plane ticket for the entire circuit I decided to remain and not fly back home because I would not have had enough money to pay for another ticket two or three weeks later.

I called my distant aunt in Cleveland and asked her if I could stay with her for two to three weeks. She was delighted and invited me to come at once! As soon as I arrived at her doorstep I asked her: "Do you have some tennis courts close-by?"

She did not know much about tennis, nevertheless she started calling around the local clubs and found out that there was a professional coach by the name of Jack March in one of them. She drove me to meet him. He introduced himself as an ex-tennis player who, by his own words, never achieved much but knew who I was.

"Oh yeah, you are Kodes who beat Ashe and Smith? That is remarkable; I'll do whatever

I can for you here. You'll play with our juniors. We have a narrow singles court on top and you can just stand there and feed the balls to them from the spot even with your cast on." - That was how I became a coach of the juniors!

From the next day on I came to the court even with my "plaster hoof" and played with the kids from a stationary spot just to keep my arm in shape and not loose my touch.

My aunt Mary lamented: "How can you play with it on? You should be lying in bed with your leg up!" She did not see the sense of it...

Two weeks later the cast came off and was replaced by bandage. As soon as the leg got stronger I was

Fred Kodes, my father's cousin teaching me to drink „bourbon and ginger ale".

back playing on the Circuit. We played on concrete in Caracas and I just walked through the first match against the Hungarian Szöke still hesitant to engage full force. The ankle was sore and I was afraid. I continued with the rehabilitation, I iced the ankle and bathed the leg in the pool.

I started playing at full force on red clay in Barranquilla, Colombia, where my sister and her husband and my wife joined me. I won three matches but an unpleasant thing took place in the semi-finals. I came across a Yugoslavian player Nicola Spear, the kind of a player that I always had profound difficulties playing. He was an unbelievable retriever; every point consisted of drop shots and lobs – he knew how to work me over. We played for close to four hours when at 5:5 in the fifth I got dizzy, my legs cramped up and I do not remember what followed. Apparently, my brother-in-law ran onto the court, defaulted me and pulled me into the locker-room. It might have been sun stroke or total exhaustion. I lost a good deal of my stamina during the ankle injury rehabilitation month; the additional heat was too much for me to endure. It was a drastic switch from snowy Cleveland to "burning" South America.

In the following weeks Kodes completed the Caribbean Circuit. With the exception of some tournament venues the circuit was similar to the previous two. First, there were two hard surface tournaments in Curacao and San Juan, where he took it somewhat easy and looked forward to the green clay tournaments in Florida.

One of the last stints took place in St. Petersburg where, coincidentally, my aunt Mary had moved to after her husband's death. My ankle was fine by then. I was more confident and did not hesitate to run at full speed. I felt that my performance was gaining momentum which was an uplifting realization just before the Italian Open in Rome.

As I arrived in the local club and found the draw I could not believe my eyes! There was a draw of 128 players and I was not seeded! As I stared at the draw my brother-in-law remarked: "I can't believe this!? You defeated Ashe and Smith and they did not even seed you? Who are these people who direct the tournament?"

Some tournament official came by and my brother-in-law nudged me: "Tell him; don't be stupid!"

Shyly I blurted out: "Sir how is it possible that I am not seeded?"

He looked at me and only God knows what he was thinking at that moment.

Carefully I carried on: "I thought that since I defeated Ashe..."

"What? You beat Arthur Ashe?"

Mr. Johns, Tournament Director at St. Petersburg, Florida.

"Yes; and Smith too."

"Don't say! You defeated even Stan Smith?"

He pulled down the draw and redid it in its entirety. Subsequently, he seeded me as number one and only then I realized that I put myself in big trouble. What if I lose in the first round? I shuddered!

On the way to the finals I eliminated Mike Belkin from Canada. I felt very content when I crushed the Mexican Joaquin Loyo-Mayo three times 6:3 in the finals.

Years later, while visiting my aunt Mary in a retirement community in St. Petersburg in Florida, I met the local pros who knew the tournament director Mr. Johns. He remembered me well and recounted the story: "Kodes? – Oh yes; in the seventies I had to redo the entire tournament draw because of him!"

I am told that my aunt Mary was proud of me ever since I spent those two weeks with her nursing my ankle. She and all the other relatives then followed my tennis career closely. She had five grandchildren and eleven great-grandchildren living all over the United States. Mary had been an active member of Christ Lutheran Church and volunteered on various committees.

She voluntered for many years at Bayfront and Edward White Hospitals and at Menorah Manor Nursing Home.

Mary was just a great woman, she was 98 and still won the prize in "New York, New York" party in May just before she died July 20, 2005.

FIRST BIG FINALS

Kodes left for Rome shortly after his return from the Caribbean Circuit. He was received warmly by the officials there, still remembered for his outstanding performance against Newcombe the year before. The excellent Australian as well as other five superb players from Lamar Hunt's group were absent from 1970 Foro Italico; due to some financial disagreements with the tournament organizers Lamar Hunt did not allow them to enter the tourney. In spite of it the competition was tough and it was delightful to watch Jan Kodes make his way all the way into his first grand final.

The first round went smoothly against Juan Gisbert from Spain: 6:3, 6:3, 6:1. However, I had a narrow squeak with Charlie Pasarell in the second round match. He did not let me catch my breath; he must have noticed that I was having stamina problems. I tried to disguise the way I really felt but I was truly exhausted. Roman clay was slower than the American and the

Italian balls Pirelli were heavier. One had to exert more effort during the rallies and especially trying to put the ball away than playing with the American Wilson balls.

Each and every shot seeped much energy out of me. The last point? My shot landed close to the line and Pasarell's racket got there a split of a second too late. I won 6:4, 5:7, 6:0, 6:3. I don't even know how I managed to get to the locker room. All of a sudden I blacked out.... That was the second time in a short span.

The doctor described it as "heat exhaustion collapse". "You'll be fine from now on!"

And he was right. The next day the British player Mark Cox left the court with his head slouched after Kodes defeated him 5:7, 6:3, 6:2, and 6:2. Cox' efforts to overcome fatigued adversary ended futile. The news of Kodes' fainting spell in the locker room had filtered out to everybody in no time at Foro Italico. However, the Czech player did not allow any adverse sensation to follow.

During the finals with Nastase the dry red clay stuck to my „Spring-court" canvas shoes.

In the semis I faced my agelong rival Alexander Metreveli. I took a stroll through Rome the night before. As I roamed the streets I kept mulling over: Why do I have to play Metreveli again? We know each other's game since junior years. In my mind I kept replaying some points from his matches against Tiriac and Lewis Hoad, who was the top seed. Alex played an excellent game against him... Tomorrow I'll battle for my first grand final. My gargantuan dream....

Italian newspapers debated the odds of the situation that popped up for the first time in the history of the Italian Open. In the past semifinal matches the contestants were primarily either American or Australian. In 1970 they were all players from behind the Iron Curtain. The other semifinal match was between the Romanian Ilie Nastase and Yugoslav Nikki Pilic.

Kodes' dream came true the next day – he advanced into the finals of one of the biggest world clay court tennis tournaments after defeating Metreveli 6:3, 8:6, and 6:4!

The three sets to love victory sounds trouble-free but it was anything but easy. It was a battle field. I was nervous at the start but once I shook off the jitterbugs I played fantastic!

Italian Open 1970. Illie Nastase beat Jan Kodes in the Eastern European finals.

Nicola Pietrangeli, probably the greatest Italian won in Monte Carlo three times: 1961,1967,1968 over Darmon, Mulligan and Metreveli. Received the Cup from Princess Grace of Monaco in 1967.

I faced another agelong rival in the finals - Ilie Nastase from Romania. I lost 3:6, 6:1, 3:6, 6:8 but it was an enormous fight. The Roman crowd cheered like in the times of gladiator games; unfortunately they were entertained on my behalf. I was losing 2:5 in the fourth but I still managed to inspire more drama. I tied the score 6:6 however Ilie did not allow me to take him into the fifth. Pity! Who knows what would have happened?

Jan Kodes faced another difficult joust shortly after the tournament in Rome – a Davis Cup match against Italy. He left the "city that never sleeps" and headed several hundred miles North to the foothills of the Alps where Fiat originated and where the "old lady" Juventus Turin dwells till today. There he experienced something that he never again confronted.

Davis Cup; Czechoslovakia vs Italy at Turin in 1970. Before the doubles: Massimo Di Domenico, Adriano Panatta, Jan Kodes and Jan Kukal (from left).

We all feared that match. The Italians took the aging Nicola Pietrangeli out of the team and selected Panatta – Di Domenico. They put their chances in Adriano Panatta.

At that time I was also taking exams at the College of Economy and I dragged my lecture notes and study materials everywhere with me. I fooled myself into believing that it calmed me down.

The first day passed – a tied score at 1:1 as expected. I defeated Di Domenico only after a five-set battle. It took a lot out of me. Kukal lost to Panatta. Though odds were on our side to win the doubles we ended up losing it in five sets! As soon as the Italians won the match-point the crowd started to throw the chair cushions onto the court, some of them landed on top of our heads, shoulders....

We started the third day at team score 1:2 and I thought to myself: Well, Kukal will lose to Di Domenico and the stress will be over! Our doubles loss would haunt us! - They scrambled for each and every point and all of a sudden Jan Kukal started to play better and turned things around. I was on the site premises sitting in the locker room and fear took over me! I did not see any point of the game but they kept me informed about the development of the game in stark detail.

The crowd roared on every Di Domenico's point won. When they did not roar I knew that Kukal made the point. I sat on the toilet seat, staring into my lecture notes hardly perceiving the content – something about commodities. The clamor of the crowd was overwhelming but then a loud groan echoed, followed by chilly silence that was broken only by placid applause. Composed, showing good manners. I then realized that Jan won!

Pavel Korda ran into the locker room his eyes popping out. "Lets hit quickly! You must warm up!"

By then I was dripping with sweat – from fear!

After a twenty minute break I went onto the court to play the decisive match against Panatta. I felt butterflies in my stomach. But what followed inspired in me a reaction that prompted me to dash onto the court like a hurricane and I never gave my opponent a chance to fight back in that match.

We all know what kind of atmosphere soccer fans "tifosi" can incite. The Turin center-court had pretty good capacity; there were four to five thousand spectators in the crowd. As soon as we stepped onto the court the people got up and started singing. Probably like in the British soccer league when Manchester United plays Liverpool!

As we were warming up the crowd was singing one chant or another. Once we began to play the game they all quieted down but my senses were so activated and energized by then that I hardly missed a shot! While this never happened to me ever again it inspired a real barrage in me there and then. I swept him off the court 6:3, 6:2, 6:2!

When we returned to Prague we saw newspaper headlines peering at us from the daily press: "They fought and they conquered", "Kukal generated drama as well as rescue!"

Pavel Korda, who had returned from his coaching engagement in Luxemburg, acted as a new Davis Cup coach for the first time in Turin.

He took up cooperation with Jan Kodes from the years 1966 to 1969, when he was helping Jan primarily during his winter preparation. With the Tennis Federation's consent Korda became Jan's personal coach. While neither one of them knew it then the fruit of this cooperation was going to be reaped very soon...

FRENCH OPEN

There is no other tournament that would be as physically demanding as Roland Garros. The slow heavy clay and tough competition, as well as the assumed significance of the World Clay Court Championship in addition to the Grand Slam status elevate it to one of the most challenging tennis events in the world. Several hours long marathon matches are not exceptions and startling surprises are not in short supply.

In 1970 many astonishing results cropped up. Arthur Ashe arrived as a fresh Australian Open champion hoping to go after the Grand Slam title like Laver in the previous years. His hope was crushed by the Yugoslav Zeljko Franulovic. The winner of the Italian Open, the Romanian Ilie Nastase, who was also one of the favorites in Paris, exited Paris after his quarterfinal with the American Cliff Richey. Two more tremendous achievements were accomplished by the host country's player, a spectacular youngster, Georges Goven. He defeated first his countryman Francois Jauffret and afterwards the Spaniard Manuel Santana!

Jan Kodes won three rounds and made it past the Frenchman Jean Batiste Chanfreau, the Australian Bob Howe, and the Czech Stepan Koudelka, who he beat with a merciless score of 6:0, 6:1, 6:2! That was a sweet revenge for all those defeats during junior years....

At that point Stepan was traveling from tournament to tournament with his South African girlfriend and was trying to decide where to settle down. Ultimately, he received a contract in Osnabrück and stayed in Germany. I steamrolled him and realized that I was playing at a different level than in Pardubice a few years previously.

In the fourth round Jan Kodes beat Ion Tiriac, a shrewd Romanian, 4:6, 7:5, 4:6, 6:2, 6:2.

At a set score 1:2 we had a break and went to the locker room. There were wooden lockers there and all of a sudden I heard a horrific bang! Tiriac slammed his fist into one of the lockers and punched a hole through it!

Players asked in wonder: "What is the matter? Have you lost?"

"No, I am ahead 2:1 in sets."

"So what's this madness for?"

"Because I was up 4:2 in the second set and we could have been done by now!"

The quarterfinal duel with the naturalized Australian Martin Mulligan, three times the winner of the Championship in Rome, was a sure victory for the Czech player: 6:1, 6:3, 7:5. The above mentioned Georges Goven then awaited Kodes in the semifinals! The sold out Centre Court pushed forth their favorite. This would have brought the third surprise, of Kodes' accord, and the French audience would have loved it because their own player would become the "dark horse" of the tournament.

Martin Mulligan won in Rome three times: 1963, 1965, 1967 over Jovanovic, Santana and Roche. In Paris was beaten by Jan Kodes (left).

I sensed it was not going to be an easy match but Goven surprised me with everything. He played brilliantly! The first set went to him and I only shook my head in disbelieve. I felt like he manipulated me any which way he wanted to. He ran me on the court and made no unforced errors! There was plenty of wind and I could not find a weapon against the misery he created for me! The wind was taking balls off my racket, and they landed everywhere and anywhere only not where I wanted them to. I played quick points largely out of control. I did win the second set but Goven took the third in no time and was ahead 2:1 in sets.

Thank God there was a 15 minutes break....

During the break Karel Sulc came up to Kodes in the locker room. Yes, it was the same Karel Sulc, who Jan met for the first time in 1965 during the Coupe Michel Bivort in Paris, and who offered Jan his help whenever he would be in France.

He suddenly appeared in the locker room and said: "Jaroslav Drobny is sending you a message: do not keep approaching the net after a topspin backhand."

Goven played a great defense and our rallies usually took place first from the baseline; when I could no longer stand that I approached the net after a topspin backhand. However, he found a faultless counter weapon that he used consistently and that was almost hundred percent effective: he tackled my topspin and

FRANULOVIC OU RICHEY; GOVEN OU KODES
(Dessin de Luc VINCENT).

Semifinal prognosis by the cartoonist Luca Vincent...

Sold out centercourt for semifinals with Georges Goven.

executed a chopped passing shot down the line. He took it soon after the bounce and pulled it down with a low under-spin! If I caught the passing shot with my forehand volley I would be forced to lift it which, in turn, would make it easy for Goven to put away with the next shot.

It did not occur to me that I should change my strategy; his forehand was strong and I was hesitant to play that side. I kept banging the ball from the baseline, then I approached the net with a backhand topspin... and his unreachable down-the-line passing shot flew by me. Over and over again....

"So, Jaroslav suggests to play an under-spin instead of top-spin approach because then he won't be able to play an under-spin passing shot."

I was taking a shower and lamented: "It is easy for Jaroslav to know what to play; he is sitting somewhere in the audience! I am not able to hit an under-spin backhand as well as the topspin. I am not as consistent with the slice; it is not so simple to change one's game." I kept grumbling to myself...and Karel Sulc stopped persuading me. He passed the message and was done with it.

The fourth set was on the way: Goven 2:0! And again a long exchange! I was close to the end of my strength and knew I must do something. Drop-shot him, approach the net, or... whack, beautiful top-spin backhand! I was dashing to the net and before I knew it the ball passed me down-the-line! I was at the end of my wits!

All of a sudden, I raised my eyes – I don't even know why, perhaps I was trying to beg somebody up above for help – and I looked into the audience, that great anonymous mass of people. And what did I see? There was Jaroslav Drovny, sitting almost at the top of the players' section, and with him Karel Sulc, and some others. At that moment I internalized what Karel Sulc had told me in the locker-room: "not top-spin but under-spin!"

Well, smart Jaroslav! How am I going to be able to do that with the wind blowing? Nevertheless, since the bright minds above advised it, I was going to try it out. Right at the first opportunity!

With a shaking hand I attempted to hit a slice, a careful but deep slice. He ran to it but it bounced considerably lower than the top-spin. He tried to slice is back and pass me but... it hit the tape! Gee! Is it going to work for real? I'll try it again.

The next good moment came a few seconds later. I sliced the ball, and so did he and passed me but it landed an inch outside! The battle continued; I felt revived whereas he lost confidence. I won the forth and fifth sets 6:2, 6:3!

We finished and I succumbed to the most magnificent feeling at Roland Garros, when skilful hands of the masseur Robert Laurens, my friend, drew the exhaustion out of my legs, arms, and the entire body after the five-setter while I was lying on top of the massage table. I experienced it several times over....

He kneaded my calves and commented: "Jan, you are ok. Look at these muscles; they aren't even stiff!"

All of a sudden the doors burst open and in walked Karel Sulc. He patted my shoulder and said: "Jaroslav sends his congratulations, you played magnificently!"

"And where is he?" I asked.

"On a plane! When you were ahead 3:0 in the fifth he left for the airport saying: It's all his now!"

"Well, but I play the finals tomorrow with Franulovic! And he beat Richey in the semis!"

"He is confident that you'll win that too!"

I only shook my head in disbelief. That was Jaroslav Drobny.

Jan Kodes competed with Franulovic ever since his junior years. However, they became close friends only during the Caribbean Circuit and occasionally played doubles together. Now these two friends had to play each other in Roland Garros finals. In Kodes' first grand slam final! The American Cliff Richey had needed very little to reach that final.

Generally speaking, the Americans did not do well on the Parisian red clay but Cliff was one who knew how to handle the game on clay. I must admit that I did not like playing against him and it was lucky that I didn't have to face him here. If he had made it to the finals I wasn't sure what my chances to victory would have been. But that was just my speculation....

Richey was ahead 2:1 in sets against Franulovic and 5:1 in the fourth with two match-points. The sold out Centre Court wasn't yet ready to see the end of the match. Only one more

I was down two sets to one and 0:2 in the forth set...

American „number one" Cliff Richey lost to Zeljko Franulovic having a few matchpoints.

point could have ended the tennis show. Throughout the years I realized that the Grand Slam finals were won by the player who was supported by the spectators. It was hard to believe but it was so.

Final matches, specifically at Roland Garros, often turn out to be long exhausting marathons. When the fifth set comes around and one of the players is not French, the audience seems to root for the player who is trailing behind at any given moment, which may be the other player five minutes later. They want the match to go on and on; they want to make the best of every minute of it. And in that instant, when there is a line controversy and the players begin to argue with the umpire, the audience knows how to make their stance stick. And that is what happened at the moment of Richey's double match point.

There was a controversial line-call and Cliff began to argue; in so doing he inflamed people against him. The umpire ordered to play the point over.... I was up in the stands and, naturally, rooting for Franulovic. But Richey was winning and I started to calm myself with thoughts like: if I play against the American at least the audience will be on my side cheering for me.

However, after that controversial line-call the atmosphere in the stadium changed as if some magic wand had been waved. Franulovic battled back both of the match-points, his game caught on fire, and he diminished Richey's lead to 2:5; from that point on the crowd pushed Zeljko to an amazing performance and final victory. Richey got so unnerved that he lost the fourth and fifth sets identically 5:7!

The Yugoslav Franulovic was a much nicer opponent than Richey would have been; to some extent, because Kodes knew him well, and to another extent because he was not as dogged a player as Richey. Kodes also knew that he was more unsteady mentally and his backhand passing shot was not as lethal. They played each other quite often and there were many times when Franulovic had the edge. But the Grand Slam final was altogether another matter! The sold out "furnace" of the Centre Court, the June heat and the very tense atmosphere...it was all a play of nerves.

Initially, Kodes' legs were stiff, his hands were a bit off, and he had a hard time getting into the game. He was arriving a few hundreds of seconds late to strike the ball than he needed to. On the contrary, Franulovic was light on his feet, broke Kodes' first serve and subsequently won his own, and in no time he was leading 2:0. In the next game he needed only two more points to raise the score to 3:0!

Jump over the net for the first Grand Slam title.

That would have put me in a real jam. I kept telling myself "there must come a point that will help me catch on and all will turn around". I knew that he held high respect for my game. When we were entering the court I looked into his face and sensed that he was somewhat fearful.

Suddenly, he hit a sloppy shot, possibly he felt overconfident. More importantly, I noticed that he stayed behind the base line. Drop-shot him! I scaled down the power of the ball and pushed it onto his side. The ball slid on the clay, Franulovic had no chance to catch it. The audience roared and I lost the initial inhibition!

My first Grand Slam
title – it's hard beating
a friend...

President FFT Marcel Bernard presented the „Pierre Gillou Cup" to Jan Kodes. Bernard was also a great champion, winning Roland Garros in 1946, by beating Czech Jaroslav Drobny 3:6, 2:6, 6:1, 6:4, 6:3.

From that moment on I believed in myself; I was more forceful at the net and hit harder from the baseline. I often pulled him out to the forehand side and approached the net hitting to his backhand. The subsequent volley or smash finished off the point!

The third set closure – Kodes' backhand landed in the open space on Franulovic' side. Zeljko resigned himself and did not even budge... The score board read: 6:2, 6:4, 6:0.

Jan Kodes was jumping over the net... Marcel Bernard, the former notable player and present day chairman of the French Tennis Federation was walking in with the Cup for the Champion.

It flashed through my head that last year he presented that cup to Laver, now my name would be added. Even if I didn't win any other tournament in my entire career this moment was worth all the effort I have put into my preparation so far! The crowd was applauding and it sounded like the most beautiful melody to me. I felt a bit sorry for Zeljko; after a few years nobody would remember the runner-up...

Roland Garros and Wimbledon. Only three weeks separate the two Grand Slams! As soon as the Parisian clay courts orphane the tennis circus transfers to the lawn. The tournaments in Nottingham, Halle, Rosmalen, and Queen's Club offer good opportunities to adapt to grass. Originally there were three of the Grand Slam grass tournaments but only one remains today; it is the most prestigious and famous one – Wimbledon.

Thirty five years ago, during the peek of Jan Kodes' tennis career, there was only one opportunity to practice and play on grass, and that was during the London's Queen's Club tournament. However, a Davis Cup round needed to be squeezed into the schedule before the Queen's Club tournament!

It was terrible to play Davis Cup between Paris and Wimbledon. The matches were tough and furthermore the outcome depended on my performance; I had to put all I had into them. Immediately afterwards came the Queen's Club and then Wimbledon. It was hard to rege-

The first player from Eastern Europe to win Roland Garros in 1947 was Josef Asboth from Hungary. He beat Eric Sturgess from South Africa 8:6, 7:5, 6:4.

nerate and for that very reason I had a tough time in the opening rounds of the All England Club during the first few years.

In 1970 Kodes flew from Paris directly to Moscow to take part in a Davis Cup match. The encounter took place outdoors in a Small Athletic Arena in Luzniky. As soon as Kodes, the new Roland Garros Champion, arrived, the Russians sought him out and wanted to show off their match venue to him.

Our coach, Pavel Korda, and I came and we were taken around by the non-playing Davis Cup team captain Andrejev: "Jan, what do you think about the courts?"

I looked and uttered: "Well, they are ok."

The clay was not of the best quality, it wasn't as red as the type I was used to, and it reminded me of the courts in the Czech countryside that were not maintained well. Compared to Paris they were considerably inferior!

When we arrived the following day the courts were not red but yellow! They sprinkled them at night with sand! Two courts were done and the third was almost finished. I thought it was a bad dream! Old ladies with aprons and with scarves on their heads, and with wicker baskets swung over their shoulders were marching up and down the court and tossing about sand. As if sowing the grain! And in the sand there were big rocks.

Korda was livid and stormed in: "What are you doing here?" He pulled out his camera and started taking photos.

Two officials ran in, seized Korda and drove him to the director of Luzniky, where the two had a chance to confer. It so happened that Pavel had started to filter out the rocks before the two bouncers came out to get him; he wasn't going to have his players compete on rocks! However, that action prompted the bouncers to stop him. He had no official business to be there.

Korda quarreled with the director but, in the end, we still ended up playing on the yellow sand and the photos were not to be presented anywhere! Though the ITF rules stated that clay was the surface to be played on, the quality of the clay had not been specified; course or fine, hard or soft. Not even the color was stated. Thus it was difficult to argue, and I don't think our leadership wanted to challenge them.

The match ended with a 2:3 defeat, when Kodes lost to Metreveli with the score at 2:2. Both Czechoslovak players defeated Lejus, the decisive turning point was the doubles.

At 6:5 in the important fourth set the umpire made an unfair call. Jan Kukal and I had a match point when we hit Metreveli, who happened to play the ball with his head. It

Men's Singles *Holder* R. G. Laver

FIRST ROUND	SECOND ROUND	THIRD ROUND	FOURTH ROUND	QUARTER-FINALS	SEMI-FINALS	FINAL

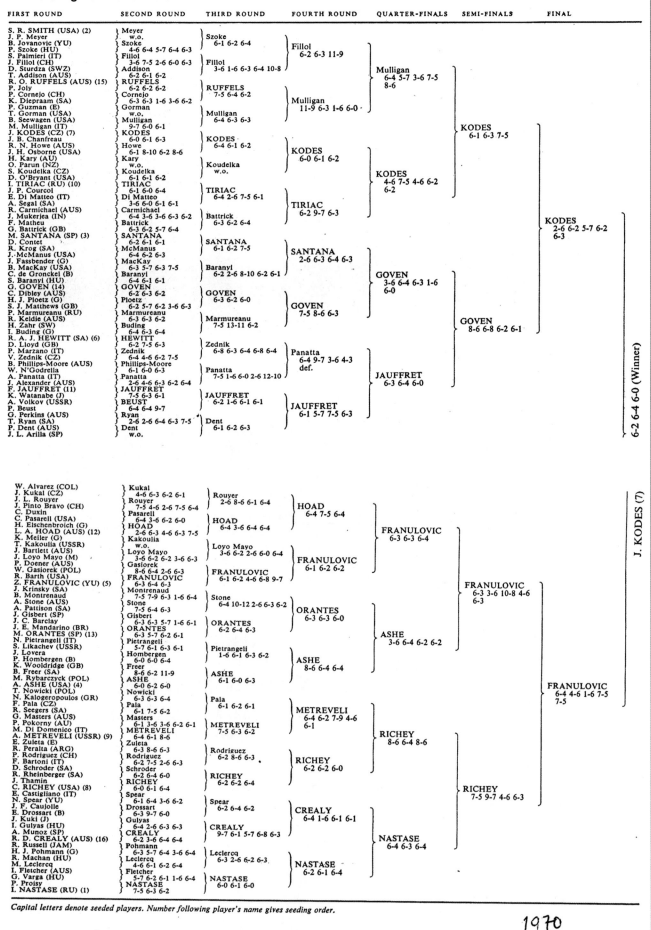

S. R. SMITH (USA) (2)
J. P. Meyer — Meyer w.o.
B. Jovanovic (YU)
P. Szoke (HU) — Szoke 4-6 6-4 5-7 6-4 6-3 — Szoke 6-1 6-2 6-4
S. Palmieri (IT)
J. Fillol (CH) — Fillol 3-6 7-5 2-6 6-0 6-3
D. Sturdza (SWZ)
T. Addison (AUS) — Addison 6-2 6-1 6-2 — Fillol 3-6 1-6 6-3 6-4 10-8 — Fillol 6-2 6-3 11-9
R. O. RUFFELS (AUS) (15)
P. Joly — RUFFELS 6-2 6-2 6-2
P. Cornejo (CH) — Cornejo 6-3 6-3 1-6 3-6 6-2 — RUFFELS 7-5 6-4 6-2
K. Diepraam (SA)
P. Guzman (E)
T. Gorman (USA) — Gorman w.o.
B. Seewagen (USA)
M. Mulligan (IT) — Mulligan 9-7 6-0 6-1 — Mulligan 6-4 6-3 6-3 — Mulligan 11-9 6-3 1-6 6-0 — Mulligan 6-4 5-7 3-6 7-5 8-6
J. KODES (CZ) (7)
J. B. Chanfreau — KODES 6-0 6-1 6-3
R. N. Howe (AUS) — Howe 6-1 8-10 6-2 8-6 — KODES 6-4 6-1 6-2
J. H. Osborne (USA)
H. Kary (AU) — Kary w.o.
O. Parun (NZ)
S. Koudelka (CZ) — Koudelka 6-1 6-1 6-2 — Koudelka w.o. — KODES 6-0 6-1 6-2
D. O'Bryant (USA)
I. TIRIAC (RU) (10) — TIRIAC 6-1 6-0 6-4 — KODES 4-6 7-5 4-6 6-2 6-2 — KODES 6-1 6-3 7-5
J. P. Courcol
E. Di Matteo (IT) — Di Matteo 3-6 6-0 6-1 6-1 — TIRIAC 6-4 2-6 7-5 6-1
A. Segal (SA)
R. Carmichael (AUS) — Carmichael 6-4 3-6 3-6 6-3 6-2 — TIRIAC 6-2 9-7 6-3
J. Mukerjea (IN)
F. Matheu — Battrick 6-3 6-2 5-7 6-4 — Battrick 6-3 6-2 6-4
G. Battrick (GB) (3)
M. SANTANA (SP) (3) — SANTANA 6-2 6-1 6-1
D. Contet — SANTANA 6-1 6-2 7-5
R. Krog (SA) — McManus 6-4 6-2 6-3
J. McManus (USA) — SANTANA 2-6 6-3 6-4 6-3
J. Fassbender (G) — MacKay 6-3 5-7 6-3 7-5
B. MacKay (USA)
C. de Gronckel (B) — Baranyi 6-4 6-1 6-1 — Baranyi 6-2 2-6 8-10 6-2 6-1
S. Baranyi (HU)
G. GOVEN (14) — GOVEN 6-2 6-3 6-2 — GOVEN 6-3 6-2 6-0 — GOVEN 3-6 6-4 6-3 1-6 6-0
C. Dibley (AUS)
H. J. Ploetz (G) — Ploetz 6-2 5-7 6-2 3-6 6-3 — GOVEN 7-5 8-6 6-3
S. J. Matthews (GB)
P. Marmureanu (RU) — Marmureanu 6-3 6-3 6-2 — Marmureanu 7-5 13-11 6-2
R. Keldie (AUS)
H. Zahr (SW)
I. Buding (G) — Buding 6-4 6-3 6-4 — GOVEN 8-6 6-8 6-2 6-1
R. A. J. HEWITT (SA) (6) — HEWITT 6-2 7-5 6-3
D. Lloyd (GB)
P. Marzano (IT) — Zednik 6-4 4-6 6-2 7-5 — Zednik 6-8 6-3 6-4 6-8 6-4
V. Zednik (CZ)
B. Phillips-Moore (AUS) — Phillips-Moore 6-1 6-0 6-3 — Panatta 6-4 9-7 3-6 4-3 def.
W. N'Godrella (AUS)
A. Panatta (IT) — Panatta 2-6 4-6 6-3 6-2 6-4 — Panatta 7-5 1-6 6-0 2-6 12-10
J. Alexander (AUS)
F. JAUFFRET (11) — JAUFFRET 7-5 6-3 6-1 — JAUFFRET 6-3 6-4 6-0
K. Watanabe (J)
A. Volkov (USSR) — BEUST 6-4 6-4 9-7 — JAUFFRET 6-2 1-6 6-1 6-1
P. Beust
G. Perkins (AUS) — Ryan 2-6 2-6 6-4 6-3 7-5 — JAUFFRET 6-1 5-7 7-5 6-3
T. Ryan (SA)
P. Dent (AUS) — Dent w.o. — Dent 6-1 6-2 6-3
J. L. Arilla (SP)

W. Alvarez (COL)
J. Kukal (CZ) — Kukal 4-6 6-3 6-2 6-1
J. L. Rouyer — Rouyer 7-5 4-6 2-6 7-5 6-4 — Rouyer 2-6 8-6 6-1 6-4
J. Pinto Bravo (CH)
C. Duxin
C. Pasarell (USA) — Pasarell 6-4 3-6 6-2 6-0 — HOAD 6-4 3-6 6-4 6-4 — HOAD 6-4 7-5 6-4
H. Elschenbroich (G)
L. A. HOAD (AUS) (12) — HOAD 2-6 6-3 4-6 6-3 7-5
K. Meiler (G)
T. Kakoulia (USSR) — Kakoulia w.o. — Loyo Mayo 3-6 6-2 2-6 6-0 6-4
J. Bartlett (AUS)
J. Loyo Mayo (M) — Loyo Mayo 3-6 6-2 6-2 3-6 6-3 — FRANULOVIC 6-3 6-3 6-4
P. Doener (AUS)
W. Gasiorek (POL) — Gasiorek 8-6 6-4 2-6 6-3 — FRANULOVIC 6-1 6-2 6-2
R. Barth (USA)
Z. FRANULOVIC (YU) (5) — FRANULOVIC 6-3 6-4 6-3 — FRANULOVIC 6-1 6-2 4-6 6-8 9-7
J. Krinsky (SA)
B. Montrenaud — Montrenaud 7-5 7-9 6-3 1-6 6-4
A. Stone (AUS) — Stone 7-5 6-4 6-3 — Stone 6-4 10-12 2-6 6-3 6-2
A. Pattison (SA)
J. Gisbert (SP) — Gisbert 6-3 6-3 5-7 1-6 6-1 — ORANTES 6-3 6-3 6-0
J. C. Barclay
J. E. Mandarino (BR) — ORANTES 6-3 5-7 6-2 6-1 — ORANTES 6-2 6-4 6-3
M. ORANTES (SP) (13)
N. Pietrangeli (IT) — Pietrangeli 5-7 6-1 6-3 6-1 — Pietrangeli 1-6 6-1 6-3 6-2
S. Likachev (USSR)
J. Lovera — Hombergen 6-0 6-0 6-4 — ASHE 3-6 6-4 6-2 6-2
P. Hombergen (B)
K. Wooldridge (GB) — Freer 8-6 6-2 11-9 — ASHE 8-6 6-4 6-4
B. Freer (SA)
M. Rybarczyck (POL) — ASHE 6-0 6-2 6-0 — ASHE 6-1 6-0 6-3
A. ASHE (USA) (4)
T. Nowicki (POL) — Nowicki 6-3 6-3 6-4 — ASHE 3-6 6-4 6-2 6-2
N. Kalogeropoulos (GR)
F. Pala (CZ) — Pala 6-1 7-5 6-2 — Pala 6-1 6-2 6-1
R. Seegers (SA)
G. Masters (AUS) — Masters 6-1 3-6 3-6 6-2 6-1 — METREVELI 6-4 6-2 7-9 4-6 6-1
P. Pokorny (AU)
M. Di Domenico (IT) — METREVELI 6-4 6-1 8-6 — METREVELI 7-5 6-3 6-2
A. METREVELI (USSR) (9)
E. Zuleta (E) — Zuleta 6-3 8-6 6-3 — Rodriguez 6-2 8-6 6-3
R. Peralta (ARG)
P. Rodriguez (CH) — Rodriguez 6-2 7-5 2-6 6-3 — RICHEY 6-2 6-2 6-0
F. Bartoni (IT)
D. Schroder (SA) — Schroder 6-2 6-4 6-0 — RICHEY 8-6 6-4 8-6
R. Rheinberger (SA)
J. Thamin — RICHEY 6-2 6-2 6-4
C. RICHEY (USA) (8)
E. Castigliano (IT) — Spear 6-1 6-4 3-6 6-2 — Spear 6-2 6-4 6-2
N. Spear (YU)
J. F. Caujolle — Drossart 6-3 9-7 6-0 — CREALY 6-4 1-6 6-1 6-1
E. Drossart (B)
J. Kuki (J) — Gulyas 6-4 2-6 6-3 6-3 — CREALY 9-7 6-1 5-7 6-8 6-3
I. Gulyas (HU)
A. Munoz (SP) — CREALY 6-2 3-6 6-4 6-4 — NASTASE 6-4 6-3 6-4
R. D. CREALY (AUS) (16)
R. Russell (JAM) — Pohmann 6-3 5-7 6-4 3-6 6-4 — Leclercq 6-3 2-6 6-2 6-3
H. J. Pohmann (G)
R. Machan (HU) — Leclercq 4-6 6-1 6-2 6-4 — NASTASE 6-2 6-1 6-4
M. Leclercq
I. Fletcher (AUS) — Fletcher 5-7 6-2 6-1 1-6 6-4 — NASTASE 6-0 6-1 6-0
G. Varga (HU)
P. Proisy — NASTASE 7-5 6-3 6-2
I. NASTASE (RU) (1)

FRANULOVIC 6-3 3-6 10-8 4-6 6-3

RICHEY 7-5 9-7 4-6 6-3

FRANULOVIC 6-4 4-6 1-6 7-5 7-5

KODES 2-6 6-2 5-7 6-2 6-3

J. KODES (7) — 6-2 6-4 6-0 (Winner)

Capital letters denote seeded players. Number following player's name gives seeding order.

1970

KODÈS a surclassé l'ombre de Franulovic

Françoise DURR et Gail CHANFREAU ont remporté le double

JAN KODES sortit de sa poche un petit carnet rouge et il inscrivit: « 6 juin, Paris, victoire sur Franulovic 6-2, 6-4, 6-0 en finale des championnats internationaux de France. »

Depuis ses débuts, Kodes note ainsi tous ses résultats sur des petits carnets. Cette fois, pourtant il aurait certainement pu s'en passer : il ne risque en effet pas d'oublier la première grande victoire de sa carrière.

Jan Kodes est devenu ainsi, dix-huit ans après Jaroslav Drobny, présent sur les gradins de Roland-Garros, où s'entassaient environ dix mille personnes, le deuxième Tchécoslovaque à remporter ce championnat.

Une victoire totale dans une finale courte (1 heure 05) et décevante, justement parce que Kodes était pratiquement seul sur le court.

Le merveilleux Franulovic, si brillant vainqueur de Ashe auparavant, n'était que l'ombre de lui-même.

Il mena 2-0 pourtant dans le premier set. Mais ce fut en raison de fautes de Kodes qui ne s'était pas encore réglé.

La fragilité de « Franu »

Dès que le Tchécoslovaque trouva sa cadence, il n'y eut plus de match. Franulovic ne pouvait rien contre le « pressing » constant de Kodes, qui le poussait régulièrement à la faute.

Si le Yougoslave tentait de monter au filet, il était irrémédiablement transpercé par les passing-shots de Kodes, en superforme et dans un jour de grâce.

« Jamais de ma vie je n'avais joué aussi bien, dira plus tard Kodes. Sauf peut-être cette année contre Newcombe, l'an dernier, à Roland-Garros. Mais, ce jour-là, je n'avais pas eu de réussite. »

Et de 2-0 en faveur de Franulovic, le score passa à 6-2 et 1-0 pour Kodes. En quelques

nèrent, bien qu'il ait sauvé trois balles de set :

« Alors, à deux manches, j'étais sûr que j'allais gagner », avoua Kodes.

Il n'avait pas à être inquiet en effet. Très confiant, il montait au filet à la moindre occasion, certain de finir le point.

En face, Franulovic paraissait perdu, désemparé. Rien à faire contre ce Kodes-là, qui ne laisse pas une seconde de répit à l'adversaire, ne lui donne jamais la moindre occasion de se reprendre. On ne refait pas tous les jours le coup du match contre Richey.

Une exécution

Et le troisième set fut une triste exécution. Cette fois Kodes gagna 8 jeux consécutifs.

Une preuve de sa domination : Franulovic n'eut pas une seule balle de jeu dans les 18 que gagna Kodes.

« Tel qu'il a joué aujourd'hui, estimait Franulovic, Kodes est du niveau de Laver et des autres meilleurs joueurs du monde. »

Ce que Kodes confirmait peu après :

« Aujourd'hui je pense que j'aurais pu gagner également contre n'importe qui. »

Aucune prétention chez Kodès. Ce n'est pas le genre de ce garçon aux yeux bleus, au visage émacié et triste d'où émerge sous la chevelure blonde et frisée, un nez à la Bourbon. Mais, à vingt-quatre ans, Jan Kodes a effectivement atteint le niveau des meilleurs, du moins sur terre battue.

Sur herbe, le Tchécoslovaque est nettement inférieur. Il s'en explique :

« Nous, Européens, nous jouons trop peu sur herbe. Nous n'avons aucune expérience. »

Jan Kodes n'en est pas moins un grand champion. On ne gagne pas par hasard les championnats de France.

Son plus difficile adversaire :

« Ce fut Tiriac. D'ailleurs, lorsque j'avais vu le tableau, je m'étais dit, si je passe Tiriac, j'ai une chance de gagner. Mais contre Goven, j'étais contracté parce que j'étais favori, et je savais qu'il y avait la finale au bout de ce match. Et ce fut également difficile. »

Kodès, tout sourire, c'est le premier grand succès de sa carrière.

all happened just in front of the main umpire, referee and the entire audience! The referee from Poland allowed the point to stick, and instead of it being our match point, it was advantage to Soviets.

We lost 5:7, 6:1, 6:2, 6:8, 4:6.

Immediately afterwards I lost to Metreveli in five sets 2:6, 5:7, 6:3, 6:2, 5:7 in the first round of Wimbledon! The match was suspended for darkness at 2 sets all; the fifth set got finished the following day. I remember it as if I played it today. I was leading 4:3 and he hit the tape twice in a row with the ball rolling over to my side. I thought I was going to go mad but there was nothing one could do about such shots.

Tony Trabert was the first American to win on clay in Paris. He took the title twice: over his compatriot Arthur Larsen in 1954 and Swede Sven Davidson in 1955.

CONFLICT BEFORE THE MASTERS

While on the world tennis scene The International Tennis Federation began eliminating areas of friction slowly but surely, domestically, in Czechoslovakia, there were more and more opinions and newspaper articles deprecating professionalism and tennis itself! The reasons were clear enough: the superseding cause was the rigid period of political "normalization", closed borders, hence difficulties to travel out of the country and, especially, to the West. All of a sudden it was pointed out that there were individuals in the country who spent more time in "capitalist" countries playing tennis than at home, who made their living playing tennis, a bourgeois and privileged sport of the "crème de la crème" society, and who earned their living in dollars! At that point of time all that was something utterly unthinkable!

Typical Czech jealousy began to work at full speed. Vaclav Svadlena, for instance, wrote:

I do not wish to argue the debate between Jiri Fabinger and Antonin Bolardt, however, some points claim clarification or explanation. For example, why should we be concerned with semi-professionals, I mean "our" semi-professionals, and consider revision of their contracts. Wouldn't it be more correct simply invalidating them? It is beyond comprehension that our players are available to the Union only for ten instead of contractual sixteen weeks. Are we going to allow and support this aftermath of Prague Spring 1968?

Rude pravo – Communist press

Such and many other similar articles appeared with more frequency. That was troublesome. At that moment I was afraid to oppose anything. I was under constant pressure, yet I wanted to satisfy all sides. Unfortunately, I could carry on that way only at the expense of missing tournaments with world competition, where I could have reached more points and achieved a better final ranking at the end of the year.

Jan Kodes and his success was a sore in many people's side. It is evidenced by the following extempore that occurred in connection to the departure to the first Masters' Cup in Tokyo. The tournament took place in December, shortly before Christmas. . One day the Kodes' received an envelope in which they found return air-tickets for Jan and his wife from Prague to Tokyo, fully paid by Pepsi Cola, the main tournament sponsor; enclosed was an invitation letter signed by Jack Kramer.

In view of my preparation I started working out on wooden surface of RH Praha in Vrsovice, where Jiri Hrebec approached me the first day and apologized for hurting me with the affair. I accepted his apology and tried to forget it...

Lenka conveyed that she would like to fly to Tokyo with me, and to my mind that was a sure thing – I was going to Tokyo with my wife. Same as all the other entrants. But, a problem arose. My wife, also a tennis player of higher standing, had a "business" passport that she used numerous times to travel with Sparta club team. I had my personal private passport in addition to the "business" passport. Before traveling to the West the "business" passports had to be collected from the International Department of the Central Committee of Czechoslovak Union of Physical Education and Sport, headed by Dr. Frantisek Kroutil. In addition to having a passport we also had to have an exit visa; that was given, customarily, before the first trip out of the country at the beginning of the year. We did not have any complications with visas to Tokyo; we were told that we should obtain those upon arriving at Tokyo airport; that had been arranged by the tournament organizers.

The departure date was fast approaching and there was not enough time to issue a personal passport for Lenka. I took Jack Kramer's invitation letter and rushed to the International Department of our CUPES. With the letter in hand I asked to borrow her "business" passport with the exit permit in it. But, I only came across blank stares!

They refused to let us use her passport, and they would not arrange her exit visa! Why should my wife travel with me when there was no reason for it? She was not representing the country!

I could not believe my ears! She had been with me for twelve weeks during the Caribbean Circuit; we had traveled back and forth in the United States, why should she not be allowed to join me now?

Her father, Dr. Jiri Rössler, almost suffered a heart attack: "Why is she not allowed to go? What a blunder! It is a formal affair and you'll be there huddled and the only one without a wife during their social functions?"

He sent me to a vice-chairman Oldrich Hradec. I attempted to explain to him the reason why my wife should join me on this trip; as my discourse went on I got so wrapped up in persuading him to meet my wishes that I ended up telling him details from tournaments I had played and the overall events of the tennis season. It was quite embarrassing since he had little knowledge of tennis and, obviously, little interest in it. In other departments I was pretty much unknown too. They did not know how or where I played, how I was ranked, or what the Grand Prix was...

Hradec called up Dr. Kroutil and collectively they declared that Lenka could not go along with me. I wanted to know at least one good reason for their decision! Why not? Why couldn't they let us use her "business" passport for a week?

Dr. Kroutil eluded: "It can't even be considered! In no time everybody would want to travel with their wives!"

He was not a very likable person; though he knew several languages and was intelligent, he was conceited; by this time I was loosing my cool but I had to hold myself back.

Later Hradec said: "You know, if somebody from the Committee ever found out that we paid your wife's trip to Tokyo, how do you think that would look?"

At that point I could not stay calm any longer and I exploded: "I am not asking you for anything. Not even for one "koruna" (Czech currency)!

"So who is going to pay your trip?"

I have received the prize from Ivan Lichner, who was the director and founder of the Czechoslovak International Championhips at Bratislava.

I put my hand in my jacket-pocket, pulled out the plane tickets and said: "Here is a plane ticket for me, and here is one for my wife. The sponsor, Pepsi Cola, is paying for it all. They pay for the plane tickets, room, and board. I don't want anything from you, not even a "koruna"! Only let us use my wife's business passport and exit visa!"

Hradec stiffened and looked at Kroutil, who uttered: "Well, it is all the same; since you are a semi-professional what more would you want from us?"

I said: "Dear comrades, do you know what? I recognize why you do not desire that my wife travels along with me. You think that if we both travel out of the country at the same time we might decide to stay there! You are afraid that we would do that! But I'll tell you something! My wife was with me twice on the Caribbean Circuit. Twelve weeks this year and last year. We have criss-crossed parts of the Americas - Curacao, Caracas, Columbia, and the United States. Thus, we could have defected a long time ago. I do not need to go to some damn Tokyo to do so! If this is your only reason for prohibiting my wife from traveling with me then it is totally pitiful".

Hradec was visibly upset: "Do you know what? Allow us to go over things; meanwhile wait in the corridor!"

It was such a mortifying situation that I felt like a piece of dirty rag. After our Davis Cup victory with Brazil, Denmark, Italy, France, and my personal victory at Roland Garros – I never expected anything so humiliating. I was standing in the hall and grunted under my breath: "If they don't let her go – I'll defect! If they do let her go – I'll stay!"

For a while thoughts were racing in my head, but then the door opened and obviously irritated Dr. Kroutil came out and said: "Well, come along!"

We descended to the floor below and he pulled out the passport with the exit permit from a file cabinet and handed it to me saying: "Here, cheerio!" He was flustered and talked to me like to a little boy.

Such was my first introduction to the leadership of our athletics. Only with time I realized that I had been pretty brazen. I was twenty two, and in front of me stood a highly ranked vice-chairman of the Central Committee of Czechoslovak Union of Physical Education and Sport; only a chairman was ranked above him. They held distinguished positions, they were members of the Communist Party, they could have done with me anything they pleased; I must admit that I dreaded a bit what was to come. On the other hand, I also realized that this incident could build respect for me in the future.

A few days later Lenka and I were sitting on a plane in the direction of Tokyo. By this time calm and collected, I thought about the passport episode during the flight and decided that their behavior seemed like an alibi-building affair. The vice-chairman Oldrich Hradec impressed me quite positively, but Dr. Kroutil affected me negatively. It was my conception of the issue that he was terrified that they would face repercussions if I did not return from abroad. It was further interesting that, subsequent to that whole affair, my wife never again experienced any more problems with exit permits to the West.

After a long exhausting trip the Kodes' landed in Tokyo. It turned out to be quite challenging to get to the hotel since the taxi-driver spoke no English.

"You have Kramer's business card" remembered Lenka "so show it to him".

Nothing! Only after I repeated the hotel's name "Okura" he finally understood.

At the reception I bumped into Jack Kramer. "Hello, Jan, how was your trip? A bit long, right? Well, rest a little and come to the press conference in the evening. Don't forget!"

In the hotel lobby there was a table with American, Australian, Czechoslovak, and Yugoslavian flags, a flock of journalists and photographers. There was no end to questions. Then the anxiety continued – a formal party followed, all players were introduced, and the director of Pepsi Cola made a speech.

I was so tired that my eye-lids were drooping while I sat on the podium. Fortunately, very soon dinner was served; the famous Japanese delicatessens. I almost laughed out loud when I saw Stan Smith struggling with chop sticks. The next moment, however, I lost my laugh when I bit into a raw fish!

Our visit of the historical Kyoto was an experience that one hardly ever forgets. The next day, however, we had to return to tennis again. I went to see the opening match.

"How do you like it here?" the director asked me.

A carpet similar to our "kovral" covered the wooden floor. I came to find out very soon how fast the surface was. Six years earlier Vera Caslavska fought here for Olympic medals in gymnastics. That was in August when weather was still warm. But this was December, and only

Jack Kramer, won Wimbledon in 1947 and two US titles in 1946-47. He later became as manager and spokesman on behalf of all players.

the Lord knows how the cold wind made its way inside. It seemed like they had no heating in the tennis hall but they had gas heaters in the locker rooms. When Arthur Ashe and Ken Rosewall started the opening game the stands were full to the maximum. Those spectators must have felt like sitting in a refrigerator!

The competition was played as a Round Robin and that was a terrific practice for me on the fast surface, even though I lost all singles: 3:6, 2:6 to Rosewall, 3:6, 5:6 to Smith (at 5:5 we played a tie-break), 4:6, 3:6 to Laver. But that did not bother me. They were all the best players of the world! I was practicing with the professionals Laver and Rosewall. The mere fact that I was on the same court and could play with them every day absolutely fascinated me. It was a lifetime experience. Moreover, Laver was my doubles partner! That was a complete bomb! We defeated Rosewall-Franulovic 3:6, 6:5, 6:4 and we lost to Smith-Ashe 3:6, 4:6.

Eighth place in the first Grand Prix, 33 points, and $7,500 for Kodes plus his participation in the Masters tournament in Tokyo. In addition victory at Roland Garros, reaching finals in Rome, and defeating Italy in Davis Cup on hot home Italian turf. Besides placing in the Grand Prix also achieving high ranks in other rankings that were popping up spontaneously in agreement with various experts.

In Europe, for instance, Kodes placed third. The Americans ranked him ninth in the world. And at home? The seventh place in an opinion poll "Athlete of the Year"; the weekly Mlady svet (Young World) ranked him even first! That seems like a very good record, doesn't it? In spite of it there were great many people who could not swallow his success, and in general, they were bothered by the existence of circumstances that dominated tennis then: the existence of semi-professional and

Marie Neumannova (2nd from the right) won both major Czechoslovak tournaments in Ostrava and Bratislava in 1971. But, the most valued victory of her career was the 6:4, 6:3 conquest of Billie Jean King on Virginia Slims tour in Jacksonville finals in spring 1972. That year B. J. King won three Grand Slam titles - the French, Wimbledon and the US Open!

professional contracts, the ease of traveling anywhere in the world, and the ability to earn hard currency.

The vice-chairman of the Central Committee of the Czechoslovak Union of Physical Education and Sport (CUPES), Oldrich Hradec, said in an article in Rude pravo at the beginning of January 1971 "It is Time For Tennis Overhaul". The article was written in the spirit of rehashed reality, that "the first and foremost importance to represent the country is threatened by an agreement of a few contractual players, who are the only athletes to have such an agreement with the tennis association". "How will the committee representatives solve this conundrum?" asked Jaroslav Stanek, the ex-table-tennis national player and the author of the article. "Czechoslovak physical education and sport will develop unambiguously on amateur principles. Gradually we shall oversee all sport sectors. And soon we'll also deal with tennis. We know that there is much to repair since a whole range of things got out of hand in this sport", affirmed Hradec, and he continued: "Representing our country abroad stands above all; the individuals' club and personal interests must conform to that. The accent will be on Davis Cup that is the most important tennis team contest in the world... Our participation in this most popular European team contest is more important than individual entries in some inconsequential tournaments in Argentina or Chile. Another negative feature of the tennis routine is the domestic league. It should be, and in most sports it customarily is, the main and the pivotal content of the competitive season... But, in tennis, there are cases, when a league match is played continuously because a player finishes his games ahead of time in order to be able to travel out, while the rest of the team play their matches later, on a different day. We must believe now that the Tennis Federation will revise their practices and will draw some consequences. We must bring our "white sport" to the levels that are true to the principles of socialist athletics."

The objective of this article was clear. Clip the tennis players' wings. Stop them from traveling around the world – particularly the Western part of it; limit their entry in the most prestigious tournaments of world significance and with that spoil their chances to earn some dollars.

They did not want us to travel abroad; on the contrary, they encouraged us to play perhaps twenty matches for the club teams because that would limit our foreign contacts to a minimum. Naturally, I had a contradictory opinion on this issue.

1971 was my year of immense education; I felt that I succeeded in entering the cluster of the world best tennis players. I realized that they respected me because I was able to play even leveled matches with them. I decided to try to strengthen that standing in the coming year and make an effort to reach the absolute pinnacle.

CONTRACTS WITH PRAGOSPORT

The 1971 agreement between a group of selected tennis players Kodes, Kukal, Holecek, Pala, Zednik and Vopickova and the tennis association was mentioned earlier. A firm by the name of Pragosport that dealt with business matters of the Central Committee of Czechoslovak Union of Physical Education and Sport existed already then. In order to clarify the new trends in Czechoslovak tennis it is necessary to look a few months back.

On October 28, 1968 a new law about federal configuration of the country came in force. According to its directive Czech, Slovak and the Federal Czechoslovak Tennis Federation were founded. Principle of equal opportunity was to be observed, meaning that there should be equal representation of Czechs and Slovaks in the all federal athletics unions. If the first chairman was Czech, then the vice-chairman had to be Slovak, and visa versa. The chairman of the Slovak TF, Jozef Jedlovsky, came to an accord with the candidate for the post of a federal chairman, Stanislav Chvatal, agreeing that Slovakia would forego its parity representation in the Federal TF if the Slovak members took on some other important posts. It is to be mentioned that shortly before this situation came up the post of a Davis Cup team captain was freed when Dr. Rössler, a Davis Cup team captain and a long-time chairman of the Central training committee for top tennis players was struck by a heart attack. Antonin Bolardt substituted him only temporarily and the post was now free and waiting for a new candidate.

Federal Chairman Stanislav Chvatal and the Czech TF accepted Jozef Jedlovsky's suggestion. Dr. Ivan Lichner became the new chief of Central training committee and Slovakia took on the post of the chairman of technical committee. But Slovaks held only four or five out of twelve positions in the executive committee.

This arrangement was endorsed by the General Assembly in January 1969 in spite of Antonin Bolardt's protests.

The new chairman of the CTC Dr. Ivan Lichner become automaticaly Davis Cup captain. But Lichner was a realist. He understood that his time was limited due to his work responsibilities in Bratislava and he would not be able to perform his duty at high level and intensity; thus he presented a proposal with a new concept. As a chairman and chief executive was to be responsible for all actions and events of all top teams and therefore consulting with Dr. Rössler who was not returning to his post of a Davis Cup team captain for health reasons they suggested Bolardt, Kavanek, Rampas, or Vera Sukova to take place as captains for important team competitions. TF board accepted the suggestion, but later Ivan Lichner admitted that great mistake was made due to Dr. Rössler's recommendation in reference to the first name of Antonin Bolardt.

After Kodes's victory in Paris Ivan Lichner went through the most uncomfortable experience in his life when all players were given prize money in cash except for the champion, Jan

Kodes; Dr. Tyra, the group leader received the money and passed it onto Lichner. Immediately upon return home Ivan Lichner went to the TF chairman, Stanislav Chvatal, and convinced him that something must be done about it because our players feel discriminated against and are agitated. This was not only about Roland Garros but also about all Grand Slam tournaments.

The Chairman asked Ivan Lichner to present the issue at the executive cabinet. Dr. Hubler gave some resistance but under the leadership of Stanislav Chvatal the majority voted for an institute of "statutory players", who were then allowed to receive prize money with a promise of turning in a percentage (as taxes) to Pragosport. The road to this achievement was long and thorny.

Right from the beginning of the following year, in 1971, a very lively debate took place about the issue of tennis semi-professional players; should they be contractually bound only to the Czechoslovak Tennis Federation or should Pragosport take them under their wings?

Pragosport was a firm of the Czechoslovak Union of Physical Education and Sport for the "pros". I believe that the chess player Hort and some equestrians were associated with this firm already then. Those were the types of sports in which prize money had been awarded. Pragosport also serviced veteran athletes, for instance figure skaters, who performed in foreign revues after concluding their competitive careers, and coaches, who coached abroad.

There were squabbles among the Tennis Federation representatives but the final decision determined that the tennis semi-professionals would play under the Czechoslovak Tennis Federation for part of the year, and the tournaments that they played on their own account and without an appointed coach they would enter into the Pragosport books.

Many conferences and proceedings took place between the Tennis Federation chairman, Stanislav Chvatal, and the Central Committee of CUPES vice-chairman Oldrich Hradec, resulting in a compromise. That was favorable to us, players, but the leadership still insisted that we had to spend a specific number of weeks each year available to the Czechoslovak Tennis Federation in order for them to draw percentage of our prize money and use that for sending other worthy players to world tournaments.

I signed a contract with Pragosport to try it out. The Federation enforced some conditions like having to be available for Davis Cup matches, the National Championships, Czech Championships, Club League Play-offs, Collegiate Championships and other possible events. Again they tried to resolve the question of "how many weeks" but we were faced with a done deal.

I have saved my first receipt from the levy to Pragosport. It is dated March 24th, 1971. Up until that time we had very little money left after we had purchased our plane tickets, paid for hotels and all other miscellaneous expenses that we had to pay for ourselves. The important thing was that we earned our living now and we were free to choose entry in tournaments that were not within the ambit of the federation.

The mentioned contracts were annual, thus every following autumn the same difficulties arose: Tennis Federation tried to discontinue the contracts with Pragosport for good, Pragosport showed enormous effort for the contracts to be maintained.

My contract with Pragosport gave me one significant advantage. There were many tournaments that took place in the socialist bloc and I was always invited to participate in them - Bulgarian, Polish, Romanian Championships. However, there was no prize money, and only amateurs took part in them. Thanks to my contract that did not include those tournaments I was free to enter Open Grand Prix tournaments in the West!

I am convinced till today that the Tennis Federation believed only one thing: "Kodes desires nothing else but money!" That was not the case at all! I wanted to play on the world platform, not just some amateur tournament in a place like Leningrad! Soon it proved possible even in the USSR. The Russians came to Philadelphia and played the Open as well, and later they played the entire WCT Circuit financed by Lamar Hunt. Sometimes I thought that we, the Czechs, were more "popish" than the Pope himself.

★ 75¢ | December 1970 | World's Largest Tennis Magazine

WORLD TENNIS

AGAINST PROFESSIONALS

It was early spring of 1971. On the other side of the Atlantic Ocean ITF Pepsi Grand Prix will start very soon. This particular U.S. Indoor circuit was played exclusively on "Supreme" surface for the first time. The new surface was laid by tournament organizers of U.S. Nationals in Salisbury, then in Macon, and Hampton. Since the Czech players did not continue that year on with the Caribbean Circuit Kodes returned home right after the American tournament series. He like to get ready for European clay court season, specialy for Grand Prix events.

An unpleasant incident transpired in Macon, Georgia. We were playing a doubles semifinal match with Zeljko Franulovic against Spaniards Orantes-Gisbert. The game took place at some university; its main court was full to the capacity with about 1500 spectators. I took a second serve practice shot with a lot of topspin on it which resulted in the ball bouncing up high. At the same instant Juan Gisbert was getting ready to take his practice serve on the other side of the net. At the very moment when he tossed the ball up my ball arrived and struck him squarely in the eye! His knees buckled and he came down and stayed down as if dead. The emergency crew took him to the hospital, the match was terminated. I was beside myself because I found out that evening that he might need to undergo eye surgery. He spent four days in the hospital, canceled the Caribbean Circuit and then was transferred to Barcelona. We saw each other again two months later and I was thankful to find out that surgery was not necessary. Nevertheless, I felt anguished, though glad when Juan's doctor explained to me that thanks to the spin on the ball the melton surface hairs damaged only his cornea.

So, the semifinal match never took place and what made me really unhappy were accusations of some silly Americans that I had done it on purpose.

This time I didn't achieve any remarkable results on the circuit. Out of five tournaments I made it to the quarter-finals only once and that was rather bleak before the upcoming difficult season. There were Davis Cup matches ahead of me, the Italian Open, defending my Paris title, then Wimbledon, Forest Hills, Grand Prix and my obligatory home tournaments. I wanted to succeed everywhere.

I decided to visit Zeljko Franulovic and spend a few days with him in Split. The idea behind that decision was to practice in a pleasant climate out-of-doors. It also gave me an opportunity to recharge emotionally. I stayed at his home, and as I was resting in the evenings after the daily workouts I pondered over the upcoming "merry-go-round" of tournaments and Davis cup matches. Occasionally, I wondered about the gossip the tabloids were spreading at home about my stay in Split. Travel to Yugoslavia was viewed with certain bias then...

Popularity abroad was often interchanged with backstabbing and disgrace at home. Many Czechs, who represented the country successfully and reached notable results in a variety of disciplines all over the world, faced scowl internally. Soon after Kodes arrived in Split there was an extensive write up about him in the local newspaper. He practiced with his friend Franulovic for several days, and met Zeljko's parents and girlfriend, as well as his club buddies. There was peace and harmony, and Jan felt like in a dream. However, everything idyllic ends at some point, and tennis responsibilities called Jan back to reality.

He headed to Nice on the French Riviera. His preparation in warm Adriatic climate and on clay proved to have been very helpful. Jan advanced all the way to the finals already in his first Grand Prix event that year! Progressively he dispatched of the Spaniard Moreno, Hungarian Baranyi, the French Barthes, and then fellow countryman, Frantiek Pala, in the semifinals. In the finals he faced his peer and rival, the Romanian Ilie Nastase.

A fearsome match opened up; the spectators witnessed a formidable battle and a fight for each point. Kodes was up 5:2 in the first set but lost it 8:10! The Czech player reigned again in the second set and was leading 5:2. Nastase, fearing a loss of the second set, started disputing calls and argued with the umpire.

At one point it took him close to ten minutes to settle an argument. I stood on the other side of the court and thought to myself: "No, I mustn't get involved in this! That is exactly what Ilie is waiting for!" Nonetheless, I grew nervous and did not succeed in turning seven set points into a set under my belt. In the end, the Higher Power decided the outcome – as I was running up to catch a drop shot I slipped on the sideline that was made of harder lime material!

I felt a sharp bolt of pain shoot through my knee. The first thing that came to my mind was a problem with my meniscus! In spite of it I wanted to finish the match. I lost the remaining sets 9:11, 1:6. Fortunately, my own diagnosis I mentioned before was not confirmed by the medical team. The tournament physician pronounced it as a pulled interior ligament and that put my mind at peace.

That night, as I lay with a sore knee in my room applying healing liniment to it, I swore under my breath: "Damn, Ilie, I am going to pay you back for this very soon!"

Kodes tried to come back to play already the following week in Monte Carlo but lost to the Frenchman Patrick Proisy but he could not yet succeed.

He returned home, where he was to take part in a weeklong training camp at I.CLTK Stvanice before the first round Davis Cup encounter with Egypt. Before the depature to Cairo he entered another Grand Prix series tournament in Catania. He struck another stringent battle with Proisy in the semifinals and repaid him the Monte Carlo loss with a 6:3, 6:2, 5:7, 6:3 win.

I beat George Goven easily in the finals 6:3, 6:0, 6:2. It is close to unbelievable what an amazing difference half a year or a year of training can make. It is, seemingly, a long time during

which a player is capable to make terrific changes in his game. Nine months before I struggled with Goven through a five-set match whereas here I totally dominated him. Other players had to get past such phase too, for instance Bjorn Borg and later Boris Becker.

In the tropical heat of Cairo Czechoslovakia defeated Egypt 4:1. Vladimir Zednik lost the only point at the time when the final victory had already been secured.

I played an important match for the first time with a hat on. The heat was so intense that I had doubts I would be able to get through

Training camp of the Davis Cup team selection at Stvanice before their encounter with Egypt. From the left: Jan Kodes, Pavel Hutka, Frantisek Pala, Jiri Hrebec, Vladimir Zednik, and Jan Kukal.

the match on that court. The hat was in my way during the serve and overhead. I then decided to put it on only during his serving games and I took the hat off before my serve and poured water over my head. This was an excellent preparation for the upcoming Italian championship in Rome.

It is not far from the Egyptian pyramids to the metropolis of the ancient Rome via the Mediterranean Sea. The 1971 tournament in Rome carried some unique significance. Based on the agreement between the WCT and the Italian Tennis Federation, all the best professional players from Lamar Hunt's group showed up – Rosewall, Laver, Roche, Newcombe, and the organizers completed the draw with several selected non-professionals and host country players. Jan Kodes was the only Czechoslovak among them.

And rightly so! His performance on the Roman red clay downright shocked the tennis world; he proved that his victory in Paris the previous year was no fluke! He eliminated three Australians in succession – Stolle, Roche, and Newcombe, and then the Dutch Okker in the semifinals, and it was only the "divine" Laver who stopped his poised advance in the finals.

I lost 5:7, 3:6, 3:6 but it was an amazing experience for me. I came to recognize the left-hander's power and his amazing technique. We played in front of famous Foro Italico sold-out audience.

The day before the final match I received an interesting phone call. It was George McCall, Lamar Hunt's henchman, who was passing me a message from Lamar Hunt: " Jan, I want to talk to you in Paris; Lamar wants to know if you would like to join the professionals; we are ready to offer you a contract."

I was speechless; I had no idea what to answer. I had learned via the grapevine that Lamar Hunt was in the process of discussing the future of tennis with the ITF; which tournaments would be open to all players and which only to the professionals or the amateurs. His intention was obvious – draw the best players over to his group. It was only a question of time when he would succeed in that. However, the ITF was still resisting his pressure at that point of time time: "You, professionals, are not unbeatable, since the likes of Kodes and Nastase are able to defeat you..." Obviously, we created a very strong argument for the ITF!

But, let's do not get ahead of time... The names of opponents who arrived in Rome inspired anxiety. However, Kodes proved round after round that his focus was very clear: win the International Italian Championship! Fred Stolle, former high-ranking star, did not pose much resistance. This Australian celebrity was three times the Wimbledon finalist in the years 1963-1965 though he never won the trophy. He was the uncrowned prince of the most famous world championship – how many have entered tennis history as such!? Jan Kodes did not anticipate yet that practically the same fate was to haunt him on Roman clay... At that point he did not entertain a notion that he would not win in Rome.

He faced Tony Roche in the second round. As the match progressed into the third set the Czech player had a match-point. However, the ball off his racket ended out. Roche took this opportunity and tied the score; he even got ahead. On Kodes' serve Roche was two points from victory! And it was at that moment that he got to feel the deeper sense of "Jan Kodes' unceasing fighting spirit". A ball that many players would have let go, Kodes reached and returned. The battle came to a tie-break.

It was the serve that decided the match. Generally, Tony's serve was better than mine. However, in the close of this match it wasn't so. After the two-and-a-half hour battle I was so worn out that I barely made it to the locker room. It was lucky that I had experienced this heat in Cairo during our Davis Cup match a week before and was able to deal with it better in Rome.

Two days later the Italian newspapers wrote that "John from Bohemia" would confront the menace of all players, the Wimbledon champion, John Newcombe.

On the way to the centercourt we bumped into Lamar Hunt. He patted John's shoulders frankly and he tossed in my direction "good luck!" as if he wanted to say: "Boy, you don't stand a chance!"

The match progressed similarly to the one with Roche. I lost the first set but

The sold out 1971 Foro Italico during the quarter-finals with the Australian John Newcombe.

my serve got better in the second, so did the volleys, and my backhand was effective. I won 6:1! I anticipated real pandemonium in the third set, Newcombe's unbelievable pressure.

And it came! The Australian was ahead 3:0 but Kodes bravely resisted and tied the score at 3:3. He was down again 3:4 and on his serve Jan gave Newcombe a chance to break. Newcombe was ahead 5:3 and serving two points away from the victory. It would require a miracle to win his serve at this point. But, miracles happen from time to time! Two risky returns raised the white chalk off the lines.

In the next rally I noticed that he stayed back. "Drop-shot him" rang through my head. - I hold this shot in front of my eyes till this day. John did not even react. He only turned and faced Lamar Hunt with distressed eyes as if he expected help from that direction.

I was flying high at this point and felt that I could not lose. Newcombe messed up the last two points; he was, evidently, stressed out.

Tom Okker came to see Kodes in the locker room after the match; he was to face Kodes in the semifinals: "I rooted for you dreadfully and am glad we'll play each other next. I am confident against you!" he said presumptuously.

"Well, I'll take at least a set from you" laughed Kodes.

I felt the previous two difficult matches in my legs, whereas Tom was covering the court like a gazelle. He was true to his nickname "Flying Dutchman". However, he lost his lead and force in the second set, and the tide slowly changed.

I did not play any extraordinary tennis but I tried to hit harder in the exchanges and make no unforced errors. During the changeover in the third set Tom took sugar and some pills. "Aha, you too have had enough! Well, friend, I can beat you! I only need to win the third set. Then we'll have a break..."

Cold water on my head and a little leg massage helped me immensely. After fifteen minutes we were back on the searing clay. Okker trailed behind and tried to pull up but I never let him get ahead.: 4:6, 6:3, 7:5, 6:4!

In the tunnel toward locker-rooms Tom stayed silent. Only when we reached the changing room he exclaimed: "That can't be for real!"

It made me smile; defeats are part of athletic competition. How many have I had to swallow!? Once I even discussed this topic in the Czech newspapers: "Every defeat definitely rattles me up to a degree; nobody likes to lose, even if it is just an exhibition. However, I believe that it is important to stay sane through the present-day long season and one has to economize with physical and mental strengths. So, I divide tournaments as to the degree of importance. I cannot always play the maximum; not even Laver, Rosewall or Newcombe do that; when I come across somebody who strives to shine and puts maximum effort forth I don't always play to the point of spilling my guts on the court. I try to play to survive; I don't want to go into extremes, nor do I want to risk ultimately my health..."

I clarified that in order to help people understand why I would lose in the first or second rounds of a couple of tournaments following a Grand Slam in which "I made the finals". Seeing the reaction of some people at home it was obvious that many people could not fathom that: "He is in the finals of a Grand Slam and bombs out of the first round in the next tourney he enters; how is that possible?"

Kodes upsets Newcombe

ROME, May 8 (UPI) -- Jan Kodes of Czechoslovakia won the last four games in his quarterfinal match against John Newcombe to upset the top-seeded Australian 2-6, 6-1, 7-5, in the 28th annual Italian tennis championships today.

Kodes, who also ousted Australian Tony Roche in an earlier upset, took the match on his third match point after the tournament referee overruled a linesman, for the second overruling of the day, in the 12th game of the third set.

Earlier, Arthur Ashe of Richmond, Va., moved into the semi-finals with a victory over Roy Emerson of Australia, 6-4, 3-6, 6-4, with the match point coming on an overruling by the umpire of a linesman.

Kodes won the last five games of the second set, then fought back against a 3-0 game lead by Newcombe in the third, to break the Aussie's ninth and 11th game serves and hold on for the match. Kodes went ahead 40-15 in the final game, the last point on the referee overruling a linesman who failed to call a Newcombe volley out, but only took the match when Newcombe failed to return a sizzling serve at advantage out.

Newcombe entered the Rome turnament leading the million dollar World Championship Tennis competition. Kodes, still playing as an amateur, was a finalist in the 1970 men's singles at Rome.

In the womens singles, first seeded Virginia Wade of Britain reached the finals by defeating Helga Hosl Schultz of West Germany 6-4, 6-3 and Helga Niessen of West Germany won a place in the finals by beating Gail Chanfreau of France 6-3, 6-2.

IL CECOSLOVACCO GRAN PROTAGONISTA DELL'«OPEN» ROMANO

Kodes in finale con Laver

It is close to impossible to stay in the top condition for very long; the inevitable lows must come at some point. Geographical changes, different climate, dissimilar ball quality...make an impact on one's game. The worst rounds are the first rounds. I have never given any match for free, without a fight, but I have had days when my concentration wasn't fully there, when I was impatient, inconsistent, and made too many unforced errors even with seemingly easy shots. Even a tennis player is only human and not an unfailing machine. I came to understand that in world tennis everything revolves around the Grand Slams. Only the Grand Slam results will give player

Kodes drapes his arm around Newcombe after upsetting the Wimbledon Champion in the quarter-finals, 2-6, 6-1, 7-5.

I wasn't happy – I lost without taking even a set!

singolare maschile

1971

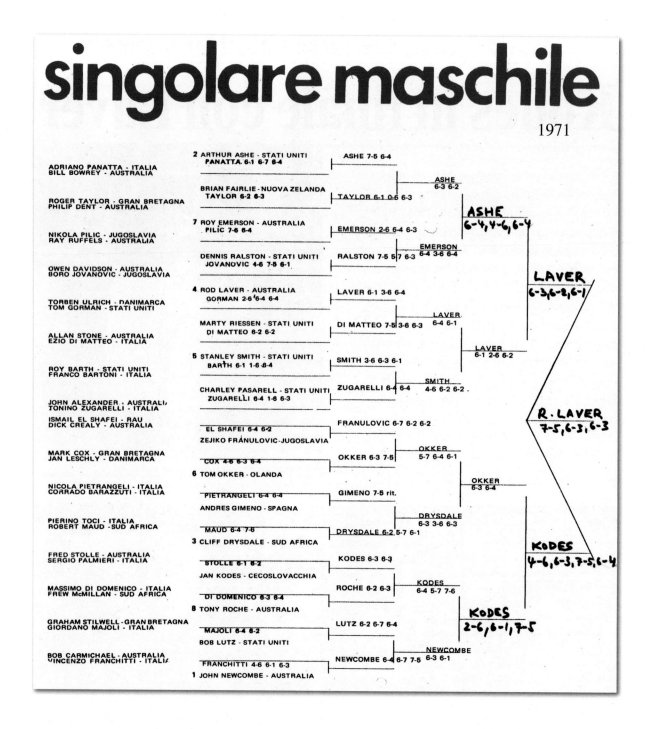

recognition based on his performance under such pressure. Other tournaments do not enjoy such esteem. I am sitting in the locker-room, and next to me, stretched on the masseur's table, is Rod Laver. Today this short freckled Australian, eight years my senior, swept Arthur Ashe off the court 6:3, 6:2, 6:1. The eight years are represented by two Wimbledon victories," two Grand Slams" 1962 and 1969 and five years from 1963 through 1967 of world professional tennis competitions.

Do I have a chance to surprise him with anything? Perhaps with my confidence, my combative spirit and hope that he doesn't know me yet. Am I going to be able to stand against his deathly left-handed offense?

In no time Laver was ahead 5:2! He did not leave anything to chance. I had no idea he knew of me and what kind of a player I was; he fought for every point right from the start. But I could not allow to be swept off the court like some rookie! I too, fought for every point and in time the score board read - Laver vs. Kodes 5:5.

In spite of Laver's momentary letdown, when he lost his serve and Kodes was playing out of his mind flailing risky shots without fail, the Australian brought the first set to a winning close, followed by the next two successful sets to a final 7:5, 6:3, 6:3 victory.

The locker-room was like a madhouse; there were photographers and journalists everywhere.

"Mr. Laver, what do you think about your opponent's game?"

"He displayed a host of spectacular shots!" He patted Kodes' shoulders, picked up a towel and headed for showers.

That kind of valuation boosted up Jan's ultra ego; it made him feel real good. Tennis world was coming to reckon with Jan Kodes!

After several hard matches I am in the finals and getting the feel of Rod Laver's true mastership!

However, I was not too happy. I was hoping to take at least a set from him and make him put out his maximum effort. Instead, I arrived at the understanding that Laver had something that others did not possess. He was able to fake you out with his body and after a long exchange you could not predict his next move or intention.

During his stay in Rome Kodes was able to arrange an exhibition at Stvanice Island. The Czech tennis fans were hungry to see world class players with their own eyes; so far only Davis Cup matches gave them that opportunity and each time that took place the old Stvanice was bursting in seams, for instance against Australia, Spain, USSR, and Sweden."

"They kept pressing me: "Hey, you must bring in some decent players! We don't get to see much quality play otherwise."

I wanted to stop this constant nagging and, at long last, I came to an agreement with Smith and Gorman. The one thing I had not predicted was my advance to the finals in Rome! That caused me to arrive a day late and play only the doubles. Smith played singles against Pala, and Gorman faced Zednik. The event was definitely a sensation for Prague in spite of my absence the first day. I must admit with all honesty that I would never exchange any exhibition for the final match with Laver!

Jan Kodes was the only Czechoslovak in Rome in 1971 and, in addition, he was there without a head-coach. After the finals with Laver he went to the cashier's to pick up his prize money. After taxes his net income was about four-and-a half-thousand dollars.

When I arrived in Prague I didn't know what to do with the money. It was a considerable amount then. Up to that tournament I was earning significantly less and spent it at once paying for plane tickets and hotels. This was the first time I retained some extra cash.

I called Dr. Tyra, the Tennis Federation secretary, and asked him what to do.

"Wait, I'll call Chvatal." The result of his conversation with the Tennis Federation chairman Stanislav Chvatal was an order: "Keep it at home and wait till we resolve all the issues; only then we'll advise you on how to proceed!"

This process related to their endless discussions on the topic of semi-professionalism and professionalism.

The Czechoslovak Union of Physical Education and Sport then made out an endorsement for me with the Czechoslovak National Bank, assuring them that I had earned the money.

Laver and Wade take Italian titles
Kodes takes W.C.T.
But who paid whom?

By LANCE TINGAY

Rod Laver

Virginia Wade

THE Italian meeting this year moved into the main stream of events. It was, save for the women, the biggest and best event yet staged amid the marbled grandeur of the Foro Italico. It lost a little of its serenity and peace, as indeed did Rome itself with its strikes—garbage collectors, hotel staff, traffic police, airport luggage loaders and doubtless others made their social protest—and its four day absence of water. But it gained record crowds (about 35,000) and

record revenue (something like £53,000) which if not much by Wimbledon standards was splendid for Rome.

All this was the outcome of a marriage between World Championship Tennis (Lamar Hunt himself graced the scene) and the Italian Federation. It was in fact a W.C.T. tournament, the 6th of their world series. But it was also the old Italian Championships though not, inevitably, anything to do with the Grand Prix.

How they contrived the combination I do not know. There was, for instance, W.C.T. men like Dick Crealy, Bill Bowrey, Phil Dent, Ray Ruffels, Owen Davidson, Torben Ulrich, Allan Stone, John Alexander, Frew McMillan, Graham Stilwell, Bob Carmichael, Brian Fairlie, Nikki Pilic, Marty Riessen, Roy Barth, Ismail El Shafei, Mark Cox, Bob Maud, Fred Stolle—what a long list that is!—who under the terms of W.C.T. events must have earned at least 600 dollars

in singles. But none reached the last 16 to qualify for the starting prize money of 750 dollars under the terms of the Italian Championships. So who paid whom I do not know.

That is all by the way. The big thing about the Italian meeting was that Rod Laver won it, that Jan Kodes popped off good W.C.T. players right, left and centre and was stopped only by Laver from taking a W.C.T. event from under the noses of the official union. And, of course, there was Virginia Wade winning the women's singles.

Patriotic result

Let me deal with this patriotic result first. Leaving out the British Hard Court meeting at Bournemouth, which impinges domestically more than it does abroad, this was the finest title gained by Miss Wade since her U.S. Open victory in 1968. She played well to win, having already won a couple of Italian tournaments before she came to Rome. In her last two matches, where she beat the German number one Helga Hoesl in the semi-final and the German number two, her old rival Helga Niessen-Masthoff in the final, Miss Wade never played more consistent, firm and solid hard court games in her life. Her major difficulty was in the quarter-final against the Czech gymnast, Marie Neumannova, who often delivers her first serve right handed and the second left handed. That match she pulled round after a poor first set and a tie break second.

Yet one needs to be honest and admit that the women's events in Rome this year were very much a throw away event compared with the men. The field was only 16 with Miss Wade the top seed and Mrs. Masthoff the second. It was a pity because Miss

Wade played well enough to triumph in a stronger field.

Nor would the women's lib enthusiasts have approved. There was 1,000 dollars top prize for the women. The men's was 10,000 dollars.

This ten grand was filched by Laver to add to his enormous earnings. Because the seeding was done on W.C.T. lines, being based on points earned in the previous W.C.T. events, Laver had only fourth seeding. It hardly mattered. He paced his effort nicely. Tom Gorman took the middle set from him. So did Stan Smith in the quarter-final. In the semi-final he demolished Arthur Ashe in intimidating fashion, for if he played immaculately then Ashe could only perform like a no-hoper who had tried and failed against his man all too often before. As for the final Laver I thought was rather nervy against Kodes but after the indigestion of the first set, where he lost a 5-2 lead and seven set points in all, he showed his class and saved the reputation of W.C.T.

Kodes last year took the French championship. One could not but say then that it was a fine effort but not what it might have been. There were no contract pros in the field. But in Rome in 1971 there were not only contract pros in the field, 31 out of the 32 of them, in fact, Ken Rosewall being the only absentee, but it was W.C.T.'s own tournament.

Gentle

The Czech, a gentle personality but not half so gentle a player, went through the big reputation men like a scythe through grass. Lamar Hunt was there to see him do much of it and seemed not to mind in the least.

The first for Kodes was an ex-Wimbledon finalist, Fred Stolle. That

was in two sets. The second for Kodes was another Wimbledon finalist, Tony Roche. That was a pulsating contest and Kodes nosed home in a tie break third set.

Number three for Kodes was the Wimbledon champion himself, John Newcombe. This was the finest match of the meeting and a tremendous one. Kodes lost the opening set and won 7-5 in the third. Newcombe led 5-3, 15-love on his own service, in the decider. All of the next 13 points were won by Kodes, with Newcombe going into the same kind of daze as he did in the Wimbledon final last year against Rosewall when he lost rather more points than that on the trot. But this time Newcombe had no lee-way for recovery and out he went.

Master man

The semi-final, the stage at which the best of five sets came into operation, had Kodes winning against Okker after losing the opener. The crowd wanted him to win against Laver in the final but not even their clamorous and vibrant emotion could bring that one off. Laver was the master man of the tournament. The hero was Kodes.

Three British men were there. Graham Stilwell began against the Italian Giordano Maioli and that was that. Mark Cox beat the Dane Jan Leschly and then lost to Okker. Roger Taylor beat Phil Dent, then Brian Fairlie but made no showing of significance against Ashe.

Neither W.C.T. nor the Italian Federation had cause to regret their marriage of convenience. Indeed both were so pleased with their bedding down that they arranged for the 20th and last in the W.C.T world series to be staged in Turin or Milan in November.

Only thanks to such endorsement the Commercial Bank was able to open a foreign currency account for me, in which I deposited my money. However, I was not permitted to withdraw dollars from the account, only dollar store coupons or vouchers, that I could use in a special Tuzex store, where foreign products were being sold (products that were impossible to buy in common street stores). When I think about it all and my mind considers all that was involved in these transactions, I arrive at a conclusion that I was, most likely, the first Czechoslovak professional!

From that point on I always deposited my hard currency earnings in that account upon return from a tournament. I was allowed to use the coupons for my personal necessities within the country. When I needed to travel out to a tournament and obtained an exit permit from the CUPES only then I was permitted to withdraw a fixed amount of dollars per day from my

I played only the doubles match with Jan Kukal against Stan Smith and Tom Gorman during the exhibition in Prague.

account. They gave me a "standby" for my trip and dictated to me how many dollars I was allowed to use per day from that account! They had a specific quota of how many dollars could be used for tennis and the fact that it was my money that I had earned earnestly made no difference; I was not allowed to go over that limit.

I took the money I won in Rome to the Tuzex coupon store and bought my dad a car, Fiat 850. Besides all the Renaults, it was the only other possible vehicle I could buy there. I felt I needed to do that so that my dad could commute easily to see my practices at Sparta club in Stromovka Park.

SECOND GRAND SLAM TITLE

In the second round of Davis Cup we defeated Portugal easily 5:0 at Stvanice Island. Next on the agenda was Paris and Jan's defense of the title from 1970. As the previous year champion Jan Kodes was seeded as number one. Several professionals from Lamar Hunt's group ignored Roland Garros and the organizers decided to make the draw for the remaining favorites very challenging. Fortunately, neither the first round opponent Pole Wieslaw Gasiorek nor the third round opponent Australian Bob Carmichael gave Kodes much resistance. But the host country players did.

The French thought highly of me after the 1970 French Open. Within a couple of days Pierre Darmon met me on the way from practice and said: "Jan, we are well aware of the difficult political atmosphere in your country. Under the authorization of the president of the French Tennis Federation I want to relate to you one thing; should you need help we are prepared to offer you an asylum and accept you in our tennis training camp. If you would like to stay in France we'll get you an apartment, you'll receive appropriate salary, and we'll help you with everything you should require."

I thanked him and responded with fleeting indecision and vacillation. I did not say yes or no. At any rate, it planted a bug in my head. I felt that in spite of the 1968 Invasion by the Warsaw Pact Armies the situation at home was not so terrible. That is to say that I traveled abroad most of the time playing tournaments thus I was unaware of the country's developments. However, conditions began to worsen. Personally, I lucked out in a way that I won Roland Garros twice at the time when "normalization" was taking place full speed. It would have been difficult, I imagine, to get rid of someone who becomes twice the Grand Slam champion...

For me the Roland Garros matches were immensely taxing in the sense that the French players mustered up amazing performance in front of their home audience and other favorites thus faced tremendous challenge. That year I met a host country's player three times! I played Jean-Pierre Courcol in the second round, Francois Jauffret in the sixteenths, and Patrick Proisy in the quarter-finals.

It was Jauffret who tormented me the most; he was ahead two sets to one but I won in the end in five sets. It was a very difficult match and after the finals with Nastase I considered it the second most challenging match

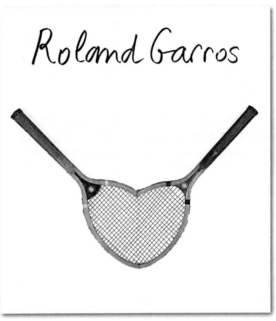

I have never played with such a racket.

Roland Garros clay demands immensely hard work.

The "Hot Box" No: 54 in Roland Garros. Seated, the millionaire Lamar Hunt (with glasses); directly behind him John McDonald is pointing at me during the finals with Nastase and suggesting to Mike Davis that signing us up with the professionals would probably pay off...

I played there. I surrendered one set even to Proisy. The French thought out a strategy against me that proved to be effective. They wore me out first and then they attacked me in the middle of the court which eliminated me from hitting sharp angles. They made me work dreadfully hard!

The following story proves how popular Jan Kodes was in France already after his first triumph in 1970; it transpired a year later about the time when Pierre Darmon offered Jan asylum.

Benny Berthet, the ex-player and official of the French Federation, decided to make a gesture of offering all seeded players a car. Customarily, the players used taxis or subway to move around; there was no official form of transport. The organizers found a sponsor and all of us, seeded players, obtained car keys. We were free to travel around Paris any way we wanted to and the organizer did not need to worry about us. It was a nice development; no more walking to and from the subway with a tennis bag full of rackets over the shoulder. Once, with my coach returning to the hotel from dinner at around 10:30 pm

I crossed the intersection at Place de Ternes on orange light - not yet red. I got pulled over immediately by the traffic police and I felt my heart sink. Korda advised me: "Say that

The natural gut strings by the French company Babolat have always been and will most likely continue being the best!

Good concentration during the match is crucial.

adidas
chausse tous
les "GRANDS"
du tennis
mondial

LAVER   NEWCOMBE   ASHE   KODES

adidas
R. HAILLET

Robert Haillet leader shoes from Adidas existing till today with the name: Stan Smith.

Jan Kodes vs. Ilie Nastase, Eastern European finals again at 1971.

you are Kodes." I opened the door but I knew very little French, only a couple of words. The policeman started telling me something so I pulled out my passport and he peeked inside and said: "Tchecoslovaquie? Kodes? C'est vous?" "Oui, c'est moi. Joueur de tennis!" He saluted, returned my passport and we drove off. Korda uttered: "You see, moron!" - It proved that my victory in France had multi-effects.

Zeljko Franulovic had no chance against Kodes in the semifinals. Just like after the finals the year before he left the court with his head lowered after only three sets. Kodes won 6:4, 6:2, 7:5 and was on his way to face the old rival, the Romanian Ilie Nastase, in the finals.

We met in front of the locker-room and he appeared poised and confident. When I looked at him I was struck by an audacious thought: pull it off like last year! - This was the third time we would meet each other in Paris. Beat him...and show him some revenge compounded with "interest" for the shameful five set defeat in 1966, when I played in Roland Garros for the first time.

Ilie was then among the absolute world top players. In 1969 he and Tiriac comprised one of the best and most success-

It is more difficult to defend a title than to win it; this is the second trophy from the hands of Marcel Bernard the winner at 1946. He beat Jaroslav Drobny in the final, the year I was born.

ful European doubles teams in Davis Cup competition. They beat the US team in the finals that year and repeated the triumph again in 1971 and 1972.

Jan Kodes competed with Nastase numerous times in his career and in most of those encounters the battles were exhausting and frightfully difficult. The 1971 finals in Paris was

My coach Pavel Korda who represented in DC 1960-62, with both finalists.

Donald Dell, the ex-player, the captain, the manager and lawyer with his clients during Roland Garros in Paris. From left: Tom Gorman, D.Dell, Charlie Pasarell, Stan Smith, Arthur Ashe and Bob Lutz. Europeans Zeljko Franulovic and Jan Kodes are missing.

no exception. Kodes won the first two sets 8:6 and 6:2, Nastase took the third 6:2. A particular point in the fourth set most likely decided the outcome of the entire match.

I must state here that I was physically well conditioned in 1971. All of a sudden, it was all the same to me whether the match would stretch out only to two or to five sets. Yes, the rallies were grueling but I felt much better than in the previous years. And the final with Nastase was a perfect example of that.

Nastase will never forgive me a situation that popped up then. I was up two sets to one, and in the fourth set he was leading 3:1 and had three breakpoints to 4:1 on my serve. If he had turned one of those chances into a game won we would have, most likely, gone into the fifth set.

He drop-shotted me and I ran it down; however, in order to play it back successfully I had to dive for the ball in the style of later Boris Becker. I hit a very difficult volley in flight and landing on my knees. I remained lying on the ground and he must have thought that I would not get up again thus he hit a dinky shot right next to me. However, I sprung up, leaned into the shot, and put the ball away. The stands went crazy!

That turned things around. I broke Nastase's serve and won the fourth set 7:5. With it I triumphed in the final match. Ilie has not been able to swallow that till today. Whenever we meet he calls me a "trickster" because I had acted like I was worn out, yet I had enough vigor to play the point.

"You whimper all the time and yet you continue to play!" I heard this sentence from him perhaps a thousand times.

And then it was over. The racket flew up in the air; Kodes jumped over the net and extended his hand to frowning Nastase.

I realized at that moment that I defeated a very formidable opponent. And here, at Roland Garros! On Parisian clay that I liked so much and where I always felt I could perform my best.

Jan Kodeš - Roland Garros title
defender. Over Ilie Nastase.

Rex Bellamy – The Times.

My coach, Pavel Korda, was running towards me and we plunged into an embrace. Then the rest of my supporters came up. I wasn't taking notice of what my coach was telling me, and I wasn't conscious of the photographers either. I was only soaking up the fact that I won here for the second time!

A forty minute press conference followed and only after that a massage at last. The skilful hands of my friend Robert Laurens, French masseur kneaded and rubbed my weary muscles.

He was still lying on the table when Ivan Lichner walked in. "Jan, do you even fathom what you have accomplished?" he addressed directly Kodes' fresh achievement. "Only four players won Paris twice in succession since the end of the Second World War! The American Frank Parker in 1948 and 1949, our Jaroslav Drobny in 1951 and 1952, then another American Tony Trabert in 1954 and 1955, and Nicola Pietrangeli in 1959 and 1960. Not even Lew Hoad, nor Ken Rosewall, nor Rod Laver pulled it off. Only now – you have!"

Solid and unflinchingly single-minded, Kodes was just to good for the flamboyant and gloriously gifted Nastase in a final that made tennis look the loveliest of games.

Rex Bellamy, The Times

Kodes' victory and above all his defense of the French International Championship title aroused due respect all over the world. French press raved about the popular Czech player's performance; the Romanian newspapers insisted among others that the Czechoslovak defeated Nastase thanks to his tenacity and his net play intensity… We are not sure who in the world could beat Kodes playing the way he did today." The Romanian television station purposefully inserted live broadcast from the entire match. On the other hand, the Czechoslovak fans were out of luck…

At least the press paid attention to Kodes' achievement. The daily as well as the weekly periodicals offered extensive dialogues with the Roland Garros champion.

UNE PASSIONNANTE FINALE ET KODES vainqueur de NASTASE conserve son titre

EXTRAORDINAIRE apothéose. Les championnats internationaux de France de tennis se sont terminés au stade Roland - Garros de fastueuse manière. Le match gagné par le Tchécoslovaque Jan Kodes au détriment du Roumain Ilié Nastase restera comme un des grands moments de sport, comme un exceptionnel événement. Les dix mille spectateurs réservèrent d'ailleurs aux deux héros de cette finale hors série par sa richesse et son intensité, une longue et vibrante ovation. A maintes reprises, ils avaient eu l'occasion par de chaleureux applaudissements, de manifester leur satisfaction car les péripé-

Le premier ministre M. Jacques Chaban-Delmas n'a pu, associé avec Henri Pellizza, conserver le titre de champion de France de double des vétérans : il a été battu (6-3, 6-3) par Robert Abdesselam et l'Australien Howe.

les auxquelles ils assistaient se révélaient d'une rare qualité : atteignaient souvent la perfection technique, donnaient lieu à des échanges pleins d'imprévus.

Il faut même mentionner tout particulièrement ce passionnant duel au filet lors du sixième jeu du quatrième set. Après plusieurs volées aussi surprenantes les unes que les autres, Jan Kodès, pris à contre-pied, voulut tenter de renvoyer, tomba sur le court et, dans un sursaut désespéré, parvint, par miracle, à renvoyer la balle du revers et à prendre, à son tour, son adversaire à contre-pied.

Ce point devait d'ailleurs revêtir une importance capitale : il permettait à Jan Kodès, qui avait été mené 3-1 puis 3-2, de rejoindre à 3-3, alors que, si Ilié Nastase l'avait inscrit à son actif, il eût compté 4-2, et le match pouvait alors basculer :

« Si j'avais remporté ce set, je crois que j'étais capable de gagner la finale », estimait Ilié Nastase, qui manifestait souvent son sentiment sur les appréciations des juges. La réflexion de Nastase semble d'autant plus vrai-

semblable que Kodès laissait apparaître une grande fatigue, qu'il avoua.

« C'est le match le plus difficile que j'ai eu à livrer tout au long de ce tournoi après celui qui m'a opposé à Patrick Proisy. »

Une fois de plus, Jan Kodès fit apprécier sa concentration de tous les instants, ses revers tran-

Les stands de l'Est à Roland-Garros.

(Dessin de Luc VINCENT.)

chants, ses volées, ses balles lourdes. Quand il eut inscrit deux sets à zéro, l'affaire sembla aller rapidement vers sa conclusion.

Mais, dans la troisième manche, Ilié Nastase, grâce à ses retours croisés, sa faculté d'anticipation, sa vivacité de déplacement, réussit à remettre en question l'issue de la rencontre et, quand il mena 3-1 dans le quatrième set, tout un chacun pensa bien que l'on s'acheminait vers un cinquième et ultime épisode.

Kodès sut alors exploiter, comme il l'avait fait la veille, contre le Yougoslave Franulovic, sa combativité et sa faculté de hausser le ton au moment voulu. Nastase tenta bien de retarder l'échéance, mais Kodès était le plus fort et, quand il marqua le point gagnant, il bondit de joie pardessus le filet pour embrasser son rival, puis serrer dans ses bras son aîné Jaroslav Drobny, en 1951 et 1952, de gagner le titre de champion du monde de tennis sur terre battue, pour la deuxième fois consécutivement.

Auparavant, la jeune Austra-

lienne Evonne Goolagong avait obtenu sa première victoire, en battant sa compatriote Helen Gourlay. Elle n'offrit pas une démonstration aussi brillante qu'à l'habitude et elle éprouva certaines difficultés à maîtriser une rivale qui se montrait fort habile à la volée.

Françoise Durr, éliminée par cette même Evonne Goolagong en simple, devait obtenir, en guise de compensation, deux titres : celui du double, avec Gaïl Chanfreau, et du double mixte, en compagnie de Jean-Claude Barclay.

Gérard du Peloux.

SIMPLE MESSIEURS. — Demi-finales : Nastase (Roum.) b. Froehling (E.-U.), 6-0, 2-6, 6-4, 6-3 ; Kodes (Tch.) b. Franulovic (Youg.). 6-4, 6-2, 7-5.

Finale : Kodes (Tch.) b. Nastase (Roum.), 3-6, 6-2, 2-6, 7-5.

SIMPLE DAMES. — Finale : Miss Goolagong (Aust.) b. Miss Gourlay (Aust.), 6-3, 7-5.

DOUBLE MESSIEURS. — Finale : Ashe-Riessen (E.-U.) b. Gorman-Smith (E.-U.), 6-8, 4-6, 6-3, 6-4, 11-9.

DOUBLE DAMES. — Finale : Mlle Durr-Mme Chanfreau b. Miss Gourlay-Miss Harry (Austr.), 6-4, 6-1.

DOUBLE MIXTE. — Finale : Mlle Durr-Barclay b. Miss Shaw (G.-B.)-Lejus (U.R.S.S.), 6-2, 6-4.

SIMPLE JEUNES GENS. — Finale : Barazutti (It.) b. Warboys (G.-B.), 2-6, 6-3, 6-1.

SIMPLE JEUNES FILLES. — Finale : Mlle Granatourova (U.R.S.S.) b. Mlle Guedy, 2-6, 6-4, 7-5.

Men's Singles *Holder* J. Kodes

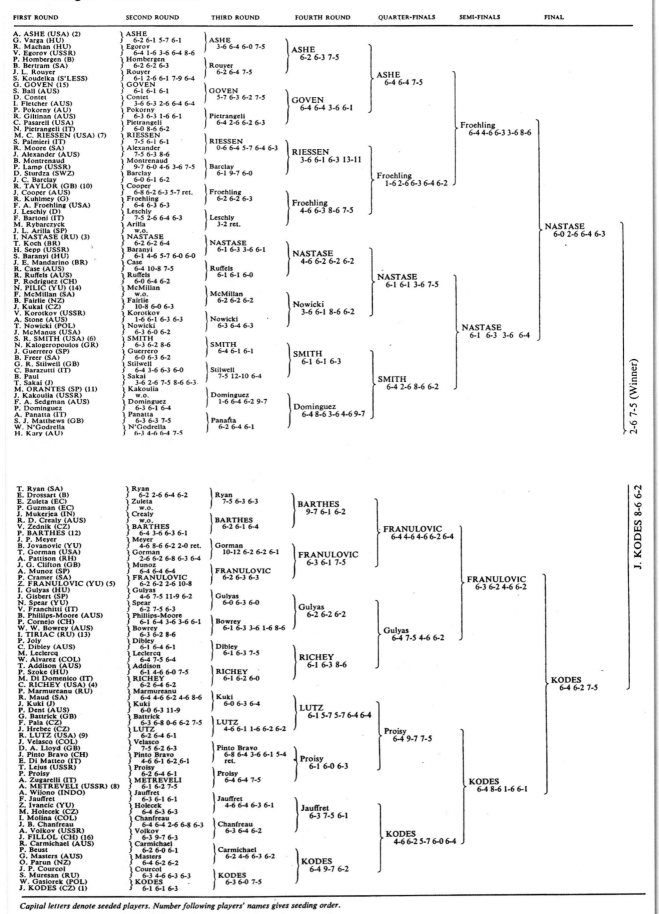

FIRST ROUND	SECOND ROUND	THIRD ROUND	FOURTH ROUND	QUARTER-FINALS	SEMI-FINALS	FINAL

Top half

FIRST ROUND:
A. ASHE (USA) (2)
G. Varga (HU)
R. Machan (HU)
V. Egorov (USSR)
P. Hombergen (B)
B. Bertram (SA)
J. L. Rouyer
S. Koudelka (S'LESS)
G. GOVEN (15)
S. Ball (AUS)
D. Contet
I. Fletcher (AU)
P. Pokorny (AUS)
R. Giltinan (AUS)
C. Pasarell (USA)
N. Pietrangeli (IT)
M. C. RIESSEN (USA) (7)
S. Palmieri (IT)
R. Moore (SA)
J. Alexander (AUS)
B. Montrenaud
P. Lamp (USSR)
D. Sturdza (SWZ)
J. C. Barclay
R. TAYLOR (GB) (10)
J. Cooper (AUS)
R. Kuhlmey (G)
F. A. Froehling (USA)
J. Leschly (D)
F. Bartoni (IT)
M. Rybarczyck
J. L. Arilla (SP)
I. NASTASE (RU) (3)
T. Koch (BR)
H. Sepp (USSR)
S. Baranyi (HU)
J. E. Mandarino (BR)
R. Case (AUS)
R. Ruffels (AUS)
P. Rodriguez (CH)
N. PILIC (YU) (14)
F. McMillan (SA)
B. Fairlie (NZ)
J. Kukal (CZ)
V. Korotkov (USSR)
A. Stone (AUS)
T. Nowicki (POL)
J. McManus (USA)
S. R. SMITH (USA) (6)
N. Kalogeropoulos (GR)
J. Guerrero (SP)
B. Freer (SA)
G. R. Stilwell (GB)
C. Barazutti (IT)
B. Paul
T. Sakai (J)
M. ORANTES (SP) (11)
J. Kakoulia (USSR)
F. A. Sedgman (AUS)
P. Dominguez
A. Panatta (IT)
S. J. Matthews (GB)
W. N'Godrella
H. Kary (AU)

SECOND ROUND:
ASHE 6-2 6-1 5-7 6-1
Egorov 6-4 1-6 3-6 6-4 8-6
Hombergen 6-2 6-2 6-3
Rouyer 6-1 2-6 6-1 7-9 6-4
GOVEN 6-1 6-1 6-1
Contet 3-6 6-3 2-6 6-4 6-4
Pokorny 6-3 6-3 1-6 6-1
Pietrangeli 6-0 8-6 6-2
RIESSEN 7-5 6-1 6-1
Alexander 7-5 6-3 8-6
Montrenaud 9-7 6-0 4-6 3-6 7-5
Barclay 6-0 6-1 6-2
Cooper 6-8 6-2 6-3 5-7 ret.
Froehling 6-4 6-3 6-3
Leschly 7-5 2-6 6-4 6-3
Arilla w.o.
NASTASE 6-2 6-2 6-4
Baranyi 6-1 4-6 5-7 6-0 6-0
Case 6-4 10-8 7-5
Ruffels 6-0 6-4 6-2
McMillan w.o.
Fairlie 10-8 6-0 6-3
Korotkov 1-6 6-1 6-3 6-3
Nowicki 6-3 6-0 6-2
SMITH 6-3 6-2 8-6
Guerrero 6-0 6-3 6-2
Stilwell 6-4 3-6 6-3 6-0
Sakai 3-6 2-6 7-5 8-6 6-3
Kakoulia w.o.
Dominguez 6-3 6-1 6-4
Panatta 6-3 6-3 7-5
N'Godrella 6-3 4-6 6-4 7-5

THIRD ROUND:
ASHE 3-6 6-4 6-0 7-5
Rouyer 6-2 6-4 7-5
GOVEN 5-7 6-3 6-2 7-5
Pietrangeli 6-4 2-6 6-2 6-3
RIESSEN 0-6 6-4 5-7 6-4 6-3
Barclay 6-1 9-7 6-0
Froehling 6-2 6-2 6-3
Leschly 3-2 ret.
NASTASE 6-1 6-3 3-6 6-1
Ruffels 6-1 6-1 6-0
McMillan 6-2 6-2 6-2
Nowicki 6-3 6-4 6-3
SMITH 6-4 6-1 6-1
Stilwell 7-5 12-10 6-4
Dominguez 1-6 6-4 6-2 9-7
Panatta 6-2 6-4 6-1

FOURTH ROUND:
ASHE 6-2 6-3 7-5
GOVEN 6-4 6-4 3-6 6-1
RIESSEN 3-6 6-1 6-3 13-11
Froehling 4-6 6-3 8-6 7-5
NASTASE 4-6 6-2 6-2 6-2
Nowicki 3-6 6-1 8-6 6-2
SMITH 6-1 6-1 6-3
Dominguez 6-4 8-6 3-6 4-6 9-7

QUARTER-FINALS:
ASHE 6-4 6-4 7-5
Froehling 1-6 2-6 6-3 6-4 6-2
NASTASE 6-1 6-1 3-6 7-5
SMITH 6-4 2-6 8-6 6-2

SEMI-FINALS:
Froehling 6-4 4-6 6-3 3-6 8-6
NASTASE 6-1 6-3 3-6 6-4

FINAL:
NASTASE 6-0 2-6 6-4 6-3

(right margin: 2-6 7-5 (Winner))

Bottom half

FIRST ROUND:
T. Ryan (SA)
E. Drossart (B)
E. Zuleta (EC)
P. Guzman (EC)
J. Mukerjea (IN)
R. D. Crealy (AUS)
V. Zednik (CZ)
P. BARTHES (12)
J. P. Meyer
B. Jovanovic (YU)
T. Gorman (USA)
A. Pattison (RH)
J. G. Clifton (GB)
A. Munoz (SP)
P. Cramer (SA)
Z. FRANULOVIC (YU) (5)
I. Gulyas (HU)
J. Gisbert (SP)
N. Spear (YU)
V. Franchitti (IT)
B. Phillips-Moore (AUS)
P. Cornejo (CH)
W. W. Bowrey (AUS)
I. TIRIAC (RU) (13)
P. Joly
C. Dibley (AUS)
M. Leclercq
W. Alvarez (COL)
T. Addison (AUS)
P. Szoke (HU)
M. Di Domenico (IT)
C. RICHEY (USA) (4)
R. Marmureanu (RU)
R. Maud (SA)
J. Kuki (J)
P. Dent (AUS)
G. Battrick (GB)
F. Pala (CZ)
J. Hrebec (CZ)
R. LUTZ (USA) (9)
J. Velasco (COL)
D. A. Lloyd (GB)
J. Pinto Bravo (CH)
E. Di Matteo (IT)
T. Lejus (USSR)
P. Proisy
A. Zugarelli (IT)
A. METREVELI (USSR) (8)
A. Wijono (INDO)
F. Jauffret
Z. Ivancic (YU)
M. Holecek (CZ)
I. Molina (COL)
J. B. Chanfreau
A. Volkov (USSR)
J. FILLOL (CH) (16)
R. Carmichael (AUS)
P. Beust
G. Masters (AUS)
O. Parun (NZ)
J. P. Courcol
S. Muresan (RU)
W. Gasiorek (POL)
J. KODES (CZ) (1)

SECOND ROUND:
Ryan 6-2 2-6 6-4 6-2
Zuleta w.o.
Crealy w.o.
BARTHES 6-4 3-6 6-3 6-1
Meyer 4-6 8-6 6-2 2-0 ret.
Gorman 2-6 6-2 6-8 6-3 6-4
Munoz 6-4 6-4 6-4
FRANULOVIC 6-2 6-2 2-6 10-8
Gulyas 4-6 7-5 11-9 6-2
Spear 6-2 7-5 6-3
Phillips-Moore 6-1 6-4 3-6 6-1
Bowrey 6-3 6-2 8-6
Dibley 6-1 6-4 6-1
Leclercq 6-4 7-5 6-4
Addison 6-1 4-6 6-0 7-5
RICHEY 6-2 6-4 6-2
Marmureanu 6-4 4-6 6-2 4-6 8-6
Kuki 6-0 6-3 11-9
Battrick 6-3 6-8 0-6 6-2 7-5
LUTZ 6-2 6-4 6-1
Velasco 7-5 6-2 6-3
Pinto Bravo 4-6 6-1 6-2 6-1
Proisy 6-2 6-4 6-1
METREVELI 6-1 6-2 7-5
Jauffret 6-3 6-1 6-1
Holecek 6-4 6-3 6-3
Chanfreau 6-4 6-4 2-6 6-8 6-3
Volkov 6-3 9-7 6-3
Carmichael 6-2 6-0 6-1
Masters 6-4 6-2 6-2
Courcol 6-3 4-6 6-3 6-3
KODES 6-1 6-1 6-3

THIRD ROUND:
Ryan 7-5 6-3 6-3
BARTHES 6-2 6-1 6-4
Gorman 10-12 6-2 6-2 6-1
FRANULOVIC 6-2 6-3 6-3
Gulyas 6-0 6-3 6-0
Bowrey 6-1 6-3 3-6 1-6 8-6
Dibley 6-1 6-3 7-5
RICHEY 6-1 6-2 6-0
Kuki 6-0 6-3 6-4
LUTZ 4-6 6-1 1-6 6-2 6-2
Pinto Bravo 6-8 6-4 3-6 6-1 5-4 ret.
Proisy 6-4 6-4 7-5
Jauffret 4-6 6-4 6-3 6-1
Chanfreau 6-3 6-4 6-2
Carmichael 6-2 4-6 6-3 6-2
KODES 6-3 6-0 7-5

FOURTH ROUND:
BARTHES 9-7 6-1 6-2
FRANULOVIC 6-3 6-1 7-5
Gulyas 6-2 6-2 6-2
RICHEY 6-1 6-3 8-6
LUTZ 6-1 5-7 5-7 6-4 6-4
Proisy 6-1 6-0 6-3
Jauffret 6-3 7-5 6-1
KODES 4-6 6-2 5-7 6-0 6-4

QUARTER-FINALS:
FRANULOVIC 6-4 4-6 4-6 6-2 6-4
Gulyas 6-4 7-5 4-6 6-2
Proisy 6-4 9-7 7-5
KODES 6-4 8-6 1-6 6-1

SEMI-FINALS:
FRANULOVIC 6-3 6-2 4-6 6-2
KODES 6-4 6-2 7-5

FINAL:
KODES 6-4 6-2 7-5

(right margin: J. KODES 8-6 6-2)

Capital letters denote seeded players. Number following players' names gives seeding order.

MILLIONAIRE HUNT'S OFFER

Winning the French Open twice in succession drew much respect from my opponents. In addition, it motivated Lamar Hunt to recruit the Roland Garros "King of Clay" to his "stable" of professionals. He presented his offer already in Rome.

He declared that he would enlist Nastase and I "cost what it may"! The same included Franulovic. We were very important for his motive to own all the best players in the world. At the same time, we represented a threat to his professional players when we started defeating them. In Rome they were perplexed by Nastase and me and disliked getting their behinds kicked.

Via his assistant, Hunt invited me to meet him in Paris. He arrived for the finals; he greeted me casually and assured me that his offer was still in effect. I kept postponing my ultimate response. In part, I sensed that it could cause problems for me at home, and secondly, following the development of the world tennis I anticipated that soon all players would be competing together. It was a battle between the ITF and Lamar Hunt. The ITF allowed the financial purse to enter tennis competition and consented to accepting not only the amateurs but also the professionals, whereas Lamar Hunt desired only the professionals. This issue incensed a long hard fight between them. And I waited patiently in the background...

It was customary to play another Davis Cup round between Paris and Wimbledon. This time it turned out to be already a semifinal match of the European Zone A. We played it, again, on Stvanice Island against the traditional opponent – the team from the Soviet Union.

It was an unbelievably difficult match but the Czechoslovak players finished on top. The first day Frantisek Pala defeated Korotkov easily 6:3, 6:4, and 7:5. However, Kodes lost to Metreveli in five.

In the crucial set, I was leading 2:0 and yet I botched it! I was too nervous and Alex recognized it. He played without fail and that decided the outcome.

I knew one thing – should we lose to the Soviets, the fight about professionalism would flare up again.

The next day, Jan Kukal and I engaged in an immensely difficult doubles match that was suspended for darkness at 5:3 in our favor in the fifth set, and I was to serve for the match. We were well aware that at a tied score the doubles generally decided the overall outcome of the encounter. The side that wins the doubles will have a psychological edge over the other. Furthermore, we did not foresee that Frantisek Pala would make a point against Metreveli.

On Sunday morning we entered court number 1 at Stvanice Center, about an hour before the match resumed, and we practiced just about every possible variant of play while I served. Serve, approach, and volley directed there or there. I knew precisely that I had to serve into Metre-

This is what the invitation to the official Davis Cup dinner looked like.

Our captain, Antonin Bolardt, came across seemingly calm no matter what the score was like.

veli's backhand. He would then return a low slice to my forehand volley, which was not my strength. It was imminent that I should not mess up that volley!

We practiced it till we could do it no more. When we entered the Centre Court I was pretty solemn. But, we played the ball exactly the way we had practiced. We won my serve, and with that the game we needed to win 6:3 in the fifth!

I still shiver when I picture it all. I did not sleep well that night and kept waking up because my mind was busy contemplating the play for the following day. Suspended matches always took the better of me; it was my incubus.

About an hour after the conclusion of the doubles match, Jan Kodes was back on the court. He defeated Korotkov 6:0, 6:3, and 7:5; there was no doubt about his victory at any given moment of the match.

I felt great after conquering the doubles. Only in the third set of the singles match my legs started to tighten. It was the responsibility more than anything else that weighed me down...

The triumph determined our advance into the European finals. However, the fact that I lost to Metreveli at home while I was leading 2:0 in the fifth was good enough reason to stir things

**With Jan Kukal before the doubles match against the team
of Alexander Metreveli and Sergiy Lichacev.**

up again by those who begrudged us. They roused up full speed the debate about semi-professionalism and professionalism!?

I overheard the rumble like: "You see, Metreveli, an amateur! He doesn't need any contact
with the world top to win."

Euphoric Stvanice Center roared!

TO BRAZIL VIA SPAIN

In mid-July Jan Kodes headed across the English Channel to Wimbledon before welcoming fervent Spaniards at Stvanice for the Davis Cup European Zone finals. He lost in the first round – again!

Time and again my draw was not favorable to me – I faced Tom Okker! He dealt me three times 6:3. However, I played on Centre Court for the first time!

It is immensely difficult to succeed on Centre Court the first time. It feels like stepping into a holy shrine. The crowd, the Brits, the overall atmosphere, inspire a curious sense of magnitude. Centre Court is considered, righteously, a sort of tennis temple. It is terribly difficult to cope with it. Every player who steps onto Wimbledon's Centre Court for the first time loses a bit of confidence and courage. Simply put – he is unable to play his normal game. He is afraid to dare and feels constrained. He can't concentrate and observes the crowd to see if they like his game or not; he looks for excuses. Tom Okker had played on Centre Court various times and felt comfortable.

My consolation was our doubles advance with Jan Kukal into the third round. We were knocked out by an Australian team Bill Bowrey – Owen Davidson in four sets.

Before the Davis Cup encounter we had to fulfill our "traditional" duty at home. Kodes won the Czech Championships in Litvinov easily when he defeated Kukal in the finals 6:2, 6:3, and 6:2. He did not really understand why he was required to take part in that tournament. He then succeeded in accomplishing a double-whammy in the International Championships in Bratislava. In singles final he outplayed the Hungarian Stabholcs Baranyi after a five-set battle 4:6, 6:3, 5:7, 6:4, and 6:3 and together with Jan Kukal they defeated Hrebec – Pavel Hutka 6:2, 1:6, and 6:3.

He was further obligated to play the European Tennis Club Masters Competition between Sparta and Schwechater Vienna with an 8:1 overall victory, in which he outplayed Blanke from Austria 6:1, 6:2.

It seemed like the leadership was punishing us for playing abroad for US dollars and wanted to squeeze as much play out of us for nothing!?

The Spaniards arrived with their strongest team: Manolo Orantes and Juan Gisbert. The legendary Lewis Hoad came with them as their advisor. Manuel Santana, the best Spanish tennis player of recent past, commentated the European Davis Cup final for television.

Stvanice witnessed a memorable encounter that entered history of Czechoslovak tennis.

The score after the first day was tied at 1:1. Pala lost to Orantes 6:2, 4:6, 2:6, and 5:7. Kodes defeated Gisbert in spite of trailing behind 0:5 in the fourth! He managed to turn it around and win 7:5...

Juan Gisbert, a Barcelona Lawyer, arrived as a fresh champion from Munich. He was a very tenacious, smart and patient player. He was a clay-court specialist and embodied a tough adversary especially in

Czechoslovakia vs. Spain. From left: Jose Guerrero, Antonio Muňoz, Manuel Orantes, capt. Jaime Bartroli, referee Heidrich, capt. Bolardt, Kodes, Pala, Zednik, Kukal, (Juan Gisbert missing).

Davis Cup; he had defeated a number of excellent world players like Martin Mulligan or Christian Kuhnke.

Kodes took the first set and was leading 4:2 in the second but lost four games in a row. The same situation repeated itself in the third set: from 3:0 up he was, all of a sudden, 3:4 behind.

I didn't know what was happening to me. I nabbed the set with much hardship. Darkness enveloped us fast and the referee decided to suspend the match at 6:3, 4:6, 9:7. I often pondered over the game suspension; is the night recess beneficial or detrimental? Most likely the reaction is individual. The player who is "on-the-go" may get thrown off by the forced break. On the other hand, the one lagging behind may pick up renewed strength and motivation. In my case – I hardly slept. We had played three physically strenuous sets.

The next day Gisbert opened the fourth set serving. He hardly saw three of the returns that came back.

I took the lead 0:40 quickly but - tennis is an unpredictable game. One can win a seemingly lost match but also lose a match seemingly going the right way. I lost five points in a row in the

With Juan Gisbert (left) was never easy match.

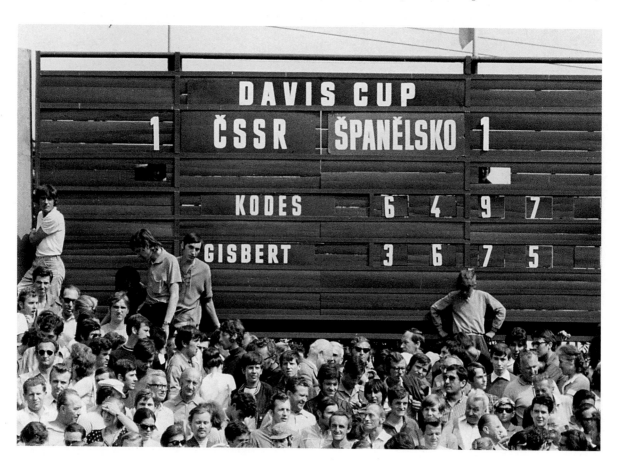

next five minutes I was 0:5 down! I was unable to settle down and committed many unforced errors. He, on the other hand, put in force excellent passing shots and top-spin high bouncing serves. I resigned myself to thinking in terms of the fifth set and started contemplating about how to open it. At that instant tension fell off my shoulders.

That moment as if injected new blood into Kodes' arteries and Gisbert could not fathom what the trick was that altered the subsequent play.

All of a sudden my shots were accurate and I was able to put the ball away successfully. I started to battle again for that osten-

The Czech disappointing doubles.

sibly lost fourth set. It was a pity to let it go. I was playing out of my mind, as if someone had swung a magic wand, and I won 7:5. An hour later we were able to play the doubles!

Horror! Nobody can describe the course of that encounter with Spain in any other fashion. Not even Alfred Hitchcock would have thought it out any better. Kodes – Kukal received a brutal lesson from Gisbert – Orantes in doubles: 4:6, 9:11, 4:6. The Spaniards demonstrated tennis tricks in front of Stvanice crowd with phenomenal returns and grand style that had helped them win several tournaments in the United States and in Munich the previous week.

The players from the Pyrenees peninsula were on top of the ball. They led 2:1 in points and it did not even cross their minds that Gisbert could be defeated by Pala at the start of the closing day. But everything turned out unpredictably!

Gisbert was evidently exhausted. He tried to stay away from long exchanges and pressed to attack; Frantisek tormented him with precise lobs. He allowed him only two games and game him no chances: 6:0, 6:1, 6:1. Stvanice roared with enthusiasm! It was one of Pala's best career performances!

The decisive point would come out of the duel between Kodes and Orantes.

After the turn-around against Gisbert I felt stronger, especially mentally. I believed I would make that third point. I determined to fight till I drop.

After just a few points I realized that I did not feel stiff or tense the way I did the days before. I enjoyed the adrenaline pumping excitement; my reaction was swift. Yet, the task at hand was nothing close to easy. That match was mentally draining for I never felt as much responsibility for the outcome. The first set was over in 48 minutes, the second took 34 minutes and the third lasted three-quarters of an hour: 7:5, 4:6, 7:5.

At 3:3 in the third I felt cramps creeping up on me. Fortunately, they did not take hold of me until that night, when they woke me up from my restless sleep.

A ten minute break was over in no time; I did not have time to even lie down on the massage table and had to get back to the court. A very important game-point arrived in the eighth game. He played it cleverly – it barely rolled over the net. However, I ran it down and played it resolutely and with confidence. It translated into a 5:3 lead and I served for the match.

Second match-point. The projectile of the serve lands exactly in the corner close to the service line. Ace! The crowd explodes! Kodes leaps over the net and together with Frantisek Pala they are raised above the heads of the fans who burst upon the court.

Frantisek Pala was a great surprise... won 6:0, 6:1, 6:1!

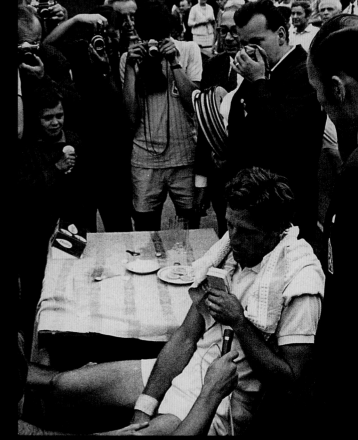

Exhausted Kodes after his last day victory over Orantes at 2:2, I could hardly walk...

Great time for the Czechs. Pala´s unexpected victory over Gisbert resolved.

Should we really fly to play in Brazil?

I was totally spent but Frantisek Pala was the one most responsible for the outcome because it was he, who rescued the match with his outstanding performance. I was expected to deliver two points no matter what.

From the newspapers Kodes found out that the next opponent was going to be Brazil. They beat Mexico 3:2. However, it was the non-playing captain, Antonin Bolardt, who informed him that the encounter was going to take place in Brazil, the opponents' home.

According to the set laws Koch and Mandarino were supposed to come to Europe since they signed into the European Zone and with that gave up their rights and, instead, agreed to play all matches in Europe.

Our captain, supposedly, argued with the ITF but was informed by the secretary, Basil Reay, that we must travel to Brazil since we played at home twice while they played in Mexico...

It suggested that captain Bolardt was not handling the situation effectively. It appeared that he was conducting shady politics with the ITF. We even suspected that he not only did not achieve but did not want to achieve home advantage for us! Until the last moment we did not know where or on what surface and with what kind of balls we would play. Only the day before our departure things cleared: Porto Alegre.

Wow! We'll arrive there on Tuesday after three transfers and thirty hours in transit to play that coming weekend; that was close to suicidal! I knew from my personal experience how many days acclimatization to South America took. It pointed exactly to the fact that we would feel the strongest need to sleep at the time of the matches!

We arrived there bushed, crabby and tired. On top of it, we were welcomed by rain. Petrol Tennis Club where the encounter was supposed to take place had only four courts. On two courts the organizers erected stands; the other two were available for practice. It rained cats and dogs.

We practiced in a gym because they told us they had no indoor tennis hall! We pressed Bolardt to demand a court somewhere else for practice. Not possible... Yet we later found out that the Brazilians practiced outside of town – while we had nowhere to go! Bolardt was unable to arrange the same conditions for us. When the rain subsided we got onto the Centre Court

Arrivals to Porto Alegre two days late...

Training at the „gym-room".

that was as hard as concrete. We found out that they did not practice there at all. They gave us hard balls but the Brazilians received different, soft ones. Our coach, Pavel Korda, also pressed Bolardt to protest. But he brushed him off saying that he knows what he is doing and he put forth no protest.

The disaster struck on the day of the match. The organizers spread the Centre Court with fresh clay that had no time to combine with the old surface. They also pulled out their Mercury balls.

When Mandarino hit drop-shots to me the ball hardly bounced up! There was nothing I could do with it. The balls were soft, flat, did not fly and they helped Edson stay in the rallies longer and eliminate my shot winners; my game lost its zip.

The crowd was crazy; I felt bemused. At the net the surface shifted under my feet while Mandarino passed me well down the line. I lost two sets 6:8, 4:6.

I had guessed the acclimatization timing correctly.

I woke up in the third set and Mandarino let up. I still did not play well but I won the set 6:4. The break usually helped me but not this time. I started to make unforced forehand errors again after the break and I could not cope with the low sliced shots.

"I drag myself here such a distance and for nothing"- flashed through my mind as Mandarino converted the match-point at 6:4. In the following match Pala lost to Koch easily 4:6, 4:6, and 2:6.

I talked to myself: Oh well! Now we know what to expect. "We'll win the doubles, Frantisek; you'll beat Mandarino and I'll defeat Koch. I know how to handle left-handers!"

However, we did not win the doubles with Jan Kukal and, instead, were sent packing. The third day matches could not alter anything. Pala beat Carlos Kirmayer in five sets and the match between Zednik and Tavares did not get finished. At home many polemics took place over the reasons of our demise. I had my own opinion – just sticking to the rules would have helped! For that we needed a different captain. I was disgruntled by the whole affair.

We practically accepted everything! We played with Brazilian Mercury balls that aren't used in any other big tournaments. It was, really the ITF's fault; there was poor communication and nobody could reach anybody by phone. On top of it all, I had a feeling that nobody really cared though it was an Inter-Zonal semi-final match! In the following Inter-Zonal round final the Romanians, Tiriac and Nastase, defeated Brazil in Sao Paolo playing already with regular Slazenger balls and reached the Challenge Round against the US to whom they succumbed 2:3 in Charlotte.

Antonin Bolardt - Flexible rules: "We presumed that the encounter with Brazil would take place in Prague. Since the rules literally claim: if one of the protagonists had an option of playing at the venue of choice in the span of the last five years then this up-coming match will be played at the venue of the other. According to the draw CSSR should have been given the choice and the rule of five years did not apply since Brazil from South America entered the European group in 1968 giving up all its rights to home matches. There was a basic disagreement that was quickly resolved by ITF secretary Basil Reay who decided to place the encounter in Brazil since CSSR played at home already twice, while Brazil competed in Mexico. However, still before then, during Wimbledon where I met with Brazilian representatives they agreed to come to Prague should we end up playing each other."

Ceskoslovensky sport – Czechoslovak press

The thing that was most curious was the fact that nobody tried to resolve the Czechoslovak protest before the encounter.

Only after the match was over we received a copy of a letter from Mr. Reay from ITF to the Brazilian Tennis Federation, in which he communicated to the Brazilians that our protest was valid. There had been clear discrimination against us since we were not informed of the court surface, quality of balls, team roster, name of the referee or the venue of the encounter in timely manner prior to the match as rules dictated. Those shortcomings had a profound negative effect on our team's preparation. The closure of the letter stated: "If Brazil were to conduct itself the same way in the following year Davis Cup competition it would be disqualified". However, that was not going to help or solve our cause.

BREAKTHROUGH AT THE US OPEN

The year 1971 brought on a significant turning point in Jan Kodeš' career. He placed himself most definitely among the best tennis players of the world with his amazing achievements during that year. It was not just his success in Paris and Rome - after all, he grew up on red clay and knew how to complicate the game even for the best players - but he triumphed even on grass at the West Side Tennis Club, Forest Hills.

From the Davis Cup encounter in Brazil I flew directly to the US, to a tournament in Cincinnati. We went to the indoor tennis hall straight from the airport since it had been raining for several days. I lost easily 3:6, 4:6 to the American Jeff Borowiak but it didn't really bother me.

The 1971 U.S. Open

Reunion with a figure skater Bohunka-Muki Sramkova, remembered as a sibling partner of our champions from Ostrava.

All that week I was nursing the hurt from the Brazilian blow and I played doubles with Franulovic. After two successful rounds we lost to Gorman – Connors 6:2, 3:6, 6:7 and immediately took off for the American clay court championships in Indianapolis.

The heat in Indianapolis was unbearable and we hardly felt like practicing. We drank tea or Gatorade, the drink of the American Olympians. It contained electrolytes, minerals, salts, and vitamins replenishing what the body had lost in the heat through sweating. It has been popular till the present day.

Heat or no heat, we had to play. Kodes started wearing a hat in order to get used to it for the US Open.

I advanced to the quarter-finals but a young American, Roscoe Tanner, eliminated me there. I was unable to break his serve; the American's cannon-ball serve did me in. It rattled me to lose to him but, on the other hand, all I now remember is that I became the official doubles champion of the United States. Zeljko and I had to win five matches to make it to the finals where we defeated an American team Clark Graebner – Erik Van Dillen 6:7, 7:5, 6:3. By the time I boarded the plane for New York I felt like the Davis Cup loss to Brazil was long time in the past.

Kodes made it to the US Open venue a week ahead of time, thus he had plenty of time to prepare for another Grand Slam event. Milan Holecek knew a Czech coach about an hour by train outside of New York. It was then only a few minutes on foot from the Station to the Rockaway Hunt Club.

There were beautiful grass courts there and Milan started to search for the Czech coach, ex-hockey player Stanislav Nepomucky.

"Oh, do you mean Stan Nielsen? Yes, he is here!"

In walked a chap, who used to play ice hockey for us in Czechoslovakia. He emigrated in early fifties, and since most hockey players then also played good tennis, he made a living for himself teaching tennis in New York.

"Well boys, come early in the morning and I'll let you use a court. I don't want any money; use the court as you please, but as soon as the club members appear you must let them play."

Milan and I practiced there daily, taking the train from New York and then whacking the ball for five sets. Subsequently, the day came when we transferred to the official US Open hotel close to the Madison Square Garden.

When I entered the hotel lobby with my suitcase, I saw Ion Tiriac with a group of players standing at a distance. Ion shouted at me: "Where are you going with that suitcase?"

"Well, to check in."

"You had better pack up and go back to the airport and home!"

"Why?"

"Don't you know who you play in the first round?"

"No, I don't."

"You face Newcombe in the first round!"

That was twice the Wimbledon champion, who grew up on grass! It was the worst draw I could have.

The next day at noon – scorching heat and only a couple of hundred people in the audience.

Who was interested in watching some unknown Czech getting whipped off the court by a Wimbledon champion?

The Australian won the toss and let me serve first. It was very clear that he was underestimating me.

But Kodes did not take the "offer" and lost his serve as well as the following game. He worked hard, ran everything down, but his movement on grass was still uneasy.

The grass was fresh, moist and slippery. The heat and humidity were so oppressive that it was hard to breath. Twice I fell down. Somebody laughed in the audience. I saw a smirk even on John's face. He took the first set 6:2.

But the situation reversed in the second set. Kodes played doggedly; he won his own serves and returned hard Newcombe's serves to the point of risking unforced errors. An unbelievable point decided the outcome of the tiebreak. Newcombe hit a perfect shot and followed it up to the net. Kodes barely reached the ball but returned it backwards from a reverse position and into the court. The Australian did not expect that and literally froze – that cost him the tie-break! A little more than an hour into the match, at a set score 1:1, the stands were almost full. Several thousands of spectators sensed that something big was brewing.

I realized that I could make it past that round but I would have to succeed holding my serve. I took risks, without those I had no chance. This was not clay, the surface on which I defeated Newcombe in Rome, but grass, my least favorite surface.

I attempted very risky returns that put him under pressure. Hard shots aimed at his feet, to intimidate him.

Newcombe's weaker second serve progressively became ammunition for Kodes' brilliant backhand return. Under its pressure the Australian's volley started to fumble.

NEWCOMBE OUSTED BY KODES

Number one seed ousted by Jan Kodes.

Newcombe lamented shortly after the match: "He did not give me many chances at the net; his serve returns were struck with such power and so close to the lines that I could not even touch many of them." And "I kept holding my serve often thanks to the drop-volleys that I played in crucial moments when Newcombe least expected them."

It was well known that Kodes hardly used a lob in his match repertoire.

I don't remember how I got the idea but I suddenly recalled that, on several occasions, Jaroslav Drobny suggested to me: "In the most important moments you must play what nobody expects."

In the third set tie-break a very important point decided the outcome. John hit a volley and followed it up very close to the net; I made a backswing as if I was about to hit a passing shot but, in fact, I played a lob. It was not the best one but it came as such a surprise that he had no chance of getting to it in time. He smashed the racket to the ground (as if it were the racket's fault).

In the fourth set Newcombe started to feel sorry for himself whereas Kodes' confidence grew stronger; in the end there was no necessity for another tie-break. Jan Kodes won 6:3 providing tennis fans with a first class sensation. He edged out this year's Wimbledon champion and the first seed in this tournament in the first round! Last time that happened was in 1930 when the Frenchman Jean Borotra was defeated in the first round by Berkeley Bell!

World Tennis

Jan Kodes, the Czechoslovakian who has twice won the French Championships on slow Paris clay, was induced into playing the U. S. Open although he has always detested grass. He had regularly lost in the first round of Wimbledon. When he found his first opponent at Forest Hills was to be John Newcombe, he was hardly the happiest feller in the tournament. He rolled up to the clubhouse like a ship in a storm, rocking with the waves and wearily thrusting his head against the winds. He was, naturally, complaining about the grass which, as he said predictably, "is not for tennis. The ball bounces high or low. Sometimes it does not bounce at all. You don't know what's happening."

No one expected Kodes to beat Newcombe. When he did, it was the biggest opening round upset since Jean Borotra lost to Berkeley Bell in 1930. Kodes blitzed the mighty Australian with a free-hitting display of power tennis that earned him a 2-6, 7-6, 7-6, 6-3 victory. Newcombe won the first set 6-2 but dropped service early in the second. In the sixth game he missed an overhead. It was not unlike the famous overhead that Billie Jean King msised against Nancy Richey in the Garden when leading 6-1, 5-0; it showed a chink in the supposedly invulnerable armor. Kodes, who had beaten Newcombe in the Italian Championships on clay the previous May, did not miss the significance of that badly bungled overhead. Newk had moved back slowly for it, and it was a tired-looking stroke that plopped the ball into the bottom of the net. It gave Jan the incentive to go on the attack.

Kodes ignored the hazards of an uneven bounce and reverted to his normal clay court game. He let fly with his service returns and soon Newcombe's below-par second serve was feeding him all the ammunition his powerful backhand needed. The Australian's volleying started to fall away under the pressure but, as Newk remarked later, "He didn't give me much to volley. He was teeing off for the lines with such power that I couldn't even reach most of the returns, let alone get them back."

Kodes was getting his first serve in court—a big plus for the Czech as his second delivery sits up and begs for annihilation on grass. He served an ace to win the first tie-breaker and the second set by 5 points to one, and when he took the third also on the tie-break, the solid structure of Newcombe's game was tottering. A series of hammer blows from the Czech's backhand gave Kodes the 4th set and the match 6-3.

John Newcombe threw his racket four times during the match. He could not come to terms with the match development and it drove him crazy.

Kodes' first round win created an upheaval! How come the Roland Garros champion was not seeded? Who made the seeding? Journalists questioned: "How can two Grand Slam champions play each other in the first round? Is that a cliché of amateurism?"

Frank Svehla, the publisher of the Czech newspaper in the US was asked more than two hundred times – "Who is Jan Kodes?"

It seems that the Americans did not even know that I had won the French Open in Paris. However, they should have received some warning after I beat Arthur Ashe and Stan Smith in Philadelphia. But, such is ignorance...Perhaps they noticed my Roland Garros victory but deduced: "He doesn't know how to play on grass! He lost in the first round of the previous year's Wimbledon, and again this year..."

They did not realize who I lost to - players like Roche, Drysdale, Okker, or Metreveli (undoubtedly the best East-European grass court player). He had won several tournaments in Australia but that remained un-noticed!

The following day was a rest day for Kodes and he anxiously waited to find out who he would meet in the second round. From the tabloids he perceived that most of the American public assumed his first round victory to be a fluke. They looked forward to further development in the subsequent rounds.

Kodes' next victim was going to be yet another member of Hunt's professional group, the French Pierre Barthes. He was a very tenacious player, who knew well how to play on grass. In view of Kodes' first round success, the organizers set the match again on the Centre Court.

Pierre played well; he put super top spin on his serve so the ball bounced high and he then followed it up to the net, where he volleyed soundly. He was also an effective doubles player.

Jan Kodes.

Glimpses from the semi-final match with Jan Kodes.

A television station CBS' picture of the historic West Side Tennis Club house at Forest Hills.

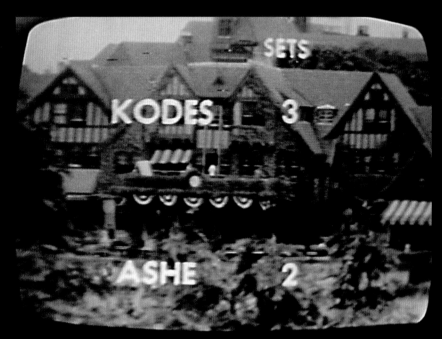

The CBS commentator, Jack Kramer two times the US Open champion – 1946 and 1947, and 1947 Wimbledon champion interviewing Jan Kodes after his victory over Arthur Ashe.

For the longest time, I did not know what to do against his cool calculated game. I tried all kinds of play but the result was pitiful – I was down 0:2 in sets, and 2:4 in the third. The Frenchman was about to take the next serve game and advance to 5:2; I started seeing the worst. "How can an experienced player like me allow this match to slip away this easily?"

But that is why tennis is such a marvelous contest. Until the umpire announces "Game, set, match Barthes!" the game can always turn around and reverse.

Most likely, he lost concentration for a couple of points; he double-faulted two times, and that was a moment when I turned things around! I broke his serve and then won the next game and subsequently the whole match in five sets.

Kodes salvaged a match that was almost lost; after that he took off on a winning streak. He defeated three Americans in a row – Butch Seewagen, Frank Froehling, and Bob Lutz..

They all knew how to play well on grass; Froehling had reached Wimbledon quarter-finals in 1963, Bob Lutz in 1969! Somewhat easy three-set victories against them gave me confidence. I grasped self-belief and a sublime desire to conquer.

In 1969 Kodes lost to Bob Lutz in Wimbledon but here he caught Bob on one of those days that all players want fast to forget. Kodes' backhand and especially his backhand return reached amazing proficiency: he destroyed Lutz 6:4, 6:2, 6:4.

Froehling exhibited a close to demonic serve. Yet, I did not let that throw me off. I killed him 6:0, 7:6, and 6:3. Next round was the semifinal match. There I faced another American, the outstanding Arthur Ashe. He possessed one of the most potent serves in the world, the kind that could be classified as a super serve.

It started to rain again in New York and the wait for the play to resume was exhausting. Even the spectators were restless and ready to see the battle between America and Europe. The other semi-final match was between Stan Smith and Tom Okker. The fans were happy since Smith defeated the "Flying Dutchman" in spite of pulling from behind in the last fifth set when the score was 1:3 in his disfavor.

In U.S. Tennis Finals

Smith vs. Kodes

FOREST HILLS, N.Y. (AP) — Giant killer Jan Kodes of Czechoslovakia stunned favored Arthur Ashe Jr.. 7-6, 3-6, 4-6, 6-3, 6-4, yesterday and went into the men's singles final of the rain-plagued U.S. Open Tennis Championships against big Stan Smith, the American soldier from Pasadena, Calif.

The 6-foot-4 Smith, serving 16 aces, turned back speedy Tom Okker of The Netherlands in a match of sporadic brilliance and letdowns, 7-6, 6-3, 3-6, 2-6, 6-3.

SMITH AND Kodes meet today for the $20,000 first prize. Also today, top-seeded Billie Jean King of Long Beach, Calif., and second-seeded Rosemary Casals of San Francisco play for the women's crown—the f i r s t time since 1958 that two U.S. women competed in this final. That was the year that Althea Gibson defeated Darlene Hard.

An erratic service, producing a dozen double faults, was the undoing of Ashe, the s k i n n y Negro young man who won the inaugural Open in 1968 with a five-set victory over Okker.

The last two and a half sets of the Ashe-Kodes semifinal was played in a drizzling rain and Ashe repeatedly had to stop to wipe off his fogged up spectacles.

KODES IS the first East European-Iron Curtain competitor—to reach the finals of the U.S. Open. Jaroslav Drobny, a self-exiled Czech beat Ken Rosewall of Aus-

★From First Sports Page

tralia for the Wimbledon title in 1954.

Kodes, 25, a graduate of the University of Prague, entered the tournament unseeded and unnoticed, having never gone further than the second round in a grass court event.

It's the first U.S. Open title shot for Smith, who won the U.S. Amateur in 1969 and who went into the Wim-

bledon final this year against Newcombe.

AS WIMBLEDON runner-up, Smith was seeded No. 2. Ashe was placed No. 3 after the withdrawal of Rod Laver and Okker was No. 4.

If Smith should win the $20,000, he has announced the purse will go to the U.S. Lawn Tennis Association for the D a v i s Cup fund. If Kodes wins, as an independent pro, he collects $15,000 and $5,000 goes to his country's tennis association.

It is quite a distance from the Clubhouse to the Centre Court, a little over a hundred and fifty yards. Both Stan and I carried a pair of "spike" shoes besides our rackets. An ex-icehockey player Miloslav Pospisil lived in New York, joined us.

In the course of the Forest Hills final Kodes converted into a surprisingly effective volleyer. He approached the net so closely that it often appeared that he would fall over it. He either reached the ball or he put it away, playing the volley with a straight arm and a firm wrist.

The match stretched out and that was the reason why the second semi-final match started relatively late. Kodes won the first set in a tie-break but the onset of the set was pretty intimidating. Ashe targeted Kodes' serve and attacked it with three beautiful returns as if he wanted to let Kodes know that he, too, had splendid returns! Ashe won his own serve as well and led 4:2. However, he then double-faulted twice and allowed Kodes to tie the score at 4:4. It cost him dearly. Ashe thus allowed him to fight for the set in a tie-break that he was never fond of himself. In spite of Kodes winning the tie-break, the American took the next two sets. And in the fourth Ashe was 3:1 ahead!

At this point it started to drizzle, or better to say that the fog was very thick and moist, it was not raining. The humidity was bothersome and Arthur's glasses were fogging up; however, the umpire rejected his appeal for game suspension. I did not like playing on wet grass either. I lost balance in several instances.

Heavier balls and fogged up glasses befuddled Ashe's biggest weapon – his hard serve. At the moment of tossing the ball and looking up at it, he was almost blinded. Kodes tied the set score 2:2 and opened the fifth set by breaking Ashe's serve and soon leading 2:0. However, Ashe was not giving up; he had won Forest Hills once before and wanted the championship again. He broke Kodes back, tied the score at 4:4, and was serving. Kodes provoked himself to take some risk and at deuce he pressed Ashe to botch a backhand volley; in the subsequent advantage point he produced a lethal return wining the game and bringing the score to 5:4.

I pulled out similar arsenal I had used to overwhelm Newcombe: risky returns placed close to the lines. I also attempted several successful drop-volleys.

At 5:4 Kodes served for the match. Ashe passed him twice during that game but when the first match-point came up Kodes turned it into a match won! He was only the third European since the World War II to reach the Forest Hills finals.

We finished around 8 pm. The dusk set in and, in those days, there was no car that would take me to the hotel. I had to pack up my bag and take the subway; it was midnight by the time I reached the hotel. The next day at mid-day I was to play the finals against Stan Smith.

Insane heat and humidity reigned over New York again. Before they hit the first point of the game both protagonists had already had enough of it after the weeklong marathon matches. After their five-set semi-final matches the players did not have even a day off.

I felt sore all over; my calves, knees, shoulders... In the locker room I realized that Stan did not feel much better..I warmed up into the game sooner and won the first set 6:3. Stan had problems returning my first serve and confronting my sharp returns. However, at deuce and

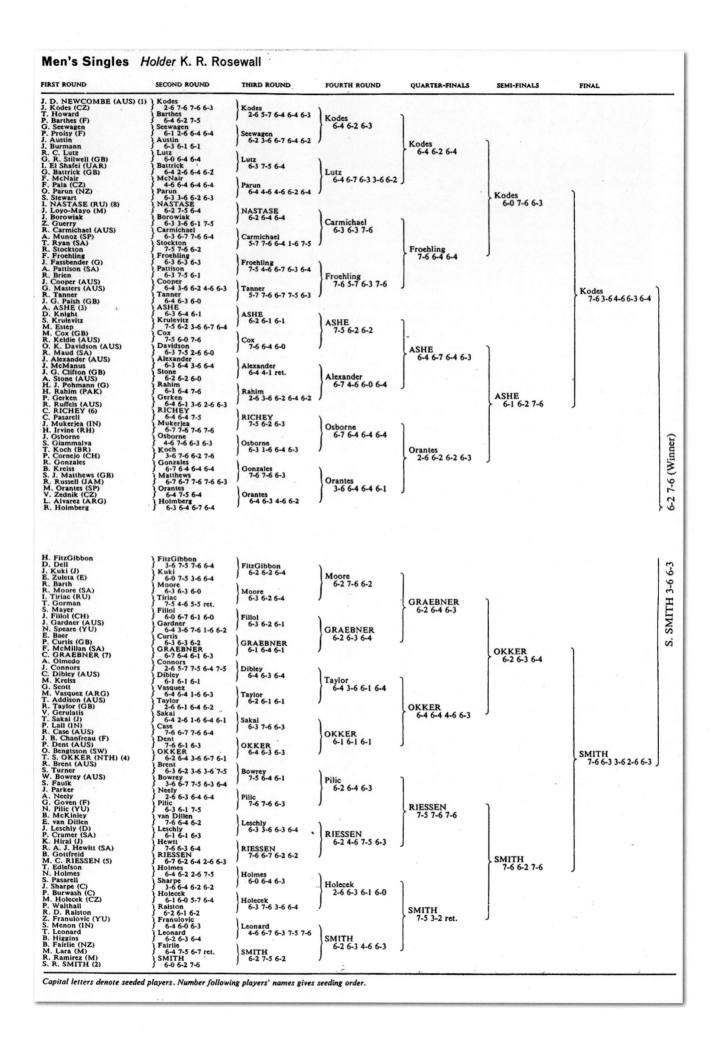

FIRST ROUND	SECOND ROUND	THIRD ROUND	FOURTH ROUND	QUARTER-FINALS	SEMI-FINALS	FINAL

Top half

First Round:
- J. D. NEWCOMBE (AUS) (1)
- J. Kodes (CZ)
- T. Howard
- P. Barthes (F)
- G. Seewagen
- P. Proisy (F)
- J. Austin
- J. Burmann
- R. C. Lutz
- G. R. Stilwell (GB)
- I. El Shafei (UAR)
- G. Battrick (GB)
- F. McNair
- F. Pala (CZ)
- O. Parun (NZ)
- S. Stewart
- I. NASTASE (RU) (8)
- J. Loyo-Mayo (M)
- J. Borowiak
- Z. Guerry
- R. Carmichael (AUS)
- A. Munoz (SP)
- T. Ryan (SA)
- R. Stockton
- F. Froehling
- J. Fassbender (G)
- A. Pattison (SA)
- R. Brien
- J. Cooper (AUS)
- G. Masters (AUS)
- R. Tanner
- J. G. Paish (GB)
- A. ASHE (3)
- D. Knight
- S. Krulevitz
- M. Estep
- M. Cox (GB)
- R. Keldie (AUS)
- O. K. Davidson (AUS)
- R. Maud (SA)
- J. Alexander (AUS)
- J. McManus
- J. G. Clifton (GB)
- A. Stone (AUS)
- H. J. Pohmann (G)
- H. Rahim (PAK)
- P. Gerken
- R. Ruffels (AUS)
- C. RICHEY (6)
- C. Pasarell
- J. Mukerjea (IN)
- H. Irvine (RH)
- J. Osborne
- S. Giammalva
- T. Koch (BR)
- P. Cornejo (CH)
- R. Gonzales
- B. Kreiss
- S. J. Matthews (GB)
- R. Russell (JAM)
- M. Orantes (SP)
- V. Zednik (CZ)
- L. Alvarez (ARG)
- R. Holmberg

Second Round:
- Kodes 2-6 7-6 7-6 6-3
- Barthes 6-4 6-2 7-5
- Seewagen 6-1 2-6 6-4 6-4
- Austin 6-3 6-1 6-1
- Lutz 6-0 6-4 6-4
- Battrick 6-4 2-6 6-4 6-2
- McNair 4-6 6-4 6-4 6-4
- Parun 6-3 3-6 6-2 6-3
- NASTASE 6-2 7-5 6-4
- Borowiak 6-3 3-6 6-1 7-5
- Carmichael 6-3 6-7 7-6 6-4
- Stockton 7-5 7-6 6-2
- Froehling 6-3 6-3 6-3
- Pattison 6-3 7-5 6-1
- Cooper 6-4 3-6 6-2 4-6 6-3
- Tanner 6-4 6-3 6-0
- ASHE 6-3 6-4 6-1
- Krulevitz 7-5 6-2 3-6 6-7 6-4
- Cox 7-5 6-0 7-6
- Davidson 6-3 7-5 2-6 6-0
- Alexander 6-3 6-4 3-6 6-4
- Stone 6-2 6-2 6-0
- Rahim 6-1 6-4 7-6
- Gerken 6-4 6-1 3-6 2-6 6-3
- RICHEY 6-4 6-4 7-5
- Mukerjea 6-7 7-6 7-6 7-6
- Osborne 4-6 7-6 6-3 6-3
- Koch 3-6 7-6 6-2 7-6
- Gonzales 6-7 6-4 6-4 6-4
- Matthews 6-7 6-7 7-6 7-6 6-3
- Orantes 6-4 7-5 6-4
- Holmberg 6-3 6-4 6-7 6-4

Third Round:
- Kodes 2-6 5-7 6-4 6-4 6-3
- Seewagen 6-2 3-6 6-7 6-4 6-2
- Lutz 6-3 7-5 6-4
- Parun 6-4 4-6 4-6 6-2 6-4
- NASTASE 6-2 6-4 6-4
- Carmichael 5-7 7-6 6-4 1-6 7-5
- Froehling 7-5 4-6 6-7 6-3 6-4
- Tanner 5-7 7-6 6-7 7-5 6-3
- ASHE 6-2 6-1 6-1
- Cox 7-6 6-4 6-0
- Alexander 6-4 4-1 ret.
- Rahim 2-6 3-6 6-2 6-4 6-2
- RICHEY 7-5 6-2 6-3
- Osborne 6-3 1-6 6-4 6-3
- Gonzales 7-6 7-6 6-3
- Orantes 6-4 6-3 4-6 6-2

Fourth Round:
- Kodes 6-4 6-2 6-3
- Lutz 6-4 6-7 6-3 3-6 6-2
- Carmichael 6-3 6-3 7-6
- Froehling 7-6 5-7 6-3 7-6
- ASHE 7-5 6-2 6-2
- Alexander 6-7 4-6 6-0 6-4
- Osborne 6-7 6-4 6-4 6-4
- Orantes 3-6 6-4 6-4 6-1

Quarter-finals:
- Kodes 6-4 6-2 6-4
- Froehling 7-6 6-4 6-4
- ASHE 6-4 6-7 6-4 6-3
- Orantes 2-6 6-2 6-2 6-3

Semi-finals:
- Kodes 6-0 7-6 6-3
- ASHE 6-1 6-2 7-6

Final (top half): Kodes 7-6 3-6 4-6 6-3 6-4

Bottom half

First Round:
- H. FitzGibbon
- D. Dell
- J. Kuki (J)
- E. Zuleta (E)
- R. Barth
- R. Moore (SA)
- I. Tiriac (RU)
- T. Gorman
- S. Mayer
- J. Fillol (CH)
- J. Gardner (AUS)
- N. Speare (YU)
- E. Baer
- P. Curtis (GB)
- F. McMillan (SA)
- C. GRAEBNER (7)
- A. Olmedo
- J. Connors
- C. Dibley (AUS)
- M. Kreiss
- G. Scott
- M. Vasquez (ARG)
- T. Addison (AUS)
- R. Taylor (GB)
- V. Gerulaitis
- T. Sakai (J)
- P. Lall (IN)
- R. Case (AUS)
- J. B. Chanfreau (F)
- P. Dent (AUS)
- O. Bengtsson (SW)
- T. S. OKKER (NTH) (4)
- R. Brent (AUS)
- S. Turner
- W. Bowrey (AUS)
- S. Faulk
- J. Parker
- A. Neely
- G. Goven (F)
- N. Pilic (YU)
- B. McKinley
- E. van Dillen
- J. Leschly (D)
- P. Cramer (SA)
- K. Hirai (J)
- R. A. J. Hewitt (SA)
- B. Gottfried
- M. C. RIESSEN (5)
- T. Edlefson
- N. Holmes
- S. Pasarell
- J. Sharpe (C)
- P. Burwash (C)
- M. Holecek (CZ)
- P. Walthall
- R. D. Ralston
- Z. Franulovic (YU)
- S. Menon (IN)
- T. Leonard
- B. Higgins
- B. Fairlie (NZ)
- M. Lara (M)
- R. Ramirez (M)
- S. R. SMITH (2)

Second Round:
- FitzGibbon 3-6 7-5 7-6 6-4
- Kuki 6-0 7-5 3-6 6-4
- Moore 6-3 6-3 6-0
- Tiriac 7-5 4-6 5-5 ret.
- Fillol 6-0 6-7 6-1 6-0
- Gardner 6-4 3-6 7-6 1-6 6-2
- Curtis 6-3 6-3 6-2
- GRAEBNER 6-7 6-4 6-1 6-3
- Connors 2-6 5-7 7-5 6-4 7-5
- Dibley 6-1 6-1 6-1
- Vasquez 6-4 6-4 1-6 6-3
- Taylor 2-6 6-1 6-4 6-2
- Sakai 6-4 2-6 1-6 6-4 6-1
- Case 7-6 6-7 7-6 6-4
- Dent 7-6 6-1 6-3
- OKKER 6-2 6-4 3-6 6-7 6-1
- Brent 6-3 6-2 3-6 3-6 7-5
- Bowrey 3-6 6-7 7-5 6-3 6-4
- Neely 2-6 6-3 6-4 6-4
- Pilic 6-3 6-1 7-5
- van Dillen 7-6 6-4 6-2
- Leschly 6-1 6-1 6-3
- Hewtt 7-6 6-3 6-4
- RIESSEN 6-7 6-2 6-4 2-6 6-3
- Holmes 6-4 6-2 2-6 7-5
- Sharpe 3-6 6-4 6-2 6-2
- Holecek 6-1 6-0 5-7 6-4
- Ralston 6-2 6-1 6-2
- Franulovic 6-4 6-0 6-3
- Leonard 6-2 6-3 6-4
- Fairlie 6-4 7-5 6-7 ret.
- SMITH 6-0 6-2 7-6

Third Round:
- FitzGibbon 6-2 6-2 6-4
- Moore 6-3 6-2 6-4
- Fillol 6-3 6-2 6-1
- GRAEBNER 6-1 6-4 6-1
- Dibley 6-4 6-3 6-4
- Taylor 6-2 6-1 6-1
- Sakai 6-3 7-6 6-3
- OKKER 6-4 6-3 6-3
- Bowrey 7-5 6-4 6-1
- Pilic 7-6 7-6 6-3
- Leschly 6-3 3-6 6-3 6-4
- RIESSEN 7-6 6-7 6-2 6-2
- Holmes 6-0 6-4 6-3
- Holecek 6-3 7-6 3-6 6-4
- Leonard 4-6 6-7 6-3 7-5 7-6
- SMITH 6-2 7-5 6-2

Fourth Round:
- Moore 6-2 7-6 6-2
- GRAEBNER 6-2 6-3 6-4
- Taylor 6-4 3-6 6-1 6-4
- OKKER 6-1 6-1 6-1
- Pilic 6-2 6-4 6-3
- RIESSEN 6-2 4-6 7-5 6-3
- Holecek 2-6 6-3 6-1 6-0
- SMITH 6-2 6-3 4-6 6-3

Quarter-finals:
- GRAEBNER 6-2 6-4 6-3
- OKKER 6-4 6-4 4-6 6-3
- RIESSEN 7-5 7-6 7-6
- SMITH 7-5 3-2 ret.

Semi-finals:
- OKKER 6-2 6-3 6-4
- SMITH 7-6 6-2 7-6

Final (bottom half): SMITH 7-6 6-3 3-6 2-6 6-3

Winner: S. SMITH 3-6 6-3 6-3 6-2 7-6 (Winner)

Capital letters denote seeded players. Number following players' names gives seeding order.

0:1 in the second set the umpire called a foot-fault on my second serve! Stan received the ad and caught on. He won the second set 6:3 and tied the set score 1:1. I lost my confidence for a while and he took the third set 6:2. It seemed that the fourth set and the match was going to be his as well but, all of a sudden, I started to play much better again and tied the score in spite of the fact that the umpire called about five foot-faults against me throughout the match, which drove me crazy. I never had problems with it in previous tournaments! Was it intentional? Who knows?

At any rate, at 2:3 Kodes broke Smith's serve with his fast powerful yet controlled returns from both sides and tied the score at 3:3. He lost his next serve, however, and the score stood 3:4. At this he broke the opponent again in the following game and evened the score at 4:4. Heavy balls and relatively slow court helped him carry on all the way to the five-

Friendly finals: Jan and Stan.

point tiebreak, where he had a chance to rally and, perhaps, win.

I suddenly felt that I was able to sway even the fifth set my way. Perhaps, I got overconfident. I was ahead 3:1, and at 3:2 I had two serves. Generally, that would have given me the decisive edge but there was Stan Smith on the other side of the net, a player of the world class caliber. He punched two ferocious returns by me before I even saw them and tied the score 3:3. In next two points he delivered such fierce serves that I barely touched them; Stan converted his first match point to win the tie-breaker 5:3, and thus he became the new US Open Champion!I have the entire match taped and I watch it from time to time to see where I faltered. Basically, I did not make any mistakes. It was the third set that decided the outcome; for a while

Stan Smith, the U.S. Open (Navy) Champion with Jan Kodes.

TENNIS U.S.A.

Official publication for the
United States Lawn
Tennis Association
NOVEMBER, 1971   50¢

PACIFIC SOUTHWEST OPEN

JAN KODES

CLAY-COURTER KODES TAKES TO GRASS

I suffered from a physical weakness and I lost the touch. In the fourth set tie-break Stan hit some remarkable returns from my good first serves; he took some risky shots and closed the match with two aces.

VICTORY OVER ROD LAVER

Kodes had a chance to face the best players of the world one more time this season. In the Fall, Sweden hosted their traditional Stockholm Open. It took place in the Royal Hall, where Kodes would play the Davis Cup finals four years later.

In 1971, all of Lamar Hunt's champion players entered the tournament: Rosewall, Okker, Ashe, Laver, Drysdale... I defeated the Swede Lars Ölander 6:2, 6:0, Bob Lutz 6:4, 6:2, and then, in the quarter-finals, I came across Rod Laver. By this meeting we had played only twice – once in the Grand Prix Masters in Tokyo in 1970, and this year in Rome - I lost both times. Would the third encounter turn out differently...?

The outcome was decided in the third set tie-break. His left-handed serve was enigmatic. Few players ever anticipated where he would place it. Jan Kodes had observed him for years and had a trifle of an idea about how to deal with Rod's serve by now. The ball served to the forehand side bounced on a curve into the body, whereas served into the backhand it bounced away.

It is seemingly simple and logical, but tackling it on the court is anything but that. It is not easy for a right-hander to adapt to it, and by the time one accomplishes it the match is about over. I knew that there was only one solution to confronting Rod's serve – by reacting to it a few hundredths of a second earlier, even without knowing the direction of the ball. Waiting for the ball to bounce on Stockholm's fast surface was suicidal. I moved forward already during his toss. It was terribly risky! If he served into my forehand I would totally miss it. It was impossible to change the body movement once I was on the go.

That type of gamble proved fruitful in the important moments! My backhand return made the Hunt Group's star drop to his knees. Jan Kodes defeated Laver 4:6, 6:4, 7:6! He then overcame Cliff Drysdale 2:6, 6:2, 6:4 in the semifinals, but lost to Arthur Ashe in the final.

Yet, I had a great chance in the fifth set when I was leading 4:1 and 0:30 on his serve! However, I messed up two returns in a row due to my late backswing and then lost the set 4:6. I regretted very much that I allowed the championship slip out of my grasp; I lost concentration in the end.

I still want to return to my match with Laver. When we returned to the locker-room he was taking a shower and I was just sitting around.

Sensationsseger i Stockholm Open
ROD LAVER UTSLAGEN

SÅ SER dagens finalister i Stockholm Open, Jan Kodes och Arthur Ashe, ut i närbild. Herrarna förefaller ha trevligt tillsammans. I dag slåss de om 52 000 kronor... Foto: LARS NYBERG.

Grattis-telegram från hustrun kastas in mitt under matchen

Swedish newspapers recorded with interest my victory over Rod Laver as well as later defeat by Arthur Ashe.

HERRSINGEL

BÄST AV TRE SET. FINALEN FEM SET. TIE - BREAK VID 6—6 I SAMTLIGA SET.

Segrare 1969: Nikola Pilic · Segrare 1970: Stan Smith

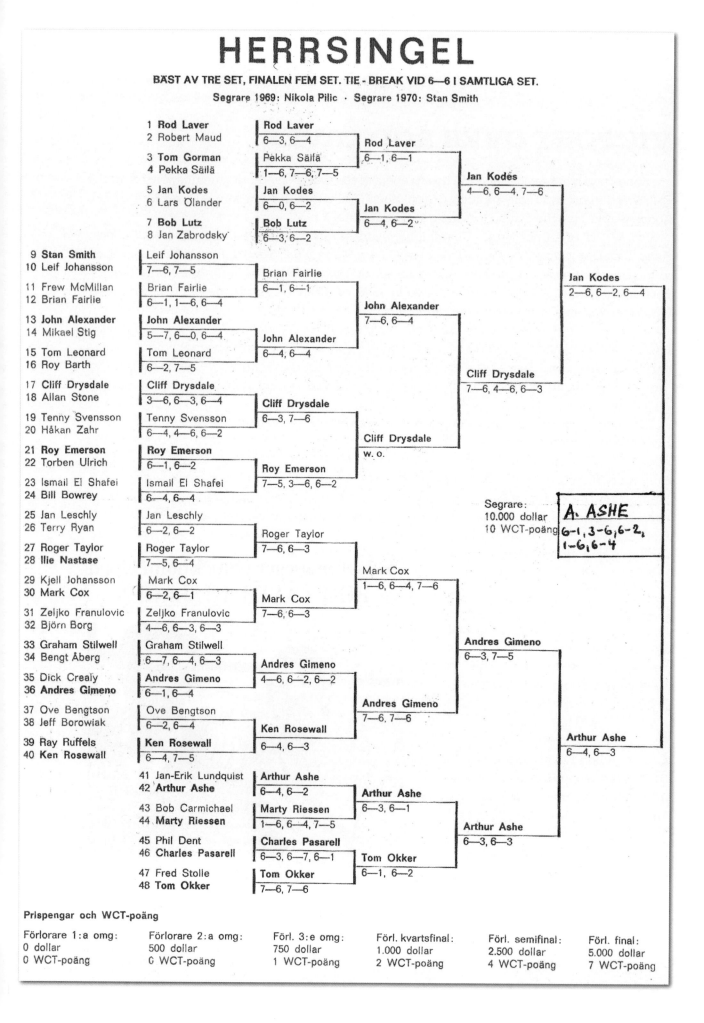

1 **Rod Laver**
2 Robert Maud

3 **Tom Gorman**
4 Pekka Säilä

5 **Jan Kodes**
6 Lars Ölander

7 **Bob Lutz**
8 Jan Zabrodsky

9 **Stan Smith**
10 Leif Johansson

11 Frew McMillan
12 Brian Fairlie

13 **John Alexander**
14 Mikael Stig

15 Tom Leonard
16 Roy Barth

17 **Cliff Drysdale**
18 Allan Stone

19 Tenny Svensson
20 Håkan Zahr

21 **Roy Emerson**
22 Torben Ulrich

23 Ismail El Shafei
24 Bill Bowrey

25 Jan Leschly
26 Terry Ryan

27 Roger Taylor
28 **Ilie Nastase**

29 Kjell Johansson
30 Mark Cox

31 Zeljko Franulovic
32 Björn Borg

33 Graham Stilwell
34 Bengt Åberg

35 Dick Crealy
36 **Andres Gimeno**

37 Ove Bengtson
38 Jeff Borowiak

39 Ray Ruffels
40 **Ken Rosewall**

41 Jan-Erik Lundquist
42 **Arthur Ashe**

43 Bob Carmichael
44 **Marty Riessen**

45 Phil Dent
46 **Charles Pasarell**

47 Fred Stolle
48 **Tom Okker**

Rod Laver
6—3, 6—4

Pekka Säilä
1—6, 7—6, 7—5

Jan Kodes
6—0, 6—2

Bob Lutz
6—3, 6—2

Leif Johansson
7—6, 7—5

Brian Fairlie
6—1, 1—6, 6—4

John Alexander
5—7, 6—0, 6—4

Tom Leonard
6—2, 7—5

Cliff Drysdale
3—6, 6—3, 6—4

Tenny Svensson
6—4, 4—6, 6—2

Roy Emerson
6—1, 6—2

Ismail El Shafei
6—4, 6—4

Jan Leschly
6—2, 6—2

Roger Taylor
7—5, 6—4

Mark Cox
6—2, 6—1

Zeljko Franulovic
4—6, 6—3, 6—3

Graham Stilwell
6—7, 6—4, 6—3

Andres Gimeno
6—1, 6—4

Ove Bengtson
6—2, 6—4

Ken Rosewall
6—4, 7—5

Arthur Ashe
6—4, 6—2

Marty Riessen
1—6, 6—4, 7—5

Charles Pasarell
6—3, 6—7, 6—1

Tom Okker
7—6, 7—6

Rod Laver
6—1, 6—1

Jan Kodes
6—4, 6—2

Brian Fairlie
6—1, 6—1

John Alexander
6—4, 6—4

Cliff Drysdale
6—3, 7—6

Roy Emerson
7—5, 3—6, 6—2

Roger Taylor
7—6, 6—3

Mark Cox
7—6, 6—3

Andres Gimeno
4—6, 6—2, 6—2

Andres Gimeno
7—6, 7—6

Arthur Ashe
6—3, 6—1

Tom Okker
6—1, 6—2

Jan Kodes
4—6, 6—4, 7—6

John Alexander
7—6, 6—4

Cliff Drysdale
w. o.

Mark Cox
1—6, 6—4, 7—6

Andres Gimeno
6—3, 7—5

Arthur Ashe
6—3, 6—3

Jan Kodes
2—6, 6—2, 6—4

Cliff Drysdale
7—6, 4—6, 6—3

Arthur Ashe
6—4, 6—3

Segrare:
10.000 dollar
10 WCT-poäng

A. ASHE
6—1, 3—6, 6—2,
1—6, 6—4

Prispengar och WCT-poäng

Förlorare 1:a omg:	Förlorare 2:a omg:	Förl. 3:e omg:	Förl. kvartsfinal:	Förl. semifinal:	Förl. final:
0 dollar	500 dollar	750 dollar	1.000 dollar	2.500 dollar	5.000 dollar
0 WCT-poäng	0 WCT-poäng	1 WCT-poäng	2 WCT-poäng	4 WCT-poäng	7 WCT-poäng

When he came out of the shower I asked him: "Rod, do you remember the 1961 Centre Court exhibition in Prague against Korda and Javorsky?"

"Yes! Prague – it was beautiful there, I loved it. I remember Stvanice Island."

"And do you remember the boy at the net post? The net ballboy? That was me!"

Kodes returned from Forest Hills as number four player in the world, and fourth in the Grand Prix. After Stockholm Open '71 the second Masters took place in Paris.

It was an amazing and evenly matched tournament. We played on "matesoft", a new artificial carpet that nobody knew. It took me two days to adjust to it. I finished fifth after three wins and three losses.

I lost to Barthes 3:6, 4:6, beat Graebner 7:6, 6:4, then I lost to Richey 2:6, 6:3, 4:6, but I defeated Smith 6:4, 3:6, 6:4, and Franulovic 6:4, 2:6, 7:5, and lost to undefeated Nastase 7:5, 2:6, 2:6. Nastase became the invincible prize winner.

At home I was voted second in the journalists' poll "Athlete of the Year" behind Ondrej Nepela. Many people were convinced that, without any doubt, I had earned the first place. It was circulated that the Slovak journalists gave me, unanimously, the tenth place in order to secure Nepela's first place. What can one do? The Slovaks always stood more together, unlike us, the Czechs....

Even the Chairman of our athletic organization, Miroslav Hlavacek, accepted me as the most successful Czechoslovak tennis player and a "Deserving Sport Champion". He congratulated me heartily but I had an impression that this charade had a whiff of some reconciliation that was initiated by CUPES. It seemed that CUPES was suddenly eager to do well by me. Up until that time articles in the press constantly smeared me. But after I won Roland Garros the second time, an accommodating hand was extended to me. Perhaps, they feared that I might defect.

All times greats: Jack Kramer, Don Budge, Fred Perry and Frank Sedgman (from left).

Tennis
DE FRANCE

**NUMÉRO
SPÉCIAL**
les tournois
que vous jouerez
cette année

**COUPE
DAVIS**
après
France-Suède

**STAN
SMITH**
un beau
champion de
Paris

**JAN
KODES**
le tenant
du titre de
Roland-Garros

ELUSIVE TITLE

He had a year left to finish studies at the University majoring in Economy. Ahead of him was defending his dissertation, passing final exams, and together with Lenka they were expecting their first addition to the family. He decided to give private life a preference before tennis! He skipped the Caribbean as well as the American indoor tennis circuits, and he postponed his departure for the Riviera. He passed two exams and little Jan (Johny Jr.) was born on March 11, 1972.

Although he studied throughout the winter season and awaited the birth of their offspring he did not just dawdle around. He worked out at Klamovka, conditioned indoors as well as outdoors cross-country running or playing little soccer in the snow. In addition to that he was one of the organizers of an "exhibition" that was a truly festive occasion for the fans. As several times in the past Sparta's leadership was the acting party that made this exhibition possible; they pushed for an international encounter and this time it was between Sparta and Bucharest. And so it happened that Kodes attracted one of the best Davis Cup doubles teams of the time – Ilie Nastase and Ion Tiriac, to come and play in Prague before the end of 1971.

We agreed on conditions suitable for them and they accepted the offer to come. Among other things they also received a gift of a beautiful crystal bowl – a classical Czech product. We also paid for their plane tickets to New York. The exhibition took place in the Basketball Hall Sparta at Letna.

However, things did not go smoothly. Both protagonists arrived in Prague on the day of the exhibition but Ruzyne Airport was enveloped in thick fog! The Hall was full to its capacity while the plane was still circling above Prague! The air-traffic controller even considered diverting the plane elsewhere. However, it all worked out well in the end and the players were transported directly from the airport to Sparta, and from the car directly to the court!

The un-traditional start of 1972 was the cause of Jan Kodes' absence from five Grand Prix tournaments where most of his rivals collected many points. He calculated that he would warm up and gain some points in the subsequent weeks when, in the previous years, he was already tired. He focused specifically on the Italian Open in Rome.

There were two tournaments that preceded the Italian Open and that he also entered – Madrid and Nice. He opened in grand style in the Spanish metropolis and defeated Bengston, Hoad, Borg, Gimeno and lost only in the finals to Nastase 6:3, 7:6, 6:7, 6:7, and 3:6. A week later he beat Smith in the semifinals 6:4, 2:6, 6:2 but turned around to lose to Nastase again in the finals, this time quite easily 0:6, 4:6, 3:6. However, he celebrated a championship victory in doubles with Stan Smith.

It was the only time in my career that I played doubles with him! We beat Nastase – McMillan 6:3, 3:6, 7:5 in the finals. If he played along with Stan Smith on the same side at least once he had no chance to do the same with McMillan, his opponent from the Nice finals. McMillan was from South Africa.

At home the comrades in athletic leadership hammered into our heads: "You mustn't play with a South-African!" – meaning that we could not partner up with South-Africans for doubles. Nastase was from Romania, another socialist country, yet he played with whomever he chose to!

In our country this issue was approached in a totally illogical way. First, we received a warning about it, then a letter informing us about countries that we were not to accept invitations to take part in their events – Israel, Chile, Taiwan, and South Africa. I do not claim that the Central Office of Czechoslovak Union of Physical Education and Sports invented it; most likely they had to respect orders of comrades from above, from the Ministry of Exterior. It did

Stan Smith with Jan Kodes won the doubles finals at Nice Grand Prix 1972 over Ilie Nastase and Frew Mc Millan 6:3, 3:6, 7:5.

not rattle me much but we faced constant questions from players on the tour who made fun of it. Even Nastase teased me: "Oh well, you Russian puppets, you can't travel wherever and play with whomever you desire!"

I conversed with the South-Africans; we were friends. We lunched together and chatted about various topics including the sights of Prague. I related to them the beauty spots of our magnificent Capital when somebody asked me: "By the way, why aren't you coming to Johannesburg?"

And I had to say: "I am not allowed to!"

"Why?"

...It was difficult to explain "why". This issue got me into uncomfortable situations; people in the free world could not grasp the mentality of our leaders who made such decisions.

I am mentioning this because I won altogether about twenty doubles titles in my career. Most of the times I teamed up with foreign partners like Stan Smith in Nice, Franulovic in US Clay Court Championship in Indianapolis, Nastase in Hamburg and Barcelona, Fibak in Madrid, Munich, Barcelona, Monte Carlo... However, I had to play Grand Slam tournaments with another Czechoslovak – in Wimbledon, Paris, and Forest Hills I played with Kukal. Together we also won tournaments in Hilversum in 1969 and in Istanbul. With Zednik we won in Palm Desert and Los Angeles but never made it past quarter-finals in Grand Slams.

I do not want to offend my colleagues unfairly but I believe that if I had teamed up, let's say, with Nastase I might have secured more titles. The officials constantly forced me to play with another Czech in order to develop teamwork for Davis Cup competition. And I obediently accepted....

After several "jousts" in the opening of 1972 season Jan Kodes realized how fragile was the pinnacle position among the tennis greats whose abilities and prowess were very even. His matches with Ilie Nastase were a perfect example of that.

We hammered at each other practically our entire careers. Naturally, it was not only with Ilie that I had a standing rivalry, I had that with several other players as well, but the chain of encounters with Nastase in 1972 was downright dominant. We played each other three times in three weeks! I lost in five sets in Madrid after failing to capitalize on two match points. I was 5:2 ahead in the fourth! A week later he swept me off the court easily in Nice. Another week after that I defeated him in Rome in four 6:4, 1:6, 6:3, 6:3.

Following that victory Kodes reached the finals in Rome for the third time. Two years previously he lost to Nastase and in 1971 he succumbed to Laver. This time he faced Manuel Orantes. Though his record against him was pretty even he lost to Manolo in a very close four-set match and the Italian Open title remained just a dream for Jan. Kodes thus became the forever Crown Prince of Rome....

Davis Cup competition was in full swing in 1972. We faced and beat Belgium in the first round.

With that victory under our belt the fans were able to look forward to seeing young Borg in person in Prague. What a prodigy! At fifteen he was already showing his teeth!

Kodes defeated him 6:2, 6:3, and 7:5. Frantisek Pala's match against Bengtson got suspended at 8:6, 2:6, 0:6 and 3:4; he lost that set the next day 3:6. Kodes and Kukal won their doubles 8:6, 6:4, 6:3 and on the closing day Pala also defeated Borg three times 6:4.

Before Jan Kodes left for the country of Gaelic Rooster he played yet another victorious match against Andres Gimeno (6:3, 6:4) as part of the European Challenge Cup between Sparta Prague and Real Barcelona.

Paris -1972. Jan was seeded as number one again. He envisioned a dream – winning the tournament the third time in succession! But making history can be a complicated endeavor. Home player Patrick Proisy played out his part in Jan Kodes' quarterfinal doom...

When I followed the last few rounds of the tournament I had a feeling that I could have won it if... However, one cannot rely on "ifs". I was in good shape and nothing hinted towards failure.

However, on the day of the quarterfinal match a number of events interloped in an unbelievable fashion. The officials set up my match with Proisy as the main attraction of the day on Centre Court. However, there was a rain shower before and the preceding women's match dragged out. Before we entered the court the weather acted up again. There was a dreadful downpour and the start of our match was further postponed.

It was about 6 p.m. when we finally began to play. A heavy, wet, slippery court suited Proisy more than it did me. He played a smart game, made no unforced errors and used sliced backhands effectively, drilling it back into the center of my court and succeeding in tiring me out with that type of play.

Three medals from Italian Open finals 1970, 71, 72.

I played him also in the quarter-finals the year before and had no difficulty defeating him. This time, however, it was altogether a different scenario. Proisy was one of the players who were tough to play against. Beside him it was also Richey, Taróczy and Metreveli. These four players knew how to play against me and I disliked playing against them. Not to mention that the crowd, naturally, cheered vehemently for Proisy.

The first set ended with my demise but I won the second 8:6 in spite of lagging behind 2:4 earlier in the set. Things turned around in the third set; I started playing well at last and took points one by one winning the third set easily 6:2. We then had a 15 minute intermission and as I was lying on the massage table having some work done on my legs the tournament director, Pierre Darmon, walked in and said: "Jan, the match is suspended for the day!"

I had no idea what time it was but it seemed like dusk was setting in.

"You would not have enough time for more than two games before darkness. We'll just continue tomorrow."

At that moment I did not realize what it meant and I approved it with a nod. I felt those three sets in my fatigued legs and it suited me well in that instant that we would not go back out to continue playing. However, after my 45-minute massage I walked out expecting dusk in full swing and I could not believe my eyes, as the sun was out and matches on some outside courts were still in progress! I am not inclined to say that the tournament directorship tried to trick me; however, the fact remains that we could have probably finished the match!

Men's Singles *Holder J. Kodes*

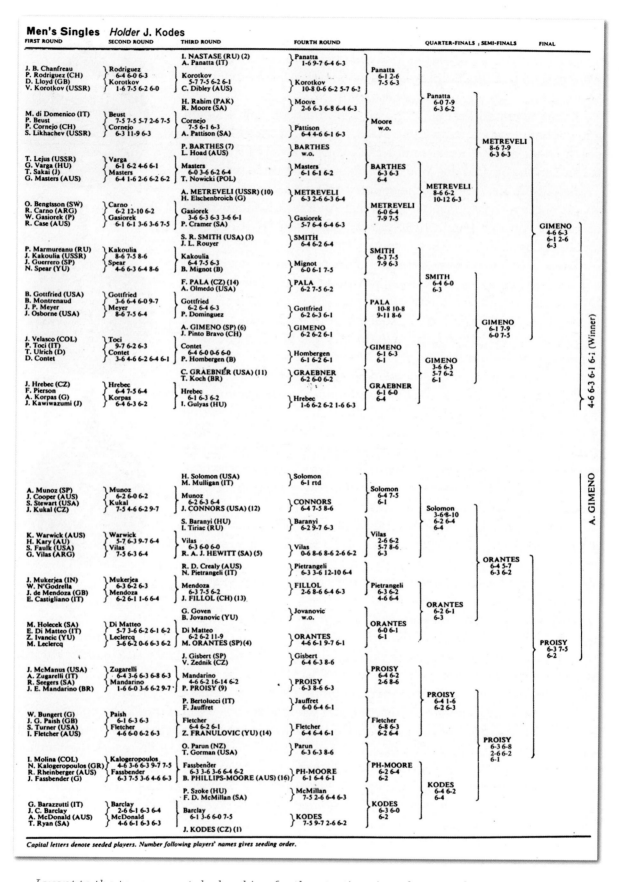

FIRST ROUND	SECOND ROUND	THIRD ROUND	FOURTH ROUND	QUARTER-FINALS	SEMI-FINALS	FINAL

Capital letters denote seeded players. Number following players' names gives seeding order.

I went to the tournament desk asking for the starting time the next day.

"We don't know yet; we'll let you know."

I was leaving the premises not knowing at what time I would play the following day. That would be unthinkable today! Generally, the suspended matches do not start at eleven the way the first matches begin that day but rather as the second matches on the court. During *dinner I found out that we would play at 10:30 in the morning. That made me feel qualmish – I have never been a morning person... I went directly to my hotel and hit the pillows. But I could not sleep, I tossed and turned. I kept contemplating - why was the match suspended?*

I was back at the courts at ten the next day. The sky was clear and low bright sun shone right into my face on one side of the court and I committed a double-fault at 1:1. The packed stadium went crazy!

Proisy whipped me like a little boy on that court.

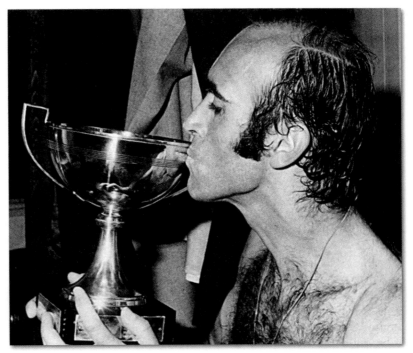

Andres Gimeno kissing the Cup from the French Open 1972. At the age of 34 years become the oldest RG champion. In 1960 PRO Tour was second only to Pancho Gonzales.

He played well and no matter what I tried to do to disturb his momentum he reacted with more confidence. He slaughtered me 6:2, 6:1!

I wished I could put on a disappearing act but, at the same time, I realized that I had to be a good sport about it. But, I missed out on a historical opportunity and I admit that it bugged me for a long time.

The French celebrated Proisy's achievement and elevated him to star rank. He defeated Orantes the next day and reached the finals. However, it was the "tennis court professor" Andres Gimeno who conquered the title unexpectedly. He was thirty-four then and he swept Proisy off the court like an inexperienced junior: 4:6, 6:3, 6:1 and 6:1! He chose a totally different strategy against him than I did. His technique was perfect, he knew how to use dropshots well and used them successfully pulling Proisy up to the net with a chop and then lobbing him.

Till this day, when I bump into Gimeno he says: "Thank you, Jan, for making it possible for me to win Roland Garros!"

RISE OF THE OPEN ERA

September 1972 was the official opening date of players' tennis association ATP. The Association of Tennis Professionals was founded during the US Open. Its first president was Cliff Drysdale and the vice president was Jack Kramer. However, the first attempts to form a "players' alliance" that would protect tennis players' interests were present since 1969 when "open-tennis" was created. Until that time there were tournaments that either the professionals or just the amateurs entered.

Already in 1926 an American industrialist C. C. Pyle gave rise to professional tennis when he signed contracts with two players: Suzanne Lenglen for $75,000 and Mary K. Browne. Soon thereafter the Americans Vincent Richards, Howard Kinsey, Harvey Snodgrass, the Czechoslovak Karel Kozeluh and the French Paul Feret also signed professional contracts. And that was how professional tennis era began with exhibitions, shows, mini-circuits and tournaments not only in the US but also in Europe.

Gradually, other Americans and Europeans joined ranks of the professionals: e.g. Ramon Najuch, Edmund and Paul Burke, Bill Tilden, Lester Stoefen, Hans Nusslein, Frank Hunter, Ellsworth Vines, George Lott, Bruce Barnes, Robert Ramillon, Martin Plaa, Henri Cochet, Fred Perry, Donald Budge, Bobby Riggs as well as Frank Kovacs. After the war, in 1946, the American promoter Jack Harris organized profi-tours of Bobby Riggs vs. Donald Budge, who were soon joined by Jack Kramer, Pancho Segura, Dinny Pails from Australia, Pancho Gonzales and Frank Parker. In 1952 Jack Kramer took over the position of a promoter while continuing to play and he was joined by players Frank Sedgman and Ken McGregor to challenge Pancho Gonzales, Donald Budge and Pancho Segura. In 1954 Jack Kramer organized a tournament of four: Gonzales, Segura, Sedgman and Budge.

Little by little new players joined the group in order to challenge Pancho Gonzales, though unsuccessfully most of the time. Those players were Wimbledon champions Tony Trabert, Rex Hartwig, Lew Hoad, Ken Rosewall, Alex Olmedo, Ashley Cooper, Mal Anderson, Butch Buchholz, Andrés Gimeno, Barry MacKay, Mervyn Rose and finally Rod Laver. By this time it was the year 1962, when Laver won his first Grand Slam, still under amateur status, and "big Pancho" Gonzales decided to retire prematurely. Debates over who was and is the best player in the world cropped up again when Laver joined the professionals. In his first professional circuit in 1963 Laver lost to Hoad as well as to Rosewall. He lost easy to Rosewall in the finals of the official Professional Championships at Forest Hills at the end of that year 4:6, 2:6, 2:6. The following year this Championship was relocated from New York to Longwood Cricket Club in Boston, where it continued until 1999. In 1964 the new main tournament sponsor, Merchants Bank of Boston, attracted again the eight-times champion from 1953-1959 and 1961 Pancho Gonzales, who succumbed only in the finals to Rod Laver 6:4, 3:6, 5:7, 4:6. New promoters and organizations expressed interest in the players and the contracts started changing or totally faded away.

In 1967, when the millionaire Hunt entered the scene and founded a professional firm World Championship Tennis (WCT), he revealed signatures of eight new players so called "Handsome Eight" – Tony Roche, John Newcombe, Cliff Drysdale, Dennis Ralston, Butch Buchholtz, Niki Pilic, Roger Taylor, and Pierre Barthes. That made the ILTF (later ITF) leadership concerned and alerted and they started to engage in further negotiations.

It was mainly the Brits Herman David, Derek Penman and Derek Hardwick, who suggested to work out the situation once and for all and who laid down a foundation of "open tennis" principle for all players. The Chairman of Wimbledon AELTC, Herman David, arranged a tournament of eight professionals on the Centre Court just about a month after Wimbledon. It was sponsored by the British television station BBC. The final between Laver and Rosewall 6:2, 6:2, 12:10 outperformed the Wimbledon final from a month before between John Newcombe and Wilhelm Bungert 6:3, 6:1, 6:1, however it did not sway the Wimbledon Club Chairman's opponents. In its summer meeting ILTF again voted against the "open" tournaments so the conflict carried on. However, Herman David vehemently declared that even if Wimbledon, the most important tournament in the world, is the only one open to all it will carry on with the professionals from now on. The English LTA headed by Derek Penman supported Herman David and voted in "open tournaments" in December 1967 for the next year.

The Americans also received a scare, when a new professional organization NTL – National Tennis League - was founded along with the WCT, and in it the Davis Cup team captain George McCall and David Dixon had already signed players like Rod Laver, Ken Rosewall, Pancho Gonzales, Andrés Gimeno, Fred Stolle and a newcomer Roy Emerson under contract!

As was mentioned above, Suzanne Lenglen and Mary K. Browne became the first female professionals in 1926. In 1950-51 Gussie Moran played Pauline Betz and Althea Gibson, the 1957-58 Wimbledon Champion, played another American Karol Fageros in exhibition pre-games for the basketball Harlem Globetrotters. Other female players that signed professional contracts with NTL were: Billie Jean King, Rosemary Casals, Francoise Durr and Ann Haydon Jones. Bob Kelleher, president of the American USLTA (later USTA) made all the other members aware of the seriousness of the situation and they supported the Brits in their quest for consent of open tournaments. In the meantime, Owen Davidson from Australia signed a several year professional contract as the main LTA coach in London. Other professional coaches, who also played tournaments, had been Karel Kozeluh, Welby Van Horn in the past and later Luis Ayala.

Derek Hardwick

Based on the decision of two tennis super-powers, the ILTF called an urgent situation meeting of tennis unions and federations of all member countries in Paris On March 30, 1968. The ILTF leadership received enough needed votes here from the representatives of 47 countries to organize 12 open tournaments that would include all players! It was not surprising that countries from the Eastern bloc were against it!

There were four classification groups voted on in Paris:

1. Amateurs – must not accept any prize money and are subject to their national unions and federations.
2. Professional teachers – can play along with the amateurs only in "open" tournaments.
3. Professionals under contract – those, who live of tennis and are not subject to their national unions/federations, are permitted to play only "open" tournaments and are prohibited from representing their countries in Davis Cup or Federation Cup competitions.

Herman David

4. Registered players – can accept prize money in "Open" tournaments after an agreement with their national union or federation and furthermore do not lose the privilege to play amateur tournaments and Davis Cup or Federation Cup competition representing their country.

Point # 4 expressed accurately Jan Kodes' status. *"I wanted to play Davis Cup for nothing, but the money I earned in world tournaments should have been mine. Yet, initially, they took it away!"*

The formation of the ATP was not as unswerving as might appear. In the United States the first signs of players' union appeared during 1969. It was said that Newcombe would be the chairman, Pasarell the vice-chairman, Ashe the treasurer, and Laver, Pilic, and Cox the committee members.

Derek Penman

In 1970 the tournaments were divided into categories of sorts. If we had a chance to peek into the calendar of the time we would find "open" by some tournaments, "amateur" by others, and "registered" by the remaining – entirely in agreement with above mentioned categories. There was a mention of two players who were, somewhat, outside the system and, in a way, made a mess of it – Kodes and Nastase. As an amateur, Kodes succeeded in defeating the absolute top in 1971 Rome and Stockholm Open. That prompted Lamar Hunt to desire that as many players sign his WCT contract and he tirelessly pressed the ITF to allow it officially. The reason was evident! When his "sheep" were being defeated by some amateurs he was losing money. That was the reason why he kept repeating: "We must get Kodes to sign with us!" *"They kept calling me and various managers tracked me down and offered me contracts: "Ask at home and see if they'll go along with it." I kept postponing the issue and from time to time I conferred with Nastase about it. I sensed that it was going to bring me problems and hoped that time would solve it one way or another. Whispers around the tournaments predicted that soon the tournaments would be open anyway."*

Tennis had a chance to take this step toward development and the future of the sport world wide thanks to the fact that it was not an Olympic sport. However, it took the ILTF, WCT and NTL four more years of struggle to win control over and manage the tournament schedule. Mike Davis, the English ex-Davis Cup player and the acting WCT Director, became also a member of ILTF commission for the International Calendar; in spite of it, the WCT announced its own 1971 circuit that signed up players like: Arthur Ashe, Charlie Pasarell, Bob Lutz and Ray Moore. That further prolonged the tennis "war". It was a reaction to the first Grand Prix attempt organized by the ILTF and sponsored by Pepsi-Cola and culminating with Masters tournament in Tokyo the year before. Other players were expressing interest in playing the WCT series, where they had a chance to confront the best players of the world and also earn higher "prize money". The dragging controversy was put to rest with finality with a peaceful settlement in American courts in March of 1972, when both sides agreed to promote and support world tennis in the interest of all players. Consequently, a meeting in Copenhagen that April agreed on a calendar schedule of tournaments – the first four months was WCT series tournaments and the rest of the year involved ILTF Grand Prix tournaments and team competitions like Davis Cup and Federation Cup. Lamar Hunt worked out two groups of some thirty two players each, and the top four then advanced into the Masters tournament in Dallas. The following year the number of players who signed contracts with him increased; there were then three groups. The first two from each group plus two players with most points from any group advanced into the Masters.

"My whole life, I've fought to open up the game for the players."
– Jack Kramer

The Founding of the players' own organization ATP (Association of Tennis Professionals) in September 1972 at Forest Hills during the US Open was the most meaningful step for the players. The still active player, Cliff Drysdale, became its first president and Jack Kramer was the executive director. His concept of World Grand Prix Series with a culminating Masters tournament was so agreeable that it has been in affect as ATP World Tour still today though with several adjustments.

After the rise of ATP and WTA the Grand Slam tournaments continued taking place simultaneously. That is true even today when the ATP and WTA mutually agree to play at the same time and in the same venue.

The players' association ATP was founded as the third entity in addition to the ITF and Lamar Hunt's WCT; they were all players' unions of sorts. From time to time tennis players gathered and discussed things that did not suit them and they did not like. *"There were instances that reminded me of factory grumbling, when people whined about having poor quality machines. "Our locker rooms are too small!" "There is no masseur!" - Players put together a committee or leadership that was a predecessor of ATP. Players started to join and also to speak up! I saw it for the first time in 1970 in Los Angeles. There was a sign in the locker room: Players' meeting! Today! - There were thirty of us. Some nagged: "It is impossible for the Roland Garros directorship to require us to start playing at 10 am! The match-start should always be at eleven!" Others complained about the tournament seeding. Granted, this was a tough issue and one of the biggest problems. For instance, Stan Smith was seeded as number one in Paris. But his clay court game did not merit that seeding; he lost in the second round and that influenced the course of the entire tournament.... The next discussion touched upon who should be the chairman, treasurer, and a member of the committee. Arthur Ashe was the most actively engaged player; suddenly I heard him say: "Well, Kodes should also join the committee!" I jumped off the chair and declined the offer saying that my English was not good enough for the honor. At that moment a voice was heard from behind: "That does not matter; you can go to school!" It was the legendary Pancho Gonzales, a well-known joker, who liked to make fun especially on behalf of the young."*

Cliff Drysdale was ranked in the World Top Ten six times (best: 4 at 1965).

A foundation of something more solid was established in the tennis system the moment the third entity entered the scene. The first Grand Prix Series of tournaments was played in 1970 under the name of Pepsi-Cola Grand Prix 1970 and it culminated with the first Masters Tournament in Tokyo. The ITF initiated tournament categorizing within the objective of this first Grand Prix. There were three categories established – A, 1, and 2; each tournament was assigned a category based on points given and the size of the prize money; tradition also played out its significance. Two years later another novelty took place. The first computerized ranking system of the world's best tennis players was put to work in August 1973. It was the ATP's creation that came out exactly on August 23, 1973, and the first world number one ranked player was the Romanian Ilie Nastase, even though he did not win Wimbledon or the US Open, he only won Paris! "Naturally, the computerized point system was imperfect and it underwent changes in the following few years."

Jan Kodes played the Grand Prix Masters four times in a row in the years 1970 through 1973. He qualified for it twice as the fourth Grand Prix position rank (1971 in Paris, 1972 in Barcelona) and once from the sixth position (1973 in Boston). In the premier year in 1970 he occupied the eighth place, but was invited to come to Tokyo as a substitute and eventually replaced Richey who had fallen ill. It is very important to mention that he took part also in 1974 WCT Masters in Dallas, Texas.

"I was always exhausted at the end of the season but I gave the utmost respect to participation in the Masters. The sad part was my realization that players seeded above me had played many more tournaments that gained them more points. I was obliged to return home and play league matches, Nationals in Ostrava, and the International Championships in

Bratislava. That caused me to lose five weeks of play on the Grand Prix circuit. In addition, we played Davis Cup matches but those I played with pleasure and so did other players. My final Grand Prix ranking was always affected by my absence from those five or six Grand Prix tournaments." How would it have turned out had he been able to play all the tournaments?

The compensation for placing among the Grand Prix top ten players was good, including the bonuses. For instance, placing 6th amounted to $8000. *"While I was abroad they often asked me: "Why do you go back? Don't return!" Donald Dell, one of the American managers, who also took care of my interests, asked me a hundred times: "Why are you going back? Simply inform them that you won't play!" But, naturally, I was afraid to do just that. I kept assuring myself that my position at home was an important one, particularly in relation to Davis Cup competition. However, I am convinced till this day that thanks to a number of petty unprofessional Tennis Federation officials I got robbed of better Grand Prix placement and higher world tennis ranking. They did not want to understand that my winning the Czech Championships in Litvinov was really meaningless from my point of view.*

Discussions at home about what, where, when and against whom I should play took no end. It is noteworthy that at this point Kodes, Nastase, Metreveli, and also Connors and Borg were among the world best players who had not yet joined the ATP because it was a professional organization. The ATP leadership, made up of active players, launched ATP registration in the United States during its first year of existence. With that they intended to create sort of "employment" positions that also included benefits. They created a status and hired lawyers to undertake the necessary steps that the US law required. *"In order to be able to collaborate with ITF the ATP had to acquire rank of a regular firm with everything included. The ATP president, Cliff Drysdale, and the executive director, Jack Kramer, were surrounded by other "officials" like Arthur Ashe and Charlie Pasarell. Players, with the exceptions of me, Nastase and Metreveli, then signed entry proclamations. I could not sign it! It would have turned me automatically into a professional player and they would not have accepted that at home. However, this condition disappeared with time and we were allowed to join the ATP without signing anything."*

The ATP got into a conflict right at the start of its existence; in tennis history it is forever known as "Wimbledon Boycott" or the "Pilic Affair". Nikki Pilic from Yugoslavia was the first European member of Lamar Hunt's professional group. The Yugoslavian tennis association supported by the "open" status required of him his participation in Davis Cup competition. The encounter in question was against New Zealand at Zagreb. Pilic refused to play arguing that he had signed a professional contract. In return, the Yugoslavian association banned him from playing in 1973 Paris and Wimbledon. The ATP then entered the dispute. As a new organization they wanted to prove validity of their existence. "The two most vocal individuals were Jack Kramer and Arthur Ashe. They declared that National Federations ought to make agreements with their players instead of just controlling them." However, it was too late for democratic solutions. Many players sided with their colleague and refused to play Wimbledon that year. *"It is also true that there were many insignificant players, who were ATP members because by then players were joining ATP in droves."* The Pilic' affair caused absence of several of the best players from Wimbledon that year; but out of the top fifteen most recent Grand Prix standings Newcombe, Smith, Pilic, Panatta, Okker, Gorman and Orantes only, stayed away from it. Jan Kodes feels consequences of this first serious tennis conflict till this day.

UNBELIEVABLE DOUBLES

West Germany and the Soviet Union. Just the mention of these country names before the Davis Cup encounter evoked waves of emotions. Stifling atmosphere and tension hung in the air.

Marathon Doubles: Hans-Jürgen Pohmann, Jan Kodes, Jürgen Fassbender and Jan Kukal (from left).

In 1972, we had never beaten the Germans and the last loss in 1968 was still a sore memory. Our 1972 match was being previewed with anticipation in the newspapers long before the start. The German press slandered me before even the first practice, journalists ignited the atmosphere and fans against us.

The third round match that decided who would advance into one of the European group's finals in rich Rochusclub in Düsseldorf entered the annals and the history of Czechoslovak Davis Cup team as one of the most dramatic ever. The Germans announced their selection of Jürgen Fassbender, Harald Elschenbroich, and Hans-Jürgen Pohmann; not as accomplished as recent players Christian Kuhnke and Wilhelm Bungert.

This selection inspired untimely optimism at home; many thought that our advancement was clear. Only few understood that given a chance of playing five matches Elschenbroich would defeat Kuhnke four of those five times!

Kodes won both singles, Pala lost, and the doubles was thus the decisive match. Kodes – Kukal defeated one of the best teams in the world Fassbender – Pohmann 19:17 in the fifth!

At 0:1 Jan Kodes entered to face Fassbender as a favorite. However, he had a hard time finding counterattack weapons in the first set against the West German's hard-hit shots. In the next two sets Kodes, luckily, found his balance and was leading 5:2 in the fourth. At 5:3 he had a match point. Botching an easy volley cost him another game and the score was tied at 5:5 with Fassbender then taking the lead 6:5.

I hurried too much and made unforced errors because the play time limit was approaching; it made me worried about the game suspended for darkness. And that is what happened anyway! Now what will transpire tomorrow? It had rained during the night before we resumed the match. As usual, I could not go to sleep. I tossed and turned, stared up at the ceiling. All of a sudden I realized that the match with Fassbender was very similar to the one I played recently at Roland Garros with Proisy. It was better not to think about it!

The situation was critical at one point in the resumed match. Kodes almost lost his serve, which would have resulted in losing the fourth set. In the end he was happy with a 3:6, 6:3,

6:2, and 10:8 victory. It was well deserved and fought for. It was far from easy and for that reason it was valued highly.

Two hours later he was entering the court again to play doubles with Jan Kukal.

They had heard constantly: "If we are to advance we must win the doubles!"

"Well, it won't be a stroll in a park that is for sure" uttered Kukal and they all laughed...

I hope that Jan Kukal won't be bothered if I reveal now, years after the effect that we got into a terrible quarrel in the locker room that day. We played an unsteady game and were down 1:2 in sets. There was absolute quiet in the locker room during our break. The non-playing captain Bolardt did not say a word and the coach Korda did not either; the others tried to comfort us saying that all would turn out ok.

I lost my cool because Jan played too hesitantly. I was losing my serves because shots were passing by him and he could not put away volleys. He let some balls go that he thought would go out, but they landed in. I then either missed some of these balls because I did not expect it to come, or I did not even reach it. In simple terms, Jan was not playing the net game he was capable of playing and knew how to play.

"Hey, Jan, you are dreadfully timid at the net and you have me play it all. We can't win this way. You have to come out of your hole, otherwise we can't win! Wake up!"

He took offense and sent me to hell... But, it did help! A different Kukal returned to the court. And he played great! I remember that with joy even though I am not sure that he recalls it with the same emotion.

The key doubles match that led to the overall victory over West Germany lasted four hours and a quarter: 4:6, 6:3, 3:6, 6:2, 19:17!

We were 5:2 ahead in the last set. Jan was serving for the match, I was standing at the net. The eyes of my opponents showed signs of accepting the fate of defeat. The first serve hit the tape, the second went out! I would have never guessed that this banal double fault could unveil a drama that followed and that one hardly ever gets to witness around tennis courts. During the match they called Jan's foot-faults in order to unnerve him. Circumstances put him in a difficult spot.

The Germans sensed a chance and came alive. They fought back two match points, the first one at 9:8, second at 13:12. Unbelievable luck was on their side. Once we were up 30:0 on Pohmann's serve but he played two such amazing let shots that everybody just froze. Each time the ball hit the tape and rolled over to our side leaving us gazing in disbelief. A moment later I triggered a volley directly at Pohmann's body. He pulled out his racket in reflex and the ball bounced off his frame. I witnessed a shot like that a thousand times; usually it slid off the racket or bounced out of the court. Not that day, however! Pohmann retrieved it and sent it into our court; we just watched it standing helplessly.

Is there no justice, I thought to myself as we were changing sides. At that point we were both suffering from leg cramps. I felt pretty awful. I don't even remember how we finally won that last point. The only thing I do remember is a thought that flashed through my mind then that there was no way we could make that point.

I also remember that my legs felt as heavy as led. We played in July and it was hot. I pulled on my sweat-suit and went to the court with Pavel Korda with the intention to genera-

te some sweat! Sweating helps muscles to regenerate; muscles lo-osen up easier when warm. I could barely move. Only after that I took a shower and had a massage.

A super-human effort went into the Düsseldorf doubles. But I remember it fondly.

After this grueling match Kodes had to beat Elschenbroich on the third day. He was surprised how well he played in the opening of that match, better than the first day. The crisis hit him in the second set at 6:4, 4:2. He botched an easy backhand volley which disquieted him. It was, after all, his best stroke that he missed! He lost four games in a row and the set. He battled for

The end of the last and deciding battle with Harald Elschenbroich.

the third set and won it but Elschenbroich gave him a lesson in the fourth.

I was unable to hit the ball over the net, I struggled physically, I had to rest in between rallies and I economized when playing the most important points. Otherwise I would not have been able to finish! I started cramping up in my legs but I did not want to give any signs of it.

At 4:5 in the fifth, at the changing table, he cried in rage as well as out of sorrow.

Bolardt was telling me something but I was not absorbing any of it. I only wished for the end to come.

But the end only comes after the last point is over! Elschenbroich double-faulted and Kodes mobilized the last bits of energy he could muster.

I hurt all over and was cramping up but I was careful not to make any error.

Then the last point came; nothing spectacular, just a half-volley but it played out! 6:4, 4:6, 6:2, 1:6, 8:6! Czechoslovakia advanced again into the European zonal Davis Cup final. I barely made it to the net to shake my opponent's hand. Only one more time I felt this decrepit and that was after my semifinal match with Roger Taylor in Wimbledon.

This was the first time ever that we defeated the Germans and in their home venue! They had a hard time accepting it. I was as happy as a little kid that we succeeded.

Perhaps the entire Czechoslovak press commented on the Düsseldorf victory. There was no end to praise about Kodes' heroic achievement:

Hundred and sixty five games in three days would leave an imprint on any player. It was an amazing effort that Kodes had to exude in the encounter with West Germany. In his match with Elschenbroich he used literally the last drop of his energy. He experienced several crisis but his willpower helped him pull through. Elschenbroich played a refreshing game; he had plenty of energy, he reached all Kodes' drop-shots, he knew how to execute backhand passing shots and played mainly from the baseline. Kodes' words after the match: It was terribly tough but I am happy that I won. It cost me a lot of energy; it was a pity that I did not manage a 5:2 lead in the second set; in a way, that broke me. However, I kept telling myself: you must, you must, you must! I am glad it is over. We are now in the finals.

Vecerni Praha – Czechoslovak press

Murtas Churchilava? He must have two hearts at least!

Those were the words of a surgeon and a team-mate of a well-known Soviet soccer player, the legendary goalie Lev Jasin. He wanted to express his admiration for his friend's accomplishment. Those who saw Churchilava on TV live from the final game of the European Championships between West Germany and the Soviet Union certainly understands that he merits such distinction. Jan Kodes is the most amazing tennis laborer I know – declared his doubles partner Jan Kukal with deep respect and bowing to Kodes' unparalleled relentless effort that our player exhibited in the encounter against Germany. It would have been the same if he also said: "Jan Kodes must have at least two hearts!" Everybody, who watched the Düsseldorf match and Jan Kodes' achievement, must be in agreement with that statement.

Ceskoslovensky sport – Czechoslovak press

Davis Cup accomplishments, the Stvanice ecstatic crowd, the delighted Nation in front of TVs, the euphoria and jubilation that arose from overcoming the world best tennis players was only one side of the coin. On the other side I came to realization that I was being presented as a typical product of socialist athleticism. The comrades started introducing me to communist youth, the pioneers, and the budding athletes as an example to follow.

What he said about Jan Kodes
Jan Kukal

Jan Kodes was a key player of a whole generation of players who paved the way for the likes of Martina Navratilova, Hana Mandlikova, Ivan Lendl, Milos Mecir and others. Without him all who followed would have had much more difficult conditions. Kodes has done tremendous work in the way of advertising Czechoslovak tennis and he led tennis out of the years of darkness. The year 1948 was a tragic turning point not only for the rich and intellectual crème de la crème of our Nation but also for the "white sport" that fell under the accusation of a decadent bourgeois pastime.

Close to ten years passed from the famous blow to Jaroslav Drobny in early 1950s in Gstaad, Switzerland, when a Czechoslovak consul Jan Zelenka, future Czechoslovak Television director general, did not allow him to play in the finals against a South African opponent. At the beginning of the dark Czechoslovak tennis period this was not just a blow, it also generated emigration exodus of Davis Cup players like Drobny and Cernik.

Vera Puzejova and Jiri Javorsky also accomplished much hard work for our tennis but Jan Kodes was the main protagonist in the struggles of advancing the popularity of tennis. He was a fighter with a heart of a warrior who did not withstand defeats easily and was ready to spill his guts out on the court in order to achieve the ultimate. He personified integrity and traits of perseverance.

Jan's "apprentice" years were strongly influenced by his father, who was persecuted by the communist regime that disallowed him to run his own law practice and who then had to labor for years. He had more free time that he dedicated to his son Jan and daughter Vlasta.

Jan is four years my junior. I did not come from a tennis family thus I did not have the background and took some time for me to decide whether I should follow basketball or tennis. It might have been Jan's father's positive relationship with me that encouraged that we started practicing together in early 1960s. He helped me considerably;

I was like a training "horse" and he was a typical determined fighter with strong will-power.

During the melting period of our icy totalitarian regime in the years between 1968 and 1969 we received an invitation to play the Caribbean Circuit that only the best players of the world participated in; for us it was the utmost event then! Neither the Czechoslovak Union of Physical Education and Sport, headed by Dr. Richard Nejezchleb, nor the Tennis Federation had financies to cover the plane tickets. However, the Vice-Minister of Culture, Josef Rehak, offered to look for sponsorship. In the early 1970s a number of controversies led to a historical event: establishment of Czechoslovak Professional Tennis under the sponsorship and rules of Pragosport. Stanislav Chvatal, the Tennis Federation Chairman, was the main force responsible for this important step. With it tennis became a forerunner of all other sports by some twenty years! It came about out of anguish over the 50% value of purse that we had to turn in to the authorities.

The accomplishments would not have taken place without Jan Kodes. It was his Davis Cup achievements that made the "white sport" popular again. The entire country participated through the Stvanice tennis events. Davis Cup became the most important competition for the fans to follow. We were not driven just by patriotism alone; we also knew that once we lost in Davis Cup we also lost exit visas without which our passports were good for nothing.

In Davis Cup competition "Little Jan" (as he was nicknamed) guaranteed two points. The rest of us, Holecek, Pala, Zednik, Hrebec, and me, had to come up with one more point to win. Some key doubles matches with Jan have turned unforgettable for me. One of those was the first Davis Cup point I made in Copenhagen in 1969, when we defeated Leschly – Ulrich. In Düsseldorf we won 19:17 in the fifth set after more than four hours against the West Germans and Jan added the decisive point the next day after another five-set battle with Elschenbroich in spite of being totally physically spent.

As far as the Grand Slam tournaments go I remember specifically Jan's two consecutive Roland Garros triumphs there in 1970 and 1971. During the first final against Franulovic from Yugoslavia I got so involved in his match cheering for him that I even changed sides in the audience as he changed sides on the court.

Jan and I fostered a special relationship; we practiced together and we traveled around the world together. We did not part even after leaving the professional circuit. When Jan became the non-playing Davis Cup captain he chose me as the team coach. He lived through the matches as if he played them himself. If it were possible he would even breath for his players. The team did not win much but we reached the world semifinals twice. Part of the problem was the fact that Ivan Lendl was not returning home much after the historical Davis Cup triumph in 1980. It was understandable though because the time of the country's normalization process was not conducive to achieving tennis goals. Ivan became the world number one player in 1983 and with that he achieved more for Czechoslovak tennis than all our ambassadors together.

Kodes was not dormant either. He realized his life dream in the way of Stvanice Tennis Center construction. I'll never forget his crouched silhouette dragging the tennis center model from one byrocratic office to another trying to find support with his usual and typical Kodes resolve.

Jan affected my life positively one more time when he worked on my behalf during my desired transfer to Austria while neither the CUPES Chairman Himl nor the Tennis Federation leadership supported that move.

Jan Kodes played a very important positive role in my life and I am for ever grateful to him.

Jan Kukal

June 1972 – Jimmy Connors receives the Rothmans London Grass Court Trophy at Queens Club from LTA President Judge Carl Aarvold. Turning professional that year, Jimmy won his first title in January at Jacksonville, Florida over Clark Graebner 7:5, 6:4 and as unseeded player made an impressive Wimbledon debut – reaching the quarter-finals, losing to Ilie Nastase.

WIMBLEDON "SEMIS"

After his successful performance in 1971 US Open at Forest Hills Jan Kodes decided to work systematically on adjusting his game to the grass court surface: improving his net-approach after the serve, following the serve at least three feet beyond the "T", and above all executing the first volley successfully! It was the toughest period of his career.

The Americans had difficulties moving on clay, the Europeans on grass. Arthur Ashe would have preferred the grass-court-like foot "stutter" on clay to actual sliding, which was impossible. I felt the other way.

My Forest Hills achievement gave me a boost and, at the same time, it made me aware of a certain falsehood. I always heard around and read in newspapers that Continental Europeans would never do well on grass; it was generally accepted that grass-court dominance was the Americans', Australians', and South Africans' hegemony. Suddenly, I realized that it was not so. I recognized that one could compete on a level with the best players even on grass.

I did not grow up on grass and so I did not know how to move productively on that surface. I fell numerous times in my matches against Newcombe and Smith...Now I wanted to prove to myself that I could put up such strong challenge that I would become their equal foe.

Five times he returned from Wimbledon after the opening round, each time having faced a tough draw: Drysdale, Roche, Riessen, and, in 1969 after his first round five-set victory over Pato Cornejo, he lost to the American Bob Lutz in five; that was followed by another five-set first round loss to Metreveli the following year after he had won the French title!

Jan Kodes during the semifinals with Stan Smith.

Few months later Onny Parun reached the Australian Open final in 1973. He was defeated by John Newcombe 3:6, 7:6, 5:7, 1:6.

He always lost on court #1 or #2. In 1971 he entered the "Tennis Dome" for the first time; he lost quite easily again in the first round to Tom Okker 3;6, 3:6, 3:6 but, finally, he was able to play on Centre Court. The following year, in 1972, he played on Centre Court for the second time and this time it was in the quarter-finals. His opponent was a New Zealander Onny Parun, the 1971 quarter-finalist and a solid grass-court player who had advanced over such seeded players as: Andres Gimeno, the recent Roland Garros champion, and the German Wilhelm Bungert, a Wimbledon finalist from 1967.

I won in straight sets 6:2, 6:3, 6:4 playing well; with that I proved to myself that I had nothing to fear even on Centre Court. When you enter it the first time you experience goose-bumps. There is a special, almost spiritual atmosphere. One has a unique experience playing there. All best players had already played there many times – Laver, Newcombe, Ashe, Smith.

And it was Smith who stopped the Czech player's delightful Wimbledon advancement.

For a long time I could not shake off the feeling that I could have won. I was 6:3 and 4:3 ahead; it was deuce on my serve that Stan had no chance breaking until that point. I hit an "ace", white chalk lifted upwards, but the umpire called "fault"! There was no correction; I argued

Event 1.—THE GENTLEMEN'S SINGLES CHAMPIONSHIP

The Winner will become the holder, for the year only, of the CHALLENGE CUP presented to the club by KING GEORGE V, and also of the CHALLENGE CUP presented by The All England Lawn Tennis and Croquet Club. The First Prize is a piece of silver, known as "The Renshaw Cup" annually presented to the Club by the surviving members of the family of the late ERNEST and WILLIAM RENSHAW. Details of Prize Money, will be found on page 37. The Winner will receive silver replicas of the two Challenge Cups. A Silver Medal will be presented to the Runner-up and a Bronze Medal to each defeated Semi-finalist.

FIRST ROUND	SECOND ROUND	THIRD ROUND	FOURTH ROUND	FIFTH ROUND	SEMI-FINAL	FINAL
1 S. R. Smith ①.........(U.S.A.)	S. R. Smith ① 6–1 6–1 6–3					
2 H. J. Plotz...............(G.)		S. R. Smith ① 6–4 9–8 6–3				
3 A. R. Gardiner...........(A.)	D. Irvine 6–2 7–9 6–2 5–7 6–4		S. R. Smith ① 6–3 7–5 3–6 9–7			
4 D. Irvine................(R.H.)						
5 P. Cornejo...............(CH.)	T. Sakai 6–4 9–8 6–3......	A. Mayer 8–9 6–3 6–2 6–4		S. R. Smith ① 8–6 4–6 6–2 6–4		
6 T. Sakai.................(J.)						
7 S. J. Matthews..........(G.B.)	A. Mayer 4–6 6–3 6–3 5–7 6–3					
8 A. Mayer................(U.S.A.)						
9 I. G. Fletcher..........(A.)	I. G. Fletcher 6–4 6–3 6–3	I. G. Fletcher 6–0 6–4 1–6 6–3				
10 J. L. Rouyer...........(F.)			I. G. Fletcher 6–1 6–0 6–1			
11 A. Olmedo............(PERU)	A. Olmedo 4–6 6–3 6–3 6–4				S. R. Smith ① 6–2 8–6 6–2	
12 J. Ulrich..............(D.)						
13 W. R. Durham...........(A.)	F. Pala 6–8 9–8 6–4......	F. Pala 4–6 7–5 2–6 7–5 6–2				
14 F. Pala................(CZ.)						
15 H. Kary...............(AU.)	H. Kary 8–6 6–3 8–9 3–6 6–0					
16 P. Szoke..............(HU.)						
17 A. Metreveli ⑧.......(U.S.S.R.)	A. Metreveli ⑧ 6–2 8–6 6–4					
18 P. Marzano............(IT.)		A. Metreveli ⑧ 7–9 6–1 6–4 6–4				
19 J. Simpson............(NZ.)	P. Dominguez 6–3 4–6 6–1 7–5		A. Metreveli ⑧ 7–5 6–3 3–6 6–4			
20 P. Dominguez..........(F.)						
21 T. Ulrich.............(D.)	T. Ulrich 6–2 3–0 rtd......	J. G. Paish 6–3 7–5 6–2		A. Metreveli ⑧ 6–3 6–1 6–3		
22 J. G. Clifton........(G.B.)						
23 J. G. Paish..........(G.B.)	J. G. Paish 7–9 6–4 9–8 6–3					
24 E. L. Scott.........(U.S.A.)						
25 P. Proisy............(F.)	P. Proisy 6–4 9–8 8–9 6–4	P. J. Cramer 6–3 7–5 6–4				
26 S. Likhachev.......(U.S.S.R.)			P. J. Cramer 9–8 6–4 9–7			
27 P. J. Cramer........(S.A.)	P. J. Cramer 6–4 7–5 6–4					
28 I. Gulyas...........(HU.)						
29 J. C. Barclay........(F.)	M. Estep 6–3 7–5 6–8 6–4	M. Estep 6–4 6–2 6–2				
30 M. Estep............(U.S.A.)						
31 P. R. Hutchins......(G.B.)	J. Kamiwazumi 6–3 8–6 7–5					
32 J. Kamiwazumi.......(J.)						
33 A. Gimeno ④.........(SP.)	A. Gimeno ④ 6–1 6–2 6–4					
34 K. F. Weatherley....(G.B)		O. Parun 6–4 8–6 6–8 8–9 6–4				
35 A. Van der Merwe....(S.A)	O. Parun 6–2 7–5 6–2......		O. Parun 6–4 4–6 9–7 9–7			
36 O. Parun............(N.Z.)						
37 J. de Mendoza.......(G.B.)	J. R. Cooper 2–6 6–3 6–2 7–5	W. P. Bungert 5–7 6–4 0–6 6–2 6–3				
38 J. R. Cooper........(A.)						
39 E. Di Matteo........(IT.)	W. P. Bungert 6–3 1–6 4–6 6–4 6–3			O. Parun 8–9 6–4 6–4 rtd.		
40 W. P. Bungert.......(G.)						
41 T. Kakoulia......(U.S.S.R.)	T. Kakoulia 9–7 7–5 7–9	T. Kakoulia 9–8 4–6 6–3 6–4				
42 R. F. Keldie........(A.)						
43 R. D. Knight........(U.S.A.)	D. A. Lloyd 9–8 9–8 6–4...		J. Hrebec 4–6 6–3 8–6 6–1			
44 D. A. Lloyd.........(G.B.)						
45 G. Vilas...........(ARG.)	J. Hrebec 7–5 7–5 7–5...	J. Hrebec 6–2 6–2 6–4				
46 J. Hrebec..........(CZ.)						
47 P. Marmureanu......(RU.)	S. Baranyi 6–3 6–4 6–0....				J. Kodes ⑤ 6–2 6–3 6–4	
48 S. Baranyi.........(HU.)						
49 J. Kodes ⑤........(CZ.)	J. Kodes ⑤ 6–1 4–6 6–1 6–1					
50 P. H. Rodriguez....(CH.)		J. Kodes ⑤ 6–0 6–1 6–2				
51 P. M. Doerner......(A.)	G. Seewagen 6–2 7–9 9–8 6–4		J. Kodes ⑤ 6–0 6–3 6–2			
52 G. Seewagen........(U.S.A.)						
53 J. P. Meyer........(F.)	M. Holecek 6–3 3–6 9–8 9–7	D. Bleckinger 6–4 6–4 1–6 9–7		J. Kodes ⑤ 6–2 6–4 6–4		
54 M. Holecek.........(CZ.)						
55 D. W. Schroder.....(S.A)	D. Bleckinger 6–2 6–3					
56 D. Bleckinger......(U.S.A.)						
57 V. Amritraj........(IN.)	V. Amritraj 7–5 9–8 3–6 2–6 6–4	J. H. McManus 6–1 6–2 8–6				
58 W. J. Austin.......(U.S.A.)						
59 P. Bertolucci......(IT.)	J. H. McManus 6–2 6–3 6–3		J. H. McManus 6–0 6–4 6–1			
60 J. H. McManus......(U.S.A.)						
61 W. L. Lloyd........(A.)	W. N'Godrella 4–6 8–9 6–4 7–5 11–9	P. Hombergen 5–7 8–6 6–3 6–4				
62 W. N'Godrella......(F.)						
63 P. Hombergen.......(B.)	P. Hombergen 5–7 6–1 5–7 6–4 6–3		C. S. Dibley 8–9 6–3 6–2 6–1			
64 R. L. Bohrnstedt...(U.S.A.)						
65 T. J. Ryan.........(S.A.)	C. S. Dibley 6–3 6–4 6–2..	C. S. Dibley 6–3 6–3 8–6				
66 C. S. Dibley.......(A.)						
67 A. Munoz...........(SP.)	R. Gonzales 6–2 7–5 6–1..		C. S. Dibley 9–8 6–4 9–8			
68 R. Gonzales........(U.S.A.)						
69 R. Tanner..........(U.S.A.)	R. Tanner 6–3 2–6 6–4 7–9 7–5	R. Tanner 6–2 6–2 6–4				
70 J. Velasco.........(COL.)						
71 J. R. Pinto Bravo..(CH.)	A. J. McDonald 6–4 3–6 6–3 6–0		R. L. Stockton 9–8 6–1 6–4			
72 A. J. McDonald.....(A.)						
73 J. H. Osborne......(U.S.A.)	C. J. Mottram 6–4 6–2 3–6 2–6 7–5	R. L. Stockton 9–8 4–6 6–3 6–2 6–4				
74 C. J. Mottram......(G.B.)						
75 T. Koch............(BR.)	R. L. Stockton 8–9 4–6 6–3 6–2 6–4			P. Barthes ⑥ 6–3 6–3 5–7 6–4		
76 R. L. Stockton.....(U.S.A.)						
77 J. Gisbert.........(SP.)	J. Gisbert 6–3 2–6 6–2 6–0	P. Barthes ⑥ 6–4 6–2 6–4				
78 H. Solomon.........(U.S.A.)						
79 J. B. Chanfreau....(F.)	P. Barthes ⑥ 7–5 9–8 6–3		B. J. Phillips-Moore 9–8 6–1 3–6 6–2			
80 P. Barthes ⑥......(F.)						
81 J. Loyo-Mayo.......(M.)	B. J. Phillips-Moore 6–3 6–2 6–2	B. J. Phillips-Moore 9–8 6–1 3–6 6–2				
82 B. J. Phillips-Moore..(S.A.)						
83 S. Ball............(A.)	S. Ball 6–4 4–6 7–5 6–3...		I. Tiriac 8–6 6–1 6–2			
84 F. D. McMillan.....(S.A.)						
85 I. Tiriac..........(RU.)	I. Tiriac 6–4 6–2 5–7 7–5.	I. Tiriac 6–4 9–7 9–8				
86 A. Zugarelli.......(IT.)					M. Orantes ③ 6–2 6–0 6–2	
87 V. Zednik..........(CZ.)	B. E. Gottfried 6–2 6–2 9–7		N. Pietrangeli 2–6 8–6 6–3 7–5			
88 B. E. Gottfried....(U.S.A.)						
89 R. Stock...........(U.S.A.)	N. Pietrangeli 6–4 6–3 6–4	N. Pietrangeli 2–6 8–6 6–3 7–5				
90 N. Pietrangeli.....(IT.)						
91 I. Molina..........(COL.)	I. Molina 3–6 6–2 6–4 6–3		M. Orantes ③ 6–2 6–2 6–1			
92 A. J. Pattison.....(R.H.)						
93 R. D. Crealy.......(A.)	R. D. Crealy 9–7 6–2 1–6 7–5	M. Orantes ③ 6–2 6–3 6–2				
94 N. Spear...........(YU.)						
95 G. Goven...........(F.)	M. Orantes ③ 8–6 7–5 6–4			M. Orantes ③ 6–4 4–6 6–3 4–6 6–3		
96 M. Orantes ③......(SP.)						
97 J. E. Mandarino....(BR.)	K. Meiler 6–4 6–2 6–1....	E. J. van Dillen 3–6 4–6 6–1 6–4 6–4				
98 K. Meiler..........(G.)						
99 E. J. van Dillen...(U.S.A.)	E. J. van Dillen 7–5 8–6 6–1		F. Jauffret 8–6 6–1 6–4			
100 S. E. Stewart.....(U.S.A.)						
101 F. Jauffret.......(F.)	F. Jauffret 1–6 7–5 8–9 6–1	F. Jauffret 6–2 6–3 6–4				
102 O. Bengtson.......(SW.)						
103 C. Barazzutti.....(IT.)	J. W. Feaver 4–6 9–8 6–2 3–6 6–0			J. S. Connors 6–2 6–3 8–6		
104 J. W. Feaver......(G.B.)						
105 J. Kukal..........(CZ.)	J. Kukal 4–6 8–9 6–4 6–4 8–6	A. Panatta 9–8 8–9 6–9 8–6				
106 M. Vasquez.......(ARG.)						
107 A. Panatta........(IT.)	A. Panatta 6–4 8–9 4–6 6–4 6–1		J. S. Connors 6–3 0–6 6–4 8–6			
108 N. A. Fraser......(A.)						
109 S. A. Warboys.....(G.B.)	N. Kalogeropoulos 6–1 1–6 6–3 6–4	J. S. Connors 6–3 7–5 8–6				
110 N. Kalogeropoulos.(GR.))						
111 J. S. Connors.....(U.S.A.)	J. S. Connors 6–3 9–7 7–5			I. Nastase ② 6–3 6–4 6–4		
112 R. A. J. Hewitt ⑦.(S.A.)	R. J. Moore 6–2 6–1 6–0..	T. W. Gorman 6–4 6–4 7–5				
113 R. G. Clarke......(N.Z.)						
114 R. J. Moore.......(S.A.)	T. W. Gorman 6–4 6–4 6–2		T. W. Gorman 6–4 7–5 2–6 4–6 8–6			
115 B. Mignot.........(B.)						
116 T. W. Gorman......(U.S.A.)	J. Fillol 6–0 9–7 4–6 6–3..	J. Fillol 4–6 8–6 7–5 6–4				
117 K. G. Warwick.....(A.)						
118 J. Fillol.........(CH.)	G. Masters 8–9 8–6 4–6 6–3			I. Nastase ② 6–3 3–6 8–6 6–1		
119 G. Masters........(A.)						
120 A. Amritraj.......(IN.)	J. Fassbender 4–6 7–5 7–5 12–10	J. Fassbender 6–4 6–8 9–7 7–5				
121 J. Fassbender.....(G.)						
122 L. A. Hoad........(A.)	P. Lall 5–7 6–3 6–2 6–4 6–3		I. Nastase ② 9–8 6–3 6–4			
123 P. Lall...........(IN.)						
124 P. Gerken.........(U.S.A.)	C. E. Graebner 6–2 3–6 6–4 6–3	I. Nastase ② 6–3 4–6 6–1 6–2				
125 C. E. Graebner....(U.S.A.)						
126 J. Mukerjea.......(IN.)	I. Nastase ② 6–4 6–2 6–2					
127 J. D. Bartlett....(A.)						
128 I. Nastase ②.....(RU.)						

Final / Winner: S. R. SMITH ① 4–6 6–3 6–3 4–6 7–5

S. R. Smith ① 3–6 6–4 6–1 7–5 *(Semi-Final/Final column)*

I. Nastase ② 6–3 6–4 6–4 *(Semi-Final)*

Heavy type denotes seeded players. The encircled figure against names denotes the order in which they have been seeded. The Matches will be the best of Five Advantage Sets. For particulars of Abbreviations see page 11.

13

26 *The Daily Telegraph, Friday, July 7, 1972*

Lawn Tennis Championships

SMITH v NASTASE A FITTING CLIMAX TO WIMBLEDON

By LANCE TINGAY

AN American-Rumanian men's singles final for tomorrow, the tall Stan Smith against the genius from the Balkans, Ilie Nastase, was duly reached in the Lawn Tennis championships yesterday.

The seeding committee have done well, forecasting right not only the finalists in the main event but in the women's singles and the men's doubles also.

Smith beat the Czech Jan Kodes 3-6, 6-4, 6-1, 7-5 in 129 minutes yesterday. Nastase beat the Spaniard, Manuel Orantes, more simply and more briefly by 6-3, 6-4, 6-4 in 74 minutes.

Both in their varying styles were good matches. They were not, however, memorable as was the women's semi-final the day before between Evonne Goolagong and Chris Evert.

Perhaps it was because reputations and standing were not at stake; all the players involved had established places in the game, and nothing transpired to disturb them.

Smith against Kodes had rather a wooden quality. The fire and sparkle of the day belonged to Nastase and Orantes, for with them the touch of ball on racket strings was more sympathetic, and though far from lacking in pace and penetration the rallies were more prone to exploit the delicate and subtle.

Forest Hills replica

Last September at Forest Hills Smith won the U.S. title by beating Kodes in the final, and the score by which he did so was much the same as yesterday's, Smith taking precisely the same number of games in the same set order and Kodes getting just one more. This was a match in replica.

Kodes's early superiority did not endure. He, far more than his opponent, was dependent for life and death in the rallies on projecting his first service into court.

Smith got better as the match went on. Indeed, in the early stages, it seemed as if some vital part were missing from the mechanism by which his backhand volley functioned.

Kodes ahead

Having lost the first set, the vital service break game being the eighth when Smith added a double fault to some volley errors, Smith fell behind in the second. Kodes was 4-3 in front with his own service to come.

Afterwards he attributed his loss to the double fault he delivered on the second point. Certainly he never subsequently looked a winner for having lost his advantage he lost his next service game also and, with it, the set.

Having saved one set point in that game Kodes was downcast by a "line" decision on his first delivery when the score was deuce. Despair and despondency enveloped him and, symbolically perhaps, two black crows chose that time to circle overhead.

Even when on top at the start, Kodes played as if he were disapproving of the whole affair. Despite his success, he has always refused to admit that grass is a reasonable surface on which to play the game.

At any rate the third set was entirely a black one for the Czech. Smith's ascendancy grew more marked and though I doubt if his forthright pressure reached his own standards of a year ago, he began increasingly to hint at a champion's quality.

Smith was denied an easy victory. It was not until the 11th game of the fourth set that the American at last broke service to stand in front, having survived a minor crisis when Kodes had one fleeting chance to lead 5-1.

Smith hiccuped on the verge of victory, double faulting on his first match ball. But he was 40-0 then and a service winner sufficed to take the American to his second Wimbledon singles final in two years.

His major strength was serving. A statistician worked out that he had 67 per cent of his first deliveries in court. That is 13 short of the percentage held as ideal but it was good enough yesterday. The measure of Kodes' serving skill was 60 per cent.

Sadness and delight (Kodes and Smith).

the call but to no avail. It was a very important moment; I lost concentration and committed a double fault on the next point. That turned the match around! I lost 6:3, 4:6, 1:6, and 5:7. In spite of it I gained confidence that I could succeed even in Wimbledon.

The Czech and British press quoted Kodes' performance in the semi-finals of the most prestigious Grand Slam tournament as: When the umpire called Kodes' serve "out" at the close of the second set it critically affected the final outcome of the match. Kodes was visibly shaken by the call and lost concentration, double-faulted to lose that game and the second set, and dropped the third set easily 1:6.

I am and I am not angry. The fact remains that I was close to the finals. I believe that I would have won the match if I turned that game at 4:3 in my favor. I felt I had it in me to defeat Smith. The 1972 Wimbledon final was interesting for two reasons. First and foremost, the final duel between Smith and Nastase that was won by the American 4:6, 6:3, 6:3, 4:6, and 7:5 was considered one of the best finals ever. In quarter-finals Nastase defeated Connors, who had been considered a possible finalist. Secondly, it was rather pungent that both finalists were army recruits at that time!

In the previous US Open at Forest Hills Stan Smith came onto the court to play against me in some Navy T-shirt. He was serving with the Navy and a year later he was still with them. The same was true about Ilie; I believe he had a rank of a captain. I had a feeling that it was that Wimbledon final between two enlisted army officers that gave ideas to Army chiefs at home, who then insisted that I should also join the army ranks. They alleged that I complained about my back problems but played world level tennis so why should I not join the Army too? After all, two soldiers reached Wimbledon finals that year...!?

THE MAYERS

The Nationals in Ostrava finished in a usual fashion with slightly extraordinary results. Jan Kodes won all three titles! This "tour de force" he accomplished only twice in his career – in 1969 and 1972.

I played three matches daily even after reaching quarter-finals, when we played three-out-of-five sets. Nowadays one could count on the fingers of one hand the number of tournaments with best of five set matches; it is only the Grand Slam tournaments that do so. But, in those earlier times, they" tortured" us in the Nationals! It is also true that they could have suggested to me: "Well, then don't play the mixed-doubles!" However, Sparta wanted all the titles. All clubs wanted them....

It was very alluring to desire and defend the US Open final. Prior to the US Open Jan Kodes played tournaments in Indianapolis and Toronto but reached no significant results – he lost to McMillan in Indianapolis, and to Vilas in Toronto. Yet, it was a good practice for the US Open in very hot and humid climate though the surface was not grass.

I reached the finals the year before and was undergoing hard-core training after those two tournaments; the quality of my game was rising. Arrogantly, I even entertained the idea that I could aspire to win the US Open....

However, tennis Gods weren't with him. Kodes came across Alex "Sandy" Mayer in the second round. He was excellent on grass; he had even mastered the return and very good volley. He was not a well-recognized player but he was hard to defeat.

The five-point tie-breaker was created and used by the Americans that year. The television broadcasters welcomed the tension and the gradation. Each player served twice, and the receiving player could choose the side where he wanted to receive, which determined where the server was to serve from, the deuce or the add court.

And what happened that day at Forest Hills? I was leading two sets to none, and the standing in the third set was 6:6 and 4:4 in the tie-breaker. That turned out to be my match point and his set point! I served a good serve placed in a corner. I then answered his return with a difficult volley deep into Sandy's forehand. He ran it down barely reaching it and, with trouble, scraped it directly to my backhand volley. I hit the volley again to his forehand.

A similar situation had come up several times during the match. Sandy liked hitting passing shots

Martina Navratilova took the Czechoslovak National title at Ostrava over my sister Vlasta in 1972.

Men's Singles   *Holder* S. R. Smith

FIRST ROUND	SECOND ROUND	THIRD ROUND	FOURTH ROUND	QUARTER-FINALS	SEMI-FINALS	FINAL

```
S. R. SMITH (1)        SMITH
W. Martin                5-7 6-1 7-5 6-3
A. Panatta (IT)        Graebner            SMITH
C. Graebner              4-6 6-3 7-5 6-2     6-1 6-4 6-7 6-0
A. Munoz (SP)          Munoz                                 SMITH
R. Holmberg              6-4 6-7 6-3 6-4                       6-3 7-6 7-5
J. Pinto Bravo (CH)    Stone               Stone
A. Stone (AUS)           6-4 6-4 6-7 6-4     6-1 6-0 6-7 6-0                      SMITH
A. GIMENO (SP) (14)    GIMENO                                                    2-6 7-6 6-7 1-6 6-3
V. Korotkov (USSR)       6-4 7-5 6-4         GIMENO
C. Owens               Davidson              6-4 4-6 6-4 6-1
O. K. Davidson (AUS)     6-4 7-6 3-6 4-6 6-3                   GIMENO
R. O. Ruffels (AUS)    Ruffels                                5-2 rt'd
F. McNair                6-2 6-3 6-4         Ruffels                                              ASHE
W. Brown               Brown                 6-3 7-5 6-4                                          7-6 7-5 6-4
J. Delaney               6-7 6-4 6-4 6-4
A. R. ASHE (6)         ASHE
H. Rahim (PAK)           6-3 6-3 4-6 7-6     ASHE
R. R. Maud (SA)        Maud                  6-4 6-4 7-6
J. Kamiwazumi (J)        6-4 6-7 6-2 6-1                       ASHE
J. D. Alexander (AUS)  Alexander                               6-4 6-4 3-6 6-1
P. Dent (AUS)            4-6 7-6 6-4 4-6 6-4 Case
R. Case (AUS)          Case                  7-6 7-6 4-6 3-6 6-4                  ASHE
F. Schunck               6-2 6-2 6-4                                             5-7 7-5 6-4 6-3
R. C. LUTZ (13)        LUTZ
C. Dibley (AUS)          6-4 6-4 6-2         LUTZ
S. Menon (IN)          Vilas                 6-3 6-3 7-5
G. Vilas (ARG)           7-6 6-4 6-4                           LUTZ
M. Kreiss              Scott                                   7-6 6-2 6-2
E. L. Scott              6-3 6-4 6-4         Scott                                                             ASHE
A. Amitraj (IN)        Amitraj               3-6 6-4 7-6 7-5                                                  6-1 6-4 7-6
D. Schroder (SA)         7-6 6-3 6-4
R. G. LAVER (AUS) (3)  LAVER
J. G. Paish (GB)         6-2 6-1 6-3         LAVER
S. Warboys (GB)        Seewagen              6-3 6-2 7-5
B. Seewagen              7-6 4-6 7-5 6-2                       LAVER
J. Fairlie (NZ)        Fairlie                                 6-2 4-6 6-7 6-1 7-6
J. Austin                7-6 6-3 6-2         Fillol
F. Pala (CZ)           Fillol                6-4 7-5 6-3                          RICHEY
J. Fillol (CH)           6-4 6-1 6-2                                             3-7 7-6 7-6 6-3
C. RICHEY (12)         RICHEY
B. Gottfried             6-2 7-6 6-2         RICHEY
A. Olmedo              Olmedo                6-2 6-3 7-6
Z. Guerry                6-3 7-6 6-7 7-6                       RICHEY
C. Hagey               Goven                                   6-7 6-3 7-6 6-7 6-4
G. Goven (F)             15-0 rtd            Gerken                                               RICHEY
P. Gerken              Gerken                6-4 6-1 6-7 5-7 7-5                                  3-6 6-1 6-4 6-2
P. Walthall              7-6 6-1 6-2
J. KODES (CZ) (8)      KODES
D. O'Bryant              6-2 6-4 6-3         Mayer
A. Mayer               Mayer                 6-7 3-6 7-6 6-3 6-1
J. B. Chanfreau (F)      6-4 6-1 6-3                           Mayer
P. Proisy (F)          Proisy                                  6-3 6-3 6-1
P. Du Pre                6-1 6-4 6-2         Ramirez
R. Ramirez (M)         Ramirez               6-2 2-6 1-6 7-6 6-4                  McMillan
J. Singh (IN)            6-4 3-6 6-2 6-1                                          6-3 6-4 3-6 6-7 6-4
M. C. RIESSEN (9)      RIESSEN
G. Masters (AUS)         6-1 6-7 6-3 6-2     RIESSEN
R. Moore (SA)          Anderson              6-3 7-5 6-7 7-5
M. Anderson (AUS)        6-4 7-5 6-7 3-6 6-1                   McMillan
F. D. McMillan (SA)    McMillan                                6-2 7-6 4-6 6-4
J. L. Rouyer (F)         7-5 7-5 7-6         McMillan
T. Leonard            Leonard               6-2 6-3 6-4
S. Higgins               6-3 3-6 6-7 6-4 7-6
```

```
R. McKinley           Pasarell
C. Pasarell             6-3 6-4 7-6         Pasarell
V. Amritraj (IN)      Gerulaitis            7-6 6-3 6-2
V. Gerulaitis           2-6 6-3 6-2 6-3                        DRYSDALE
G. Hardie             N'Godrilla             6-3 4-6 6-1 6-4
W. N'Godrilla (F)       6-2 4-6 6-3 6-4     DRYSDALE
M. Belkin (C          DRYSDALE              6-3 6-4 6-1 6-4
E. C. DRYSDALE (SA) (11) 5-5 rt'd                              Stolle
R. Emerson (AUS)      Stolle                                   4-6 7-6 6-4 7-6
F. S. Stolle (AUS)      6-7 6-4 6-2 6-2     Stolle
M. Machette           Machette              6-3 6-4 6-3
M. Holecek (CZ)         1-6 7-6 6-4 6-4                        Stolle
E. Dibbs              Dibbs                  7-6 6-4 5-7 7-6
J. Borowiak             6-2 6-7 6-3 7-6     NEWCOMBE
T. Kakoulia (USSR)    NEWCOMBE              6-3 6-4 6-2                           NASTASE
J. D. NEWCOMBE (AUS) (5) 6-1 6-2 6-4                                             6-4 3-6 6-3 6-2
R. Russell (JAM)      Kukal
J. Kukal (CZ)           6-4 4-6 3-6 6-3 6-4 Cornejo
R. Dell               Cornejo               6-3 6-4 6-2
P. Cornejo (CH)         6-4 3-7 6-4 7-6                        HEWITT
J. Fassbender (G)     Fassbender             6-4 6-4 3-6 6-1
I. Molina (COL)         6-4 7-6 4-6 6-3     HEWITT
H. J. Pohmann (G)     HEWITT                7-5 6-3 6-4
R. A. J. HEWITT (SA) (16) 6-4 6-2 6-2                          NASTASE
P. Dominguez (F)      Dominguez              6-4 6-4 6-2
R. Gonzales             4-6 6-3 6-2 6-3     Dominguez
R. Osborne            Reid                  5-7 6-4 7-5 6-4
J. Osborne              6-4 6-2 6-4                            NASTASE
R. Taylor (GB)        Taylor                 6-3 5-7 6-2 6-3
A. Pattison (RH)        3-6 7-6 6-3 3-6 6-3 NASTASE
J. Velasco (VENEZ)    NASTASE               7-5 6-2 6-7 2-6 7-6
I. NASTASE (RU) (4)     6-0 6-2 6-0                                              NASTASE
T. Sakai (J)          Sakai                                                      4-6 7-6 6-2 6-1
J. Kuki (J)             6-2 7-5 6-4         Cooper
G. D. Battrick (GB)   Cooper                6-3 6-2 6-2
J. Cooper (AUS)         6-3 6-1 6-0                            Cooper
O. Parun (NZ)         Parun                  7-6 6-4 6-3
F. Froehling            4-6 6-4 6-3 6-2     ORANTES
J. Simpson (NZ)       ORANTES               6-1 2-6 3-6 7-5 6-4
M. ORANTES (SP) (10)    7-5 6-2 6-2                            Tanner
R. Carmichael (AUS)   Carmichael             6-2 7-6 7-6
P. Doerner (AUS)        6-4 6-4 7-6         Tanner
R. Tanner             Tanner                4-6 7-5 6-3 3-6 7-6
I. El Shafei (UAR)      7-6 6-4 6-4                            Tanner
T. Ulrich (D)         Solomon                6-4 3-6 7-5 6-3
H. Solomon              6-7 7-5 6-1 7-6     OKKER
P. Cramer (SA)        OKKER                 6-1 6-2 6-2                          Gorman
T. S. OKKER (NTH) (7)   6-2 6-3 6-4                                              7-6 5-7 7-6 6-7 6-4
R. Keldie (AUS)       Tiriac
I. Tiriac (RU)          6-4 1-0 rt'd        Pilic
P. Rodriguez (CH)     Pilic                 6-7 6-4 3-6 7-5 7-6
N. Pilic (YU)           6-1 6-3 7-5                            Gorman
J. McManus            McManus                6-4 6-4 6-4
D. Birchmore            2-6 4-6 6-1 6-4 6-3 Gorman
T. Gorman             Gorman                4-6 6-4 6-1 6-3
J. CONNORS (15)         6-1 3-6 6-7 7-5 6-4                    Gorman
H. Hose (VENEZ)       Hose                   6-4 6-3 6-3
S. Faulk                7-5 4-6 7-6 7-6     Stockton
D. Stockton           Stockton              6-2 6-3 3-6 7-6
R. Barth                7-5 4-6 7-6 7-6                        Stockton
M. Cox (GB)           Cox                    6-7 6-2 4-6 6-2 6-2
M. Estep                6-4 6-1 6-3         Cox
P. Curtis (GB)        ROSEWALL              1-6 6-3 7-6 7-6
K. R. POSEWALL (AUS) (2) 6-1 7-6 6-2
```

FINAL (right margin): **I. NASTASE** — 3-6 6-3 6-7 6-4 6-3 (Winner)

Alex „Sandy" Mayer

Gene Mayer

Sandy Mayer was a confident player with Hungarian ancestry. His father used to play in Hungary but was not one of the top players. He immigrated to New York and both his sons were born already in the US. I always had a hard time playing against them. They understood our European mentality and sensed the moment when one experienced fear; they took advantage of it. They were very intelligent and knew much about Europe. Chatting with them was different from chatting with other Americans. The conversation flowed easily about anything and everything; they knew Vienna, Prague, Budapest, they recognized our borders with Poland, they were familiar with Yalta Treaty and Munich agreement. Most Americans had no idea about such things.

I also met their father who was their coach. He was excited when he found out that I came from Prague. "Ah, Prague! I know it there; it is a beautiful city!"

I befriended all the Mayers. However, that does not change the fact that I lost that match and my vision of a US Open victory remained only a dream. Nastase and Ashe reached the finals. Ashe was leading 4:1 in the fifth and had a game point on his serve to reach 5:1. In spite of it Nastase won! In a way I can say that I "let him" win Forest Hills. I strongly believed in myself against him on grass! The curious thing is that it was Sandy Mayer who defeated Nastase the next year in Wimbledon and I won the whole thing. Now, who says that there is no justice in tennis?

on the run; he hit a shot and ran back to the center expecting the next shot to come crosscourt in the other corner. With that in mind I hit the ball behind him. If I was successful in pinning him down to a spot from which he hit a shot easy for me to put away then I hit that shot exactly in the direction where it came from because I anticipated him to start moving in the opposite direction. Thus the ball was going behind him and away from the direction he was running. At this moment, I played the same backhand volley strategy as earlier in the match. But this time, on that match point, he resigned himself to the mercy of the moment and did not move; thus my shot came directly to his racket! He passed me, won the tiebreak 5:4 and the third set 7:6. After that he rolled over me 3:6 and 1:6! I lost a match that I had, practically, won. One shot decided the outcome! It was also a great lesson and experience for me; I learned what not to do on a match point!

Upon his return home Jan Kodes gave a press conference to the Czech journalists through which described the almost finished season. He also depicted the match with Sandy Mayer at Forest Hills: "I felt terribly after the match because it happened at the moment when I thought I had passed my "bad luck" period. This defeat brought back the mental qualms."

After Fred Perry won Forest Hills in 1936 it took almost thirty years before another European pushed through and won at Forest Hills – Manuel Santana in 1965. Seven years later, in 1972, Ilie Natsase joined them. He defeated Arthur Ashe 3:6, 6:3, 6:7, 6:4, and 6:3 in the finals and received $20,000 and a new car. It was a culmination of his very successful 1972 season. In addition, he represented his country only a few days after the US Open final in Davis Cup final against the team of USA in Bucharest. The opponent of one of the best European teams Tiriac-Nastase was the US selection made up of Stan Smith, Tom Gorman and the doubles player Erik van Dillen. At team standing 2:2 Tiriac and Stan Smith battled for the decisive third point. It was, again, one of the matches that entered the Davis Cup history.

When Stan Smith, who was cheated out of many points by local linesmen, sat down in his chair after losing the fourth set he muttered dejectedly in the direction of the non-playing captain, Dennis Ralston: "I can't beat him!"

"From now on play nothing close to the lines! Everything must bounce three feet inside the lines so that they can't call against you; hit hard and swift" - was the advice of the great ex-US Davis Cup player.

Smith followed the advice to a point and defeated Tiriac with a "bagel" in the fifth set!

CONDE DE GODÓ TROPHY

Upon his return from the United States Jan Kodes took a break from tennis for a few days. Badly needing some rest after such a demanding schedule, Kodes took a respite but he could not leave his racket idle for long. Together with Jan Kukal he left for Split, where he had made a promise to Zeljko Franulovic to take part in the Yugoslavian Championships. In the finals he came across the Greek Nick Kalogeropoulos. Yes, this was the same player whom he battled in Athens in 1965 in the Galea Cup semifinals winning in three sets in scorching heat.

In 1965 Nick Kalogeropoulos was a star and the champion of Junior Wimbledon but he never won anything significant after that. Nevertheless, he must have been illuminated again in Split by some Holy Spirit and we battled formidably for five sets

That tournament was not important to me since it did not fall into the Grand Prix group, but I had made the promise to my friend Zeljko and honored it. I considered it to be more of a practice tied together with vacation and seeing the sights of Split. Yet, even at such tournament, I did not want to play poorly. Ivan Lendl did not like losing in exhibitions either. In his opinion, the opponents lost fear if they defeated him in exhibitions and gained confidence feeling that he was beatable. I did not go that far in my thinking but it happened to me several

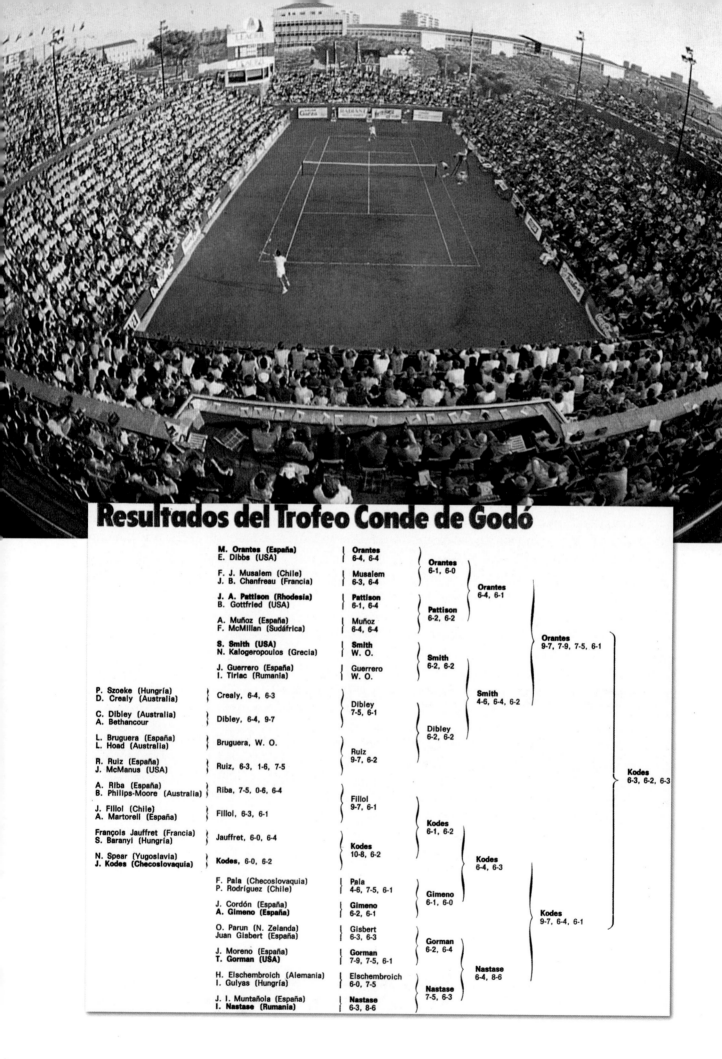

Resultados del Trofeo Conde de Godó

M. Orantes (España)	Orantes				
E. Dibbs (USA)	6-4, 6-4	Orantes			
F. J. Musalem (Chile)	Musalem	6-1, 6-0			
J. B. Chanfreau (Francia)	6-3, 6-4		Orantes		
J. A. Pattison (Rhodesia)	Pattison		6-4, 6-1		
B. Gottfried (USA)	6-1, 6-4	Pattison			
A. Muñoz (España)	Muñoz	6-2, 6-2			
F. McMillan (Sudáfrica)	6-4, 6-4			Orantes	
S. Smith (USA)	Smith			9-7, 7-9, 7-5, 6-1	
N. Kalogeropoulos (Grecia)	W. O.	Smith			
J. Guerrero (España)	Guerrero	6-2, 6-2			
I. Tiriac (Rumania)	W. O.		Smith		

P. Szoeke (Hungría) / D. Crealy (Australia) — Crealy, 6-4, 6-3

C. Dibley (Australia) / A. Bethancour — Dibley, 6-4, 9-7 — Dibley 7-5, 6-1

L. Bruguera (España) / L. Hoad (Australia) — Bruguera, W. O.

R. Ruiz (España) / J. McManus (USA) — Ruiz, 6-3, 1-6, 7-5 — Ruiz 9-7, 6-2

Dibley 6-2, 6-2

Smith 4-6, 6-4, 6-2

A. Riba (España) / B. Philips-Moore (Australia) — Riba, 7-5, 0-6, 6-4

J. Fillol (Chile) / A. Martorell (España) — Fillol, 6-3, 6-1 — Fillol 9-7, 6-1

François Jauffret (Francia) / S. Baranyi (Hungría) — Jauffret, 6-0, 6-4

N. Spear (Yugoslavia) / **J. Kodes (Checoslovaquia)** — **Kodes, 6-0, 6-2** — Kodes 10-8, 6-2

Kodes 6-1, 6-2

Kodes 6-4, 6-3

F. Pala (Checoslovaquia) / P. Rodríguez (Chile) — Pala, 4-6, 7-5, 6-1

J. Cordón (España) / **A. Gimeno (España)** — Gimeno, 6-2, 6-1 — Gimeno 6-1, 6-0

O. Parun (N. Zelanda) / Juan Gisbert (España) — Gisbert, 6-3, 6-3

J. Moreno (España) / **T. Gorman (USA)** — Gorman, 7-9, 7-5, 6-1 — Gorman 6-2, 6-4

Kodes 9-7, 6-4, 6-1

Nastase 6-4, 8-6

H. Elschembroich (Alemania) / I. Gulyas (Hungría) — Elschembroich, 6-0, 7-5

J. I. Muntañola (España) / **I. Nastase (Rumania)** — **Nastase, 6-3, 8-6** — Nastase 7-5, 6-3

Kodes 6-3, 6-2, 6-3

times that I was ahead two sets in a minor tournament only to lose the next two sets and then struggling in the fifth. I then found this strong force within me saying: "Fight, persevere! You are building your stamina for the upcoming big matches! You can lose but not without putting up a fight. Do not give even a point gratis!

In that way I was pretty pigheaded and this made me rather unpopular among my fellow players. "Oh Kodes! He drives me crazy! You think you have him down but he carries on till his last breath."

Many players break in such situations and concede. I would never succumb. I was always doggedly stubborn and determined to put up a fight to the end! My strength of will paid off most of the times. After all, Borg, Vilas, Connors and others did that too.

There were two more clay court tournaments to enter in the Fall – a very prestigious Spanish International Championship in Barcelona, and a tournament in Zaragoza that was prior to it.

I was not all that enthusiastic about the Zaragoza tournament; nevertheless, I arrived in the heart of Spain after six hours of puttering along on the train. I played the Yugoslav Nicola Spear in the semifinals. He was a clever player who knew how to play against me. Drop shot – lob, drop shot – lob! He made me grind my way through points by making me run all over the court and, if I finally approached the net, he either passed or lobbed me. Matches against him always cost me a lot of energy. In that particular semifinal match I kept telling myself: I mustn't get too fatigued for Barcelona!

Kodes won the battle! The finals took place on Sunday morning at 10:00 in order to give the players enough time to transfer to Barcelona after the match. Kodes' counterpart was a fearsome Australian, a left-hander Barry Phillips-Moore.

We played three out of five sets; I overcame him in four but only after a good battle: 4:6, 9:7, 9:7, and 6:3. The match stretched out and we hardly had time to make the express train to Barcelona that was leaving at 3pm. I threw my stuff in the bags, took a quick shower, the organizers shoved a gorgeous trophy in my arms and said: "Mr. Kodes, hurry up!"

I dashed to the platform and a minute later the train rolled in... Throughout the train ride I studied the notes from my university lectures and by that evening we arrived in Barcelona. I could not believe my eyes when I got off the train – there was a huge mob of people like on the Wenceslas Square in Prague during our Velvet Revolution! It was a Sunday evening and people were returning from their weekend travels! What chaos, yelling, scuffle for taxis! And there was I, adorned like a Christmas tree with racket bags, suitcases, and the trophy. In the end, I succeeded in getting into a taxi and made my way to the hotel.

The name of the hotel was Zenit and it was located very near the tennis courts. We all pretty much liked the hotel but it had one shortcoming – extremely soft sagging beds. Though soft beds were not uncommon in most parts of Western Europe the degree of softness in this hotel reached an acute rate. I preferred sleeping on firmer beds...

Luckily, the staff of the hotel were already familiar with me and as soon as I entered the lobby the receptionist shouted: "Ah, señor Kodes! Buenos dias! Tabla! Tabla para el señor Kodes!"

In no time two chaps hauled in a piece of plywood and followed me to the room. There they slid it under my mattress.

There are times when you have no idea who your opponent might be. Generally, that is true about the first rounds.

In my room I found a schedule of matches and when I scanned the draw I thought I was having a nightmare; first round – Spear! On Monday, Centre Court, at 11am!

I hit the pillows but did not sleep well that night. I sensed that I had another agonizing battle ahead of me.

However, it all looked differently in the morning. Kodes started the match like a machine right from the beginning. No mistakes, uncompromising, whatever he touched found its proper deathly landing spot.

I was sweeping him and soon the score was 6:0, 4:0! Then he made a game and things started going his way. He drop-shotted me and I did not reach it. Then he hit the line-chalk; the dust rose. I started to choke a bit but I still grabbed the game to 5:1 and I served for the match.

At 30:0 I tossed the ball for the first serve and I felt sharp pain penetrating my lumbar area; that forecasted worse things to come! I told myself: "You mustn't let anybody see that you are in pain!"

As soon as your opponent senses that you are not your hundred percent he makes you suffer. I managed to finish the match successfully: 6:2 in the second set. When I entered the locker room I lay down on the massage table but I could hardly move. I felt the same I had experienced the previous year in Hamburg!

One of the local officials suggested to me: "See Dr. Mario Cabañes; he'll help you."

I shuffled my feet to Orantes and asked him: "Listen, they are sending me to some Dr. Cabañes; do you know him?"

"Yes, I do. He is our Davis Cup doctor and he is great; a real expert. He'll look at you." One of the members of the organizational committee (coincidentally, that same man who is the main director of the entire Barcelona tournament today) put me in his car and drove me to the doctor's villa.

An elderly gentleman greeted me: "Ah, señor Kodes; I know you from Davis Cup! A champion! Czechoslovakia!

He spread some ointment on my back, then he applied heat from a large lamp, maneuvered my back in various ways and, at the end, he gave me an injection. "It is nothing grave. Come again tomorrow. You must rest it; I'll call and request a day off for you."

The next day he gave me another rubdown and another injection but, on Wednesday, I had to go back to play. I had a formidable opponent – the French Francois Jauffret. I was worried about the match but it turned out well. The result was 10:8, 6:2! From that point on my confidence returned and I played like a machine again and sweep away Jaime Fillol and Andres Gimeno.

I played really well at the net, and my serve and drop-shots were also successful. I won the Spanish Open Championship without loosing even a set! Nastase suffered a semifinal defeat 9:7, 6:4, 6:1, and Orantes got ousted in the finals 6:3, 6:2, and 6:3! I disposed of both in front of a packed stadium.

My back gave me no problem what so ever; señor Cabanes had golden hands and I was very much obliged to him; Manolo Orantes had been right! I dare to say that I played, perhaps, the best tennis of my career in Barcelona in 1972! Zaragoza must have been a good preparation for what I displayed in Real Tennis Club Barcelona.

In December, Kodes still entered three more tournaments in the end of that year. He lost to Nikki Pilic 4:6, 5:7 in the traditional Stockholm Open, and to Smith 2:6, 4:6 in the Paris Indoor Championship. The culmination was the Masters Tournament in Barcelona for which he qualified as number four based on the Grand Prix ranking.

We played on the new artificial " mateflex plastic carpet". It was fast and, at the same time, a bit unsafe. Bubbles popped up here and there and some places of the court were unsteady. All of us feared that we could get hurt.

I did not advance from my group; though I beat Gimeno 6:3, 6:2, I lost to Connors 4:6, 3:6 and to Smith 2:6, 6:3, 3:6. Nastase won the entire tournament defeating Smith in the finals.

That year Smith, Nastase, and Franulovic finished ahead of me in the Grand Prix ranking... However, I had played nine tournaments less than they had! The fact that I started playing tournaments later in the year and also spent time playing on the Davis Cup team till the European finals affected the number of tournaments I was able to enter.

Yet, I hoped till the very end that I would take the Masters.

The victory in Spain was very sweet and it made up, somewhat, for the loss I suffered against American Alex Mayer at Forest Hills.

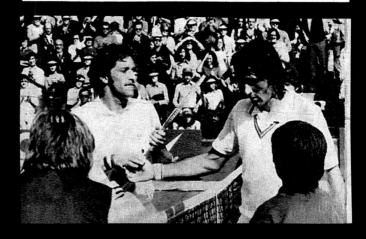

Barcelona, lunes, 23 de octubre de 1972
Segunda época ★ Año XXI ★ Número 2.400

The Spanish Open was always
a great clay-court event. I won
it without losing a set...
(pic. Kodes-Nastase).

Jan Kodes received the trophy from
don Carlos de Godó.

KODES INSCRIBIO SU NOMBRE EN EL «GODO»

El checo Jan Kodes conquistó ayer, por primera vez en su dilatada y positiva trayectoria tenística, el Trofeo «Conde de Godó», tras imponerse a Manolo Orantes por 6-3, 6-2 y 6-3. Triunfo apoteósico y absolutamente merecido, que permite a su ganador escalar posiciones importantes en el «Grand Prix». En la fotografía de Brangulí, don Carlos de Godó, Conde de Godó, creador del trofeo, este año bajo nuevo diseño y reglamentación, entrega el preciado galardón que lleva su nombre al checoslovaco Jan Kodes

...es de Godó presented me the trophy

EL MILLON FUE PARA JAN KODES

● EN SU PEOR PARTIDO DEL TORNEO ORANTES PERDIO EN LOS TRES «SETS»: 6-3, 6-2, 6-3

Jan Kodes conquistó por primera vez y con todos los honores el Trofeo "Conde de Godó" batiendo en la finalísima disputada ayer con casi lleno en los graderíos a Manolo Orantes en tres "sets": 6-3, 6-2 y 6-3 tras poco más de hora y media.

En el momento de hilvanar el comentario de lo que ha sido la brillante singladura deportiva del torneo en su XX edición, puntuable para el "Grand Prix", es para asegurar que, Orantes, ayer, proporcionó nueva ocasión, con su desangelada actuación ante el jugador checo, para ser puesto en la picota de los comentarios desdeñosos o, simplemente, en boca de quienes, tras haber pagado una entrada se consideraron defraudados al presenciar su derrota. Sí, evidentemente, Orantes y su clase volverá a ser puesto en entredicho; duramente criticado. Nos duele porque en el fondo existirá parte de razón, aunque no imputable al jugador que, sobre la pista, hizo cuanto estuvo a su alcance y no pudo. En cambio un exceso de deportividad ha sido, en nuestra opinión, lo que ha llevado al traste sus posibilidades de triunfo en el "Godó". Y, consiguientemente, en la mediocre actuación deparada en la final ante Kodes.

Discutido e indiscutible

Es lamentable lo que ocurre con Orantes. Por una serie de circunstancias, durante los últimos tiempos ha sido puesto muchas veces en entredicho ya en torneos o más allegada en ocasión de las recientes eliminatorias de Copa Davis. El caso es que, Orantes, no cuaja una buena actuación cuando las cámaras de la televisión son la ventana abierta por donde toda la nación —al menos, la parte tenística o más allegada a este deporte—, está pendiente de él. Y aunque no see ésta la verdadera cuestión, si convendrá explicar que Manolo Orantes, acusó ayer un exceso de celo demostra el domingo al jugar tres disputados «sets» después de haber disputado cuatro durísimas mangas al estadounidense Stan Smith al que venció, magis-

la pésima actuación de Orantes. Simplemente matizar unos puntos que, creemos han contribuido, bastante, a que el campeón de España no estuviera a la altura de sus reales posibilidades y, sobre todo, a lo que muchísimos aficionados esperaban.

Los excesos se pagan

Este gran error; o exceso de confianza en las propias condiciones físicas, traicionó a Orantes que, por si fuera poco, se encontró con un Kodes sensacional que le pegaba todo y, además, tenía el santo de cara pues, incluso entraba aquellas pelotas mal empaladas y, que, lógicamente, debían caer en las pistas colindantes.

Al margen de todo cuanto queda dicho, afirmamos una cuestión que, posiblemente, será desorbitada en relación a la dispar forma de actuar entre el pletórico y acertado Kodes

Jan Kodes, el brillante ganador del "Godó-72", eleva, satisfecho, el trofeo conquistado por vez primera en su pletórica vida deportiva

(Foto Brangulí)

Jan Kodes with Spanish Open trophies.

PILIC "AFFAIR"

Saturday, July 7, 1973. The All England Lawn Tennis Club's Centre Court clock read 4:35 p.m. As he was getting ready to serve at match point in the Wimbledon finals, Jan Kodes was knocking on the door of tennis immortality! He tossed the ball above his head, struck it into his opponent's court and followed it to the net. Alex Metreveli returned the serve with his backhand, and Kodes' subsequent volley sent the ball into the open court. Though the opponent reached the ball, he hit it into the net. The end! Spectators rose from their seats of the jam-packed Centre Court and applauded the triumph of their new Wimbledon champion. That applause sounded like the world's most beautiful chorus to Kodes' ears. The ball-boys lined up, and the Duke of Kent descended from the Royal Box onto the red carpet. He strode over the worn-out green grass turf and presented Jan Kodes with the trophy of the most prestigious tournament in the world.

In no time, two things, that made me immensely happy, coincided. As I made my way out of the court I was greeted by Martina Navratilova who was sitting right behind the exit doors in front of the locker room. She jumped up and gave me a hug and a kiss.

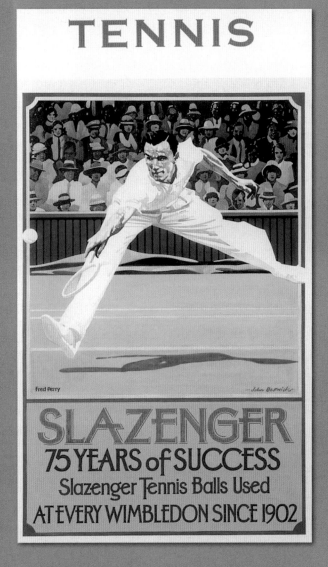

I hardly entered the locker room and there was Fred Perry. He took off the signature Wimbledon tie he was wearing and passed it to me saying: "Jan, here is a tie for you. You will receive the same tie from the All England Club. By winning Wimbledon you have become a member of the club, but this tie is from me. Remember that it is all the same whether some players entered or did not enter this championship because no weak player ever won Wimbledon!"

There are debates even today arguing that Kodes won "depreciated" Wimbledon since some players had boycotted it. A number of members of the Association of Tennis Professionals protested Niki Pilic's punishment by his National Tennis Federation for refusing to compete against New Zealand in Davis Cup and they stayed away from this most important tournament. The resulting humbug was provoked by the ATP. Nevertheless, the All England Lawn Tennis Club spectator attendance reached new records in spite of the absence of Smith, Ashe, Newcombe, Rosewall, Okker....

I had defeated Newcombe, Smith and Ashe on grass within the past couple of years, and Laver in Stockholm, Rosewall, Okker and Riessen on the indoor WCT circuit in the US. Why should I not be able to beat them in Wimbledon?

TENNIS "COUP D'ETAT"

Who would have foreseen what was to happen during the first six months of 1973 leading towards the Saturday, July 7?

Jan Kodes began to play tournaments that were part of Lamar Hunt's circuit. A contract signed between ITF and WCT signified a "turn-around" in world tennis. The significant development was represented by the fact that all best players of the world, regardless whether they were still under professional contract or not, were allowed to enter all world championships and competition, including Davis Cup team contests for their respective countries. That raised the popularity and significance of this unofficial measure of prowess, which increased the importance of those specific tournaments to the level of world championships.

Before he traveled to the WCT circuit, which started in Europe Kodes glanced back at 1972 with members of the press, and he declared: *"I do not believe 1972 was as bad as many insist it was. I reached the finals in Rome and semis in Hamburg, I made my way into the Wimbledon semifinals for the first time, and I won in Barcelona".*

That year he repeated reaching the fourth place in the final count of the Grand Prix.

He went on saying: *"Placing among the Grand Prix top players is a result of the entire year's effort, and the one who does not deliver solid performance has no chance of making in into the midst of the best ten players of the world.... If a player wants to succeed he must learn to distribute his strength through the year and, simultaneously, time his best performances for the most important events. Our public doesn't realize that the world competition is steadily escalating and that, at present day, there are some eighty players who can beat each other on any given day. The outcome depends on the momentary physical as well mental strength of each individual; that is why I appeal to people to view me not only as a man with a tennis racket but also as a fellow human being."*

It was not easy. People were not used to the amount of money that a tennis player was able to earn, even though it was a laughable amount compared to today's earnings. Too many people at home looked attennis only through the dollars.

For instance, I bought a new car in the dollar store Tuzex. The moment I drove it in public I heard: "Wow, Kodes has it easy, he can afford to buy a Saab!"

As soon as I lost in the semifinals they switched to:"Oh well, Kodes!

Legendary Fred Perry won Wimbledon three times in a row in 1934-1936. He was the first player who succeeded in winning all four Grand Slam tournaments though not in the same calendar year. Since his day only R. Emerson, A. Agassi and R. Federer accomplished it. And only two players ever achieved the classical Grand Slam: Donald Budge and Rod Laver.

Jan Kodes victory
WCT Cologne in 1973.

Ken Rosewall in the Sparta basketball hall.

He has money now so why should he bother with effort and winning?"

Yes, the money was good for that period of time; it was also significant to be earning the "greenbacks"; what people did not realize, or chose not to see, was the fact that it was all earned through daily hard work and sweat either in practice or in competition.

From Jan Kodes' point of view, his 1972 performance was nothing to fret about. There was one other issue that had hardly anything to do with the "white sport"; nevertheless, it had a flattering effect on Jan. One of the contemporary Czech periodicals published a comprehensive article about then thirty-nine year old American actor, Robert Redford, father of three children. When asked "What do you think of Czechoslovakia?" he answered: "From Czechoslovakia I know Kodes and I know of the existence of V & W **(Voskovec and Werich)** from the era of "Osvobozene divadlo";(Independent theatre) I have seen both Czechoslovak Oscar winning films (The Shop on Main Street and

Norma and Ken Rosewall with their "tour guide", Jan Kodes, in the Tower of the Old Town Hall.

Hatte keine Chance: Brian Fairlie

Gewann beim Profi-Tennisturnier ein Luxus-Appartement: Jan Kodes

Kodes war der Clou von Köln

Neuseeländer Brian Fairlie unterlag ihm im Finale der Tennis-WM 1:6, 3:6, 1:6

VON H. J. WESKAMP

Köln. Dank seiner überaus starken Rückhand ist der tschechoslowakische Tennisprofi Jan Kodes sämtliche Wohnungssorgen los. Sie vor allem sicherte ihm am Sonntagnachmittag den Sieg beim Weltmeisterschaftsturnier der Gruppe B und damit ein Eigentumsappartement im Wert von 51 000 DM im andalusischen Ferienzentrum La Parra.

In der ersten Hochstimmung über den unerwartet schnellen Triumph lud der 26jährige Prager sämtliche Mitspieler des Kölner Turniers zum September-Urlaub in seine neue Luxusbehausung ein. Möglicherweise wird dann auch sein Finalgegner Brian Fairlie (24) sein Gast sein, dem er in 85 Minuten mit 6:1, 6:3, 6:1 nie auch nur die geringste Chance gelassen hatte.

Während der kompakte Neuseeländer nach dem Finale völlig ermattet wirkte und immer wieder auf seine Oberschenkel wies, in denen er nach dem überaus schweren und glücklich errungenen Sieg vom Vorabend über das sowjetische Tennisas Alexander Metreveli

(6:2, 6:7, 6:4) „Pudding" spürte, gestattete sich Kodes erst mal ein Bier.

Zweimal habe er gegen Brian schon verloren, in London und in Kopenhagen, „aber diesmal mußte es einfach klappen". Auch er habe das Spiel vom Samstagnachmittag, das er mit 6:2, 6:7, 6:1 gegen den Engländer Mark Cox gewonnen hatte, noch in den Knochen gehabt: „Wir waren beide ziemlich geschafft, so daß wir beide nicht das beste Tennis zeigen konnten, das normalerweise drin ist. Aber die Hauptsache ist für mich, daß ich gewonnen habe."

Zumindest in der Bewertung seiner eigenen Leistung untertrieb der Tscheche. Er war taktisch und körperlich topfit in dieses Spiel gegangen. Die 3500 Zuschauer in der Deutzer Halle staunten nicht schlecht, daß das Laufwunder Fairlie aus Neuseeland, das schon bei der ersten Tennis-WM in Köln im Oktober 1971 dreimal den Pokal als bester Kämpfer des Tages erhalten hatte und auch diesmal seine Gegner, darunter den zweimaligen Weltmeister Ken Rosewall, förmlich niedergerungen hatte, keinen Stich bekam. Der ungesetzte Kodes

bewies die weitaus besseren Nerven als der auf dem zweiten Rang gesetzte Fairlie.

Kodes gewann den ersten Aufschlag sicher, und im zweiten Spiel zeigte Fairlie dann seine entscheidende Schwäche, er verlor sein Aufschlagspiel. Das tat er dann im Verlauf des Matches noch weitere achtmal. Außerdem machte er von Anfang an den Fehler, Kodes zu häufig auf dessen Schokoladenseite — der Rückhand — anzuspielen.

Was von dort an unterschnittenen oder überrissenen Schlägen auf ihn einprasselte, ließ ihn mehrfach dem Gegner Beifall spenden, dann wieder kopfschüttelnd zur Decke starren und endgültig völlig resignieren. Warum er nicht häufiger zum Netz gekommen sei, wurde er nachher gefragt.

Fairlie: „Ich wollte ja, aber er hat mich am Anfang ein paarmal mit seiner Rückhand passiert, das hat mir das Selbstvertrauen genommen."

Davon hatte Kodes nach dem Sieg genug: „Es war mein erster Sieg in einem WM-Turnier, das wird mir Auftrieb geben und mir auch beim Davis-

Pokal helfen." Kodes gehört natürlich zum Team seines Landes, das demnächst gegen Polen anzutreten hat.

Fairlie aber tröstete sich über die Niederlage mit einem 5000-Dollar-Scheck sowie sieben Punkten in der Weltmeisterschaftswertung hinweg, die in der Gruppe 3 seinen zweiten Platz hinter dem Amerikaner Marty Riessen (23 Punkte) und vor den Engländer Mark Cox (15) festigten.

Der Sieger von Köln liegt mit 12 Punkten schon auf Rang vier, zusammen mit Rosewall und dem Briten Roger Taylor.

Überraschung im Doppel

Mit einer großen Überraschung endete das Finale im Doppel. Nicht die hohen Favoriten Tom Okker aus den Niederlanden und Marty Riessen aus den USA, sondern die Briten Mark Cox und Graham Stilwell holten sich die 1800-Dollar-Prämie nach 7:6 im Tiebreak und 6:3. Riessen und Okker, die im Einzelwettbewerb jeweils am späteren Sieger Jan Kodes gescheitert waren, vermochten auch in ihrer Domäne nicht zu überzeugen.

Closely Watched Trains) and when I showed interest in French poetry and surrealism I came across something by Nezval...".

I admit that this tickled me. And plenty so!

During the first WCT tournament in Cologne Jan managed to accomplish a curious thing.

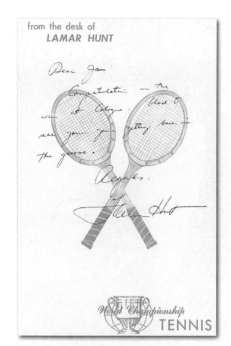

A congratulatory note from Lamar Hunt was waiting for me in my hotel in Rome.

He arranged for a Ken Rosewall exhibition in Prague! Again, it was going to take place in the Indoor Hall in Letna.

I sought Ken in Cologne and tried to persuade him to visit and play in Prague. "Emerson came, and so did Laver!" I nagged.

He shrugged his shoulders, hardly spoke and sent me to see his wife: "If Norma wants to see Prague, then why not?" I looked her up and when she heard my proposal she replied: "If Ken feels like it then I'll come along!"

And - they came!

It was the only time that the famous tennis player from the land Down Under made an appearance in Prague.

He received crystal vases; his wife accepted a fine china set from Carlsbad; and we paid for his plane ticket to New York. I showed them the sights of Prague and when we climbed up to the tower of the Old Town Hall, Norma was absolutely ecstatic! We then headed to the Castle and I was very proud of what I was showing them.

That year Kodes entered the professional WCT circuit insipidly. He lost to the New Zealander Brian Fairlie 4:6, 3:6 in Milan, and 3:6, 3:6 to Zeljko Franulovic in Copenhagen. However, by the time the third tournament in Cologne came about he was playing with all his menace! In succession he disposed off Franulovic 6:4, 6:3, Okker 6:4, 6:3, Riessen 6:1, 7:5, Cox in the semifinals 6:3, 6:7, 6:1, and Brian Fairlie in the finals easily 6:1, 6:3, 6:1; with that he became the professional champion of then West Germany.

And that was an excellent entrance into the season! The press gave him elated commentaries and, to his surprise, unlike in Hamburg spectators in Cologne supported him!

The WCT circuit then transferred from Europe to the North America continent. In Vancouver Kodes defeated Jovanovic, Metreveli 6:4, 6:2, then Van Dillen 6:1, 2:6, 6:0 and for the first time also Rosewall 7:6, 2:6, 6:3! He lost to the American Tom Gorman 6:3, 2:6, 5:7 in the finals.

It was a great achievement to reach the finals defeating Rosewall, yet I was still a bit put off by the loss to Gorman. I did not realize that Tom had reached Wimbledon semis in 1971 beating Laver! Gorman had a very unpleasant super-spin on his second serve and it bounced up so high into my backhand that I could not lean well into it.

I had to take a couple of steps back and just play the return; I could not aggressively attack it the way I normally liked to.

We then transferred to the American surprising "red" clay in Houston. Kodes overpowered the Davidson, Borowiak, and Riessen but suffered revenge from the racket of Ken Rosewall; the Australian performed better this time and won 6:2, 6:2.

As it turned out in retrospect, the next tournament was extremely important for Kodes' success at Wimbledon that year. After beating Jeff Borowiak in Cleveland he namely defeated Metreveli for second time in an exhausting battle 6:4, 5:7, and 6:3! The following day, fatigued, he succumbed to Fairlie 4:6, 1:6.

I was so bushed from the previous match that I could barely walk. In 1973 two Soviet players entered the professional WCT circuit – Metreveli and Kakulja. Unlike the Czechoslovak semi-professional players who traveled alone, the Soviets were always accompanied by a "group leader".

We knew perfectly well that it was a government snitch. They always had somebody following them; that person cashed all their prize money. On the other hand, their daily allo-

wance was higher than ours. The Americans could not figure them out and looked at them as if they were some exotic species. They drew the crowd at every tournament; wherever they played the stands were full. When I played Borowiak in Cleveland some 150 spectators were hardly visible in a stadium with 3000 seat capacity. As soon as Metreveli entered the court the stadium was bursting in seams! The long-time tradition of white tennis attire was broken during WCT circuit. All of a sudden it was permitted to play in colorful clothes and one could hardly imagine the reaction of the American spectators when Metreveli entered the stadium with a red T-shirt and white shorts! People went wild! They worshipped him and it really bothered me, especially since I knew that the red color represented the communist regime!

In spite of it Kodes beat him in Cleveland and he did not suspect yet how important this victory would be for him in very near future.

When I advanced to the finals of Wimbledon that year many people, undoubtedly, said: "Finals against Metreveli? Oh, that will be ok". However, Alex was two years my senior and had more experience playing on grass than I did. There were numerous tennis events that the Russians did not enter but they played the grass court tournaments in Australia regularly, whereas we did not have enough money to travel there. Before the 1973 Wimbledon Metreveli had won eight (!) grass-court tournaments - Adelaide in 1970, Hobart,Perth and Melbourne in 1971, and in 1972 Sydney, Hobart, Adelaide and Perth.

I lost to him twice in Davis Cup, a few times in various tournaments, and he also beat me in junior tournaments. I clearly had a negative score against him. For that reason it was so important that I, finally, defeated him a few months before Wimbledon. It was crucial for my mental strength in the decisive moments of the final Wimbledon match!

After Cleveland Kodes felt considerably worn out and he lost to the Brit Mark Cox in both remaining WCT tournaments in Charlotte and in Denver. The changing surfaces also had a role in the outcomes. They played out-of-doors on clay in Charlotte and in Denver the surface was fast indoor supreme.The WCT method of ranking was similar to that of the Grand Prix; it terminated in April with a Masters tournament in Dallas.

Lamar Hunt undertook one more issue in 1973 that is impossible to ignore. He included the Grand Slam results from the previous season, meaning 1973 (that he valued above all), when the WCT ranking was calculated for the present year. It helped me qualify even for the 1974 WCT Masters in Dallas, which was esteemed higher than the Grand Prix Masters. It was played via regular draw and three out of five sets; no Round Robins that always complicated the advancement of individuals with the most points that were often problematic to figure out.

Our national selection played a Davis Cup match in Cairo still before the second Grand Slam tournament.

The Czechoslovak Sport reported: "The host country player fought bravely under the scorching heat of around thirty-eight degrees Fahrenheit in the shade, playing a risky game but losing his serve already in the sixth game of the first set, when Kodes advanced to 4:2 and finished winning the set. In the opening of the second set, at 1:1, our player lost his serve; however, Mahmoud had no more chances at anything after that".

"In the first two sets I was battling more the heat than my opponent – 6:4, 6:4, and 6:0. Since everything is immensely exhausting in such challenging conditions one has to play economically, without any unnecessary steps." With that victory Kodes lay a foundation to the first quarterfinal victory of Davis Cup's European Zone B. In almost forty degree Fahrenheit temperatures another player successfully passed his first significant international launch – Jiri Hrebec. He did not disappoint us and conquered the best Egyptian player El Shafei 8:6, 6:4, 3:6, 4:6, and 13:11!

Why did we start off playing quarter-finals? It was a result of Davis Cup's organizational changes. All teams were divided into three groups according to the level of their performance. The best of the teams were then seeded into the third round – the quarter-finals.

"The match I should have won!" – That is how one could characterize Jan Kodes' performance in Roland Garros in 1973. The French Open practically concurred with the Davis Cup quarterfinal match in Cairo.

I flew to Paris feeling very optimistic. I won there twice, the third time it did not work out for me but why should I not succeed again this time?

However, on my return trip from Egypt, I must have left that optimism on the plane, somewhere above the Mediterranean Sea?! I survived two rounds in Paris that were played only as best of three sets. It was a request from ATP that wanted to test how the shortened matches would affect the course of the entire tournament. The organizers of Roland Garros met that request.

First I defeated Fairlie and then the South-African Pat Cramer. Only the third round was played the usual three out of five sets and there I met the Australian Colin Dibley, a Wimbledon quarterfinalist from 1971. He had a great serve and it took much effort to beat him in four sets. In the fourth round, I met the Yugoslav Boro Jovanovic, half of a very successful doubles team Pilic – Jovanovic. I was confident since I had defeated him several times. However, the weather did not cooperate and as the match was often interrupted due to rain the surface was heavy and I was glad when I brought the game to a successful end. I managed to take the match 4:6, 6:3, 4:6, 6:0, and 7:5.

In the quarters Kodes faced the American Tom Gorman, a player that he did not particularly like playing against and with whom he had a negative match record.

Nonetheless, it was the best choice of a quarterfinal opponent there was. I still remember that I was pleased to be facing a "Gringo" because clay was not the favorite surface of the Americans.

Shortly after mid-day the skies opened and torrential rain fell upon Paris. As if flood-gates had been raised, there was thunder, lightning, and sheets of water falling, even hails. I was sitting in the locker room and, deep down inside, I sort of rejoiced that we would not be able to play after the havoc produced by Mother Nature. It is to say that I was pretty sore from the match with Jovanovic and I would have welcomed having the quarterfinal match postponed.

However, as quickly as the storm came so quickly it dissipated. I walked out and the sky was as clear as it could be, the sun was burning, the court was one big pond. Half an hour later I noticed that the organizers were drying up the court and spreading fresh clay over it. And then the moment arrived to play....

The surface was slow, slippery and soft, exactly the conditions I disliked. Tom chose to serve and volley and I was unable to pass him. The patchy surface bothered me – one ball bounced fast, the next one slow; one high, the following one low, close to the ground. And Tom played well – I lost in four 4:6, 6:7, 6:4, and 1:6. I did not expect that and it greatly upset me.

At the same time it was a huge sensation for the correspondents: Kodes, the two-time champion from 1970 and 1971, knocked out again in the quarter-finals!

Nastase turned out winning French Open overcoming Kodes' conqueror in the semifinals and the Yugoslav Niki Pilic in the finals. Subsequently, Nastase became Kodes' doom in the Italian Open, a tournament that was played for the first and last time right after Roland Garros. Nastase humbled Kodes 6:2, 6:2 in the quarter-finals!

Thus, Kodes was leaving for Wimbledon with two quarterfinal losses from Paris and Rome. His spirit was further decreased when he was disqualified from doubles in Rome for late arrival...

I was scheduled to play with Arthur Ashe against the home team Pietrangeli – Di Domenico. The stumbling block was the public transport. The organizers did not have as many cars available as they do have today. In order to be transported one had to call the tennis premises and wait to be picked up. Often the best solution was to opt for taking a taxi. And that is what I chose in Rome. However, when faced with a traffic jam a huge predicament popped up.

Men's Singles *Holder* A. Gimeno

FIRST ROUND

I. NASTASE (RU) (2)
J. Pinto Bravo (CH)
T. Sakai (J)
J. Hrebec (CZ)
J. Fassbender (G)
D. Naegelen
M. Lara (M)
P. Joly
F. JAUFFRET (15)
I. El Shafei (UAR)
A. Zugarelli (IT)
Z. Franulovic (YU)
K. Meiler (G)
G. Battrick (GB)
E. Dibbs (USA)
P. Dominguez
A. GIMENO (SP) (7)
E. Di Matteo (IT)
J. Gisbert (SP)
G. Vilas (ARG)
E. Deblicker
P. Gerken (USA)
S. Siegel (USA)
T. Ulrich (D)
R. TAYLOR (GB) (10)
K. Warwick (AUS)
K. Johansson (SW)
A. Metreveli (USSR)
T. Addison (AUS)
C. Pasarell (USA)
H. Elschenbroich (G)
P. Szoke (HU)
B. Jovanovic (YU)
F. Kuki (J)
F. Pala (CZ)
S. Likhachev (USSR)
B. Montrenaud
C. Barazzutti (IT)
J. Kamiwazumi (J)
R. Chavez (M)
J. KODES (CZ) (14)
B. Fairlie (NZ)
P. Cramer (SA)
R. D. Crealy (AUS)
C. Dibley (AUS)
D. Contet
P. Cornejo (CH)
T. Nowicki (POL)
J. D. NEWCOMBE (AUS) (6)
M. Holecek (CZ)
I. Molina (COL)
J. G. Paish (GB)
H. J. Pohmann (G)
A. Amritraj (IN)
J. Borowiak (USA)
J. Haillet
P. PROISY (11)
T. Gorman (USA)
A. Stone (AUS)
J. Vasquez (SP)
T. Kakoulia (USSR)
O. Parun (NZ)
V. Zednik (CZ)
M. Mulligan (IT)

I. Velasco (COL)
J. M. Lloyd (GB)
G. Varga (HU)
N. Pilic (YU)
P. Dent (AUS)
S. Faulk (USA)
R. Ramirez (M)
J. CONNORS (USA) (12)
I. Tiriac (RU)
P. Hombergen (B)
N. Pietrangeli (IT)
F. Froehling (USA)
W. N'Godrella
T. Edlefsen (USA)
W. Lloyd (AUS)
M. ORANTES (SP) (5)
J. L. Rouyer
N. Kalogeropoulos (GR)
A. Pattison (RH)
G. R. Stilwell (GB)
J. Loyo-Mayo (M)
P. Bertolucci (IT)
I. Fletcher (AUS)
M. COX (GB) (13)
H. Solomon (USA)
F. D. McMillan (SA)
J. Kuki (J)
B. Gottfried (USA)
N. Spear (YU)
G. Masters (AUS)
I. Gulyas (HU)
A. R. ASHE (USA) (4)
J. B. Chanfreau
H. Kary (AU)
A. Munoz (SP)
D. Stockton (USA)
J. Alexander (AUS)
P. Barthes
B. Borg (SW)
C. RICHEY (USA) (9)
M. Estep (USA)
M. Rybarczyk (?OL)
N. Kelaidis (GR)
J. Fillol (CH)
R. Case (AUS)
B. Mignot (B)
R. Carmichael (AUS)
A. PANATTA (IT) (8)
P. Kronk (AUS)
B. Phillips-Moore (AUS)
S. Baranyi (HU)
R. Moore (SA)
T. Ovici (RU)
R. Machan (HU)
J. Ganzabal (ARG)
T. S. OKKER (NTH) (16)
D. A. Lloyd (GB)
E. Van Dillen (USA)
C. Drysdale (SA)
P. Toci (IT)
J. C. Barclay
J. McManus (USA)
G. Goven
S. R. SMITH (USA) (1)

SECOND ROUND

NASTASE (2) 6-1 6-4
Hrebec 6-2 6-3
Fassbender 6-2 1-6 6-1
Lara 7-6 6-1
JAUFFRET (15) 7-6 6-3
Franulovic 5-7 6-3 6-3
Battrick 6-4 6-2
Dominguez 7-5 7-5
GIMENO (7) 6-7 6-4 6-3
Vilas 6-4 6-0
Gerken 6-4 6-2
Ulrich 6-2 7-6
TAYLOR (10) 6-1 3-6 6-3
Metreveli 7-5 6-4
Pasarell 6-4 6-0
Elschenbroich 7-6 6-2
Jovanovic 5-7 7-5 6-3
Pala 6-4 6-3
Barazzutti 6-4 6-7 6-0
Kamiwazumi 6-3 6-1
KODES (14) 4-6 6-2 6-1
Cramer 3-6 7-6 6-2
Dibley 6-0 6-1
Nowicki 3-6 6-4 6-2
Holecek 7-5 6-1
Paish 7-5 1-6 6-1
Pohmann 6-4 6-2
Haillet 7-6 7-6
Gorman 6-7 6-1 6-1
Vasquez 7-6 1-6 7-5
Parun 6 4 6 0
Mulligan w.o.

Lloyd 6-4 6-4
Pilic 6-4 6-4
Dent 6-2 6-4
Ramirez 6-4 7-6
Tiriac 7-5 6-1
Froehling 6-0 6-1
N'Godrella w.o.
ORANTES (5) 6-3 6-4
Rouyer 7-5 1-6 6-3
Pattison 6-2 6-1
Bertolucci 6-3 6-1
COX (13) 6-4 6-1
Solomon 3-6 6-2 6-3
Gottfried 7-5 1-6 6-2
Masters 1-6 6-4 7-5
ASHE (4) 6-4 6-4
Chanfreau 6-4 5-7 7-5
Stockton 6-3 6-2
Barthes 6-3 6-4
Borg 6-2 6-3
Estep 6-3 6-3
Fillol 6-2 6-4
Mignot 6-1 6-3
PANATTA (8) 6-2 6-4
Phillips-Moore 6-2 6-4
Baranyi 6-4 3-6 6-3
Machan 3-6 6-2 6-2
OKKER (16) 6-1 6-1
Van Dillen 6-4 6-2
Drysdale 6-3 4-6 6-1
McManus 6-4 7-6
SMITH (1) 2-6 6-1 6-3

THIRD ROUND

NASTASE (2) 6-2 6-4
Fassbender 6-3 7-6
JAUFFRET (15) 6-4 7-6
Dominguez 7-6 6-4
Vilas 6-2 5-7 8-6
Gerken 6-2 6-3
TAYLOR (10) 6-4 6-4
Pasarell 6-0 6-3
Jovanovic 6-1 4-6 9-7
Barazzutti 6-2 6-1
KODES (14) 6-1 6-0
Dibley 6-4 6-4
Holecek 7-6 6-4
Pohmann 6-2 6-4
Gorman 6-3 6-3
Parun 6 4 7 5

Pilic 6-1 6-7 6-0
Dent 6-2 6-1
Froehling 7-6 7-6
N'Godrella 6-0 7-6
Pattison 7-5 6-4
Bertolucci 7-5 6-3
Solomon 6-4 6-2
ASHE (4) 7-6 6-2
Stockton 6-4 6-4
Borg 3-6 6-1 8-6
Fillol 6-1 7-6
PANATTA (8) 6-1 1-6 8-6
Phillips-Moore 7-5 6-2
OKKER (16) 7-5 6-3
Van Dillen 6-1 3-6 6-4
SMITH (1) 7-5 7-5

FOURTH ROUND

NASTASE (2) 6-2 6-1 6-3
JAUFFRET (15) 6-1 2-6 6-1 3-6 6-0
Gerken 6-1 7-6 6-1
TAYLOR (10) 6-2 4-6 3-6 6-3 7-5
Jovanovic 6-2 6-1 7-5
KODES (14) 6-3 6-4 1-6 6-1
Holecek 6-4 3-6 6-0 4-6 8-6
Gorman 6-4 6-3 6-3

Pilic 3-6 7-5 7-6 6-3
Froehling 6-4 6-3 6-4
Bertolucci 3-6 6-4 6-7 6-4 6-4
ASHE (4) 7-6 6-2 6-7 6-4
Borg 6-7 7-5 6-2 7-6
PANATTA (8) 6-4 6-4 6-1
OKKER (16) 6-2 6-1 6-2
SMITH (1) 6-2 6-4 6-7 4-6 6-1

QUARTER-FINALS

NASTASE (2) 6-4 6-2 6-4
TAYLOR (10) 6-4 6-4 1-6 2-6 6-4
KODES (14) 4-6 6-3 4-6 6-0 7-5
Gorman 6-3 6-3 6-4

Pilic 6-2 6-2 6-3
Bertolucci 7-6 6-3 6-4
PANATTA (8) 7-6 2-6 7-5 7-6
OKKER (16) 6-3 3-6 7-6 3-6 6-4

SEMI-FINALS

NASTASE (2) 6-0 6-2 7-6
Gorman 6-4 7-6 4-6 6-1

Pilic 6-3 6-4 3-6 6-4
PANATTA (8) 6-3 5-7 6-3 6-4

FINAL

NASTASE (2) 6-3 6-4 6-1
Pilic 6-4 6-3 6-2

NASTASE 6-3 6-3 6-0

Capital letters denote seeded players. Number following player's name gives seeding order.

Margaret Smith-Court – there has never been a tennis player to match her record; altogether she rolled up 62 Grand Slam titles in singles (24), doubles and mixed doubles. She won two Grand Slams: in 1970 in singles and in 1963 in mixed doubles with Ken Fletcher. Only two other players came close to her achievements – Martina Navratilova with 58 GS titles (18 in singles) and Steffi Graf with 22 singles titles.

I arrived about 45 minutes late and the match had been scratched by then. Was it the organizer's fault? Or, perhaps, intent? I don't know…. It would not happen today. I can't imagine that the tournament officials would default for the very same reason somebody like Federer. The tournament would be over then! I was a two time Roland Garros champion; they could have given me more time and, perhaps, fine me instead of defaulting me; it was a different era. Nowadays they switch the match to a different court, the taxi drivers inform the officials of the traffic situation via cell phones, and everybody simply waits till the player arrives. It is also true that if you get into a traffic jam in New York you have no chance making it in time to Flushing Meadows.

All tennis players' dream is to win Wimbledon. And not just Wimbledon but any Grand Slam tournament.

Winning Grand Slam tournaments is valued so highly because they are more difficult than any other tournaments throughout the year. The ATP ranking is nice to have but it is not ideal. Rios from Chile occupied the first rung once yet he never won a Grand Slam event.

Jan Kodes entered the Centre Court like a seasoned warrior to play the 1973 Wimbledon finals. Besides the double victory in Paris he had reached the US Open finals in 1971, the Wimbledon semifinals in 1972, and three Italian Championships finals in Rome.

And it was exactly that final match at Forest Hills two years previously that gave him tremendous impulse leading to the subsequent mark in his tennis history.

BATTLE VS. GRASS

Grass! Surface that is loved as well as cursed. Those, who grew up on grass do not like clay surface and visa versa. As a continental European nursed on red clay Jan Kodes made his acquaintance with grass at Junior Wimbledon. He was eighteen when he arrived in London for the first time – and before long, all of a sudden, Jaroslav Drobny appeared by his side. He always turned up at the right moment like a magic wizard, as if he knew when the every man Czech Jan was about to whip up a great performance - 1970 Paris… 1973 Wimbledon.

Already in 1964 when Kodes, then a junior, was introduced to Jaroslav Drobny by Jiri Javorsky, the former enquired: "Have you ever played on grass?" "I have not had a chance; they don't allow juniors to travel behind the Iron Curtain". "Well then, come on to Hurlingham and take this opportunity to have at least one practice session on grass. Just so that you get the feel for what it is like."

Jaroslav Drobny then acquainted us with his friend and diamond entrepreneur Milos Vainer, who lived directly by the gates of the famous Wimbledon grounds; these grounds had no practice courts in those times and players had to warm up in the historic Queen's Club with grass as well as wooden surface courts. That was hard since the few grass courts could not satisfy the demands of all players, and court reservation was very complicated…

Telephones were perpetually busy, reservations were impossible to make ahead of time, and players playing that same day had precedence before the rest. We found out the order of play from the newspapers and only then we could call to reserve a practice court; when we finally secured a reservation and arrived we were often told "sorry, there is no free grass court left"; thus we had to settle for practice on a wooden court!

Radana and Milos Vainer emigrated from Czechoslovakia in 1947; they had a weekend house in English countryside in Wargrave on the Thames, about an hour from London by car. Milos was a devout tennis fan and he always tried to set up our practices on grass at the local cricket club. Ultimately, I decided to give up on the Queen's Club tournament before Wimbledon because it got rained out often and had to be completed indoors; instead we spent that week practicing along with Holecek, Pala, and Zednik at Vainers' in Wargrave.

It was great fun there, and it felt like a training camp with all the necessary ingredients. We worked out hard several times a day, even in slight drizzle. There were no court covers and the grass was not as perfect as in Wimbledon but it was grass and for us that was as good as gold. The local population watched us running, practicing doubles, and taking turns on one of the cricket grass courts converted into a tennis court. Milos gained the custodian over by telling him how much we liked it there and that we would come back again the following year. On some days we truly lucked out because we got to practice while in London they totally rained out!!! During the weekend Radana spoiled us with strawberries and cream when Jaroslav Drobny, was in the mood he told us stories from his own experiences and illuminated us saying that grass is not just for cows but also for tennis play! - The grass practice court issue is no longer of concern since players have about seven practice courts right on the grounds of the main Wimbledon. However, I feel for ever indebted to Milos for all that he had done for us and am glad to have reciprocated by winning the title and showing him that the effort was not in vain.

In Junior Wimbledon Jan Kodes defeated a Dane, an Englishman, and an American and fought his way all the way to the semifinals in spite of the fact that he had to battle a few problems:

- because of the faster and lower bounce a player must react considerably faster and know ahead of time his next move;

- there are no long rallies on grass the way one plays on clay where a player uses strategy to prepare an attack gradually

- grass is tricky in the way that opportunities that come up once do not come up again; if the players are of the same level and both serve well then it is reflex and luck that determine the outcome.

- movement on the grass court is problematic for everyone who did not grow up on grass courts: when the grass is wet it becomes slippery, when it is dry feet sort of stumble; on clay a player can slide out, on grass one has to run it out with tiny light steps.

Five times Kodes lost in the first round of Wimbledon, but in 1972 he made it to the semifinals against the champion Stan Smith. By then he penetrated the mystique of a grass court game.

I realized that the world will never consider me as one of the top players if I don't grapple grass and conquer it, if I don't speed up my feet and backswings for each stroke, if I don't change the way of thinking and adjust my game strategy to that surface.

Clay surface tournaments became somewhat rare then. Only one grand slam was played on clay, at Roland Garros. Jan won Paris in 1970 for the first time but immediately afterward he lost in the first round of Wimbledon and was not seeded in the US Open at Forest Hills. The argument was clear: "perhaps he won Paris but he doesn't know how to handle the game on grass!"

However, Jan gave a real shocker to all and "rolled over" the Australian John Newcombe, the French Pierre Barthes, and four Americans Butch Seewagen, Frank Froehling, Bob Lutz and Arthur Ashe all the way to the finals where he was stopped by Stan Smith.

The outcome of 1971 US Open definitely convinced me that I can succeed on grass.

HARD WORK PLAYING ON GRASS

Jiri (George) Parma, our former Davis Cup player, and later one of the first coaches of Martina Navratilova who emigrated to and lived in New York, once told me: "Don't be afraid to charge to the net right after the serve. Even though your serve is no cannon ball shot it has plenty of spin on it and that allows you to approach in and hit a volley. And you know how to execute that!"

However, every volley is different! In order to hit a perfect volley on clay is a different story from punching one on grass. A spectator may not realize it but the difference in execution of strokes on different surfaces is crucial! It was a long road full of drudgery, sweat, ascetic discipline and willpower to achieve, or come close to, stroke perfection. I realized that I had to adapt my entire game to grass if I wanted to succeed on it. That was the most difficult period of my tennis career! For one, I hated playing on grass and I was one of those who claimed that it was, indeed, good just for the cows! I also complained about the bounces! It simply badgered me!

One day, it was Jaroslav Drobny who opened my eyes at Wimbledon! "Do you think that grass didn't bother me? It drives everybody crazy! You don't want to believe that only you have the bad bounces!? My friend, the guy on the other side of the net faces the same bad bounces you do!" And then he gave me the best advice: "You must start to love the grass and only then you'll begin to win on it."

"But how am I supposed to like it?" I objected. "That is a common self-reflex. You have to incite a belief that it doesn't bother you: only your opponent faces bad bounces, not you. You have to believe "I run well on this surface, my opponent doesn't.""

I took his advice to heart and, in addition, I benefited from watching the best players on Centre Court. It was during those first few years when I lost early in the draw but stayed on thanks to playing doubles that I chose to take a seat on Centre Court and just watched the best players' footwork. Often, I didn't even follow the score; that wasn't important then. Those players must have grown up on grass courts, I thought, especially the Australians. So I sat there and watched their feet!

The first thing I noticed was their fluent graduation from serve to subsequent run, when right foot stepped forward. They knew how to jump for the serve off the left foot and back to the left foot which allowed them to ease the right foot forward and run. On grass it is essential to make it at least a meter beyond the service line after striking the serve. If you get stuck too far back you have to play half-volleys then and lift the ball.

The second thing that I engraved into my mind was the fact that it is essential to know how to execute successfully the first running volley. It is possible to stop at that first volley on a clay court, when you take advantage of a slide. You can hit the volley and then continue on to the net. However, that is close to impossible on grass. The first volley must be hit while on the move forward, preferably well placed deep into the opponent's field and followed up to the net. This was one thing that Lendl never mastered and, perhaps, that cost him the Wimbledon title, the one he never reached. The player, who learns to hit this low opening volley deep into the opponent's court, and a drop-volley on top of it, has a great arsenal on grass.

The third realization: if the first serve is a fault, the second serve must be well placed. It doesn't need to be hard but rather deep and with a good spin.

It is one thing to discover grass court strategy and it is another thing to internalize and implement it. For me it was that much harder because I learned it late, at the age of 24 or 25!

The first volley on grass is crucial; you must squat down and not miss the shot...

The new asphalt court built in Sparta Club in early 1970s helped Jan Kodes practice some of the grass court antics.

I kept saying that grass court play couldn't be such unbelievable science; I also realized that play on artificial surfaces indoors was very similar to that of playing on grass. And I persuaded myself to believe that playing on grass or indoors was very much the same.

It was mentioned already how Jan and Martina Navratilova practiced in Sparta's basketball hall. Then the club constructed an asphalt court which they later covered with mateflex that created a surface with qualities very similar to grass.

I arrived at Sparta with a bag of tennis balls and rushed to the court. I was there alone and I drilled a serve, approach and fake a volley. Serve, approach, volley into forehand side. Serve, approach, volley, smash. Serve, approach, volley into backhand side. Over, and over, and over again!

But do not be fooled! It was not all that easy! After the serve one must run forward in a crouched position with the center of gravity somewhat lower. The serve return is usually low and that is why one must start getting lower in time and anticipate the lower bounce. A player who stays up will run into trouble. Before he squats down the ball zooms by; he is too late!

It was very important for me to make my way three feet beyond the service line after the serve in order to strike the ball at a decent height; I lowered my knees like a skier going into a gate and out; only then I was capable of making an effective first volley. Practicing this caused unbelievable fatigue to my quadriceps. I was as sore as if I did frog jumps all day long. However, the leg power is critical for success on grass particularly for volleys. One of our drills with Petr Korda used to be: he hit the ball at me; I volleyed and did a squat! Over and over – volley & squat, volley & squat. What a workout! Without it you can't succeed on grass. It is impossible to slide to a shot like on clay, although some players know how to. Most players still go by a principle that efficient legs rule success on grass.

Basic strategy for playing on grass is the serve & volley system. But some of the players as Rosewall, Borg, Connors, Agassi, later Lleyton Hewitt, Federer and Nadal where able to mix it up and succeed from the baseline too. A good return is very important too. It does not have to be hard but must stay low.

On grass it is a sin not to go to the net after a good serve! But it is essential that the server succeeds in executing the first volley! That is what I observed watching the best players. If they could not put away the first volley they held the opponent back with it and opened up the rally. They placed the volley close to a line and put away the next shot with a volley or overhead. In other words: the first volley must be handled in such a way that the opponent cannot strike a passing shot. The opponent must be kept off balance or out of time to move and backswing comfortably. Usually he manages to hit a higher ball that is easy to finish off.

The second principle is to hit the first serve in. It does not need to be an "ace"; as long as it sits in at least like the second serve even the best of returners will have a hard time putting it away. And if a receiver takes a risky shot the percentage of unforced errors will be high. I was never a great server and always doubted my success in comparison to Smith's or Ashe's ...

What did I need to do in such instance? Who was my role model? Ken Rosewall! He was half-a-head shorter than everyone else and yet he beat them. Why? Because his serve was deep and well placed. His serve was not very fast but it allowed him to make his way to the net and win his points with volleys. In addition he had great returns and managed to win opponents' serving games.

Based on these principles I developed my own grass court game. My return was good enough and I knew I could torment some opponents with it. The foundation of my game, however, had to depend on winning my serve." I'll win my serve as long as I place it well, even if it is not hit very hard. The main focus for improvement is my volley." And I achieved that thanks to my workouts on asphalt and later mateflex in Sparta.

WIMBLEDON VICTORY 1973

A week before Wimbledon a scandal with Pilic broke out in full force. It was a culmination of the world tennis organization's crisis, which had been lingering for some time. Since 1968, when gates of world tennis tournaments were opened also to professional players, the International Tennis Federation (ITF) faced problems with unions representing the interests of the players.

The strongest dispute flared up in the middle of 1973. Seeded Yugoslavia lost a Davis Cup match to New Zealand at Zagreb and Nikki Pilic, who refused to compete was fined by the Yugoslav tennis association with a nine months long play suspension penalty, which was announced at the start of the French Open. Pilic appealed the decision and ITF lowered the penalty to one month, however Wimbledon took place during that month. ATP board of directors than said that they had not alternative but to carry out their threat of a boycott unless Wimbledon allowed Pilic to compete. The independent Wimbledon All England Lawn Tennis Club stood by ITF decision, denied Pilic the entry and the ATP threatened to boycott.

It is my opinion that majority of players considered the issue as pointless thinking "who cares about Pilic and the Yugoslav Tennis Association?" ATP inflated the controversy further and one week before Wimbledon, during the Queen's Club tournament, the feud reached a boiling point. Jack Kramer and Donald Dell represented the players and threatened the ITF and the governing body of the All England Club with a boycott of over seventy players. Nevertheless, the organizers held their ground.

Many people felt that the situation could have been saved. If it was a battle for the control of the game, it was also a battle in which both the contending sides shared great many common interests. Wimbledon, as the most prestigious tournament in history, and the All England Lawn Tennis Club as its organizer, held tremendous influence over the course of world tennis. They hoped that members of ATP would support the tournament, but if they decided against that, the Champioships would still go on. However, the ATP, against a mounting wave of criticism, decided to continue the boycott. Later the crowd was the second biggest in the Championships history, and the British triumphantly made the best of a bad job.

The original list of seeded players was as follow:

Smith, Nastase, Newcombe, Ashe, Rosewall, Okker, Riessen, Emerson, Gorman, Richey, Panatta, Orantes, Alexander, Lutz, Kodes and Taylor.

"When this issue was under scrutiny during the week before Wimbledon began ATP representatives inquired among all players whether they would or would not play.

I was not an ATP member and neither were Nastase, Metreveli, Borg, or Connors. At that time the ATP was still in diapers - a motley organization that needed time to solidify. I do not know if players, who refused to play, later regretted their decision but it is obvious that the ATP with its actions impressed the international functionary body for the times to come. Even today, when something pops-up in tennis world, they are still able to pull out Pilic scandal with a threatening tone. It became a precedent for dealing with player frictions.

I was surprised that even some professionals turned down playing Wimbledon that year in spite of the fact that they weren't ATP members. For instance Rosewall, an older player then, and three times a finalist; I do not understand till today who managed to influence him so much that he refused to play. But, according to the Grand Prix point standings out of top 15 just prior the tournament were Newcombe, Smith, Pilic, Panatta, Okker, Gorman and Orantes, who supported the boycott.

When it was definite that an agreement would not be reached the organizers had to alter the seeding to eight players only: Nastase, Kodes, Taylor, Metreveli, Connors, Borg, Davidson, Fassbender.

I did not get emotionally involved in the turmoil of the issue and until the draw was made public I did not know who was in nor who was out. The remaining players were still strong and there were some excellent grass court specialists particularly the Indians. I was convinced that I should not choose not to boycott Wimbledon! Nastase thought similarly, Taylor was told that unless he shows up on the court the British would expel him from the club. They put it to him straight and plainly. For the Americans it was simple: "We, ATP members, can pick and choose tournaments we want to enter."

The controversy lingered in my mind: "Newcombe is not playing and that is his decision. I defeated him on grass already at Forest Hills and in Rome on clay. Rosewall, who I beat three months previously in Vancouver, will not play. In the last couple of years I did beat Ashe and also on grass. I overcame Laver in Stockholm, Okker and Riessen on the WCT indoor circuit. Why should I not beat them also in Wimbledon?" Laver chose not to enter regardless the boycott. And Smith? I could beat him last year, why not this year.

I considered that Wimbledon as any other tournament. There was nothing else I could do. Yet, many people asked me: "So, how many players actually entered it?" I answered: "As usual – 128! The same as any other Grand Slam tournament."

Jan Kodes had to win seven matches, all in three out of five sets, before he could raise the Wimbledon Trophy above his head. Those matches were far from easy. He could not take a rest in between side changeovers sitting down because there were no chairs. Wimbledon chairs appeared following year 1974!

The London spectators were wonderful! In spite of the absence of the biggest stars they supported "their" tournament spontaneously and came in record numbers almost daily. When Nastase entered the centre court to play the opening match as a number one seed the audience welcomed him with standing ovation. They repeated the same when their own favorite, Roger Taylor, came out to play. It was a common belief that the final match would be between these two players. But, there was still Jan Kodes....

I was seeded as number two. That gave me plenty of responsibility to deliver a fine performance. The previous year I reached the semifinals and I contemplated; that I could reach that far again?! I experienced something similar in Paris, when I won, and in subsequent years I was seeded as number one.

First round – Ken-Lchi Hirai from Japan.

As we were entering the court I entertained a thought "perhaps this is one of the qualifiers". I served first and twice followed the serve to the net; he passed me down one line, then the other, and before I knew it he broke my serve. I tried to get back on serve but could not do it. He was good and had excellent footwork. I lost the first set 6:4!

It shook me up; I did not anticipate much resistance! I had to work very hard to win in four sets 4:6, 6:4, 6:1, 6:3.

Second round – Pietro Marzano from Italy.

A doubles player, used to play Davis Cup for Italy, good serve and volley, not very good return. I was not afraid of him and beat him in straight sets 6:0, 6:4, 6:3. In the next round I faced a South African John Yuill who had defeated two local champs Warboys and Curtis; I eliminated him again in straight sets 6:1, 7:5, 6:2. The second set was a struggle!

In the following round it proved very helpful for Kodes to have spent some time in India. It was there he met and played an excellent pair of players and doubles partners Lall – Mukerjea, thanks to whom India often won East Asian zone of Davis Cup. It was the latter who met Jan in Wimbledon among the last sixteen and it attested to be a very tough match.

I had to work like a horse to win 6:4, 3:6, 6:4, and 6:3. We played on court number 6, I trust, but the level of the game was of championship match quality!

That day, when Kodes finished off Jaidip Mukerjea, Wimbledon experienced a big surprise. Court number 2 was jumping with excitement; it was jammed with people and every so often there were explosive reactions similar to football audiences. While lying on a massage table I inquired: "What is going on there?"

Event 1.—THE GENTLEMEN'S SINGLES CHAMPIONSHIP

Holder: S. R. SMITH

The Winner will become the holder, for the year only, of the CHALLENGE CUP presented to the club by KING GEORGE V, and also of the CHALLENGE CUP presented by The All England Lawn Tennis and Croquet Club. The First Prize is a piece of silver, known as "The Renshaw Cup" annually presented to the Club by the surviving members of the family of the late ERNEST and WILLIAM RENSHAW. Details of Prize Money will be found on page 37. The Winner will receive silver replicas of the two Challenge Cups. A Silver Medal will be presented to the Runner-up and a Bronze Medal to each defeated Semi-finalist.

FIRST ROUND

1	I. Nastase ①	(RU.)
2	H. J. Plotz	(G.)
3	I. Molina	(COL.)
4	W. L. Brown	(U.S.A.)
5	P. Siviter	(G.B.)
6	H. Kary	(AU.)
7	T. Sakai	(J.)
8	K. McMillan	(U.S.A.)
9	I. Santeiu	(RU.)
10	R. Chavez	(M.)
11	A. Mayer	(U.S.A.)
12	R. A. Lewis	(G.B.)
13	S. G. Messmer	(U.S.A.)
14	C. Iles	(G.B.)
15	G. Misra	(IN.)
16	V. Zednik	(CZ.)
17	J. Fassbender ⑧	(G.)
18	I. Gulyas	(HU.)
19	J. Moreno	(SP.)
20	M. W. Collins	(G.B.)
21	R. F. Keldie	(A.)
22	R. L. Bohrnstedt	(U.S.A.)
23	F. Gebert	(SW.)
24	T. Svensson	(SW.)
25	N. Pietrangeli	(IT.)
26	J. G. Simpson	(N.Z.)
27	N. A. Fraser	(A.)
28	J. Hagey	(U.S.A.)
29	J. G. Paish	(G.B.)
30	M. Lara	(M.)
31	C. E. McHugo	(G.B.)
32	H. J. Pohmann	(G.)
33	A. Metreveli ④	(U.S.S.R.)
34	S. J. Matthews	(G.B.)
35	R. G. Giltinan	(A.)
36	R. Machan	(HU.)
37	G. Braun	(A.)
38	A. J. McDonald	(A.)
39	J. R. Cooper	(A.)
40	H. S. FitzGibbon	(U.S.A.)
41	F. P. Walthall	(U.S.A.)
42	T. Nowicki	(POL.)
43	C. Mukerjea	(IN.)
44	H. Engert	(G.)
45	E. L. Scott	(U.S.A.)
46	J. W. Feaver	(G.B.)
47	C. L. Letcher	(A.)
48	R. H. Stock	(U.S.A.)
49	J. S. Connors ⑤	(U.S.A.)
50	M. J. Farrell	(G.B.)
51	D. A. Lloyd	(G.B.)
52	C. Barazzutti	(IT.)
53	S. Likhachev	(U.S.S.R.)
54	W. R. Durham	(A.)
55	T. B. Karp	(U.S.A.)
56	R. J. Simpson	(N.Z.)
57	J. G. Clifton	(G.B.)
58	J. R. Pinto Bravo	(CH.)
59	C. Dowdeswell	(RH.)
60	D. Joubert	(S.A.)
61	T. Bernasconi	(F.)
62	B. Mitton	(S.A.)
63	J. Hordijk	(NTH.)
64	Z. Guerry	(A.)
65	B. Jovanovic	(YU.)
66	S. Ball	(A.)
67	J. L. Rouyer	(F.)
68	S. Baranyi	(HU.)
69	K. Tanabe	(J.)
70	P. Kanderal	(SWZ.)
71	T. Kakulia	(U.S.S.R.)
72	W. J. Austin	(U.S.A.)
73	G. Peebles	(U.S.A.)
74	K. Meiler	(G.)
75	J. Singh	(IN.)
76	B. Martin	(A.)
77	P. Hombergen	(A.)
78	S. E. Myers	(A.)
79	P. Lall	(IN.)
80	B. Borg ⑥	(SW.)
81	F. Pala	(CZ.)
82	D. J. Bleckinger	(U.S.A.)
83	D. T. Crawford	(U.S.A.)
84	N. Holmes	(U.S.A.)
85	R. E. McKinley	(U.S.A.)
86	P. F. McNamee	(A.)
87	E. Russo	(A.)
88	J. Kuki	(J.)
89	J. Hrebec	(CZ.)
90	F. A. Sedgman	(A.)
91	A. Zugarelli	(IT.)
92	D. Stojovic	(YU.)
93	J. W. James	(A.)
94	H. Elschenbroich	(G.)
95	J. L. Haillet	(F.)
96	R. Taylor ③	(G.B.)
97	J. M. Lloyd	(G.B.)
98	J. F. Caujolle	(F.)
99	P. C. Kronk	(A.)
100	K. N. Hancock	(A.)
101	B. Mignot	(A.)
102	P. Pokorny	(AU.)
103	V. Amritraj	(IN.)
104	H. W. Turnbull	(A.)
105	K. Pugaev	(U.S.S.R.)
106	E. W. Ewert	(A.)
107	M. Machette	(U.S.A.)
108	D. A. Parun	(N.Z.)
109	B. J. Phillips-Moore	(A.)
110	R. W. Drysdale	(G.B.)
111	P. Joly	(F.)
112	O. K. Davidson ⑦	(A.)
113	A. Amritraj	(IN.)
114	S. S. Meer	(P.)
115	J. Mukerjea	(IN.)
116	E. A. Zuleta	(E.)
117	R. A. Buwalda	(S.A.)
118	M. Iqbal	(P.)
119	G. W. Perkins	(A.)
120	J. Kamiwazumi	(J.)
121	S. A. Warboys	(G.B.)
122	J. Yuill	(S.A.)
123	P. W. Curtis	(G.B.)
124	G. S. Thomson	(G.B.)
125	P. Marzano	(IT.)
126	R. Ramirez	(M.)
127	K. Hirai	(J.)
128	J. Kodes ②	(CZ.)

SECOND ROUND

- I. Nastase ① 6-3 7-5 6-2
- I. Molina 6-4 9-7 8-9 6-3
- H. Kary 6-4 7-9 6-1 6-2
- T. Sakai 6-1 3-6 9-8 6-4
- R. Chavez 5-7 4-6 6-4 7-5 7-5
- A. Mayer 7-5 6-4 6-3
- C. Iles 7-5 6-2 6-4
- V. Zednik 6-4 6-4 6-1
- J. Fassbender ⑧ 8-6 6-8 6-3 6-3
- J. Moreno 6-4 6-3 6-3
- R. F. Keldie 7-5 6-4 3-6 6-3
- T. Svensson 6-8 9-8 7-5 9-7
- J. G. Simpson 8-6 2-6 3-6 7-5
- J. Hagey 6-4 7-5 8-6
- M. Lara 5-7 6-4 7-5 6-2
- H. J. Pohmann 6-3 6-4 6-4
- A. Metreveli ④ 6-3 6-4 9-8
- R. G. Giltinan 6-3 6-4 6-3
- A. J. McDonald 6-4 6-4 6-2
- J. R. Cooper 6-3 8-9 6-3 9-7
- F. P. Walthall 4-3 6-6 6-8 6-3 6-2
- C. Mukerjea 6-4 7-5 8-9 6-4
- J. W. Feaver 8-9 6-3 6-8 6-4 6-4
- C. L. Letcher 5-7 6-4 6-3 6-1
- J. S. Connors ⑤ 6-4 6-4
- D. A. Lloyd 6-2 0-6 6-1 6-1
- W. R. Durham 6-3 6-4 3-6 6-4
- R. J. Simpson 6-4 8-6 6-0
- J. R. Pinto Bravo 6-4 3-6 2-6 6-4 6-8
- D. Joubert 6-3 4-6 6-4 7-5
- B. Mitton 8-6 6-1 6-3
- Z. Guerry 9-7 6-2 6-2
- S. Ball 7-5 8-6 6-3
- S. Baranyi 6-0 6-2 6-2
- P. Kanderal 6-4 6-3 6-4
- W. J. Austin 3-6 4-6 6-3 6-0 6-4
- K. Meiler 9-7 6-4 6-2
- B. Martin 6-3 9-7 2-6 6-3
- P. Hombergen 6-3 6-3 6-1
- B. Borg ⑥ 6-3 6-4 9-8
- F. Pala 6-3 1-6 6-3 7-5
- N. Holmes 6-4 6-2 6-4
- R. E. McKinley 6-4 6-1 6-0
- J. Kuki 1-6 6-2 8-9 6-4 9-7
- J. Hrebec 6-0 6-4 7-5
- A. Zugarelli 6-3 6-2 6-4
- H. Elschenbroich 5-7 6-2 3-6 8-6 6-2
- R. Taylor ③ 6-2 6-3 6-3
- J. M. Lloyd 8-9 4-6 6-3 6-4 6-3
- K. N. Hancock 7-5 6-4 3-6 6-4
- B. Mignot 6-1 6-1 6-3
- V. Amritraj 6-4 6-2 6-4
- E. W. Ewert 3-6 6-1 7-5 9-8
- M. Machette 3-6 6-4 6-3 6-1
- B. J. Phillips-Moore 6-3 9-7 7-5
- O. K. Davidson ⑦ 6-4 6-4
- A. Amritraj 6-4 6-4 9-8
- J. Mukerjea 7-5 6-1 6-3
- R. A. Buwalda 5-7 6-3 6-2 6-4
- G. W. Perkins 6-4 6-4 3-6 9-7
- J. Yuill 6-2 4-6 9-7 4-6
- P. W. Curtis 6-4 6-4 6-2
- P. Marzano 6-3 6-4 2-6 6-2
- J. Kodes ② 4-6 6-4 6-1 6-3

THIRD ROUND

- I. Nastase ① 6-2 7-9 7-5 6-1
- T. Sakai 6-1 6-3 3-6 6-3
- A. Mayer 7-9 6-1 9-7 6-2
- V. Zednik 6-3 6-3 4-6 6-2
- J. Fassbender ⑧ 6-3 6-4 6-4
- R. F. Keldie 8-9 6-0 6-4
- J. G. Simpson 8-6 6-4 8-9 6-3
- H. J. Pohmann 2-6 7-5 2-6 6-1 7-5
- A. Metreveli ④ 6-4 6-2 7-5
- J. R. Cooper 6-4 4-6 4-6 7-5 9-7
- F. P. Walthall 3-6 6-1 6-1 9-8
- J. W. Feaver 9-8 6-4 9-8
- J. S. Connors ⑤ 6-4 6-3 5-7 6-2
- R. J. Simpson 9-8 7-9 7-5 3-6 6-2
- D. Joubert 4-6 6-2 6-2 2-6 6-3
- B. Mitton 7-5 2-6 4-6 7-5 7-5
- S. Baranyi 1-0 ret.
- W. J. Austin 9-8 6-3 6-3
- K. Meiler 6-1 6-4 9-8
- B. Borg ⑥ 6-4 6-2 6-4
- N. Holmes 8-6 2-6 6-0 1-6 7-5
- R. E. McKinley 6-4 3-6 6-2 6-2
- J. Hrebec 7-5 1-6 4-6 7-5 6-2
- R. Taylor ③ 6-3 6-2 6-2
- J. M. Lloyd 7-5 6-4 6-4
- V. Amritraj 6-1 6-1 6-2
- E. W. Ewert 7-5 6-2 6-3
- O. K. Davidson ⑦ 6-3 6-4 6-3
- J. Mukerjea 3-6 6-3 6-2 6-4
- G. W. Perkins 4-6 6-3 3-6 6-1 10-8
- J. Yuill 4-6 6-3 1-6 6-2 6-3
- J. Kodes ② 6-0 6-4 6-3

FOURTH ROUND

- I. Nastase ① 7-5 6-2 6-4
- A. Mayer 8-6 7-5 6-0
- J. Fassbender ⑧ 6-2 5-7 4-6 7-5 15-13
- H. J. Pohmann 4-6 7-5 6-3 6-4
- A. Metreveli ④ 6-2 6-3 6-1
- J. W. Feaver 7-5 6-1 9-8
- J. S. Connors ⑤ 6-2 6-1 6-2
- B. Mitton 4-6 8-9 6-4 6-1 9-7
- S. Baranyi 2-6 5-7 6-3 6-4 6-4
- B. Borg ⑥ 6-4 6-4 3-6 2-6 6-3
- R. E. McKinley 6-2 3-6 7-5 7-5
- R. Taylor ③ 6-1 5-7 6-4 6-2
- V. Amritraj 7-5 6-4 3-6 2-6 7-5
- O. K. Davidson ⑦ 6-1 6-4 3-6 6-3
- J. Mukerjea 9-8 6-4 6-3
- J. Kodes ② 6-1 7-5 6-2

FIFTH ROUND

- A. Mayer 6-4 8-6 6-8 6-4
- J. Fassbender ⑧ 6-2 7-5 6-3
- A. Metreveli ④ 8-6 6-4 6-1
- J. S. Connors ⑤ 6-3 6-3 6-2
- B. Borg ⑥ 6-3 6-2 6-8 5-7 6-1
- R. Taylor ③ 6-1 7-5 6-8 7-5
- V. Amritraj 7-5 8-9 6-3 6-4
- J. Kodes ② 6-4 3-6 4-6 6-3

SEMI-FINAL

- A. Mayer 3-6 4-6 6-3 6-4 6-4
- A. Metreveli ④ 8-6 6-2 5-7 6-4
- R. Taylor ③ 6-1 6-8 3-6 6-3 7-5
- J. Kodes ② 6-4 3-6 4-6 6-3 7-5

FINAL

- A. Metreveli ④ 6-3 3-6 6-3 6-4
- J. Kodes ② 8-9 9-7 5-7 6-4 7-5

Winner: J. KODES ② 6-1 9-8 6-3

Heavy type denotes seeded players. The encircled figure against names denotes the order in which they have been seeded. The Matches will be the best of Five Advantage Sets. For particulars of Abbreviations see page 11.

13

"Nastase is having a hard time with Alex Mayer" the masseur quickly responded. "He has Mayer? I didn't know that!" At that moment I had a vision of the messed up volley a year previously at Forest Hills.

At tournaments of this caliber one paid attention to himself above all, not to others. I looked at the draw to see who I played in the first round, maybe I looked to see who I might play in the second. Who was playing in the other half of the draw did not interest me at all. After my match I laid in the tub in the locker room for good 20 minutes in warm water and some pleasant salts soothing the tired muscles and I was contemplating who I would prefer playing against – Nastase or Mayer?

Very soon Nastase walked into the locker room. He was worn out, quiet, he had lost in four sets. The previous year he needed only two more points to defeat Smith in the finals, this year he was the hottest favorite. He won Paris, Rome, and he was at the top of Grand Prix.

"Does anybody know Vijay Amritraj?" I asked the next day in the players' restaurant. Silence followed my question. Nobody knew anything about him until his compatriot Mukerjea spoke up: "He is young, plays well but he is still clueless. Even though he has good strokes, you don't need to be concerned, he is only a rookie." That quieted my anxiety.

I went to scout out my next opponent. Vijay played on court number one with the 8th seeded Australian Owen Davidson. Owen was a semifinalist here in 1966 after delivering a surprise defeat to number one seed Roy Emerson. Amritraj conquered Owen after an amazing battle. Vijay had unbelievable strokes, beautifully straight, pounded, not with much topspin. He hit the ball early which sped up the velocity. He mastered the true "grass" game and thus became a very dangerous opponent.

The remaining quarterfinalists were Taylor-Borg, Connors-Metreveli and Fassbender-Mayer. If I would win I would face the winner of Taylor-Borg.

They put us on court number one. It was faster than Centre Court, abnormally hard; I did not favor playing there. Today it does not resemble the court it was then... From the first point I knew this was going to be a hard battle. His return was superb and his serve very unpleasant, hard, flat, and it barely bounced up. More importantly, it was obvious he knew how to play on grass!

We played in gruesome heat. I won the first set 6:1 in eighteen minutes! In the second set I was ahead 2:1, and it seemed it was going to be as easy as the first set. But, after two superb returns the Indian evened the score 2:2. And slowly he took over dictating the match. He won the second and third sets and in the forth he pulled out unbelievable passing shots. He was in his element and impossible to break.

We went after each other's serve. I hit two excellent volleys but he struck a line from a totally impossible position! I started to doubt my chances, however I did manage to break one of his serves and with that I won the fourth set.

The fifth and last set was upon us! When I walked up to start the first game of that set it flashed through my mind that the outcome will reflect our physical and mental strength. Each kept winning his serve but I was the one trailing. The Indian gave an impression of confidence and his serve was terrific. At 4:5 on my serve and 15:30 I was two points from elimi-

Roger Taylor was happy to get to his third Wimbledon semifinal by beating Björn Borg 6:1, 6:8, 3:6, 6:3, 7:5.

nation! But I kept telling myself, "he will make a mistake, he is only a rookie" as Mukerjea had suggested.

That way of thinking is common among tennis players. They hope that younger players will fold in the drama of the culminating game or in the tie-break.

I knew then what Jaroslav Drobny had hammered into my head: "Alternate serving from backhand to forehand and into the body. If you try to hit it stereotypically into the same spot you'll be doomed." So, my serve zoomed perfectly into the body. Nevertheless, he must have anticipated it and he returned it with a backhand underspin directly at me, barely clearing the net and under my feet. I had only one choice: half-volley deep into his court and then a drop shot! He took off after my drop shot, I charged towards him in case that he would lift the ball because then I could put it away. Unexpectedly, he played a very good lob! I scrambled back and had no other way of hitting the ball than popping it up tremendously high. I lifted the ball as high up as I could. However, though the ball was high it landed short. It was dropping right around the service line. Amritraj wanted to put it away from the air and did not let the ball bounce. It

Jimmy Connors lost in the quarter-finals to Metreveli but won doubles teamed up with Nastase. By the end of 1973 he reached #1 US National rank along with Stan Smith.

was shortly after mid-day, the ball was very high in the air and the sun was right above our heads. He framed the ball and whacked it directly into the audience!

After the match was over I contemplated that point; if he had let it bounce "I would have gotten roasted!" Most likely, he was afraid to let it bounce since one can never predict the height and direction of the bounce on grass. He was confident! He was a great overhead hitter but, I believe, in that instant, he was a bit cocky and overconfident.

Even though it took eleven points Jan Kodes won that game at long last! The match was tied at 5:5; in the next game Jan had a break point.

Vijay served into my backhand; I had it lined up to hit down the line when I realized I was in trouble! My difficult ankle let me know that it was not feeling very well. I had sprained it a bit but I still made an effective passing shot by the Indian. Now I was 6:5 up and serving for the match. I won my serve and the match 7:5 in the fifth!

The ankle hurt. When Kodes came into the locker room he applied an icepack to it. He mentioned it during the press conference. The journalists picked up on it but did not know anything about the after-effects. He returned to the locker room and indulged himself to soaking in the tub.

Vijay Armitraj had unreal returns, especially down-the-line, and his first volleys were very effective.

About an hour later the phone rang. "Mr. Kodes, we are listening to the radio and we hear from BBC that you sprained your ankle. We have a machine called Diapolse available. If you would let us we'll take care of your injury and we guarantee that you'll be as good as new."

This player had a day of rest ahead of him so he agreed.

"OK, we'll come; just arrange that they'll let us enter the complex."

Conservative Wimbledon will not allow just anybody enter its viscera.

There were difficulties in arranging it but I succeeded in bringing the Diapolse people in. They came and placed my ankle in between two plates, from which a huddle of cables ran to something that epitomized a suitcase. How this "magic" worked I have no idea. Perhaps it worked on the principle of an ultrasound; at any rate, my ankle did not swell much, only slightly.

That night I bandaged my ankle and the following day I visited them in London. I went through the same procedure again and I must admit that those gentlemen did not lie; their treatment really helped me.

Roger Taylor became a national hero in 1970 when he beat Rod Laver and Clark Graebner to enter his second semifinal. As in 1967 against Wilhelm Bungert he led 2 sets to 1, losing to Jan Kodes in the gruelling semi-final 9:8, 7: 9, 7:5, 4:6 and 5:7.

Ilie Nastase lost his second chance by losing to American Alex Mayer in the forth round. In previous year 1972 (picture) he reached the finals, but was beaten by Stan Smith in five sets.

Roger Taylor, a member of the All England Lawn Tennis Club and a darling of the home audience, was ready for me in the semifinals. He was twice the semifinalist at Wimbledon, in 1967 and 1970. He even beat Rod Laver in the fourth round in 1970! He was a clear favorite in the eyes of the British public. He defeated Borg in a fantastic quarterfinal match, 7:5 in the fifth. Granted, Borg had had two five-set conquests in his legs from the previous rounds ...

Mayer outplayed Fassbender also in five sets, in spite of being down 2:1 in sets! To the surprise of most, Metreveli passed by Connors fairly easily.

It did not surprise me! It seemed to me that Connors lost mainly due to his inexperience. Though he was considerably younger, he was a better player and had already won several WCT tournaments. As I had mentioned, a half-a-year or a year of competitive play makes a significant difference in accomplishments of a tennis player. A year later Connors won Wimbledon, beating me in five sets in the quarter-finals.

Bjorn Borg made a big leap too; he triumphed at Roland Garros. I admit that I lucked out a bit by reaching my tennis ca-

reer peak just before this next generation of brilliant players penetrated into the forefront. Two years later I would not have stood a chance.

Semifinals, Kodes – Taylor! This was an opportunity since the era of Fred Perry that another Briton will win Wimbledon, at last!

I did not feel anything even remotely pleasant; there was tremendous pressure on me; all were against me. We played the second match on Centre Court, after Metreveli – Mayer. I did not watch their dual and was surprised that Metreveli won quite easily.

I knew I had a tough match ahead of me. Taylor, Metreveli, and Mayer were players who beat me in the past. In addition, I was concerned about the umpiring, remembering a bad call in the match against Smith the year before; if it happened last year, it can happen this year again.... And more so, since I am playing the local favorite on his home turf.

It was an amazing battle! Roger was a lefthander, which did not bother me that much on grass. From the deuce side he served into my body, from the "ad" side he served the ball away from me and that suited me well since my backhand return was my strong weapon. I was more bothered by righthanders' serves from the deuce side. I managed to return their serve but they pulled me out of the court so much that I left most of it opened. Taylor was one of those players who served the entire match with the same pace and was able to easily change direction without forecasting the target.

Most players "take a break" from serving well consistently. Ivanisevic, for instance, served like God at one moment and then, all of a sudden, was able to doublefault three times in a row. Not Taylor. He hit serve after serve evenly like a blacksmith hammers into an anvil, and, more importantly, really well. Deep, hard, into the body...

I was looking for somebody to warm up with before the match, preferably a lefthander! I searched in the locker room but found nobody. From my compatriots I would have considered Frantisek Pala, but he had lost in the second round and was gone. I must find an Englishman then!

The one who seeks also finds. An good British player John Paish had lost surprisingly in the first round. He had a great win the previous year over Stan Smith at Queens Club and his father played on the British Davis Cup team in the era of Jaroslav Drobny. I approached him with a plea that I needed to warm up against a lefthander, who would serve to me a few shots. It took him by surprise but he agreed to do it the next day.

We practiced, and I was very content; however, he seemed ill at ease. Then he blurted out: "Please, don't ever tell anybody that I warmed you up. Dad is a member of this club, he is on the board, and most likely he would not be able to swallow it. "

"Don't worry, I won't tell."

It has been more then thirty years now, his father was still among us and whenever we meet in London he doesn't fail to ask: "So, tell me, how was it then, when you beat Taylor? You warmed up with my son, didn't you?"

Oh well, those conservative Englishmen! Till today they consider it treason. I have no idea how the truth came out...

On grass my backhand was a very effective weapon.

Jan Kodes raises his right arm in acknowledgmen of the crowd's applause after his marathon semi final victory over (left) Britain's Roger Taylor.

Roger Taylor, a grass court specialist. An experienced player, who made his living playing in Hunt's professional group. He was 31 when he reached Wimbledon semifinals for the third time. The first time he lost in five sets to a German Bungert in 1967; the second time, three years later, he lost to Rosewall in four but he had beaten Rod Laver in the forth round! And in 1973 he was facing a clay court player Kodes.

All Britons, including Taylor himself, believed they would be represented in the finals.

We greeted each other in the locker room, both of us visibly nervous, both of us already on the Centre Court in thought. We both understood the weight of the occasion.

On the way to the court I kept reminding myself "Focus on your play; you must win your serve! Accept the fact that you can't win his serve! If the set reaches the final stages you can make some risky moves and, perhaps, you'll succeed in breaking his serve. The main thing is to hold your own!"

I was serving well and my volleys were effective. Fundamentally I played well and I knew that the outcome would come down to either our physical condition or mental strength!

They battled for every point and every serve. The first hour passed and they were still in the first set: 5:5, 6:6, 7:7, 8:8. Then a tiebreak! It was introduced to Wimbledon for the first time in 1971. However, Wimbledon is Wimbledon, and the committee from the All England Lawn Tennis Club demanded that it be played not at 6:6, but rather at 8:8.

In the tie-break Kodes had the second opportunity to turn the important first set in his favor. He lost the first chance at 5:4. Now he had a set-point on Taylor's serve. He was returning brilliantly all set long but it failed him in the decisive moments, (and he lost the set).

At the end of the second set, however, he did not waiver, and tied the match. In the third he was up 3:1, and 4:2. But then, a crisis. He started arriving too late to the net after his serve, his volleys lost their bite and effectiveness. He literally donated the third set to Taylor at the moment when he seemed to have almost won it!

What caused it? In a flash, he remembered his semifinal match from the year before against Stan Smith, He was ahead with the same game score but lost his serve, and then the set, and finally the match!?

This time, thank God, he lost only a set. Although, in the back of his mind, he thought he had just solidified his own doom. Yet, he soon assured himself that all was not yet lost. While Taylor needed only one more set to win the match Jan knew that nothing was final before the last point was over. He started taking risky shots and it paid off; he grabbed the fourth set.

The last and decisive set was similar to the previous sets: 1:1, 2:2, 3:3, 4:4.

At around 6:30 in the evening it started to drizzle. It was not raining but there was plenty of moisture in the air. The court got wet, both of us had a tumble, conditions became dangerous. The referee captain Mike Gibson, was checking the sky with concern; it looked like he was going to suspend further play when he urged Taylor to go on serving! The ball passed the net twenty seven times during that game; two times I had a break point but each time Taylor pulled out an excellent serve and the score went back to deuce. We both began to be tired of it.

The tournament referee captain Mike Gibson.

At 4:5 we changed sides and all of a sudden the chief umpire Gibson was down on the court checking: "is it slippery, or not?" The crowd started to whistle because they did not want the match to be suspended. However, Mike Gibson stood his ground and pronounced the court too wet to continue.

A break! I don't know if I was pleased or displeased that we got a break. I accepted the decision as it was and made my way to the locker room. There I jumped quickly into the tub with hot water and thought we would not continue until the following day. However, the chief umpire's assistant walked in and told us that the play would resume in 15 minutes. I knew that it is imperative for me not to stiffen up. I asked the masseur to massage Ben-Gay into my legs. Then I realized that I would start serving to stay in the match. "That is one of the worst ordeals! I often opt to receive if I win the toss at the beginning of a match because if I play good returns I can throw off my opponent and frequently I even win my opponent's serve." But this time I had no other choice.

Our chief Czechoslovak official, Ivan Lichner, was in the locker room with me. He made a comment with regard to my serve: "You are serving well from the deuce court pulling Taylor out of the court on his backhand side." "However, he is slicing a low return into my forehand and it is landing so low that I have difficulties scooping it down the line into the other side of his court", I responded." Taylor moves well, runs balls down and often scores with his devastating forehand."

"Jan, the first point back on the court will be crucial! Try to hit the first volley back to his backhand." I applied this during the match on several occasions but it was good to be reminded of it again by Ivan Lichner. I had a tendency to come a bit late to the net in the fifth set.

The break lasted about thirty minutes. It took four minutes to warm up. Kodes served. 15:0. It was risky but it worked 100 percent! I went for the volley ahead of time; I anticipated it and hit it perfectly crosscourt as Lichner had wanted! I held serve to tie the match and regained my confi dence. At 5:5 Taylor missed two low volleys, and I scored with a great return. His serve no longer had a sting; he played "just to get it in".

I hoped that he had stiffened more than I did and I tried to return his serve no matter what! He played a drop shot on my game point; I hustled to the ball and momentarily did not know where to place it. I felt the blood pumping in my temples and I just whacked the ball right into his body! I had no other choice if I wanted to make sure that I secured the point! He tried to get out of the way but the ball hit him in his side-hip. People started to drone but one has to focus on winning in such a situation. I know he understood and did not take it the wrong way.

I broke his serve and took the lead 6:5. Dusk was setting in and it was hard to see; I was worried but my serve did not fail me.

The first two match points in the twelfth game of the fifth set Taylor hit two brilliant passing shots; the score went back to deuce. I played my subsequent volleys with care not to botch them. Then, a let ball gave me one point! Taylor's last backhand return landed just outside the sideline. He had realized that I was anticipating his crosscourt returns and he changed his mind at the last moment to hit it down the line. He missed: 8:9, 9:7, 5:7, 6:4, and 7:5! After three hours and thirty minutes the Wimbledon final became a reality for me!

Soviet player, born Georgian Alex Metreveli gained prominence open era, beating Pancho Gonzales, Wimbledon 1968. Then he won several grass court events in Australia from 1969 till1972. Reached two Grand Slam semifinals: 1972 Australian and French Open and Wimbledon quarter-finals:1972-74.

Alex Metreveli overplayed Jimmy Connors and Ilie Nastase´s conqueror American Alex Mayer to play the 1973 Wimbledon Singles final. Lost to Jan Kodes.

WITH A RACKET

There were sixty-seven games; each point played meticulously and in tense atmosphere. I was totally exhausted, my heart throbbed. The hot tub after the match – how I remember that!

The Kodes – Taylor match was a culmination of world class tennis. It was a three and a half hour long epic, battle of strokes, rackets and hearts, three and a half hours of drama and suspense. In that fascinating battle the spectators were exposed to all that a tennis game on grass has to offer: Booming ball serves, returns and devastating volleys on one hand, and on the other hand brilliantly executed strokes and delightful rallies. On the whole, Kodes proved to be a more complete player, better composed than Taylor.

Hans Fuchs, Austrian press

Dan Maskell was the voice of Wimbledon, BBC-TV commentator from 1951 to 1991, an excellent player and professional champion of Britain.

National mourning swayed over England, people started to speculate why the semifinal match was suspended. If that had not happened, Taylor would have won for sure! Others claimed the contrary; it was unfair toward Kodes because matches are suspended, on principle, at a tie score - in this case Taylor was up 5:4. It was suspended on purpose to hurt Kodes' chances!

The conservative English public took offense: "How could anybody believe that it was done on purpose?!" And, there were voices saying: "If that daft Gibson did not suspend the match, Taylor would have won. He is older and during the break he stiffened up more than Kodes did!"

I did not let these polemics rattle me. It was all the same to me.

The following day the British press was full of articles dissecting the reasons for the defeat of the home favorite and the thrilling semifinal match was analyzed game by game.

The British praised the match as one of the best Wimbledon has ever had a chance to witness and they quoted the historically highest number of spectators on Centre Court.

At the same time, an article popped up with the headlines announcing to the world: Two players from behind the Iron Curtain would meet in the finals of aristocratic Wimbledon!

...Kodes and Taylor had to leave the court arena for 28 minutes and it then took only 8 minutes for Taylor to loose a match that lasted more than three hours. Thirty-one years old Taylor was close to the Wimbledon final, where an Englishman would have appeared for the first time in thirty-five years, but it was five years his junior, Czechoslovak Jan Kodes, who advanced to the finals after more than three and a half hours...

...Metreveli defeated Nastase's conqueror and with that nothing stood in the way of historic and purely Eastern European final... Will a Russian, and at that a Georgian, take Wimbledon title for the first time?

...Kodes seemed more relaxed and agile, while Taylor appeared to be mainly a superb server... Kodes pulled out outstanding passing shots, especially in the fifth set when he became a menace in serve returns as well as in passing shots; Taylor kept up pace only thanks to his serve...

...Taylor was very close to victory, but the better player prevailed. Kodes was faster and more aggressive on grass, the surface he is thought to dislike...

...It is hard to imagine a more dramatic, exhausting, and spectacular semifinal match than the one between Taylor and Kodes. The break was not beneficial for Kodes either. He was down 4:5, though serving. The Czech player returned confident and nothing could derail him...

British press

Realization descended on me the next day. I grasped what was ahead of me. The finals of the most prestigious tournament in the world! Playing the finals of any tournament of consequence is still very different from playing the Wimbledon finals.

Metreveli made it known that he would have preferred meeting Taylor in the finals....

Many players prompted me: "Please, don't let the Russian win! That hasn't happened here yet!" I went to lunch and heard again: "I hope you won't let the Russian win!" I arrived for practice and a Polish Englishman, an emigrant and ex-player Mr. Spychala, who was in charge of scheduling play on practice courts and passing out balls, said: Jan, tomorrow I'll be rooting for you; you won't let a Russian win, will you?" I had to listen to this all day long!

I would have preferred playing against Newcombe or Smith. That would have been a real spectacle!

And then it struck me: "What do they say at home? In Prague? The 1968 invasion of Czechoslovakia was still a fresh wound in everyone's mind. The entire nation is following this development! What if I lose? People will say: Naturally, they ordered him to lose, he had to let him win. It is the same as with the hockey team! "

This was anything but an easy situation. In front of my eyes passed all my previous encounters with Metreveli - even unsettled accounts. The Davis Cup match in Moscow 1970 – after having won Roland Garros I lost. Immediately after that Metreveli defeated me in a five-set battle in the first round of Wimbledon. I was ahead 2:0 in the fifth set a year later in Prague during our Davis Cup scuffle and I lost again! Those were years 1970 and 1971. But I beat him in Rome, where I swept him off the court 6:3, 8:6, 6:4!.

We knew each other since our youth; he understood my weaknesses, and he read my facial expressions and recognized if I was nervous or not. And I was very familiar with him. Nevertheless, it was very clear to me that he was the best European grass court player.

"What am I going to play against him?" I asked that of myself over and over again until I put a stop to it and said: "Forget the clay court, and all those matches you ever played against him on clay! Think only and retrieve the memory of the games in which you faced him on grass or indoors." Those were only three encounters! Wimbledon in 1971 and two matches on WCT Indoor circuit in spring 1973. Yes, Cleveland 4:6,7:5, 6:3 and Vancouver 6:4,6:2 I won both and indoors on "supreme" rubber carpet!!

Such was my way of thinking that Friday, a day before the most significant final match of my life. I contemplated all odds, I practiced just 30 minutes and rested; I had a massage and tried to nurse my messed up ankle.

The evening before my final match they showed clips on television from the matches played in the last few days. There was Metreveli defeating Jimmy Connors and Alex Mayer, the winner over the Rumanian Nastase, and then they showed my match against Taylor. In the train of the clips Jack Kramer and Fred Perry made their commentaries. They talked with Dan Maskell, a former Davis Cup player in the era of our Kozeluh and afterwards a Wimbledon commentator for many years: "It is the first time in the history of this championship that two players from communist countries face off in the finals. Who will prevail?"

"If I were to put money down on anybody it would be Kodes,"said Fred Perry. "Why? Because he won Paris twice and he reached the finals on grass at Forest Hills. Metreveli will be nervous, he does not have much experience dealing with the pressures of a final match."

"I was Kodes'commentator in 1971 at Forest Hills, where he defeated Newcombe and Ashe," said Jack Kramer. "He has a dangerous serve return and his game on grass improved tremendously. He is a more complete tennis player now, after winning Roland Garros twice and he showed against Taylor that his serve is adequate."

These comments made me feel very good. I persuaded myself that if experts say that I am better, it must be so.

I went to bed around 10:30 pm. I called the reception and asked not to forward any calls to me since I did not want to be disturbed in the middle of the night or early in the morning. I put cotton wool in my ears and took half of an aspirin to warm my body through. I did all that in order to have a good rest before the finals.

In the morning the receptionist woke me up as I had requested and within a minute I had four phone calls! My friend, Franta Novak, told me: "I could not get hold of you!" Others asked: "What is going on with you? It is impossible to reach you!" I only blessed my fantastic foresight that I might get disturbed by phone calls. In real terms I found myself fitting a true "professional" with all that it entailed.

On the way to Wimbledon I realized that I had not asked anybody to warm me up. But it didn't disconcert me. Just making my way to the court struggling through the crowds will tire me out! Well, I'll have a massage done and warm up in the locker room. Inwardly I decided that I did not need the on-the-court warm up.

Upon my arrival I spotted Metreveli warming up on court number two! I panicked and was overwhelmed with a feeling that I should, indeed, warm up a little. I looked around and found no players in sight; they have already left. Damn it, who shall I hit with? At that moment the veterans finished some doubles and they came to the locker room all sweaty and tired out, among them Vic Seixas, a 1953 Wimbledon champion, By the way, Vic was one of the first individuals who came to me after the match with Taylor and told me how unfair was the suspension of play at 4:5; he did not remember anything of the sort ever taking place at Wimbledon before.

I approached him: "Vic, I am due to go on the court to play the finals in a few minutes but I have nobody to warm up with. I am a bit nervous and need just a few minutes to hit the balls back and forth. Would you pop up a few balls for me? Fifteen minutes, no more than that."

"You don't think that I could warm you up? I can't take that responsibility." He knew what it entailed to be in the finals and he was afraid he could not warm me up sufficiently.

"Vic, only a few minutes; you'll serve, I'll return in order to get the rhythm going!"

"But Jan, how can I warm you up?"

"Come on, we are both changed to play..."

I talked him into it, picked up balls and we went to court number two. I started a rally but he was unable to respond successfully. Poor guy was more nervous than I was! I needed only a few hits, a return, some serves, a few volleys, just to get the timing going...

We spent about twenty minutes on the court and as we were returning to the locker room he said: "I know this did not give you much but I hope that it helped you and you'll win the first set."

I took a shower, light massage and off I went to the Centre Court.

I was immensely grateful to Vic for those twenty minutes of warm up. He knew very well the meaning of what he said when he wished me good luck in the first set. On grass, success at the beginning of the match is terribly important. If I launch the set well my opponent will "miss the train". And that is exactly what happened! I won the first set 6:1. It was my return that determined it; down the line, under the feet. Whatever I touched resulted in great outcomes! On my serve I flew to the net like a lion to approach close to the net and execute volleys. All was going well.

Metreveli was anxious to say the least; his facial expressions told me that he was overcome by crisis. He was making faults on his first serves and I capitalized on that. I noticed this

Vic Seixas won important titles as 1953 Wimbledon over Dane Kurt Nielsen and 1954 US Championships at Forest Hills by beating Rex Hartwig.

Winning the second set tie-break, which at that time, was played at 8:8, was probably the most crucial moment of our contest...It is not well known, that it was historically the first ever tie-break played in a Wimbledon singles final!

"drowning" and I pulled out effective self-talk: "The more games you make now, before he crawls out of the slump, the better. I knew that his stumble could not go on for ever.

Metreveli recovered right at the beginning of the second set.

At 0:1 he played a beautiful volley drop shot and it made the stands roar. Up until that point the audience was neutral, as if they did not want to get involved in the development of the match. But when I later renewed my lead they seemed to side with me, which helped me very much.

Metreveli caught on with that drop shot volley. The match then swayed like a swing: 0:2, 2:2. 2:4. Twice we each won serve of the other. At 4:5 Metreveli even had a set point on Kodes' serve!

Should I serve into his forehand, or backhand? I decided to go for the third alternative – directly into his body. He could have returned it with his backhand but he lacked confidence in its success. He ran around it and played it with his forehand and failed.

The set continued to 8:8 and a tie-break that I managed to win, and with that I won the second set 9:8.

Later I realized, that historically, I won the first ever tie-break played in Wimbledon singles final!!

So, I was leading 2:0 in sets but I knew that the match was not won yet. One must know himself well enough to judge what he is capable of. And in the decisive moment one must be able to play what he is capable of playing and trust that he will succeed in it. One cannot wallow when the first Wimbledon match point comes around but rather concentrate on each individual point with patience until the very end. It is the brain that directs the play.

However, we are only human. It takes a toss put up a bit too far to the left or to the right and the serve doesn't land where I intended it to. Or the arm stiffens up, legs tighten, and the confidence and fortitude vanish, cramps creep up, throat dries up, and suddenly it is over!

It hit me at 4:2 and 40:15 in the third set. I was serving and I had to wait for some lady, who

The winning matchpoint.
It is all over...
Jan Kodes became the
Boycott Champion?

Receiving the Challenge Cup – AELTC trophy – from Duke of Kent.

was making a disturbance, to quiet down. She was right behind the score board. As I lingered I looked in that direction and spotted 6:1, 9:8, 4:2. Until that point of the game I was quite unaware of the score but at that instant I told myself: "Just two more games!"

All of a sudden I felt I was getting tight. I turned toward a ballboy and talked to myself: "Relax! Don't worry! You are ahead and he has no chance today; you are better!" In that moment I must not allow the possibility of a double fault. On the contrary, I had to concentrate and even before striking the serve I had to decide on what I was going to play as the point develo-

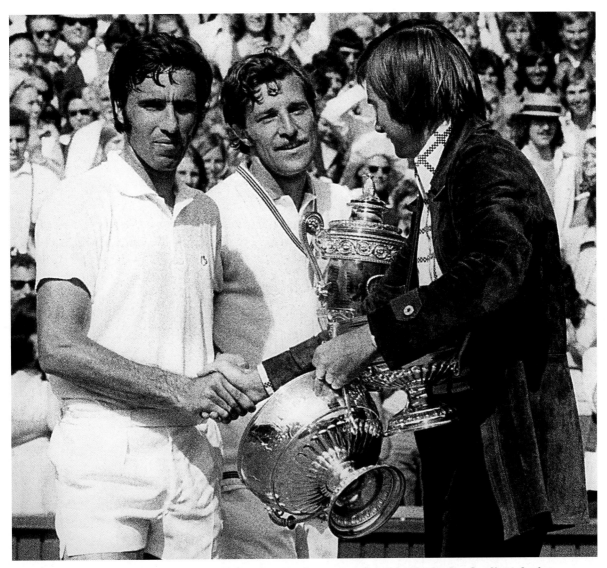

Jimmy Connors won doubles with Ilie Nastase and congratulates both singles finalists during the closing ceremonies.

ped. *"First serve into his backhand, run quickly to the net, be vigilant of a high forehand volley. If he returns to my backhand, I'll hit it down the line!"*

I extended the pause before serving, looking up into the sky and completely loosening up. I hit the first serve in and put away the volley, advancing the score to 5:2. All the anxiety fell off me!

Metreveli pulled back on his serve to 5:3 but that was the last sign of resistance from him. It was 16:35 London time when Metreveli hit the last ball into the net, and all Kodes could think of at that moment was: *"At least I won't get scolded at home for losing to Metreveli!"*

I didn't feel so much pressure because I was playing the Wimbledon final, but rather because I was playing against him. I would have been more relaxed facing Nastase or Newcombe on the other side of the net. I would not have felt such responsibility. The Wimbledon title was a reward for the extremely hard work put into my preparation, the willpower I put forth in my training in order to succeed even on grass. The essence of the victory in this match was not just the trophy; it embraced all my achievements on grass in the early 1970s. I won the dual and achieved success even on the surface that had inflicted distress to me at the beginning of my career.

As I was departing from the court I felt a hundred percent confidence that the British as well as people from the rest of the world were happy that Kodes won. I felt good that people at home would be content. I did not think in terms of "communist party and my government" but rather as a fellow countryman, who detested the Russians after what they had done to us invading in 1968.

England was also content. Their darling Taylor lost with the eventual winner. They, too, were glad that the winner was not a Russian. The world was different then. The political scene has changed by now and when Sharapova wins the audience goes wild.

The first final between representatives of two Communist countries – the USSR and Czechoslovakia was a disappointing affair with Kodes, despite having some trouble in the second set, always looking the winner. The score in his favour was 6:1, 9:8, 6:3. Kodes summed it up by saying: "This final may have been disappointing from the spectators point of view, but there have been worse." I commented at the time: " I agree. There have been worse." As a matter of fact it was the ninth time in 15 years that the loser in the final hadn´t won a set and six times that the winner had lost fewer games! Wimbledon despite all its vicissitudes attracted 300,172 spectators- the second best ever attendance.

Peter Wilson, Daily Mirror

The match for the Championships was neither better nor worse than many. It was obvious that nerves detracted from Metreveli´s best. Kodes was always competent and, when Metreveli muffed the set point he had at 5:4 for the second set, there was little to stop the Czech from taking the title.

Lance Tingay,
The Daily Telegraph

As soon as the fresh Wimbledon champion submerged himself into the lockeroom hot tub the chairman of the Czechoslovak Tennis Federation Stanislav Chvatal and Ivan Lichner came to congratulate him.

"Well, Jan, where is the T-shirt you played in?" asked the chief of the Czech Tennis. Jan gave it to him but later relented.

Stanislav Chvatal perceived it and within a few months after retiring from his position of a chairman he returned the T-shirt back to Jan.

The traditional banquet "Dinner of the Champions" took place in Savoy Hotel. He tried to dance the introductory waltz in his rented dinner-jacket with a daughter of the president of the All England Lawn Tennis Club Mr Herman F. David. The women doubles final and delayed mixed doubles matches had been switched to play on Sunday. The women's champion Billie Jean King had to play five matches in 24 hours and therefore was not able to come.

Because Jan was returning to Prague next day they met only when both played at Forest Hills two months later.

The welcome at Ruzyne airport was spontaneous. There was a large crowd, but he got to hug his parents as soon as he disembarked from the plane.

I looked forward to coming home; I could have stayed two more days in London but I felt the tug to return home; I was away long enough and I was worn out.

Dance with AELTC President's daughter, Peggy David, at the Champions Dinner. The woman champion, Billie Jean King, was unable to attend.

Arrival at Ruzyne Airport in Prague. Hundreds of welcoming fans, press and officials showed up with my wife and parents, with few receiving permission to approach all the way to the British Airways aircraft. My mother and Davis Cup captain Antonin Bolardt with my rackets are on the left, Tennis Federation President, Stanislav Chvatal, drinking champaign is on the right.

MY BRITISH CZECH ADVISOR

Jaroslav Drobny won Wimbledon in 1954. Ten years later he met then eighteen-year-old Jan Kodes, who entered the junior championships there and played on grass for the first time. Nine years later Drobny congratulated Kodes on winning his Wimbledon title.

Jaroslav Drobny
an "amphibious" athlete

There aren't many athletes in the world who have reached the absolute top in two sports. And there aren't many athletes who made two countries famous through their personal accomplishments. The hockey and tennis player Drobny, who represented Czechoslovakia and Egypt, was one of them. He was unique!

He was born on October 1921 in Prague. As a sixteen-year-old he won the Junior Tennis Nationals in Pardubice. His advancement became famous because nobody took even a set off him on the way to the finals. Only Vladimir Cernik, his future coach, took one set away from him in the finals.

At the age of sixteen Jaroslav Drobny played with a very serious face and such refined tactics and resolve that many seasoned players undoubtedly envied him. For that very reason he soon represented the country in Center-European Cup. He won his first Czechoslovak Nationals in 1938, when he defeated Roderich Menzel in the finals.

The beginning of his tennis career shows certain parallels to the professional development of Martina Navratilova. While Martina was able to shine visibly only after her defection, it was WWII that took away Drobny's best competitive years. He was eighteen in 1939; during the war fury he studied at the Commercial Academy in Prague – Karlin. In 1946 he shocked the world when he, all of a sudden, advanced into the Roland Garros finals, where he lost to the Frenchman Marcel Bernard. He was leading two sets to none exhibiting great attacking game of tennis. Bernard realized that he needed to take away his strongest weapon, the aggressive attack, and asked for the court to be soaked. Drobny could not move well on the heavy wet clay surface and lost the following three sets.

"The French headlines cried out: "Drobny did not lose on the court but rather outside its lines.

A few weeks later he stood close to the Wimbledon final. He lost in the semi-finals to the Australian Geoff Brown but along the way he defeated Jack Kramer in five to advance into the quarter-finals!

Picture from Stvanice - 1946. They all played at Wimbledon and represented Czechoslovakia in Davis Cup competition From left: Jaroslav Drobny, Vojtech Vodicka, Josef Caska and Frantisek Cejnar.

Jaroslav Drobny was a remarkable two-sport world-class athlete: As an ice-hockey player he scored three goals in the final game against the U.S at the 1948 Olympics.

Jaroslav Drobny reached Wimbledon finals three times. In 1949 he lost to Ted Schroeder in five sets and in 1952 to Frank Sedgman in four, but he eventually won in 1954 over Ken Rosewall. Drobny won twice Roland Garros in Paris (1951 and 1952) and played two semifinals at Forest Hills in 1947 and 1948 on grass, losing to Jack Kramer and Pancho Gonzales. He also took the French doubles title (with Lennart Bergelin) and mixed doubles title (with Pat Todd) in 1948. He was number one in the world rankings in 1954 and the First Wimbledon left-hander winner since 1914.

Karel Kozeluh (center) as a Davis Cup coach with Jaroslav Drobny (left) and Vladimir Cernik. Prague in 1948.

"Drobny is no transitional star that appeared on the tennis horizon just momentarily. His advance into the semi-finals was not just a lucky episode. He is a personality that will bring much good for tennis," proclaimed the official magazine of the English Tennis Association.

Jaroslav Drobny was a classical example of an athletic amphibian; besides tennis he was a terrific ice-hockey player and he reached much success in hockey long before his tennis accomplishments. He did not accept an invitation to the US Open in 1946 due to his ice-hockey obligations. The American press immediately accused him of being afraid of Jack Kramer and seemed to forget that Drobny defeated Kramer in Wimbledon... A year later he represented the country as a member of the National Ice-Hockey team that won the World Cup in Prague! In 1948 the team won silver medal in the Olympic Games in St. Moritz, Switzerland!

After matriculating from high school he accepted all kinds of positions even as a shoe salesman. He always had a job that allowed him to play sports. He was a member of the National Ice-Hockey selection from the time he was fifteen years old till 1949, and he was one of the best four Czechoslovak tennis players from 1938. By 1948 he won the Czechoslovak tennis Nationals ten times. In 1947 he was voted the best athlete of the year; he had grown very popular among the athletic public.

At the start of 1948 he recognized that things within our country were going to change. He reached the singles finals for the second time at Roland Garros losing to Frank Parker and won doubles that year teamed up with the Swede Lennart Bergelin. They defeated a highly favored Australian team Harry Hopman – Frank Sedgman! He never involved himself in politics and the February events (the communist coup d'etat) left him initially unconcerned. However, he soon realized that his life was going to be highly controlled and he would be manipulated and restricted. He had to undergo demeaning interviews each time before as well as after going abroad; they schooled him in how to behave like an athlete from a socialist country and he was told who he was allowed to compete against and who he was not allowed to face. He slowly recognized that he had to find a solution that would allow him to climb to the top group of world tennis players.

In 1949 the Czechoslovak tennis leadership talked him into abandoning ice-hockey since it held him vulnerable to injuries and it also took him away from winter preparation for his tennis competition. It was not easy for him since ice-hockey always took preference. In spite of everything he decided not to play the national hockey league for his CLTK club.

The Davis Cup debacle in Paris in 1949 marked a turning point. They reprimanded him for improper preparation and threw the guilt of defeat at him. The press criticized the tennis association and suggested: "Seek new talents among young workers! Times of prodigies are over!" All of a sudden tennis players became foes of the masses.

He advanced all the way to the Wimbledon finals, where he lost to the American

Pancho Gonzales beat Drobny at Forest Hills in 1948 semis: 8:10, 11:9, 6:0, 6:3 and won the US title for the first time over Eric Sturgess in the finals.

Frederick "Ted" Schroeder in five sets. Consequently, he and Cernik received an invitation to enter the International Swiss Championships in Gstaad. Authorities in Prague wanted both of them back. The tournament organizers received a message that repudiated the Czechoslovak players' entry in Gstaad due to the fact that German players also participated in the tournament and so did players from Nazi General Franco's Spain. On July 13, 1949 an order for the Czechoslovak players to return home immediately arrived in Switzerland!

The organizers protested because losing the top seeded player devalued the tournament. Jaroslav Drobny tried to negotiate with the Czechoslovak Embassy representatives, who arrived in an attempt to force both players out of playing the tournament. They threatened the players and a brawl broke out. Drobny recognized then that if he returned home his situation would become forever complicated and he would never get to play any more world tournaments. He never before found the strength to emigrate. However, the scuffle here changed his mind...

During the tournament an owner of one of the biggest hotels in Gstaad looked after him. All of a sudden Jaroslav became homeless; he belonged nowhere. He was welcomed at all tournaments with open arms but when the tournament was over he had to look for the next leg. He decided to stay in Europe in order to pursue his dream of tennis mastership. Australia extended a very tempting and obliging offer to him but it was too far away...

However, he could not stay in Switzerland; and the English turned their backs on him in spite of enticing him long before then to emigrate and promising him all he wanted. When he returned from Australia he played two tournaments in Egypt; in Alexandria the Egyptian King Faruk offered him and Egyptian passport during Jaroslav's visit with the entire royal family!

Drobny and Cernik with reporter Vico Rigassi announced their defection from Czechoslovakia on July16, 1949 at Gstaad to „chose freedom". Drobny going on to the final, losing to the American Earl Cochell in five sets, but winning the doubles with Cernik and mixed doubles with Miss Fry.

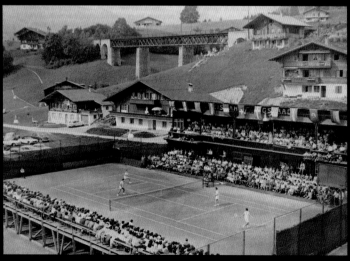

Gstaad was awarded the Swiss International Championships for second time in 1948 and made a special effort to attract the top players the week after Wimbledon. Eis skating–rink was used as tennis centercourt during the tournament.

Palace hotel Gstaad with other tennis courts.

Two great rivals of J. Drobny met in the 1950 Wimbledon final:
Budge Patty beat Frank Sedgman 6:1, 8:10, 6:2, 6:3.

His departure marked the "end of Czech tennis". Tennis disappeared from the sport arena; many tennis courts were converted into volleyball courts. Czechoslovakia stopped being represented on the international tennis scene and participation in Davis Cup was canceled...

In 1950 Drobny reached Roland Garros finals for the third time and faced the American adversary Budge Patty. Jaroslav was ranked fifth in the world that year; it was a pity that he could not play Davis Cup because match results counted for ranking. He could not play for Egypt that year since he had played already for another country.

Before long more great accomplishments started coming his way. He won Roland Garros at last and two times in a row! In 1951 he defeated his doubles partner, the South African Eric Sturgess, in the finals 6:3, 6:3, 6:3 and the following year he overcame the Australian Frank Sedgman 6:2, 6:0, 3:6, 6:4.

In 1953 he married Rita Anderson, an excellent English tennis player, and a year later they were expecting their first family addition. Jaroslav then achieved his life dream; on July 2, 1954 he defeated the Australian Ken Rosewall 13:11, 4:6, 6:2, and 9:7 in Wimbledon finals. He was thirty three and hardly anybody believed that he could still win.

The final against Rosewall was his third Wimbledon final; he lost the previous two to Schroeder and Sedgman, and three times he got defeated in semifinals. He strove for sixteen years to triumph at Wimbledon. He stepped onto the All England Lawn Tennis Club courts the first time as a seventeen year old in 1938. He used every bit of experience that he ever gathered in order to reach the ultimate glory. It is interesting to mention here that players of today earn more than half a million pounds for their victory. In 1954 Jaroslav Drobny received coupons for goods worth 20 in total.

Jaroslav Drobny with Ken Rosewall from Australia after the 1954 Wimbledon final.
Drobny is holding the silver President's Cup that was then presented to the winner.

Perhaps it was his fate that Jaroslav Drobny found the second home in England, a place that did not treat him kindly at the start of his emigration. He spent half a century in England; after his wife passed away he settled in Putney, a district close to the Wimbledon courts that he attended regularly every year. He visited Prague several times during the nineties and in 1996 he participated in the 90th anniversary celebration of the Czech Tennis Association. On that occasion he was inducted into the Czech Tennis Hall of Fame. He merited an award as one of the best ten Czech tennis players of all times and received life membership in his original I. Czech Lawn Tennis Club (I. CLTK) along with Jan Kodes and President Vaclav Klaus.

On that occasion he said: "All my life I thought I was a better hockey than a tennis player. If it wasn't so it still remains a fact that I had more fun on the ice with my fellow hockey players than I had on the courts."

Jaroslav Drobny passed away in London on September 15, 2001, at the age of almost eighty.

Serve was never my forte and I struggled with it that much more on grass. It caused me a tremendous mental strain. The point was not to avoid double-faults but rather to place the serve well.

It was Jaroslav Drobny who helped me a lot with it: "You must not serve stereotypically on grass. Even if your serve is good but you always hit it into your opponent's backhand he will adapt to it eventually. You must vary the serves – two times into the body, then into the forehand, backhand, forehand again, into the body; you must mix it up so that your opponent cannot anticipate the placement. Otherwise, he prepares for the return and either attacks it or hits it under your feet. You must understand that your opponent will serve in the same manner."

My serve return was strong. However, Taylor, for instance, tortured me with his second serve into my body with a slight twist. I did not know whether to return it with a backhand or a forehand. And that was his second serve! It bothered me more than his first serve that was hard but had less spin and was easier to return. I had to use more of my own power returning his second serve and I had to be quick getting out of its way. Either I maneuvered my feet quickly, or I was late. If I was late I only managed to return the ball in such a way that Taylor put the next shot away.

Jaroslav Drobny was a left-hander who gained much experience while traveling around various tennis facilities of the world. It was no wonder that Jan Kodes approached him before his Wimbledon semifinal match against Taylor with a question: "Jaroslav, tell me, what bothered you the most when you faced a right-hander: when he served toward forehand into your body, or into the backhand out and away to the side? He hits a low sliced crosscourt backhand to my forehand volley, and that bothers me. I have no idea where he would hit a forehand shot."

"Jan, remember one thing above all: you must hold a left-hander nice and tight, meaning that you keep on feeding the shots into his backhand because his reach is limited on that side. In order to make it look as casual as possible make sure that as soon as you know that you can put the ball away hit it into his forehand. That way he'll feel that you are hitting indiscriminately into both sides" said Jaroslav Drobny. "In the toughest moments and situations, when you are pressed only to rally, you must always target the backhand side! It is less likely that he'll hit a passing shot from that side. Lefthanders generally pass from a running forehand and they have a hard time to do the same from their backhand."

This was yet another time when his advice was very helpful. There was just one more thing I needed. When somebody gives you advice you are still dealing only on the theoretical level. You must be able to turn it into practice – you must remember to do so in a match! I re-

Having received many telegrams and letters I like this one from Stan Smith the most.

membered Jaroslav during the match with Taylor about three times. During a match one cannot concentrate only on one thing but rather it is necessary to evaluate and find weapons for all kinds of situations. However, when a match reached an important point I often bounced the ball several times before serving it and resolved: If he returns into my forehand, I'll follow Jaroslav's instructions. If he returns a low ball I'll volley it crosscourt. I approached the net determined to carry out that decision without altering it! It did not matter how the opponent moved or did not move; I played what I had decided and waited for the reaction.

As soon as one decides to change the strategy while already on the run, invariably you botch it! Such are the laws of the game of tennis that apply twofold on grass surface. You don't reach advantage on your opponent's serve, perhaps twice in a set. You either break your opponent's serve or you don't but you won't have another chance to do so any time soon. On clay you will, on grass you won't. It is in these very moments that a player must play with utmost concentration and according to those unwritten tennis rules. Even if I hit the ball out it does not bother me that much since I followed my plan; I get really unhappy if I botch a ball because I did not stick to my principles.

I had about five rackets with me in Wimbledon but I wanted to use only two of them during the finals. The leather grip was already thumbed and my fingers slid in comfortably, the string tension was just right, one slightly softer. However, I ran into a problem after the morning semi-finals. Two strings in one of the rackets started to roll. That posed a dilemma: should I ask to have it re-strung? Or should I just let it be? My rackets had been strung specifically for me in Prague and I was used to them. Naturally, they strung rackets in Wimbledon too, but each machine leaves a different touch, one is set to kilograms, the other to pounds and the pound-setting did not suit me well.

I approached Jaroslav Drobny and asked him to look at my racket. He took off his glasses, studied the strings for a while and then he said: "Play with it! Take the risk; I don't think it will break. On clay it would not survive a set because clay is coarse but it should last through a match on grass." And it lasted through the entire final match! The string burst only later, about half-an-hour into a mixed-doubles match on court number two where Martina Navratilova and I lost the quarter-final match to the future champions Davidson – King 3:6, 0:6.

...It remains to be told that Taylor did not succeed in reaching the finals at home even the third time around. In 1967 he was stopped by the German Bungert, and in 1970 the Australian Rosewall beat him after Taylor had defeated Laver. Kodes reached semi-finals the previous year when he succumbed to Smith, the eventual winner. "Reaching Wimbledon finals is yet another amazing accomplishment of Jan Kodes after his two-time victory in Paris in 1970 and 1971, reaching the 1971 US Open finals and the Roman finals three times in 1970, 1971, and 1972.

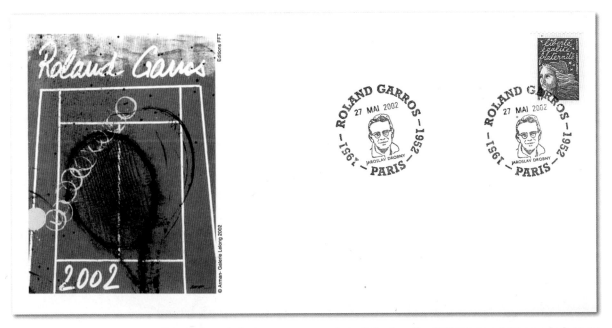

Special postal stamps were printed during the 2002 Roland Garros in honor
of Jaroslav Drobny who passed away on September 15, 2001 in London.

…Kodes' victory in the marathon match with Taylor demonstrates that he is no longer an insignificant
player… It took him years to adapt to grass; the Australian player Laver claimed that it took him four years
to get used to clay… The percentage of risk on grass
is still high; "the first serve and first volley are crucial;
my serve is not as hard as Smith's but the percentage of
well placed serves is just as high as his…" Kodes plays
today as well on grass and hard surface as he does on
clay and he has also developed the complimenting way
of tennis thinking.

Czechoslovak and British press

*In the course of the entire Wim-
bledon competition we were not
allowed to sit down during change-
overs; that got introduced only the
following year. My final with Metreveli was thus the last match when
players could not rest – there were
no chairs. We had thirty seconds to
drink, towel off and get back to the
other side of the court. It was ok with
me. The matches flowed, there was
nothing disturbing the continuity.
But what a difference a year later,
when I played against Connors in the
quarter-finals and he sat down at 2:1
in the first set and stayed there for
a minute and a half! That made a real
difference….*

Billie Jean King achieved securing equal prize money
for women for the first time at the US Open in 1973.

One of the busiest areas at the Open are the two clubhouse courts located directly in front of the clubhouse.

The U.S. Open

by F. E. Storer / Editor *Tennis. USA*

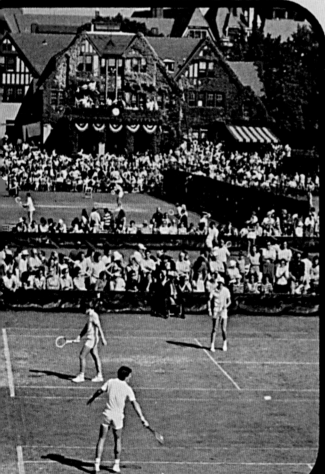

The large crowds mass around several of the outside courts with the clubhouse in the background

Here is a wide angled view of the packed Stadium with play being held on the center portion of turf reserved for the last few days

WIMBLEDON CONFIRMED

There is no tennis player who would not wish to win Wimbledon. Everybody longs to achieve that but only a few succeed in doing so. There is, however, one more triumph that every male tennis player desires to win – the "Salad Bowl", the trophy that goes to the winner of Davis Cup team competition.

Dwight F. Davis most likely did not perceive at the time what kind of prestigious competition he laid foundation to, when he suggested organization of it to the US Lawn-Tennis Association. On the Eve of the 20th Century selected players of different countries began competing for the highest tennis team conquest.

Davis Cup matches have been surrounded by specific and unique atmosphere different from individual tournament ambiance. There is hub, tension, emotion, never lacking drama, and frequent reversals. It is about team effort and national pride!

After winning the Wimbledon title it felt like somebody put a bug in my head and I could not shake it. I thought of conquering the great "Salad Bowl" on just about every step!

At that point he had no idea how close he was going to be to achieve that goal within a couple of months or how long it was actually going to take to really get hold of it.

Two weeks after Wimbledon we confronted Germany in front of a sold out Stvanice. Fassbender, Pohmann, Meiler. Everybody predicted that I would play nervously, however, I felt great. I approached the match as any other mere match; however, it was not that simple and the resulting team score of 3:2 proves that.

Kodes won the opening match against Karl Meiler 6:3, 6:4, 6:1 and Jiri Hrebec shone against Jürgen Fassbender in the following match winning the second valuable team point in four sets.

However, Jan Kukal and I lost the Saturday doubles to Fassbender – Pohmann 2:6, 6:3, 6:8, 7:9 and it prompted me to say in the press conference: "This shows you how well we must have played last year in Düsseldorf, when we defeated them!"

Davis Cup July 1973 Czechoslovakia vs. West Germany. From left: Karl Meiler, Harald Elschenbroich, Hans-Jürgen Pohmann, Jürgen Fassbender, capt. Wolgang Höfer, referee Dane P. Dählholm, capt. A. Bolardt, J. Kodes, F. Pala, J. Hrebec and J. Kukal.

Karl Mailer had already wins over Rosewall, Taylor, Connors...Australian Open 1973 semi-finalist and German Open runner-up had a little chances against Kodes in openning match, lost in straight sets.

Bungert reacted to that on television with: "Kodes was clearly the best player on the court but doubles is a team game and he cannot win it by himself." But he was able to do so in singles! He swept Fassbender off the court in three sets on Sunday and with that he gained the decisive third point.

Italy arrived in Prague to play the finals of the European "B" Zone. However, Kodes almost didn't post against Barazzutti or Zugarelli! He woke up one morning with grave problems in one of the cervical vertebra. He withdrew from the International Championships in Bratislava. After careful examination the doctor pronounced his condition so serious that he advised: "For reasons of cervical vertebra injury I do not recommend Mr. Kodes to engage in any game-play!"

The pain was so strong that he could not turn his head nor was he able to raise his arm. As usual, there were several skeptics: "Oh yeah; he won Wimbledon and now he doesn't feel like playing for the country; he feigns some neck-pain."

At the Federation the officials insisted that I finish my healing in order to be ready for the face-off with Italy. Only the Slovaks seemed bothered....

Frantisek Pala won the Czechoslovak International Championships against the Hungarian Janos Benyik in the finals. In the meantime Kodes underwent injection treatment but did not yet feel totally recovered!

Kodes practiced with Pala before the Davis Cup match. Neither his neck nor his back bothered him any more but he was very cautious serving in order to prevent re-injury. It was the two-week pause in training that worried him more than anything else.

He opened the encounter uneasily against Corrado Barazzutti and lost 5:7, 6:3, 4:6, 6:2, and 1:6. That was a shock for Stvanice crowd. The match was suspended due to rain at 4:5 in the third and was finished the following day before doubles that Kodes – Pala won 6:2, 8:6, and 6:4.

The break of Kodes' practice while healing was visible in his unconvincing performance. In spite of losing nobody could reprehend him for anything. He directed the game of doubles

Corrado Barazzutti was first Italian to win Orange Bowl Junior, later became a great clay-court player, had several good wins over top class players, surprised the Czechs with his performance in Prague, won Davis Cup for Italy later in 1976.

successfully and Pala complimented him well. The domestic press praised the strength of their teamwork...

I would classify the Davis Cup match with Italy as one of the events that brought forth the prominence of Jiri Hrebec. After my first match loss he evened the score to 1:1 by defeating Zugarelli 12:10, 6:1, and 6:1. He also reached the third team point against Barazzutti overcoming him 9:7, 6:1, and 6:4. By the time I entered the court for my last singles match the team-score had been decided in our favor; that was something I had not been used to. It felt great!

Jiri Hrebec never reached as much success in individual tournaments as he did in Davis Cup matches. The home audience succeeded in arousing him to his ultimate performance. Like with a swing of a magic wand he switched to a higher level of delivery. He was able to capitalize on his excellent forehand and quick feet. He also entertained the crowd with his concomitant comments that people enjoyed and loved him for. Though his occasional aberrations were often tolerated he proved to be a fine team player.

Consequences of the match had a sequel at the "green table". The Davis Cup organizing committee discussed the Italian non-playing captain's extempore behavior. Quick tempered Fausto Gardini, an excellent clay-court player of his era, had had problems with court behavior in the past and during the match between Hrebec – Zugarelli he offended the chief umpire to such a degree that he got himself disqualified from further competitions in any official capacity for life!

After two home victories at Stvanice the Czechoslovak team traveled to Australia to play the Inter-Zonal finals.

Forest Hills, West Side Tennis Club grass courts, and the US Open - the last of the season's Grand Slams. It never carried the ostentatious attributes so characteristic of Paris Open or Wimbledon, however, it was said to be the best attended tournament in the world. That was due to, most likely, the the high prize money!

Jiri Hrebec with Antonin Bolardt, our Davis Cup captain, after one of his acrobatic saves.

For Jan Kodes the 1973 end-of-August tournament acquired a special savory flavor. Jan arrived in New York with his Wimbledon champion glory and the first newspaper he picked up read: "Wimbledon was conquered by the least known tennis player!"

I am still sorry even today that I did not win that US Open. I was smothered by journalists and photographers from the first round on. They hung around and wanted to see me lose; they wanted to witness the Wimbledon champion on his knees.

As I was getting ready for my first round match I met my friend, the New Zealander Onny Parun on the way to the court. He nodded his head toward the mob and uttered: "They want you to lose!" It was terrible to hear but after the first couple of games I realized that he was right. There was frenetic applause when I made an error, but when my opponent fouled up the crowd just rustled disappointingly.

It inspired me, however, and I resolved: Hey, I am not going to give you this pleasure of bowing out! I faced formidable opponents and I struggled. Most importantly, I advanced.

In the first round – I played the French Wanaro Godrella. Kodes lost the first set 6:7 but he did not give his opponent a chance after that: 6:1, 6:2, 6:4. He lost a set in the second round as well against the American Jim McManus - 7:5, 6:3, 6:7, 6:1, but beat the Egyptian El Shafei in straight sets 6:3, 7:5, 7:6. He did not get stopped even by the Australian John Alexander, the grass court specialist, in the sixteens: 7:6, 7:5, 6:4. He met the culprit of the Wimbledon boycott, the Yugoslav Niki Pilic, in the quarter-finals.

The fact that he had caused the excessive uproar and misgivings at Wimbledon that year called for much attention to him here. Furthermore, our game was scheduled on Centre Court thus I faced a crowd of fourteen thousand against me. On top of all that – Pilic was a very tough opponent. He was a lefty with a very daunting serve. His first serve was later comparable to the one of Goran Ivanisevic; fast loop, vehement power, flat and bouncing out of the court. When his serve was on it was close to impossible to return. He had played with the professionals for years, and he was the only player in the Handsome Eight group who was able to beat Rod Laver! We played a challenging five-setter; as I had mentioned previously, left-handers never bothered me and I came out on top: 6:2, 4:6, 6:1, 3:6, and 7:5.

A curious thing about this match with Pilic was that Jan Kodes lost his "Wimbledon" racket, the racket he had used when he conquered Metreveli and won the Wimbledon finals.

I had a break point in the fifth set at 4:1. He hit the first serve and as I returned it the racket broke in my hand. It was my favorite...though pretty beat-up to the point that I had to string it tighter; the frame had a crack but I continued playing with it. It felt like an extension of my hand; it gave me a sense of great touch. I was sorry to lose it...

The ATP enforced two fundamental seeding changes at the 1973 US Open. It was no longer just eight but sixteen players who were seeded, and there was no tournament committee deciding who the seeded players would be but rather a computer generated ATP ranking

Smith and Kodes Reach Semifinals With Victories Over Parun and Pilic

By PARTON KEESE

Jan Kodes walking off court after breaking his racquet while returning a service to Nikki Pilic at Forest Hills.

It was a hot-and-cold day at the United States Open tennis championship in Forest Hills yesterday. Advancing to the semifinals of the men's singles were a hot Stan Smith over a cold Onny Parun, 6-3, 6-3, 6-2, and Jan Kodes over a cold-and-hot Nikki Pilic, 6-2, 4-6, 6-1, 3-6, 7-5.

Even the weather joined in, the play starting in humid air but then cooling off as rain fell in the middle of a women's doubles semifinals. Mrs. Margaret Court and Virginia Wade won that, 6-0, 6-4, over Evonne Goolagong and Janet Young.

With the top-seeded Smith serving better, returning serve better (especially lambasting Parun's second attempts), lobbying better and volleying better, it was no contest and the match was completed in 75 routing minutes. Stan was even luckier than the New Zealander, with several of his "mis-hits" falling in. The big Californian remains the lone American in men's singles.

The eastern European confrontation between the Czechoslovak, Kodes, and the Yugoslav, Pilic, provided the leading drama. There were several intriguing aspects that many in the crowd of 9,842 seemed to know.

As the winner of the recent boycotted Wimbledon championship, Kodes has been referred to as a "cheap" or "watered down" champion, terms that aggravate him greatly. Pilic, of course, was the catalyst in the Wimbledon affair when nearly 80 pros refused to play because Nikki was banned. Now here they were, the principals in that episode facing each other at Forest Hills.

Another part of the act was the 34-year-old Pilic's reputation of arguing, stalling and debating with ballboys, a problem that has followed him from tourney to tourney. There was little of that yesterday, however, though Kodes admitted "Nikki is a tough person to play because of his antics."

Kodes, 27, a finalist against Smith here two years ago, whipped through the first set but then ran into Pilic's blistering left-handed serves in the second. With a set apiece, Kodes whipped through the third. Then Pilic, playing "acey-deucey," was superb in the fourth, so it came to the decisive final set.

Pilic's serves were on target and Kodes's returns were almost perfect. Result: stalemate. "I was thinking tie-break at 4-4," admitted Kodes afterwards. "I'm afraid of Nikki when his service is on, but I like to play him because he doesn't return service so well."

With no service break in sight, Pilic had only made two volleying errors and Kodes blasted two other balls by him. Result: Czech-mate.

After the tense match (though there has yet to be a five-set tiebreaker at the Open this year) Kodes bemoaned his luck, a strange act for a winner. "Nikki was lucky in the fifth set," he said. "He didn't have much chance on my serve, and he

Continued on Page 32, Column 3

decided the order. Nastase, Smith, Ashe, Laver, Rosewall, Kodes, Okker...

Semifinal pairs were established after Newcombe defeated Connors in a great battle and with a twist of luck, Armitraj triumphed over Laver but lost to Rosewall, and Smith overcame Gorman and Parun; Newcombe – Rosewall and Kodes – Smith.

That Saturday Newcombe – Rosewall were the first ones to step onto the grass Stadium Court. John Newcombe came out the winner of the duel of the two Aussies; he defeated his fellow countryman in three sets. A few minutes after the match concluded the second semifinal match began between Kodes – Smith and that one took the crowd out of their seats numerous times with its developing drama.

It was a crazy match. I won the first set 7:5 and was ahead 4:0 in the second. However, I was forced into a tie-break. The US Open still favored the short nine-point tie-breaker then, meaning that at 4:4 we both had a set-point and the deciding point was to come. If I won the point I would lead 2:0, if he won the point he would tie the set score 1:1. Stan hit a 6 inch long double-fault. At that I started walking to switch sides but the umpire called: "Game, set, Smith!"

I stopped in my track bewildered; I was hundred percent sure he would say "Game, set, Kodes!" I started to argue, people whistled, but the umpire stood his ground. The umpire then asked the line- judge and he pointed with his hand that the ball was good. I could not believe

U.S. Open semifinals: Kodes (top) beat Smith (bottom) in five sets.

my eyes nor ears! They simply stole a set from me! The tournament referee Mike Blanchard showed on the court, but didn't do anything...

When I came close to my chair I kicked it! It fell, and since it was a folding chair it collapsed. People started to whistle that much more, the umpire gave me a warning, and I was as mad as hell. I started to lament with my arms, looked around without focus... nobody came to my aid.

It threw me off so much that I lost the third set 6:1. I was fuming through just about each and every point. Up to that double-fault I played a better game; he was the first seed but the way I played that day I could beat him in straight sets!

After the third set, as we were changing sides, I thought: "You damn Americans; I can upset you only by winning. You give me no other choice!"

I pressed hard and started to fight for every point again! Stan let up, I quickly gained a break and won the fourth set 6:1!

We started the fifth set and I hardly remember anything from that point on. All I know is that we kept our serves and at 4:5 Stan had a match point! I have a total blank about what happened after that. I have thought that he had the match point on my serve but it all remains a blur, except that I won. I was totally fatigued when we finished close to eight at night. By the time I reached the hotel it was midnight and I had to rest up for the final match with Newcombe the following day.

Jan Kodes doesn't remember the nerve wracking close of the semi-final battle with Stan Smith, however, the Boston Globe and Forest Hills television commentator Bud Collins recalls the finish of the fifth set to the last detail.

"There was a record high crowd of some 15,137 spectators at Forest Hills. Already in the finish of the second set Jan Kodes showed his soccer dexterity when he kicked a chair as a protest against the umpire's unfair call that accepted Smith's evidently long second serve as "in" and thus "granted" the home-player the set. The dusk was setting in during the fifth set and both players held their serves. At 5:4 in Smith's favor Kodes was down 0:30 while serving. With a miraculous volley he tied the score 30:30 but Smith gained the next point after a phenomenal exchange of both players when Smith forced Kodes to hit a forehand volley out and thus gained a match point. Kodes warded off the match point with an ace and with that shot he launched a string of three victorious games that brought him to a triumphant finish. At first, Kodes' put-away overhead and Smith's subsequent error tied up the score at 5:5. Kodes gained two breakpoints with his excellent backhand shots during Smith's serve but the American brought the score back to deuce after a brilliant serve and volley play. Kodes pressed ahead with two outstanding forehand returns and a successful backhand passing shot and broke his opponent's serve. He was now 6:5 in the lead. At this point darkness was setting in but it was to Kodes' advantage to go on. He played the next three points just serve and volley – 30:0, 40:0; his second volley was unreachable thanks to the auspicious nip of the net-tape. After that Smith did not even budge to return Kodes' good serve and the match was over."

Jan Kodes doesn't want to take a chance that the point isn't over even with Stan; Smith sprawled on his back. Neither player wanted to bail their match despite fading light.

I even forced him down to the ground...

The advancement into the 1973 US Open final confirmed Kodes' Wimbledon victory.

I needed to prove that my Wimbledon victory was no fluke. Defeating Smith was crucial for that very reason.

At the press conference following the conclusion of the semifinal match Jan sharply related the controversial situation that ended the second set. He flatly declared that the "Americans stole a set from him"!

They insisted that the umpire made a mistake because he missed the ball in question. I stood my ground uncompromisingly: "Umpires all over the world pay god-damn attention in such moments because they are well aware that the point in question can decide the match one way or the other. It is unacceptable to label that call a "mistake!"

With that I actually accused the umpire of making such call intentionally in order to help Smith. Our newspapers at home did not discuss the incident but the US press debated it soundly!

The press conference had repercussions. The next day, as Jan was packing his bags after the finals, the hotel room telephone rang as he was getting ready to leave New York.

"Jan, this is Donald Dell. We have a problem! The line-judge that was sitting on the line where the questionable call occurred read the interview with you in the newspapers and said that he would take you to court. You accused him of intentionally hurting you in order to help Smith! This can get you into a real jam. I recommend to you to apologize to him..."

"No way! To hell with it! Are you nuts?!"

"Well, do as you please. I am suggesting to you to iron things out."

Due to the American laws the court case would have cost a lot of money; and so, grinding my teeth, I sat down and wrote the line-judge an apology. I sent a copy to the USTA but I am convinced till this day that the call deprived me of a Grand Slam title. I was physically too tired the next day and I could not keep up with Newcombe in the end of the final match. I finished the first two sets with Smith in just about an hour! Because of the faulty call we had to play three sets more! I finished physically fatigued and mentally unstable.

John Newcombe in the semi-final made 38 year old Ken Rosewall look 38, beating him 6:4, 7:6, 6:3. It was this easy match, plus the timing of it, which gave him an unfair advantage over Jan Kodes in the final, for it was over early in the day and gave Newcombe plenty of time to unwind and get a night´s good sleep.

Laurie Pignon, The Daily Mail

Over 15,000 fans watched the match; it was broadcasted all over the United States. The match lasted 170 minutes, the last set started at 23:50 in Czechoslovakia, ten minutes to six New York time, and we finished at dusk.

Press agencies called the match a "Match of the Titans" that had several very dramatic moments. The most important one came in the second set tie-break when Smith's serve landed clearly out and Kodes just lightly stroke the ball into the net, however, the line-judge Commings did not call the fault! Kodes protested to the tournament referee Mike Blanchard, who did not honor the protest and the game went on. The crowd was up in arms because they saw the shot landing visibly out. The UPI agency stated that the ball landed at least four inches out...

Kodes claimed he was cheated, and two neutral players better placed than I , said that Smith´s serve at 4-4 in ridiculous nine-point tie-break was nine inches out. This would have given the Czech a two sets to nil lead and would certainly have shortened the match! By any standards it was a classic, and in my view the most exciting and dramatic clash of the year.

Laurie Pignon, The Daily Mail

There was the memorable semi-final match between mighty Stan Smith and Jan Kodes at Forest Hills when Kodes finally won 7:5, 6:7, 1:6, 6:1, 7:5, ending in the twilight in an atmosphere of Wagnerian drama. One may thing of some of the great contests that have marked lawn tennis history.

Lance Tingay, The Daily Telegraph
Rothmans Book of Tennis: "The best of 1973"

I doubt if, in the history of the game, a man was more inspired, more raised up to the heights of genius, than Kodes in winning his semifinal against Smith. By rights his sparkle should have been quenched for good when he was robbed, as blatantly as a player ever was, of his chance to lead two sets to love on the ridiculously hazardous circumstance of the four-all score in the American nine-point tie-break sequence. It was a memorable contest.

Lance Tingay, The Daily Telegraph
World of Tennis 74 "Players of the Year"

Forty years old Pancho Gonzales reached semis on the French Open in 1968! The picture is taken at Wimbledon.

At the US Open they still practice an exception to all the other Grand Slam events – there is no day rest between the semi and final match. Saturday is called the longest day, when the most important and entertaining matches take place. First, the first men's semifinal singles match goes on, then the la-

U.S. OPEN MEN'S SINGLES

First Round	Second Round	Third Round	Fourth Round	Quarter-Finals	Semi-Finals	Final

First Round

Stan Smith (1) Sea Pines, S. C.
Patrick Proisy, France
William Martin, Palos Verdes, Calif.
Tito Vazquez, Argentina
Hans Pohmann, Germany
Roscoe Tanner, Lookout Mountain, Tenn.
Geoff Masters, Australia
Clark Graebner, New York
Tom Gorman (13), Seattle
Eddie Dibbs, Miami
Ove Bengtson, Sweden
Arthur Carrington, New York
Patricio Cornejo, Chile
Mark Cox, Great Britain
Joaquin Loyo-Mayo, Mexico
John Feaver, Great Britain
Manuel Orantes (8), Spain
Christopher Mottram, Great Britain
Ian Fletcher, Australia
Reyno Seegers, Washington, D. C.
George Seewagen, Bayside, N. Y.
Haroon Rahim, Pakistan
Ross Case, Australia
Rolph Norberg, Sweden
Martin C. Riessen (12), Evanston, Ill.
Tom Koch, Brazil
Onny Parun, New Zealand
Jasjit Singh, New York
John Lloyd, Great Britain
Robert Kreiss, Bel Air, Calif.
Paolo Bertolucci, Italy
Jeff Simpson, New Zealand
Arthur Ashe (3), Miami
Colin Dibley, Australia
Sherwood Stewart, Houston
William Higgins, Carefree, Ariz.
Jean B. Chanfreau, France
Guillermo Vilas, Argentina
Bjorn Borg, Sweden
Roy Barth, Los Angeles, Calif.
Nikki Pilic, (15), Yugoslavia
Jeff Austin, Rolling Hills, Cal.
Anand Amritraj, India
Patrick Du Pre, Birmingham, Ala.
Phil Dent, Australia
Terry Ryan, Australia
George Hardie, Long View, Calif.
Frank Froehling, Coral Gables, Fla.
Jan Kodes (6), Czechoslovakia
Wanaro N'Godrella, France
Jim McManus, Berkeley, Calif.
Lito Alvarez, Argentina
Dick Crealy, Australia
Milan Holocek, Czechoslovakia
Frew McMillan, South Africa
Ismail El Shafei, Egypt
Roger Taylor (11), Great Britain
Antonio Zugarelli, Italy
John Alexander, Australia
Vitas Gerulaitis, Howard Beach, N.Y.
Barry Phillips Moore, Australia
Ian Crookenden, Roanoke, Va.
Cliff Drysdale, South Africa
Richard Dell, Bethesda, Md.

Jiri Hrebec, Czechoslovakia
Richard Stockton, Port Wash., N. Y.
Antonio Munoz, Spain
Raul Ramirez, Mexico
Bill Brown, S. Luis Obisop, Cal.
Brian Teacher, San Diego, Calif.
Gerald Battrick, Great Britain
Cliff Richey (16), Houston
Torben Ulrich, Denmark
Vladimir Zednik, Czechoslovakia
Jun Kamiwazumi, Japan
John Andrews, Fullerton, Calif.
Robert McKinley, St. Ann, Mo.
Bob Carmichael, Australia
Graham Stilwell, Great Britain
Ken Rosewall (5), Australia
Chico Hagey, La Jolla, Calif.
Ray Moore, South Africa
Allan Stone, Australia
Steve Siegel, New York
Tom Edlefsen, Los Angeles
Toma Ovici, Romania
Victor Amaya, Holland, Mich.
Adriano Panatta (14), Italy
Pat Cramer, South Africa
Belus Prajoux, France
Eugene Scott, New York
Vijay Amritraj, India
Karl Meiler, Germany
Patrice Dominguez, France
Harold Solomon, Silver Springs, Md.
Rod Laver (4), Australia
Georges Goven, France
Erik van Dillen, San Mateo, Calif.
Fred McNair, Chevy Chase, Md.
Charlie Pasarell, Los Angeles, Calif.
Jaime Fillol, Chile
Mike Estep, Dallas, Tex.
Herb FitzGibbon, New York
Jimmy Connors (9), Belleville, Ill.
Steve Krulevitz, Baltimore
Pierre Barthes, France
Brian Gottfried, Ft. Lauderdale, Fla.
Paul Kronk, Australia
Alex Mayer, Wayne, N. J.
Paul Gerken, East Norwalk, Conn.
Pancho Gonzalez, Las Vegas
Tom Okker (7), Netherlands
Ion Tiriac, Romania
Armistead Neely, Tampa, Fla.
Jeff Borowiak, Tiburon, Calif.
Raz Reid, Greenville, S. C.
Jim Delaney, Potomac, Md.
Ivan Molina, Colombia
Marcelo Lara, Mexico
John Newcombe (10), Australia
Owen Davidson, Australia
Jurgen Fassbender, Germany
Corrado Barazzutti, Italy
Charles Owens, Tuscaloosa, Ala.
Andrew Pattison, Rhodesia
John James, Australia
Humphrey Hose, Venezuela
Ilie Nastase (1), Romania

Second Round

Smith (1) 6-4, 5-0, ret.
Martin 6-0, 6-1, 6-1
Tanner 6-2, 7-6, 6-4
Masters 4-6, 6-7, 6-1, 6-4, 7-5
Gorman (13), 6-3, 6-1, 6-2
Bengtson 6-3, 6-4, 6-3
Cox 6-4, 7-6, 6-3
Feaver 6-1, 6-3, 4-6, 6-3
Orantes (8) 6-3, 6-1, 6-3
Fletcher 6-4, 6-1, 6-1
Seewagen 7-5, 6-4, 7-5
Case 6-4, 6-4, 6-3
Riessen (12) 5-7, 6-2, 6-3, 6-2
Parun 6-1, 6-7, 6-3, 3-6, 6-1
Lloyd 6-1, 6-7, 6-0, 4-6, 6-3
Simpson 6-3, 3-1, ret.
Ashe (3) 7-6, 6-7, 7-5, 6-2
Stewart 6-3, 6-0, 4-6, 6-4
Chanfreau 6-3, 6-3, 6-4
Borg 3-6, 6-7, 6-4, 6-1, 6-2
Pilic (15) 7-6, 6-4, 6-2
A. Amritraj 6-2, 6-1, 6-2
Dent 6-2, 6-4, 6-2
Hardie 3-6, 7-6, 6-2, 6-4
Kodes (6) 6-7, 6-2, 6-1, 6-4
McManus 6-3, 6-1, 6-2
Crealy 6-3, 6-3, 6-2
El Shafei 6-4, 6-2, 6-4
Taylor (11) 6-4, 6-4, 6-4
Alexander 7-6, 7-6, 6-4
Phillips Moore 4-6, 6-3, 6-2, 6-1
Drysdale 6-7, 6-1, 6-0, 6-3

Hrebec 6-2, 7-5, 6-2
Ramirez 7-6, 6-2, 7-6
Teacher 6-3, 6-7, 6-4, 6-0
Richey (16) 6-0, 2-6, 6-4, 3-6, 6-4
Zednik 6-4, 6-4, 6-2
Kamiwazumi 6-2, 2-6, 6-2, 7-6
McKinley 6-4, 6-3, 6-2
Rosewall (5) 6-3, 6-2, 6-2
Moore 6-3, 7-6, 6-4
Stone 6-3, 6-3, 6-4
Ovici 6-7, 6-3, 6-3, 2-6, 7-6
Panatta (14) 7-6, 6-7, 6-3, 6-7, 6-4
Cramer 7-5, 6-1, 6-2
Amritraj 6-4, 7-6, 6-2
Dominguez 7-6, 6-3, 6-0
Laver (4) 6-0, 6-2, 6-2
van Dillen 3-6, 6-3, 6-2, 7-6
Pasarell 5-7, 6-3, 6-7, 7-6, 6-2
Jaime Fillol 6-1, 7-6, 7-5
Connors (9) 6-3, 6-3, 6-2
Barthes 6-4, 3-6, 6-1, 6-2
Gottfried 6-4, 6-1, 6-2
Gerken 4-6, 7-5, 4-6, 4-1 ret.
Okker (7) 6-7, 6-3, 6-1, 6-4
Tiriac 4-6, 6-4, 4-6, 6-4, 6-0
Borowiak 4-6, 6-3, 6-2, 6-2
Delaney 6-7, 6-1, 6-4, 7-6
Newcombe (10) 6-7, 6-3, 6-3, 6-7, 6-3
Davidson 6-3, 4-1, ret.
Owens 6-2, 7-6, 6-4
Pattison 7-6, 6-2, 6-3
Nastase (1) 6-4, 6-4, 6-3

Third Round

Smith (1) 6-3, 6-2, 6-1
Tanner 6-4, 6-4, 6-1
Gorman (13) 7-5, 7-5, 6-3
Cox 4-6, 6-4, 6-2, 6-4
Orantes (8) 6-2, 3-6, 7-5, 6-3
Case 6-2, 6-1, 6-1
Parun 6-3, 7-6, 7-6
Simpson 6-3, 3-6, 6-3, 6-2
Ashe (3) 6-4, 6-2, 6-2
Borg 7-5, 2-6, 6-1, 6-4
Pilic (15) 7-5, 5-7, 7-6, 6-4
Dent 6-4, 5-7, 6-1, 6-2
Kodes (6) 7-5, 6-3, 6-2, 6-1
El Shafei 6-3, 7-5, 6-1
Alexander 3-6, 4-6, 6-4, 6-3, 7-5
Drysdale 6-3, 6-3, 6-4

Ramirez 6-3, 2-6, 6-3, 6-2, 6-4
Richey (16) 3-6, 6-3, 6-4, 3-6, 6-3
Kamiwazumi 4-6, 6-3, 6-4, 5-7, 6-4
Rosewall (5) 6-1, 6-3, 6-3
Stone 7-5, 6-1, 4-6, 7-6
Panatta (14) 6-1, 6-3, 6-1
Amritraj 3-6, 6-3, 6-7, 7-6, 7-5
Laver (4) 6-1, 6-3, 6-2
Pasarell 7-6, 6-4, 4-6, 6-3
Connors (9) 6-4, 4-6, 7-5, 7-6
Gottfried 6-1, 6-3, 6-4
Okker (7) 7-5, 6-3, 6-7, 7-6
Tiriac 6-4, 7-6, 7-5
Newcombe (10) 7-6, 6-3, 6-3
Owens 6-1, 6-7, 6-4, 5-7, 6-2
Pattison 6-7, 2-6, 6-3, 6-4, 6-4

Fourth Round

Smith (1) 6-7, 7-6, 6-4, 6-3
Gorman (13) 3-6, 7-5, 6-4, 6-4
Case 6-1, 6-4, 7-6
Parun 3-6, 6-3, 7-6, 6-1
Borg 6-7, 6-4, 6-4, 6-4
Pilic (15) 4-6, 6-3, 6-3, 6-1
Kodes (6) 6-3, 7-5, 7-6
Alexander 3-6, 7-6, 6-2, 6-2

Richey (16) 6-2, 6-4, 6-7, 7-6
Rosewall (5) 7-6, 6-1, 6-1
Stone 7-5, 6-7, 4-6, 6-3, 6-4
Amritraj 7-6, 2-6, 6-4, 2-6, 6-4
Laver (4) 6-1, 6-3, 6-2
Connors (9) 6-3, 6-4, 6-7, 6-2
Okker (7) 6-4, 3-6, 6-3, 6-4
Newcombe (10) 7-6, 6-3, 6-4

Quarter-Finals

Smith (1) 3-6, 7-5, 6-3, 6-4
Parun 6-4, 6-1, 4-6, 6-4
Pilic (15) 6-4, 5-7, 6-3, 6-4
Kodes (6) 6-3, 7-5, 7-6

Rosewall (5) 6-3, 6-4, 6-3
Amritraj 6-2, 6-2, 6-2
Connors (9) 6-3, 6-2, 6-4
Newcombe (10) 6-7, 6-1, 7-5, 6-4

Semi-Finals

Smith (1) 6-3, 6-3, 6-2
Kodes (6) 6-2, 4-6, 6-1, 3-6, 7-5

Rosewall (5) 6-4, 6-3, 6-3
Newcombe (10) 6-4, 7-6, 7-6

Kodes (6) 7-6, 6-7, 1-6, 6-1, 7-5

Newcombe (10) 6-4, 7-6, 6-3

Final

J. NEWCOMBE
6-4, 1-6, 4-6, 6-2, 6-3

KODES 46620
NEWCOMBE 61461

After winning 1973 Wimbledon Jan Kodes played a five-set final vs. John Newcombe. He led two sets to one but missed the opportunity to reach the world number one rank. Newcombe beat him 6:4, 1:6, 4:6, 6:2, 6:3 and took the US Open title for the second time. Nevertheless, Kodes proved his great performance on grass and solidified his status as a Wimbledon champion.

dies' final match, followed by the second men's semifinal singles match. The men's final follows on Sunday!

This schedule is a result of television control. TV sponsors the tournament and they dictate what they want and how they want it. Players know it and ask for change but even the ATP doesn't influence the organizer's stance. The players who are scheduled for the second semi-final match are out of luck.

If they had not taken the second semi-final set away from me and I were ahead 2:0, perhaps I would have won in three and had enough strength the following day to give Newcombe a good fight. But there is no point in speculating about it today; I would have benefited the most from a day off. I am not saying this as an excuse for my loss; I simply believe that it is unfair to all finalists who have suffered the same and who still do.

A battle for No. 1 in the world - that is what the 1973 US Open final was about! Jan Kodes and John Newcombe met previously two years earlier and, coincidentally, on the same court but in the first round. Jan Kodes then won ...

I am lucky to have the final match taped and I have watched it many times over; I did not make any fundamental mistakes. I was two sets to one ahead and in the fourth set at 1:1 I needed one point to break my opponent's serve and switch sides to have the wind behind me. But he whipped up an ace! Smack, down the middle into my forehand.

After that ace things turned around. Kodes did not have enough "fuel" in him to succeed in another five-setter. He lost 4:6, 6:1, 6:4, 2:6, and 3:6. There was no other European before him, however, who had reached the US Open finals twice in such close succession. That was, nonetheless, a weak consolation to losing the rank of the world's best player of 1973 by such a very slight margin.

John Newcombe won his first US Open in 1967, and Wimbledon in 1967, 1970 and 1971.

John Newcombe never delighted in watching my "in flight" backhand passing shot...

John Newcombe: "Jan Kodes is an excellent player and I am lucky to have played him in top form. At any rate, it was not an easy win." Exhausted Kodes said after the match: "My match against Smith cost me a lot of strength. My legs felt extremely sore in the last couple of sets against Newcombe and my serve failed me."

Newcombe Defeats Kodes for U.S. Tennis

Continued From Page 1, Col. 2

singles winners hailed from Australia, where Mrs. Court and Ken Rosewall won titles. Kodas got $12,000 as runner-up.

Foreign players also predominated in the other finals played yesterday. Mrs. Court and Virginia Wade of Britain captured the women's doubles, 3-6, 6-3, 7-5, over Mrs. Billie Jean King and Rosemary Casals.

In mixed doubles, Mrs. King teamed with Owen Davidson of Australia and defeated Marty Riessen and Mrs. Court, 6-4, 3-6, 7-6.

Just as in his semifinal victory over Stan Smith on Saturday, Kodes seemed to perform miracles. As an acrobatic scrambler, retriever and hustler with tremendous maneuverability, he represented an almost perfect contrast to the less mobile Newcombe, a serve-blaster and power-stroker with knockout punches from either side.

Though it took the 27-year-old Czechoslovak a few games to get started, Kodes came tearing back in the second and third sets just as he had with Smith.

Kodes, this year's Wimbledon champion, sent Newcombe's powerful serve back twice as hard as it arrived. Not only did Kodes blunt Newcombe's big weapon, he placed the return so unerringly out of his reach that Newcombe could only stare at Kodes as if he were superman.

Down two sets to one, Newcombe was frantically searching for something new and his bag of tricks was low. The leaping, diving, sprawling Kodes was not only reaching everything, he made winners out of unbelievable retrieves.

The New York Times/William E. Sauro
Jan Kodes of Czechoslovakia serving to John Newcombe in yesterday's men's final at Forest Hills.

Jan Kodes, right, and John Newcombe congratulate each other after the final match
The New York Times

"Everything Jan touched turned to gold," said Newcombe afterward. "Everything I did he had a counter for. When you're down like that, the thing to do is not panic. If you do, you're in trouble. With momentum going for the other guy, you wait it out and wait for it to swing to you."

"Hitting his second serve deeper and harder — "I thought that to be my main problem" — Newcombe suddenly shot out to a 4-1 lead in the fourth set. When his first serve wasn't nipping the line for an ace (He served 14 aces to Kodes's five), his second serve still kept Kodes back.

That's when Kodes started running out of miracles. And miracles were what the audience had come to expect of the seemingly indefatigable Czechoslovak, who had been

seeded No. 6. He had won from Nikki Pilic and Stan Smith the last two rounds, both tough five-setters, and here he was again going to five sets.

Blistering serve after serve through, by and over the leaping Kodes (Kodes was marked with chalk on his legs, green on his shorts and dirt on his brow), Newcombe won the fourth set in bizarre fashion. The final two winning strokes were returned from sliding, sitting positions, which Newcombe may have copied from Kodes himself.

The decisive set was almost the same. Was Kodes

tired from his exhaustive matches? "Not tired," he said, "but it is hard to play semis and finals on successive days."

Kodes found fault only with Newcombe's serves. "They were unbelievable," he said, "especially on the crucial points when they hit the corners. They're difficult enough to return when I can reach them."

Newcomb, 10th seeded, had devoted much of his time to his ranch in Texas and his tennis camps in the last two years.

"But now I'm out to prove I'm the best player in the

world," Newcombe said. "No more kidding around."

Newcombe had played in only nine tournaments this season before coming to Forest Hills, but in his career he has won three Wimbledon titles, two United States and one Australian title, and has taken the national championships of Germany and Italy once each.

Yesterday's match lasted 2 hours 20 minutes and was considered by many who saw it to be one of the most brilliant ever played on the grass at the West Side Tennis Club.

The signal that the end was near came in the fourth game of the fifth set when Newcombe scored the only service break of the set. He hit a sharp backhand angle shot to make it 0-15. Then he passed Kodes with a forehand shot. Kodes evened the score with two strong serves, but Newcombe scored with a sideline shot then forced Kodes to bloop a volley into the net.

The match followed service to its conclusion. Newcombe quickly ran up a 40-0 advantage with his serve in the ninth game. After a winning shot by Kodes, Newcombe put all his power into a final serve, which kicked up a cloud of dust on the backhand service line. Not even the leaping, sprawling, diving Kodes could return it.

Profile of John Newcombe appears on page 46.

Mrs. B
Fores

The New York Times

Newcombe's victory over Kodes gave him confidence to forecast assuredly: "We are determined to not only make our way to the Davis Cup finals but also win the legendary "Salad Bowl". Kodes is a formidable opponent, we mustn't underestimate Czechoslovakia!

I served exceptionally well this time and felt very confident. That gave me the nerve to take a risk in the fourth set at 1:2. That was the only way I could finish off the match successfully. Taking the risk paid off. On the other hand, Kodes burned off too much of his energy in the heat of his previous two battles leading up to the finals; one against Pilic and then, especially, the one facing Smith. Twenty hours was too little to regenerate for the final match against Newcombe. And that much more we should appreciate Kodes' effort; he still took Newcombe to five sets!"

"Kodes seemed to be performing wonders the same way he did in the semi-final match against Smith. Like a mercurial acrobat with an amazing agility he was a complete contrast to the less vibrant Australian. Kodes darted one unbelievable shot after another to his opponent's side. Only virtually thunder-bolting serves and merciless attacks could break him – and that is what Newcombe accomplished."

The New York Times

In the final Kodes, grey faced and as eager as a starving ferret, led Newcombe two sets to one – and up to that stage played better tennis than any time at Wimbledon. In the last two sets it was almost as if a tap had been opened inside Kodes: slowly the man who had given so much for so long became drained of inspiration. But, he came as a discredited Wimbledon champion, he departed as a worthy one.

Laurie Pignon, The Daily Mail

Rankings started to emerge soon after the US Open; one of the first ones came out in the British Daily Telegraph. His author was Lance Tingay, a well-known British tennis expert: 1. Newcombe, 2. Smith, 3.Nastase, 4. Kodes, 5. Ashe, 6. Rosewall, 7. Laver...

There was no one player who could be seen as world champion in 1973, but certainly three, perhaps four, merited world championship status. Even so the status of Wimbledon men´s singles was not weakened. The Czech Jan Kodes, proved, by his subsequent exploits at Forest Hills, where he dramatically beat Smith and lost, but narrowly, in the final to Newcombe, that the 1973 Wimbledon champion was illustrious as most of his predecessors. He led two sets to one, and it was then that the strain of his previous match, less than 24 hours before, took its toll. An exhausted Kodes did not become US Champion. He had though, without doubt marked himself as player of the year.

Lance Tingay, The Daily Telegraph

"Jan Kodes, the Czechoslovak Wimbledon champion and US Open finalist is ranked only forth. Newcombe's first rank is, surely, overestimated; he had no other significant results besides the US Open title." Antonin Bolardt added to this absolutely correct statement: "We are not trying to diminish Mr.LanceTingay's expertise, nevertheless, his published ranking does not seem to reflect fairly achieved results and may thus affect the estimation of other creators of important rankings. The Wimbledon title was always considered as the ultimate accomplishment of the year. This was not the first time that a number of players did not enter it. Jan Kodes confirmed his superior performance at the second most important world tennis championsip at Forest Hills, and reaching quarter-finals in Rome and Paris. None of the players – Newcombe, Smith, or Nastase – can show such results in so many of the most significant tournaments. Newcombe was eliminated in the second round in Rome and the first round in Paris by fairly unknown players but he won the Australian Open against Onny Parun in the finals. Neither Smith, nor Nastase, nor Kodes entered the Australian Open. Nastase did not make it even to the quarter-finals in Wimbledon or Forest Hills. Smith reached only the quarter-finals in Rome, and the sixteens in Paris. Not even the overall Grand Prix standing could negatively affect Jan Kodes' rank. We express our opinion that Jan Kodes' achievements have not been appreciated enough. The same holds for the Dutch Tom Okker, who eliminated Smith in Rome and Paris, and the Yugoslav Pilic, who reached the finals there."

The Daily Telegraph

Peter Wilson and Lance Tingay

"Even the players were forced to admit that Kodes' volley was nothing to be sneezed at and that he was a great deal more then just a clay-court specialist who could play a bit on grass. If one looks back at his record, Kodes was probably the most underrated player of his era."

Richard Evans, The Times

These blunders and curiously put-together rankings were a result of feuds between ITF and ATP. Between 1970 and 1975 Lance Tingay worked out critical evaluation of the Grand Prix system and then speculated whether the going system assessed truly the best player. He lined up all winners of the biggest world championships during those years and their Grand Prix ranking. Besides other interesting findings he also discovered that the Argentine, Guillermo Vilas, won the Grand Prix twice in 1974-75, but had never reached the finals of any of the big Grand Slam championships!

In the past, the Grand Prix point system appreciated the number of tournaments each player entered; the more tournaments you participated in, the better chance you had to be ranked higher because you collected more points by becoming a frequent tennis tourney traveler.

The Grand Prix ranking was unreliable also for another reason; it did not take into consideration the significance, or worth of each tournament. There were instances when a player won two small tournaments and collected the same or almost the same amount of points as if he won Roland Garros! The point system of today is much more just; it shaped itself around the end of the 80s and beginning of the 90s.

Stan Smith, co-seeded No. 1, went down with all flags flying in the semis to Jan Kodes.

Runner-up Kodes proved his Wimbledon crown a worthy one.

There was no way to beat the heat!

Playing his finest tennis in a long time, champion John Newcombe repeated his 1967 triumph. His powerful serving was the key.

The ageless Ken Rosewall, 39, went to the semi-finals, enthralling everyone with his dazzling strokes and speed.

MILITARY SERVICE

After the US Open Jan Kodes left for California to take part in the traditional hard court Pacific South West Championships in Los Angeles. However, he lost to Pat Cramer from South Africa in the first round. His biggest problem was his physical fatigue as well as the difficulties related to the transfer from grass to hard-court. He was almost sorry to be there at all.

However, after several days of adjustments they won a very strongly attended doubles tournament with Vladimir Zednik. In the finals they "gave a lesson" to an overly confident team Nastase - Connors 6:2, 6:4. Other strong teams like Smith - Van Dillen, Alexander - Dent, Ashe-Tanner, Emerson - Rosewall also participated in the tournament. It was only with luck that they defeated Olmedo-Ramirez 3:6, 7:6, 7:6 in the semi-finals overcoming several of their opponents' match-points.

Despite looking like David and Goliath we were a good team with Vladimir. His stature of over six feet made him look like a giant on the court. We were warming up before the final and Connors and Nastase, who were good friends, were merrily joking around. Nastase lighthe-artedly called in our direction: "Tarzan and the Russian!" He called me that to make light of my country of origin as a Soviet colony.

"And you, Romanians? Aren't you their colony too?"

"No, we are Romanians; we come from Rome..."

He tried to aggravate Vladimir by calling him Tarzan...

We finished a few games and as we were changing sides Vladimir Zednik suddenly uttered: "That Nastase really gets on my nerves! Do you know what? If you can reel the serve into Connors' body and if he consequently lifts the return then I'll run across and "smoke" a bullet into Nastase to stop his annoying tattle!"

We delivered as he had suggested. The serve went to Connors' body, he lifted a crosscourt shot, Vladimir ran over and hit Nastase straight into his chest. The audience rustled but the game went on peacefully from that point on! Lads on the other side quieted down and we reigned over the court. Beating them was a real achievement since they won Wimbledon that year.

Rejoicing with Vladimir Zednik after conquering the Wimbledon champions Connors – Nastase 6:2, 6:4 in 1973 Pacific South West Championships in Los Angeles.

Barcelona came soon after and with it Kodes' defense of Spanish Championship title. Nastase avenged the doubles debacle in grand style by defeating Kodes in his favorite tournament in four sets in the semifinals!

Upon return home Jan Kodes found an envelope at home with a stamp of the sender as: District Military Unit – Prague 7. Enlist in Ruda Hvezda (the Red Star)! The next league match Jan entered already in uniform.

"Years later I found out how I ever happened to join the military ranks. The day of my Wimbledon final there was a Cabinet Council meeting and many comrades, the ministers, watched my match during their breaks! Supposedly, Chairman Lubomir Strougal turned to the Minister of Defense, Army General Martin Dzúr: "Well, Sir, what are we going to do with Kodes? He is beating Metreveli!"

By then Major General Professor Dr. Zdenek Kunc had written a report on my behalf declaring me "unfit to enlist" and advocating an issue of a "Blue book" that would officially render me unable to engage in military service for reasons of poor health. The issue was not getting resolved and only in early Fall I received a notice from the Arm Forces that requested me to come to the Ministry of Defense!

I arrived there, announced myself at the Gate and a guard guided me in. He then phoned somewhere and in no time an officer came to pick me up. I followed him through a long corridor, first bars, second bars, passing by more guards, up the stairs till we reached a spacious office.

"Comrade General, recruit Jan Kodes is here" announced my guide, who was soon bid to take leave.

An elderly general, whose name I no longer remember, was sitting behind an enormous desk. I stood there, stared, and waited. After a while he raised his head and said: "Come closer! I want to look at a Wimbledon Champion. Hmm, you suffer from lower back spondylolysis?"

"Well, that is what was discovered by Professor Dr. Kunc in the Central Military Hospital…"

"Right, he writes that here, in this document. But I'll tell you something. I have had the same condition and I made it walking from Buzuluk (USSR) back to Prague!"

I looked at him bewildered. Then I gazed more closely at his scars here and there and everywhere.

"Listen, if you give up playing competitive tennis you won't have to enlist in the Army. But if you intend to go on playing then you must join up."

And that was it. A few weeks went by and I received a draft card; only for a six-month reserve service, stationed with Ruda Hvezda Prague. With that they reassigned me to a Ministry of Interior unit.

It took no time from Sparta to Ruda Hvezda; it was right across the street. He reported for duty exactly as the draft card had ordered him to. The commanding officer was Major Snajdr.

He explained to me the regimen at Ruda Hvezda and told me where to collect my uniform. He sounded quite all right.

I slept in barracks for the first time; the climate was dreadfully hot. All recruits slept in one room, the other was half-empty because the athletes were away; so I slept there. Mosquitoes ate me alive; blankets had moth holes; I woke up with mosquito bites everywhere. It was awful! I hardly slept.

I feared that this was the end of my tennis. Wake-up time was at six, I hardly slept a wink and woke up tired – I could not imagine training under such conditions. When I entered Sparta Club across the street with dark circles under my eyes Dr. Rössler stared at me alarmed. "You must approach the colonel Mudra and ask him for some concessions! After all, you are a Wimbledon Champion and they should not treat you like this! This is not normal!"

I took it to heart, picked up my things and left for the secretariat to see Colonel Vaclav Mudra.

"What do you want here?!" came brusquely from the lips of the secretary.

"This is a private matter; I'd like to talk to the executive officer Vaclav Mudra." She briefly disappeared before she came out again and behind her entered Colonel Vaclav Mudra, who was in charge of all Ruda Hvezda Clubs in the country. He was a robust man with salt and pepper hair and with a broad smile from ear to ear.

"Well hello, Jan! What have you got; what's going on? Come on in!"

I started timidly and formally: "Comrade Colonel, I have been here five days and I find it impossible to practice. First of all, it is very hard to sleep due to the mosquito infestation. And the air is so oppressive that it is hard to breathe; I don't get to sleep more than five hours a night. I can't go on like that! In addition, Davis Cup match is right around the corner and I need to be in tip-top shape!"

"Well, you know, this is military service! How else would you imagine things to run in the Army?"

"I have no idea; I am almost twenty seven..."

"Well, what's with you? You are here only for six months!"

Major General Professor Dr. Kunc' report accomplished its intent - for health reasons I was not allowed to go through Boot Camp, nor was I supposed to lift or carry heavy objects.

"Well, it seems to me that I just have an administrative position here..."

"Well, guess what?" he interrupted me. "We'll make the following deal. You'll sleep at home returning directly here for morning roll call; you must make sure that you report on time; I'll have a word with Snajdr. You must promise me just one thing. You got your uniform and you will wear it at all times."

Normally, we were permitted to be dressed as civilians for certain occasions. "Let's shake hands on that and you can go home to sleep!"

Roll call took place at seven in the morning. It made little difference whether I got up at six in the barracks or half an hour earlier at home to make it to Stromovka on time. It was better to sleep at home in my own bed than in that bed-rack in the barracks. Moreover, it was unbearable going to practice tired and with bites all over me.

Thus I extended my hand to solidify his offer of our broad-minded pact. That was also the reason why I always appeared in uniform during that time-period: at my graduation, the Blossom Ball, the Best Athletes' Banquette and the Grand Prix tournament in Prague....

However, the telephone rang one morning in the Kodes' residence.

"Is private Kodes there? This is Ruda Hvezda's duty-officer. Come at once! Fast! Move it! Important event!"

"Oh, Sweet Jesus! I must be in some jam! - I did not even have time to eat breakfast; I cranked up the car and made my way to Stromovka the fastest way possible.

"What is going on?"

"You are to go to study-hall at once."

Evidently nervous Major Snajdr was waiting for me in front of that room: "Where have you been, man? It has taken you eternity to get here!"

I walked in and there sat three dudes in civilian clothes. One of them was, obviously, the leader. The other two looked sort of strange...

They sat me down in the front bank and positioned themselves opposite to me on their chairs. One of them started rather gruffly: "Well, comrade Kodes, do you realize that your position has changed? You are now a Czechoslovak Army recruit and that obliges you to stay away from elements that could harm the interests of our country and of our socialist constitution."

I stared at him as if he were a ghost and thought: Oh, oh; here it is! I am no longer seventeen but twenty seven. I stayed quiet, staring at him and saying nothing.... "Do you realize that?" he thundered on.

"Yes; oh yes, I do. I have just joined Ruda Hvezda."

"And do you know that you cannot discuss anything, anywhere, with anyone? If somebody asks you how many soldiers are there in this unit or where this unit is located you are not allowed to answer. Has anyone ever asked you anything before?"

"Beg your pardon! I go from one set of tennis courts to another and move around tennis players from the entire world; nobody is interested in such matters...."

I tried to make light of the issue but, at that point, the other younger guy pulled out a notepad and started to recite: "Comrade Kodes, on April 2-8 you were in Milan; you then flew to Rome and on April 30 you left for Paris." He read my precise itinerary.

Deep down I thought that it was easy to find out all that information. After all, one could read where I had visited in the passport. - I nodded that it was true. There have been many tournaments spread out all over the world. I often traveled directly from one to the other.

But sometimes you travel alone, without an escort, right? What does the name of an emigrant Holecek mean to you? Have you been in contact?"

At that moment my adrenalin level rose and I exclaimed: "Naturally we are in contact; he was my team-mate who represented Czechoslovakia along with me! We played Davis Cup together and won many matches. You bet I see him and I talk to him! All players are in the same locker room; you don't expect me to jump out the window when he enters, do you?"

He considered me impudent after my outburst and raised his voice. "Haven't you even attempted to sway him from emigration?"

I, too, turned up the voice volume: "Let me tell you something. I am one of those who tried to persuade him to stay until the very last moment; I wanted him to go on playing Davis Cup doubles with me. However, he got worried when our captain Bolardt gave signs that Milan would not be selected any more. That was the reason why he emigrated!"

He quieted down then but started anew a little while later: "And what is the name Jaroslav Drobny to you?"

"I met him in London when I was eighteen!"

His eyes looked like they were going to pop out.

"I played Junior Wimbledon then. It so happened that an older bespectacled gentleman appeared in front of me surrounded by several Englishmen who introduced him to me: "This is Mr. Drobny, the 1954 Wimbledon Champion." We shook hands, made an acquaintance and that was it."

"Well, what is your opinion of Mr. Drobny?"

"You should not ask me that! I look at him as a tennis player. Mr. Drobny won Wimbledon and that is all I needed to know. He was a man who achieved the same that I accomplished as well. We both know how much effort it took. When we have a chance to talk he congratulates me, gives me advice, and sometimes he brings to my attention the mistakes I commit. And that is all. Nothing less, nothing more!" - I was respectful but held my own.

Suddenly the young one said: "And what about the other emigrants in the United States?"

"I have no idea what you want me to say. There are times when somebody shouts words of encouragement in Czech to me during practice from behind the fence; that is all."

"We are just warning you and want you to know that as soon as you meet somebody you should inform us about it. You should identify the individuals you meet and above all you should let them know that you aren't willing to see them! Do you understand?"

"I understand and it's ok with me."

By then I was quite peeved but, unexpectedly, the older comrade gave a sign to the younger that it was enough. "Thank you." They shook my hand and left.

Major Snajdr ran in to see me at once, distressed and flustered: "You should not have said that you met Drobny."

"Comrade Major, I am not a little kid. If another world war broke out do you think that anybody would care whether I sleep on a bunk-bed in the barracks or in my comfortable bed at home?"

He laughed at that and the issue was closed. I was then left alone. However that interrogation was unpleasant for another reason. Major Snajdr explained to me that all recruits had to undergo the interrogation. "That is done routinely with all new recruits. It is not some special fabrication against you."

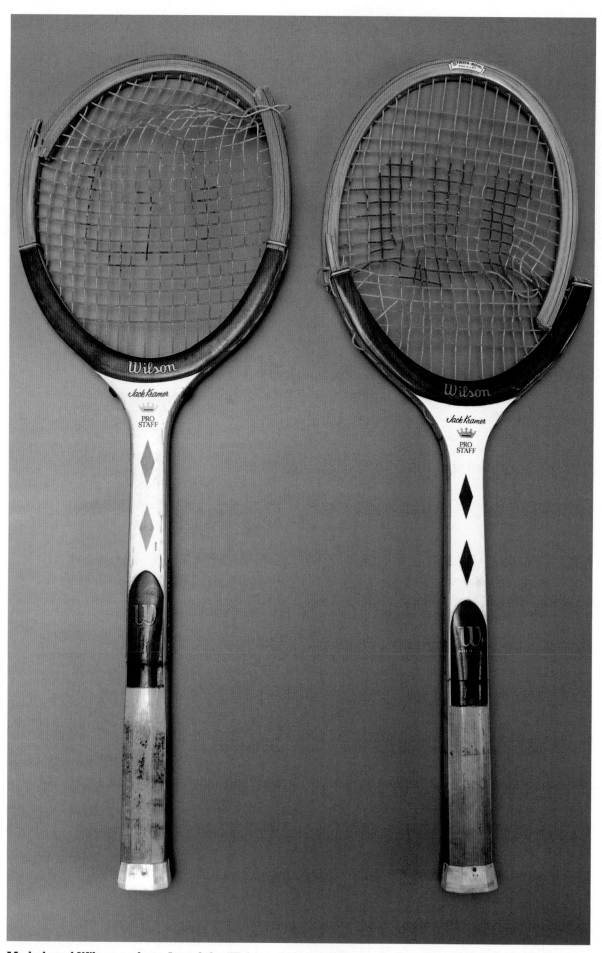

My beloved Wilson rackets. I used the "Fairway" brand grips on the handles of my next rackets...

WITH A RACKET

Nevertheless, it all felt denigrating. They did not treat me as a player who won Wimbledon but rather as any other seventeen year old head-shaven chap at Sumava frontier. I excused it only as a necessary formality.

Prague experienced its first Grand Prix event soon after Jan Kodes captured his Wimbledon title. Pragosport's director, Jaroslav Maly, was the main initiator of the tournament and Antonin Bolardt directed it. Rudolf Bara from Pragosport, the main tournament sponsor, managed the organizing committee. Thanks to Jan Kodes' exhibitions with Tiriac, Nastase, and Rosewall in Sparta Hall at Letna gave inspiration to organize a Grand Prix tournament in Holesovice became reality.

The Tennis Federation tried to clear its conscience. Most members realized that there were no other opportunities for the tennis fans to see the world's best players outside of Davis Cup encounters.

The Grand Prix was listed as a category C with $25,000 purse. Borg, Vilas, Taylor, Pilic, Tanner, Parun, and Taróczy participated. Kodes was seeded as number 1, Roger Taylor as number 2. The tournament ended up like a "small Czechoslovak championship". From the foreigners only the Swede, Ove Bengston, advanced to the semifinals.

The final was purely a Czech affair; Jan Kodes lost in five sets to Jiri Hrebec, who played an outstanding game: 4:6, 6:1, 3:6, 6:0, and 7:5. At 4:4 in the fifth Kodes botched an easy put away on his game point and then tensed up. He finished the match with a double-fault.

"It has been my life goal to defeat Jan Kodes; after all he has been among the world's best players for several years," said Hrebec after the match. "However, I always kept in mind his perseverance and willpower to win and I thought I would never succeed in breaking through it. I came close several times in our home matches. I had set points and match points that I never turned into matches won. For that reason the five sets in Prague had such significance not only as a win but also as a break-through the mental barrier. I received a trophy and prize money and, in addition, badly needed self-confidence."

Kodes' confidence based on his Wimbledon and US Open achievements was gone and that was not an optimistic realization before the upcoming Inter-Zonal Davis Cup semifinal match.

I truly did not want to lose in Prague but Jiri played really well while I was tired at the end of that season. He played his best tennis that year and he confirmed it consequently during Davis Cup matches in Australia.

Publicity poster of the first tennis tournament ever played for "prize money" in Czechoslovakia! It was held in Prague in December 1973 as part of the ITF Grand Prix.

HEADING DOWN UNDER

"Australians fear nobody but Kodes" read the Australian headlines. However, those three days, for which the group of eight Czechoslovak players hauled themselves all the way to the other side of the world, belonged to Jiri Hrebec. He played better than ever before! The inter-zonal semifinal match in Melbourne was the only trip Down Under that Jan Kodes took there in his entire tennis career!

Before the take-off for Australia. From the left: Vladimir Zednik, Jan Kodes, Frantisek Pala and Jiri Hrebec.

Even though I did not succeed there I remember it fondly. We were well aware that the Australians considered us with utmost respect right from the moment of our arrival.

In 1921 Czechoslovakia participated in Davis Cup for the first time and the inter-zonal final in 1973 was the fourth in its history. The first time they played in Canada, the second time in The United States, and then in Brazil. In mid-November of 1973 the strongest Australian selection awaited us at the famous Kooyong Stadium, the venue of Grand Slam events. The team was made up of Laver, Rosewall, Newcombe and Anderson.

The Australians wanted to break the chain of five consecutive Davis Cup wins of the United States and for that reason the non-playing captain, Neale Fraser, called back the legendary "old guards" to play. Laver had not played Davis Cup for the last eleven years, Rosewall was somewhat senior as well, and Newcombe...?

The journey from Prague to Melbourne took us thirty three hours. We experienced a "trifle" of an excitement in Singapore as if some force wanted to spice up the long flight; we had to en-gage in an emergency landing since the landing gear suffered hydraulic failure. I felt pretty queasy when I looked out of the window and saw emergency forces, ambulances and fire engines ready for action just a few hundred feet below me. The moment we touched down Pavel Korda was visibly relieved and uttered: "Next time I am coming by boat!" I felt pretty much the same way.

Soon after landing the players learned from Antonin Bolardt that the referee was going to be an Australian! An older

View of the Kooyong Stadium in Melbourne during the Davis Cup match with Australia.

The singles stories

KODES ANGERED BY REFEREES

By SCOT PALMER

JAN KODES, Czechoslavakia's No. 1 player, yesterday urged neutral referees for future Davis Cup matches with Australia.

Kodes was well beaten yesterday in straight sets 6-3, 7-5, 7-5 by Australia's left hander, Rod Laver.

But he complained after the match about decisions that went against him during the massacre.

Kodes has little to complain about.

The crowd was with him, and Laver, at 35, was returning to Davis Cup play after 11 years' absence, and supposedly was "under done" for this match.

But Laver demonstrated he had lost none of his artistry and cunning.

Laver, after a nervous start, stood back near the centre court base line and attacked Kodes' service as if it was a piece of blancmange.

He punched the ball almost at will past the desperate outstretched racquet of Kodes to touch the side lines and the base line.

Kodes and Laver were involved in two disputed points during their match, but neither occasion deserved Kodes' reaction.

He said after the match: "We thought when we came here we would have no trouble.

"But we have learned from experience."

Kodes said that in Czechoslovakia's two other Davis Cup ties this year neutral referees had been in charge.

He would like one to be in charge next time the Czechs meet Australia.

Kodes was angered by two calls in the first set which enabled Laver to gain a 4-3 break and take control of the set.

Czech captain Antonin Bolardt got off his chair to speak to the linesman as Kodes stood fuming.

But Laver never lost his composure and his confidence soared as the match progressed.

He admitted he had never served better for three years and his volleying, especially down the line, was vintage Laver.

There was another disputed moment in the fifth game of the third set.

This time Kodes, who had already had been given the game, had to walk back on court and serve again, after the referee ruled a let.

JIRI HREBEC shows his big striding style in this forehand return.

'ACE' HREBEC BLASTS NEWK OUT

HIS name is a tongue twister — "Year-Jee Sheb-Betz" is the best you can do with it.

By SCOT PALMER

But yesterday, good looking Czech Jiri Hrebec, 23, blasted Australia's top singles player John Newcombe off Kooyong's centre court.

His success will also mean a red letter day for the Czechoslovakian Ministry of Sport and its Tennis Federation which "adopted" Hrebec at the age of nine years.

Then he was a skinny legged kid kicking a soccer football in the streets of Prague.

At the request of his father Joseph, the State took Hrebec to tennis and said that one day he

would play Davis Cup for the nation.

He has done this for the first time this year against Germany and Egypt.

But in his own words, he's never played a game like the four sets he rolled out yesterday against Newcombe.

Hrebec, 6.2 (183cm) and 11.7 (72kg) who has walked in the shadow of his countryman Jan Kodes for a fortnight because no one could pronounce his name, crushed Newcombe 6-4, 8-10, 6-4, 7-5, in 196 minutes of glorious tennis.

Fourteen times, more times than he'd ever dreamed, the emotional Hrebec aced Newcombe.

In one game in the first set four smashing services left the Australian stranded in quick succession.

The others always seemed to come at crisis points during the long exhausting match and slowly but surely helped to reduce Newcombe's game to mediocrity.

Hrebec jumped in the air and shouted loudly after he had put his country on level terms, one rubber each, with Australia.

Up to now the only Australian scalp that Hrebec really had to his credit was that of veteran Frank Sedgman whom he beat in the first round at Wimbledon this year.

"I wanted so badly to win one rubber at least for Czechoslovakia and now I have done it," said Hrebec.

"I will relax a little now and will try my best against Rod Laver on Sunday."

Hrebec, married, with a six-month-old daughter Andrea, has never worked at anything but tennis.

When other young Czechs were out joining in the socialist scheme of things in Prague Hrebec was working on his superb volley and cannon serve.

Unlike his countryman Jan Kodes, Hrebec has not qualified for army duty because of stomach trouble.

Hrebec' ace sent Newcombe to the locker room.

gentleman, Jim Elthing. Supposedly, the host country wanted to save money on bringing in an umpire from abroad. True to the matter remains that it was a very important match and the only one that precise year without an impartial umpire.

We were very unhappy with Bolardt to have allowed that to pass. It beats me why he always wanted to ingratiate himself with everybody. Was it because of his friendship with Basil Rey, the ITF secretary? Or was it for another reason?

The Hotel Palm Lake Motor was about four and a half miles from the Kooyong Stadium. It was springtime in Australia; the weather was pleasant, training conditions were perfect.

I was intrigued by the Aussies' very different way of practice. We came out with our classical two-phase training: an hour and a half in the morning, and two hours in the afternoon. We interchanged several different game combinations and we also practiced doubles that we deemed very important.

The Australians arrived at 10 a.m. and drilled two against one in

You must be kidding!

Laver in the back, Rosewall at the net, Zednik up front, and Kodes on the ground.

twenty-minute segments. I watched them intently; it was very interesting. For instance, Laver worked out alone opposite two other players, and by the time he finished he was totally spent. In a day he must have played about eight of these extremely rigorous twenty-minute segments.

When I came across the Aussie team's captain, Neal Fraser, after one of these practices I asked him, kidding: "Who will you put in the line up?" Laughing heartily he answered: "The heavy duty weapons! - By the way, we almost lost Rod! His wife did not want to let him come but, supposedly, he slammed the table with his fist and insisted that he would play!"

At that point, Laver had been living in California for several years; however, he made it to Melbourne in time. Similarly, Rosewall and Newcombe had migrated to Texas. Australian fans condoned these world top players for deserting their home country in order to earn their living in the United States, Australia´s tennis arch-rival number one.

It is my humble opinion that it did not matter who Neale Frazer named in the line up. The team that consisted of Laver, Newcombe, Rosewall and Anderson was a "Dream Team"! It is also interesting to mention that we faced the best but, at the same time, the oldest Australian team ever. There was no shame losing to the best team ever.

The toss up between the presidents of both Federations clearly decided the order of matches. Kodes played Laver in the opening match, followed by Hrebec with Newcombe. The first day the Aussie press asked: "What will happen after Newcombe secures a win?" They expected to be leading 2:0 at the close of the opening singles, or tie at 1:1 in the event that Kodes beats Laver and Newcombe defeats Hrebec. However, Jiri Hrebec beat all odds!

Kodes lost the opening match to Laver 3:6, 5:7, and 5:7.

It was the first time ever that I played him on grass. We both started out nervously and, in addition, a strong wind was blowing. It was difficult to break each other's serve. The linesman made a few mistakes right from the start. He called foot-faults on me several times yet they disregarded Laver's double-fault at 3:3 and 0:40. It truly angered me because the referee showed no interest in correcting the mistake.

Jim Elthing was an old man. When there was a questionable call he did not even bother to get out of his chair to verify. His lack of action threw me off balance and I was even more surprised when our captain Bolardt just sat there doing absolutely nothing to help me out. The match could have gone differently... My frustration intensified.

Laver did not play anything spectacular but as the game progressed he played better. He was returning well, and he hit effective passing shots and volleys. I did not succeed in repeating my great play from Forest Hills. I did not play aggressively enough and my volleys did not have the usual bite. I expected more of myself, especially when I was leading 5:2 in the second set; I should not have squandered that. After all, we played on grass!

A significant surprise came out of the second singles game. Jiri Hrebec staged the most spectacular match of his life and defeated John Newcombe 6:4, 8:10, 6:4, and 7:5!

He gave a truly superb performance; in some moments he seemed like in a trance. He noticed nothing and nobody and just concentrated on each and every ball. Melbourne grass had a different quality to the one at Wimbledon; it was a bit slower and Jiri moved extremely well.

In the tenth game of the forth set, at 4:5, Hrebec battled to hold his serve. He was cramping up and had to be massaged during the previous change over; he also gulped down a salt tablet. When Newcombe served the next game Jiri hit two out-of-this-world returns. The Aussie just shook his head in disbelief and fifteen thousand spectators applauded Hrebec, as if they had forgotten that their own player was being overpowered. Jiri finished off his brilliant performance in a classic manner – with two aces.

The Davis Cup encounter had inspired much interest among the public and all three days were quickly sold out. Hrebec's first day performance must have complicated the Aussies' planned line-up for the rest of the matches. While the Czechoslovak doubles team,

This is what Laver's behind-the-back shot looked like at a crucial point of the match.

Kodes – Zednik, came out in pretty good spirits in the second-day doubles, Rosewall replaced Newcombe in the doubles with Laver..

Only after the match concluded we found out that Newcombe had been so thrown off by the singles defeat that he refused to play the doubles. Supposedly, he did not want to take a chance in losing another point!

It was a battle of nerves and serves. Vladimir Zednik proved that his serve was one of the deadliest in the world.

If we only lost two fewer of our serving games, perhaps, we might have won by the same score that we lost – 1:3. It was the return that the Aussies performed better than we did. Our only chance was breaking Rosewall´s serve, however, Laver poached so masterfully at the net that he created confusion for us, while they complimented each other and showed terrific teamwork.

Short of one minute the dramatic battle lasted three hours in oppressive, above a hundred degree Fahrenheit (40°C) heat! Team Kodes – Zednik delivered an excellent effort, nevertheless, they succumbed to the legendary team 4:6, 12:14, 9:7, and 6:8.

I knew the outcome was nothing to be embarrassed about.

...Australian press correctly noted that the host team had luck on their side because Jan Kodes, the Wimbledon champion, was not in his best form. Had he been in tip-top shape the Davis Cup final could have ended up very differently that year. Some twelve thousand spectators watched the matches....

...A crowd of about eight and a half thousand people watched the Saturday three hours long thrilling doubles battle. Both teams displayed excellent tennis. Particularly Laver was outstanding never loosing his serve; Zednik lost only one, Rosewall three, and Kodes four.

Czechoslovak press

Czechs lost the important battle. From left: Laver, Rosewall, Kodes and Zednik.

The third day Hrebec could have tied the score but he succumbed to Laver after five unbelievable sets 7:5, 3:6, 4:6, 6:4, and 4:6 ... Without strong motivation Kodes then surrendered to Newcombe 2:6, 2:6, and 4:6.

Jiri engaged in a masterful game with much finesse. Both players were worn-out by the time the fifth set came around. Unfortunately, Jiri lost his serve in the opening of that set and later got broken again. The score was 2:5; at that point I was sitting in the locker room nervous and wondering whether I was going to go onto the court to fight for the deciding point. Our masseur, Joseph Stejskal, periodically informed me of the running score standing.

Jiri must have gathered his last physical and mental strengths and managed to lower Laver´s advance to 4:5. At that point, the Aussie did not allow his serve and his team´s chance to slip any further. He was up 40:0, Jiri pulled up to 40:30 but his next shot ended up in the net. We lost 1:4, nevertheless, if luck had been on our side it could have been our team fighting in the final against the USA.

Laver – Newcombe – Rosewall.

It is my opinion that this Davis Cup exemplified the pinnacle of Jiri Hrebec's tennis career; he played sublime tennis against Newcombe. - By the way, Australia later beat the USA 5:0 in Cleveland!

It was not the first time that the strange and hard-to-believe "diplomacy" of our non-playing captain, Antonin Bolardt, negatively affected the outcome of our Davis Cup encounter.

When we played in Brazil I reproached him for allowing the match to be played with Brazilian balls Mercury. Davis Cup has always been played with neutral balls! A very similar situation popped up again Down Under. We arrived there and he agreed to an Australian to be the referee!

Bolardt was an OK captain at home; though, even there, he concentrated his energy on the "behind-the-scenes" exploits. When we played abroad he was useless! First of all, his English was close to non-existent, and secondly, he tried to elevate his image to some sort of a sophisticated "diplomat" that he was not. When we complained about the linemen's calls he did not protest, he did not stand up or plead for us; instead he brushed off our requests with words like: "The Australians would not cheat; they don't need that!" Five or six bad calls in the first set of my match against Laver showed him the reality.

I argued and I protested but it was to no avail! The referee sat there like a sack of potatoes and did not interfere in the game, did not alter anything. He pretended that there was nothing wrong. At one moment I shouted: "Don't make me think that the best player in the world needs help from the Umpire!" Naturally, I screamed that in English for all to hear. The Aussies did not like it.

The 1973 Inter-Zonal final match in Australia was lost, unfortunately, due to failed Czechoslovak tennis diplomacy even before the first point was played.

I could not imagine that the Italians or the French would ever accept playing with any but the official Davis Cup balls! It simply would not happen! Nor would a host country national be nominated and accepted as the referee of the match. Do you think that the Australians would accept a Czech referee if the match were to be played in Prague? No way! They would laugh at such proposition! Bolardt allowed it; I have no idea why but he did. Our coach, Pavel Korda, vehemently disputed these decisions too.

"The Aussies don't need it". What a naive excuse from captain Bolardt! As if he had never come across anything like that before! It has always been a sort of unwritten and generally accepted rule in Davis Cup competition that, to some degree, line judges favored the host country. It is for sure that they wouldn't take points away from their own team. When there was doubt the point went to the host country. For that reason the referees have always been from neutral countries to decide disputes objectively. Today, besides the referees, even neutral chair umpires are appointed.

BOSTON MASTERS

From the smallest Continent Jan Kodes headed alone to North America, specifically to Boston, to take part in the end-of-the season Grand Prix Masters.

The Tennis Federation paid for our Prague – Melbourne – Prague air-ticket. I bought another ticket for myself from Melbourne to Hawaii to Boston and to Prague but when I was making the reservation to Boston with British Airways I found out that the price was the same. It made no difference if I was flying to Prague eastwards or westwards, the price was identical.

It occurred to me that my coach, Pavel Korda, who was also the Davis Cup team coach and an employee of CUPES, could fly with me to Boston to the Masters: "Pavel, you don't need to return to Prague with the rest of the team; come along with me to Boston! That way I won't be there all alone!"

That got him thinking and he kept asking me how would we take care of the room and board?

"Don't worry about it; I'll take care of the hotel as well as regular board allowance for you; the only difference will be that you'll return home ten days after the others."

Two days later he came up to me and told me that he would not fly with me to Boston. He was afraid that Bolardt would use it, in some form or another, against him.

"How would he use it against you?"

"Don't you know Antonin? He has created loony atmosphere around us. As a communist he is capable of anything!"

I took it almost personally that Pavel did not try hard enough to stand up for himself and was giving up. "So, I'll approach him and explain to him the situation."

When I met with Antonin he assured me: "No problem; he is free to go with you!"

Yet, he did not join me! Only much later I found out that Bolardt prohibited Pavel to travel with me but was afraid to tell that to me squarely face to face!

Unfortunately, such was the relationship of a top Czechoslovak official with the best player in his care! The Boston Grand Prix Masters tournament was played in two groups. Kodes faced in sequence Nastase, Newcombe and Gorman.

I lost to Nastase in a very tight match 4:6, 6:2, 4:6 and then I lost easily to Newcombe 4:6, 1:6 but defeated Gorman 6:3, 3:6, and 6:3. I did not advance from this group that Nastase won in spite of losing to Gorman in his first match. Due to total number of sets won Nastase advanced and won the entire Masters tournament.

For a week, the Boston Garden arena, home of the Boston Bruins hockey players, transformed into a tennis arena with Matéflex surface. Jan arrived on Monday and checked into a hotel next to the arena. Since the tournament did not start until Wednesday he took advantage of the two free days for practice. After practice he joined others to eat and drink in a small bar opposite to the Garden.

Apparently, it was a popular meeting place of professional hockey players and that was exactly what I was seeking. It so happened that my brother-in-law, Milan Vopicka, gave me a task of buying him skates. He represented our country as a junior and later played hockey league for Sparta.

"You must buy me skates – Takabery; and also good boots. The best ones are CCM," he requested of me before my departure.

We entered that bar after practice; we sat down and chatted, I ordered a light meal and a drink. At the bar a chap was sitting next to me who suddenly turned to face me and asked: "You are a tennis player, aren't you? Where are you from?"

"From Czechoslovakia; I am here to play the Commercial Union Grand Prix Masters."

"Oh, that is great! We would like to watch some tennis. I am Derek Sanderson, a Boston Bruins hockey player." He was one of the NHL's most productive offensive players of that era, won Stanley Cup twice in 1970 and 1972!

I thought to myself: "Gee, this is unbelievable; such a star is sitting next to me!" We engaged in a conversation and discussed many topics – hockey, tennis... and suddenly I remembered: Damn, my brother-in-law and the skates! Should I ask Derek about it or should I not? Wouldn't it be embarrassing?

At last I pulled the courage and asked:"Listen, would you be able to help me with something?" "What do you need?"

I explained to him that my brother-in-law was also a hockey player and needed some decent skates; at that he said: "Look, that's not a problem. You give me your racket, I'll give you skates."

As I envisioned what he had just said I laughed; does he really mean it? At that point he already knew that I had won Wimbledon, but new boots with mounted skates on them cost then about five hundred dollars or more! That was not an inexpensive item!

We remained chatting there till about half past ten. Finally, we got up to take leave since our matches were going to start the following day. In the meantime, he ran off and sat at another table with some girl but as soon as he noticed that I was about to leave he yelled: "Hey guys! There will be tickets and hockey sticks for you, ok?!" Then he turned to me: "Come to the Garden tomorrow at eleven with the racket still in it's wrap; take the elevator to the fourth floor and find the door that says "Boston Bruins"; somebody will be there and will give you the skates and boots."

I restrained myself from getting too excited, nevertheless, I took the racket the next day after practice, got in the elevator on the second floor where our locker-room was, and rode the elevator up to the fourth. The door slid open and I felt like Alice in Wonderland! Wherever I looked there was red carpet...In other places there were tiles but Boston Bruins had red carpets in front of each office and changing room....

I knocked on the door with the racket in my hand. Somebody opened; from his attire I thought he might be a custodian. "I am Jan Kodes..."

I did not manage to even finish a sentence "You are Jan Kodes! Do you have the racket?"

"I do; here it is." I passed him the racket and he gave me a box. The original, still sealed box. Skates, boots CCM, size eight and a half! I took it and left. "Golden" Derek saved me from having to run from one store to another in search of the skates. Additionally, I found out that it was not possible to find this brand in regular stores; they would have had to be ordered. For a long time this episode seemed to me like a dream that has passed by.

After Jan's return home he was finally able to participate in his graduation that had been postponed twice. Jan met with his closest family and friends in the lounge of the School of Economy building and received his diploma from the hands of the University President.

It was a modest private celebration but I was very pleased with it particularly on behalf of my father. He was immensely proud and happy that I finished my university studies.

At the end of the year Jan Kodes was voted the Best Czechoslovak Athlete of 1973. The fact that it was not an Olympic year made it easier for him to come out on top....

It was the most successful year of Kodes' career.

The Boston Masters 1973

STATE DECORATION

In winter of 1974, before the start of a new season when gaining strength and stamina was paramount, Jan participated in a training camp in the mountains with his Sparta team. Soon after that the WCT tournament circuit started in Philadelphia and he advanced all the way to the semi-finals. There he met the eventual winner, Rod Laver, and battled with him for four sets. The press commented on the match with much respect and admiration. Upon his return to Europe he entered three tournaments – Bologna, London, and Barcelona. He advanced to the semi-finals only in London; everywhere else he dropped out earlier and returned home in between tournaments. While at home, he obtained the news of being awarded a National Distinction for his merit in Development. He was pleased with the recognition however, there was something "fishy" about the presentation of it.

Customarily, the President presents Decorations for Outstanding Work in the Prague Castle Hradcany on October 28, on the occasion of celebration of the origin of Czechoslovakia as a country. However, Jan Kodes was not invited to the Castle in 1973. Only a few months later, in early spring of 1974, he was presented that honor in the Central Office Building of the Communist Party without any journalists or television crews present; it was, as if it was a secret ceremony.

State Decoration presented in Frantisek Ondrich's office. Only Antonin Himl could be present.

I could only guess why I was not invited to the Castle in October 1973. I had no idea that I was going to receive that recognition. I would have, however, flown in from anywhere in the world to receive the honor. The CUPES proposed my nomination and it was approved; but, it must have been held up and signed with delay. Reason? I was a "tennis" player! Tennis was not an Olympic sport and for that reason many representatives of our politburo did not relish it.

Only later the CUPES Chairman, Antonin Himl, injected a bit of light into the whole affair: Jan, we are content that, in the end, the proposal was signed and you were awarded the honor. Let's be happy with the outcome."

There was an International AIPS congress of journalists in Spanish Malaga around that same time. Kodes was voted fourth among the world's best male athletes in 1973! Formula 1 pilot, Jackie Stewart, was selected for the top spot, Dwight Stones, the superb American high-jumper took the second place, and the phenomenal Belgian cyclist, Eddie Merckx, took the third.

His Wimbledon title was valued more abroad than at home. Hardly any mention appeared in the press about his fourth best athlete in the world place ... Jan's most difficult moments in his life happened during the mentioned European tournaments. His father fell ill with leukemia while his son continued playing the WCT tournament series in South America and in the United States.

I did not want to depart. I got myself into the frame of mind that I did not care to play in Brazil or the other tournaments in South America. My dad took precedence! However, it was

Matches with Rod Laver always had a special motivation. This time I lost at „Spectrum"– NHL Philadelphia Flyers home in four sets. (pic.Laver in blue).

his explicit wish that I continued playing and so, in the end, I flew to Sao Paolo and there I "helped" the young Argentine, Guillermo Vilas, become famous. I did not take advantage of two match-points at 6:1, 5:3 and 40:15 and, instead, I lost the match 6:1, 5:7, and 3:6!

The WCT circuit continued on in Palm Desert, where Jan received the shocking news – his father passed away! A distressed journey home followed, then the funeral, his mother drowning in sorrow, grief...

Soon afterwards he traveled via Siberia to Tokyo where he lost to Taylor, and from there he headed to Houston, Texas. In the first round he came across Vilas again and lost to him 6:3, 3:6, 2:6. He then continued on to Denver to play in the last but important tournament of the circuit.

It was here where they would determine whether I advance into the final WCT Masters in Dallas. I knew I needed to reach at least the semis; anything less would have meant that I was out of luck.

He beat the first seed, Rod Laver, 6:2, 6:4 in quarter-finals! With that he acquired the longed for points; he then succumbed to Roscoe Tanner's deadly serves.

Denver is located in higher altitude and the balls were flying faster and further, which helped my serves when I played against Laver. However, it gave that much more advantage to Roscoe Tanner with his bomb-like serves. Nobody was even surprised when he defeated Arthur Ashe in the finals.

The 1974 WCT circuit was the most difficult one that Kodes ever participated in. He was placed in a green group – Laver, Ashe, Borg, Panatta, Taylor; Tanner, Solomon, Tiriac, Vilas, Dibbs, Cox.... Each opponent was more difficult than the next. And what distances they had to travel - USA, Europe, Brazil, Japan, and back to the US! From the three groups the following players advanced into the WCT Masters final event: Laver, Ashe, Borg, Kodes, Nastase, Newcombe, Smith and Okker. Jan Kodes defeated his life-rival Nastase 7:6, 6:1, and 7:5 deli-

Moody Coloseum at Dallas. The court was marked with singles lines only.

vering a very good performance. However, in the semifinals he came short against Borg, ten years his junior, 6:4, 4:6, 3:6, 2:6!

I realized that Borg was beginning to be beyond my capability. I won the first set 6:4 and I felt that if I did not win the second set I would not have a chance against him. Borg played from the baseline, hit no unforced errors, forced me to stay back and if I approached the net he passed me with artistry. My serve was inconsistent and that decided the outcome. Nevertheless, the game was more even than the result suggests.

In the course of the tournament several interesting and surprising outcomes came out of a number of matches. Ashe lost to Borg, Laver to Smith, Okker to Newcombe, who came out as the Champion in the end when he overcame Borg in a surprising 4:6, 6:3, 6:3, and 6:2 victory. Kodes succumbed to Smith 4:6, 5:7 in a battle for the third place.

By then both of us had had enough of tennis and physical strain. We were glad it was coming to an end.

SCANDAL IN ROME

Undoubtedly, the "marble courts" at Foro Italico have soaked up not only sweat but also many tales. However, Kodes' 1974 extempore during the Italian Open topped them all. The Wimbledon champion was seeded second. In the second round he was to play the second or third best player of Italy, Antonio Zugarelli, on Centre Court. That year the first two rounds were played best of three sets. Kodes lost the first one 6:7, and won the second 6:3. In the third set and serving at 4:5 and 30:30 he hit a winning volley that bounced squarely on the line...

I visually checked and saw that the line-judge indicated with both hands that the ball was good. At that I turned around and walked to the baseline to serve for the next point, when I heard: "Advantage Zugarelli!" That gave him a match-point! I stopped short and walked over to the umpire asking: "Beg your pardon? That is incorrect! Advantage Kodes, eh? It bounced on the line!"

He shrugged his shoulders: "The referee claims that it was out."

"What referee?"

In that instant a man got up in a box and walked over to us saying: "Kodes, Kodes; that was out and it is advantage Zugarelli."

"What advantage Zugarelli; the line-judge clearly indicated it as an "in" shot."

"No, no, no, no! I saw it and it was out, resulting in advantage Zuragelli!"

That was the referee of the tournament, Michele Brunetti. *I walked around the net and pointed at the imprint. It was beautifully clear and right on the line; the ball was obviously good. I said: "You can order the point to be played over; you can't just give him a point that he did not win! A match-point is in the works here. I won that point, not he."*

"I am the tournament referee!"

Slowly, I started seeing blood: "Mr. Brunetti, you are confused with Davis Cup! Only there a referee is permitted to change the line-judge's call; not in a tournament like this one! Here the referee is the Umpire.

The tournament referee Michel Brunetti was in the wrong. He had no right to change the linesman's and chair umpire's call.

With a frozen expression in his face he responded: "I am the referee here and I can do as I want!"

That was too much for me! I pushed him and he staggered. The crowd hummed. "Go away!" I yelled. "You have nothing to do here! This is not a Davis Cup match!" I pushed him again. The crowd roared.

At that moment another chap got up from the box, Gianfranco Cameli, the tournament director, and announced: "Game, set, match, Zugarelli!" The audience whistled and hollered, the whole place broke into crazy chaos. People wanted to see tennis; they wanted the outcome to be decided on the court.

I was afraid that the ITF was going to punish me with a suspension but during press conference journalists stood up for me! They did not defend my unsportsmanlike actions and the fact that I pushed the referee twice but they accentuated the whole egregious situation.

After this unprecedented event the ATP enforced a rule that a domestic national cannot occupy

Bertie Bowron

the post of a referee at any tournament and they created a new position of a "tournament Supervisor".

After many years I became a member of the Davis Cup commission. Brunetti represented Italy in the same commission! Ten years had gone by since the incident and we came face to face at one of the meetings. At first we just gaped at each other and did not converse but in time the ice was broken; we just laugh about it by now.

One day Panatta and Bertolucci told me: "Do you know what is really paradoxical? - The fact that the guy Brunetti is, fundamentally, a terribly nice and just person. We have no idea what prompted him to come out with that ridiculous call in his capacity of a tournament referee. Most likely he confused the Davis Cup rules with the tournament rules; he is a bit of a moron. Since he worked as a Davis Cup referee for so many years he must have gotten mixed-up and applied the same rules to a tournament."

The ITF was benevolent and Kodes lucked out without any punishment. He left worriless for Paris. At 1974 Roland Garros they tried out playing on Centre Court at night under lights. The weather was awful and cold. Kodes lost to Jauffret 6:7, 5:7, 5:7. The night lighting was not very good and since only few people sat in the audience the organizers decided to discontinue the night play from the next year on.

WIMBLEDON AND US PRO 1974

As tradition dictates, as a winner of the preceding Wimbledon Kodes opened on Centre Court against an excellent doubles player, Sherwood Stewart, from the United States.

It reminded me the circus-like atmosphere of the previous US Open at Forest Hills. The stadium was bursting in seems, there were journalists, photographers, and everybody who was seeking a sensation. What bothered me the most was the fact that even players gambled money that Stewart would beat me in the first round.

Everybody looked forward to the match with eagerness and anticipation but - there was no sensation. Kodes won persuasively 6:3, 6:4, and 9:7!

It rained cats and dogs in London and the tournament started sliding.

After three five-set victories against Lief Johansson from Sweden, Dick Crealy from Australia, and Tom Gorman I was really tired. Especially the third match was full of drama. I was down 2 sets to none yet I won after forcing back several match-points that Tom had at 6:5 in the fourth set. It was an exhausting battle with a triumphant end 6:8, 2:6, 6:3, 9:7, and 6:4.

Due to the adjustments caused by rain-delays Kodes had to play the quarterfinal match against Jimmy Connors the following day. The match against Gorman concluded in the late afternoon, and the quarterfinal match was pushed two hours ahead and started at noon. There was very little time to rest up well, or go through a common recovery treatment. On top of everything the match was set to court number 1 that Kodes never really liked.

I believe we played an amazing five-set match worthy of a status of a final match. I lost 3:6 in the fifth. I did not take advantage of a chance I had after winning the first set and having a break point in the second at 3:2. It did not bother me much at the moment when it happened but in retrospect it dawned on me and I regretted it a lot. In the semis I would have met Dick Stockton, who I had never lost to, and in the finals I would have met Rosewall, who got swept away by Connors 6:1, 6:1, and 6:4. It was the same Rosewall, who reached the finals for the fourth time and lost again. In his first Wimbledon final he lost to Jaroslav Drobny in 1954! Connors was two years old then. In a way I felt sorry for Ken. If I had made it to the finals for the second time I might have let him win...

But these are all speculations; I see things clearly today. As luck was on my side in 1973 so it was against me in 1974. At any rate, I believe that my "balance sheet" from 1972 to 1974 was

MEN'S SINGLES 1974

FIRST ROUND	SECOND ROUND	THIRD ROUND	FOURTH ROUND	QUARTER-FINALS	SEMI-FINALS	FINAL

Top half

J. D. NEWCOMBE (AUS) (1)
G. Goven (F)
B. Mitton (SA)
G. Masters (AUS)
N. Pilic (YU)
N. Estep (USA)
H. J. Plotz (G)
E. Dibbs (USA)
V. Zednik (CZ)
G. Vilas (ARG)
M. C. Riessen (USA)
T. Nowicki (POL)
H. Elschenbroich (G)
J. E. Mandarino (BR)
E. J. van Dillen (USA)
J. Singh (IN)
A. R. ASHE (USA) (8)
H. Kary (AU)
T. I. Kakulia (USSR)
W. W. Martin (USA)
R. P. Dell (USA)
R. Tanner (USA)
V. Gerulaitis (USA)
K. Meiler (G)
K. R. ROSEWALL (AUS) (9)
B. J. Phillips-Moore (AUS)
R. C. Lutz (USA)
V. Amritraj (IN)
W. N'Godrella (F)
R. G. Giltinan (AUS)
M. Lara (M)
P. Kanderal (SWZ)
S. R. SMITH (USA) (4)
G. E. Reid (USA)
B. Taroczy (HU)
R. R. Maud (SA)
N. A. Fraser (AUS)
D. A. Lloyd (GB)
U. Pinner (G)
J. Borowiak (USA)
I. Tiriac (RU)
P. Dominguez (F)
P. Cornejo (CH)
R. Ramirez (M)
G. Seewagen (USA)
J. B. Chanfreau (F)
D. E. Deblicker (F)
H. Rahim (PAK)
B. BORG (SW) (5)
G. R. Stilwell (GB)
J. G. Simpson (NZ)
R. L. Case (AUS)
J. Fassbender (G)
M. Cox (GB)
I. El Shafei (UAR)
O. Parum (NZ)
M. ORANTES (SP) (12)
H. Solomon (USA)
J. F. Caujolle (F)
T. Koch (BR)
O. K. Davidson (AUS)
A. D. Roche (AUS)
J. G. Alexander (AUS)
P. Szoke (HU)

SECOND ROUND (top):
NEWCOMBE (1) 6–3 6–2 8–6
Masters 6–4 6–3 7–5
Pilic 4–6 6–3 6–4 6–2
Dibbs 2–6 6–1 6–4 6–2
Vilas 6–2 9–8 6–4
Riessen 6–2 6–4 7–5
Elschenbroich 7–5 6–2 6–1
van Dillen 7–9 6–3 4–6 7–5 6–3
ASHE (8) 6–4 6–2 6–4
Kakulia 8–6 6–1 5–7 6–4
Tanner 6–4 6–3 6–4
Meiler 6–8 6–4 6–2 6–1
ROSEWALL (9) 6–4 6–3 6–3
Amritraj 7–5 6–4 8–6
Giltinan 6–3 3–6 6–4 6–2
Kanderal 4–6 8–6 6–2 ret'd
SMITH (4) 6–3 6–3 6–2
Maud 4–6 4–6 9–8 6–2 6–4
Fraser 4–6 8–9 7–5 6–4 11–9
Borowiak 6–3 6–3 9–8
Dominguez 6–3 6–0 8–6
Ramirez 9–7 8–9 6–4 5–7 6–3
Chanfreau 9–8 5–7 9–8 1–6 9–7
Deblicker w.o.
BORG (5) 6–1 4–6 6–4 6–1
Case 6–3 9–8 6–3
Fassbender 6–2 6–4 7–9 7–5
El Shafei 4–6 4–6 8–9 7–5 9–7
ORANTES (12) 6–3 6–2 6–1
Koch 6–4 1–6 4–6 6–4 8–6
Roche 6–2 6–4 7–5
Alexander 6–2 7–5 8–6

THIRD ROUND (top):
NEWCOMBE (1) 9–8 6–3 8–6
Pilic 6–4 8–6 6–4
Vilas 7–9 6–1 6–4 3–6 6–1
van Dillen 6–4 7–5 6–4
ASHE (8) 6–1 6–4 6–3
Tanner 8–6 6–4 8–6
ROSEWALL (9) 6–2 5–7 9–8 6–1
Kanderal 7–5 9–8 7–5
SMITH (4) 6–4 6–1 6–2
Borowiak 8–9 6–3 8–6 1–0 ret'd
Dominguez 3–6 9–7 6–3 7–5
Chanfreau 2–6 7–5 6–3 9–8
BORG (5) 3–6 6–1 8–6 7–5
El Shafei 7–5 8–6 6–4
ORANTES (12) 6–2 6–4 4–6 6–2
Roche 8–6 6–4 4–6 8–9 6–3

FOURTH ROUND (top):
NEWCOMBE (1) 6–2 7–5 7–5
van Dillen 6–3 6–4 1–6 7–5
Tanner 7–5 6–3 8–9 6–3
ROSEWALL (9) 6–2 6–3 6–3
SMITH (4) 8–9 6–3 6–4 8–6
Dominguez 7–5 6–1 6–4
El Shafei 6–2 6–3 6–1
ORANTES (12) 2–6 5–7 7–5 6–4 8–6

QUARTER-FINALS (top):
NEWCOMBE (1) 7–5 6–3 6–4
ROSEWALL (9) 2–6 9–7 6–3 7–5
SMITH (4) 6–3 6–4 7–5
El Shafei 6–4 3–6 6–3 7–5

SEMI-FINALS (top):
ROSEWALL (9) 6–1 1–6 6–0 7–5
SMITH (4) 9–8 7–5 6–8 7–5

FINAL (top):
ROSEWALL (9) 6–8 4–6 9–8 6–1 6–3

Bottom half

F. D. McMillan (SA)
A. Mayer (USA)
R. Thung (NTH)
R. Seegers (SA)
J. M. Yuill (SA)
R. R. Dowdeswell (RH)
A. Amritraj (IN)
T. W. GORMAN (USA) (11)
R. D. Crealy (AUS)
R. Taylor (GB)
R. A. J. Hewitt (SA)
J. R. Pinto Bravo (CH)
J. M. Lloyd (GB)
L. Johansson (SW)
S. E. Stewart (USA)
J. KODES (CZ) (6)
A. Zugarelli (IT)
J. Higueras (SP)
K. G. Warwick (AUS)
A. C. Neely (USA)
J. Fillol (CH)
F. Pala (CZ)
J. I. Muntanola (SP)
J. R. Ganzabal (ARG)
H. J. Pohmann (G)
A. Panatta (IT)
P. C. Kronk (AUS)
P. Proisy (F)
C. S. Dibley (AUS)
P. C. Dent (AUS)
O. Bengtson (SW)
J. S. CONNORS (USA) (3)
J. G. Paish (GB)
A. J. Pattison (RH)
K. Johansson (SW)
P. R. Gerken (USA)
S. Krulevitz (USA)
R. I. Kreiss (USA)
J. W. Feaver (GB)
A. METREVELI (USSR) (10)
W. J. Austin (USA)
M. J. Farrell (GB)
I. Molina (COL)
E. C. Drysdale (SA)
S. Baranyi (HU)
P. Barthes (F)
R. D. Ralston (USA)
T. S. OKKER (NTH) (7)
T. Svensson (SW)
G. Battrick (GB)
T. Sakai (J)
R. L. Stockton (USA)
C. M. Pasarell (USA)
C. E. Graebner (USA)
S. Ball (AUS)
C. J. Mottram (AUS)
I. G. Fletcher (AUS)
S. A. Warboys (GB)
F. Jauffret (F)
M. Holecek (Stateless)
B. E. Gottfried (USA)
R. J. Moore (SA)
J. Hrebec (CZ)
I. NASTASE (RU) (2)

SECOND ROUND (bottom):
Mayer 3–6 9–7 5–7 6–2 6–4
Thung 6–1 6–4 6–4
Yuill 6–3 6–2 4–6 3–6 6–3
GORMAN (11) 6–4 7–5 3–6 4–6 8–6
Crealy 4–6 9–8 6–3 9–8
Hewitt 6–4 6–1 2–6 6–3
Johansson 6–3 6–3 6–2
KODES (6) 6–3 6–4 9–7
Higueras 4–6 6–2 6–3 4–6 6–1
Warwick 9–8 7–5 6–1
Fillol 6–4 6–1 6–4
Ganzabal 9–7 9–8 6–0
Panatta 4–6 6–2 6–3 6–3
Proisy 6–3 6–4 6–4
Dent 4–6 4–6 9–8 6–4 11–9
CONNORS (3) 6–1 7–9 6–2 6–4
Pattison 6–2 6–3 6–8 6–3
Johansson 7–9 3–6 6–2 6–1 14–12
Krulevitz 6–3 3–6 7–5 4–6 6–4
METREVELI (10) 6–2 6–3 3–6 6–1
Austin 5–7 6–3 6–2 6–0
Drysdale 6–0 6–3 6–3
Baranyi 6–2 6–2 6–0
OKKER (7) 6–1 6–3 4–6 6–3
Battrick 9–8 6–4 6–2
Stockton 6–4 6–3 6–2
Pasarell 6–3 0–6 6–3 4–6 6–3
Mottram 6–4 6–3 7–9 6–3
Fletcher 7–5 3–6 6–3 6–3
Jauffret 1–6 4–6 6–4 8–6 6–4
Gottfried 6–3 4–6 7–5 2–6 10–8
NASTASE (2) 8–9 6–3 6–4 6–2

THIRD ROUND (bottom):
Thung 9–7 6–2 6–3
GORMAN (11) 6–3 7–9 8–6 6–3
Crealy 2–6 0–6 6–4 6–4 6–4
KODES (6) 3–6 7–5 6–3 4–6 6–4
Warwick 6–3 6–0 8–6
Fillol 6–4 6–3 6–4
A. Panatta 6–4 7–5 4–6 6–2
CONNORS (3) 5–7 6–3 3–6 6–3 10–8
Pattison 6–2 6–3 6–4
METREVELI (10) 6–1 1–6 6–3 6–4
Drysdale 0–6 6–2 6–4 6–3
OKKER (7) 6–2 6–2 6–4
Stockton 3–6 6–3 6–4 4–6 6–4
Mottram 6–2 9–8 9–7
Fletcher 6–3 6–4 9–7
NASTASE (2) 6–3 6–2 9–8

FOURTH ROUND (bottom):
GORMAN (11) 8–6 6–1 6–1
KODES (6) 4–6 6–4 6–3 2–6 7–5
Fillol 6–3 4–6 6–1 6–4
CONNORS (3) 6–2 7–5 6–2
METREVELI (10) 3–6 6–4 7–5 4–6 6–3
OKKER (7) 4–6 6–3 6–3 6–3
Stockton w.o.
NASTASE (2) 7–5 6–3 6–4

QUARTER-FINALS (bottom):
KODES (6) 6–8 2–6 6–3 9–7 6–4
CONNORS (3) 6–3 5–7 6–0 6–1
METREVELI (10) 9–8 3–6 6–4 6–2
Stockton 5–7 6–4 6–3 9–8

SEMI-FINALS (bottom):
CONNORS (3) 3–6 6–3 6–3 6–8 6–3
Stockton 6–4 7–5 6–1

FINAL (bottom):
CONNORS 4–6 6–2 6–3 6–4

WINNER: J. S. CONNORS (3) — 6–1 6–1 6–4 (Winner)

Capital letters denote seeded players. Number following player's name gives seeding order.

pretty good: semifinals, championship victory, quarter-finals. When I lost it was to the eventu-al winner.

Wimbledon was always marked by tradition of conservative England. Establishing changes or modifying what was firmly rooted was very challenging. Nevertheless, the organizers acted quite quickly in 1974 and within six months of 1973 US Open they permitted chairs at change-overs even at this most prestigious tournament.

I was used to the classical side-changing: a game finished, I took a sip, wiped off sweat and walked back to the other side of the court. It took a few seconds and the game kept its momentum. However, after the changes and introduction of chairs Jimmy sat down every time for a full minute and a half. I was already hopping on the baseline while he took his sweet time on the chair! It bothered me. With a slight exaggeration I can say that besides a Wimbledon trophy replica I also earned two other supreme achievements. In 1973 I was the first finalist playing a tie-break, and a year later I experienced the introduction of chairs at change-overs.

Czechoslovakia defeated Germany 3:2 in Davis Cup in Munich, where Jiri Hrebec got injured during a match-point against Pohmann. The weakened team was then defeated in Donetsk in Ukraine in spite of leading 2:1 after the doubles. On the final day Kodes lost to very well playing Metreveli even though he was ahead 4:1 in the fifth set!

From the leading score of 4:1 in the fifth set they cheated me out of one point after another; the match then turned around and I lost.

During the flight home one of the Czech newsmen from Rude pravo (the official daily of the Communist Party) patted me on my shoulder: "Jan, I was in Wimbledon this year and saw all your five-set matches. I was again in Donetsk now and after all that I have seen I promise to you that I will not write a negative word about you till the end of your career!"

I responded: Well, why don't you write the real story from Donetsk right now?" He froze. "Jan, I can't do that..."

After that frustrating Davis Cup match Kodes had to take part in the National Championships in Ostrava. He pulled his gluteus maximus muscle in the finals against Zednik and had to retire from the match at 1:2 in sets. Because of that injury he then missed three Grand Prix tournaments – Toronto, Washington, and Indianapolis. He returned to play the US Pro circuit event in Boston, he beat Arthur Ashe in the quarters 6:3, 6:2. The rising star of the next generation and the female

U.S. Pro Championships semifinals at the Longwood Tennis Club, Boston in 1974. Björn Borg overcame Jan Kodes 7:6, 6:0, 1:6, 2:6, 7:6. Kodes led 5:1 in the fifth set!!

fans' idol, Bjorn Borg, the Roland Garros champion that year, awaited him in the semis. *The surface that we played on in Boston was green-gray clay "hard-thru" that resembled sand. We played for more than three hours and everybody rooted for Borg.*

I was 2:0 down in sets; lost the first one in a tie-breaker but in the second Bjorn bestowed me a "bagel". I tried to play from the baseline, prepare the ball and wait for an opportunity to approach the net, rather than attacking with uncontrolled haste. After I received the "bagel" I got mad and decided to take risks. Now I'll approach everything and press forward to the net no matter what; I'll try to speed things up so that he can't develop his machine-like game. I was successful and won the third 6:1, fourth 6:2! I was well ahead even in the fifth – 5:1 ...but he passed me with a ball that bounced off the tape. I was right there but the ball sprang up over my racket! Then came another shot off the tape and things turned around. Borg then woke up!

I tensed up and lost 6:7! From 5:1 in the lead I did not produce a match-point. Unbelievable! I had 30:0 or 30:15 several times; always just two points away from the match. I did not make any obvious mistakes but he was passing me with amazing precision. My serve was not strong enough; Borg returned it effectively. It was impossible to hit an "ace" against him for he stood way back. Perhaps I should have switched back to baseline game but I was too tired for that.

Two opponents hit a peak together. From 1:1 in the third Kodes, leaping like a gymnast, sometimes throwing himself lengthwise at the ball like an acrobatic goal-keeper and doing everything except rupture himself, won nine games in succession to reach 4:0 in the fourth and soon levelled the match at two sets all.

Then came the excitement of that final fifth set. Admittedly service was of small account in this thriller, there being 23 breaks in 46 games. Nonetheless Kodes served three times for the match at 5:2, 5:4, and 6:5 but still lost.

This glorious three-hour struggle in which there deserved to be no loser, ended appropriately with a tie-breaker and the unyielding Borg fired just enough of those fireball double-handed backhands to win 7:4!

Frank Rostron, The Daily Express

US OPEN 1974

The 1974 US Open followed. It was memorable mainly for the fact that it was played for the last time on grass! Kodes lost to Connors in the quarter-finals 5:7, 3:6, 7:5, 2:6. After his Wimbledon victory Jimmy also won the US Open sweeping Ken Rosewall off the court 6:1, 6:0, and 6:1.

Both, Borg and Connors, played in Wimbledon in 1973; one lost to Metreveli, the other to Taylor. A year later I was losing to them! They progressed immensely during that one year. Borg won Roland Garros, Connors took Wimbledon and US Open titles. At that level the technical side of a player stays more or less the same but it is the mental strength that matures. It shows particularly in crunch moments when their self-esteem and confidence help them through.

For me it was important to know that they were still afraid of me and held due respect for my game. The Fall started with traditional tournaments in Spain.

I came across Borg again in the quarter-finals in Barcelona.

We played the best of three sets: I won the first 6:0 and led 5:3 in the second but lost it 7:9; I led again 5:3 in the third and lost it 5:7.

Time and again I was so close to winning but had no match-points! It was exhausting; we had long exchanges through which he moved like an agile cat always meeting the ball with perfect timing. It drove me crazy!

During one of the last tournaments, in Stockholm, I called my wife and she read to me a recent telegram:

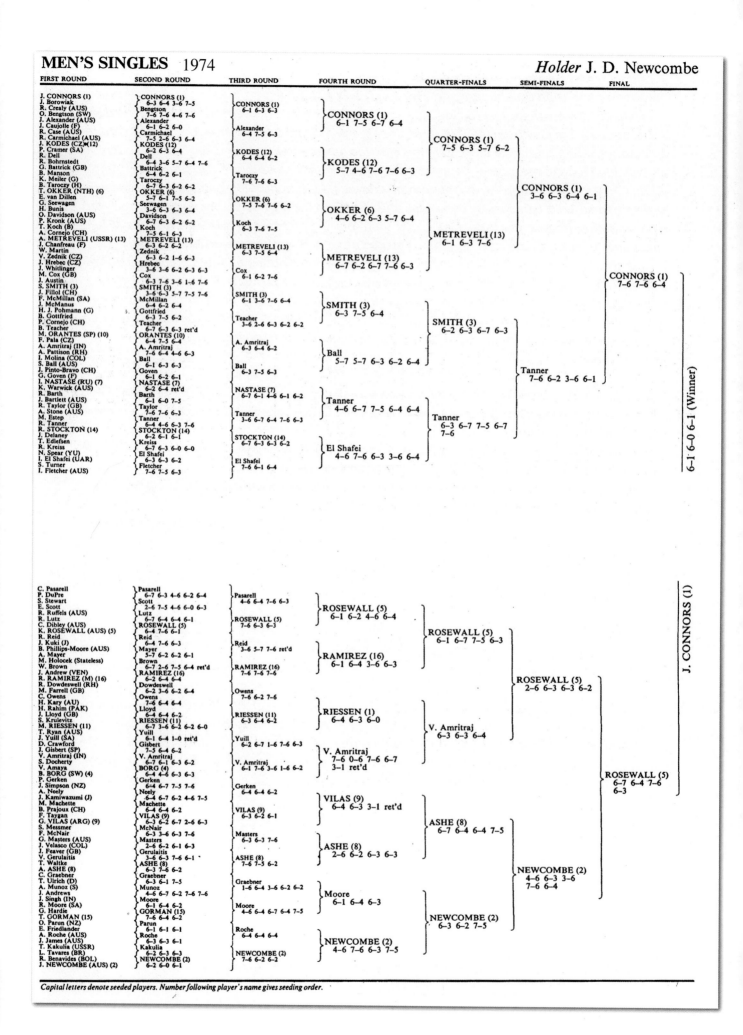

FIRST ROUND	SECOND ROUND	THIRD ROUND	FOURTH ROUND	QUARTER-FINALS	SEMI-FINALS	FINAL

Top half

- J. CONNORS (1)
- J. Borowiak
- R. Crealy (AUS)
- O. Bengtson (SW)
- J. Alexander (AUS)
- J. Caujolle (F)
- R. Case (AUS)
- R. Carmichael (AUS)
- J. KODES (CZ) (12)
- P. Cramer (SA)
- R. Dell
- R. Bohrnstedt
- G. Battrick (GB)
- B. Manson
- K. Meiler (G)
- B. Taroczy (H)
- T. OKKER (NTH) (6)
- E. van Dillen
- G. Seewagen
- H. Bunis
- O. Davidson (AUS)
- P. Kronk (AUS)
- T. Koch (B)
- A. Cornejo (CH)
- A. METREVELI (USSR) (13)
- J. Chanfreau (F)
- W. Martin
- V. Zednik (CZ)
- J. Hrebec (CZ)
- J. Whitlinger
- M. Cox (GB)
- J. Austin
- S. SMITH (3)
- J. Fillol (CH)
- F. McMillan (SA)
- J. McManus
- H. J. Pohmann (G)
- B. Gottfried
- P. Cornejo (CH)
- B. Teacher
- M. ORANTES (SP) (10)
- F. Pala (CZ)
- A. Amritraj (IN)
- A. Pattison (RH)
- I. Molina (COL)
- S. Ball (AUS)
- J. Pinto-Bravo (CH)
- G. Goven (F)
- I. NASTASE (RU) (7)
- K. Warwick (AUS)
- R. Barth
- J. Bartlett (AUS)
- R. Taylor (GB)
- A. Stone (AUS)
- M. Estep
- R. Tanner
- R. STOCKTON (14)
- J. Delaney
- T. Edlefsen
- R. Kreiss
- N. Spear (YU)
- I. El Shafei (UAR)
- S. Turner
- I. Fletcher (AUS)

Second round (top half):
- CONNORS (1) 6–3 6–4 3–6 7–5
- Bengtson 7–6 7–6 4–6 7–6
- Carmichael 7–5 2–6 6–3 6–4
- KODES (12) 6–2 6–3 6–4
- Battrick 6–4 3–6 5–7 6–4 7–6
- Taroczy 6–7 6–3 6–2 6–2
- OKKER (6) 5–7 6–1 7–5 6–2
- Seewagen 3–6 6–3 6–4
- Davidson 6–7 6–3 6–2 6–2
- Koch 7–5 6–1 6–3
- METREVELI (13) 6–3 6–2 6–2
- Zednik 6–3 6–2 1–6 6–3
- Hrebec 3–6 3–6 6–2 6–3 6–3
- Cox 6–3 7–6 3–6 1–6 7–6
- SMITH (3) 3–6 6–3 5–7 7–5 7–6
- McMillan 6–4 6–2 6–4
- Gottfried 6–3 7–5 6–2
- Teacher 6–7 6–3 6–3 ret'd
- ORANTES (10) 6–4 7–5 6–4
- A. Amritraj 7–6 6–4 4–6 6–3
- Ball 6–1 6–3 6–3
- Goven 6–1 6–2 6–1
- NASTASE (7) 6–2 6–4 ret'd
- Barth 6–1 6–0 7–5
- Taylor 7–6 7–6 6–3
- Tanner 6–4 4–6 6–3 7–6
- STOCKTON (14) 6–2 6–1 6–1
- Kreiss 6–7 6–3 6–0 6–0
- El Shafei 6–3 6–3 6–2
- Fletcher 7–6 7–5 6–3

Third round (top half):
- CONNORS (1) 6–1 6–3 6–3
- Alexander 6–4 7–5 6–3
- KODES (12) 6–4 6–4 6–2
- Taroczy 7–6 7–6 6–3
- OKKER (6) 7–5 7–6 7–6 6–2
- Koch 6–3 7–6 7–5
- METREVELI (13) 6–3 7–5 6–4
- Cox 6–1 6–2 7–6
- SMITH (3) 6–1 3–6 7–6 6–4
- Teacher 3–6 2–6 6–3 6–2 6–2
- A. Amritraj 6–3 6–4 6–2
- Ball 6–3 7–5 6–3
- NASTASE (7) 6–7 6–1 4–6 6–1 6–2
- Tanner 3–6 6–7 6–4 7–6 6–3
- STOCKTON (14) 6–7 6–3 6–3 6–2
- El Shafei 7–6 6–1 6–4

Fourth round (top half):
- CONNORS (1) 6–1 7–5 6–7 6–4
- KODES (12) 5–7 4–6 7–6 7–6 6–3
- OKKER (6) 4–6 6–2 6–3 5–7 6–4
- METREVELI (13) 6–7 6–2 6–7 7–6 6–3
- SMITH (3) 6–3 7–5 6–4
- Ball 5–7 5–7 6–3 6–2 6–4
- Tanner 4–6 6–7 7–5 6–4 6–4
- El Shafei 4–6 7–6 6–3 3–6 6–4

Quarter-finals (top half):
- CONNORS (1) 7–5 6–3 5–7 6–2
- METREVELI (13) 6–1 6–3 7–6
- SMITH (3) 6–2 6–3 6–7 6–3
- Tanner 7–6 6–2 3–6 6–1

Semi-finals (top half):
- CONNORS (1) 3–6 6–3 6–4 6–1
- Tanner 6–3 6–7 7–5 6–7 7–6

Bottom half

- C. Pasarell
- P. DuPre
- S. Stewart
- E. Scott
- R. Ruffels (AUS)
- R. Lutz
- C. Dibley (AUS)
- K. ROSEWALL (AUS) (5)
- R. Reid
- J. Kuki (J)
- B. Phillips-Moore (AUS)
- A. Mayer
- M. Holocek (Stateless)
- W. Brown
- J. Andrew (VEN)
- R. RAMIREZ (M) (16)
- R. Dowdeswell (RH)
- M. Farrell (GB)
- C. Owens
- H. Kary (AU)
- H. Rahim (PAK)
- J. Lloyd (GB)
- S. Krulevitz
- M. RIESSEN (11)
- T. Ryan (AUS)
- J. Yuill (SA)
- J. Crawford
- J. Gisbert (SP)
- V. Amritraj (IN)
- S. Docherty
- V. Amaya
- B. BORG (SW) (4)
- P. Gerken
- J. Simpson (NZ)
- A. Neely
- J. Kamiwazumi (J)
- M. Machette
- B. Prajoux (CH)
- F. Taygan
- G. VILAS (ARG) (9)
- S. Messmer
- F. McNair
- G. Masters (AUS)
- J. Velasco (COL)
- J. Feaver (GB)
- V. Gerulaitis
- T. Waltke
- A. ASHE (8)
- C. Graebner
- T. Ulrich (D)
- A. Munoz (S)
- J. Andrews
- J. Singh (IN)
- R. Moore (SA)
- G. Hardie
- T. GORMAN (15)
- O. Parun (NZ)
- E. Friedlander
- A. Roche (AUS)
- J. James (AUS)
- T. Kakulia (USSR)
- L. Tavares (BR)
- R. Benavides (BOL)
- J. NEWCOMBE (AUS) (2)

Second round (bottom half):
- Pasarell 6–7 6–3 4–6 6–2 6–4
- Scott 2–6 7–5 4–6 6–0 6–3
- ROSEWALL (5) 6–4 7–6 6–1
- Reid 6–4 7–6 6–3
- Mayer 5–7 6–2 6–2 6–1
- Brown 6–7 2–6 7–5 6–4 ret'd
- RAMIREZ (16) 6–2 6–4 6–4
- Dowdeswell 6–2 3–6 6–2 6–4
- Owens 7–6 6–4 6–4
- Lloyd 6–4 6–4 6–2
- RIESSEN (11) 6–7 3–6 6–2 6–2 6–0
- Yuill 6–1 6–4 1–0 ret'd
- Gisbert 7–5 6–4 6–2
- V. Amritraj 6–7 6–1 6–3 6–2
- BORG (4) 6–4 4–6 6–3 6–3
- Gerken 6–4 6–7 7–5 7–6
- Neely 6–4 6–7 6–2 4–6 7–5
- Machette 6–4 6–4 6–2
- VILAS (9) 6–3 6–2 6–7 2–6 6–3
- McNair 6–3 3–6 6–3 7–6
- Masters 2–6 6–2 6–1 6–3
- Gerulaitis 3–6 6–3 7–6 6–1
- ASHE (8) 6–3 7–6 6–2
- Graebner 6–3 6–1 7–5
- Munoz 4–6 6–7 7–2 7–6 7–6
- Moore 6–1 6–4 6–2
- GORMAN (15) 7–6 6–4 6–2
- Parun 6–1 6–1 6–1
- Roche 6–3 6–1
- Kakulia 6–2 6–3 6–3
- NEWCOMBE (2) 6–2 6–0 6–1

Third round (bottom half):
- Pasarell 4–6 6–4 7–6 6–3
- ROSEWALL (5) 7–6 6–3 6–3
- Reid 3–6 5–7 7–6 ret'd
- RAMIREZ (16) 7–6 7–6 7–6
- Owens 7–6 6–2 7–6
- RIESSEN (11) 6–3 6–4 6–2
- Yuill 6–2 6–7 1–6 7–6 6–3
- V. Amritraj 6–1 7–6 3–6 1–6 6–2
- Gerken 6–4 6–4 6–2
- VILAS (9) 6–3 6–2 6–1
- Masters 6–3 6–3 7–6
- ASHE (8) 7–6 7–5 6–2
- Graebner 1–6 6–4 3–6 6–2 6–2
- Moore 4–6 6–4 6–7 6–4 7–5
- Roche 6–4 6–4 6–4
- NEWCOMBE (2) 7–6 6–2 6–2

Fourth round (bottom half):
- ROSEWALL (5) 6–1 6–2 4–6 6–4
- RAMIREZ (16) 6–1 6–4 3–6 6–3
- RIESSEN (11) 6–4 6–3 6–0
- V. Amritraj 7–6 0–6 7–6 6–7 3–1 ret'd
- VILAS (9) 6–4 6–3 3–1 ret'd
- ASHE (8) 2–6 6–2 6–3 6–3
- Moore 6–1 6–4 6–3
- NEWCOMBE (2) 6–3 6–2 7–5

Quarter-finals (bottom half):
- ROSEWALL (5) 6–1 6–7 7–5 6–3
- V. Amritraj 6–3 6–3 6–4
- ASHE (8) 6–7 6–4 6–4 7–5
- NEWCOMBE (2) 4–6 6–3 3–6 7–6 6–4

Semi-finals (bottom half):
- ROSEWALL (5) 2–6 6–3 6–3 6–2
- ROSEWALL (5) 6–7 6–4 7–6 6–3

Final:
- CONNORS (1) 7–6 7–6 6–4
- ROSEWALL (5)

J. CONNORS (1) 6–1 6–0 6–1 (Winner)

THE NEW YORK TIMES, SUNDAY, OCTOBER 6, 1974

Jan Kodes of Czechoslovakia returning service by meeting ball in front of him and leaning into the stroke.

"Based on the decision of the Coaches Council further International entries are denied for the rest of 1974 with the exception of Stockholm. Signed – Coaches' Council."

I returned to Prague and wanted to find out what it was all about. Every one tried to dodge my questions and said: "That has nothing to do with you. It is just that there have been too many tournaments already this year and CUPES' financial quota for foreign travel has been exhausted."

Strange… We, the players, received no money from them! How did this come about?…

In 1974 there was a definite change of players at the top. Names like Smith, Nastase, Newcombe, Kodes no longer rang as much as in the past two years. New names appeared – Connors, Borg, Vilas, Ramirez and others who flashed up like comets in the sky. Czechoslovak tennis fans started to view Jan Kodes' performance as if he were on the way-out…

It seemed to me that many people did not fathom how much my father's passing away affected me. During that year a new Sparta Indoor Hall began to be constructed and all believed that it was for Kodes. Perhaps it was so; if I had not performed so well abroad we would

have never achieved having the second indoor hall built in Prague. – For some time I toyed with the idea of rehabilitating in a spa. My back that gave me first signs of problems two years earlier, bothered me from time to time and usually so in the most inopportune moments.

For years doctors recommended him spa treatment but he never had enough time that he could afford to take off his busy schedule. In the close of 1974 he finally decided to go to Piestany in Slovakia.

It was fantastic. Their procedures really helped me regenerate; I also slept like a log. Only one morning I woke up at five and could not return to sleep. I kept tossing and turning in bed, I stared at the ceiling, all kinds of thoughts were flashing through my head. Eventually, I dosed off only to be woken up by a ringing phone. It was my sister Vlasta: "our mom passed away this morning at six thirty!"

I lost both parents in a span of nine months. Dad died on March 27th, my mother on December 11th. They were sixty-five and sixty-three years old! My aunt Mary in Florida lived till recently; she reached the age of ninety-eight…

How to Improve Chances On Your Return of Serve

By SHEPHERD CAMPBELL

The serve, as almost any tennis player can tell you, is the most important shot in the game. But what's the second most important?

Not many recognize that it's the return of serve—the stroke that all players have to hit on about half of all the points they play. Yet, important as it is, the return of serve is one of the most underrated shots in tennis. Few club players spend much, if any, time practicing it and the inevitable result is that they seldom hit it as well as they could.

A player who wants to work on this decisive element of the game should keep three things in mind, according to Jan Kodes, the Czechoslovak star, who is one of the masters of the stroke:

1—Watch the ball from the moment it leaves the server's hand during his delivery.

2—Meet the ball out in front of the body and lean in to the stroke.

3—Stay with the percentage shot by concentrating on keeping the ball in play.

Probably the biggest mistake the average player makes on returns of serve is to watch the server and not the ball. But the object of the game, after all, is to hit the ball (not the server). So the ball should be watched, beginning at the point when the server begins his toss. By observing whether the toss goes to the left or right, it's often possible to detect whether the serve will be coming down the center or angling across the service box. And keying on the ball from the outset means a re-

ceiver doesn't put himself at the disadvantage of trying to pick it up in mid-flight. How deep in the court you stand depends upon the anticipated velocity of the serve. But on the first serve, it's generally best to stand about at the baseline, a couple of feet from the singles sideline, and then move up a step or two for the second serve. Kodes says, "I prefer to wait for the serve in a pronounced crouching position and then bounce up in the air as the ball is served so that I am really on my toes to move to the ball."

This technique helps keep the weight forward so that a player can move toward the ball in short, rapid steps and then hit it out in front of the body. Hitting out in front is essential to get the proper control and power into the shot. The ball should be met about waist high, if possible, and stroked with the body leaning into it.

In placing a shot, it doesn't pay to go for spectacular, outright winners. The basic objective of service returns should be a conservative one; just try to keep the ball in play. Then a player can decide whether to attack the server's second shot or to lay back for a ground stroke. "Stick with the high-percentage shots you know you can make well when returning serve," Kodes advises, "and resist the temptation to try for nearly impossible winners."

●

Shepherd Campbell is editor of Tennis Magazine.

Jimmy Connors, with the Australian Open trophy, enjoyed one of his finest seasons ever in 1974. After defeating Ken Rosewall in Wimbledon and US Open finals he beat Phil Dent at Kooyong, Melbourne. Besides the three majors he also won in South Africa (over Ashe), the US Clay court Championships (over Borg) and the US Indoor events.

VLASTA AND MARTINA

She captured thirteen National and five International championship titles. She reached Roland Garros quarter-finals twice (1968, 1970), and Wimbledon sixteens in 1970; in Rome she advanced into the quarters in 1972 and a year later she reached the semis, where she was stopped by Evonne Goolagong from Australia. In all she won fourteen tournaments: Berlin, Halle, Split, Ljubljana, Zagreb, Palermo, Pescara, Kitzbühel, Milano, Monte Carlo, four times in Bratislava, Vienna, Munich. In 1969 she became the European Amateur Champion in Turin. She even beat two Wimbledon champions – Margaret Smith-Court in Munich in 1965 and Virginia Wade in Rome in 1973. She challenged other excellent players like Billie Jean King. They were, perhaps, better but she always gave them a good run for the money. Her matches at the highest level were usually hard-fought three-set encounters. She had strong will-power, high moral values and unceasing fighting spirit. "One has to be born with such characteristics. Most likely, I inherited them from our father just like Jan did" said Vlasta Vopickova.

She grew up on the same courts as her brother Jan – in Dukla Karlin, where her parents were members and also played. She showed up at the courts daily, and spent vacations there as well. At home she played against the wall on the balcony, and with Jan they played table

My sister Vlasta Kodesova-Vopickova defeated Margaret Smith-Court, the greatest Australian who won three Grand Slam titles in Wimbledon, US and Australia that year. It was on clay in quarter-finals at Munich, in 1965. Later in semis she was defeated by best German Helga Schultze.

tennis. They hammered a ball with anything they found around, hitting it even with a cutting board. Doing sports was part of their lifestyle, tennis took the top spot. At Dukla Club she usually practiced with Jan. Their father insisted: "It is the best for the two of you to practice together; you accommodate each other."

Up until the age of fourteen she beat her two years younger brother Jan. She was better, her strokes were more fierce. Jan fumed and fretted. She competed with him from very early age and that helped them both. In club tournaments she often competed in boys' categories; she was their even rival. From the baseline she played an excellent solid game; she hit superb ground strokes, down-the-line as well as cross-court. Above all, her strokes were deep, they created pressure. She was capable to hit shots exactly into the corners and such hits were difficult to retrieve. When Frantisek Pala played mixed-doubles with her in later years he often commented: "When Vlasta starts feeding the opponents with her corner shots nobody can get to them!"

Her fighting spirit and "Kodes-like" willpower were proverbial. She made herself known among the girls at the age of fourteen, and at sixteen she won the Nationals in Pardubice; at seventeen she literally popped into the national selection. The only time that she played mixed-doubles with her brother Jan was at the Nationals in Pilsen in 1967. She then accomplished a unique feat: she reached three championship titles. There was a period of time when the Kodes siblings were winning almost everything – singles, doubles, and mixed doubles; they won many titles on behalf of Motorlet Prague. Together they played tournaments all over the world; Vlasta played along with Puzejova-Sukova, the 1962 Wimbledon finalist, and later with Jitka Volavkova. Eventually, she was overshadowed by her brother's fame but it remains true that from 1964, when Vera Puzejova-Sukova retired, till 1972 she was the only Czechoslovak player among top ten female European players and top twenty world-wide. Only in 1973 Martina Navratilova replaced her, when she ranked sixth at the age of seventeen... but Vlasta Vopickova-Kodesova still maintained her eighth European rank!

What she said about Vlasta Kodesova - Vopickova
Martina Navratilova

The Kodes family had a tennis monopoly! Their mom could also play, and Vlasta was our number one. She played tournaments against top world players and withstood competition at that level pretty well. For me, personally, she was an indicator of my tennis self-evaluation. When I, finally, defeated her, I felt I truly improved and it gave me confidence to bring my game to the next level. Then, in semi-finals, I overpowered Renata Tomanova, who I had lost to numerous times before. In Junior tournaments she always beat me but I beat her easily in this semifinal match. It suddenly flashed through my head: "Oh God, perhaps I'll win even the finals." But, I came down with the flu and felt sick through the match; I drank tea and water on change-overs. I would not recommend it to people as a weight loss recipe but it is true that I lost quite a few pounds during that match. I was glad that it lasted only two sets; I would not have lasted through the third. I did not even register that I took away from Vlasta and assumed the number one rank. I used to be in fifteenth position and suddenly I climbed up to the top. That helped in the coming year when I was allowed to travel to the US for the first time. It was a leap upwards that launched me into the world tennis scene.

Life presents moments that act like catalysts; they change course or speed up things. Changes in my tennis life would have come no matter what but, perhaps, not as fast. From that point of view the final against Vlasta was crucial. It was that much more important that it was her, Vlasta. That victory had a unique flavor. Vlasta Vopickova, Jan Kodes' sister! Did I, indirectly, beat him too?

Martina Navratilova

The tennis world was offering much to Vlasta Vopickova during the peak of her tennis career. It would have taken very little impetus in the course of her first trip to the United States in 1970 when she was joined by her husband Milan as well as Jan, her brother; they could have stayed "over the other side of the Atlantic". They met Czech Americans in Florida who suggested to them to remain there. All of them! The two siblings could play tennis, and Milan ice-hockey. But, they did not take that step; first and foremost because of their parents. Vlasta knew what would have resulted from their defection. There was yet another important point. Czech tennis was not directed from abroad but from within! If everybody decided to seek freedom and money abroad, what would have happened to tennis at home?

Very few people in far away lands know where Czechoslovakia was, and where the Czech Republic of today is. In reference to the names of our politicians some foreigners may be familiar only with Vaclav Havel. In the arts industry Milos Forman is known as a Czech-American film director and screenwriter and Rafael Kubelik and Karel Gott are known to music lovers; few individuals may know that Otto Wichterle invented modern contact lens. However, names of outstanding athletes that our small country gave birth to are familiar to many! Older generations may remember Olympic gold medalists like Emil Zatopek, Vera Caslavska, Jan Zelezny and most recognize names of Roman Sebrle, as well as NHL player Jaromir Jagr, Golden Soccerball winner Josef Masopust or Pavel Nedved. And the entire tennis world is familiar with names of Jaroslav Drobny, Vera Puzejova-Sukova, Jan Kodes, Martina Navratilova, Ivan Lendl, Hana Mandlikova, Jana Novotna, Petr Korda, Helena Sukova...

Vlasta was a great competitor and fighter. Picture from 1959.

Czechoslovak National Doubles Champions 1962-63. Vlasta Vopickova and Vera Puzejova-Sukova.

Czech tennis has had good reputation in the world. In 1993 top ten Czech players of all times reunited in Prague's Sport Hall on the occasion of an exhibition between Petr Korda and Jimmy Connors. However, still many more successful tennis players were missing from that reunion. Vlasta Vopickova was one of them and so were all her rivals like Jitka Volavkova, Alena Palmeova, Marie Neumannova, Renata Tomanova and Regina Marsikova. Czech tennis always abounded with players that brought fame to our small country. It is difficult to compare achievements from the nineteen fifties to nineteen seventies. In those times there was no computerized ranking system; that innovation has been effectively in use in ATP and WTA only in the last three decades. European and world ranking used to be set by polls in reputable magazines, or by journalists and experts. Some eminent tennis personalities were among those who constructed ranking of the top players. Yet, each based their ranking input on different criteria....

Tournament organization and purpose differed from present day function of tournaments. There were fewer tournaments and best players played them all; it was practically impossible to purposefully avoid playing a particular player. A player reaching the quarter-finals or semi-finals always had to put out maximum effort.

Czechoslovakia instigated an additional handicap to its players and that was the unwillingness to allow players travel worldwide – it was a limiting factor. Tennis was predominantly an outdoor sport that was practiced from spring to fall; only gradually indoor halls started to spring up. Very few players were able to afford traveling to other continents. Domestically they all had the same conditions and only the best reached the top rung. Nobody was restricted in any way traveling around tournaments within the country.

In 1996 forty-four players were inducted into the Czech Tennis Hall of Fame in Prague during the 90th anniversary celebration of Czech Tennis Federation foundation. Vlasta Kodesova-Vopickova was one of the inductees. There have been no other best tennis players' reunions since.

EMIGRATION DILEMMA

The 1975 year turned out to be the year of the highest triumph for the Czechoslovak Davis Cup team to date. The proof of that was the final match against Sweden in Stockholm at the end of that year.

It was also the year where the most talented female player born in Czechoslovakia left only to become the best dominant player of the world a few years later. Martina Navratilova asked for asylum during the US Open at Forest Hills.

Furthermore, it was a year of Jan Kodes' repeated comebacks. He won against a great field in Madrid and reached the finals in Hamburg, Düsseldorf, and Kitzbühel; in addition he won three tournaments in doubles – Munich (with Fibak), Düsseldorf (with Jauffret), and Madrid (with Nastase). However, the Davis Cup final was the most significant.

The year started the same as the previous ones: practice at Klamovka indoor courts or in the basketball hall in Korunovacni Street, little soccer games in snow, jogging in Stromovka, swimming and conditioning in Podoli; all was geared to gain strength.

Life in Sparta was very pleasant. My running in the beautiful nature of Stromovka Park was peaceful. Track and Fielders resided opposite to the tennis courts and they always joined us in the soccer scrimmage fun; we did not need to beg them twice. I enjoyed the few winter weeks that I spent at home.

Jan Kodes' season started with a series of six tournaments in the United States organized by Jimmy Connors' manager Bill Riordian. He no longer felt like flying around the world the way he did the years before; he was perfectly content playing tournaments along the East coast of the United States. He returned to the "good-old-places" like Salisbury, Maryland, and New York. However, his results were lukewarm. He lost to Mayer and then to Taylor.

In Hampton, Va., he reached the finals against Connors. In spite of leading 6:3 and 3:0 he lost the second and then the third set 3:6, 0:6. The sold out Hampton Hall saw a tremendous match. Jan lost to the American also in New York's MSG Felt Forum 5:7, 6:3, 1:6.

We struck battles every time we played each other and it is hard to believe that Connors is one of the players I never defeated! He is seven years my junior but I never believed that the age difference had anything to do with the outcomes. There were other factors that affected the results. He had a great return and so did I; my serve was somewhat weaker and so was his. We killed each others' serves with aggressive returns. In situations like these each point was gained through rallies. Our games were similar, though he played a two-handed backhand. He produced a very aggressive game preparing for each shot with an enormous backswing and hitting the ball on the rise soon after it bounced. He hardly let me catch my breath. Time and again we both ended our rallies totally spent. If I were to defeat him I needed a better serve. I also believe that he had even more dogged willpower than I. He was the most dogged player of us all!

People rose from their seats during our matches. Deuce, ad-in, deuce, ad-out, deuce...over and over again. Though the score from Hampton seems pretty clear – from 3:0 in the second set I lost twelve games in a row – in reality it was not so unequivocal. It was my physical condition that deteriorated; I was not in the best shape then and he wore me to death. His passing shots were excellent and I could not approach the net after just any shot. These matches did not take place on clay and I wonder how we would have grappled in Paris, Rome, or Barcelona; The outcome would have certainly been different. We played all our matches on grass or on rubber Supreme. Only once we played on grey clay at the 1976 US Open; I lost that match as well.

All our encounters were "razor-sharp" and I remember them fondly. Getting ready for a match with Connors inspired adrenaline; I always knew we were going to battle till the last breath.

In May, after the series of six tournaments in the United States, Jan Kodes participated in European tournaments – Munich, Bournemouth, Hamburg, and Düsseldorf. He lost to the New Zealander Parun in quarter-finals in Bournemouth in Southern England.

A strange thing happened to me then. Subconsciously, I sensed that things were going to turn troublesome. The first signs of it appeared at the end of 1974 – receiving a telegram from the coaching council that I was not allowed to play abroad. After losing to Parun I was truly upset. Jaroslav Drobny, who came to spend a tennis weekend in the seaside resort, showed up soon after the match. We sat down among the Centre Court audience and watched the next match. I was not really noticing what was going on on the court because we discussed all sorts of topics. Above all we dissected the political atmosphere in Czechoslovakia and talked about issues surrounding tennis.

I asked his advice as to what I should do: "Jaroslav, I am anxious. Situation at home is getting more and more complicated. It seems that I'll face great difficulties."

Now I must return by the date that I had set up to commence construction of my family residence. I applied for a piece of land in Prague 6 in the middle of 1973. They assigned it to me but I had to wait for a permit to build. I did not receive that until April 23, 1975! The Bournemouth tournament took place shortly after that, in May 12-18, 1975.

So, I now had the permit but I had not started with the construction. I was in a great dilemma: should I start with the construction or should I not? My parents' passing away the preceding year as if broke my spirit. In the past, when I had a problem, I sought my father and he helped me resolve it. Now I juggled with: what am I going to do if I am not allowed to play abroad? I have my degree and I have completed military service as well! I was not allowed to compete against the South African McMillan, Milan Holecek emigrated; I had gone through the unpleasant talk with the military counter-intelligence; everything was sitting in my mind weighing on my conscience.

I remembered how Darmon approached me in Paris and offered me help after my second victory in Paris should I have chosen to stay in France. All these thoughts were floating in my mind and messed with my head. What should I do next?

It was an eerie situation. I did not want to defect; at the same time I needed to assure myself that if I stay I'll be content with the decision. I had traveled in the United States and noticed how people lived there: in beautiful residences with pools, tennis courts, gorgeous gardens; such awesome homes! But I also realized that Prague is not in Florida and our climate is different. Yes, I wanted a pool and even constructed it at first, but I got rid of it in time...

I abandoned youthful dreams; though I was no longer a youngster – I was pulling twenty nine. My wife Lenka did not want to even hear about emigration. Once in a while I nudged her in that direction but she had her friends at home who she did not wish to leave.

So we sat there with Jaroslav and I asked him: "Jaroslav, please, tell me what I should do."

At that point he told me his story. "You know, Jan, it was a terrible life that I led then, in 1949, after I emigrated. You can't fathom what I had to endure. Yes, everybody abroad promised much including nationality but when the moment of truth came they did not fulfill the promises and left me alone; whether it was the English or the French. At one point I had to travel with so called "white" passport – "stateless". In the end I had an Egyptian passport but I still was not permitted to enter several countries that did not want to issue me visas. For that reason I could not take part in a number of tournaments."

Drobny also recalled the finals in Gstaad that transpired to be the last straw that evoked his emigration. The doors swung open, he said, and two embassy officials entered and told him that he was not to play the finals. Jaroslav objected: "You can not be serious! The Stadium is sold out and I am supposed to enter in an hour; what am I to tell the organizers? That I cannot play? That is absurd!"

One of the two officials was Jan Zelenka, the subsequent director of Czechoslovak Television. It was he who said: "If you enter the court, don't return to Czechoslovakia!" And Jaroslav, indeed, did not return.

I listened to his tale and wanted to believe that these were not the fifties and times were, hopefully, a little better.

We discussed the issue a while longer. He said: "Look, if I were you...Tell me, are you missing anything in your life? - You won Wimbledon, you triumphed twice in Paris – they can't afford to touch you!"

"Well, Jaroslav, can they or can they not... You never know. I have a feeling they can."

"You are a Wimbledon champion and that means something in this world. And consider the prize money. Even when they take away percentage of it you still hold the status of a professional and you retain a decent amount. It is not like in the fifties. If I were you I would stay there. If you don't take charge of tennis in Bohemia who will? You are destined to lead tennis in some fashion even after you retire from active competition."

I repeat again that I never resolved to emigrate; I played with the idea and needed somebody else to give me his honest view of things. And he was the one who had gone through the act of emigration. With that discussion he cleared the differences in our situations; times were profoundly more severe at his moment of decision. "You don't need to do that today. You can wait and see."

I held great respect toward and regard for Jaroslav Drobny. He was able to judge and address things with precise expressions. He was tough and confident!

As he spelled it out to me I based my decision on it: Ok, I'll stay in Prague, I'll start the house construction and if something happens I'll just have to write off the investment. With that I resolved to let go of the worry.

Hamburg was one of the tournaments that Jan Kodes did not like - slippery clay, hard courts, problematic motion.

I had to use special tennis shoes that we called Adidas-Tractors. The soles were rougher, something like winter tires on cars.

By then he reached semifinals in Hamburg three times. In 1975, however, he defeated the first seeded player, Guillermo Vilas, 6:2, 6:3 in the quarter-finals, which was a great accomplishment. Six years separated them – Kodes was twenty-nine, Vilas twenty-three.

I played well the entire tournament; aggressively and without hesitation believing that Guillermo was really the favorite. I took risks and maximized on them. The last two rounds were played best of five sets and in both I battled hard for five sets. In the semifinal match I outlasted Bertolucci from Italy, in the finals I lost to Orantes 6:3, 2:6, 2:6, 6:3, and 1:6 after an extremely long tough fight. We both struggled with physical condition and the final outcome was decided in the start of the fifth set. The Germans remained true to themselves and, as usual, they cheered for my opponent.

At that time Guillermo Vilas was already among the absolute clay-court top players. He was like a machine with

Hamburg 1975. Number one seed Guillermo Vilas was eliminated by Jan Kodes in quarter-finals.

excellent concentration, great stamina and determination. His baseline strokes were very good and he possessed a powerful passing shot. He also had an amazing topspin lob that he often turned into a deadly weapon. Kodes knew that approaching the net after shoddy shots would cost him points. - In no time Vilas avenged the Hamburg defeat and beat Kodes at the next Roland Garros championship.

He beat me easily in the fourth round. I lost badly 1:6, 4:6, and 2:6. I had no chance against him on the slower clay!

Kodes then lost in the second round of Wimbledon to Geoff Masters in five sets despite of having two match-points!

I was beaten again, Manolo Orantes won in five sets.
Right: TD Mr.Abendroth.

MARTINA

The Czechoslovak International Championship in Bratislava finished without its main star. The Centre Court second round match between Kodes and Sevcik had to be suspended at 7:5 and 2:1 in Sevcik's favour. Kodes misstepped and sprained his ankle. The result was a rupture of the right ankle capsule that precluded him from further play.

Default and several days of complete rest followed. How many times has something of the same sort happened? He has dealt with sprained ankles numerous times!

"What a pity that Dr. Slava Rybin is no longer here; he would be able to confirm it!" – thought Kodes when accusation started to spring up.

Doesn't injury always come at the most inopportune moment? Jan dazzled fans in the Davis Cup match against France, his performance was on the rise and his chances of success at US Open were promising. It was obvious that the culprit of his injury was an overall fatigue; his body needed a let-up.

It often happened to me when I was under enormous strain for a long period of time that I got injured. Then, in 1975, I had two Davis Cup matches behind me. And what made me very unhappy were some people's suspicions that I "did not feel like playing some ordinary matches". I considered that very unfair. There was no reason "not-to-want-to battle". On the contrary, I was eager to do so!

He gave himself two weeks of rest; he skipped two Grand Prix tournaments and started a new in Toronto, Canada. However, he had to retire again in the second round when he played Colin Downdswell. His ankle still wasn't in good enough condition. Subsequently he won two matches in Boston but lost the third easily to Laver on the American clay!

The US Open at Forest Hills was played on grey clay for the first time that year and, surprisingly, Manolo Orantes became the champion. In the semifinals he defeated Vilas in five sets in spite of the fact that the Argentine was leading 2:1 in sets and 5:1 in the fourth! In the finals he outplayed Connors easily 6:4, 6:3, 6:3. Kodes fought his way to the fourth round where he played with Guillermo Vilas on Centre Court in the evening under the artificial lighting.

I really disliked playing under the lights and got hammered quite badly! Vilas punished me with amazing passing shots and lobs. I packed up my gear and left quickly. I was quite glad to have finished with the US Open and be able to fly home. Though we defeated Metreveli – Taylor 6:2, 6:1 in doubles with Wojtek Fibak we had to retire from the remaining matches because of Wojtek's injury.

After the match with Vilas I took a cab to the hotel. I was tired, and started snoozing. It was around eleven at night when I was already half-dozing and the radio station was broadcasting the news. In a flash I came around. The radio broadcaster was declaring that Martina Navratilova announced at the press conference that she would not be returning to Czechoslovakia!

View of tennis courts at Sparta Tennis Club in Prague. The venue where Kodes', Navratilova's, Mandlikova's, Sukova's, Tomanova's and others' world tennis careers began.

Tennis club Sparta had the most national players playing for its team
– Kodes, Pala, Tomanova, Holubova, Pisecky, Navratilova... In our club
matches, many times the final results where determined by the last two
mixed doubles matches. This is exactly what happened in a memorable
match in 1973 against Ostrava. Sparta was leading 8:7 but the Ostrava team
had a tremendous mixed doubles team of Necas – Lendlova.
"Jan, how shall we put together the mixed doubles teams?" the coaches and
club officials asked me before the decisive matches. Then they answered
their own question with: "The first mixed doubles team will be you and
Tomanova, second Pala and Holubova."
I objected and said that I didn't want to play with Tomanova. "If you want us
to grab the point then I'll play with Navratilova!"
"Wait a minute; how come with Navratilova?"
"Do you want a point? With Tomanova I can't guarantee the point!"
"But Martina is only fifteen!" they argued.
"Well, fifteen she is, but she is not afraid at the net, and whatever is within
her reach she executes. Renata has terrific baseline strokes but she is fearful
at the net. She will let those balls go by for me to hit. I want to play with
Martina!" They argued with me, and officials as well as Dr. Rössler tried to
persuade me to play with Renata. In the end I had my way. I played with
Martina, Renata played with Frantisek Pala and we won 9:8.
Martina came to Sparta as a young girl. Most of the time she worked out
on the court next door but right from the beginning I noticed that she
was pressing forward and approached the net; with that she produced an
aggressive, attacking game. I remember her Dad, Mirek Navratil, who sat in
between the courts on a bench and observed what was going on on both
courts. After our practice was over he came up to me and asked: "So, what
do you think about Martina's game?"
I passed much time with her at Sparta; we practiced together and we played
mixed doubles together, we had lunch in our local canteen together. I see it
as if it were today – the clubhouse, wooden cottages, the Perny family who
cooked great... There was that little window where daily menu was attached
and from which the meals were passed. It is no longer true...
Martina had a fantastic friendly disposition. She was into everything – she
skied, played little soccer with us on Letna field, we played chess and
checkers. Already as a young girl she was fun, really. However, it never even
crossed my mind that she would win Wimbledon nine times...

Wimbledon 1975. The mixed-doubles semifinal match on Centre Court between Kodes-Navratilova and Riessen-Court came to a close. The Czech team lost to the future Wimbledon champions 7:5, 0:6, 2:6.

It was a pity; we had several breakpoints on Riessen's serve at the beginning of the third set. I just did not succeed in hitting an effective return – and that decided the outcome. It was a double pity since we would have had a good chance in the finals against Stone-Stove after Roche-King defaulted in the third round.

As they departed from the court it did not even cross Jan Kodes' mind that it would be the last mixed doubles match with Martina.

I returned home and worked out at Sparta when Mirek Navratil approached me after a few days: "Martina is facing problems; they want to "discipline" her for having stayed in a hotel in Paris with other foreign players, and for making friends with American players. It bothers them, they constantly harass her, and they create problems around her."

I did not pay much attention to it for I had heard much gossip and rumors during my career. However, a few days passed and they forbade Martina to travel to the United States. That angered me and I approached the CUPE chairman Antonin Himl: "Mr. Chairman, I found out that.... supposedly, Navratilova is not permitted to travel to the United States? How much truth is in that?"

He started our quite calmly: "You know, I have some news here from the Tennis Federation that Navratilova is getting too Americanized and doesn't stick to the group of our players".

Mr. Chairman, these are good for nothing statements! I played Wimbledon with her this year; I can't go to the US Open without her! How would I explain it there? Do I say that she has a flu and that is why she is not present? Or do I say that you did not let her go? Explain to me what sense does it make to prohibit her from entering the US Open entry?" He just gaped at me so I continued. "If you don't permit her to go now she'll defect at the next opportunity when you send her out! If you hold her back you are guilty of killing a great talent, perhaps the greatest in the world!"

He left and at that moment, I must admit, there were two things I did not surmise. First, that Antonin Himl was familiar with the letter that Antonin Bolardt had delivered to the personnel office of the Central Committee of Czechoslovak

Martina Navratilova and Renata Tomanova at Sparta Prague.

Jan Kodes with Martina Navratilova in 1973 before their mixed doubles match in extra-league Sparta vs. Ruda Hvezda. From left: the team leader Karel Melichar, on the bench sitting Jiri Hrebec, the chair umpire Stanislav Prada.

Union of Physical Education. In it he declared that "in the course of recent Wimbledon Championships he arrived at a conviction that Martina Navratilova was getting ready to emigrate and most likely would not return from her family trip around Europe"! Second, it did not even cross my mind that she would emigrate! Though, I believe, they had threatened her at home.

In 1975 Martina Navratilova entered the world tennis scene with confidence. She reached two big finals in Paris and Rome losing to Chris Evert and she represented the country with great success in the Federation Cup, which the Czech players won for the first time. Under the leadership of Vera Sukova the team of Navratilova, Tomanova, and Kozeluhova gradually defeated Ireland, the Netherlands, West Germany, and France. It was Martina Navratilova and Renata Tomanova who played all the matches. In the finals against Australia they did not give away even a set to the favored Goolagong and Gourlay!

Inevitably, Martina became a target of attention and in Wimbledon reached the quarter-finals, losing to Margaret Court. She was now among the world's top players. It was there where problems started to sprout, problems that eventually caused her flight from Czechoslovakia.

She started to entertain the idea of emigration in the autumn of 1974. She strove to become the world's top player, she desired to live in the United States of America, and she wanted to become a US citizen. But, she hesitated too long. Each time she thought "this is the right moment to do it" she recoiled from it. The prick of conscience told her "your home is in Czechoslovakia: Revnice, Berounka, Praha..." She realized the enormous consequence of fleeing.

The comrades in the leadership of Czechoslovak athletics made the decision for her. Imposed hardships, false rumour-spreading inspired largely by Antonin Bolardt, one of the communists in then leadership of Czechoslovak tennis, impinged on her. It frightened her that she might no longer get the exit permit to the West.

After the Federation Cup victory her fate was sealed. "We'll clip Martina's wings" proclaimed Antonin Bolardt.

Harmful gossip accelerated, intensified, and transformed into threats. "Either you follow what we dictate, or we'll destroy you."

Vera Sukova, the national coach and a captain of the Federation Cup team realized that the situation was turning critical and with a frank chat she attempted to help Martina. She took Martina aside and explained to her how to behave in order to be left alone: "Martina, you have got to slow down or you will get yourself as well as me into trouble. Be smart, play along with us!"

Even her parents advised her to cool down. But, Martina was eighteen, she was at the brink of her world fame as a tennis player, yet, in her own motherland that she has represented so well, they were trying to squeeze her neck.

In spite of the strained atmosphere she was allowed to enter the Virginia Slims Circuit. Following her victory in Boston she was going to fly home but, she decided to extend her stay in the United States by one more tournament on Amelia Island without informing any officials at home about it. This gave rise to a reason to "clip her wings"!

Before her final-round match, she received a telegram from the Czech Tennis Federation requesting her to return at once. She would not risk defaulting from a finals match of a world tournament. In a very nervous performance she succumbed to Chris Evert and took the next plane over the Atlantic only to be called to account in Prague. They accused her of being conceited and ordered her to associate only with the Czechs or players from other socialist countries when playing abroad.

Based on this condition she was permitted to enter Roland Garros. In Paris she shared a hotel room with Chris Evert! And on top of it she played doubles with Chris.

This went round and round. Upon her return troubles continued. Before Wimbledon, after Wimbledon... She requested a permit to enter the 1975 US Open. Thanks to Jan Kodes' and Stanislav Chvatal's initiative there was a meeting at Antonin Himl's. The debate was long; Martina could not understand why there was so much fuss when she did not intend to emigrate. And, at that moment, that statement was true. All she wanted was to play tennis and she felt she had the right to decide where, when and with whom. Kodes and Chvatal succeeded in persuading Himl in granting the permission, though with a condition that she would return immediately thereafter.

As she was departing she felt that outside forces had the power to control her ever so much more. She realized that she could not live happily in such a system that would not

**The 1975 Federation Cup champion team upon return from Aix en Provence.
From the left: Martina Navratilova, non-playing captain Vera Sukova,
Renata Tomanova and Miroslava Bendlova-Kozeluhova.**

permit her to make her own decisions. Her final resolution ripened during her stroll with her Dad along the river Berounka on the eve of her departure to the United States. She recognized that staying under the watchful eye of the Czechoslovak athletic authorities would bring the end to her ambitions.

In 1990 Stanislav Chvatal, a Chairman of Czechoslovak Tennis Federation from 1969 to 1976, wrote: "The state of Martina's affairs frightened me; again and again I contemplated the situation from 1949, when everything good in Czech tennis was lost in a scope of a few days and the resulting emigration of Drobny and Cernik literally erased our tennis." By his authority he vouched for Martina before her planned trip to the United States. "Prior to her departure I invited her to my office. We had an odd conversation. We both knew where we stood in our understanding of the circumstance. I repeated several times that she had the power to decide about her fate in her own hands now. She gave me her photograph with a dedication; it was touching. When she was gone I did not know what to think about that lapsed moment; on the other hand I sensed I knew it very well."

Stanislav Chvatal was recalled from his post of a chairman of our Tennis Federation in 1976 and Miloslav Janovec was voted in his stead...

I did not vouch for her but I stood up for her. It was impossible to vouch for Martina or anybody else that they would not defect. But I tried to explain to Antonin Himl and others that they would not gain anything by prohibiting her to play a tournament. I tried to persuade them to allow Martina to fly to the United States...

When I heard the radio news that she announced her defection the first thing that entered my mind was to call her and discuss the issue. When I arrived at the tennis courts the next day I was told: "Don't call her, she is gone. She does not want to talk to anybody. They grabbed her and took her god-knows-where. Perhaps to Chicago and then to Los Angeles."

At that moment I remembered my recent conversation with Jaroslav Drobny in the Bournemouth stadium. Deep down inside I realized: I am twenty-nine and my case is different. She is only eighteen; she has her life ahead of her.

I did not blame her but I did not say it out loud. I do not know how I would have answered if anybody asked me then whether I indorsed her emigration. Martina simply wanted to rule her own life. But nobody asked me so I stayed quiet. I was busy with the upcoming Davis Cup at Stvanice against Australia so, perhaps, they were afraid to ask me for that reason; they did not want to rattle things further.

Vera Sukova tried to contact Martina still in New York with the intent of changing her mind. It did not work. There was a US Open Newsletter at Forest Hills that made comments about events around the courts; they also published an article that stated: "On Sunday an eighteen-year old Martina Navratilova announced in the middle of the championship: "I have applied for a political asylum!" Various officials from her home country accused her of being too Americanized and requested her to spend more time at home than abroad. "I realized that I would not be able to become the best player in the world if I am not allowed to play the important tournaments. That was crushing my tennis ambitions." At the age of eighteen she is considered one of the top five players in the world. She has earned $135,000. Her emigration from Czechoslovakia does not have a political reason. "I am only concerned with my tennis career" she said. Since she comes from a communist country processing her request has been a routine job for the immigration officials. They made a statement that her visa would be extended without a problem."

Obtaining a "Green Card" and thus legalizing her residency in the USA was a question of mere few weeks. Before the Green Card was granted Martina managed to play several tournaments in Atlanta, Charlotte, and Denver.

There she came face to face with Vera Sukova, who was sent there officially from Prague to try once more to persuade Martina to return. She was accompanied by a Czechoslovak Embassy official who tried doggedly to convince Martina to come home. He promised that if she returned she would not be persecuted and that he himself would make sure that she would be treated better. All that only refreshed her memory of communist antics and that further confirmed her certainty that if she returned, more trouble would result.

Her Dad's words from their stroll along the Berounka before her departure flashed through her head: "Do not come back no matter what! They may make us beg you to return but you must not listen to us. Do not return home!"

Vera Sukova realized that nothing would change Martina's decision. She suffered for it; she was fond of Martina. She suffered also for the reasons that authorities at home would pester her while she wanted to continue to hold a strong women's team together. They shook hands after two hours of discussion and they parted peacefully.

Publicly, Martina Navratilova ceased to exist in Czechoslovakia. About two weeks after her announcement in New York the Czechoslovak Tennis Federation made a proclamation: "Martina Navratilova suffered a defeat in the face of our proletarian public. Czechoslovakia offered her all the means for her development but she gave preference to a doubtful career of a professional and a fat bank account."

What she said about Jan Kodes
Martina Navratilova

I remember the day when I was Jan's ballgirl at a winter tournament at Klamovka. I was so happy to be on the same court with him that I was beside myself. He was my hero! He was not only our national number one player but he reached achieved success around the world. Even before winning Wimbledon! He won Paris and several other world tournaments; he established his place among the world's best players.

When the name Kodes pops up I add – a champ! And in the best meaning of the word. He has always been great with me; when I was still a school girl or later as a junior. He has never disappointed me as a human being, and that doesn't happen often. Too many times individuals who reach the imagined "throne" turn around and let you down. You realize that he is not worth much as a human being and it takes you by surprise. Jan never surprised me in that way; he always confirmed my initial feeling that he is a solid tennis player and a solid person. I was lucky to have gotten to know him still before I myself became famous, and before he won Wimbledon.

I reminisced about all that recently. He reached the finals at Wimbledon and won it, and then he still played mixed doubles with me! He always gave his maximum, played till he dropped. Yet he did not have to; by then he was a Wimbledon champion. Even on the court, when we played as partners, I addressed him in a formal way that is unique to our language; to my mind he was always Mr. Kodes.

In those times we all did our utmost all the time. Nowadays? I frequently notice that players who advance further than they had anticipated at the start of the tournament sometimes default from the doubles or mixed doubles in order to be fresh for the later rounds of singles.

We then lost in the semi-finals to the eventual champs King-Davidson. It was my first Wimbledon. I played singles, doubles, and the junior tournament...And with my hero I played mixed doubles! My schedule was loaded. In the junior championship I reached the finals where I lost to the American Ann Kiyomura 4:6 and 5:7 in spite of leading in both sets! I was up 4:2 in the first, 5:3 in the second.

I was upset that I lost to Kiyomura, but it was more important to me that Jan won at that time! If somebody asked me then what would make me happier, me winning the Junior Wimbledon and him losing the main final, I would have said the reverse; the

Since 1975, when Jan and Martina played together at Wimbledon for the last time, 24 years elapsed before they teamed up again to play a mixed doubles exhibition in June 14, 1999 at their old club Sparta in Prague.

way it turned out! It was clear! I was ecstatic for his triumph. I waited for him as he departed from the Centre Court and planted a congratulatory kiss on his cheek!

I watched all his matches; his five-setter with Roger Taylor in the semifinals was a real nerve-wringer. Following his Wimbledon matches was an unbelievable experience for me! It was delightful! I watched other players religiously as well – King, Margaret

Sparta had finally the new club-house building. Martina and Jan played against Hrebec – Sukova.

Court ... I was absorbing everything like a sponge. For me that was the best Wimbledon ever! Nobody knew me, I was free to move about any which way. I saw many matches and played many of them too. And it all ended beautifully. It was a Wimbledon of dreams. Naturally, it would have been even better had we won the mixed doubles...

Only upon my return home I learned about a story that took place at Ruzyn Airport. Jan was accompanied on the plane by our group leader, if I remember correctly his name was Lichner. As soon as the plane landed he stepped out of the plane in front of Jan, most likely to "enjoy his 15 seconds of fame". Coincidentally, he had left me in London alone; my Junior Wimbledon finals match was to be played the following day. I was sixteen and he should have taken care of me. I had been to the USA before and it did not rattle me, but my father was quite furious with him.

Subsequently, I transferred from Slavia VS to Sparta. We trained together, played the league, traveled to tournaments, even to the US Open. Our whole crew – Jiri Hrebec, Renata Tomanova... I no longer remember when I started addressing him in the familiar fashion; was it then or after I had defected and our paths later crossed again? It is serious business when you relate to somebody in a familiar way... I guess I was over eighteen by then. During those two years we spent a lot of time together and also with Renata Tomanova. We had a crush on Jan; he was good looking but already married. Renata had eyes just for him and whenever we sat somewhere she always squeezed herself next to him. I was jealous of her; I did not dare do that.

The men's game appealed to me; most likely I picked that up by watching their game so much. My role model was, naturally, Jan. His forehand was weaker, but his backhand was that much stronger; it was exceptional. I represented the reverse and I admired his backhand! How can he execute it so beautifully and yet a bit atypically? He had an unbelievable feeling for the ball; it was amazing what shots he was able to come up with! As I was observing his technical craft I also came to admire his fighting spirit. I lived through a few of his Davis Cup matches that he played at Stvanice. For instance, in 1971, when we defeated the Spaniards. I used to sit in the first or second row under the railway tracks; I went through a lot of emotions at those matches. When I was nine I saw Laver there twice. But for me "live tennis" in Prague was represented by Jan Kodes.

I did not begin to travel until 1973 so only then I was able to start comparing. Jan confirmed that my game was the right game; it was good to attack and go to the net. I did it subconsciously; it was not that I talked myself into it; I always liked approaching the net. Since Jan was successful with it I presumed that it was the style to play. When various experts tried to advice me to stay back more I did not listen to them.

Jan was my role model not only for his tennis but mainly for his fighting tenacity. I have never seen him slack away; even when he got sore over something he became that much more unyielding and battled on. He was a superb tennis and human role model. The more I got to know him the more he represented the human ideal of completeness. I don't talk about him often but when I think of him now I realize that he was more of a model for me than Laver, for instance, who won the Grand Slam, Wimbledon, and who was the star of the 1960s. When I later lived through the world tennis mania myself I found Jan Kodes to be my ultimate model.

I am also aware that he played his role in my favor during my emigration from the country in 1975. He put in his word for my liberty to travel. That took place even before the Forest Hills tournament. I was playing the doubles quarter-finals at Wimbledon and my parents and my sister came to watch me; we then traveled to France on vacation. We returned via Plzen, where there was some tournament. When we came to watch the matches everybody looked at us as if we were some illusion. We asked what was going on and were told: "there was a rumor here that you have defected; the entire family!" It is true that we thought about it and we discussed it on the way back home.

But we never planned anything, and we never told anybody; it was just a family matter among us, my mother, father, me, and my sister. But my father did not have the guts to do it...

We returned and about three days later I was supposed to fly out to the Annie Soisbault Cup. I normally trained with the team but the day before the departure I received a call from Mrs. Sukova, the national coach and the team captain. She told me that I was not going anywhere!

I asked what kind of nonsense that was; I was all packed and ready to go?!

"We want to give a chance to younger players!" She wasn't able to tell me directly what was behind that decision, and I believed her then.

But my Dad sensed that the problem was elsewhere. They did not want to let me out; I was too uncomfortable for them.

However, I was made to go to Vienna a few days later to the amateur championship. They wanted me to go there because there was a chance that I could win something for the Tennis Federation there. I played terribly. The first or second round match was the worst of my career. I also misbehaved and threw my racquets all over the place, breaking almost all of them. I returned home and about two weeks later I was supposed to fly to the US Open. All of a sudden they did not want to give me an exit permit, and I did not even have a passport. One was expired; the next was being held somewhere and it started to dawn on me that they did not want to let me out.

My Dad took it on himself and called everybody who might have some pull. I did not know that even Jan got involved. Later my Dad told me how much Jan helped out. Also Mr. Chvatal, the federation chairman helped; it was the two of them. Years later, I was able to thank them. At that moment I still did not know that I would later defect.

That decision took form at the airport. My Dad was telling me: "Look, if you decide to stay there, don't listen to us if we call you and try to persuade you to return; even if we repeat it a thousand times. You must not return! Don't worry, I won't tell Mom anything for the time being. If you decide to stay in the US it is just fine!"

By then I knew I would most likely do it but only in New York I decided it for sure. I realized that if I return I will face more problems. The same will go around and around and I will suffer for it. I knew that my decision would not affect Jan. At the most somebody would scold him but would they refuse to allow him to travel? I was sure they would not go that far. He was too much of a star for them to limit him. However, I sensed that my family would be negatively targeted.

My Dad was no longer allowed to go on with his work so he had to switch and work somewhere else as an unqualified worker in Tatrovka in Dejvice. My sister Jana was not accepted to study, and, more over, was expelled from the Sparta Club.

I met Jan only three years later at Wimbledon in 1978. I admit that I don't clearly remember that meeting. We just said: "Hi, how are you?" Not much of a reunion. I only remember one thing for sure. Neither then, in Wimbledon, nor any other time later he did tell me that my defection caused him hardship. I am for ever grateful to him that he stood up for me, and as I think about it after all these years I am not surprised that he did so. I do not know till today what went on behind the scenes then and we have never talked about it much.

Martina Navratilova

Bronze medal for 1975 mixed doubles semi-finals at Wimbledon.

FINALS AT THE ROYAL HALL

Preparations for the Inter-Zonal Davis Cup finals were fast underway. Prague has never before experienced a tennis celebration of such caliber; it was the first time in history that such an important match was taking place at home. Vera Sukova returned into these feverish preparations from the United States – alone! Without Martina Navratilova whom she had chaperoned during the US Open. Before long, Stanislav Chvatal was recalled from his function as a Tennis Association Chairman. He later remembered this controversial period and affirmed: "There was nothing more one could do. The situation became hopeless. Drobny and Cernik had been, literally, banished without any remorse, and a quarter of a century later the "Martina case" took up the same character of misery and despair. The leadership of the Czechoslovak Union of Physical Education and Sport and the Communist Party had not learned anything. I never understood why Antonin Bolardt had written the letter that started the entire crisis with Martina Navratilova. Martina is the best player in the world in tennis history and it is a pity that she did not achieve her best accomplishments under our flag."

The Australians arrived with their line-up of Tony Roche, John Alexander, Ross Case, Phil Dent and non-playing captain Neale Fraser.

Their number one was Tony Roche who had won Wimbledon doubles already five times. Besides that he was in Grand Slam singles finals six times: three times at Roland Garros, but only once winning the championship in 1966, twice in the US Open, and once in Wimbledon. For two years he occupied the second position among the world's best players.

"We are not afraid of playing on clay; those, who want to play in Davis Cup finals must be ready to win on any surface," declared Neale Fraser before the draw at Prague's Town Hall. He was even more content after the toss: "Alexander may bring a surprise against Kodes, and Tony will surely beat Hrebec."

Davis Cup vs. France.
From the left: capt. Antonin Bolardt, Jan Kodes, Pavel Hutka, Frantisek Pala a Jiri Hrebec.

After opening match victory over Alexander, Kodes received congratulations from Prime Minister Lubomir Strougal (left) and Antonin Himl (Chairman of CUPES).

When we walked out of the Town Hall after the Inter-Zonal Davis Cup final draw a group of chimney-sweepers were passing by. I chased them down and asked them: "Wait, I would like to touch you for good luck; we'll need it if we want to beat Australia in the weekend final! I touched them; and after we won I received a telegram: Congratulations on your huge Davis Cup victory! The Town Hall chimney sweepers.

Alexander composed half of an excellent doubles team Alexander-Dent. Kodes never had any trouble with him in singles and had defeated him four times until then.

He played a typical Australian game. Hard flat strokes, good net play, good volleys. There was nothing tricky like the ferocious top spins produced by Borg or Vilas. I was not too afraid of him, however, a different problem popped up. Since the match took place late in the autumn, on the last September weekend, the matches started very early, I believe even at ten in the morning, which was utter horror for me. I really disliked playing early. The toss decided that I played the first match thus I was not spared of the early morning angst. I entered the court knowing too well that defeating Alexander was going to be a key to overall team success.

I could not sleep my fill and woke up early, around five, with butterflies in my stomach. That match turned out to be more difficult than I had anticipated; I was spent after the four

sets! He used a strategy against me that I had used in Boston against Borg. He attacked my second serve with a slice and rushed to the net; I either passed him or I missed and lost the point. In the third set when the match could have gone either way, I had a lot of luck on my side as I pulled out several amazing passing shots, short and angled out of the court. This decided the match. I won 6:4, 2:6, 7:5, and 6:4.

In the second match, a curious tennis drama unfolded that led to a great surprise. Tony Roche clearly won the first two sets against Jiri Hrebec 6:3, 6:4. It looked like there were no doubts about his soon coming victory; however, Hrebec rose up to the occassion and delivered an unbelievable turn around. The audience drove him to battle, Kodes motivated his buddy from the court-side bench to simply persevere, and all of a sudden the tide changed! Hrebec prevailed in the next two sets 6:1, 6:3. Roche obviously tensed up and the non-playing captain Neale Fraser started checking his watch periodically throughout the fourth set. He realized that his player had a chance only if the game got suspended because

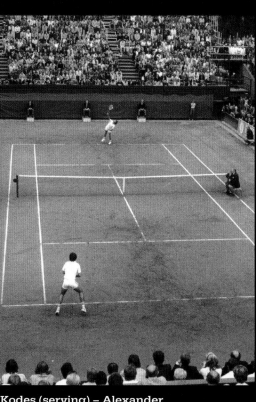

Kodes (serving) – Alexander

John Alexander

Jiri Hrebec won matchpoint with
Roche. We are leading 2:0...

Tony Roche

From left: Tony Roche, Ross Case, John Alexander, capt. Neale Fraser, referee De König from Belgium, capt. Antonin Bolardt, Jan Kodes, Jiri Hrebec, Frantisek Pala and Vladimir Zednik.

Vladimir Zednik

John Alexander and Phil Dent had no difficulties to beat the Czech team Pala-Zednik, to save the tie and hope for third day play.

Jiri Hrebec was in a trance at that point and everything he touched was successful. Nature was merciful to Fraser and the match was suspended for darkness till Saturday at two sets all, and 1:0 in Hrebec' favor in the fifth set.

The game resumed at eleven in the morning before the afternoon doubles match. It was over in no time – Jiri Hrebec won the final set 6:3!

The Davis Cup leadership then decided that Kodes would not play the doubles; instead they appointed Zednik – Pala to take the challenge.

The reason behind this tactical decision at 2:0 was to give Kodes time to rest up in order to make the third point against Roche the next day. That turned out to be completely reasonable. However, as soon as the Czechoslovak doubles team was announced, voices were heard among the Stvanice crowd that the team Zednik - Pala was sacrificed by the leadership, that they were left at the mercy of the Australians. It might have appeared so but it was understandable from the tactical point of view. Pala – Zednik lost 3:6, 6:3, 2:6, 3:6, and Alexander – Dent thus lowered the score difference to 1:2.

On Sunday Kodes raised the spectators from their seats numerous times! He defeated Tony quite easily 6:3, 6:1, and 6:4!

Since I did not play doubles I was rested and I trusted myself to beat him. In that match my passing shots were brilliant. I totally unnerved him with my backhand crosscourt passing shots that won many points for me. I felt tremendous confidence and ease playing the match.

Roche was unable to develop as much pressure as Alexander had and Kodes played a truly outstanding game.

The last match, Hrebec – Alexander, did not get finished. At set score 2:1 and tied at 6:6 in the fourth the match was suspended for darkness and simultaneously concluded. The final score between Czechoslovakia and Australia ended at 3:1.

There was a a lot of interest to watch the Czechoslovakia vs. Australia match at Stvanice that temporary stands had to be raised behind the baselines. The Centre Court capacity was thus increased by two thousand seats and even so the tickets were sold out immediately for all three days. Jan Kodes himself was more than a trifle responsible for that.

Like after winning Wimbledon in 1973, he was received by the Prime Minister Lubomir Strougal in Hrzansky Palace, where he came in closer contact with people from the government and the Central Committee of the Czechoslovak Union of Physical Education and Sport.

It gave me courage and confidence to address them at times fearlessly and say things that an ordinary athlete would not muster up the courage for. I often spoke my mind honestly and squarely. Before the Davis Cup final I insinuated that all over the world stadiums were being enlarged and spectator capacity increased such as in Bucharest before the finals with the USA; why not do the same here, where the interest of the public was so high?

The business department of the Central Committee of CUPES and the Tennis Federation originally approved the proposal but quickly retreated from the intent saying that the whole matter was way too complicated. Another impediment was the question of construction financing; who would cover the bills? When I remarked at CUPES that the additional stands would, most likely, never be constructed a sudden mandate befell the relevant office that the Centre Court capacity must be raised.

The new stands underwent a stress test performed by the army soldiers who stamped and jumped on the new stands in order to assure the organizers that no catastrophe would take place and the safety of the audience would be guaranteed. Although it was only a temporary structure the Centre Court looked snug and appeared much better on television screens. The Stvanice capacity was thus raised to six thousand seats.

Our victory was rewarded by thunderous ovations that I had never had a chance to experience before. No wonder – it was the first time ever that we reached the Davis Cup final!

Kodes Puts Czechs in Cup Final

PRAGUE, Sept. 28 (AP)— Jan Kodes propeled Czechoslovakia into the final round of the 1975 Davis Cup against Sweden when he beat Tony Roche of Australia, 6-3, 6-1, 6-4, today.

The victory gave Czechoslovakia an insurmountable 3-1, lead in the three-of-five match tennis series.

In the last singles match, John Alexander of Australia was leading Jiri Hrebec, 8-6, 6-, 1-6, and the fourth set was tied, 6-6, when play was halted by darkness. The match will be completed tomorrow.

Czechoslovakia's victory sets up the first Davis Cup final between two nations from the European continent. Sweden earned a berth in the final, to be played later this year, by beating Chile, 4-1, a week ago.

Kodes and Hrebec had won the opening singles matches, but Australia kept its hopes alive when Alexander and Phil Dent won yesterday's doubles.

Kodes, a former Wimbledon champion and his country's top player, was in complete contro. of his match against Roche.

Roche, plagued by double-faults, managed just one point in the second set.

Our victory against the Aussies was well presented...

Hard work for masseur Josef Stejskal (left) and Federation treasurer Vilem Chadima.

What else appeared in our press after this fantastic achievement?

Jan Kodes: "It was my dream to play the Davis Cup final at least once. That dream has now been fulfilled. I immensely longed for this opportunity. In my match with Tony Roche I totally spent myself especially in the first set. By the third set I was close to feeling incapacitated. However, it was also a mental affair and the knowledge of the soon approaching conclusion. There were moments when I did not think I could play a decent stroke any more but adrenalin must have kicked in and I gathered the remaining strength. I trust that the first set decided the outcome. It confirmed again my belief that the opening set is crucial in important matches and highly strung atmosphere just like here or in the 1973 Wimbledon."

Antonin Bolardt: "Kodes has never played a better match in Davis Cup than today."

Bolardt was no Bergelin nor Darmon; his statement shows how little he understood tennis because I played better in a number of previous matches that I had played at a tied score 2:2. For instance with Panatta, in Turin, on the opponent's turf. At home the audience drove me, and conversely, they rocked Tony Roche out of balance. Similarly, in Dusseldorf in 1972, when I played the deciding match against Harald Elschenbroich after a physically enormously draining doubles match that finished 19:17 in the fifth set. Bolardt must have made the com-

ment just for the press because if he considered the other circumstances he would not have been able to put it that way. Making the third point in front of the home crowd can't be any more difficult than winning the third point on the opponent's turf at 2:2!

Davis Cup's General Secretary Basil Rey: "I have never seen better tennis in Davis Cup competition. The entire athletic performance as well as that of linesmen and the main umpire was accomplished at a hundred percent level..."

Prime Minister Lubomir Strougal, Vice-Premier Vaclav Hula, Communist Party Chairman Milous Jakes, Party Secretaries Jan Fojtik and Frantisek Ondrich, Prague's Mayor Zdenek Zuzka and the CUPES Chairman Antonin Himl were all present in the audience.

Communist "Royalty" watching tennis! Tennis had a label of a "bourgeois" sport! It was Antonin Himl who succeeded in bringing these government potentates to Stvanice. As CUPES Chairman he understood that any good athletic achievement in any sport brought positive contribution for the entire country. It did not matter that it was not soccer, or ice-hockey, even tennis was acceptable. It became obvious that individual sports could attract world prestige too, whether they were Olympic or non-Olympic. In our country the old belief still persisted that only the Olympic sports had value and importance, followed by mass exercise called "spartakiada", then soccer, ice hockey, and team sports. And suddenly, tennis changed the old conviction; the nation fell in love with tennis and, at long last, the officials started paying some attention to it. That was extremely important. Granted, Davis Cup was still different from individual tennis competition. My reaching finals at Forest Hills or in Hamburg still meant little to them but the Davis Cup team reaching the final was hugely celebrated!

In connection with the Prime Minister's reception of the Davis Cup team members the players also received a financial reward. The CUPES had put together a key for rewards for athletes in Olympic sports. Gold, silver, bronze medals were appreciated with graduated amounts. Tennis, at that time a non-Olympic sport, had a level of reward that was very inferior. While the players could have received it it became to be understood that seeking a reward directly from the government would grant them a higher amount of status and other perks.

Considering the day and age we collected a very decent amount of money; I received eighty thousand Czech "Crowns-Korunas", Hrebec sixty thousand, and Pala and Zednik forty each, and we were all thanked for representing the country superbly.

Few days after the victory with Prime Minister Lubomir Strougal (center). Capt. Bolardt, Kodes, Hrebec and Federation President Stanislav Chvatal (right), who was later revoked due to Martina Navratilova's defection.

Lubomir Strougal was very pleasant at that gathering; he spoke intelligently and made a positive impression on me. He was no "hick" as some other communist officials were. It was obvious that he had his head screwed on right. He did not use the trite phrases as was customary with many party officials but rather acted natural and friendly. He assured us that he appreciated our performance and would be happy to help us whenever help was needed. I had a good feeling about him.

The victory over Australia had an affect on yet another thing. As Jan Kodes expressed some fears at the beginning of the year, when he took Jaroslav Drobny into confidence and shared some problems and difficulties with him, he now gained a feeling that all was turning out well and nobody would neither prohibit nor order him around. He felt content. It was the end of September... However, only a few days later everything turned around again!

SECRET EVENT

After the Davis Cup final he stayed at home for a few days, worked out and played in the league play-offs at Sparta. Sparta did not defend its title and ended up second trailing CLTK. They missed Martina...

Tournaments in Madrid and Barcelona were ahead of him, both were very important for final Grand Prix points standings. This was where the overall ranking was definitely decided and from it one could deduce who would qualify for the Masters.

However, during the time of the league play-offs events in Spain took on a political intent. Several members of the Basque separatist organization ETA instigated trouble in the Northern provinces. A number of them were taken into custody and imprisoned. Domestic press printed a detailed account of the events with a shocking postscript – prohibition of cultural

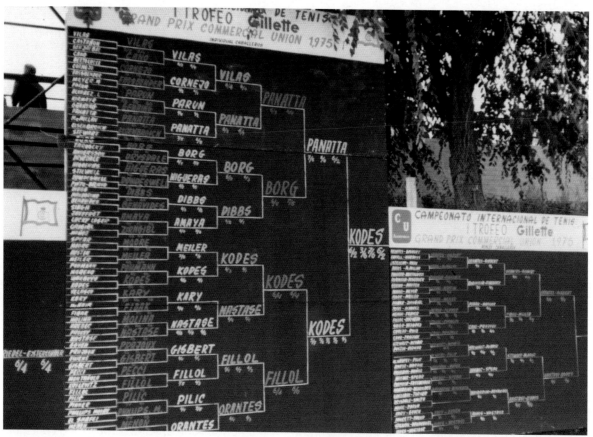

Grand Prix Madrid 1975. The draw of 64 players.

Adriano Panatta and Jan Kodes at Grand Prix Madrid in 1975. Panatta reached the finals after defeating Vilas and Borg but succumbed to Kodes in four sets.

and athletic events; prohibition of relations with the outside world on any level. That was implemented just a couple of days before our departure to Madrid! What had to happen – happened; we were not allowed to fly!

I felt like somebody poured boiling water over me! I looked forward to the tournament; it was an important one for me. As soon as I mentioned it at home old Dr. Rössler (my father-in-law) released a torrent of suggestions: "You can't leave it at that! What kind of nonsense is that? They can't manipulate you this way!"

I tried to explain to him how difficult the situation really was; since they canceled all cultural and athletic affairs nothing could really be done.

"That is impossible! Tomorrow Inter Bratislava is supposed to play soccer there against Barcelona! You must do something! They can't just forget it! You still have Davis Cup finals ahead of you!"

Upon learning that Inter Bratislava was, indeed, going to be playing in Barcelona, I calmed down a little. The first tournament did not take place in Barcelona but rather in Madrid! I needed to get to Madrid.

In the end Dr. Rössler egged me on: "Call Strougal at the secretariat!"

I nodded but thought that calling Himl would do just as well. The next day I called the Central Committee of CUPES – "Chairman Himl is on a business trip and will be out of office for several days!"

Slowly, I was giving up but my father-in-law urged me again: "What's wrong with you? Are you a moron to throw in the towel this easily?" Again he pressed to call the Prime Minister.

So, I sat down and dialed the number for Eva Janouskova, Lubomir Strougal's daughter and a wife of an editor Jiri Janousek, who I knew well: "Eva, I have a problem and need ten minutes of your Dad's time. We are not permitted to travel to Spain."

It was 6:30 pm. She called back shortly: "You are in luck; he is, presently, at the Presidium. On your way from Sparta stop at Strakovka; he'll give you five minutes for sure."

It was the first time that I entered that building. I announced myself at the reception and stated that I was going to the Presidium to see comrade Kryslova. She came down and led me to her boss.

It was a spacious room and he was sitting in a leather armchair behind a large table: "Hi, Jan, what's up?"

"We were told that we were not to fly to Madrid because of the highly tense political atmosphere in Spain. But I must go there because the Grand Prix Series continues and in a month and a half Jiri Hrebec and I will be playing the Davis Cup finals in Stockholm. We cannot afford to stay on the sidelines at this point. This is one of the last opportunities for quality preparation. The departure for Madrid is scheduled for the day after tomorrow and I see no reason why we should not fly there. What has really happened in Spain?"

He listened in silence and oddly looked me over, to the point that I suspected that he did not know anything about the issue! I don't mean about the situation in Spain but rather about the restriction to travel! "Hm, wait; something happened there, didn't it? Hold on, I'll find out what the matter is."

He picked up a phone and called Lubomir Prochazka, who was the Communist Party chief for people's committees and social organizations. He was among those, who presented me with a National Award in the spring of 1974. "Lubomir, what is going on in the case concerning our athletes and the situation in Spain?"

He listened for a while and then said: "Well, but these things should be reviewed individually and with sensitivity! Our tennis players Kodes and Hrebec have important tournaments to enter and it is necessary to take into consideration the fact that they have the Davis Cup finals against Sweden ahead of them!"

He listened again for a moment and then he laid the receiver down. "Don't worry, that will get resolved; you'll be able to go."

The next day, in the morning, they called me from CUPES to come at once. Antonin Himl was still away and it was Vice-chairman Julius Chvalny who received me. A Slovak. There was also Libor Batrla, at one point the director of Czechoslovak Television. And it was he, who gave me a lecture! "Comrade Kodes, you want to take a trip to Madrid!? But you ought to respect.... Do you even understand what happened there?"

"I am aware of some problems and demonstrations but I do not understand how that relates to my tournament entry in Madrid and my representing Czechoslovakia?"

He burst out at me: "You must realize that you, the athletes, demonstrate your affinity to what goes on in the West!"

It seemed to me that he was trying to sway me to give up my desire to go to Spain. We carried on a debate for a while that was going nowhere until he said: "Even you, tennis players, must respect other athletes, and must take a stand on that serious political problem!"

"Then explain to me, comrade Batrla, how is it possible that Inter Bratislava is playing a soccer game there tomorrow?" He froze because, evidently, he had no knowledge of that! Astounded he gazed at Chvalny, who started explaining with embarrassment: "Well, you know comrade Batrla, the team was there, in Barcelona, already before the troubles started and it was impossible to call them back." Under normal circumstances they would have had to call them back and they would not play. But since it was soccer they were afraid that they would be fined by UEFA. And handsomely at that!

"Oh yeah, I forgot – we are "only" tennis players!" I said.

At that moment Batrla again turned to Chvalny. "How is that possible?" Chvalny started to stutter and discharged some lame excuses but Batrla stopped him: "So, make another exception!" And he turned to me: "We'll make that exception for you but you mustn't feel hurt that the media will not mention a word about it in the newspapers."

They stuck to that to the letter. Not a mention appeared in our domestic press about our performance in Madrid.

Only those who lived through that period of time can understand the absurdity of those actions. All those things that comrades in top positions managed to manipulate, conceal, or forbid?

But what was all that fuss about? CUPES received notification from the Communist Party's Central Committee to limit relations with Spain for a period of time. Representative at CUPES fulfilled that request so eagerly that they went overboard and stopped travel altogether. Nobo-

KODES,
VENCEDOR DEL GRAND PRIX DE MADRID

(Reportaje gráfico de MACARIO.)

Pese a la baja temperatura, el Club de Campo de Madrid registró una gran entrada, que puede calcularse en 4.500 espectadores. He aquí un aspecto de los graderíos durante la disputa de la final.

A sus veintinueve años, el checoslovaco Jan Kodes ha vuelto por sus fueros. Tras derrotar a Fillol, en semifinales, supo solventar, en el encuentro decisivo, la oposición de un Adriano Panatta en espléndida forma. He aquí, en acción, al ganador del I Trofeo Gillette.

Kodes y Nastase consiguieron la victoria en el doble, batiendo en la final a Gisbert y Orantes, actuales líderes del Grand Prix en la modalidad. En la foto, Nastase ensaya una dejada ante la mirada de su compañero.

Sin lugar a dudas, Juan Gisbert fue el mejor de los cuatro protagonistas de la final de dobles. Sin embargo, al final, la suerte sería adversa a la pareja española. Este «smahs», de impecable ejecución, quedó fuera del alcance de Kodes y Nastase.

Jan Kodes y Adriano Panatta enarbolan los trofeos conseguidos en esta prueba madrileña, puntuable para el Grand Prix Internacional. El checoslovaco y el italiano brindaron un magnífico partido.

dy bothered to examine the significance of individual athletic events and travel departures. As it turned out, we, the tennis players, broke through their stiff practices.

The following day we flew with Jiri Hrebec in the direction of the Pyrenees Peninsula. Frank Pala and Vladimir Zednik were a little hurt that everybody forgot them. The exception was made only for two names, that of Kodes and Hrebec. And that decision was defended by the fact that a month and a half later we were to play the Davis Cup finals. Did the Tennis

Grand Prix Madrid 1975. Jan Kodes with the Gillette Trophy.

Federation act on Pala's and Zednik's behalf? Why not? What about the Davis Cup team captain? Did he bother to stand up for them? All these unanswered questions pointed only to one realization that followed tennis ever since tennis players became semi-professionals – our individual entries in tournaments did not interest them. I doubt they ever knew where we were going to play next week.

Our arrival in Madrid came as a great surprise. As soon as Jan Kodes entered the grounds of Club di Campo, he was met by ATP Tour Manager: "Jan, you are here, you came? That is fantastic!"

I looked at him spiritedly and he explained: "We've heard that you and Nastase would not be coming! It made us all distressed! The organizers and sponsors are really frustrated."

"Well, as you see, I am here."

At that moment, as a representative of ATP interests, he wasted no time and called Nastase in Romania. "When are you arriving?"

"We are prohibited to travel to Spain!"

"But Kodes is already here!"

Nastase did not want to believe it so Vittorio passed me the phone: "Hey, Ilie, I am here!"

"Russian!?(his nickname for Kodes...) How did you manage to get to Madrid?"

"They gave me a special permit."

At three o'clock that afternoon we were working out on a court and Nastase was already landing in Madrid!

The category A tournaments in Spain were Kodes' favorite; fine clay was as if "tailor-made" for him. Traditionally, there was very strong competition in Madrid; it was one of the most popular Grand Prix clay court tournaments. And it was just like that in 1975. The number one seed was Vilas, two Orantes, three Nastase, four Borg, Kodes was the sixth seed. Besides those mentioned above there were also Dibbs, Fillol, Panatta, Gisbert, Pilic...

Kodes' sound Davis Cup mastership continued and luck was on his side this time...

The enormous championship trophy from Madrid was soon placed next to his most valued trophies from Wimbledon and Roland Garros in his home mantelpiece.

After easy victories over the Germans Pohmann and Meiler I shamed Nastase 6:4, 6:4 in the quarter-finals. In the semi-finals, however, I squeezed by Fillol by "the hair of my chiny-chin-chin" after a five set marathon. I was trailing 5:7, 2:6, and 3:5 but I managed to turn the game around and won the last three sets 7:6, 6:2, 6:3.

The Chilean Jaime Fillol was one of my peers, who was not afraid of me. He hit very fast approaches followed by good net play. His second serve was unpleasant; it bounced up high. He even managed to eliminate my good aggressive return particularly from the backhand side.

Adriano Panatta, who previously conquered Vilas and Borg, awaited me in the finals.

That was a tremendous battle. I had to attack constantly and prevent Panatta from appro-aching the net. I broke him down with my serve in the third set tie-break. I won 6:3, 3:6, 7:6, and 6:2. Adriano was feeling on top of his game after his victories over Vilas and Borg. He was confident that he would beat me but he had forgotten my effective play at the net.

For Jan Kodes this was one of the last big tournaments of his career where he was able to achieve some great victories.

It is rather paradoxical since I almost missed it because of some absurd prohibition to tra-vel. In addition to my success in singles I also won the doubles with Nastase, when we defe-ated Orantes – Gisbert 7:6, 4:6, 9:7 in the finals. Even today I am still baffled as if it were some unbelievable story. And considering the circumstances under which I succeeded to travel to Madrid I can proclaim that it was my "incognito" tournament.

From Madrid the Grand Prix Series I traveled to Barcelona, where the International Spa-nish Championship took place. Kodes lost to Borg in quarter-finals 1:6, 6:2, 4:6. The blond Swe-de then defeated Panatta in the finals 1:6, 7:6, 6:3, 6:2. And the doubles team Kodes -Nastase lost in the semis to Borg - Vilas.

After that match we feared we would have nightmares about topspin lobs till Christmas-time...

At the close of the season the Masters tournament in Stockholm evaded Kodes by a very small margin; Nastase won it defeating Borg in the finals. In Czechoslovakia Kodes was voted the second best athlete of the year. The best athlete was a ski jumper Karel Kodejska who became the world champion in Ski Flying that year.

DAVIS CUP FINAL IN STOCKHOLM

The Davis Cup finals took place in the Royal Hall in Stockholm, Sweden. Jan Kodes played there many times and knew every corner of it, and thus he understood what awaited his team.

The fast rubber surface called "Holmsunds-plattan" was familiar to all of us, since we play-ed there regularly; thus the territory was not totally unknown to us. I myself played there only shortly before the Davis Cup finals in the Stockholm Open tournament.

When we were leaving for Stockholm, Antonin Bolardt could hardly bear that Jaromir Tomanek would follow us there as a team leader. Tomanek, the future Chairman of the Soccer Association and the editor in chief of the Czechoslovak Sport Daily, came and did not interfe-re in anything. But Bolardt was furious: "Tomanek is coming with us to watch over us. He is coming to keep an eye on me. He is a secret police agent!"

It was only another signal about an obvious rivalry among two of them who would watch over everything during our match with regard to their future political ambitions at home. But Tomanek was a passive observer in Stockholm while Bolardt could not stop himself from talking about him every single day: "Tomanek! What is he doing here? He will just lull around the Centre Court box!" He kept on making belligerent remarks on behalf of Tomanek. We paid no attention to it.

The two nations prepared differently for the final. While our players practiced painstakingly twice daily, Björn Borg, then the two times Roland Garros champion and the fourth best player in the world, left for a safari in Africa with his coach Lenart Bergelin... to rest up mentally and emotionally. However, the Swedes as a team did not leave things to chance either; they invited Ilie Nastase to be their sparing partner during the last week of training before the match. And why not, since Ilie knew Kodes' game almost as well as his own?! His presence during practice sessions was certainly felt – he turned the work outs into full-blown entertainment!

With a dead-serious face he told Kodes: "Borg is out of shape."

Our player number one thought to himself: "Who do you think you are trying to fool? – You don't think I know where you are coming to me from?... This is just a build-up stunt. Who would pull out a trump card ahead of the action?"

A propos Bjorn Borg! That chap had everything ahead of him while the Swedish tennis fever was reaching its climax. The streets of Stockholm swarmed with youngsters with long blond hair and short leather jackets. One could almost miss the real Borg. Hordes of female fans started to shriek as soon as Borg made an appearance, similarly to the British devotees during "Beatle-mania" more than a decade before.

When Jan Kodes met him for the first time in front of the Royal Hall a mob of female admirers hardly let his idol leave. The American television commentator and a tennis expert Bud Collins made up a nickname for him – "Davis Cup Killer". It might sound a bit stilted but it was truly enviable and amazing what Borg accomplished in Davis Cup in 1975. He was undefeated in twelve consecutive matches regardless of who his opponent was ...Orantes, Fillol, Meiler, Metreveli...

In the Swedish camp everything revolved around Borg and the clown Nastase dispensed good humor.

The highly anticipated match was inaugurated by the Swedish King Gustav Charles XVI on Friday, December 19, 1975. It was expected that the score at the end of the first day would be tied at 1:1, and that is exactly where it stood. Hrebec easily lost the opening match with Borg easily 1:6, 3:6, 0:6.

Hrebec met up with Kodes in the locker room; one just finished the other one ready to go onto the court. Kodes tried to find out about Borg in order to have an idea what to expect on Sunday: "Was it so bad, or is he really so good?"

"I don't even know what to tell you; I have never in my life been this nervous", Hrebec answered. "Just figure – I chose two out of my three rackets that I was going to use but I played with the third and did not even know it until after the first set!"

In the second singles Kodes evened the score; he defeated the huge Ove Bengtson 4:6, 6:2, 7:5, and 6:4. It was not an easy match. Out of five serves the Swede hit four first serves, and three of those were "aces"! What is the poor guy on the other side supposed to do when the cannon ball serve is coming at him?

"There are times when I didn't even see the ball coming" said Kodes during a change-over shaking his head in disbelief. *"I am worried to lose my serve, yet he double-faults twice a game with three aces to follow! Thus he holds his serve. We hardly carry on any rallies; what should I play against him?"*

Swedish stamp printed for Davis Cup finals 1975.

Frantisek Pala, who was seated right behind the player's chair, overheard that question. "What bothers you? A hard powerful shot or a spin?"

"Power."

"So, step back about a meter!"

In extreme situations one often forgets to think about simple solutions. The game turned around once Bengtson lost his serve. Giants like him do not like when their major weapon stops performing. It then affects the rest of the strokes and it rattles their confidence.

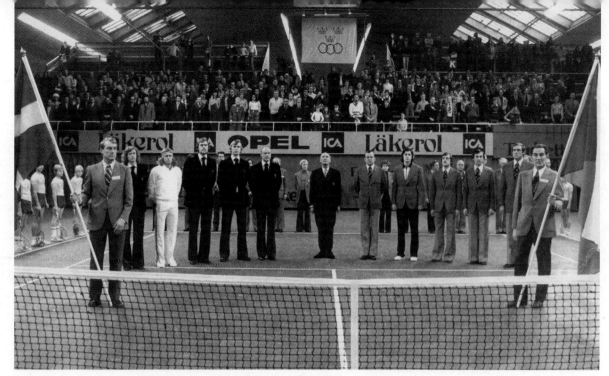
Opening ceremony of Davis Cup finals 1975 at Stockholm, Sweden.

Kodes started to direct the match. Slowly he gained confidence that he would succeed. A match-point came and he realized that he had not yet used his most lethal weapon – the backhand return down-the-line. Most likely, the Swede realized that too and he sent a booming serve to Kodes' backhand. Undoubtedly, he did not think that Kodes would hit a risky shot like that at this moment... it was not a powerful but rather a precisely placed shot in a spot where the opponent least expected it.

"With Bengtson each and every indoor match is difficult. I was under a lot of pressure and I knew that if I lost my serve I would hardly catch up to him later. Besides, we were down 0:1; I had to tie the score. It is always difficult to play when the score is unfavorable; but we managed to succeed," Kodes said to journalists.

Next on the program was the doubles, the match that created an odd atmosphere among the Czech players. By contrast to the previous matches it was obvious this time that Kodes – Hrebec should play all the matches. Generally, they played the singles, and only occasionally also doubles. In principle, the doubles team was made up of Kodes plus "somebody". Lately, only in Prague against Australia, the doubles team was not the standard one but rather Pala – Zednik, and we already know why it was so.

When we practiced among ourselves Jiri and I lost to Pala – Zednik several times. Jiri could not take it and flared up because Frantisek and Vladimir stopped being just sparing partners and rather tried to prove that they were better than us. We had singles practice behind us and felt tired; doubles work out was only an addition to our overall preparation.

However, Jiri lost his cool and started to swear: "To hell with this! I won't play the doubles! Who do they think they are? Let somebody else play it!"

It was further exasperating that Antonin Bolardt and Pavel Korda were uncertain and did not yet identify who to nominate for the doubles. Bolardt advocated Zednik, Korda pushed forward Hrebec. I admit that I had no idea who to go for. Indeed, in 1973 in Australia I played with Zednik, and subsequently we won tournaments in Los Angeles against Nastase – Connors, and also in Palm Desert. We played plenty of good matches like the one in Doneck.

It is true that Vladimir played great in practice – he served hard and punished us with "ace" after "ace". The court was very fast so I had difficulties with returns as well as the recovery after the return. Jiri was, perhaps, more daring. We knew it was going to be a battle of nerves! Hrebec in 1975 was not the same as Hrebec in 1973.

The entire week in Sweden was taken up by our debate over who should play the doubles.

Kungligahallen at Stockholm

Even just before the match started we all gathered for a long discussion that was to decide the final nomination.

Jiri Hrebec vehemently argued and declared: "I am not going to play!"

Bolardt continued to say that it hasn't been decided and "we shall see"... Then somebody got an idea to draw the names from a hat. That was absolute idiocy! It put me in such a dilemma that I could hardly sleep. As soon as I hit the pillows all the pros and cons came forth and started to disturb my peace. "It makes no sense to press Jiri to play if he is refusing to do so!? On the other hand, I told myself, considering that Bengston is on the other side of the net, Jiri returns better and our success depends on that. Borg is not a great doubles player. If we return well we'll pressure the opponents and they may tense up. The counterargument was that Zednik would hold his serve confidently but we would not threaten them with returns because Vladimir's returns are not so effective." Then I also remembered that Jiri and I lost here, on this very court and surface, just before this Davis Cup the Stockholm Open against Borg – Bengston 4:6, 3:6.

Björn Borg

I did not want to flatly interfere and mandate who I wanted to play with. The loss in the Davis Cup match in Munich against Fassenbender – Pohmann flashed through my mind. Jiri impinged on me with his negativism and I thought it would be better to play with somebody who wanted to come out and play rather than somebody who was pressed to do so. I knew that if things started going wrong Jiri would erupt with: "I warned you that I should not play!"

In the end, there was no toss up and, instead, we waited for the score at the close of the first day.

SVERIGE BORG·BENGTSON 4
CSSR KODES·ZEDNIK 2

Giant Ove Bengtson gave his partner a great
performance.

I will always remember this doubles match
because it decided everything.

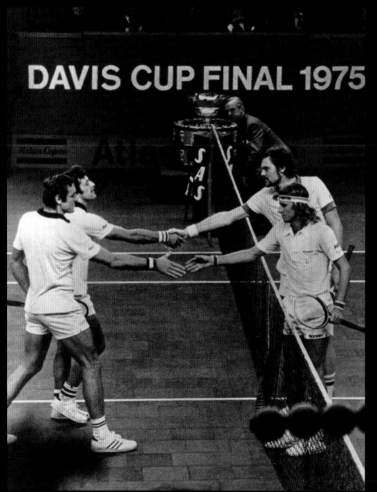

DAVIS CUP FINAL 1975

Jan Kodes - third day no chance
against excellent game by Borg.

Czechoslovak team with Davis Cup trophy. From left: masseur Josef Stejskal, Zednik, Hrebec, capt.Bolardt, Kodes, Pala and coach Pavel Korda.

By then only two names were considered: Pala and Zednik. Hrebec was no longer mulled over after his debacle with Borg; he eliminated himself. In order to refresh his spirit after the devastating loss to the Swedish number one, the coach Pavel Korda took Jiri to play some mini-tennis and let him win 3:2. Secretly he still hoped that Hrebec would play the doubles.

Evidently, Jiri lit up and burst into the room, where we were meeting after the first day's matches, and reported: "I smoked out the coach!" At that point Bolardt had already passed out pieces of paper where each one of us wrote the name of a proposed partner for Kodes. Pala or Zednik? I put down Zednik. And it was he who got the majority of the votes.

However, the trouble started right from the start. Vladimir Zednik served first and started the match with two double-faults; we lost that game. He tensed up, lost his confidence and we lost the doubles three times 6:4. That created a difficult situation since we knew that it was the doubles that would decide the outcome of that overall final. We could not envisage that I would defeat Borg. Though, granted, there was still a tiny shred of hope in our souls...

Till today I think that it would have been better if Hrebec played the doubles. The fact that it was our first Davis Cup final and fans from Czechoslovakia came to cheer us on created, naturally, extra pressure on us, players; inevitably nerves set in. However, as I look back, I still believe that Jiri would have been a better choice from a tactical point of view. There would have been more rallies. The surface was fast and everything reeled out after the serve. The side that lost serve decided the outcome. Borg held his, I held mine, Bengston held his, but Vladimir, unfortunately, tensed up and always stumbled; that was why we lost.

After the match Bjorn Borg said: "The score might indicate that the doubles match was an easy affair; but it was not so. Our opponents always won the important games. We expected Zednik to serve better. When his serve deserted him he tensed up."

Third day ceremony: Borg, Bergelin, Belgian referee De König, Kodes and Bolardt (from left).

Vladimir Zednik: "I was happy to reach a very solid, confident and promising form in Stockholm. On the other hand, I am sorry that I was unable to demonstrate that form in the doubles."

It is curious, and somewhat hard to understand, how much the power of one's mental state affects the outcome in critical moments.

Vladimir was a huge guy; physically he looked like a bouncer, outwardly confident but inside his heart sank during those crucial moments. Jiri, on the other hand, always reminded me of a little lion. He fought, he gnawed, and he battled. Naturally, the age-old law is still in place – a doubles game is played by two players and a pertinent loss cannot be blamed on just one player. It is my opinion that in Stockholm Antonin Bolardt's fundamental incapability and indecision were on full display. He would not let even the coach, Pavel Korda, make sense to him. It was difficult; as number one I always tried to do the maximum for the benefit of the team but Bolardt's handling the situation created a rift within the team and the resulting strained mood. If Bolardt and Korda said on Tuesday during practice: "Hrebec plays the doubles regardless the outcome of practice games!" all would have been accepted and acted upon!

I had to make similar decisions when I later became the Davis Cup team captain. And I always made them in good time! Sometimes it was complicated and difficult but there was no way around it. Vacillating and tacking around until the last possible moment, practicing and observing all players till the very end, did not help our players preserve their calm. It is the leadership that has to take upon them the responsibility to lead the team. And, naturally, it must be done in time!

The pre-game predictions were clear: Kodes as well as Hrebec would beat Bengtson, both would lose to Borg, and the doubles would decide the overall outcome. This was exactly the assumption that held true to the point. Deep down inside some might have hoped that Kodes would defeat Borg but the young Swede convinced everyone that he would soon become the world number one. He gave Kodes no chances and after the straight set victory 6:4, 6:2, and 6:2 he secured the third point.

I had no chance against him. Only the first set was somewhat even.

In addition, Kodes did not have luck on his side. On an easy overhead his racquet touched the tape of the net. Some perfect shots that Borg had no chance reaching because he set out in the opposite direction, ended up in the tape. And the most important points the Swede made were miss-hits. Luck favors the better player...

The last shot from Kodes' racket ended up in the tape – the game was over. Borg's racket flew up high towards the ceiling, and the Royal Hall exploded into mass roar. A splendid silver cup was standing in front of the Royal Box. When Kodes glanced in its direction the contours slowly blurred away.... "Damn, this surely can't be the last chance gone!"

Jiri Hrebec defeated Bengston 1:6, 6:3, 6:1, and 6:4, however that only adjusted the final score to 2:3. This victory gave provided an impetus to the development of the "golden years" of Swedish tennis.

The following year, Borg started his five-year run as Wimbledon champion, Mats Wilander followed him, Stefan Edberg and others came after him. The Vikings conquered the world!

Cheerful time with Davis Cup trophy. Birger Anderson, Ove Bengtson, capt. Lennart Bergelin, Bjorn Borg and Rolf Norberg.

If we had played on clay with the Swedes, I am convinced we had a seventy percent chance of winning. We beat them at Stvanice in 1972! And they played with the same team Borg – Bengtson. Though, granted, Borg was a less experienced youngster then.

The 1975 Davis Cup final with Sweden was the first all-European final since 1933. In 1933 it was England vs. France.

The final inspired immense interest among fans at home; it stimulated the nation and drew perhaps hundreds or even millions of fans to their television screens. On such an occasion the matches were watched even by those individuals who normally do not follow sports.

A group of fans, some of them being popular and well known celebrities, came all the way to Stockholm to support the tennis players – Slava Simek, Mirek Palecek, both actors from Theater Semafor and both tennis enthusiasts, journalist Jiri Janousek... Their cheers had no chance against the loud Swedish crowd but our players appreciated their presence very much.

"I relish the honesty in sport," quoted famous Czech actor Jiri Sovak in one of his interviews. "When somebody jumps, daresay ten meters and wins then he merits the medal. Nobody can later approach him and allege: You took off with more power than the others, so your victory is invalid. I really admire the top athletes. When the final in Stockholm took place I was with Kodes in spirit; he is an exceptionally brave man. The likes of him in Ancient Rome wore laurel wreaths on their heads and they held seats in the Senate."

Jaromir Tomanek, the team leader, returned to Prague with a cheerful and optimistic spirit: "Perhaps next time we'll finish on top. Afterall – reaching the finals in such an event is a great success in itself! Remember how much we still celebrate soccer success in Rome in 1934, or in Chile in 1962; one day we'll be proud to remember this tennis final in Stockholm."

Pavel Korda, the national coach: "This is a sad return home for me for we had an excellent chance to triumph. It is beautiful to be second, but the final loss still feels irksome. The Swedes had the edge on us and handled the indoor game better."

Grand Prix Madrid event "Trofeo Gillette" 1975. Jan Kodes reiceived the trophy from the President of Spanish Tennis Association Mr. Pablo Llorens Raňaga.

MERCILESS TIMES

In 1976 Jan Kodes returned to the US to play the WCT Indoor Circuit, however, he found himself losing sooner than he had been used to. Only sporadically he advanced to the final rounds...

In March he won a Swiss Indoor tournament is Basel where he defeated his Davis Cup partner and Tom Okker's conqueror, Jiri Hrebec.

He also battled his way into the finals in Nice, where the Italian, Corrado Barazzutti, overcame him in five sets. Unfortunately, Jan botched several match points in the fourth and fifth sets! In the next WCT tournament in Monte Carlo he was crushed by the Italian Panatta and in Stockholm by Nastase.

At Roland Garros he got overwhelmed easily by the Hungarian Taroczy in the early third round! He decided to leave Wimbledon out of his schedule and, instead, he concentrated on his preparation for Davis Cup in Budapest. After the very unpleasant 1:3 Davis Cup defeat by the Hungarians in which he lost a point against Taroczy again, he played a semifinal match in Gstaad against the Mexican Raul Ramirez; he also reached his almost traditional final in Kitzbüehl, Austria, and lost to Orantes from Spain 6:7, 2:6, 6:7. However, together with Hrebec they won doubles title against a German team Fassbender-Pohmann 6:7, 6:2, 6:4.

In early September he was the oldest US Open quarterfinalist at Forest Hills; he got knocked out by Jimmy Connors, the eventual champion. In the finals Jimmy defeated Bjorn Borg on that gray-green hard-thru surface in four sets.

WCT Stockholm 1976. W.Fibak from Poland beat Ilie Nastase 6:4, 7:6 in the finals. B. Borg lost to A. Panatta in the quarters.

Even though Jan Kodes defended his top position nationally for another two years he began to realize that he was not going to be able to retain that post indefinitely. More and more frequently he was plagued with injuries and after the Davis Cup loss to Hungary the media began its pressure against him: "Why is Kodes still playing? He is too old and no longer deserving to represent the country at the highest level!" At that point he was "only" thirty...

Jan played the WCT tournaments again throughout 1977 and again with little success. However, it should be noted that he crushed Nastase in an indoor tournament in Rotterdam and reached his personal best results in Monte Carlo defeating Orantes 6:3, 6:4 and Wojtek Fibak 6:4, 6:4 but losing to Barazzuti in the semis after botching three match-points, when the umpire asked to replay one of the match-point ace-serves at 6:5 in the tie-breaker! The Italian then succeeded in hitting a passing shot by Kodes, which made Jan tense up and, in the end, he lost the match 7:5, 6:7, 5:7 and with that he

MEN'S SINGLES US Open 1976

Holder M. Orantes (SP)

Top half

- J. S. CONNORS (1)
- R. A. J. Hewitt (SA) — CONNORS 6–3 6–3
- J. Ganzabal (ARG) — Fleming
- P. Fleming — Fleming 7–5 7–6 — CONNORS 6–1 6–0
- F. McNair — McNair
- T. Gullikson — McNair 6–3 2–6 7–5 — McNair 6–7 6–1 6–0
- M. Cox (GB) — Cox
- J. L. Haillet (F) — Cox 6–3 6–7 6–2 — CONNORS 7–5 6–3
- V. GERULAITIS (16) — GERULAITIS 6–4 6–1
- B. Manson — GERULAITIS 6–2 6–2
- B. Taroczy (HU) — Krulevitz
- S. Krulevitz — Krulevitz 7–6 7–5 — GERULAITIS 4–6 6–3 6–2
- G. Mayer — Mayer
- P. Bertolucci (IT) — Mayer 6–4 6–1 — Franulovic 6–3 6–4
- B. Prajous (CH) — Franulovic
- Z. Franulovic (YU) — Franulovic 7–6 6–1 — CONNORS 6–4 6–3 6–1
- A. R. ASHE (7) — ASHE 7–6 6–3
- J. James (AUS) — Kodes
- P. Dent (AUS) — Kodes 6–2 6–2 — Kodes 6–1 6–2
- J. Kodes (CZ) — Gottfried
- C. Dibley (AUS) — Gottfried 7–6 6–3 — Kodes 6–2 7–5
- L. Gottfried — Richey
- V. Amaya — Richey 6–4 7–6 — Richey 6–0 6–2
- C. Richey — Martin
- H. SOLOMON (10) — Martin 7–5 6–4 — Kodes 6–4 7–6 2–6 7–6
- W. Martin — Waltke
- F. Pala (CZ) — Waltke 6–4 6–3 — Waltke 6–3 6–3
- T. Waltke — McMillan
- F. D. McMillan (SA) — McMillan 7–5 6–1 — McMillan 6–4 6–1
- B. Teacher — Ruffels
- M. Cahill — Ruffels 7–5 6–1 — McMillan 3–6 6–1 6–4
- R. Ruffels (AUS) — VILAS 6–4 6–4
- G. VILAS (ARG) (3) — VILAS 6–2 6–4
- D. Schneider (SA) — Case
- R. Case (AUS) — Case 2–6 6–3 7–5 — VILAS 6–3 ret'd
- Z. Guerry — Caujolle
- J. F. Caujolle (F) — Caujolle 6–1 6–1 — Johansson 6–4 5–7 6–4
- J. McManus — Johansson
- A. Pattison (RH) — Johansson 6–1 4–6 6–3 — VILAS 7–5 6–4 6–0
- K. Johansson (SW) — BARAZZUTTI 6–4 6–0
- C. BARAZZUTTI (IT) (13) — Yuill 6–3 7–6
- P. Kronk (AUS) — Yuill
- J. Yuill (SA) — Yuill 6–1 6–2 — Kakulia 6–7 7–6 6–3
- S. Turner — Gardiner
- R. Benavides (BOL) — Gardiner 6–3 2–6 6–3 — Kakulia 6–4 6–4
- A. Gardiner (AUS) — Kakulia
- M. Edmondson (AUS) — Kakulia 7–5 7–6 — VILAS 6–1 2–6 7–6 7–6
- T. Kakulia (USSR) — RAMIREZ 7–6 6–0
- R. RAMIREZ (MEX) (8) — Dowdeswell 6–4 6–4
- P. Proisy (F) — Dowdeswell
- B. Fairlie (NZ) — Dowdeswell 6–0 6–4 — Dowdeswell 7–6 6–2
- C. Dowdeswell (RH) — Seewagen
- M. Meyers — Seewagen 6–7 6–3 6–1 — Lutz 6–1 6–4
- B. Seewagen — Lutz
- P. DuPre — Lutz 6–4 6–2 — DIBBS 6–2 6–4 6–2
- R. C. Lutz — DIBBS 6–2 6–2
- E. DIBBS (9) — Bunis 6–2 6–1
- C. Pasarell — Bunis
- E. Friedler — Bunis 6–2 5–7 6–4 — DIBBS 8–2 6–1
- H. Bunis — Winitsky
- S. Stewart — Winitsky 6–3 1–6 7–5 — DIBBS 7–6 7–6
- V. Winitsky — Alexander
- J. Alexander (AUS) — Alexander 6–4 6–2 — Alexander 6–1 6–3
- C. J. Mottram (GB)

Bottom half

- K. Warwick (AUS) — Warwick 6–4 6–4
- V. Amritraj (IN) — Warwick 6–4 7–5
- V. Pecci (PAR) — Pecci
- J. Gisbert (SP) — Pecci 7–5 6–3 — TANNER 6–2 6–4
- I. Molina (COL) — Delaney
- J. Delaney — Delaney 6–3 7–6 — TANNER 7–6 7–6
- M. Estep — TANNER
- R. TANNER (11) — TANNER 6–3 6–4 — NASTASE 7–5 6–7 1–6 7–6 6–4
- N. Holmes — Holmes
- D. Bohrnstedt — Holmes 6–0 6–7 6–1 — Riessen 6–3 7–6
- M. Machette — Riessen
- M. C. Riessen — Riessen 4–6 6–4 6–3 — NASTASE 6–2 7–5
- E. Van Dillen — Pohmann
- H. J. Pohmann (G) — Pohmann 7–6 6–3 — NASTASE 7–6 4–6 7–6
- O. Parun (NZ) — NASTASE
- I. NASTASE (RU) (5) — NASTASE def. — NASTASE 4–6 6–4 6–2 6–3
- B. Bertram (SA) — Stockton 6–3 6–1
- R. Stockton — Stockton 6–1 6–2
- J. Bartlett (AUS) — Menon
- S. Menon (IN) — Menon 6–3 7–5 — Stockton 6–2 7–6
- G. Masters (AUS) — Masters
- R. D. Crealy (AUS) — Masters 7–6 6–2 — Moore 3–6 6–2 7–5
- R. J. Moore (SA) — Moore
- W. FIBAK (POL) (14) — Moore 7–5 6–7 6–2 — Stockton 6–3 7–5 6–4
- J. Velasco (COL) — Velasco 6–2 6–3
- F. Taygan — Velasco 2–6 6–3 6–1
- B. Phillips-Moore (AUS) — Phillips-Moore
- T. Giammalva — Phillips-Moore 6–2 6–2 — Velasco 6–4 6–2
- B. Scanlon — Scanlon
- M. Mitchell — Scanlon 6–2 6–1 — Scanlon 6–3 7–6
- O. Bengtson (SW) — PANATTA
- A. PANATTA (IT) (4) — PANATTA 6–1 7–6 — SMITH 6–0 6–1
- A. Betancur (VEN) — Battrick
- G. D. Battrick (GB) — Battrick 7–6 7–5
- R. Cano (ARG) — Cano
- J. Whitlinger — Cano 7–5 6–4 — Cano 7–6 5–7 6–3
- T. Moor — Moor
- R. Norborg (SW) — Moor 6–4 3–6 6–3 — SMITH 6–0 6–1
- S. Ball (AUS) — SMITH
- S. R. SMITH (12) — SMITH 6–3 6–4 — SMITH 6–0 6–1
- I. El Shafei (UAR) — El Shafei
- E. Dublicker (F) — El Shafei 4–6 6–3 6–4 — Stone 6–0 6–1
- A. Stone (AUS) — Stone
- H. Kary (AU) — Stone 6–2 6–2 — ORANTES 3–6 1–6 6–2 7–6 6–1
- J. Andrew (VEN) — Andrew
- B. Mitton (SA) — Andrew 7–6 6–3 — ORANTES 6–2 6–4
- J. Kuki (J) — ORANTES
- M. ORANTES (SP) (6) — ORANTES 7–5 6–1 — ORANTES 7–6 6–2
- N. Spear (YU) — Okker
- T. S. Okker (NTH) — Okker 6–3 6–3 — ORANTES 6–2 6–4
- B. Walts — Higueras
- J. Higueras (SP) — Higueras 4–6 7–6 6–4 — Okker 6–3 7–6
- A. Metreveli (USSR) — Metreveli
- R. Thung (NTH) — Metreveli 6–1 6–3 — GOTTFRIED 6–2 6–2
- J. Hrebec (CZ) — GOTTFRIED
- B. GOTTFRIED (15) — GOTTFRIED 6–1 6–1 — GOTTFRIED 6–4 7–5
- P. Cramer (SA) — Lloyd
- J. M. Lloyd (GB) — Lloyd 6–3 6–1 — Lloyd 6–4 6–0
- G. Reid — Saviano
- N. Saviano — Saviano 4–6 6–3 6–1 — BORG 6–3 6–3
- J. Diaz — Fillol
- J. Fillol (CH) — Fillol 6–4 6–3 — BORG 4–6 6–2 7–6
- C. Letcher (AUS) — BORG
- B. BORG (SW) (2) — BORG 6–2 6–2

Quarter-finals / Semi-finals

- CONNORS 7–5 6–3 6–1
- VILAS 6–1 2–6 7–6 7–6 → CONNORS 6–4 6–2 6–1
- NASTASE 4–6 6–4 6–2 6–3
- BORG 4–6 6–0 6–2 5–7 6–4 → BORG 6–3 6–3 6–4

Final

J. S. CONNORS — 6–4 3–6 7–6 6–4 (Winner)

Bjorn Borg won his first Wimbledon final in 1976 over Ilie Nastase 6:4, 6:2, and 9:7. It was Nastase's second Wimbledon final – in 1972 he was defeated by Stan Smith in five sets.

lost the opportunity to confront Borg in the finals. However, he won doubles together with Jauffret overpowering the team Okker - Fibak 2:6, 6:3, and 6:2.

Romania inflicted a devastating Davis Cup defeat 3:1 upon the Czechoslovak team in Bucharest. An awkward and embarrassing situation transpired during the match between Hrebec and Nastase, when the non-playing captain Bolardt recalled Hrebec from the court and the match was defaulted.

The year 1977 was the last year when WCT and ITF Grand Prix circuits were played separately. Kodes achieved a distinct result in doubles with Fibak when they defeated the very best American team Smith – Lutz 6:4, 6:4 and reached the Roland Garros finals. They were overcome by Brian Gottfried and Raul Ramirez in four sets 7:6, 4:6, 6:3, and 6:4. In singles he was edged out by Nastase from Romania in the fourth round 6:4, 7:5, and 6:3.

The new Roland Garros champion, Guillermo Vilas from Argentina, knocked him out of the Wimbledon first round 9:8, 7:5, and 6:4 on Centre Court.

A couple of weeks later he played against him again in the Kitzbüehl finals and lost for the third time. After an even four hour battle, when Kodes was ahead 2:1 and 40:15 in the fifth set, he left the court defeated again 7:5, 2:6, 6:4, 3:6, and 2:6. However, he delivered an excellent performance.

After two successful rounds at the US Open Brian Gottfried, the Roland Garros runner-up, defeated him quite easily 6:4, 6:2.

In the close of that year a step was taken that Jan Kodes had envisioned already a year before. He returned from Sparta club back to I. CLTK at Stvanice, the place where his tennis journey began…

In the course of 1978 a new generation of players began to appear. In the Davis Cup series against the Netherlands Tomas Smid came out for the first time in doubles next to Kodes. That was where the splendid tennis partnership of Kodes - Smid started. They won crucial Davis Cup matches between 1978 – 1980 and they also advanced into the finals of many Grand Prix tournaments – Stuttgart, Hamburg, Rome, Nice, Hilversum, Aix en Provence, Indianapolis and Köln on Rhine. After defeating the New Zealander Fairlie in singles in the French Open and

Roland Garros doubles finals 1977. From left: Jan Kodes, Wojtek Fibak, Brian Gottfried a Raul Ramirez.

Brian Gottfried and Raul Ramirez (front) reached the title. Jan Kodes at the net.

then Pilic from Yugoslavia, Kodes was surprisingly overwhelmed by Arthur Ashe 6:4, 2:6, 6:7, 3:6. Jan faltered in the third set tie-breaker, when Ashe was already cramping. Inste-

Renata Tomanova's best year was 1976, when she reached the Australian and French Open finals, also won Barcelona and Baastad. In 1978 she won the Australian Open doubles with Betsy Nagelsen from the United States.

ad of taking advantage of the situation he got nervous and committed uncalled for unforced errors. He considered that defeat the worst of his Roland Garros performances. The doubles finalists from the previous year, Kodes – Fibak, had split up; the former teamed up with Smid, the latter with Okker, and neither team advanced into the finals. The Americans, Gene Mayer and Hank Pfister took the championship.

Kodes came down with high fever and flu that year in Wimbledon and pulled out of his first match against Jaime Fillol.

At home, in Prague, Czechoslovakia defeated the Netherlands 3:1 and Poland 3:2 in Davis Cup. However, Kodes lost to Okker and Fibak in the two encounters and the team captain Bolardt nominated, surprisingly, the fresh national champion from Ostrava, young Ivan Lendl, in his stead for the next Davis Cup match against England.

I was surprised since I had decided to skip the US Open in order to practice at home as much as possible and on grass. I also opened my court to all to practice on before the trip to England. As our players returned one by one from the US Open I gained a feeling that we had a great chance to succeed.

Upon their arrival in England Antonin Bolardt decided that Ivan Lendl would play

Jaroslav Drobny came to Eastbourne with our mutual friend Frank Novak (right). Unfortunately, even their support did not help, we lost the doubles in five sets.

in Kodes' place. However, in the windy seaside encounter Ivan did not manage to win even a set, and Hrebec lost both of his singles in five sets to John Lloyd and Buster Mottram. The Czechoslovaks failed to win the doubles too. The favored team Kodes – Smid lost the third point to Mark Cox – John Lloyd 4:6, 15:13, 4:6, 6:2, and 4:6. In spite of leading 3:1 in the fifth they were unable to secure a winning point that would have given them a chance to reverse the outcome of the match the last day of the encounter.

Thus, England won 5:0! The British press did not believe that replacing Kodes by a young inexperienced "debutante" Lendl in such an important encounter was a smart decision. They pronounced it a rash and unfortunate choice, especially since the match was played on grass.

The overwhelming defeat in Eastbourne showed that Ivan Lendl who, at the age of nineteen, had taken over the top spot in Czechoslovak tennis, was not yet as beneficial to the Davis Cup team as some wanted to believe. Euphoria over "Lendl has overtaken Kodes" remained unfulfilled.

Granted, my performance was no longer impressive. My tennis proficiency was still good, but my stamina and mental endurance were in shortage. Even my coolheadedness wasn't the same as before. Still, the fact that Ivan defeated me did not assure that he would defeat everybody.

In 1979 everything was different. The rising generation, Ivan Lendl and Tomas Smid, grabbed the opportunity and their Davis Cup team selection advanced into the Inter-Zonal semifinals against Italy. On the way to the city that never sleeps they had to overcome France and a very challenging team of Sweden.

DROWNING INTERMEZZO

In order to stay on course of events we must head toward the Equator, further South of Europe, before we get tangled up in this year's Davis Cup battles! In his career Jan Kodes' tennis travels took him only three times into the heart of equatorial Africa. Curiously, it was in the last three years of his tennis career. In 1979 he visited there twice, first Nigeria, and then

Cameroon. He liked it more in Nigeria and for that reason he repeated his trip there again two years later.

The year 1979 started out with an indoor exhibition tournament in Spanish Mallorca, where he beat Nastase 4:6, 6:3, 9:7. He then tried to improve his computerized ATP standing and took part in a tournament in Lagos, Nigeria.

Nigeria impressed Jan with its mega-contrasts. On one hand he saw a modern airport, super-highways into the city, grandiose and imposing buildings that adorned the down-town with its incredible architectural styles, and also a nice looking tennis club.... On the other hand he saw shocking poverty: shanty towns, slums, people living in conditions that we could never imagine possible.

A German player also played the tournament in Nigeria. His name was Reinhart Proobst and a few years later he would be my teammate in Amberg, at the end of my career. We played each other in dreadful heat; I felt sorry for the local children, who were the ball-boys. They were malnourished, one had a bulging tummy, another had had polio, yet another suffered from rickets. It was a heart-wrenching sight. After the match they ran to us and all they desired was something to drink. We had been used to giving out head bands, wristbands, balls, and signatures and it took us totally by surprise that they did not care to get those popular items and the only item they truly craved was the life-saving liquid – water! I opened up the fridge and gave out a few bottles of Coke. I also gave them my own bottle and it was emptied in no time.

I took a shower, packed my bags, and as I was getting dressed a distraught ATP supervisor walked in and said: "Mr. Kodes, we have a problem; please, follow me to see the tournament director!"

I walked into the office and waited a while before the tournament director appeared: "We are truly delighted to have you here but you mustn't do again what you have done today."

"What have I done?"

"You opened the fridge and gave out about ten Coke bottles!"

"For God's sake, is that a crime? A few bottles of Coke!" I reached into my pocket and wanted to give him ten dollars.

"It is not the dollars that we are concerned with. In this country Coca Cola is like ...how should I explain?" and he started fishing for the appropriate words. "As if I offered them some Whiskey. Coke is luxury! Since they are poor they can drink only water. The tournament budget would not be able to afford a Coke for each ball boy after each match!"

"And why not?"

"Because their mentality allows them to accept Coke only when their family reaches a certain standard of living."

So, it was not that I robbed the club of a few dollars but rather I disturbed their ingrained customs.

"Beg your pardon; the boys were terribly thirsty!"

"That is not true because they have their own ball boys' quarters where they keep jars of water that are exclusively for them!"

I remember the jars; large and made of clay, with a narrow spout; it was difficult to pour water into cups from them because they were rather heavy. Those narrow openings had their purpose – thanks to the small hole the water kept nicely cool even in the height of the heat.

In Lagos Jan Kodes advanced to the semifinals, where he lost to Hans Kary from Austria 5:7, 7:6, and 8:10. The next plane to Europe did not fly till Monday so he took advantage of an invitation from the Czechoslovak Embassy officials, who had watched his matches, and gladly took a trip with them to the seaside.

We arrived at the beach that was reserved primarily for Embassy personnel use. I struck up a conversation with a lady who explained to me where there was a section for the Germans, the Dutch, and the other diplomatic core; she also talked about their life in Nigeria; it was good to hear how pleased they were that I came and through me they got news from home. We were just lounging and chatting and every so often one of her colleagues, an Embassy doctor, urged me: "Jan, let's go in the water and take a swim!"

"Ok; give me a second."

He would not leave me alone and, finely, the lady companion exclaimed: "Don't go with the nutty doctor; look at the high waves – it is dangerous behind them!"

But, when I could stand the heat no more I went in the water. It was delightful and warm, soothing for my sore ankles and back! It was easy to get onto the other side of the waves, there and back. I jumped through them back and forth having fun like a little kid. For periods of time I basked in the sun and then I got lured into the water again; in the meantime the doctor left.

It was later in the afternoon, a bit after four. I got in the water, swam a short distance, and here came one wave and then another...Suddenly, a disaster struck! I felt powerful force pulling me out into the sea. Only moments before the doctor instructed me that I should not try to swim perpendicularly back to the shore after I jump through the wave and it washes over me because that creates these tongues that pull one out to sea; he told me to swim along, parallel to the beach. But by this time I was so far away that I hardly saw the shoreline!

I tried to swim forward but I was pulled backwards! I sensed that this was my last hour, my death bed! Every time the wave washed over me and the water level dropped I could see the shore-line and I waved my arms madly. But then the next wave shrouded the view again.

Nobody on the beach had any idea where I was. I ran out of steam and just lay on my back to rest and regain some strength. However, as soon as I did that the force pulled me another hundred feet out. What horror of horrors! I was on my last leg! I mobilized the last bits of strength and started treading water and waving my arms again.

Then I noticed commotion on the beach. People were running here and there and were pointing toward the sea. I lay on my back again and comforted myself with a belief that they now noticed where I was. In no time some twenty Africans plunged into the water and headed toward me. Rescuers! It could not have taken them more than thirty seconds. They encircled me and slowly started pulling me toward the shore.

I was totally exhausted and could not even swim any more. It seemed like eternity before we got back to the beach. It took some forty five minutes. They could not go straight for the beach but rather had to pull me to the side and in the direction to the shore; that prolonged the rescue effort. In some spots the tide was making its way out to sea, in other spots it was coming back to shore. A person unfamiliar with such phenomena was in great danger. Time of day was also important. Conditions were different at two in the afternoon than at four, which was caused by changing tides.

By the time we reached the shallow waters I was hardly able to move. I stood up but my knees buckled. I must have fallen six times before I passed the few feet out of the water! I staggered utterly spent. They pulled me to the spot where I had left my stuff; I felt like I was dying. Only at this point I realized that my gold necklace with a lucky charm of number 1 was gone. The sea took its tariff, most likely in exchange for my life.

The woman I had been talking to was still sitting there and when she saw me she laughed unkindly: "I told you not to go over to the other side of the waves!" She almost turned my demise into horseplay!

This incident had yet another consequence. About quarter of an hour later embassy officials came and brought me a form with the International Red Cross insignia: "Mr. Kodes, this will cost you a hundred dollars! Please, fill out this form and pay up. You must pay otherwise they'll let others drown next time. This happens here every weekend! The Dutch, the Bulgarians, the Germans. The Red Cross is on duty here around the clock with binoculars. Please, pay for it."

"That is not a problem but why did they leave me out there for so long?" - They shrugged their shoulders.

This was one of the worst experiences of my life. I admit that I am not a strong swimmer and I was truly petrified. In my mind I saw the tide pulling me further and further and imagined that nobody would get to see me ever again.

In spite of this horrible experience Jan Kodes returned to Nigeria once more. In 1981 he traveled there with Stanislav Birner.

We flew from Paris and, coincidentally, Francois Georges Goven and Christophe Roger-Vasselin were on board with us. Upon arrival in Lagos we had to go through passport control when we got off the plane. We had no problem but those two?

"Are you French?" asked the officials and they took them aside at once; we hardly had a chance to say good bye. We went directly to the club, worked out and played around...There was still no sign of Goven and Vasselin. They reached the club some six hours later! – They were held by the custom officials at the airport all that time; they did not want to let them enter the country.

I did not understand the situation then; the political landscape was very complicated in those times of the 20th Century when most African countries were trying to free themselves of the Colonial rule. When I came just on my own two years previously I was not alert to political complexities but this time the incident of the French players reminded me that Nigeria was a British Colony for great many years and its Independence was granted only in 1960. Two decades after the overthrow of the British was not such a long time to presume that the extempore at the customs office was anything but a demonstration of long standing aversion between the British and the French.

Jan Kodes experienced yet another interesting episode from this second visit to Nigeria.

There was a party at the Czechoslovak Embassy. Food supplies arrived from Frankfurt – Czech bread, horseradish mustard, canned frankfurters... There was great atmosphere at the Embassy that evening and much fun. Some fifty people attended and I whirled around. Kodes here, Kodes there. They started serving frankfurters and I tasted one, then another and more – they were delicious. About ten minutes after I took a break from my food consumption I started having cramps. Progressively I was feeling so dreadfully ill that I thought my end was near. The interesting thing was that nobody else got sick but me.

I retched and retched yet I felt even worse the next day; I had to take "kinedryl" when I boarded the plane. It took three weeks in Prague of going from doctor to doctor before they found the culprit; I was diagnosed with salmonella. I was so weakened that when I got up from bed I had to support my-

Arrival from Lagos before the league match with NHKG Ostrava. I played again for I. CLTK, in cold climate, at Stvanice. I lost to Ivan Lendl 4:6, 1:6.

self touching the walls with my hands as I made my way to the bathroom. It took another five days before I started to feel better; doctors told me that the frankfurter I ate was bad. It was bad luck that I ate just the one that was rotten.

Let's go back to 1979. During the Davis Cup tournaments that Jan Kodes took part in that year his tennis elbow problem gradually grew to mega strength. That November it culminated in an operation theatre "Na Bojisti" (On the Battlefield) in Prague. The tennis elbow problem must have been brewing for quite some time. But he must have dreadfully aggravated it playing with a metal racket. True, his shots were more penetrating and faster; however the elbow was suffering further damage. That was the reason why he switched back to his beloved Wilson wooden racket upon return from Lagos the following year. Nevertheless, the operation could not be evaded, only postponed.

When he returned from Africa he started the European Circuit. He beat Pavel Slozil in the indoor Grand Prix in Linz 4:6, 6:3, 7:5. But he was no match for the French number two player, Giles Moretton, and lost 7:6, 6:7, 3:6. He completed a series of tournaments in Ger-

many before playing the French Open. He played indoors at Stuttgart, and on clay in Hamburg and Munich. It was in Hamburg where he won the German doubles championship title with Tomas Smid for the second time after defeating Okker-Fibak, Gottfried-Case and in the final the Aussies Edmonson-Marks 6:3, 6:1,7:6! They continued with their winning streak even at Roland Garros, where they were stopped in semis by the brothers Mayer in a four-set battle 6:7, 7:5, 3:6, and 6:7.

He also played a marathon singles match opposite Dick Crealy from Australia and won 7:6, 6:7, 3:6, 6:4, 8:6 but his advance was thwarted in the second round by Victor Pecci from Paraguay.

The 1973 Champion no longer dazzled with his performance on Wimbledon grass. He lost in the first round to Hank Pfister from USA but he carried out another marathon doubles with Tomas Smid in the first round. They defeated Warwick-Ball only after a five-hour battle 4:6, 5:7, 7:6, 6:4, and 14:12! They disposed of Clerc-Rodriguez 6:0, 6:3, 6:3 in the second round, but succumbed to the Aussies Case-Masters 4:6, 6:4, 5:7, and 6:7 in the next round.

Regina Marsikova won Czech Nationals four times (1975, 77, 78, 84). She won the Italian Open title in 1978 over Virginia Ruzici 7:5, 7:5. Three times she advanced into the French Open semifinals (1977-79) and won doubles with Pam Teeguarden from the US in 1977. She also won several other events - Toronto, Madrid, Barcelona, Avon Masters act. She had wins over Evonne Goolagong, Wendy Turnbull, Mima Jausovec and Andrea Jaeger.

Ivan Lendl powered the Czechoslovak team to win Davis Cup in 1980.

Lendl held number one tour ranking 8 times for a total of 270 weeks at the peak during 13 seasons in the Top Ten between 1980 – 1992.
Won 8 Grand Slam Singles titles.

He is the only a player, who played 8 consecutive US Open finals between 1982-1989, won 3 times in 1985-1987 over McEnroe, Mecir and Wilander.
Ivan captured also 5 ATP Masters Cup&Year-end event titles in the years 1981-82 and 1985-87.

ROAD TO DAVIS CUP VICTORY

Yannik Noah was not able to stop the Czechs from winning the doubles. The Czech team Jan Kodes – Tomas Smid overwhelmed Noah – Moretton in four sets.

Three European metropolises witnessed the Czechoslovak Davis Cup team's performance in 1979. Hardly anybody thought that the match on Seine would be decided already after the doubles. It was especially the home fans and tennis experts who were shocked. Ivan Lendl surprised Yannick Noah in the opening match with a 6:3, 6:3, 3:6, 9:7 victory and Tomas Smid followed suit in the next match overpowering Giles Moretton in five 4:6, 4:6, 6:3, 6:3, and 8:6. On Saturday Kodes-Smid defeated Noah-Moretton 7:5, 6:4, 5:7, 6:2 and the advance of the Czechoslovak team was secured! The last singles were played to complete the matches. Both were three-setters. Lendl took the first one beating Moretton 6:1, 6:2, 6:2; in the second match Noah averted the humiliating score of five to nothing by defeating Smid 7:5, 6:1, and 6:2.

The French were surprised by my performance in the doubles. On the other hand, they expected more from their darling Noah.

The US Open was fast approaching and prior to it there were four warm-up tournaments on American hard surfaces. Still before leaving for the US Jan Kodes played the Dutch Championships in Hilversum, where he battled and succumbed to Taróczy in five 6:4, 3:6, 5:7, 7:6, 3:6 and with Tomas Smid they advanced to the doubles finals. They played another doubles final in Indianapolis, on the other side of the Atlantic, where they lost to John McEnroe-Gene Mayer 4:6, 6:7. In the subsequent tournament in Toronto Kodes provided a surprise when he defeated the American Victor Amaya 0:6, 7:5, and 6:0 on a concrete surface and then played an even match with several years his junior and a number one seed, the "Big Mac" John McEnroe, resulting in a 5:7, 3:6 loss.

Jan Kodes' first and last entry at Flushing Meadows hard courts turned into the longest match of the first tournament day; Jan defeated the South-African David Schneider only after a heroic effort 4:6, 5:7, 6:4, 6:3, 6:1. However, the aftermath of that match left him depleted of strength that he lacked in the second round. He received a three set lesson from a Brit Buster Mottram – 3:6, 6:7, and 3:6.

The Davis Cup directorship set the date for Zonal finals to be in the middle of September. Stvanice welcomed Sweden in the "B" Group headed by Bjorn Borg, who had won Wimbledon and Paris four times by then! The Centre Court capacity was increased by a thousand seats and even that was not enough to satisfy all tennis fans in their desire to get in.

Everybody wanted to see the world number one player with their own eyes, including the Chairman of our government Lubomir Strougal and the CUPES Chairman Antonin Himl, the vice-president of the Central Committee of Narodni Fronta (National Guards) professor Tomas Travnicek and others. The ITF president, Philippe Chatrier from France, was also in the audience. The 1956 Wimbledon Champion Lew Hoad oversaw the smooth flow of the encounter as a referee.

As usual, the key to the eventual Davis Cup victory was the doubles. Was there anybody between Lendl and Smid who could defeat Borg? That was very unlikely. The fair Swede was celebrating his absolute tennis dominance.

The 1979 opening ceremony of Davis Cup encounter with Sweden at Stvanice. From the left: Per Hjertquist, Kjell Johansson, Björn Borg, Ove Bengtson, captain Anders Sjögren, referee Lewis Hoad, non-playing captain Antonin Bolardt, Jan Kodes, Pavel Slozil, Ivan Lendl, Tomas Smid.

"Doubles will decide the outcome; I do not believe that Johansson will score any singles point," announced the non-playing captain Antonin Bolardt after the draw. The opening match turned out perfectly; Tomas Smid gave Kjell Johansson no chances: 6:4, 6:3, 6:2. The second match also delivered the expected outcome – Lendl lost to Borg 4:6, 5:7, 2:6.

The match was suspended for darkness at 2:2 in the third set and was completed the next day before the doubles. Ivan Lendl demonstrated several times over what tennis fans could expect of him in the near future. He managed to play a great many unbelievable shots that showed his huge potential.

The Saturday doubles was definitely the key to advancing into the Inter-Zonal finals. Borg-Bengtson were on the Swedish side – the same two who took away the Czechs chances in Davis Cup finals in Stockholm four years earlier. This time Kodes-Smid took revenge on them in Prague and won in four: 2:6, 6:3, 6:4, 6:0!

One directed the game, the other played it. Kodes' experience and Smid's attacking euphoria did the job. Borg tried to dictate the play on their side and with that he also assumed the responsibility but he was not successful. It was clear that he was an exceptional singles player but he was not as successful in doubles.

A merciless battle developed between Lendl and Johansson to seize the third point. The Swede took the first set 10:8 and in the process he worked himself into a trance-like condition. However, he soon sobered up from his tennis intoxication, when Lendl turned the game around with two successful sets 6:4, 6:4. However, after a break the Swede came back in big style and won the fourth 6:4. At two all in sets the Swedish contingent was reasonably sure of their success. The Northerners were confident that Borg would make the third point if the overall score was 2:2 before the last singles. Conversely, they did not yet know the tremendous strength, moral and physical, that Ivan Lendl would bring into the fifth set. He literally swept Johansson off the court 6:1! After five hours and fifteen minutes the advancement into the European final remained at Stvanice Island.

Tomas Smid played the last match against a substitute Per Hjertquist, and at 3:5 in the first set he defaulted for injury. Domestic press evaluated Jan Kodes' doubles performance very positively and they discussed his tremendous contribution to our young and promising Davis

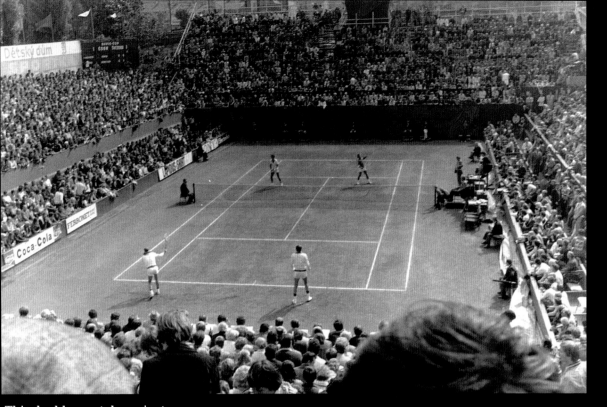

This doubles match against Borg and Bengtson decided the outcome of the encounter that we won 3:2. I played really well, however I would still have been happy to exchange the success in this doubles with the overall Davis Cup final victory at Stockholm in 1975.

Jan Kodes and Tomas Smid in Prague after their important doubles victory over the Swedish team Borg – Bengtson.

Björn Borg

Cup team. Jiri Nejedlo wrote the following in Lidova demokracie, and Pavel Vitous in Mlada Fronta:

Last Saturday Jan Kodes showed again the benefit of his tennis experience that brings us back to the peak of his career. It is amazing how he managed to fire up our doubles team after the first lost set. It is a proof of his immortal strength of character. Simply put, he is a personification of a true "champ" as he is nicknamed by Tomas Smid.

We must acknowledge that the team veteran, Jan Kodes, was the most significant force in the successful defeat of the Swedes. It was not only due to his perfect strategy and technical delivery but, literally, thanks to his inspiration and injection of victorious fire and force into his teammate Smid. He embodies a priceless source of positive influence on the entire team spirit as an advisor and coach, and he has a gift to propel them to higher achievements. The team will still need him for some time ahead!

Mladá fronta – Czechoslovak press

Naturally, our preparation for the European finals with Italy took place on clay. Kodes lost in the quarters of the traditional National Championship in Bratislava to Jiri Hrebec 3:6, 6:1, 3:6 but together with Smid they delighted in beating Slozil-Hrebec 6:0, 6:0, 6:4 in doubles! Even the third set score started out 2:0!

The Czech team was optimistic when they traveled to Rome and they felt they would succeed there. They presented the well established line-up of Lendl and Smid in singles, Kodes-Smid in doubles. The home team was made up of Panatta, Barazzutti, Bertolucci, and Zugarelli.

The participants in this encounter were met by scorching heat, rowdy frenetic "soccer-like" audience, unfair line-judges who even great referee Frank Hammond could not control... We lost 1:4, nevertheless, we still left with one advantage that we were not aware of at the moment – the possibility of playing Italy at home, in the case that we meet them again.

The Tunel at Foro Italico, through which we see Tomas Smid walking after his victory over Barazzutti, is a world rarity. It is about sixty meters long and it leads from changing rooms directly to the Centre Court. Wow, how much have I walked there! And often triumphant. Unfortunately I did not get to "taste" it after any of my three Italian Open finals.

In the opening match Tomas Smid beat Corrado Barazzutti in five sets 6:1, 3:6, 6:1, 3:6, 7:5. As it turned out, it was the first but also the last point the Czechs made in Rome. The host team's player was leading 4:1 and 5:2 in the fifth set. At this score the match was suspended for rain. It was a nerve-wringer the next day but Tomas Smid lucked out in the end, took some risks and it panned out!

The second singles Panatta-Lendl was suspended for darkness at 6:4, 1:4. However, Ivan Lendl won only the first two games the next day and the rest of the match was a total fiasco.

Bolardt described Lendl's performance as a good second set but Ivan went home with a 4:6, 6:1, 0:6, and 0:6 defeat! I must say for myself that I have never lost two "bagels" in Davis Cup! I guess Ivan was not mature enough yet. Especially a backhand passing shot was a real problem for him. Panatta was the type of a player who constantly pressed forward. He beat even Borg in Paris with that when he won Roland Garros. He served and volleyed! He put pressure on Ivan over his backhand and Ivan could not muster up a passing shot.

One of very good officials Frank Hammond from the United States.

At 1:1, the team of Kodes-Smid lost the doubles. After winning the first set 8:6, when the Italians had two set-points at 4:5, the team received a wash-out: 2:6, 1:6, 2:6.

We did not play very well, the scorching Roman heat got to us. It was a bit breezy. The score looks pretty grim but we played long even games. We were also nervous in front of the passionate Italian audience. Panatta dominated the net; he was the most high-powered pla-

We did not win the doubles... After we secured the first set under our belt the Italians swept us off the court; Tomas and I did not expect that.

player on the court. Bertolucci returned well and played smart lobs. They both switched well and created confusion on the court. We had no chance to break Panatta's serve. He was like a hurricane after he delivered the two bagels to Lendl and he never lost his serve. Bertolucci lost his serve once, and both Tomas and I three times.

The crowd went literally crazy. The turning point came in the second set when we did not deliver on the breakpoints at 1:1. Tomas appeared tired; he did not have the spark or force and I just could not hold him any more. We played without much oomph but during our serving games there was plenty of battle going on. Long games were the order of that match. It was a strange ineffective contest.

On Sunday Barazzutti defeated Lendl in five sets: 4:6, 6:1, 6:2, 3:6, 7:5. Upon the captains' agreement the last match was played two out of three sets and Panatta crushed Smid 6:3, 6:2.

Lendl's game did not go well at Foro Italico and he lost both matches, to Panatta and Barazutti; in addition we did not succeed in doubles either. Overall losing score was 1:4.

Lendl was leading 3:0 in the fifth against Barazutti and lost! That was a pity! God knows what might have happened if Ivan had won and the score were 2:2; perhaps Panatta would have felt uncomfortable in front of his home audience playing for the decisive point! Too much responsibility sometimes plays wonders with players' heads...

The Czech players' tennis performance in Rome stirred up certain resentment. We took it hard especially during the doubles when our team experienced unprecedented decline in technical and mental potency. It is possible that they got disarmed when facing an opponent on the other side of the court, who was gifted with unusual performance and mental disposition in front of his home audience. That does not happen often. Kodes and Smid appeared weakened from the beginning as if they had no chance against the like of Panatta.

Lidová demokracie – Czechoslovak press

Panatta was at the pinnacle of his career then and delivered an outstanding tennis performance; however, the match was a humiliating wash-out for us. That was already the third one! The first was in Hungary, second in Eastbourne, and now in Rome.

To some extent even these losses were in some sense beneficial. They confirmed how difficult it is to win on the opponent's home courts. In the last two encounters Lendl was maturing and at the same time realizing that the responsibility of the first player is not, and never will be, trouble-free.

"CANNIBALS" IN THE JUNGLE!

Spicy and at the same time exotic! That was an offer that Tomas Smid received in the fall during the indoor championships in Paris, France, from a line-judge Kemadjou, Cameroon.

One day Tomas approached me to find out if I would like to play an exhibition in Cameroon. The invitation was for Lendl, him, me, and one French player. Naturally, they were mostly interested in Ivan Lendl, and the other player who fascinated audiences was Yannick Noah. They were obviously attracted to Yannick, since he grew up in Cameroon and started to play tennis there. In addition, Lendl and Noah were great rivals.

It was autumn and we thought – why not? We'll take a trip to Cameroon!

Kemadjou, my good old French friend Georges Goven and I met at the Orly Airport. Noah did not appear but promised to arrive in his native land later. Lendl and Smid did not come either because they were playing elsewhere and also agreed to come a day or two later directly to Cameroon.

Once we touched down the "main organizer" Kemadjou immediately pulled out an ingenious idea: "Hey lads, since Lendl and Smid aren't here yet they won't play the first exhibition in Mahroua. We'll take off early in the morning, and since the courts are only so-so, make sure you come already dressed in your tennis gear."

The next morning we got into a jeep and took off. After five minutes of driving the paved road disappeared and all we saw was a green "screen". Equatorial jungle! I have never in my life seen so much greenery. Only one lonely dusty road headed into its interior.

"What a neat experience!" We got tossed and jostled, there was dust all around and my stomach got queasy. But we carried on through the rainforest, a living soul nowhere to be seen, no structures anywhere, nothing. Just trees, shrubs, lianas, blossoms of all different quaint shapes and colors, greenery all around. And unbelievable humidity. It was an exhausting long road like from Prague to Brno. I don't even remember how long it took before we came out of the forest at last.

Something like a larger village extended in front of us. Here and there appeared better quality houses, mostly made of wood. There were no cars, only bicycles and a few wheel-barrows. The first place we visited was the City Hall where we were received by the Mayor. We pulled up in front of the City Hall, walked in, and Mr. Mayor came out to greet us in his shorts, slippers, and half naked. It helped us relax and laugh. I did not understand French; Goven interpreted and translated for us. The official formalities took about ten minutes and off we went to play!

There was a concrete court, with about five hundred spectators around it. I had a sore ankle from our soccer play in Prague and I told Goven about it stressing that I could not run much. He took that in mind:

"Don't worry; I'll play it to you. Let's make it look dignified."

We played three sets to everyone's delight. The dusk was setting in and we loaded the jeep and got on our way back. Naturally, we had to cross that deep forest again. As soon as we entered it it got pitch dark. Soon we started to hear all kinds of sounds, screeches, howls, and shrieks. The forest inhabitants were waking up to their nocturnal life. I soon had the willies but it was still nothing compared to what was ahead.

I took a little snooze as my head started to nod under the influence of inconceivable heat and humidity that were accentuated under the dome of the trees. I was stirred up to consciousness by a strange sound. All of a sudden our car acted up; it coughed sputtered and went dead. It was empty – no more gas! At that very moment I panicked. How are we going to be able to continue? Where are we going to get gas?

I looked around and noticed that the driver was searching for something under his seat. He then looked in the trunk of the car and pulled out a jerry can. For God's sake, where is

Line-judge Kemadjou organized the exhibition in Cameroon.

he going to get gas here? I tried to look around me but there was only darkness; I felt like I could cut through it too! Suddenly, on the right hand side, in the forest, as if fire-flies were flying around. There were tiny moving glimmers of light. And the lights were coming towards us! "Jesus, what is that?"

Imagine it was people! They were coming out of the jungle! God only knows what they were doing there! Ten, twenty, they were multiplying. They had beams of light... hard to describe them but they looked like torches. They started to communicate with the driver but could not understand each other. Soon we came to realize that those people lived somewhere near!

A few hundred meters parallel with our dusty road there was another road. On the side of that road there were slums and shacks where these people lived. We had no idea about it because even in daylight it was close to impossible to penetrate through the green huddle. We saw no houses and definitely no other road.

The most terrifying thing was that there were more and more people coming out of the forest. I was at the end of my wits and my heart was racing; it even crossed my mind that these people could be cannibals! But no, they were not cannibals, and they did have gasoline! Where they got it from I have no idea but they filled up the jerry can! I could not believe my eyes.

We arrived at the hotel with great delay and the next day "Sirs. Lendl and Smid" made their appearance.

"Where have you been, knuckleheads? I was dying of fear in the jungle and couldn't even share the experience with you!"

I then told them the whole story while we had breakfast; Lendl teased me mercilessly. You wait, I thought to myself, you'll get enough taste of what I already went through. And that came true!

In a short while Kemadjou came and said: Messieurs, here is your program for the entire stay. Check out everything you are going to play!

Up until that point we were all jokes and fun... Cameroon, what could that surprise us with? And here we had it! The following day we had an exhibition in the Capital Yaoundé! An hour long trip – by plane!

We also played in the club where Yannick Noah grew up. And he, who it was organized for, did not show up! His father was very apologetic saying that Yannick had a shoulder problem. So the three of us Czechs and Goven played all the exhibitions.

In Yaoundé we were invited to visit the university. We checked out the classrooms, the study halls, the campus, and at one moment a lad joined us. Kemadjou was busy translating because all that was spoken was French and none of us knew French. We walked up and down and all around and my ankle started to act up. In view of that they changed the order *down and all around and my ankle started to act up. In view of that they changed the order and make up of matches: Lendl and Smid were going to play singles, and Goven and I would play only doubles.*

But, going back to the university – we came to a beautiful soccer field. It was on campus and it was very attractive! Several players were training there and our guide informed us: "That is our junior varsity team, most of them from our university. They are the players who you will soon hear about because they will be great."

He was right. Remember the soccer World Cup five years later? Cameroon shocked the world!

Cameroon was an eye opening experience for me the same way Nigeria had been the spring before. Events in this part of the world usually took place in Egypt, or in Casablanca in Morocco, and close to the end of my career I played a tournament in Tunisia. That was it. I covered only the North African countries. Playing in Equatorial Africa was a novelty, and I did it twice in a row.

JAVELIN ELBOW

A number of tennis enthusiasts called our office and demanded to know what has happened with Jan Kodes. He missed several international tournaments, however the forced break was due to elbow problems and it is finally coming to an end. "I tried it out in doubles in a league game against Ruda hvezda. I must make the come-back step by step and not overload the arm."

Ceskoslovensky sport – Czechoslovak press

Tennis elbow, the scarecrow of all tennis players, recreational or professional! It must have gotten its name for the high number of occurrence among the white sport enthusiasts. Many will say that it is a consequence of a technically incorrect backhand or forehand or because of a particular racket grip. The shooting pain is so intense and bothersome that you can hardly stand holding a pencil, let alone a pint of beer. In legendary Czech actor Jan Werich's words you must sip off beer half way in order to be able to finish it, and all you should do about tennis is dream about it. You feel like climbing the walls if it were to help but nothing is seems to work.

The reason for a tennis elbow is very prosaic. A whole line of patients diagnosed with a "tennis elbow" never played tennis. Tennis elbow is a disorder from a group of so called "entezopathy", and it is an inflammation in the area of attachment of a tendon to the bone. These problems can spring up elsewhere as well, not just in an elbow. Overuse leads to changes in the given area and then discomfort starts appearing even during minimal stress that would not provoke pain under normal circumstances.

And where does "tennis elbow" hurt? One can feel two bumps (epicondyles) on the outer and inner side of the lower end of the humerus, one on each side. These are bone structures where forearm muscles attach via tendons. The muscle of the posterior side of a forearm attaches to the outer bump, and that is the incriminating place of a tennis elbow. Muscles of the inner or foreside of the forearm attach to the inner bump of the humerus. That spot becomes sore or painful when a person suffers from so called "javelin elbow", and that is the type that tormented Jan Kodes.

I labored with a painful elbow for a long time; I received injections but the intervals became more and more frequent. At first it took half a year after the injection before I felt pain again but periods between applications got shorter and shorter and finally the pain became continuous.. In this condition I played Davis Cup against Sweden in the middle of September 1979. I knew that I was going to have to face surgery one day and the elbow would have to get opened up.

He tried to delay surgical intervention for as long as he could. His elbow was very painful even after he changed to the metal "Head" racket that he had used since the middle of 1978. He did, however, play with his classic wood racket during his Lagos trip in the spring of 1979. It was excruciating especially on a serve, and also hitting forehand and forehand volley. He knew then that surgery was inevitable. He underwent the procedure in November 1979.

He prepared for it like for any tennis match. He did not want to leave anything to chance. He visited several surgeons during tournaments in the United States throughout 1979. Generally, a fellow tennis player recommended him a doctor with whom he had had some experience. Once it was in Houston, another time in Washington... He also purchased a professional publication that he studied carefully at home.

In the end, our Davis Cup team doctor Michael Kopriva introduced me to Dr. Miroslav Stryhal, elbow specialist. I visited him for several consultations in a hospital on Karlovo namesti. He asked where it hurt, and how the pain manifested itself. By that time I could hardly lift a glass of drinking water. I had a terrible pain shooting through the elbow every single time. He explained to me exactly where the cause was, how to treat the condition, he even explained that dentists have similar troubles. Simultaneously, he showed me what he would do, step by step, if I decided to undergo the surgery. His arguments persuaded me and I agreed to go ahead with it.

He was still worried because he knew that many of these procedures ended unsuccessfully. There is a difference between a person who wants to be able to use the arm for common functions and a person who wants to compete in tennis with it.

"Sir, please, realize that it must be hundred percent successful; that arm may be my bread winner when I finish playing competitively. What do I know today? Perhaps I'll turn out to be a tennis pro!" I told him.

He kept calming me down: "I know, I know, do not worry. It'll all turn out well." I even brought him the book I purchased in the States. "Don't worry; I'll research all this well, the x-rays as well as this publication. Everything will turn out well, you'll see."

Prague Hospital Na Bojisti (On the Battle Field), D-Day, H-Hour.

"I'll schedule you as the first one in the morning at eight so that you have it over with early." said Dr. Stryhal. Even Dr. Michael Kopriva attended the consultation and the day of the procedure he accompanied Jan in.

"Michael, what happens if he oversleeps that morning? I asked Kopriva. Or he gets himself involved in a car accident? Or simply is not here at eight that day?"

"What of it? Nothing happens! Somebody else will do it in his stead. The timetable has an assistant surgeon scheduled, who should be helping Dr. Stryhal. If Dr. Stryhal is not here the assistant takes over.

"You must be kidding! We agreed that only he would do it. Nobody else!"

I compelled him to come to the hospital with me. There I put him in a chair and commanded: "Sit here and be vigilant!! Your responsibility is to oversee that nobody else cuts into me but Dr. Stryhal!"

I was already in the operating theatre readied for the surgery, received the shot and my eyes were darting around looking for Dr. Stryhal; he was nowhere to be seen! "Where is Dr. Stryhal?"

"Don't worry, he'll be here at the last minute" the nurses consoled me. I was drenched in sweat from anxiety. Suddenly they placed a gas-mask over my mouth and in no time I was asleep. Thank God that they told me he had come before I fell asleep...

The first thing I did after I woke up was vomit! One of my fellow patients advised me that the best thing is to drink a beer after such a procedure. I only took a sip and all hell broke loose! And my arm? It was throbbing like crazy! A nurse had to shoot me some morphine. Dear God, that worked like a charm! The moment she injected the stuff in my vein I felt this unbelievable warmth spreading through my body. I felt totally blissful. The arm was no longer hurting.

In a short while Dr. Stryhal and Dr. Kopriva walked in. "Well, invalid, how did you sleep?

"It was ok, but could you inject the morphine one more time?"

"No, no. That is not allowed! We can do that only in exceptional cases." They still gave me one more shot and I slept beautifully but then.... I felt the pulses in my arm and brutal pain!

Eventually, Dr. Stryhal came to recognize that the cause of all those problems was periostitis, a medical condition caused by inflammation of the periosteum, a layer of connective tissue that surrounds the bone. The surgery required opening up the elbow, removing the damaged tendon, cleaning and grinding down the bone and reattaching the tendon a little lower. The tendon was thus seemingly shorter. While the operation was simple even the slightest inaccuracy could have led to interminable implications. After a surgery of this type one is never able to stretch the arm all the way.

After a couple of weeks I was supposed to come and have the cast removed.

"Well, nurse, take it off! Our tennis player surely sees himself back on the court", teased my doctor. The cast came off and what did I see? The arm was bent! "Well, engineer, stretch it out!"

I stretched it about half-an-inch! Tears filled my eyes – I thought this was my end! But he was delighted: "That is good! You are able to move it! Now move the fingers!"

I moved the fingers. "That is astounding!"

I shivered with fright and lamented how terrible it was, while he was extremely satisfied: "Very good then! We won't put the cast on any more but you will carry your arm in a sling. Then you need to start warm water treatment and we'll begin rehabilitation."

I commenced seeing Milada Vrbicka at Sparta soccer stadium. She was great; she inspired optimism in me again and she was very pleasant. She exercised my arm, gradually stretched and extended it. The arm was like a bubble gum; my anguish was excruciating. I placed my hand on the table, gently pressed down but it sprang back to its original position. I exercised faithfully for a year and a half before I was able to stretch the arm all the way!

They operated on me at the end of the year and in May I started playing tennis again. I could play basic strokes with ease but serve was still problematic at first. I was afraid to hit even the forehand with full force.

I met with Dr. Stryhal several times during the following year during my regularly scheduled visits. The elbow was getting better, my doctor was pleased, and then he said..."This is just fine, my engineer; your arm is as good as new. Now you will please your wife. Tell her that you'll do the housework. Wash windows, tiles, take the brush and scrub-scrub-scrub – all that will do you good!"

As I bid him farewell I also thanked him sheepishly for the spring-cleaning he had recommended I should get involved in. - He was a wonderful man!

A come-back from an injury is always difficult. And it is that much more difficult when one was not able to play for so long. The surgery took place in November 1979 and Kodes returned to the courts in May 1980. The National league, a tournament in Munich, the International German Championships in Hamburg, and then Roland Garros were all ahead of him.

There is no point in flattering myself - I played nothing miraculous! Nevertheless, I wanted to get back to tennis. I managed that but it came with a label – Kodes is after a surgery; we can write him off! My age also had an effect; I was thirty-three.

Though he defeated poorly playing Tom Okker in Munich 7:5, 1:6, 6:3, he then lost to Roger-Vasselin from France 1:6, 7:5, 0:6. In Hamburg he succumbed to Hans Gildemeister from Chile 4:6, 0:6 and in Roland Garros, after overcoming the American Chris Mayotte 4:6, 6:4, 6:4, 6:4 he lost easily in three sets in the second round to his compatriot Stanislav Birner.

Still before the Davis Cup match in Romania the Czech players headed to Wimbledon.

Smid and I had agreed to play doubles together but he injured the ligaments in his ankle in the finals of a tournament in Vienna, which resulted in his absence from not only Wimbledon but also from our Davis Cup match in Bucharest.

Kodes made it at least through the first round of Wimbledon beating the American Tony Giammalva 7:6, 5:7, 6:3, 6:3 but Victor Pecci from Paraguay beat him quite easily in the second round 6:3, 6:4, and 6:4.

He came back to the tennis courts, and he rejoined the Davis Cup team. And it was in the nick of time! According to the scoreboard and predictions on paper the Italians were considered sure Davis Cup winners for that year; however, Kodes created an interesting Davis Cup "hat-trick" and after seventeen years of playing for the team he finely had a chance to touch the "salad bowl". This time he did not touch it as a defeated finalist, the way it was five years earlier in Stockholm, but rather as a winner himself! And it happened after the final with none other than Italy.

He was missing from the team for the first time in his career in the semifinal match of the European Group B at Stvanice against France. In the European final in Romania he played the last match of his very rich Davis Cup presence – he played doubles with Lendl.

In Prague the French played without Yannick Noah, who was injured. They came with a young team of: Pascal Portes, Roger Vasselin and Dominique Bedel. They were crushed "5:0"! Jan Kodes' elbow was not yet properly healed and for that reason Smid played doubles with Slozil. And they won convincingly.

Ilie Nastase was absent from the team in Bucharest during the European finals; he was serving a disciplinary penalty for his temperament in England, where he threw a wet tennis shoe at the umpire during a rain spell. The punishment was harsh – no play in Davis Cup for two years!

Without him the Romanians were badly weakened. The team of Haradau, Segarceanu, Pana, and Dirzu had no chance against us. In the opening singles Lendl swept Haradau off the court 6:4, 6:1, 6:3. Pavel Slozil, who substituted for injured Tomas Smid, played also very

Stvanice - Pavel Slozil and Tomas Smid during the Davis Cup match with France. They reached the Roland Garros finals together and lost only to Noah-Laconte in five sets. They won several international tournaments. In 1978 in Paris Pavel Slozil reached his only Grand Slam title in mixed doubles with Renata Tomanova.

and easily defeated Segarcea-nu 6:3, 6:3, 6:1. We led 2:0 after the first day. The new doubles team Kodes-Lendl delivered expected result with a 6:3, 6:2, 6:4 victory. Only Stanislav Birner lost the last match a bit unfortunately to Segarceanu, thus the team left Bucharest with a 4:1 victory.

That doubles match in Bucharest was my last performance in Davis Cup, which I did not realize at the time. We won 3:0 but I was slightly nervous. When we were trying to strategize prior to the match I asked Lendl how we should play. "Ivan, you are used to playing backhand and so am I! What shall we do?"

He let me choose. I took backhand and he took the forehand side. His returns were great throughout the entire match. Haradau and Segarceanu had no chance.

The July 1980 doubles with Ivan Lendl in Bucharest was my last Davis Cup match. At the team score 2:0 after the first day we won easily.

After the night storm the air was considerably cooler. Four thousand people watched a relaxed doubles match the result of which was just a question of time. The Romanian team, in which Haradau substituted for injured Dirzu, had no chance against the Czechoslovaks. On the courts of Progress Kodes confirmed that he is still a noteworthy player with an excellent backhand and volley. Lendl was unperturbed and neither had to extend an utmost effort. In the first two sets Segarceanu seemed to be a better player of the two but he served too many faults in the third set. Haradau could not keep up with his weaker shots; he botched volleys and our players passed him easily.

Ceskoslovensky sport
Czechoslovak press

CRUCIAL VICTORY

Twelve years ago, when Jan Kodes' headed beyond the European borders for the first time, his initial trip led to Buenos Aires in South America. It now appears as if a seasoned publicist created a script of Jan's career knowing exactly what the task necessitated: a dramatic loop that sent the hero out and then brought him back to where it all had began.

As a tennis novice Jan accepted an invitation of his friend, the Chilean Pato Rodriguez, and flew to the Argentine metropolis in the fall of 1968 in order to familiarize himself with the world. In 1980 Jan went back as an experienced veteran and matador-like Davis Cup fighter, who still had the ability to be of help as a player and also a role model to his younger team-mates. On top of everything, he was playing on the same Centre Court where he had played against his role models – Rod Laver and Roy Emerson.

As soon as he found out that their Davis Cup opponent in the Inter-Zonal competition was

Argentina, he recalled the 1971 Davis Cup match against Brazil in Porto Alegre. Their unsuccessful performance was largely predisposed by utterly untimely arrival on the South American continent, which had affected adversely their acclimatization.

This time we wanted to arrive sooner in South America so we had arranged to play a tournament in Sao Paolo on the way to Buenos Aires.

The tournament of "8" was played as a Round Robin in two groups of four. Kodes lost to Nastase 4:6, 4:6, then Lendl 4:6, 2:6, and also to the Brazilian Carlos Kirmayer 7:6, 2:6, 3:6. Gene Mayer, Eddie Dibbs, Thomaz Koch, and Smid were in the second group. Tomas Smid was visibly not well yet. He limped his way through the matches and lost them all.

Ivan Lendl arrived in Buenos Aires two days later from Sao Paolo. In contrast to the others, who had obtained their visas in Prague, he had to resolve the visa issue there. When he turned up in the hotel he announced: "I am here at long last, and I am going to win both singles; it is up to the captain to secure the third point for us." However, it was he who earned us even that point with his essential share...

We flew to Brazil from the United States, where we had played tournaments in Indianapolis, Toronto, Cincinnati and the US Open in New York. I no longer took part in the US Open...

The official part of our group arrived in Buenos Aires directly from Prague. The main official was Cyril Suk, who had been appointed to that capacity in September 1979 by the Tennis Federation committee. He replaced Miloslav Janovec, who had resigned. Cyril Suk was elected to the post of the Chairman of the Tennis Federation in 1981.

Argentina was an immensely strong opponent; they had defeated an excellent team of the United States 4:1, and they were the favorites of the encounter with us. The Argentine Federation, however, had serious problems with Guillermo Vilas and Jose-Luis Clerc. They must have realized their high value, especially after their victory over the American team, and they started requesting higher financial rewards. They must have presumed that the Czechoslovak team was going to be an easy win and with that their road to Davis Cup finals would be opened. Vilas requested $65,000, Clerc $35,000. Nobody knows how much they received when all negotiations were finished and done with, nevertheless the Argentine Tennis Association leadership must have anticipated the investment in the players to bring corresponding returns. It is pertinent to mention here that our non-playing captain Antonin Bolardt faced no such problems...

The Buenos Aires Centre Court was totally sold out for September 19–21, 1980. An

Guillermo Vilas could not beat the great Ivan Lendl.

easy win by the host team was predicted and the fact that Tomas Smid was unable to play all three matches due to his foot injury played in their hand.

"We sensed that under certain conditions we could win the match but it would be very difficult. In my judgment, it was here, where Ivan Lendl proved his true qualities for the first time. We were no dark horses and that suited us well. Ivan "smoked out" Vilas 7:5, 8:6, 9:7 in an amazing, end to end, fight. That staged a huge blow to the Argentines because Vilas was at the peak of his career then. We entered the match weakened since Tomas Smid was still sidelined; his ankle ligament injury from Vienna persisted. I thought he should play because he seemed to practice well in Sao Paolo. In the end, Bolardt and Korda surprised us all when they put Pavel Slozil in the line up!

The main focus of the strategy was a point to be won in the doubles, and Ivan would try to win both singles.

But, even Pavel Slozil played an excellent game. He lost the first match against Clerc in five sets. He was leading two sets to one (3:6, 6:3, 6:4) but, unfortunately, he was no match for Clerc in the last two sets and lost 2:6, 1:6.

Jose-Luis Clerc beat Pavel Slozil in five sets, but also lost to Lendl.

Coach Korda said after the match: "The play could be characterized as long exchanges with many unforced errors, especially in the first half of the match. It was a tense atmosphere. Slozil must have suffered the jitters of the being a Davis Cup debutant leading two sets to one. Clerc took perfect advantage of it. - *In spite of the loss I commend our player; he played the best he could."* The second singles remained unfinished that day; *Lendl was ahead of Vilas 7:5, 8:6, and 3:1. Guillermo was unequivocally perplexed by Ivan. He was accustomed to long rallies from the back court and, naturally, tried to engage in that strategy on clay in Buenos Aires as well. It was critical that Lendl did not let himself be provoked to rushed actions and with that to error making; he did not mind engaging in those endless rallies.*

He demonstrated to Vilas that he didn't mind that kind of play and that he was able to carry on with it physically and mentally. Most importantly – Lendl was fiercer in finishing off the points! When it looked like both of them were fading Ivan delivered the final blow.

Vilas based his strategy on his belief that Ivan would not withstand the long exchanges mentally and would try to approach the net, where Vilas would pass him. If that did not happen Guillermo would approach the net only if he was sure he could be successful in putting the ball away. In most matches he did not approach often. Ivan was ready to spend four or five hours on the court with him playing the very same game; that came as a surprise to Vilas.

On Saturday Ivan Lendl brought the match to a triumphant end with a 9:7 victory in the third set and with that he tied the team score to 1:1. As soon as the match-point was clin-

Happy arrival for Smid, Lendl and Kodes to Prague-Ruzyne airport.

ched upon the captain Antonin Bolardt and coach Pavel Korda sat down to compose the doubles team. One of the options they busied themselves with was Kodes – Smid.

Since Lendl had played so extraordinarily and confidently in the singles he was also the one who went onto the court with Smid to play the doubles. It is my belief that it was that match that decided the outcome of the inter-zonal finals.

As an eye witness from the bench I could say only one thing: Ivan played out of his mind! As a doubles player Tomas played what he knew best; he put away shots that were well set up for him - overheads, difficult volleys, shots that had been prepared by Ivan. Ivan's returns were unbelievable, he was calm and collected.

He was not overburdened by such responsibility that weighed on him before. It was also easier for him to play away from home. If the match had taken place at home he would, very likely, have felt the stress more. The pressure would have been more taxing. The score 6:2, 6:4, 6:3 speaks volumes.

Ivan Lendl played another monstrous match on Sunday against Clerc. The Argentines were very confident until Lendl defeated Vilas. That defeat broke them.

Everything revolved around Vilas; workouts, press conferences, toss. We constantly heard: Vilas, Vilas, Vilas. When Ivan beat Vilas the Argentines got a scare; the doubles defeat brought yet another distress.

Lendl defeated Clerc in four sets 6:1, 7:5, 6:8, and 6:2. At a decisive score of 3:1 in our favor Vilas beat Slozil twice 6:2 only changing the final winning numbers to 3:2.

Our return home was accompanied with much ado: after five years Czechoslovakia would be playing the Davis Cup finals again – this time on home turf! Jan Kodes' delight was spoiled by a shocking realization that somebody stole a significant amount of his cash from the locker room!

Even today it makes me sick just thinking about it. Twelve hundred dollars! I went to the shower and left the money in my racket case. When I returned it was all gone! Vilas told me that it simply would not happen in Argentina because if they found the responsible culprit they would nearly kill him. I am dead sure that neither Ivan, nor Tomas would have anything to do with it. It was not a major tragedy but it has left a lasting affect on me whenever I remember Argentina...

There was no way that Kodes would not play in the end-of-the-season's traditional tournaments in Madrid and Barcelona. In the former he fought his way into the doubles finals together with the Hungarian Taróczy; they lost in a tight battle to Gomez–Gildermeister 6:3, 4:6, and 8:10. In the Catalan metropolis Kodes gave one of his last memorable performances. He came across Tomas Smid in the second round.

At the close of my career Tomas and I engaged in a splendid duel out of which I lost 6:1, 6:7, 8:10.

In Spain Jan Kodes personally witnessed Ivan Lendl's best doubles performance; Ivan's returns were close to unreal.

Tomas and I met Lendl–Denton in the doubles quarter-finals; we lost in two sets 2:6, 3:6. At times, Ivan's doubles performance was somewhat "moody"; but when he was "with it" and got into the game his returns were terrifying. Irretrievable!

PRAGUE, DECEMBER 1980

The 1980 Davis Cup final with Italy was fast approaching. The players entered three indoor tournaments (in Bologna, Vienna, and Köln) as part of their preparation for the big final in Prague. In Köln Kodes-Smid fought their way to the doubles finals. They defeated in sequence: Lacek–Pimek 6:4, 6:3, Curren–Denton 4:6, 6:3, 6:3, Taróczy–Slozil 7:6, 6:4 and only in the finals they lost to Pattison–Mitton 4:6, 1:6.

It is at this point where I need to broach the subject of speculation and slander that circulated about my relationship to Ivan Lendl. Very few individuals know today, and most likely nobody knew then, that Ivan asked me to come to his room in Bucharest during our Davis Cup match. He offered me coaching cooperation.

"Jan, I want to have a coach, who would be willing to travel to, at least, eight to ten tournaments with me; I would like you to be the one!"

At that point I had already received an offer from the West-German Amberg and I knew that, most likely, I was going to be playing the "Bundes league" for the next two years. "Ivan, I would love to do that for you but I must take my family into consideration."

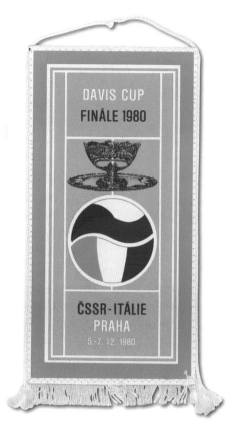

The process of the toss was rather nerve-wrecking. Who is going to play with whom the first day? From the left: Cyril Suk, Philippe Chatrier, capt. Antonin Bolardt, Czech actress Andrea Cunderlikova – performing the draw, ref. Derek Hardwick, umpire Libor Siblik, and capt. Vittorio Crotta.

In the last few years we often worked out together at tournaments. I remember, for instance, in the spring 1979 in Hamburg; Ivan was immensely ambitious and hardworking and he came up to me: "Hey, Jan, I booked a court for an hour at ten."

I asked him what it was that he wanted to practice.

"Well, let's play backhand crosscourt; I must pick up that chop."

So we drilled: I executed a top spin, he chopped it; then I chopped the ball and he played the top spin. Ivan's topspin backhand passing shot was excellent but he did not have a good under-spin. Above all, he was not successful in following up his chopped backhand to the net and due to that he could not change the rhythm of the game. When Vilas or Borg lifted the ball up high against him he needed to acquire a quick chop that would pull the ball down. And that he was what he lacked.

We played half an hour, and then an hour and I said: "Ivan, it is past eleven and you are supposed to be playing your first match at 1:00 P.M. on Centre Court."

"To hell with my first match! If I master that under-spin backhand I'll become the world's number one!" Thus we continued playing. At one o'clock he just changed his T-shirt, went onto the court, and overpowered his opponent.

It was then that I realized how incredibly ambitious he was and that he had his resolve all lined up in his head.

So, he offered me a coaching partnership before the match with Romania. I presume that he would not have done that if he had some aversion towards me.

I did not like discussing that episode and in public I never mentioned it. Ivan understood my responsibility to my family. If I had become his coach I would have had to travel with him everywhere, yet I would not be able to play the same tournaments myself since my ranking had dropped too low. I came to terms with the decision to stop tournament play by the end of 1980 and for two years I would just compete in the Bundesleague for Amberg, as I had promised. The agreement was final.

Still that year, during the US Open at Flushing Meadows, Ivan Lendl made a partnership contract with Wojtek Fibak from Poland. That was very shortly before the Davis Cup tie with Argentina, and it gave a cause to the tennis lobbyists to start the type of gossip that had driven away Martina Navratilova several years earlier. "Lendl is making friends with an emigrant in New York! He is now living most of the time in America!" – The following year Lendl bought a house in Connecticut which resulted in further never-ending rumors around his persona.

It was obvious that Ivan trusted me; otherwise he would not have approached me in the first place. In 1979 I helped with a financial contract in Basel between him and the tournament organizers who really wanted him to play in their event. The director, Roger Brenwald, asked me to mediate. I trust that our relationship was very positive in spite of my lasting belief that he should not have played in Eastbourne in 1978. That had nothing to do with anything. It was not Ivan's doing. It was one of Bolardt's rubbish ideas.

However, the historic Davis Cup final with Italy in Prague was fast approaching and, just a few days before, Ivan Lendl announced: "Yes, I am coming in time for the training camp and my coach, Wojtek Fibak, is coming along with me."

Nobody can imagine how indignantly that was accepted! Petr Hutka, who led Lendl and Slozil that year to victory at the King's Cup, was the team's captain. Pavel Korda was the Davis Cup team's coach. And now, imagine – we arrived in the Sport Hall and there were more coaches around the court than players! Hutka, Korda, and Fibak! We started to joke about it with Slozil and Smid!

Yet, the situation made good sense. There was no doubt that Ivan advanced after our performance in Argentina! We then heard nothing else but: "Wojtek! Ask Wojtek about everything!"

I know that many people in our close circle were bothered by it, be it Hutka or Korda. They won't admit to it today but it was so. I won't mention the other Federation or CUPES officials including the team captain Bolardt...

A handful of spectators were watching the preparation of our Davis Cup players on Sunday afternoon. They were far from bored because following the workout between Smid and Kodes entertained them as if it were a top tennis exhibition. However, they were all anxiously awaiting Ivan Lendl, our number one player. From a telephone message they found out that Lendl had left his native Ostrava at eleven in the morning. The trip was challenging due to bad snow that limited visibility to just a few feet. He skidded a few times but only the car carried the scars of that.

Ceskoslovensky sport
Czechoslovak press

Prague was overwhelmed by tennis euphoria. The famous "Cup" was exhibited in a department store Kotva on Republic Square. There were a hundred thousand applications for tickets. The Sport Hall capacity of fourteen thousand was lowered by two thousand for security purposes. The Italians received two thousand tickets. Many official guests arrived in Prague, including the ITF President Philippe Chatrier. A supreme surface was laid down for the tennis court. As is typical for our Czech character there were many voices for and many agai n s t the surface. Jan Kodes soothed the debate: "Many tournaments are played on supreme carpet yet each surface is unique. In some places the balls bounce faster, in others slower. Here the bounce will be a bit lower. However, it remains within the margin of players' adaptability. If the surface triggers a handicap for the players it will be the same for both teams."

At any rate, the surface was quite fast which suited us well. On the contrary, it did not suit the Italians. We all carried in our heads the memory of our defeat in Rome in 1979, when Ivan received a double "bagel" from Panatta. But in Prague, this was a different Lendl! Furthermore, we were going to play inside, on the supreme... and Ivan had prepared well to play his best tennis in the final..

Besides his new coach Wojtek Fibak, Ivan also arrived with his manager Jerry Solomon, from the sports agency ProServ.

Tomas Smid's health failed him the night of Thursday to Friday. He suffered from wicked nasty diarrhea.

Tomas' wife called me up around midnight: "Jan, I have no idea what more I can do for Tomas. He is dreadfully sick!"

I called Dr. Kopriva at once. In the morning Tomas headed to Dr. Rybin's in the Army hospital. They didn't know what to think of it and thought of pumping out his stomach. Most likely, the source of the food poisoning was a fish fillet that he had eaten.

In the course of the morning they thought of placing me in Tomas' stead in case that he was incapacitated. It did not frighten me since my record against Panatta was reasonably good.

Around eleven Smid arrived at last and without

From the left: Libor Siblik (chief of umpires), Paolo Bertolucci, Corrado Barazzutti, Adriano Panatta, Gianni Ocleppo, capt. Vittorio Crotta and the referee Derek Hardwick.

Tomas Smid (serving) won openning match over Adriano Panatta from two sets down.

any warm up proclaimed that he was ready to play. I was not aware that anybody knew what exactly had happened to him; he looked unbelievably debilitated. That added to the reason why one had to appreciate his performance that much more. He put everything he had into that match and won 3:6, 3:6, 6:4, 6:4, and 6:4.

I suspect that Adriano Panatta underestimated the development of the match when he was leading two sets to love. Tomas was a "holder". It was a battle of serves. Tomas played the serve and volley game well, but so did Panatta. Panatta started out very well and did not leave any room for further improvement, whereas Tomas started out so-so and gradually improved his game. Step by step they reversed roles and, at the end, Smid was in charge. He also showed a stronger heart.

Tomas was always able to deliver. Considering the variety of shots he possessed he definitely made the best of his arsenal. And since he played serve and volley effectively he chose that as his strategy against Panatta: serve – approach – volley to Panatta's backhand. A passing shot from the backhand side was Panatta's weakness.

The match was played in a tense atmosphere, mainly due to the Italian contingent in the audience. One of the drunken fans shouted at the officials, and was subsequently removed from the arena. The Italians then removed themselves from the court as well and refused to continue play until the drunken fan was allowed to return! In the end, the fan turned out to be a leader of the Italian Communist party and all charges against him were dropped. Antonin Bubenik, the umpire, tried to calm the unruly mob to no avail. His words "Silenzio prego! Silenzio prego!" drowned in the noise.

The mania reached its climax during the decisive set. Tomas Smid valiantly ran down his opponent's drop shot but the Italians claimed it took a double bounce. Referee Hardwick awarded the point to the host team but the Italians protested the call and left for the locker rooms. When they returned to the court the "tug-of-war" continued. Tennis fans, who watched

The Italians complained repeatedly. Captain Vittorio Crotta in dispute with the Czech captain Antonin Bolardt (sitting).

Derek Hardwick, a referee from England, was a great and typical diplomat. When in doubt he always asked to play the point over...

The Italian number one player took advantage of each disputed point to take a rest.

the television broadcast of the match, may remember the moment when Adriano Panatta verbally assaulted the chair umpire Bubenik after an objectionable call. From the television screen it was easy to recognize the abusive English language verbal tirade with which Panatta regaled one of our best umpires: "You are a big Czech pig!"

Below are some authentic quotations collected right after Smid's victory:

Tomas Smid: "Naturally, I am happy to have won. I believed in me and my team and I did not allow anything to get me down, not even the weak start when my opponent took the lead. Now I am going home to sleep because I have been up since two a.m. due to intestinal problems."

Adriano Panatta: "I played two sets in great form; in the third, and especially in the fourth set Smid took the stage and everything he touched turned out to be lethal. The fifth set was influenced by the mental concentration and also the umpire. It is my belief that Davis Cup final matches should be umpired entirely by a neutral party."

Wojtek Fibak: "Panatta played the first two sets really well, however, he later started losing his stamina. Smid, on the contrary, started out nervously but picked up his game beautifully as the match progressed."

Jan Kodes: "The fans got their money's worth thanks to the drama of the first match. Smid could not find his rhythm, while Panatta took off at once; however, things reversed and Smid was luckier in the fifth set especially at 1:2. Had Panatta taken the 3:1 lead, Smid would not have won. I was a bit disappointed by our audience. Exclamations like: "Fight! Lob! Don't give up!" made players somewhat nervous."

In the second match Lendl lost the first set to Barazzuti 4:6, but the next three sets were an unambiguous winning venture for him: 6:1, 6:1, 6:2.

The captain of the Italian team, Vittorio Crotta: "It is very likely that the end result has been decided... There were too many questionable calls and Smid's foot faults remained unobserved in Panatta's match. Under no circumstances do I want to presume that the lead of the Czech team was affected by the disputed calls."

The Italians kept protesting Tomas' uncalled foot faults. It is true that at home the players test the boundaries because they rely on the home advantage of line-calls. We went through the same treatment in Australia, Russia, and Italy.

Keeping in mind Ivan Lendl's excellent performance the Davis Cup team leadership stuck to their principle of "not changing the winning line-up" and put Lendl in Saturday doubles team with Smid.

Panatta and Bertolucci were well known to be an excellent team and they displayed their confidence to everybody around

Tomas Smid – though he was behind two sets to love he saved the match against Adriano Panatta and finished victorious.

Who says that Ivan Lendl didn't show emotions?

them. Particularly Bertolucci was brilliant, his returns were low and precise, and he reigned at the net with outstanding volleys and overheads that he played with exceptional lightness. He also demonstrated incredibly good hands and touch for the ball.

The host team started out in "Smid-like" spirit of his opening singles match – lifeless. They gave an impression of being out of fuel, without energy to give them the necessary spark to ignite a real doubles "concert". They were unable to put away the decisive shots. Fortunately for us, Panatta did not compliment Bertolucci's phenomenal effort and with his double fault he gave us the second set.

However, our team's performance did not improve even at that tied score. At moments it seemed like there were two singles players on the court playing a game of doubles. There was little teamwork on the Czech side of the court. After a break at 3:6, 6:3, 3:6 specifically Lendl's performance improved. Smid then got into the game too and that resulted in the fourth set victory 6:3.

A longstanding dream came true at last for generations of Czech tennis enthusiasts when Ivan Lendl secured the match at 5:4 in the fifth set with his clean effective game! For the first time in history they conquered the Davis Cup!

The doubles game was a nervous performance of ups and downs. However, the important thing was that, in the end, the guys won in five! The final victory was not secured even when we were 2:0 ahead. Who knows how the matches would have turned out the third day of competition if the score had been only 2:1 after the doubles! Maybe Smid would have lost to Barazzutti and then the match between Lendl and Panatta would have been the decisive one at 2:2... I am sure that would not have been an easy task. Panatta would then have played bang-bang without the pressure and responsibility of having to secure a point; that would make him feel more at ease playing Ivan. So, the doubles was crucial and it was wonderful that the score was 3:0 in our favor at its conclusion. Smid later lost to Barazzutti 6:3, 3:6, 2:6 which only points out that, most likely, he would have lost to him at 2:1 as well.

The question of referee's age limit popped up at the press conference after the doubles match. Should the Davis Cup organizing committee consider imposing an age limit of the referee the way it is in other sports? The issue was opened up, most likely, due to the British referee, Derek Hardwick's, questionable calls affecting both teams. The ITF secretary David Gray said in his response that the requested age limit would not be imposed any time soon and the choice of the chief referee would depend on the two teams' agreement.

Ceskoslovensky sport

Czechoslovak press

This is exactly what caused the problem in Davis Cup – as long as the choice rested on an agreement of both teams there was friction. For instance, in Australia our Antonin Bolardt

Ivan Lendl proved his high level of performance; he swept Barazzutti off the court and he also delivered a solid performance in doubles.

allowed the referee to be an Australian. But if he insisted on a neutral referee he would have achieved it. When we later played against Australia in Prague we also wanted the agreement of our local referee but their captain Fraser categorically insisted on: "Neutral referee only!"

Today there are no more discussions. Three neutral referees are nominated for each encounter: one chief referee and two umpires. This solution has helped the present day Davis Cup tremendously. There is no doubt that we met with questionable calls in many countries, just about everywhere in fact. It was not funny. The crowd was behind the home team, and umpires and referees too!

The problematic issue of chief referees in the most popular tennis team competition came up often in Prague since it affected the smooth course of Davis Cup matches. One of the best referees I have ever experienced in this position was an American by the name of Frank Hammond, who had directed the inter-zonal finals in Rome the previous year. He was absolutely resolute with his decisions. He did not let anything influence his decisions and soon he earned the respect of the players as well as of the hot-blooded Roman audience. In the finals in Bucharest in 1972 the Argentine Morea did not dare to even get out of his chair to correct line-calls after the "soccer-like" mob reactions of the local crowd. Even the Belgian De König, who refereed to the satisfaction of both teams the inter-zonal final against Australia in Prague in 1975, allowed the local line-judges total liberty during the finals in the Royal Hall in Stockholm some time later. Luckily, they took advantage it infrequently, but it was always in crucial moments. The British referee, Derek Hardwick, did not give an impression of a man comfortable and competent in his position during the Prague final either. The Italian segment of the audience could attest to that. Had he been firmer the match would have passed in a calmer atmosphere.

Ceskoslovensky sport
Czechoslovak press

Nothing will ever take away the advantage of the home turf...

The outcome of the match was decided; the third day matches were played only as the best of three. First, Smid lost to Barazzutti when he did not put out much effort in the last two sets. Nobody reproached him because he was very fatigued; he was still celebrated like a hero. Gianni Ocleppo played the last match instead of Panatta; Ivan Lendl beat him convincingly 6:3, 6:3.

The Italians could not withstand the weight of defeat and they left the venue immediately following the last match. After half an hour of waiting for them the closing ceremony proceeded with only a fragment of the Italian team in attendance - the non-playing captain and the substitute player Ocleppo, and our triumphant team. The ITF president, Philippe Chatrier, then handed over the famous "salad bowl" to Antonin Bolardt and said: "On behalf of myself and fifty four participants in this year's competition I am passing the Davis Cup bowl to the team of Czechoslovakia. It is a grand and well deserved victory that was achieved over such a talented and experienced Italian team that won this most famous trophy in 1976. I congratulate your captain and your team, especially then the formidable players Ivan Lendl and Tomas Smid. Your team with such young outstanding players will be hard to beat in the near future."

I am holding the "Salad Bowl" that we took turns passing around during the ceremonies.

What more could we have wished for than playing Italy at home after we passed over Argentina playing their best team of Vilas–Clerc on their home turf? And we really won that final. History is not interested in what happened in the background, did Smid have health problems or did he not, did the umpire make the right decisions or did he make bad calls? It is not relevant; we had a chance and we grabbed it; we went for it!

The same opportunity opened up in Stockholm in 1975. It was then the Swedes' historic chance. They played at home, in Stockholm, against Czechoslovakia! We beat the Australians for them and they now had a chance to be the overall winners; they grabbed that opportunity, just like we would a few years later in Prague. When you play the Davis Cup finals on home turf you must not waver. We didn't hold back and thus we triumphed at least once! I trust we'll remember Prague in 1980 for a long time because the next victory is not coming any time soon.

For me, personally, it was something totally fantastic because I had wished very much to win the Davis Cup competition and I was with the team for great many years; practically seventeen years - from 1964 to 1980! We did not triumph in Stockholm but we accomplished it in Prague... Even though I did not play, I was a member of the team and it tickles me that I lived to experience it. I always gave my maximum in my efforts to conquer the "salad bowl" and bring it home. That was my dream!

Representing your country in Davis Cup is the utmost privilege. The selected team cooperates and deals with pitfalls and traps. It is a lingering competition and players have to time their performance accordingly. For instance, I was in great shape after the grueling ten day advance and winning the French Open.

In the final match against Italy we had to deal with Smid's indisposition caused by intestinal problems from food poisoning, in Romania we had to play without him altogether due to his ankle injury. Yet, the team achieved the goal – that is our historic triumph.

I knew it was going to be difficult and dramatic... the Italians were upset before it even started and they tried to find excuses. At the tournament in Bologna they were already saying

„The Salad Bowl"at the Official Dinner! Coach Pavel Korda, Jan Kodes, Cyril Suk and Stanislav Chvatal.(from left).

that there was no way they could win in Prague. That weakened them!

I have always admired Bjorn Borg, who won Wimbledon five times and always engaged himself again and again with the same resolve, same desire and vehemence. That I call athletic grandeur! I played Davis Cup for seventeen years and somewhere, deep in my soul, I believed that one day we would succeed in winning the "salad bowl." The moment it actually happened, all the difficult moments we had along the way flashed in front of me; the chances when everything could have turned against us, the instances when we felt defeat frigidly near. Just recalling the final itself – what if Tomas did not beat Panatta? What if Ivan failed to muster better mental strength in the close of the doubles game than this formidable Italian player? Who knows? It was our willpower and strength to give out everything we had that was our strongest weapon over our opponent; in the end, it gave us with the most fantastic feeling – the Davis Cup triumph.

Discussing sportsmanship is in order; one must be a gracious winner and also a good loser. The Italians did not convince us of that in the last few days in Prague. Their defeat was the third defeat in the finals in the last few years. Our team also experienced a very disappointing defeat in their premier Davis Cup final by the Swedes in Stockholm five years before. However, they participated with dignity in the Sunday closing ceremony. When the Royal Hall broke into roaring applause during the presentation of the trophy, our players joined in. It is not surprising that our players felt a tad upset by the Italian team's attitude. It should go without saying that athletes pay tribute to the winners. But only the captain Vittorio Crotta and the substitute player Gianni Ocleppo dressed in dark sweater participated in the trophy presentation.

Ceskoslovensky sport
Czechoslovak press

I consider this unacceptable and embarrassing that they did not know how to deal with their defeat. They did not show up even at the final dinner for all participants in spite of their leaving Prague the following day. Only the captain Vittorio Crotta came, and the Federation representatives; none of the players made an appearance.

RELEASE FROM THE TEAM

Soon after the Davis Cup victory Kodes' long time friend Jan Kukal approached him and conveyed the team's opinion that Jan should retire from the team.

It was clear to me that even if I stayed with the team I would no longer play. My successors were obvious – Lendl, Smid, Slozil, I would only be the fourth and it was better to let another young player enter in my position. If I were to stay with the team I would do so only in the function of the captain or coach. I was not keen on that because I felt I still had enough in me to play matches effectively.

However, while meeting with Antonin Himl, I made sure to level things with him squarely. I let him know that I had an opportunity to play team matches for TC Amberg in Bundes-league, West Germany, and I would like to take it. I felt hurt that the Tennis Federation opposed it! How interesting! I could hardly believe it!

All of a sudden people came up with notions like: "Why should Kodes go abroad? And why, in particular, to the West? He should work at home!" Yet, they did not have an appropriate designation for him!

They could not offer me a post of the National Head Coach so I have no idea what they had in mind then; did they want me to feed balls to people or what? I must say that Antonin Himl resolutely impacted this issue when he declared: "It is with our thanks for his long time dedication to representing our country that we release Jan Kodes to take part in German tennis league."

However, there was a glitch. Antonin Himl told me right from the start of the negotiations: "I'll allow you to play for Amberg but if we happen to need you, you must return! Make that promise to me right here and now!"

Thus, as I was leaving his office, I knew that I could go abroad but I could not sign a specific contract let's say for two years, the way soccer players did.

I felt very comfortable in Amberg because they accepted me with great enthusiasm. Our ex-Davis Cup player, Petr Strobl, was the team captain and the main club tennis professional. I commuted every weekend and stayed in a borrowed apartment; my main task on the court was to win in doubles with Karl Meiler when the score was tied at 4:4!

In bundes-league they had a system of six singles and three doubles. I played the fourth position and they always told me: "Jan, don't worry about the singles; there is no problem if you lose, we do not expect you to win; but you must win the doubles with Meiler."

And – we never lost a doubles match! The decisive one was always played on Centre Court. Since all other matches have finished the audience on Centre Court was full. The atmosphere was almost as compelling as during the Davis Cup matches!

I once confided to Petr Strobl how happy I was in Amberg and suggested that it must be very pleasant to live there; but he set me right: "It is just an illusion, my friend. They love you here now, because they know that you'll be gone and on your way to Prague on Monday. But if you decided to open a Sport Shop on the Main Street you would not believe what they would do to you. At that very moment all those who love you so much now, would fear you because you would become their rival in business."

Amberg is not a large city; nevertheless its tennis team won the German championships in 1981 and 1982. The city lived and breathed tennis; the mayor attended the finals, and each match was celebrated and became a social event. Those who did not come to the tennis club didn't really exist in society.

It was always like a big show with a party afterwards. A band played, local folk instruments roared, and we sat and celebrated with the fans till the wee hours. Everybody drank and sang; it was jolly nice time. We defeated great many strong teams; the matches were never an easy ride. Our opponents had many strong foreigners in their midst. For instance, the Brits Mortram and Cox played for Essen, Chris Lewis and I played for Amberg. A number of Swedes, Spaniards, and Brits played on teams, and it was never a simple fight to play against them.

The Bundes-league was not a year-round competition; it was played on six weekends of the year. That suited me really well because I did not want to stop competing altogether. I still played well enough to enter smaller European tournaments and no longer needed to fly long distances over the Ocean. I played in San Remo, Stuttgart and Hilversum.

Mook, Holland. With the three-times Wimbledon doubles champion South African Frew McMillan playing the Senior tournament. By this time he held a British passport.

In 1981 Jan played doubles with Tomas Smid in Hilversum, with Meiler in Köln, and with Lendl in Stuttgart. However, that year proved to be Kodes' final year of playing in the Grand Slams. Vijay Amritraj literally swept him off the court in Wimbledon, and in Paris he lost to Diego Perez from Uruguay.

Doubles dominated Kodes' tennis calendar in 1981 and 1982. He alternated a great many doubles partners during those two years: Meiler, Fibak, Smid, Navratil, El Shafei, Lendl, Birner, Drew Gitlin...

The latter was his doubles partner at ATP Kenya Open in the spring of 1982. Kodes lost to him in singles in second round but together they won the doubles. He played several more European tournaments that year and when he arrived in Hilversum he won the Dutch doubles championships with Tomas Smid.

It was my last victory in an ATP tournament... We defeated Nastase–Teacher 6:4, 3:6, 6:2 in the semis, and the Roland Garros champions Taróczy-Günthardt in the finals 7:6, 6:4!

At the same time Jan Kodes started playing veteran tournaments for players over age 35. The South African Frew McMillan, now with a British passport, was his partner in the Dutch Mook. They overcame Laver–Rosewall 7:6, 6:3 and Okker–Fillol 6:4, 3:6, 6:3. However, he lost to Okker in singles 6:4, 4:6, 1:6.

More veteran tournaments followed in the United States, in Chicago and Stratton; here he got to taste doubles victory with his partner John Newcombe, when they beat Emerson–Stolle 7:5, 6:4 and Drysdale-Davidson 6:3, 6:3.

I remember Stratton fondly. It is a small town in Vermont up high in the mountains, similar to Gstaad or Kitzbühel. I drove there from New York, which was quite demanding. Frustrated, after losing to Newcombe 4:6, 7:6, and 6:7, I was returning to my hotel room when I bumped into Laver.

"How did you play?"

"Well, I lost 6:7 in the third!"

"So what are you going to do now?"

"I'll spend the night and leave for New York in the morning; I have a plane to catch to Prague."

"Wouldn't you like to get to New York today?" – asked Laver. "A helicopter will pick me up in half-an-hour. If you want, you can join me. I have a free seat." And he added that I should be ready in front of the hotel in twenty minutes. Within the next fifteen minutes I threw all my stuff in my suitcase and out I went to wait in the parking lot full of cars and surrounded by trees. In no time there was such loud roar that one could not hear his own words. Dust got stirred up and with it all other garbage rose upwards. A helicopter sat down in the middle of the parking lot. We boarded; Laver and his friend, I, and two pilots. The flight was to take about forty minutes. I thought: "Gee-whiz! It is 4 o'clock and the next CSA plane to Prague is leaving at 17.45! Rod, where are we going to land?"

"At JFK; special runway for small planes and helicopters; at about ten to five."

We landed; I ran into the airport lounge without any reservation but I did have a plane ticket to Prague. Fortunately, CSA had a few empty seats. I made it and arrived home a day and a half earlier!

Nobody can imagine how thrilling all that was for me! It was an unbeatable experience, and on top of it with Laver! It was very nice of him; he did not need to extend that offer. But even such seemingly minute gestures showed his character! Would anyone do it today?

When Antonin Himl permitted me to go abroad I had no idea how soon I would see him again. I left thinking that I closed a "gentlemen's" contract with Amberg to play for them and see what happens next. It could turn out to be a year, or perhaps four.

However, when I met the CUPES Chairman again I sensed, just like many times in the past, how much the tremendous tension between him and Antonin Bolardt was growing. In the backstage everybody was whispering that Bolardt would like to push himself into the Chairman's position. I now understood why he wanted me to promise that I would return if need be.

"You must work for Czech tennis; who else should do it?!" he told me then. I nodded. I just wanted to get out at that moment and it did not even cross my mind that in less than a year I would receive a message: "Come back, we need a non-playing Davis Cup captain!"

1982 German Team Champion - TC Amberg am Schanzl, from top-left: Jan Kodes, Karl Meiler, Petr Strobl (coach), Chris Lewis, Reinhart Probst, bottom: Helmut Fickentscher, Max Wunschig, Christopher Zipf and Werner Zirngibl.

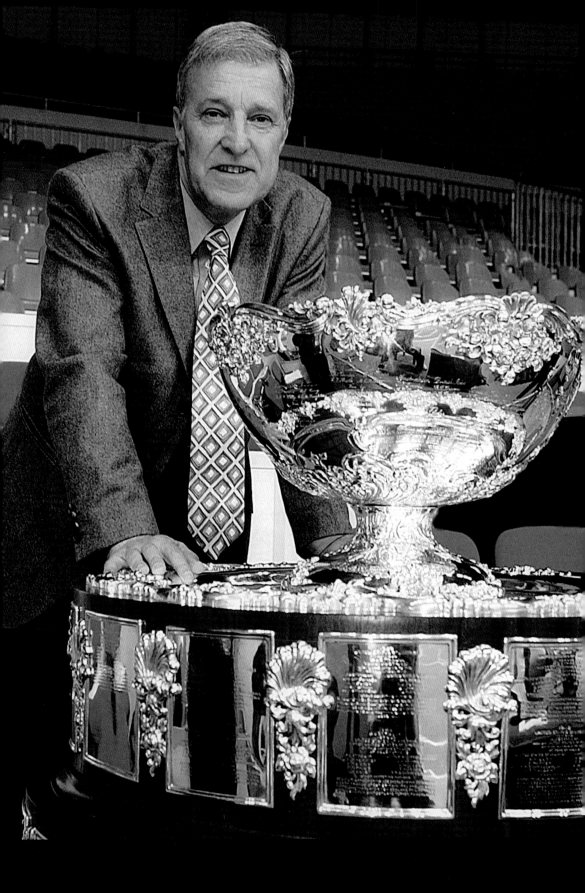

WITHOUT A RACKET

DAVIS CUP CAPTAIN

The Central Committee's order was clear: "From the next year on you are the non-playing Davis Cup team captain!" Kodes' objections that he was under contract in Amberg till the end of 1982 were futile. Antonin Himl said it was a "fait accompli": "It is confirmed and final that the present captain, Bolardt, will not continue in that position! We do not have anybody else to replace him but you. You are well familiar with everything it involves, you have the personality that fits the position, and players respect you!" The most curious point of this entire bickering affair was the fact that Jan Kodes did not care for the position. However, he did realize that before signing the contract in Germany he agreed to: "Yes, if necessary I'll return!"

It was paradoxical that CUPES (Czechoslovak Union of Physical Education and Sports) forced Kodes to accept the post of a Davis Cup captain as of 1982 while the Tennis Federation did not agree with it and did not recommend Kodes for the position! Their argument was that the players would not take him seriously since there was very little age difference. The Tennis Federation communist board members added fire to the argument saying that Kodes should be out of question for the position since he chose to play for a team outside the communist bloc, in the West German city of Amberg!

I was surprised by all of it! There were people at the Federation who would go along with my nomination provided that: Kodes must stop his competitive career! He must not enter any tournaments! He must not participate in German "Bundes-league"! Only then he can take on Davis Cup captainship.

Naturally, I did not want to give up my active tennis playing entirely. Frankly, I must admit that the financial income that I was able to secure in the Bundes-league as well as through tournament entries was one of the reasons why I did not want to stop playing. In addition, many organizers still wanted to see me enter their tournaments in spite of my age of thirty five.

The Tennis Federation officials, who agreed with Kodes' appointment into the post of a Davis Cup captain, counter-argued and pushed for nominating him as a playing captain the way Vijay Amritraj was in India or Pato Rodriguez in Chile. They both played for, as well as captained, their teams. But then a good reason against his nomination popped up: "Kodes cannot fill the post of a Davis Cup team captain; he has not taken the highest tennis coaching certification course! He has fulfilled only the 2nd level coaching certification." Fortunately, the CUPES Chairman Himl reacted readily with: "Granted, Kodes does not have the highest certification but he won Wimbledon and twice Roland Garros and that is enough for me!"

The first encounter in which Kodes participated as a Davis Cup captain was in January 1982. It took place in the Ice Hockey Arena in Prague against the team of West Germany. Czechoslovakia beat the West German team, represented by Rolf Göhring and Uli Pinner, comfortably 5:0. The closing official dinner also took place in the Sport Arena. Everybody was present and everybody anticipated Kodes committing some faux pas since he was not used to giving public speeches, especially in front of such an elite audience.

I prepared my speech according to common practices including welcoming the guests, thanking the opponents, players, organizers, umpires and ball-boys. I inserted everything that was supposed to be said. As we were taking leave after the function was over Antonin Himl approached me and said: "Thank you ever so much. You have done a great of a job!"

Those few words made Kodes feel good because Antonin Bolardt was still plotting against him at that point from a position of a Tennis Federation Board member. He kept insisting on persuading everybody that Jan was not capable of captainship. In addition, Kodes was not a party member! In spite of those two shortcomings – not being a communist and not owning the higher coaching certification – Antonin Himl believed in him.

I must make a brief comment here. As unbelievable as it might sound, nobody ever requested of me to join the Communist Party. I believed that they simply did not desire anybody with my background in their midst. Or, they were worried that I would give them a negative response and they did not want to be faced with a refusal. They knew well that I would have never joined the party bearing in mind what they had done to my father; and they were right. At the same time, they recognized my strong sense of patriotism, which I proved many times over on and off the court.

When Bolardt realized that he lost the battle with regard to the Davis Cup team captainship he tried to complicate his successor's work at hand as much as possible. As a chief of the Department of Athletics for the potential best athletes in the country he created a document called: Scope of the Davis Cup Realizing Committee's Work. In it he specified duties of each individual member, including the non-playing captain's.

Basically, the non-playing captain always fulfilled all those individual points of the written duties but this way, Bolardt was going to have a written document supervised by yet another person higher up. In that way the document was wildly inflated.

After reading through the document I realized that many of my "duties" fell under the incumbency of the team coach; and whatever Bolardt specified for the realizing committee's officer was the job of the non-playing captain! I strongly disputed this "job description" scheme; a realizing committee officer never existed before! In the end, I succeeded in persuading the Tennis Federation Board that the new office of a realizing committee head officer was unnecessary. It is obvious that entering the position of a non-playing Davis Cup captain was not an easy ride.

I was surprised by all the obstacles, especially since I had been part of the Davis Cup team for many years already (17). Moreover, I did not care for the post in the first place. I would have remained in Amberg another two or three years.

So, besides being a Davis Cup team captain in 1982 Kodes also played some tournaments. He entered Madrid, Barcelona and Hilversum for the last time in his career and with Stanislav Birner he also played the last Wimbledon doubles. He teamed up with Tomas Smid they even won doubles 7:6, 6:4 against Taróczy – Günthardt in the finals in Hilversum. Similarly, he won the title in Nairobi, Kenya, pairing with Drew Gitlin from the United States.

However, the Czechoslovak Tennis Federation did not favor his own competitive playing. They said repeatedly: "He mustn't play as long as he is a team captain!" Fortunately, the Federation Chairman, Cyril Suk, went along with Kodes' tournament entries.

In 1981 Davis Cup competition underwent organizational changes. A World Group of best sixteen teams was established. The other teams competed still in European A, European B, American and Eastern zones. That created additional unwelcome long distance travel in between continents for all players. The first round winners automatically secured their place in the World Group for the following year. Losers had to compete in Relegation rounds. This format of Qualification was later changed several times since more zones, including African zone, where appointed, due to the number of new countries entering e.g. from past USSR! The main Davis Cup sponsor that year was the Japanese Nippon Electric Company (NEC).

Kodes' Davis Cup captainship era lasted five and a half years (1982-1987). Out of fourteen encounters his team lost six and "his" players performed in great many amazing matches. They always stayed in the group of the sixteen best in the world. Czechoslovakia reached the semis three times during those years, once they advanced into the quarter-finals; only twice they lost in the first round but won the relegation match to stay in the "World Group of sixteen"!

As a captain I valued the wins away above all others; the most valuable victories, in my opinion, were abroad like in Guayaquil against Ecuador as well as other places. We had complicated situations in difficult conditions in Tbilisi vs. USSR, and then in Calcutta against India, and in Sarajevo against Yugoslavia; all three without Lendl playing for us. The team struggled

**Davis Cup Czechoslovakia vs. Germany, Prague 1982.
Among the ballboys were a few future tennis names, such as - front row: Petr Korda (1st left),
Jan Kodes, Jr (center) and in back row: Vojtech Flegl (3rd left), Cyril Suk (4th from right).**

*there and wanted to win no matter what; they wanted to prove that they could succeed even
without Ivan; and they did.*

Gradually, other players joined the experienced trio – Lendl, Smid, Slozil: Miloslav Mecir
came out in Hradec Kralove in 1983 against the USSR, Milan Srejber came out three years later
in Yugoslavia, and Karel Novacek got initiated in Hradec Kralove in 1987 playing against Israel. At the end of 1983 Frantisek Pala took over the coaching post from Jan Kukal, who returned
to his work in Austria.

Nevertheless, those were not easy years; in spite of Davis Cup victory tennis came under
tremendous pressure again. More frequent attempts of several party officials to constrict the
sport the way the East Germans had done took place. In their eyes tennis was still a sport of
the bourgeoisie and the undeniable success in the early 1970s and 1980s presented a sore in

**Czechoslovakia vs Germany 5:0. Jan Kodes as Davis Cup captain with Ivan Lendl. Behind them is masseur
Pavel Chvojka, great friend, who passed away in September 4, 1984. His tragedy saddened all the players.**

the backside of many. Basically, it was the same old story – jealousy! The tennis players traveled the world over and earned hard currency. Ivan started making big money and it was printed in the daily press. Up until that time the "prize money" amount was not public knowledge.

In the early 1980s Ivan Lendl's era took off. In 1981 he already won nine Grand Prix tournaments, lost four times in the finals, and advanced into a Grand Slam final for the first time – at Roland Garros. He lost it to Björn Borg 1:6, 6:4, 2:6, 6:3, and 1:6. That year he won the culminating ATP Masters tournament for the first time. Madison Square Garden in New York witnessed him play in grand style beating Vitas Gerulaitis in a five-set battle, when he was two sets to none down but came back: 6:7, 2:6, 7:6, 6:2, 6:4.

During one-party supremacy in the country tennis had no bed of roses for progress. Consistently, something bothered people in power, consistently party apparatus tried to "clip the wings" of our players, limit their entries in tournaments abroad and complicate their lives by demanding their participation in obligatory events at home.

There was no end to all kinds of debates, discussions, arguments and feuds in tennis circles. Over the years a number of lesser or more serious allegations against us, tennis players, surfaced. I am going to point out one example here for illustration - the statute of a professional tennis player.

The Central Committee of CUPES imparted a tennis player statute based on Tennis Federation committee's proposal for entries in foreign tournaments.

In case of Ivan Lendl, among others, it stated:

In accordance with the "Player Statute Guidelines" the Tennis Federation committee sets the following duties for the player:

■ Turn $3000.00 to the Tennis Federation Committee from each prize money reward from tournaments abroad in addition to the compulsory financial surrender to Pragosport

■ Besides the compulsory financial surrender to Pragosport turn in 30% of all monetary rewards, provided the player has not reached the age of 21

Must achieve the following goals between November 1, 1984 and October 31, 1985:

ATP – 3rd rank, Grand Prix – 3rd place, Davis Cup – 3rd place...

■ Must be available for Davis Cup competition.

■ Must enter minimum of two Grand Slam events: French Open, Wimbledon, US Open and other Grand Prix tournaments depending on the annual schedule.

■ Must participate in Czechoslovak Nationals provided that he is not released according to the ATP performance criteria – ranked in top 10!

■ Must participate in the National team league provided that he is not released according to the ATP performance criteria – ranked in top 20!

Additional responsibilities in 1985: must conduct himself in the spirit and demeanor worthy of representing the CSSR, must be politically engaged – participate in talks, forums, and seminars, must complete health check-ups, and within a week from Davis Cup competition is permitted to participate only in tournaments on the same surface.

These contracts were renewed annually and the fundamental criteria for each were the previous year performance.

"Pragosport – Player Agreement" was also a component of the "Player Statute Guidelines". The object of it was "player participation in Open tennis tournaments and exhibitions abroad, where prize money and compensations were set by the organizers." From the player's view several points of the agreement were important; besides others: "Player promises to represent CSSR honorably.... not participate in any political, religious, or other affairs of the host country; player also pledges to adhere to the exchange and customs regulations, specifically article # 142/1970 referring to exchange management; upon each return from abroad a player is obliged to: make a breakdown of rewards received and consign US $ amount to Pragosport according to a table approved by CUPES; after each return a player is bound to write a brief report in reference to his time abroad, he must attach official tournament rosters specifying the prize money rewards. Player must understand that if he/she does not comply with these responsibilities he will not receive travel documents for the next travel out of the country."

What is there to add? The comrades faced dilemma; they had to solve their inner conflict between their longing to hold control and longing to have Uncle Sam's green-backs that they could earn without actually working, only thanks to being as nice as to letting a few players play abroad for the "prize money."

Nobody ever checked how much of the money collected from the players' purses was injected into the youth programs and their participation in tournaments abroad and, most likely, nobody will ever find out. These officials quoted empty phrases and policy lines characterizing a socialist athlete on one hand but looking after their own interests on the other. These were individuals who advocated their own travel as chaperones to significant tournaments in the West either with adults or with junior teams. At the same time, they had no shame letting Martina Navratilova at a very young age and on her first trip to the US travel with only a few dollars in her pockets and take care of herself entirely ....

I need to point out this information in order to portray the characteristics of the time when, in 1980, we reached Davis Cup victory and with that we initiated a new era; an era that proved to be, without any doubt, the most successful time in our tennis history. A string of players like Lendl, Smid, Mecir, Mandlikova, Sukova, who reigned during that time period, made it possible for the next generation of players like Novotna, Korda and others to follow. It was Lendl and Smid who were the most responsible individuals for our first and last Davis Cup victory; regretfully, a few years later the pressure on them was too much to bear. Why?

This was the kind of a situation that also affected Jan Kodes. Though Davis Cup captainship seemed to be a "cushy" position, it got clouded by a constant conflict with regard to Ivan Lendl.

PARAGUAY VS. CZECHOSLOVAKIA 1983

The Davis Cup draw sent the team led by Jan Kodes to an exotic opponent in far away Asuncion. Only just before the departure did the players learn that they would play on fast indoor surface, which made Victor Pecci and Francesco Gonzales inscrutable and tough adversaries. In addition, Lendl and Smid, bound by their contracts with Lamar Hunt, the WCT founder, were committed to play a tournament in Houston on slow clay just before this Davis cup match. That resulted in the fact that both of them went out without the needed acclimatization to the fast surface.

For Ivan Lendl this was altogether a very unpleasant affair. Not so from the tennis standpoint; Ivan was a hundred percent professional and it was not a problem for him to adapt his game to new surfaces and/ or environment within a couple of days. However, it was the domestic press that for weeks had been disputing his "affinity to socialist Czechoslovakia," and his late arrival to the Davis Cup venue only stirred up further the individuals who had spoken ill of him for months.

I knew that they reprehended him for spending little time on home turf, for not communicating with the Davis Cup team outside the matches, for arriving late to the matches... But it would not make sense for him to fly to Prague only to shake hands with everybody, then turn around and board the plane back to South America! What nonsense! We simply agreed to meet in Asuncion after the tournament in Houston.

We played an unbelievable match in Paraguay that had an incredible prelude. The play took place indoors in a hall that reminded us of our Sparta basketball court in Letna, only it had more surrounding space, and the stands went up high along the sidelines holding about four thousand seats.

Our guys were practicing while I went to the traditional captains' meeting. Paraguay's tennis federation secretary presented a program for the next three Davis Cup days: "There will be a formal opening ceremony on Friday before the game starts, attended by the president of our country, Strossner. Since we have no diplomatic relations with Czechoslovakia our federation leadership decided to run the ceremony without flags or your national anthem."

I got up and protested vehemently: "If the ceremony is to be without flags or our national anthem, which is against the ITF rules, then we are flying back to Prague in the morning and I'll file an official complaint with the ITF!"

At that moment they all swooped down on me. "Wait, sit down!" and they started explaining what a difficult situation they were in.

"Look," I protested, "the ITF rules clearly state that every international competition must be accompanied by a flag and national anthem."

They just nodded their heads and then they got up and left saying that they would discuss it within their camp and, "we'll meet again tomorrow." The next day drew close: "It is all set. The assembly will take place with the flags but we won't play the anthems... because we do not have yours." I reached into my jacket pocket and pulled out a cassette with our anthem. "Here you are" I handed it to them. They were dumbstruck, but accepted it. With this episode, I am demonstrating that a non-playing captain must protect and fight for everything! It is not only to dispute controversial calls or umpires' decisions at court site or to counsel the players during changeovers. Everything is important; it is a question of representing our country! We show our opponents that we won't accept a back seat on the court or off the court! I informed my team about it which excited them that much more.

However, nothing helped us and we left Asuncion with a 2:3 defeat. Ivan Lendl overcame Gonzales 6:4, 6:4, 10:8 in the opening match but a five-hour battle followed between Tomas Smid and Pecci from which the host country player came out victorious 6:3, 3:6, 6:4, 5:7, and 6:1. The score was tied at 1:1 after the first day. The doubles game was dictated purely by the Paraguayans. Lendl-Smid succumbed to Gonzales-Pecci thrice 6:4; Gonzales sealed the Paraguayan triumph on the third day when he defeated Smid 6:3, 12:10, 3:6, 6:3. Navratil beat Caballero in the substitute's duel 6:2, 6:0.

LENDL DILEMMA

In September 1983 the team was getting ready for an extremely important match to retain position in the world group; the importance was multiplied by the fact that the match was against the Soviet Union. Since the construction of the new stadium on Stvanice Island was in full swing the team found its training haven in the Ice Hockey Stadium in Hradec Kralove; that became a future stronghold of our tennis. After our dialogue with the Mayor all local officials met our requests with maximum goodwill; they let us bring in red clay and spread it on top of the ice ring surface. Jaroslav Kott and Petr Jurosz were in charge of clay court preparation. The Soviets arrived with a team that truly concerned us: Andrei Chesnokov, Aleksander Zverev and Andrei Olhovskiy. In the opening match the Soviets proved that the encounter would not be an easy stroll; Tomas Smid conquered Zverev in a grueling five-setter 4:6, 8:6, 4:6, 6:4 and 6:4! Milos Mecir came out as a singles rookie in the second match. He was down against Andrei Chesnokov 8:10, 1:6, 0:3 showing his "apprentice" jitters with careful play and nervous serves that did not give much hope for victory.

Tennis "a la Playa"

In 1983 I was invited by Manolo Galé, the President of a Spanish club in Avilés by Oviedo, to play an exhibition with Avendano in Luanco. He assured me that many other famous players played there since it attracts crowds as it is played on the beach, on sand....
I boarded the plane with my wife and kids and three hours later we deplaned in Asturias airport in Northern Spain that services Oviedo as well as Avilés. As soon as we landed the President vowed that I had never experienced anything comparable to what was ahead of me. "Come and see where you'll play tomorrow!" We came to the location and there was a wall, the sea, the beach, and much debris in the form of discarded cans. A little distance away there were bleachers standing about half-way in the water. "Well, this is where you'll be playing tomorrow", said Manolo. Shocked I exclaimed: "Here?" "Yeah; you'll see what it looks like tomorrow at 10 a.m.; you'll be surprised!" I went to look at the place after breakfast. There was a brown surface court, all packed by a heavy roller. And there was no water to be seen! Only a moment later I realized: the tide was out! We started to play singles at eleven. The way they rolled the sandy surface it held surprisingly well and the balls bounced fine. In the afternoon we returned to play doubles. Everybody kept urging us: "Get going! At ten to three the water will be back." We started to play and, all of a sudden I noticed that the water level was coming closer and closer. Soon the bleachers were buried in the water and gradually the court got flooded. When the level of water reached as close as a few feet from the lines we packed up and left.

Exhibition court on the beach the night before...

Playing on the sand... Luanco, Spain in 1983.

A few minutes before we ran off the court...

Ivan Lendl won twice
Trofeo Conde
de Godo in 1980-1981. It was
before he reached his first
Grand Slam title at Paris (1984).
Trophy was given by Carlos de Godo
and Tournament Director Miguel Lerin
(center).

Milos seemed to be like in wonderland. I often remember that match. I had no idea what more to advice him. At this score I told him: "Milosku (endearment), I know exactly how you feel. In my first singles match against the Austrian Blanke I, too, was down 0:2 and 0:3; then captain Rössler told me: "You can't play this carefully, don't be afraid! Play your own game even if it results in a defeat. The score is 1:0 in our favor since Tomas won his match. It is no big deal if you loose." - Milos stared me down and went to serve. During that game he hit two passing shots and from that moment on he whipped Chesnokov off the court 6:3, 6:4, 6:2. I always appreciated that I managed to wake him up.

The following day Libor Pimek and Pavel Slozil beat Zverev-Olhovskiy surprisingly easy 6:0, 6:4, 6:2. That left Vaclav Svadlena without further ado to write...

The Hradec spectators proved to be jolly, they created a wonderful atmosphere and the local organizers tirelessly satisfied our needs. The following year we returned to Hradec but this time we destroyed Denmark on a rubber carpet without even a loss of a set! It was Libor Pimek who came out to play singles then.

In the course of May 1983 the foreign press, particularly West German press, started to publish information about Ivan Lendl's involvement in South Africa. Soon our home athletic and communist party authorities learned about the forthcoming exhibition, mainly thanks to the campaign launched among the North-European countries against his association with a country where apartheid ruled. They employed the Olympic charter to make their statement. Jan Kodes and Ivan's father Jiri flew then to Wimbledon to persuade Ivan not to travel to South Africa. Ivan reacted with an argument that his agency ProServ received a very attractive invitation to take part in an exhibition tournament in Sun City in South African Bophuthatswana. It surprised him that there was such an upheaval around it at home, since it was not hosted by South Africa but rather by a country with a black president, and, moreover, where the organizers demanded that all players coordinate a tennis clinic for the benefit of children of their black neighborhoods.

In addition, he wanted us to explain at home that the country in question is not a country where apartheid rules. He maintained that he was not sure how far the arrangements stood but he thought that the contract had already been signed. He promised to find out if anything could still be done in this affair. In the meantime, the organizers drafted a written complaint and a threat of a huge fine, which unsettled the managerial firm ProServ as well as Ivan himself. Thus, Ivan Lendl ultimately played the tournament in Sun City. What were the consequences? – Catastrophic from the point of view of Czech tennis...

The leadership of TF and the CC CUPES (Ministry of Sports) suspended Lendl from Davis Cup competition and fined him an amount of $150,000. The player himself disagreed with this decision insisting that he never signed to play in South Africa. After the exhibition tournament Lendl indicated that Bophuthatswana was an independent state that also condemned apartheid.

It is necessary to recall a fact here that voices at the ministry of foreign affairs in Prague were not united in their estimation of the given situation at the time of the verdict. Subsequently, it was found out that the state of Bophuthatswana was neither a member of the United Nations nor of the International Olympic Committee. As an aftermath of this entire scandal media reporting about Lendl and his tennis achievements abroad was stopped, and with it the news about Czech tennis subsided altogether. Lendl refused to accept the penalty and during the US Open in September 1983 he implied that the tone of his country's mass media showed that the country was not interested in having him represent Czechoslovakia.

The CC CUPES delegated Jan Kodes, Jan Kukal, Frantisek Pala, and Jiri Lendl to negotiate problematic topics and further development with Ivan Lendl at the tournament in Luxemburg. A contract about representing the nation was signed there between the CC CUPES, the Tennis Federation and Ivan Lendl on November 16, 1983.

However, Ivan Lendl signed this agreement only with a comment, in which he asked for a lega-

Miloslav Mecir won his first Davis Cup match from two sets down over Andrei Chesnokov, as did his captain Jan Kodes over Ernest Blanke back in 1966.

lized residence abroad in a form of emigrant passport with a condition of retention of Czechoslovak nationality in order to be able to represent the country in Davis Cup competition.

Andrei Chesnokov.

From our Luxemburg negotiations Ivan sent a check for $60,000 to Pragosport as an advance from his 1983 prize money earnings. After the Masters event in December he sent a letter to the Ministry of Interior, the Central Committee of the Communist Party, and the CC CUPES, in which he explained and defended his participation in Bophuthatswana. At the same time he infused that he disagreed with the media stance relating to his representing Czechoslovakia abroad and he asked for solution. This letter had other bearing on the development of this situation and later turned out to be the focal point of a dispute since Lendl never received the response that he had expected. His return to representing the nation was conditioned by paying up the remainder of the fine, and only then the demands stated in his letter would be addressed and dealt with.

In May 1984, based on a dialogue with Jan Kodes, Ivan Lendl wrote a letter in which he expressed his respect for the penalty since he was placed on a United Nations' blacklist (from which he was later taken off). The check for $150,000 was received from Jan Kodes by a representative in the office of financial management on June 19, 1984.

This created a similar environment at home to the one around Martina Navratilova several years earlier. The difference was that Ivan Lendl was already a world class player, was a few years older, and there was no threat that he would want to emigrate.

Draft of a contract between the Central Committee of the Czechoslovak Union of Physical Education and Sports (CC CUPES) and the leadership of the Tennis Federation (TF) and Ivan Lendl

The administration of the CC CUPES is interested in Ivan Lendl representing the Czechoslovak Socialist Republic in tennis for the reason that his representation in tournaments abroad has a positive athletic as well as political significance for CSSR. In light of the fact that Ivan Lendl is a statutory player of TF and the CC CUPES, which may pose specific problems when playing overseas in reference to his national representation and/or his own, the following contractual agreement is being drawn out between Ivan Lendl and the governing body of the CC CUPES:

Ivan Lendl, as a representative of CSSR, is covenant to:
1. behave and perform abroad in accordance with the interests of CSSR and the Czechoslovak socialist idea of sports;
2. representing CSSR in Davis Cup team competition and possibly the Nations Cup (ATP event) in all encounters at home and abroad in the years 1984-1994, if he is so appointed;
3. absence from participation in any competition or exhibition in the following countries: Chile, Israel, Thai-wan, South Africa, including any satellite states in their territories. If a new state emerges, or if a state with which Czechoslovakia holds diplomatic relations or any form of cooperation undergoes political changes, the player must consult the Czechoslovak authorities before signing a contract of entry in competition in that country;
4. is bound to turn in annually, by December 15, an amount of his Prize earnings according to his statutory contract with CC CUPES;

The administration of the Central Committee of Czechoslovak Union of Physical Education and Sports (CC CUPES) pledges to:

1. allow Ivan Lendl legal permanent residency abroad and entry in all international tournaments and exhibitions everywhere in the world with the exception of the countries mentioned in point #3 above.
2. ensure cooperation with offices of internal affairs in relationship to his frequent exit, entry and re-entry from and to CSSR, including the defense of his rights and repeated travel in agreement between him and the ambassador to the USA Mr. Suja;
3. facilitate travel for Ivan's parents as his escorts.

11. 16. 1983
PS – Comment to 2/1 is noted in the record of the meeting

Připomínka k bodu 2/1 je uvedena v zápise z jednání.

16.11.1983

IVAN LENDL

185

June 9th 19 *84*

1-131
210

PAY TO THE ORDER OF *Czechoslovak Tennis Association* $ *150 000 °°⁄₁₀₀*

One hundred and fifty thousand and ⁰⁰⁄₁₀₀ ⎯⎯⎯⎯⎯⎯ DOLLARS

U.S. Trust UNITED STATES TRUST CO.
OF NEW YORK
45 Wall Street
New York, N.Y. 10005

MEMO

⑆021001318⑆ 61 3836 5⑈

He did not desire emigration. Neither was it true, that we had to travel to see him abroad. Only later, when the situation around him became acute, we could communicate only by traveling to him. At the start we had an easy contact via his parents. They lived in Ostrava and Ivan always came for the national championships there. Before each Davis Cup match I called him up and we agreed on his date of arrival, who with and where he would practice, and what the training camp would be like. It is true that he often presented special demands, and he held special privileges. His Davis Cup match preparation was sometimes two days shorter than for the others, usually because he reached the finals of a recent tournament and needed time to rest up. Thus, he sometimes joined the team on Tuesday, while the others arrived on Sunday and started training on Monday. The media crews immediately reported from Stvanice: "How come Lendl is not here; where is he?"

There wasn't much I could do; as a captain I had to accept things the way they were and had to differentiate among my "wards". I hope that nobody will be angry with me if I simply say that Smid and Slozil did not equal Lendl.

Moreover, and I stress this, Ivan always honored our agreements. There was not even one time that he would not keep his promise. Our discussions about individual details of the terms and arrangements were always complicated but we came to an accord at all times. He knew that if he comes to play Davis Cup he wants to play well and win. It was not difficult to negotiate with him as long as all sides played fair. However, that was not always the case.

When we lost to France 2:3 in 1982, and a year later to Paraguay with the same score, people started to whisper that the captainship is beyond me, that players do not listen to me, and Lendl does what he pleases. Two camps developed within the Tennis Federation – one stood behind me, the other against me.

The chairman of the Tennis Federation, Cyril Suk, knew well that I was the right candidate for the post of a non-playing captain. He saw all the matches, and because he understood tennis, he was able to argue when others criticized the team's performance; he simply declared "the opponent was better." However, those who were against me and knew Ivan's inflexibility demanded that I command Ivan to arrive at the training camp before our Davis Cup matches the same day as the rest of the team. I knew this would be a close to impossible task. Then the headquarters stipulated – either Ivan arrives on schedule as everybody else, or he is out of the team!

I had to look for compromises constantly because I knew that Ivan had his rightful place on the team but I also knew he would not change his attitude. As I think back to all our Davis Cup matches I don't remember him ever losing a match because he was ill prepared. I always stood behind him, I acknowledged his professionalism. Perhaps, that was one of the reasons why I tolerated his attitude – his work out ethics and game readiness were superior.

Lendl was one of the top five players in the world. Playing Davis Cup matches was an obvious duty inherent to the game at the top. I agreed with him that preparing for a Davis Cup match does not need to be different from preparing for any well attended tournament. It was sufficient for him to arrive on Saturday and start a tournament on Monday. Furthermore, he always stressed that he was to play only two singles that he will be ready for and win, while Smid and Slozil would take care of the doubles. He stuck to what he had promised and there was nothing I could complain about.

CZECHOSLOVAKIA VS. FRANCE 1984

We had one opportunity to discuss Ivan Lendl's problems at Davis Cup quarterfinal match against France in July 1984 in Hradec Kralove.

I found out from Antonin Himl that the Prime Minister and the Minister of Interior Vratislav Vajnar would be coming to watch the Saturday doubles match. "Jan, that is an ideal opportunity for Lendl to resolve all his issues with the minister and have it done and over with once and for all."

I told Ivan that if he doesn't play doubles he is invited into the government box. Minister Vajnar will be there so "run up there and settle your differences with him!"

During Davis Cup in Hradec Kralove excellent conditions always prevailed. The Federation chairman Cyril Suk managed the steering committee. The organizers did their best to accommodate the players. Only once we came across a situation that nobody could do anything about.

Each time we came to Hradec Kralove we were put up in the hotel Chernigov. After the first practice before our match against France our players started to grizzle about the noise coming from the restaurant as well as from the street, since there was a railway station close by and buses were stopping there frequently; the players wondered if we could be switched

Davis Cup tie Czechoslovakia vs. France at Hradec Kralove in 1984.
L.Siblik (ch.umpires),Thierry Tulasne, Pascal Portes, Henri Leconte, Guy Forget, coach Patrice Hagelauer, capt. Jean-Paul Loth. Chair umpires from Sweden, Kurt Magnusson and Ove Lindh, Norway referee CatoVik (center), J.Kodes, P.Slozil,T.Smid, I.Lendl, M.Mecir.

Tomas Smid – Pavel Slozil won WCT Doubles Masters in 1984 at Royal Albert Hall, London overcoming Jarryd - Simonsson, the Gullikson brothers and Fleming – Buenning.

from the first floor higher up. Tactfully we were told that it was impossible since the entire floor was bugged! There were listening devices everywhere! Tomas Smid grew pale in view of the fact that the night before he let his tongue slip away and trashed the Russians! Ivan Lendl, on the other hand, thought it was funny: "So, they are going to listen to the sounds in my room if I have a girl here, right?"

However, a couple of days later reasons to laugh about stopped.

Instead of Noah the French team came with Henri Leconte.

In the opening match he held Ivan pinned back with his serve into the backhand and played very aggressively. I knew Ivan was worried about Leconte; he never liked playing against lefthanders. He succumbed to him easily 3:6, 6:8, 4:6.

In the following match Smid was down 6:4, 2:6, 3:6 against Guy Forget and our chances of victory looked shaky at that moment. However, Tomas proved himself again to be an amazing fighter and overwhelmed Forget in five sets after an unbelievable battle. He won the last two sets 6:1 and 6:4 and with that he evened out the overall score to 1:1.

The doubles game was played on Saturday. The vital second point was fought for three hours. Smid with Slozil pulled off a five set victory over Leconte-Portes 6:2, 5:7, 7:5, 4:6, and 6:2. The game was highly strung for the players on court, the spectators in the stands, the supporting team on the bench, and above all for Jan Kodes.

I was sitting on the captain's chair directly opposite to the governmental box. I could not concentrate. Something was happening on the court but I did not know what because I kept looking up. There was Ivan, sitting with the minister Vajnar. I kept saying to myself: "Oh God, please let Ivan resolve all his problems up there so that I can relax once and for all!"

I believed that with this team we could win Davis Cup perhaps three times. Everything was working out in our favor, Miloslav Mecir was making his way into the team and it seemed that soon he would take over Tomas' singles spot. Our doubles team Slozil-Smid was one of the best in the world! Who could beat us?

The Sunday program started with Ivan Lendl vs. Guy Forget. He beat him 11:9, 6:4, 6:2, thus we advanced into the semifinals. Smid lost to Leconte 6:3, 6:3 but that no longer altered anything. About two hours later Lendl got into his car and left for Vienna.

He was in a hurry to get to the airport; only an hour later I found out that Lendl and the minister Vajnar did not exchange even a word during those three hours of doubles game! Allegedly, they both waited for the other to start. Therefore nothing got resolved! Additionally, I found out that Vajnar was afraid to stir things up because somebody from above advised him not to interfere in Lendl's case!

There was always good cooperation with Tomas Smid and Pavel Slozil.

The key moment presented itself at the time before the subsequent Davis Cup match, the semifinals in the Swedish city of Bastad.

The whole circus started all over: When will Lendl arrive? When will he start training with the team?

Our Davis Cup player Ivan Lendl arrived in Prague yesterday in the morning. Soon after a short press conference he worked out under the guidance of the headcoach Ing. Pala and the non-playing team captain Jan Kodes… Following his tremendous achievement in Flushing Meadows where he battled his way to the finals, he canceled his entry in Grand Prix in San Francisco, in order to be able to adapt to the clay surface on which the next Davis Cup encounter against Sweden will take place next Friday.

Ceskoslovensky sport – Czechoslovak press

What happened then should not have happened; it is my opinion that it wronged Ivan and scarred him psychologically. Originally, he wanted to fly from the United States directly to Bastad. I approached Antonin Himl and requested of him: "Mr. Chairman, please, resolve the issues surrounding Lendl one way or the other! We keep going in circles and nothing is clear; say "yes" or "no"! The way you are dealing with Ivan is unfair and undignified."

It is my hundred percent belief that Antonin Himl himself was interested in working out the situation encircling Ivan Lendl and a few days later he phoned me: "Have Ivan fly to Prague before he goes to Bastad; we'll set up a meeting with Prime Minister Vajnar and we'll settle the matter once and for all. We'll legalize his emigrant status in the USA and resolve his Czechoslovak standing."

All was set and promised and with that in mind I called Ivan. He reacted with an edge in his voice: "Damn it, I want to be assured! I don't want to fly to Prague for nothing!"

Only when I swore that Himl promised to work things out he agreed to fly in. I went to meet the plane; though it was due at 7 am it was delayed and I had to wait. As I waited I started feeling more and more uneasy. My head was spinning with doubts; what am I going to tell him? It so happened that at 6:30 am I received a phone call from the CC CUPES (Ministry of Sports) informing me that the meeting with Prime Minister Vajnar scheduled for 10 am was canceled and asking me to call back upon Lendl's arrival in Prague.

I felt terribly and progressively still worse. From the airport I drove Ivan to my house and shortly after nine I called the office of the CC CUPES. I was then told that there would be no meeting; no questions asked and no explanations given! Only Antonin Himl was willing to face up to Lendl.

He invited us to dinner at the restaurant Nova scena in the National Theatre. Himl and I came with our wives plus Ivan. We were having a reasonably good time, Ivan was subdued.

He stayed at my house and the next day we worked out at Stvanice before flying to Sweden. I recognized then that he was in a foul mood. I knew he felt that Himl and I played a trick on him. But it wasn't our fault. He spent an additional day in Prague; I have a hard time believing that any minister is that busy that he could not spare ten minutes to resolve a nagging issue! If there was an emergency he should be able to act even at midnight!

I should say that Ivan's request to retain his Czechoslovak nationality was fair and realizable. In public it could be called a "permanent residence abroad necessitated by professional engagement". However, Ivan Lendl became a tool of political battle. In the background of this conflict was also a position of Antonin Himl, whose chair stood on very shaky ground, and "case Lendl" was most likely helpful to those, who were trying to seize Himl's position .

Himl suffered plenty of scorn for standing behind Lendl. However, Czech tennis suffered even more. Lendl paid the penalty for his Bophuthatswana entry and he was promised that the signed agreement from Luxemburg would be honored. Nonetheless, the president of our republic, Gustav Husak, was against it. And that was absolutely unfair to Ivan Lendl.

Later I found out, that the Cabinet Secretary of the Central Committee of the Communist Party Vasil Bilak spoke ill of Lendl in front of the president. Most likely that was the case because Antonin Himl had once uttered: "Jan, all is lost! Everything would be different if Ivan were Slovak. In that case he would have a go anywhere and everywhere with any kind of passport he would ask for. But, he is Czech!"

Senior „35" and over event at Bornemouth in 1983. From left: Roy Emerson, Fred Stolle, Colin Dibley, Ismail El Shafei, Manuel Santana, Tom Okker, Mark Cox, Nikki Pilic, Bob Hewitt, Owen Davidson, Sherwood Stewart, Charlie Pasarell, Jan Kodes, Neale Fraser, Roger Taylor, Cliff Drysdale, Ray Moore and Jaime Fillol.

The ATP team competition, the World Cup is played at Dussledorf's Rochus Club. Eight teams can enter according to the best players ranking. Czechoslovakia won the cup twice: 1981 over Australia 2:1 and 1987 over USA 2:1. In the years 1984, 1985, 1992, 1996, 1998 and 2003 we lost in the finals with USA 1:2 (1984, 1985), Spain 0:3 (1992), Switzerland 1:2 (1996), Germany 0:3 (1998) and Argentina 1:2 (2003). Picture from 1984: from left: Pavel Slozil, captain Jan Kodes, Ivan Lendl, Tomas Smid, Peter Fleming, John McEnroe a Jimmy Arias.

I could not believe my ears! And I did not react to that. Later, however, I learned that the figure skater Ondrej Nepela, a Slovak, also had a contract with Pragosport and accepted a contract with Holiday on Ice. He emigrated and only then asked for and received an emigrant passport. When that became known many people, Himl including, were unhappy since the passport had been issued without the knowledge or approval of the Central Committee.

If it was ok to issue a passport for Nepela, it should have been ok to issue it for Lendl as well. Or? It is said that Nepela was no longer at the top nor was he representing the country but....
(Comment: Then president Husak as well as Vasil Bilak were both Slovak...)

SWEDEN VS. CZECHOSLOVAKIA 1984

The second easy defeat was very much talked about. The Swedes presented a very strong team. Mats Wilander and Henrik Sundstrom in singles and Stefan Edberg with Andres Jarryd in doubles. In the opening singles match Smid lost easily to Mats Wilander in three sets 5:7, 5:7, 2:6. Everybody believed, however, that Lendl would even out the score to 1:1 by overcoming Sundstrom.

There was a relatively large entourage with us in Bastad – media men plus other individuals like Ivan's father. Why Bolardt was there I have no idea... The fairly slow clay convenienced Sundstrom, who had achieved some excellent results on such surface, for instance in Monte Carlo, where he reached the finals. He was a player who could hold long exchanges and also knew how to pass his opponent at the net. Ivan was leading 6:4, 6:3, 3:0 and at 40:0 had three gamepoints to be 4:0 ahead. Sundstrom dropshotted him, Ivan took off after it and could have played it anywhere in the court but chose to dropshot him back; Sundstrom ran it down and won the point; the match turned around and Lendl lost the remaining three sets 3:6, 1:6, 1:6!

When the turning point occurred I realized that Ivan was strained. He cursed, he mentioned the passport problems, his concentration and patience were gone; from that moment on he was close to impossible to coach.

At 3:0 in the third set Lendl was up 40:0. Unfortunately he did not turn the fourth game in his favor and at that moment the challenge visibly started to break down our player. In the first two sets both players maintained long rallies from the baselines. Both players played cautiously, each waited for the other's mistake and did not take the risk of changing the rhythm. Why were they both so cautious? Because the second team point was at stake! In the first two sets Lendl showed how unfailingly he took on that responsibility to defend the second point and won them not only by overcoming his opponent but himself too. Even though he did not possess the best Davis Cup performance day he flashed his most reliable weapons – the serve and forehand. In the fourth set, however, Sundstrom caught on and everything he touched won him a point, while Lendl was committing one mistake after another. It was almost hard to believe how a world class player was able to allow his game slip away. Sundstrom gained confidence, he was fast and he won the forth set and then turning the second match point into the victorious fifth set he won the match. Ceskoslovensky sport – Czechoslovak press

So, instead of a tied score at 1:1 Czechoslovakia was down 0:2. "Unfortunately, one can lose a match even with a big lead," said disappointed Lendl when so many people accused him of not delivering his best effort.

The live television transmission was commentated by Jan Slepicka and Igor Teleky. Our phone suddenly rang in Bastad. Tomas Smid answered it and a moment later related to us in consternation that Slepicka was bad-mouthing Ivan and was creating an exaggerated inflated story.

The following day Smid and Slozil lost their doubles match in a very unfortunate manner. They won fast and easy the first two sets; then at 6:2, 7:5, 1:6, 5:3 Slozil was serving for the match. Up until that game he always won his serve but.... The Swedes won the important fourth set 10:8 and they dominated the fifth – 6:2. On the closing day the Swedes dispatched us with finality. Wilander beat Lendl 6:3, 4:6, 6:2 and Sundstrom defeated Smid twice 6:4. The Czechs returned home with the unpopular "5-zip" score.

The media criticized the defeat. There were opinions relating to poor preparation and that Lendl did not fight. The leadership of the CUPES disagreed with the chairman of the Tennis Federation Ing. Suk who maintained that "no player ever gave up fighting."

It wasn't written anywhere that we should defeat Sweden on their home turf; it was a very difficult match. But the atmosphere in Prague was merciless: Lendl "threw in the towel! Perhaps he was glad that we lost."

It is my opinion that in the fourth and fifth sets Sundstrom played in a way that really bothered Lendl. Perhaps Lendl could have won a couple of games more if he persevered and didn't allow that fourth game point in the third set bother him, but he was broken after that drop shot. In addition, his psyche had been eroded by the unresolved negotiations about his passport and emigration status.

Upon our arrival at home I stood behind Ivan. I proclaimed the reports in newspapers as untrue and I appealed to the journalists to recognize that the partnership Wilander – Sundstrom is possibly the strongest doubles in the world and the Swedish team might win the entire Davis Cup competition that year. And they did! In the finals they defeated the team of USA made up of John McEnroe, Jimmy Connors in singles, and the doubles team John McEnroe – Peter Fleming 4:1! And the one point that the Americans achieved they won after being down 3:0!

In the wake of the Bastad disaster Antonin Himl sprang at me mandating to fire Lendl from the team because he did not show interest in representing it. I opposed that decision since he was one of the best players in the world then. What was the point of it?

"You are the captain! If you don't agree with his dismissal then you must explain yourself in the newspapers. The entire nation is against you."

So this is what Slepicka's television commentary stirred up. I sensed that Himl was infuriated. Rude pravo published an article "The Impact of Representing One's Country," in which I stood up for my players.

I tried to defend my team because, simultaneously, I was defending Czech tennis. I had a feeling that somebody was interested in disturbing not only our tennis harmony but also

Himl and his position. Ultimately, the ministry double-crossed Himl in setting up a meeting between Lendl and the minister Vajnar and then canceling it...

For the longest time I believed that Lendl's emigration status would be resolved but, in the end, I realized that the government intended to destroy Himl as a chairman of the Czechoslovak Union of Physical Education and Sport via the "case" Lendl.

The chief of our top quality athletes Antonin Bolardt traveled around the country and organized debates through which he condescended upon Himl's shortcomings: he is weak in leadership, the athletes do as they please.

It is my honest belief that Antonin Himl was one of the best chairmen I ever knew. Naturally, there were some weaknesses but I can't name many. In the early 1980s he was one of the first to sign the anti-doping program; in 1984 he sharply criticized the boycott of the Olympic Games in Los Angeles. He was not a political figure but rather he had profound knowledge of problems related to athletics; sports were his life around the clock. He stro-

Ivan Lendl with his first Grand Slam trophy at Roland Garros 1984. He won from two sets down 3:6, 2:6, 0:3 over John McEnroe. He dominated here again beating two Sweds: in 1986 won over Mikael Pernfors and in 1987 over Mats Wilander.

ve for success and inspired go-getter atmosphere among the players.

He often took the athlete's troubles upon himself. I remember when our national soccer team played a game and he asked me: "Jan, what is your opinion about Antonin Panenka? Do you think that even though he is in Rapid Vienna he could still play for our national team?"

"Why not?"- I asked

"Well, the soccer association keep upholding that he can't fit the team since he plays in Vienna; that he should not play on the national team. The coach wants him, but the association is against it saying that the players oppose it."

"Mr. Chairman, what kind of nonsense is that? Panenka is of such soccer caliber that any national team would grab him! The team should be grateful to have a team-mate who knows how to pass the ball, has great game-sense, and on top of it is a thinker."

But, he carried on: "They say that once Panenka plays on a foreign team he should not be allowed to play on our national team." - "Look how it is in Poland; Boniek plays for Juventus, Lato for AC Milan and, simultaneously, they both represent the national team. And how well!" That was how I managed to sway him; two days later I opened the newspapers and read the headlines: "Panenka will represent us as the only compatriot on the national team."

I also remember Vera Caslavska, who signed "2000 words" in 1968; as a punishment imposed by the authorities she was condemned for many years. When she was invited to coach the Japanese gymnastics team our gymnastic association briskly refused to grant her the permission. Himl once confided in me that the Japanese ambassador continued to call him and unceasingly asked for Caslavska to be allowed to travel to Japan.

"What do you want of her here? If you let her go there she will represent our country with flying colors! Nobody in Japan knows about or understands the meaning of "2000 words" so there is nothing at stake."

His eyes popped out and a week later I read in the press that Vera Caslavska would coach the Japanese team.

What he said about Jan Kodes
Ivan Lendl

As a little boy I was a ballboy for Jan Kodes at the nationals in Ostrava, or during the league games there. I also rooted for him when he played in Rome or Paris, and I pestered my parents to find out the results of his matches. At that time one could not commonly find tennis results in the newspapers. So, as a young chap I was his huge fan. And when I started to play, we often worked out together and then went out to eat.

I was thirteen in 1973 when he won Wimbledon, and I remember clearly where I was the day he beat Metreveli – playing a tournament in Frydlant. I kept my fingers crossed tightly... Five years later I beat him in Ostrava and took over the top championship position that he had held for twelve years. I enjoy remembering that, naturally...

I don't know if Jan remembers it with as fond memories as I do, but that is part of the "ordeal" of succession in sports. He wanted to win but so did I. When I think back today I realize that the point is not who won but rather how many people came to watch. I represented the young generation; he was a Wimbledon and French champion and a long time number one in the country.

We chatted about it recently, how the audience was bursting at the seems. There were five thousand spectators while the capacity was only about fifteen hundred! I won, and perhaps that saddened him a little, but it did not change things between us. We continued playing against each other as well as along side as doubles partners.

Two years later he no longer played in the Davis Cup final against Italy in Prague, but we had still played doubles in Romania. Tomas Smid was injured, Pavel Slozil played singles. It was invaluable to have an experienced player on the team. Nobody can assess how much Jan has devoted to the team, things I wasn't even aware of. He kept the media at a distance, and when necessary he calmed his teammates. The one who plays on the court often doesn't surmise what others around him do to benefit him. Jan with his experience knew, for sure, how and when to help.

Later we saw each other usually during our Davis Cup matches, when Jan was in a position of a non-playing captain. Then my exhibition in South Africa occurred and that was blown up into a "case Lendl"...I must admit that I know very little of its background. It was in different times; today it would not have taken place. It is a pity that it ever happened. He came to see me in Luxembourg and we put together conditions of my further representation of Czech tennis in Davis Cup. I had no idea what was going on at home...

I admit that I don't know much about Jan outside of his tennis life. After all, we are a generation apart. There are fourteen years between us and we each live on a different side of the globe. But I am always happy to see him, I enjoy our talks and we reminisce, how it was then.

Ivan Lendl

One of the great tennis fans was professor Tomas Travnicek, vice-chairman of the Federal Assembly. When Jan Kodes tried to figure out how to obtain the emigrant permit for Ivan Lendl and thus favorably secure the situation for Czech tennis he also approached professor

Travnicek and asked him: "Is there an option how to bring a proper closure to "case Lendl?" And he answered that the only person who could help it was Lubomir Strougal.

I did my utmost to arrange a meeting between Ivan and the Prime Minister Strougal. In the end it was lucky that the Strougals had a villa also in Prague 6 - Hanspaulka, a short distance from us, where the Premier took his Alsatians for strolls. I don't remember exactly when they met, perhaps sometimes before Davis Cup in Hradec Kralove. I managed to have the two of them meet in my house but afterwards I felt that even Strougal could not help the cause. Voices behind the scenes let it be known that the issue was commanded by two people in power – Vasil Bilak, who had shockingly badmouthed Ivan, and the nation's president Husak, who refused to solve Ivan's application positively. For that reason finding a positive outcome to Ivan's application was close to impossible.

Lubomir Strougal and Antonin Himl, two fervent fans of tennis and sports on one side, and political and communist party apparatus led by Bilak, Fojtik, and other obstinate hardliners on the other side. Two wings and their mutual battle that was stretched like a red tape along the history of "professional" tennis in Czechoslovakia during the communist regime. It culminated when our Davis cup captain Antonin Bolardt, in a role of a chief and a leader of the pinnacle of our country's sports programs, turned around and proclaimed inexorable war. We can only speculate what might have led him to it; perhaps his enormous political ambition to spring up in the hierarchy of political functionary?

It happened some time at the beginning of the 1980s when the old Stvanice tennis club was still in existence. Himl was in the hospital Na Bulovce. Being a strong smoker he had gone through an operation to remove a lung tumor. At the same time Czechoslovak Tennis Federation was sitting down to start their board meeting and Bolardt, who was, presently, a member of the executive committee, put forth a suggestion to deal harder with statutory players. "They should hand over their prize money not only to Pragosport but also more money back to the Tennis Federation. Even more than to Pragosport."

Jan Kodes found out about the proposed suggestion with a little time in anticipation. Supposedly, it came up in the coaches' meeting and Bolardt was determined to ask for it to be approved at the executive committee meeting.

"I could not believe it! Are they trying to send us into exile or what? When I found out at the CUPES (Ministry of Sports) that the chairman Himl was in the hospital I called up his wife and asked if I could visit him in the hospital.

Antonin Himl was glad to see me. He was evidently bored in his recovery period and was eager to find out what was going on.

"Mr. Chairman, I am so sorry to bother you, but there is an tennis federation executive committee meeting tomorrow in which they'll deliberate actions against us, players. They want us to turn in more prize money; this time not only the amount to Pragosport but also an even higher percentage to the Tennis Federation. Supposedly, it is the wish of the CUPES and approved by its committee."

He looked at me in disbelief. "I can barely believe that! What nerve does he have! None of it is true. Inform all the other members that it is total nonsense. I know nothing about any changes, nobody informed me. It must be all Bolardt's work."

The next day I arrived at Stvanice and looked up Bolardt immediately: "Antonin, please, I understand that you are presenting some suggestion to the committee..."

He did not let me finish! "You know how it is; impossible to prevent it. People at the CUPES and the Communist Party made it up. Nobody can deal with all your unjustifiable money."

I responded: "We are all statutory players with contracts signed and approved by the secretariat of the CUPES – what gives you the right to change that?"

Similarly, I succeeded to talk to other members and explained to them the order of things... the "suggestion" did not get approved. It was yet another example of the insane conflict of interests between Bolardt and Himl.

SOVIETS VS. CZECHOSLOVAKIA 1985

The Czechoslovak team opened the 1985 Davis Cup competition in Tbilisi against the Soviet Union.

I appealed to Ivan Lendl in the United States numerous times but his stance towards participation in Tbilisi was definite: "There is no way I am going to Russia! I am just getting over my middle ear infection."

I argued that we were not going to Russia but to Georgia. "No no; you don't need me there; you'll win without me! I'll start playing from the next round on."

So, I made an excuse for him at the Federation and stopped pressing him. I did not want to invite additional confrontations.

Tbilisi turned out to be quite a memorable event! We arrived there on a Sunday and Cyril Suk suggested: "Kodie, (his nickname for me) let's go and check out the Hall." - It was beautiful; built under Stalin's rule. It looked more like a concert hall - all wood, beautifully decorated, carved boxes. The surface was wooden but there was no court line-ed up! Suk wondered: "Damn, where are we going to practice? This is not ready for the match!"

I called Alexander Metreveli, who was then a vice-minister of sports in Georgia: "Alex, we are here but we see no court! Where are we supposed to practice tomorrow?"

"Don't worry; by 5 o'clock tomorrow afternoon it will be ready for you."

I could not imagine how they could ready it in time but we checked into the rooms by then and another sort of problems turned up. There was no heating and the temperature outside was 10 degrees Fahrenheit! The room felt like an ice box. I raised a protest with the reception of the hotel and told them that it was impossible to stay in such conditions.

Their response was: "We have a political order – not to start the heater for the reason of conservation."

I called Metreveli again: "How are we supposed to function in this?"

"We'll try to get radiant heaters for your rooms." They brought five of them and I thought that the players and I will each get one and the rest will have to do without a heater. A new worry popped up now – the danger that something could catch fire. Tomas slept with his hat and gloves on, and scarf around his neck.

At one point we all came out into the passageway. People were gathered there and kept pointing at something. One of us called out "Look at that huge cockroach!"

Somebody from the crowd shouted: "That is a Russian, that is a Russian – kill him!" Then the housekeeper leaned over us and said: "This is not a Russian cockroach, it is French!"

In the next instant Cyril Suk came up looking a bit pale: "Kodie, I have either a rat in my room or just a mouse running around!"

I complained again at the reception and they said: "That is not a problem!" and they planted a cat in his room....

The next day we went to the Hall. Cyril Suk declared: "We must check if there is any progress with regard to the surface transformation to a tennis court; if there is no progress we'll have to file a complaint with the ITF."

There were two army trucks parked in front of the Hall and we could hear pounding from within sounding like a gun battle. We entered and could not believe our eyes. There was Supreme carpet surface laid on top of the wood. Normally, supreme must be sealed to the underlining with special adhesive belts but here – some thirty soldiers in their camouflage suits and boots were running to and fro with hammers and were banging 1¼ inch long nails into that beautiful wooden floor! Metreveli arrived a few minutes later and nonchalantly asked: "So, how is the court? Pretty good, eh?"

It was a hard to forget Davis Cup encounter. We were ahead 2:0 after the first day; Mecir defeated Konstantin Pugayev and Smid trounced Alexander Zverev – both won easily in three sets without any problems. But, Smid and Pimek lost doubles against Zverev – Leonyuk in spite of leading two sets to none and reaching several match-points. Their final score was 6:3, 6:4, 9:11, 6:8, and 5:7. Milos Mecir was in the team's 1st position and was expected to win both singles in this very challenging atmosphere.

On the third day of the encounter Mecir was winning against Zverev 6:3, 8:6 and from the start of the third set the linesman kept calling foot-faults against him, sometimes even on his second serve; that terribly demoralized him. He stood two feet behind the baseline and they still called a foot-fault!

During a change-over he sat down on his chair and asked me: "Mr. Kodes, why are they doing this to me, why? I can't carry on like this!"

"Milos, they are doing this to you on purpose; take your stance still father behind the line and persevere."

"No; I can't take this any longer."

"Hey, you must persist and I'll talk to the umpire during the break. He took a stance about ten inches behind the line and they called – "foot-fault" on his second serve! Since it was his "ad" and a game-point the score went back to deuce.

The neutral referee was from Sweden; I approached Magnusson during the break. "I can't do anything about a linesman's call!"

"But don't you see Mecir standing almost two feet behind the line?"

"I still do not have the authority to change the call from the chair."

"Ok. Perhaps you can take that linesman out of there and put somebody else in his stead; like one of you, a Swede. Then it will all be fair. If you don't do that then I'll have no other choice but file a complaint with the ITF!"

That helped!

They started the fourth set, first game, Mecir's first serve – foot-fault! The umpire turned around and called – "linesman replacement!" and installed a Swede in his stead.

During the next changeover I tried to lend him support: "Milos, now you have a neutral linesman in place; I guarantee that they won't call another foot-fault against you." And they did not! He won the fourth set 8:6 and with that we reached the decisive third point. Instead of Smid I was able to let Libor Pimek play the last match. He lost 6:8, 2:6.

They traveled to far away Ecuador for their next Davis Cup victory. The surface this time was red clay and the team arrived in their complete formation, including Lendl who turned up in timely fashion as he had promised. In the opening match Andres Gomez suffered problems with his shoulder and decided to retire from the match at 5:3 in the first set in Lendl's favor. In the second match Mecir delivered an amazing performance and crushed their second player, Raul Viver, 6:0, 6:1, and 6:3. We reached the third point in doubles when Lendl and Smid beat the team of Ycaza – Aquirre convincingly 7:5, 6:4, and 6:4. The third day matches were only best of three sets contests to finish the encounter. The 5:0 victory advanced CSSR into the semifinals against West Germany in Frankfurt.

GERMANY VS. CZECHOSLOVAKIA 1985

The German press discussed the issues of the Czechoslovak Authorities relationship with regard to Ivan Lendl for several days leading into the semifinal match. They talked about the rivalry between Becker and Lendl and in the process they depreciated the positions of Eastern countries in the hierarchy of world tennis. During the press conference following the draw there were insinuations and unpleasant questions made with regard to Jan Kodes. His reaction was very open: "If it weren't for the Eastern European countries, German tennis itself would not be at the level where it is today." He followed that proclamation with several examples - Nikki Pilic in a position of their Davis Cup team captain,

Ion Tiriac managing Boris Becker's affairs, another Romanian, Günther Bosch, Becker's coach, and Czechoslovak Richard Schönborn in the position of a German National coach. Altogether four "Easterners"!

Hearing those words the German public took offense and their attacks in the press strengthened and, simultaneously, the Frankfurter Festhalle crowd got incensed against the Czechoslovaks.

Lendl's participation with the Czechoslovak Davis Cup team was further complicated due to his shoulder problems that made it difficult for him to serve. He underwent a fairly intricate examination and about two weeks before the encounter he called Kodes to let him know that doctors would not allow him to play in the matches. At the same time, they also discussed the question of his emigration permit.

I explained to him that the issue stagnated and that Antonin Himl was unable to advance it because people around him stalled the matter. I still appealed to him to play against Germany. But I came across a lot of resistance and we had the longest serious debate that resulted in a partial agreement. He promised to play only doubles should his shoulder be able to withstand it. However, the situation changed again two weeks later. He called again and said he would not be coming to Frankfurt. In the end, he ended up coming, but it did not help the team. His parents came to see the match and they talked him into playing the doubles; however, his performance did not help to make that point.

I noticed his dejected disposition. He did not even want to come out for the opening ceremonies; every word he said indicated his disgust with the way his issue was being dealt with, or better to say – not dealt with.

Davis Cup vs. BRD at Frankfurt in 1985. From the left: capt. Jan Kodes, coach Frantisek Pala, Tomas Smid, Ivan Lendl, Milos Mecir, Jaroslav Navratil a Libor Pimek. This was Lendl´s last Czechoslovak representation.

The outcome in Frankfurt was, practically, decided after the first day. Boris Becker overcame Milos Mecir 6:3, 7:5, and 6:4 followed by, perhaps, one of the longest singles matches in the history of Davis Cup between Michael Westphal and Tomas Smid.

During practice on Tuesday before the encounter players detected that the firm that laid the rubber carpet surface had made mistakes in measurements. One of the serving courts was three feet longer. When they realized it the Germans were truly mortified and at the captains' meeting it was decided that the entire court would be redone. All that needed to be done was to lay one-half of the court anew. However, it was not accomplished. Nobody knows why. Did the organizers feel that they were running out of time? Did they want to save money or work? They only cut out a four-inch belt with the incorrectly drawn line and inserted a new green belt; they then painted the line in the correct place.

Kodes alerted the referee to possible complications and injuries. And, unfortunately, that is exactly what happened… In the fourth set of the match between Smid and Westphal, Tomas had a breakpoint to reach 5:3. He hit a passing shot that Westphal retrieved with a volley. However, he simultaneously tripped over a slightly loose belt that had been added and where an air bubble developed. Smid passed him with the next shot that he put away and should have reached the score of 5:3 in his favor.

However, the umpire decided to call for new point which was absurd in that situation since Westphal had reached the volley in a normal fashion and Smid simply put away the next shot and won that point. There was no reason to play the point over in that instance! I protested; walked over to that belt, pulled on it gently and it came off easily – exactly as I had warned them!

The court had to be repaired and it took about three quarters of an hour; the break did not benefit Tomas. He lost the repeated point and that game and the score was 4:4. I protested again to no avail! An unbelievable battle unleashed and it did not end until way past midnight. Regrettably, it was the host team that celebrated after 6:8, 1:6, 7:5, 11:9 and 17:15 (!) match score victory.

The doubles match that Becker – Maurer won against Lendl – Smid 6:1, 7:5, 6:4 signified not only the end of our participation in Davis Cup that year but also the final termination of Ivan Lendl's participation with the Czechoslovak Davis Cup team. In Frankfurt Ivan said he would not play Davis Cup unless the emigration passport case was solved by December 15, 1985. That did not happen; in fact, nothing was ever accomplished with regard to that matter!

WITHOUT LENDL

The first round of 1986 brought us to the grass courts of Calcutta, where we played against the ambitious and enigmatic team of India. Vijay Armitraj, the playing captain of the host country, declared that he would take both points; but he only wished that was true. He did not get even one. We won 4:1, only Ramesh Krishnan defeated Smid in the opening match.

At the committee meeting I made a team nomination proposal: Smid, Srejber, Slozil and Mecir. Immediately, I was attacked! "Are you crazy?" They claimed that Mecir was not playing well and should not be considered at all since he was not in good condition altogether. As a proof they held his defeats versus players that he should not have been defeated by….

The meeting intensified but Cyril Suk terminated that debate with: "Kodes is the responsible party; he wants Mecir in, so let it be! You can cut his throat upon our return!"

I took a risk. Milos played very well in practice and so I told him even before the draw that I was nominating him to play singles. He could not believe his ears!

Tomas Smid did not measure up to the excellent Ramesh Krishnan in the opening match and lost 4:6, 2:6, 5:7. Mecir got on the court for the second match of the day and I thought to myself: If this doesn't work they'll fry me at home upon return.

But Mecir demonstrated a flawless "concert" on the court in the first set and delivered his opponent a "bagel"! On grass! Vijay Amritraj just rolled his eyes in disbelief and the crowd was forced to clap also on Milos' spectacular shots. He was decimating his opponent with unbelievable returns and lobs. He was sweeping with him in such fashion that it made our players on the bench chuckle. Milos won the remaining two sets 7:5 and 6:4.

I knew that doubles was going to decide the outcome of the encounter, as was generally the case. I also knew that it was going to be a fight.

And it was! However, the team Pavel Slozil – Tomas Smid overwhelmed the Amritraj brothers 6:2, 9:11, 6:4, 6:4 playing exceptionally well in very windy conditions in a battle that was harder than the score indicated. Tomas Smid then made the decisive point on the third day when he reached the third point defeating Vijay Amritraj 3:6, 6:3, 6:1, 6:2. After the lost doubles and the first set against Smid the Indian champion looked like a child whose toys got buried in the sand. Mecir secured the final 4:1 score when he killed Krishnan easily 6:3, 6:2.

Upon our return to Prague nobody said a word; as if defeating India should have been as easy as a walk in a park. There was not even one official who would give the non-playing captain a call to say: "Well, Jan, congratulations! You sensed it well and your selection proved successful!" Nobody said anything even at the next committee meeting!

An even more difficult opponent awaited us in the quarterfinals. Yugoslavia felt very confident on their home turf in Zetra Hall in Sarajevo. And they had the right to feel that way. Their top player, "Bobo" Zivojinovic, advanced to Wimbledon semi-finals just a few days before, where he was stopped by Ivan Lendl after a five-set battle.

Czechoslovak Davis Cup team after the arrival in Calcutta, India. F.Pala, Indian official, M. Kopriva M.D, capt. J.Kodes, Pres.C.Suk, masseur F.Kratochvil, M.Srejber, T.Smid, M.Mecir and P.Slozil.

However, the very important opening match suppressed their hopes. After a fiery battle Mecir overcame Zivojinovic 6:4, 4:6, 10:8, 6:4. Kodes then gave Milan Srejber his first chance to play singles in Davis Cup competition and he defeated Bruno Oresar convincingly 6:2, 6:3, and 6:4. At 2:0 the captain took yet another risk and selected Milos Mecir next to Tomas Smid to play the doubles! And that was a good move also – the Yugoslavs Zivojinovic – Flego did not have a chance!

We dealt the Yugoslavs the merciless 5:0 and we got particularly excited about the fact that we would face the next opponents in Prague.

Should we play outside on clay? But we are playing against the Swedes! Should we then play indoors? Or in the new Tennis Center? Since it is finished we could also baptize it on the occasion of Davis Cup! - The Swedes had one great advantage: they had clay-court specialists as well as hard-court specialists. The Northerners have always had to luxury of picking from a fine stable of players good on all surfaces.

In the end, the new Stvanice Center was chosen as the venue of the encounter. After all, Mecir was a clay-court specialist and appeared in good form.

It turned out to be an oversight! In the dreary Fall weather the Swedes pulled out their trump card - Kent Carlsson, the latest clay court winner from Barcelona! He was an unbelievably amazing defensive player who overcame the nervous Mecir quite easily with long rallies while Mecir tried to attack but committed too many unforced errors.

That was an unexpected defeat for us; we counted on making that point!

In the second match the sold out Stvanice witnessed an incredible five-set battle between two offensive players who liked to charge the net; Stefan Edberg swayed it his way with a luckier finish. Srejber was leading 4:3 in the fifth but tensed up after an erroneous line call and lost 5:7!

ATP World Cup at Rochus Club Dusseldorf, Germany. In 1987 Czechoslovakia beat USA 2:1 with John McEnroe, Brad Gilbert and Robert Seguso! Above: T.Smid, M.Srejber, M.Mecir and capt. F.Pala.

Tomas Smid injected great spunk into the doubles and it inspired Mecir to deliver a spectacular performance. Unexpectedly, our team defeated the seasoned and proven doubles team of Edberg – Jarryd, 7:5, 6:2, 6:4. With that we had a glimpse of hope that the final outcome could be swayed.

The third day, it was very close to the start of the match, the Swedes claimed that Carlsson suffered from a back injury and Mikael Pernfors would play against Milan Srejber. Pernfors was a Roland Garros finalist; after beating Becker and Leconte that year he then lost to Lendl in the finals.

After winning the first set 7:5 Milan realized that he would hardly be able to succeed by constantly attacking the net because Pernfors was playing brilliantly and devastating him with precise lobs. Srejber did not yet have enough confidence in the rallies nor did he move well to resist his opponent for long. The slow court favored his opponent and Milan lost the last three sets 0:6, 2:6, and 5:7.

Czechoslovakia lost 1:4, since Edberg defeated Mecir 6:4, 9:7 in the last match when nothing could change advancement of the Swedish team. A victory baptism of the new Stvanice Center did not take place!

The year 1987 did not start out well for the Czechoslovak team. They came out in Hradec Kralove against Israel that nominated fine players, Shlomo Glickstein and Amos Mansdorf, for their team. It was impossible to predict winning points against Mansdorf in particular; he played an amazing attacking indoor type of game. The key to advancement would be, again, the result of the doubles as well as the singles games against Glickstein. Everybody was optimistic and counted on winning points from matches played by Milos Mecir. There was no surface advantage for anybody since the matches were played on Supreme rubber carpet that everybody was familiar with from world circuit tournaments. Milos, however, appeared somewhat foggy in the first opening match and lost to excellent Mansdorf easily 4:6, 2:6, 6:3, 3:6. Milan Srejber retired from his match in the fifth set at 5:7, 4:6, 6:3, 6:4, and 2:3 because of an ankle injury that had happened in the first set as a result of wrong-footing. He continued to play but the ankle condition deteriorated. And suddenly, the team score was 0:2!

The next day the team of Mecir – Smid beat Mansdorf – Glickstein after an exciting battle 6:2, 4:6, 8:6, 8:6. The last day Mecir swept worn-out Glickstein easily off the court 6:3,

Kent Carlsson surprised the Czechs with his style and the first day victory over Miloslav Mecir. His triumph was too painful since he was replaced by Mikael Pernfors on the last day of play.

6:1, 6:2. Unfortunately that was the end of our chances.

Karel Novacek, who came out for the first time, faced a very difficult task at hand: winning at 2:2 against the 27th player in the world. No miracle took place that day; Mansdorf was too experienced and too good. While Novacek gave quite some resistance he lost 3:6, 6:4, 2:6, and 0:6.

Suddenly the team of CSSR was destined to fight for its place in the World Group competition.

Stefan Edberg beat Milan Srejber, with great luck, in the fifth set.

The defeat broke me a little; I would have never defaulted in the fifth set in Davis Cup. Milan sprained his ankle already in the first set and continued with it; yes, the condition was worsening but he still won two sets against an opponent whose physical form was deteriorating. When he lost his serve at 2:2 in the fifth set he could not take it any longer. I wanted him to continue and try to play at least another game since Glickstein was visibly exhausted. But Milan started to yell at me that he was not going to destroy his ankle and become a cripple because of me. I simply could not hold him on the court any longer.

Basically, I did not succeed in persuading him and I could not reconcile with that! Do I have to beg players to play Davis Cup?

Based on my discontent due to many surrounding circumstances I approached the CUPES Chairman Himl before the July Relegation match at home with Argentina and requested to be released from the Davis Cup captainship. My wishes were met without further questions but I had to find my replacement. I recommended Frantisek Pala because I believed him to be a good conscientious successor. He hired Vladimir Zednik as a coach. Our team then defeated Argentina at Stvanice 5:0....

It is possible that my resignation came in good time also for poli-

Milan Srejber defaulted against Shlomo Glickstein due to his ankle at 2:3 in the fifth set.

tical reasons surrounding problems around Ivan Lendl. Antonin Himl was, himself, showing signs of fatigue. It came as a shock to me when he passed away suddenly and unexpectedly during a business trip to China. He had done immense amount of good work on behalf of Czechoslovak tennis.

Tennis became a political tool in the 1980s and "case Lendl" converted to a battle of political powers. One side wanted everything to be resolved; the other was fundamentally against it. My captainship took place during this era of political clashes and those weren't enjoyable times for sure. And it was not only the issue of Ivan Lendl....

Similarly, the issue of open discussion of professionalism, or participation in the Olympic Games challenged my fortitude. The governmental group was for it, the party faction was against it. I am adding two sentences with regard to Ivan Lendl. I admired his patience over a long period of time. It is great pity that things turned out the way they did; I am surprised Ivan stuck with us for as long as he did considering the way some individuals treated him and ignored him.

Pat Cash took his chance and triumphed in 1987 Wimbledon. His victory disappointed most fans in Czechoslovakia. The final score over Ivan Lendl was: 7:6, 6:2, 7:5.

I have spent over twenty years engrossed in Davis Cup; seventeen as a player, five and a half as a non-playing captain. I was the one who decided to resign. Nobody fired me, nobody offered me something else. Nobody forced me. It was purely my decision and only mine.

The 1988 Olympic Games in Seoul. Jana Novotna (left) and Helena Sukova took silver medals in doubles. The exhausting doubles final was captured by Pam Shriver and Zina Garrison from the United States with a score 4:6, 6:2, and 10:8!

Miloslav Mecir, the only player from Czechoslovakia won the gold medal at Olympic Games. In Soul he reached the finals with victory over Stefan Edberg 3:6, 6:0, 1:6, 6:4, 6:2 and there destroyed Tim Mayotte 3:6, 6:2, 6:4, 6:2.

Mecir played in his career three grand finals - all with Ivan Lendl. At 1986 U.S. and 1989 Australian Opens was defeated, but at Key Biscayne, Florida in 1987 celebrated his victory in straight sets 7:5, 6:2, 7:5. He underlined his versatility by winning another five Grand Prix titles on four different surfaces including WCT finals over John McEnroe in Dallas.

My backhand, my weapon!
remember it?

TECHNIQUE AND METHODS

The amazing achievements of a two-time Roland Garros champion, the only Czechoslovak Wimbledon champion, and one of the best players in the world in the early 1970s, were founded on hard and determined efforts. Jan learned with diligence in his youth; he later labored till the point of utter exhaustion and was willing to spill his guts out on the court in order to succeed.

He had a number of role models among the coaches who worked with him. He listened to them well, and took over from each of them something new that he assimilated into his own arsenal.

He could write a textbook on how to train tennis and become a top player. Kinograms (photo-sequences) of his strokes, particularly of his world class topspin backhand, appeared in many tennis technique manuals. The point of this chapter, however, is not to introduce Jan Kodes as a tennis professional, but rather to illustrate those, who he drew the important advice from and whose experiences he held in such esteem that he tried to make use of them for his own benefit. It contains only some observations, principles and thoughts of various coaches, tennis experts and famous players from the era of his youth, when he was still an age-group, then junior, and finally senior player that became accomplished in his own time. Nobody is ever perfect; the learning goes on and on all through one's life. Even a Grand Slam champion keeps on learning because there is always something more to improve and master.

Today's young players would do themselves a favor if they tried to learn from his self-discipline, his attitude toward tennis, and his going after set goals. Even in this day and age they would learn much from him, in spite of the fact that much time has passed since his time of glory and some may think that he is no longer "in touch".

We used to work harder for points. If I wanted to put a ball away I had to work harder to do so with my wooden racket. I had to prepare the ball, open up the rally, before I could slam it, which I had to repeat sometimes twice or three times to really win the point. The rackets that players use today are made up of various materials and titanium compositions that enable players to hit faster and with more power. On the other hand, they often commit faults because the materials allow them to hit beyond control; they allow them to take chance-shots at the expense of game strategy and tactics.

The strategy of using the opponents' weaknesses has almost disappeared; stamina has been transferred into higher explosiveness and dynamic agility. Today's game is a power game; players try to finish off the point quickly. But among the best tennis players, same as before, power is not the decisive feature; their footwork is, hitting shots on a run is, precision and placement of the balls is, swiftness to cover the court and timing is. The serve is also very important. There have always been big servers, and always will be. Today it is Roddick, some time ago it was Sampras, Ivanisevic, and Becker, and still before them Gonzales, Smith, Ashe, Tanner or our Zednik. On grass, a surface on which three of the four Grand Slams were played, a big serve is a powerful weapon. And it is still today, even though only one Grand Slam is played on grass and that is at Wimbledon.

The serve-boomers have a hard time in Paris; they have a great attack, but they lack defense and confidence in a rally that is essential for clay court play. They are unable to withstand long rallies physically and/or mentally. On fast surfaces, on which they are most successful, they do not need to be as fit. And they do not need to be technically strong either. Fast surfaces somewhat obliterates technical requirements. You have less time. The surface has a crucial significance when same level players play against each other.

Tennis is not like ice hockey that is always played on "the same" ice. Clay, concrete, grass, rubber, carpet.... Each one of these surfaces is favored by some. Lendl never conquered Wim-

bledon because he had a hard time with a low volley on his approach to the net. Sampras fell short in Paris, because he did not know how to capitalize on his "ace" serve on clay the way he did on grass and concrete. Why did Lendl, Wilander, Bruguera, or Kuerten succeed at Roland Garros? Because they were patient, consistent, and they had amazing rallies combined with terrific passing shots. They were able to use strategy to prepare the ball for a final put away.

I bow to Agassi and Santana, who won Grand Slam tournaments on all surfaces despite of the fact that they did not possess a "killer" serve. They were capable to adapt their total game to the different surfaces and they had no obvious weakness. The less weaknesses a player possesses the more chance he has to succeed on more surfaces. In important moments the basic stroke confidence and accuracy is the most significant factor that decides the outcome of a match. Laver, Rosewall, Santana, Borg, Wilander and Connors had that. It still stands that the one who botches less in crucial moments usually wins.

The new materials used to manufacture modern rackets, play their role, in my opinion a negative one. Average players turn into better players thanks to the new racquet characteristics. They play risky tennis, meaning that they finish off the rally fast; they make mistakes but they also make points. They have become a menace for the top players in the first and second rounds. It happens that an unknown qualifier, who has only a cannonball of a serve, appears from nowhere and nobody knows what to play against him. He "whacks" the ball from left and right, he takes risks, and when the game goes his way he beats two seeded players early on but he doesn't have enough finesse to win the whole tournament.

Modern rackets also permit a player not to be in a perfect stance in relationship to the ball. Unfortunately, many young players use bad form, and they blast the ball from one side to the other only with their arms. However, a player who does not have the footwork has no chance against those who do. Consider Laver, Borg, Nastase in the past, later Agassi, Hewitt, and today unrivalled Nadal, when it comes to footwork.

Czech paddle tennis during 50s and 60s...
Regular rackets for the children were not available...

So, the guaranteed recipe for success is in being a well-rounded player. In my opinion the most well rounded player of today is Roger Federer. Looking for a weakness in his game requires much scrutiny. He is well conditioned, has equally leveled brilliant basic strokes, plays with sufficient consistency as well as "bite". He can play effectively from the baseline, he knows how to move forward to the net, how to execute volleys as well as passing shots, and he hits very good serves. He is a quick focused thinker – he is strong physically as well as mentally. It is impossible to deny that success in tennis rests on aptitude and character of the player!

Let's turn back a few decades with Jan Kodes and remember all those famous as well as the nameless that helped him even in the slightest way on his journey to the absolute world tennis peak. Perhaps some present day tennis beginners will also find inspiration in the following lines.

COACHES AND ADVISORS

At grade school age I met the artist Marcel Niederle, who showed me many photographs from the rich tennis history. The next in line who I learned much from at early age was a long time member of CLTK (Czech Lawn Tennis Club) in Stvanice, Frantisek Stejskal senior, and Milos Solc, the late player and later coach of Prague's selection of talents in Klamovka. I was always keen on finding out more information so it was no surprise that I soon started reading the few books about tennis that one could find in the Czech bookstores. They were good, though there were not many, and it was not astonishing that I read them over and over again. The book "How I Can Learn to Play Tennis Sooner than Others" authored by the DC player Ing. Karel Ardelt in 1936, presented one fundamental principle that I etched into my head: "It is a grave mistake to bury your feet in the ground during the execution of a stroke. A beginner is bound to do so but it is up to the teacher to guide his pupil player to transfer the weight effortlessly from the back foot to the front during the execution of a stroke; it means to run or dance through the ball. It is not easy but very necessary. It accelerates the speed of the ball as well as the progression of the player to the net." - The next publications I read were - one by W.T. Tilden "Tennis from A to Z", which I shall refer to later, and "Paddle Tennis" by Frantisek Burianek. In the past, most players started out playing with wooden paddles learning the fundamentals, whereas today they make mini-racquets and children play mini-tennis. A mini-court is a reduced court, the net is lower, the balls are lighter and softer, and the racquets are shorter and lighter. Mini-tennis empowers even small children to practice all strokes and game play, which was impossible on a regular size court and with regular balls.

The main advantage is the fact that children have the same court perspective with regard to their height as adults do on a regular court. Can you imagine playing a game of tennis over a net at your eye level? Well, that is the case of a child on a regular tennis court.

Most children are able to play fun games after just several weeks or months of practice. That is a great motivational tool for them and it raises the likelihood that children will stick to tennis rather than desert to other sports.

As in all sports, one learns by watching others play. I largely benefited from closely observing the older and more experienced players. As a ballboy in Stvanice I learned much by watching Javorsky, Krajcik, Puzejova, Benda, Emerson, Fraser, Stolle, Bungert, Nielsen, Pietrangeli and later, as a junior player, even Laver, Rosewall, Darmon, and others. I never underestimated nor refused to listen to advice of older players. I often learned very little but even the little came in handy at some point. Some of the "immortal" sentences that I heard from their lips I remember till today.

Karel Semerad

During primary school years as well as in high school he devoted much time to me in Prague's Stvanice; he stressed hand development and wrist conditioning through playing against a wall and simultaneously working on footwork – so called "little dance".

He said: "Accuracy of placement of a ball is more important than power; when the game is not going your way never commit faults at the expense of power."

The other sentence I still remember is: "Short crosscourt shots pull the opponent out of the court and the subsequent long down-the-line shot destroys him."

Or: "Only masters can perform early backswing and contact with the ball in front of the body!"

Jan Krajcik

He worked with me during my junior years, but later emigrated.

He insisted on the depth of basic strokes and shifting of the weight into the ball. We must have played countless hours on Centre Court – figure eight drills and triangles into the mar-

Jan Krajcik playing in Davis Cup 1957.

ked targets. Each individual stroke was counted how many times it hit the target.

We did the same with serves – I "fired" balls at boxes of balls strategically placed in different areas. He taught me to be patient during baseline rallies.

Josef Caska

He coached me during the sixties and early seventies, especially after I transferred to Sparta in Stromovka. In 1965 and 1966 he was a Davis Cup coach for a short while.

Prague exhibition on May 28,1956. Jan Krajcik lost to Wimbledon Champion Lewis Hoad 1:6, 6:4, 3:6. Krajcik was top Czechoslovak at 1950.

He taught me to take over and control rallies and stressed speeding up the game in timely fashion before it is too late. He made me return aggressively and put away my opponent's serve.

"Your opponent must be afraid to make a fault on the first serve, and you have to be ready to kill the ball when returning the second serve!" (That is the way they play today but with different rackets!)

"You must not give your opponent time; don't let him catch a breath!"

Pavel Korda

He was my coach for the longest period of time. After our return from Luxemburg in December 1969 he became the National and Davis Cup team coach; he devoted his coaching time to me personally till 1975. Regular and purposeful preparation on court was aimed particularly toward physical conditioning and stamina in ball exchanges resulting in following up to the net and successfully putting the ball away.

He stressed agility at the net and had a notable merit in improvement of my volleys, low and high, and my overheads that became my significant weapon. He also helped me with physical preparation for the big matches in Grand Slam tournaments and Davis Cup competition.

He was able to psyche me up to the point of utter exhaustion even in practice.

I would like to bring up some additional players and individuals who alerted me to some shortcomings in time and without whose advice and help, most likely, I would not have achieved the top.

Frantisek Cejnar (right) with Baron Gottfried von Cramm in Berlin in 1937. Cejnar reached quarter-finals in Wimbledon 1938 and lost to Donald Budge.

Frantisek Cejnar

"You can't succeed on the court without thinking during the important moments of the game."

Milos Solc

He was the first person who brought to my attention to the importance of developing larger chest volume – push ups and exercises with spiral stretch bands that I incorporated into my daily routine.

"Inhaling and exhaling while serving and smashing the ball is a necessity!" he said.

Josef Siba

"Mostly one, who doesn't miss, wins the match!"

"By trying to go after even impossible-to-retrieve drop-shots you gain the growe for the next matches!"

Henri Cochet

One of the legendary French "musketeers" was the first who predicted at the Galea Cup that I would win Roland Garros in Paris.

"You must learn to play economically during the big matches at Roland Garros and use more of the backhand underspin. Otherwise you won't hold up physically!"

Jaroslav Drobny

He advised me: "You can't play like this on grass; are you crazy? You must get the return into the court, not boom it out! Return it anywhere into the court, and keep it low – then react to what happens next. And when he lifts it then you have a chance to do something with it! You must keep a lefthander to his backhand; it is more laborious for him on that side. Keep sending it to him there with counter-punches, and remember not to hit to his forehand while on the move, or he will pass you. You must keep altering your serve; do not let him guess where he'll receive it, make a cocktail of it, and when it comes to the point serve it into the body; that is always the safest! During crunch situations remember to play what you know how to; do not make up some rubbish! More than anything avoid making double-faults; all opponents love that!"

Jiri Parma

"Your second serve on grass has depth as well as plenty of spin; do not be afraid to follow it up to the net. Once you get to the volley you know what to do!"

Jan Kukal

In tournaments he always made me try to better myself, he wanted me to work on improvement at all times and under any circumstances. He was able to rouse me up and persuade me about the importance and necessity of perpetual progress.

"When you don't know what to do with the ball, put it away. You can do it!"

Josef Síba with Australian Jack Crawford, who won three GS events in1933! Síba was the national coach for several years.

Jiri Parma represented in DC 1956-58 and become a great coach for Martina Navratilova, who won nine Wimbledon singles titles.

BILL TILDEN – OUR FIRST TEACHER

The unrivaled king of tennis from the years after the 1st World War, Bill T. Tilden was nick-named "Big Bill." The "big" did not refer to his high physical stature; the athlete Tilden was also "big" in many other ways. Above all it was his grand personality and tennis prowess that made him "big".

He did not start playing tennis before he was fourteen and few believed that he could turn out to be but an average player. However, after several years, he accomplished winning the US Championships, thanks to his immeasurable willpower and study of other players' game. At first, he was not highly-regarded as a player, but Tilden worked very hard to improve his game. Losing for him meant more than winning because he learned from it more than from victory; self analysis of his game was his personal rule. Eventually, it paid off for him. He won six straight US titles and won fifteen Davis Cup matches in a row.

He used anything and everything to improve his game, even his unfortunate accident in which he lost the last middle finger digit on his right hand while climbing a chain link fence. Instead of his game being hampered by the injury, Tilden changed his grip and actually improved his game.

He was about six and a half feet tall, lean and lanky. At the beginning he came across as rather clumsy but through his training regimen he corrected this shortcoming and achieved remarkable speed. He carried out each stroke on the move. It seemed as if he could cover the entire court with two long steps. He mastered several styles of serving: the first, powerful cannonball serve, the customary second with strong American twist that he knew to interchange so that it bounced differently each time. He dominated with his forehand and, in his early days, hit a relatively weak slice backhand. When he recognized his backhand weakness he withdrew from competition for two years and totally redid it. When he returned he was able to hit backhand any which way – top spin, underspin, or as a flat drive. He was able to play equally well at the net and from the baseline by constantly changing the type of stroke from spin to flat, short to deep, defensive to offensive, and with that he drove his opponents totally crazy!

The power of his personality pressed his opponents into the background on and off the court. He affected his audience in the same fashion. When he lost, nobody believed he actually lost. He surpassed his opponents even at the moment of defeat, which is, perhaps, the ultimate compliment one can make about a tennis player.

Tilden did not play for the audience, he played for the game itself, and he did not care if the audience cheered for him or not. He intended to gain their respect only through his game. For that reason the public did not particularly worship him. In the years 1920 to 1926 it was almost monotonous to see him win over and over again. The spectators often applauded his opponents more. It was only when he started to lose that the audience started to recognize his greatness. He did not show even the least temper upon a defeat; on the contrary, he accentuated the merit of his opponent. And only when people realized that Tilden was able to be not only a self-assured winner but also a humble loser, did they become truly fond of him.

In his time period W.T. Tilden elevated tennis to new heights that had never before been achieved. With his writings, where he addressed tennis theory and practice and their application to on-court play, he created modern tennis. His departure to professional competition in 1931 was the greatest loss for amateur tennis.

I read Tilden's manual "Tennis from A to Z" several times and my coach, Karel Semerad, often drew my attention to it. Tilden was the first who turned tennis into science, who perfected individual strokes, and who worked out a tactical plan or strategy. He knew how to respond to each shot in three different ways, and for each attack he boasted a defense.

The one player who tyrannized him the most was the French player Henri Cochet, who hit each and every shot on the rise, which meant that he played the ball sooner, before it bounced all the way up. Today it could be compared to the game of Connors or Agassi. Tilden used only sliced backhands for a long time; he picked up a flat backhand drive later. That required a different grip, different backswing, and a new way of thinking.

I must mention here that, reversely, Ivan Lendl worked patiently on his sliced backhand, a stroke with an under-spin, without which he would not have succeeded, as he later admitted.

In essence, Tilden was a loner, who spoke of alcohol to be "poison that damages eyes, head, and breath". I wish young players would accept that as an advice and take it to heart! He favored being honest and resented cheaters; he placed honor and virtue on the top rung and perhaps for that reason he was not as vulnerable as others.

"Play tennis without fear to lose, because the game should be fun; or don't play it at all. It is no disgrace to lose! True champions are born from the pains of defeat!" Tilden's principles still hold. Today, age-group competitions boil too often with bad calls; cheating has become part of youngsters' development and sometimes even their tactical alternative!

Rene Lacoste studied Tilden and arrived at a conclusion that to beat him means, first, "to break through his way of thinking". He maintained a diary of Tilden from his individual matches. Tilden had amazing finesse in his hands; he created and improved a drop shot as part of the offensive arsenal.

He also stressed tennis psychology, and in his essays he put much thought to the strategy of the game. In addition, he elaborated on key moments of each of his matches. He determined that the most important or decisive games are the fourth, seventh, and ninth. The crucial points are at 30:15 and 15:30 and the first ball that opens up the game and can calm the player. When young John Newcombe won Wimbledon in 1967 he answered the question "where did you learn to play tennis" with: "I read Tilden's book."

Tilden believed that a match should be played "defensively with an offensive plan". The basic principle is: Do not make mistakes! "There is nothing else that throws off a player as much as his own mistakes! Each time a player sees that an important point ends up in the net or out of the court he becomes more agitated, he loses hope and his confidence that he could win the match."

It is important to interchange rotation and velocity of the ball. The outcome is more important than style, playing a beautiful stroke is sometimes ineffective. Tilden believed that ninety eight percent of players were morons! He did not hold very kindly words for the next generation with the exception of Sidney Wood. A duel is ultimately won by the player, who directs the tempo of the game and holds it through, thus imposing his own character onto his opponent – he injects his opponent with an understanding of the soon coming defeat.

I introduced here several insights from the "old" era on purpose, because their transcendence is still vivid and applicable today. It is not true that tennis is entirely different because, in that case, Andre Agassi would not have been able to shine until recently, and fifty-year-old Martina Navratilova and John McEnroe would not have won doubles tournaments on 2006 World Circuit.

Sidney Wood was the only Champion to be given a walkover in the Wimbledon final in 1931. His Davis Cup colleague, Frank Shields, had hurt his ankle. Sidney had played in Wimbledon already at the age of 15. In 1935 he was also in the U.S. finals - lost to the Aussie Wilmer Allison.

BACKHAND CHOICE?

Should we teach one-handed or two-handed backhands right from the beginning? The debate of this topic carries on among tennis experts, methodologists and coaches ever since the two-handed stroke became fashionable at the onset of Bjorn Borg's success. It is essential to mention, however, that two-handed strokes are not a novelty.

The Australian left-hander John Bromwich, a Wimbledon finalist, used a two-handed backhand already in the years between 1938 and 1950. Others came after him: Pancho Segura, Cliff Drysdale, Frew McMillan, who gripped the racket with two hands from the backhand side. Only the fair-haired Swede mentioned previously raised the popularity of two-handed backhand to the point of a fad. Let's mention a few players who emerged with or after him: Jimmy Connors, Andre Agassi, Mats Wilander, Gene Mayer, Jim Courier, Yevgeny Kafelnikov, Lleyton Hewitt, Rafael Nadal and many others...

However, nowadays two-handed backhand has become so important because young children at the age of four or five do not have the strength to carry or swing the racquet with one hand so they opt to use both hands.

When I began playing tennis "paddle tennis" was the way to start. I used an adult-like racket from the age of eight but I cut off part of the handle to shorten the racket lever, and thus lower the stress on my young arm. Today we advocate "mini-tennis" that I had mentioned before. I strongly recommend to start with a short racket because a child can control it better and both, the forearm as well as the wrist have a chance to develop and strengthen gradually.

Wimbledon champion Stefan Edberg switched to one-handed backhand late, when he reached the age of thirteen much like Tomas Smid. Though, theoretically, both types of backhand are very good, I do not believe that two-handed stroke is better than one-handed. Borg, Connors, and Agassi were rare exceptions in their footwork – as is Nadal or Djokovic of today. It was their velocity, agility, and skill that allowed them to apply the two-handed backhand in its highest measure and with it they reached their tennis climax.

I have no idea if anybody tried to find out how many two-handers out of the masses of tennis players have reached, statistically, the top rung? Perhaps the percentage is slightly higher among women. They play a slower and not so aggressive game, which gives them more time to prepare for each stroke.

In conclusion, let's remember the best players ever with one-handed backhand: Kozeluh, Tilden, Lacoste, Cochet, Gonzales, Perry, Budge, Kramer, Sedgman, Drobny, Hoad, Olmedo, Trabert, Laver, Rosewall, Emerson, Santana, and, in later years, Newcombe, Ashe, Smith, Nastase, Orantes, Panatta, Vilas, Lendl, Noah, McEnroe, Edberg, Becker, Stich, Sampras, Rafter, Kuerten, and Federer. Even the latest numbers show that the two-handed "mania" is not dominant or critical in contemporary tennis. Some players today besides Federer have excellent one-handed backhands, including Almagro, Blake, Gonzales, Gasquet, Haas, Robredo and Wawrinka. There are many other factors that influence game progression and outcome: the serve and the skills at the net, patience during the rallies on slower surfaces, reaction time and quick decision-making during the point interchange. Physical and mental strengths are, undoubtedly, crucial.

JAN KODES' STROKES

In the 1970s Jan Kodes' stroke technique appeared often and was discussed among tennis experts in foreign publications. Particularly his passing shot from the backhand side or his topspin backhand drive and approach shots, as well as the serve return, volleys and overheads, were all presented in newspaper articles and in periodicals.

Here we present two examples from foreign publications that portray kino-grams especially of his backhand strokes, volleys, and half-volleys.

Glasbrenner and Reetz: "Perfect Tennis Training Tips for All", published by BLV Sport, Verlagsgesellschaft, Munich-Bern-Vienna:

"Tennis Strokes and Strategy" published by Simon and Schuster, New York.

That publication was presented with instruction series by: Jack Kramer, Margaret Court, Ken Rosewall, John Newcombe, Don Budge, Tony Trabert, Roy Emerson, Rod Laver, Arthur Ashe, Fred Perry, Vic, Seixas, Chris Evert, Pancho Segura, Cliff Richey, Jan Kodes, John Alexander, Tom Okker and Marty Riessen. Besides others it contains a chapter by Jan Kodes "What You Need to Know about Returning a Serve." Since that stroke was Jan Kodes' biggest weapon beside the topspin backhand we decided to discuss it more in detail.

Jan Kodes: „To reach the ball by the net at such a difficult position and be able to hit an drop-volley is almost always a winning shot, specialy on the grass courts..."

What you need to know about the Serve Return

The return of serve is, most likely, the most neglected stroke in one's practice schedule. When you realize, however, that you use it fifty percent of the times when you play shots coming from your opponent you conclude that it is the second most important stroke in a match! Strategically, it is a very important shot that you can plan ahead and choose from several variations depending on the situation! It is a bit like playing chess because you, as well as the server, have enough time to prepare, set up, and predict the next movement as well as the outcome that may or will follow. You just have to accept the fact that the one thing you cannot foresee is the type of serve that the server will use and thus what kind of a shot you'll be confronting. From the point of view of the receiver it is just as important to vary the type of return and thus make things more difficult for the server. That way neither player knows what he might expect throughout the match.

Basic Stance

When receiving a serve it is essential to assume a correct basic stance, or so called "ready Position," a position that doesn't really exist! Everything depends on your choice of a returning stroke; which one suits you better – forehand, or backhand, and how do you know to cover the space of your weaker stroke? You must cover the side of the weaker stroke better; at the same time you must take into account whether you are receiving the serve in the deuce court or on the add side, and whether your opponent is a lefthander or a right-hander because all those variants affect the bounce of the ball.

If you know your opponent you can predict his play and attempt to put away the return. However, in general, it is a good strategy to return the serve to" open up" the rally and concentrate on the server's next move - read how well he handled the return. Does he choose to be defensive and stays in the back court, or does he choose to attack and comes to the net? Those facts should determine the type of serve return you pick out of the arsenal of different options.

Surface Quality

Surface quality is a very important factor when deciding how to return a serve. If the surface is slow and the opponent tends to stay back you should try to hit a deep return either down

John Bromwich, 1948 Wimbledon finalist, 1939 and 1946 Australian Open Champion. Captured altogether thirteen doubles Grand Slam titles. This kinogram reveals that the precision of his two-handed backhand resulted from the shoulder-turn, timely back-swing and contact of the ball in front of the body.

Aggressive backhand drive performed by Ken Rosewall. These frames show the evident early backswing, shoulder turn and weight shift into the ball followed by an approach to the net.

the line, or crosscourt. On fast surfaces, when an opponent attacks and runs to the net you must try to hit a low shot, possibly crosscourt. It is very difficult for the opponent to hit a good volley from such position. And for you too, this situation is difficult but by playing the ball very low anywhere in the court you give yourself a chance to create a condition that may give you an opportunity to hit a passing shot with the next play. At any rate, even before your opponent serves, you should be clear about the different alternatives you might play in case that your opponent returns your return.

Predicting your Opponent's Serve

When you have a definite plan you can concentrate on your opponent's serve. You try to "read" his intentions; where will he serve to - into your forehand or backhand, so that you start the backswing with anticipation, which will help you; even one hundredth of a second will better your chances considerably! If your opponent is a total stranger you must observe him patiently during the first few games and try to uncover his tactics. Watch closely his ball toss while serving. Concentrate primarily on the ball, not on the opponent, which is the most common mistake of less experienced players! As soon as the ball leaves the opponent's hand follow the ball and don't take your eyes off until the rally is over.

Correct Racket Grip

Each player has a different opinion about a racket grip when awaiting the serve. I used continental grip with a very slight modification. But players, who change grip, must make the decision about which type of grip to use in time. It is necessary to make the change during the backswing but if you do not start the backswing with enough anticipation, especially on a fast surface, then you do not have a chance to return the serve.

Striking the Ball in front of the Body

The key to a successful serve return is well-known: hit the ball on time and in front of the body. The racket must contact the ball quickly, and that will be possible only if you react fast and do the backswing in time. Your reaction depends on your body's balance, your position and your ability to move towards the incoming ball.

Many players shift their weight back, which reduces the speed of their movement towards the ball. I used to bounce up at the moment of my opponent's serve instead of leaning forward on the balls of my feet; with that I made sure I was on my toes. In order to hit the return in front of the body and in time one needs to shorten the backswing a little, which does not mean to shortchange the follow through that is very important. It is essential to keep your eyes on the ball the entire time; and if you shift your weight into the ball at contact then your return has enough power, and with that you have a chance to hit a winner.

It is not possible to return every type of serve with the same return. You'll be forced to adapt to a high bouncing second serve like the ones of Edberg or Gorman. You must either back up a coup-

Guillermo Vilas did not hit only top spin shots but, when necessary, he also used backhand with under-spin rotation.

Flat Backhand Drive with a slight Topspin

My most formidable weapons were the baseline backhand drive with a slight top-spin, backhand return and backhand passing shot. The timely backswing and significant shoulder-turn were a premise to successful disguise of the intended stroke direction – cross-court or down-the-line. When the ball was struck in front of the body one could send it in either way. Coordinated footwork and weight transfer into the ball were a must.

Low Backhand

This sequence points out that the ball was struck with a slight delay when it was already descending. It was imminent to get the head of the racket under the ball in time and that necessitated lowering the center of gravity and extending a longer follow-through. Efficient footwork aided the successful completion.

Backhand Drop-shot

It is possible to deceive an opponent when approaching a backhand and surprise him with an unexpected "drop-shot". In such an instance shortening the follow-through at the right moment is necessary. If it is performed with precision it is sure to produce a winning point.

Backhand Volley

I played it with a continental grip. Motion towards the ball starts with a short step with the left foot and simultaneous should turn and reaching out; elbow is slightly flexed. Racket head adjusts to the level of the incoming ball and at the moment of contact weight is transferred from the back foot (left) to the front (right). It means to step into the ball and strike it way ahead of the body with the wrist nice and firm.

Forehand Volley

During preparation for the stroke a sideway position is essential; it starts the movement towards the ball with a short right-foot step. That initiates a backswing with the elbow slightly bent. Racket head is above the firm wrist. During the contact with ball weight is transferred from back to the front foot in order to give the stroke more force.

Forehand Drop-volley

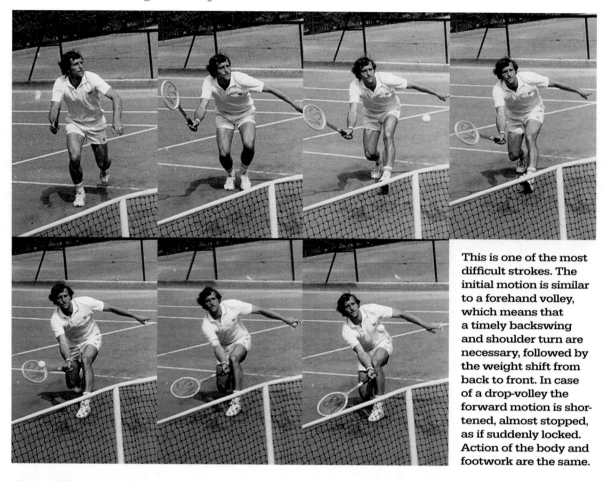

This is one of the most difficult strokes. The initial motion is similar to a forehand volley, which means that a timely backswing and shoulder turn are necessary, followed by the weight shift from back to front. In case of a drop-volley the forward motion is shortened, almost stopped, as if suddenly locked. Action of the body and footwork are the same.

Smash

A vital "put-away" shot. The most important point to remember is to react quickly and position yourself under the ball that is up high. It requires fast footwork. Left hand points up to the ball and the eyes follow the course of the ball. The backswing must be well-timed in order to be able to reach up for the falling ball. It is advantageous to shift the weight from back to front while jumping up to strike the ball.

Backhand Smash

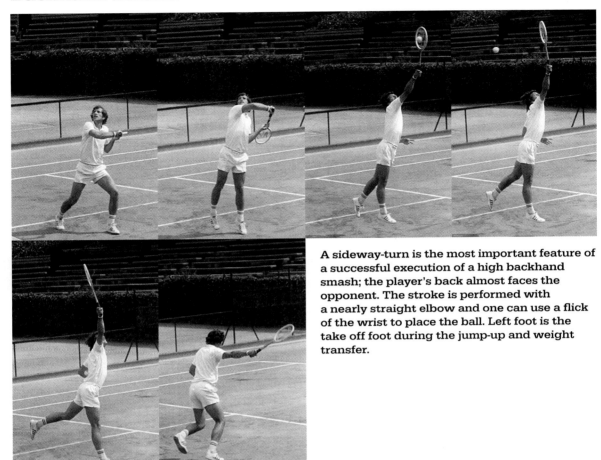

A sideway-turn is the most important feature of a successful execution of a high backhand smash; the player's back almost faces the opponent. The stroke is performed with a nearly straight elbow and one can use a flick of the wrist to place the ball. Left foot is the take off foot during the jump-up and weight transfer.

le of steps, or step into it shortly after the bounce and hit it on the rise before the top spin draws you out of the court. It is a constant battle for time and space, especially on fast courts. On slower clay, where your feet as well as your racket arm have more time to prepare, you have many more possibilities to show the serve-sluggers the power of your return, and make them feel it.

Alternating Returns

It is very important to vary your returns during a match. In so doing you put your opponent under psychological stress. The server must feel constant pressure and mustn't anticipate what will come next. On slower clay, for instance, when your opponent often stays back, it is a good idea to play a surprising drop shot from time to time, or run around your weaker stroke, like a backhand for example, and attempt to hit a forehand winner. An element of surprise disrupts your opponent's concentration and he starts making errors in situations in which he had not faulted before. It turns into a battle of nerves especially during prolonged games. In order to learn to play successful returns one also has to engage in player intelligence, strategy, self-confidence, and experience.

In conclusion, I would like to present four basic principles that will help you keep high percentage of successful returns if you stick to them:

1. Watch the ball well from the moment when your opponent contacts the ball.
2. Shift your weight into the ball and strike the ball with enough control and power right in front of the body.
3. Remember that the foremost rule is to get the ball in play. Maintain a high percentage of returned serves, do not try to kill a ball unreasonably – that would lead to a high number of unforced errors.
4. Concentration, a fighting spirit and patience are essential for a successful serve return.

Jaroslav Drobny's Left-handed Serve

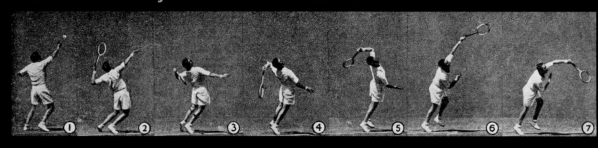

Pancho Gonzales' Right-handed Serve

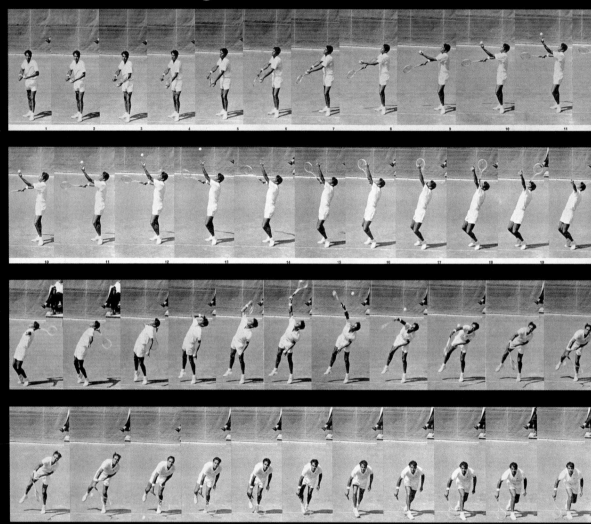

The serve was not my most formidable weapon though, I trust, I won many critical points thanks to good serve placement. At the same time it is for sure that if somebody had developed my serve well right from the beginning and perfected it further with time I might have won a few more big tournaments. The serve is one of the most challenging strokes, as it involves coordination of many movements. I chose deliberately kinograms of two excellent servers, one left-hander – Jaroslav Drobny, and one right-hander - Pancho Gonzales, who I played against in Madison Square Garden in New York. I was astonished by the impression of lightness that his serve exuded; it was effective not only for its power but also its precision and placement. Many servers, me included, tire with each serve and that may affect the outcome of our matches.

The kinograms show clearly the good toss, body turn and reach, the loop drop and acceleration from it, as well as the weight transfer of the entire body up and over the ball. The ball is struck in front of the body which permits the eyes to follow it even during the follow through. Wrist action, or snap, aids success of the serve; it controls the rotation and placement of the ball.

398

WITHOUT A RACKET

Arthur Ashe

Pete Sampras

ABOUT DOUBLES

In the last few years doubles has often been pushed into the shadows of singles, and it became almost customary that many top players would not enter doubles on the world circuit, or they would do so infrequently. Some players choose not to play doubles because they do not favor net-play or they feel uncomfortable playing frequently at the net.

There are fewer spectators watching doubles finals, yet a good doubles match is almost more fun watching than singles that sometimes can be monotonous. I am convinced that a young player who also plays doubles improves his singles game because he develops an attacking game that is essential for overall tennis mastery.

Proficiency in doubles is also important for team championships like Davis Cup. Tennis federations or team captains often persuade their best singles players to play the important and decisive doubles matches. Such examples would be the final Davis Cup match in 1975, when Bjorn Borg was asked to play in Stockholm, or in 1980, when Ivan Lendl played against Italy in Prague, or the finals in Moscow in 1995, when even Pete Sampras played for the US! At present time it is Federer, the world's number one player, who repeatedly comes out to play the doubles.

In spite of the fact that these players do not normally play doubles, or they do only sporadically, they are still able to sway favorably those important matches particularly thanks to their sharp returns or exceptional service. As long as they win the team point it does not seem to matter that a doubles team put together this way, just for that one match, doesn't show much team-work.

Playing a good doubles game requires great artistry in terms of team-work and strategy. Many players became famous just for that: Bob Hewitt – Frew McMillan, Peter McNamara – Paul McNamee, John Alexander – Phil Dent, Scott Davis – David Pate, Jacco Eltingh – Paul Haarhuis, Todd Woodbridge – Mark Woodforde, Ken Flach – Robert Seguso, Rick Leach – Jim Pugh, Bob Bryan – Mike Bryan, Daniel Nestor – Mark Knowles and others.

John Fitzgerald and Tomas Smid won two Grand Slam titles: US Open in 1984 and Roland Garros in 1986. In both finals they beat Edberg – Jarryd.

I would also like to mention some excellent doubles players, who earned Grand Slam titles with a variety of partners, and who were picked by top singles players as partners: Jacques Brugnon, Bill Talbert, Adrian Quist, Ken McGregor, Gardnar Mulloy, Ken Fletcher, Owen Davidson, Marty Riessen, Peter Fleming, Bob Lutz, Sherwood Stewart, Wojtek Fibak, Anders Jarryd, John Fitzgerald, Leander Paes and others.

From among the Czech players who won Grand Slam titles in doubles are the following: Jaroslav Drobny, Tomas Smid (2), Petr Korda, Cyril Suk, Daniel Vacek (3), Martin Damm, Lukas Dlouhy (2). It is interesting to note that they all won the titles with foreign partners! Jaroslav Drobny, Jan Kodes, Tomas Smid, Pavel Slozil, Petr Korda, Karel Novacek, Jiri Novak, David Rikl, Pavel Vizner, Petr Pala and Radek Stepanek reached doubles finals.

Peter Korda and Stefan Edberg (left) after their doubles victory in the 1996 Australian Open.

Czechs triumphant in Doubles Teams

Jaroslav Drobny – Lennart Bergelin (Roland Garros 1948), Tomas Smid – John Fitzgerald (US Open 1984, Roland Garros 1986), Petr Korda – Stefan Edberg (Australian Open 1996), Cyril Suk – Sandon Stolle (US Open 1998) Daniel Vacek – Yevgeny Kafelnikov (Roland Garros 1996-97, US Open 1997), Martin Damm – Leander Paes (US Open 2006), Lukas Dlouhy – Leander Paes (Roland Garros 2009).

Ken McGregor and Frank Sedgman from Australia were the only team in tennis history who achieved a Grand Slam in doubles in one calendar year in 1951.

Leander Paes and Martin Damm kissing the 2006 US Open trophy after their victory over Jonas Björkman and Max Mirnyi.

The most doubles grand slam titles were won by John Newcombe – Tony Roche (12), Todd Woodbridge – Mark Woodforde (11), Adrian Quist – John Bromwich (10), Neale Fraser – Roy Emerson (7), Ken McGregor – Frank Sedgman (7), and John McEnroe – Peter Fleming (7).

One of the outstanding doubles players, the American Bill Talbert, who won the US Open four times, later created ostensible "Ten Tennis Commandments" that doubles players should stick to:

1. Play as a team, think as a team
2. Doubles is won at the net; in any situation try to come closer to the net than your opponent
3. Play high percentage of first serves
4. The effectiveness of the first volley is related to the preceding serve
5. Try to foresee your opponents' intentions
6. Execute the highest possible percentage of low returns
7. The player coming up to the net must guard the center of the court
8. Cover the court together, move at the same level
9. Play forcefully; weak volley results in a loss of a point
10. Meaningful lobs over the server's partner weakens your opponents' aggressiveness

Daniel Vacek reached three Grand Slam doubles titles with Yevgeny Kafelnikov from Russia. They accomplished their victories at 1997 US Open and twice at Roland Garros in the years 1996-1997.

GAME PSYCHOLOGY

There are many manuals on psychology and how to react to different situations during a difficult match. One could always discuss these topics with individual authors of the manuals, or with coaches and other players, nevertheless, I would like to introduce a few of my own observations based on many years of my particular experiences on tennis courts worldwide.

First of all, I always tried to concentrate on myself during the matches – meaning that I focused on my play, I wanted to have a feeling of satisfaction

Cyril Suk was one of the best Czech doubles players. He took the 1998 US Open doubles title with Sendon Stolle from Australia over Mark Knowles and Daniel Nestor. In Wimbledon he won two mixed-doubles titles with his sister Helena in 1996 and 1997.

with my performance. It did not really matter to me who was on the other side. I wanted to play my game and not adjust it to my opponent's. I tried to stick to seemingly simple principles that turned out immensely significant in tight moments of some important matches: you alone must make the critical points! It was altogether different if I played against an opponent with whom I had played many times and we knew well each other's moves. In that case, I played some points contrary to the usual, in order to surprise my opponent or to break up his anticipation.

Weaknesses of some players are often known but they become obvious gradually as the match progresses, under pressure in critical moments, or during the pivotal points that influence development of the victorious sets.

I PLAYED WITH THEM...

He met them many times during his career. They fought each other as juniors in Galea Cup, and later in Davis Cup, they battled in Grand Slam tournaments, as well as in Grand Prix or Masters or in the Swedish King's Cup... During their time they were among the best not only in their respective countries but in the world. Thanks to his tennis artistry, training diligence, willpower, discipline, and desire for fair combat Jan Kodes broke into their ranks. In spite of having reached the world peak he still continued to learn. It was exactly from them – the world's best players that he drew more proficiency from. Even the top player knows that there is always space to improve further.

Arthur Ashe
(*July 10, 1943, Richmond, USA, died NYC, February 6, 1993)

In his time he was, possibly, the biggest crowd favorite! First of all because he was black, secondly, because he won the first US Open at Forest Hills as an amateur playing against players that *included all the professionals. He was a natural grass-court player who grew up on the turf and thus played good two levels better on grass than on other surfaces. When playing on clay in Paris he complained that it was slippery. His biggest weapon was his serve that he knew to place with unbelievable precision. It was very difficult to read his physical condition. He did not allow anyone to recognize any change and impressed his opponents and spectators with absolutely the same upfront at the beginning of the match as in the fifth set.*

Arthur was an exceptional player, and an excellent speaker, one of the most intelligent players I have ever met. He was also a thinker off the court, very much concerned with the world around him. Contrary to many, he was capable of brilliantly verbalizing the issues on his mind, without any stammers or papers in his hands. He became a role model for the blacks of the United States similarly to Cassius Clay.

Once, I caught him in the reading room devouring all kinds of articles from the many world magazines there. He looked almost bothered when they called him to play, as if someone just interrupted his most important pursuit.

I always thought that he would become a politician when his tennis career came to an end. He was one already at the time when our paths crossed on the world tennis circuit. It is unfortunate that fate dealt him otherwise – he fell gravely ill and passed away at the age of fifty.

Björn Borg
(*June 6, 1956, Södertalje, Sweden)

An unbelievably tenacious warrior who never let anybody know how he felt. One could not infinitely resist the consistency of his strokes during long rallies. High bounces of his top spins were interchanged by lethal forehand drives. A combination of such forehand and consistent precise two-handed backhand passing shot in addition to a cannon-ball serve elevated him to the status of immortality among the best players of all time. He had the fastest and most agile legs of all tennis players. Perhaps only Connors and Nastase came close to him in this characteristic. He was physically and mentally strong even in the most critical moments of his matches. His patience in the long rallies had no limits. He gained fame for that particularly after his matches with Guillermo Vilas, who, also, built his success on baseline play consistency.

Jimmy "Jimbo" Connors
(*September 2, 1952, Belleville, Illinois, USA)

If Nastase was born to be the most talented tennis player among the Europeans, then Connors was blessed with such talent in America. A left-hander with a well-rounded technical arsenal he grew up on hard surface courts which led him to concentrate on refining his basic strokes. He hit balls on the rise and devastated his opponents with precise deep returns of serve. His passing shots were hard because his quick feet facilitated early preparation. He knew how to come up to the net at the most opportune moment and finish off the point with a volley.

He was among the best already as a junior. I played against him several times but never managed to defeat him. Our matches were merciless several-hours long battles that pulled spectators out of their seats. We broke each other's serves and we fought to win our own in long exchanges that generally decided the outcome of the match. His combat engagement throughout the match was admirable. Like I, he finished matches almost totally spent, he fought till utter exhaustion. Sometimes I regret that we never had a chance to size each other on clay, at Roland Garros in Paris; Jimmy reached the semi-finals four times there – in 1979, 1980, 1984, and 1985. When he reached the semi-finals at US Open in 1991 at the age of thirty-nine the media asked him why was he still playing? He answered: "I enjoy the drudgery! And the spectators like it too!"

Mark Cox
(*July 5, 1943, Leicester, England)

A left-hander and a number one British player in the years 1969-1972. It is notable that he finished his studies at the University of Cambridge! He was equally proficient on all surfaces though the faster ones suited him better. He brought fame to himself when, as the first amateur, he defeated Gonzales and Emerson at an Open Tournament in Bournemouth in 1968! That later aided the proceedings between ITF and the professionals about the future of tennis. He played Davis Cup for Britain in 1967, 1968, 1969, 1973, 1978, and 1979; in 1978 he helped Britain to the final He advanced to the quarter-finals in the Australian and the US Open. He and Bobby Wilson beat Ron Holmberg and Charlie Pasarell in an epic doubles in the U.S. Indoor Championships, the longest on record! The match of 144 games that lasted over six hours!! Mark hit hard basic strokes, and, for a left-hander, he had an excellent backhand return. However, in crucial moments he often hurried too much and some time made mistakes.

Roy Emerson
(*November 3, 1936, Black Butt, Queensland, Australia)

One of the best physically conditioned players of all times, the last great champion of amateur tennis era. He dominated on all surfaces and won all Grand Slams several times. His strokes were powerful, particularly his exceptional serve returns. He was very athletic, quick at the net; he personified a tiger in a rink. Many considered him the best doubles player of all times. He won practically with all partners, reaching sixteen Grand Slam titles in doubles! He trained more than any other player at any time and with whomever. Running and frog-jumping during tournaments was his routine. His serve was not anything special but his net-play and low and high backhand volleys can never be forgotten.

Jaime Fillol
(*June 3,1946, Santiago de Chile, Chile)

An aggressive tennis player who knew how to handle the game on all surfaces. He played his baseline strokes immediately after they bounced. He badgered many world class tennis players particularly with his aggressive approach shots resulting in superior net play. His high bouncing second serves "a la" Edberg or Gorman created much problem for many of his opponents. Before he joined professional tennis he gained much game experience at the University of Arizona in the United States.

Zeljko Franulovic
(*June 13, 1947, Yugoslavia)

He was my frequent doubles partner and a close friend. A fine chap with the happiest tennis temperament I have ever seen. He was an ever-smiling champ from Split. For the most part we called him "Franulka". He did not get frazzled even in the thickest of battles and carried on with good humor spitting out funny remarks like a conveyor belt. He never searched for excuses. When he lost – his opponent was simply better... If he won – his opponent probably had a bad day...

On the court we got along really well. When I beat him in the finals of Roland Garros many people did not think he was much of a player. But that was only an illusion. His topspin forehand forced his opponents into the corners which resulted in tiring and losing stamina. He was somewhat weaker from the backhand side if his opponent pressed him with power. "Franulka" was truly a good tennis player, I'd say more unpleasant as an opponent than possibly Nastase. Ilie used to have his ups and downs whereas Zeljko kept his standard of play constant and fought under any circumstances. Thanks to that he often won even seemingly lost matches. Similarly to the game of Ken Rosewall or Tom Okker his game also impressed one with total lightness. His rise and best years were affected by his shoulder operation.

Vitas Gerulaitis
(July 26, 1954, Brooklyn, NY, USA- died September 17, 1994, NY)

One of the few Americans who were able to succeed even on the clay courts at Roland Garros. He was a well liked player with great footwork on the court. His fast light-footed movement reminded me of the "Flying Dutchman" Tom Okker. His strongest weapons in his tennis arsenal were his talent, agility, perception and reaction. He was able to speed up the game; he played the baseline strokes on the rise with a very short backswings and his backhand under-spin approach shot was a fearsome weapon. Thanks to his agility and quick reaction time he was able to volley effectively at the net. He nullified his opponents' passing shots due to his intuitive actions that won him great many important points in tough situations. He was one of very few of my peers who succeeded in adapting his game to any surface. He won the Australian Open on grass in 1977 and reached two other Grand Slam finals. On red clay in Paris he eliminated Connors in the semis in a five-set duel but lost to Borg. At home, in Flushing Meadows, NY, he then wiped out the 1979 Wimbledon finalist, Tanner, but lost to his friend, John McEnroe, in the finals. He also won Wimbledon doubles with Alex Meyer. He was extremely popular among players but, regrettably, he was also one of few players who met a tragic death.

Andres Gimeno
(*August 3, 1937, Barcelona, Spain)

Andres was nicknamed the "tennis professor". He was an excellent tactician with a phenomenal touch for the ball. He was able to bring his opponent to despair with his precise and unreachable drop shots and lobs. He was a respected member of Kramer's professional group. When I meet him today he still thanks me for letting him win Roland Garros in 1972 when he was thirty five. He whipped my conqueror, Patrick Proisy, in the finals there, when he ran him almost to death in front of the sold out stadium. Today he is a tennis commentator for Spanish television.

Andres Gomez
(February 27, 1960, Guayaquil, Ecuador)

Another fearsome and smart left-hander with a very good serve, who grew up on clay courts of South America. His first serve and his forehand were often impossible to retrieve. In rallies he knew how to interchange top-spin and under-spin shots in order to throw-off his opponent's game and prepare the ball to approach the net, where he applied vehement and sharp volleys. He was able to execute unreachable backhand drop-shots with remarkable precision. He proved to be one of the world's best clay-court players when he won at Roland Garros in Paris defeating Muster from Austria and the favored American, Andre Agassi, in the finals. He won a number of other significant clay-court tournaments as well as two Grand Slam doubles titles at Roland Garros and US Open.

Ricardo "Pancho" Gonzales
(*May 9, 1928, Los Angeles, CA, USA, died Las Vegas, July 3, 1995)

A legend with many tales. 1948 and 1949 US Championships Singles champion. A player who dominated even among the professionals. He won the US professional championships eight times in the years between 1953 to 1959, and in 1961. I played him only once in Madison Square Garden. He was forty one and today I would most likely compare him to "old" Pete Sampras. He played aggressive straightforward strokes; precise, hard, contacted with ease in front of the body. His serve was executed with a beautiful loop, "aces" just poured. Deep shots were placed in the corners, no topspins and no long tiresome baseline exchanges. Serve and volley, or approach drives or returns. I felt constant pressure that was difficult to withstand.

Tom Gorman
(*January 19, 1946, Seattle, Washington, USA)

A tennis player who superbly mastered the serve & volley system. An excellent doubles player. He was dangerous for his second serve with a high bounce after which he often approached the net and made points by forcing punishing volleys. He was a menace for many seeded players. In 1972 he won Davis Cup with team USA, however, in the victorious final on clay in Bucharest he lost both of his singles matches.

Francois Jauffret
(*February 9, 1942, Bordeaux, France)

One of the Davis Cup heroes and France's most dependable players. Exceptional clay-court player. During five-setters he was able to change his tactics and his game rhythm: defense into offense, vary the power of his shots. He always came up with something! An excellent athlete who could withstand marathon matches to utter exhaustion. Playing him in Roland Garros during his peak form was excruciating for many. He managed to beat even Roy Emerson there in 1966 and ten years later he lost to Borg 10-8 in the fifth set. He hardly ever made an unforced error; his opponent had to force the points if he wanted to win!

Rod Laver
(*August 9, 1938 Rockhampton, Queensland, Australia)

World player number one. The only player in history who won the Grand Slam twice! It is my opinion that Laver has something that no other player has – he does not allow the opponent predict where he'll place the next shot. He positions himself as if he would be aiming down the line but he sends off the ball crosscourt. He fakes out his opponents with his body. When he was playing against me he hit unbelievable and unexpected shots from totally absurd positions. He destroyed me even with a backhand lob because it was impossible to read his intention; even a split second before hitting his shot, it was impossible to detect from his backswing whether he would play a lob or a passing shot. I was always a hundredth of a second too late hitting the ball.

For a left-hander he possessed a superb backhand, actually two of them: sliced as well as top-spin. It was his backhand that made him the best player in the world. He attacked with a sliced backhand but if his opponent attacked first then he passed him with a top-spin that was unbelievably precise. He was a player who had hardly any weakness.

I remember him with great respect and admiration. The red-haired Laver had a monstrous left arm that gained him reputation of the best player in history, a chap with enormous willpower, who never tired of making up something new and astonishing, a man who seemed to have the capacity to read other people's thoughts and intentions. For sure he belongs to category of : "Greatest Players of All Time."

Ivan Lendl
(March 7, 1960, Ostrava, Czech Republic)

He was a ball boy who watched my matches during the Nationals and who followed closely the results of my international encounters. In 1978 he took over my 12-year long reign as the top Czech player. At the Nationals in Ostrava, which he entered as the best junior in the world, his delivery of strokes did not allow me to catch my breath. His intelligent self-discipline, perseverance, ferociousness, hard work and desire to become world's number one brought him to the pinnacle itself. He played basic strokes with much power, his "killer" forehand drive was particularly superb. His top-spin passing shots, excellent physical condition and exceptional

concentration resulted in great achievements on clay as well as on hard surfaces. He never favored grass. Though he reached Wimbledon finals twice he never won even a set! His hard serve and excellent returns were not enough to defeat grass-court specialists. In 1986 he lost to Becker from Germany, a year later he succumbed to Pat Cash from Australia. However, that does not diminish the fact that he was one of the best players of his time. He reached the US Open final eight times in a row; he won eight Grand Slams – three times at Roland Garros, three times the US Open, and twice the Australian Open. In addition, he won the culminating Masters tournament five times and reigned over the men's top ATP rank for 270 calendar weeks. Before he immigrated to the United States he helped his birth country win the 1980 Davis Cup; in total he played 37 Davis Cup matches in 17 encounters in the years 1978-1985.

John McEnroe
(*February 16, 1959, Wiesbaden, Germany)

An outstanding player, very technically proficient especially at the net, where he was capable to predict his opponent's target and win points thanks to his foresight, volley craft, and finesse even during seemingly lost points. His biggest weapon was his cannon-ball serve, and more so his second serve with his left-hander super-rotation, thanks to which he won many important points. His court temperament and obstinacy helped him deliver his maximum effort. He won Wimbledon three times and the US Open four times. During long rallies on European clay he lacked consistency and patience – he dashed to the net too quickly. He reached the finals at Roland Garros only once, in 1984, against Ivan Lendl. He was ahead 2:0 in sets and 3:0 and lost in spite of it!

Alexander Metreveli
(*November 2, 1944, Tbilisi, Georgia, Soviet Union)

The most outstanding and best player of the former Soviet Union. He was very good physically as well as technically and he was able to adapt his play to all surfaces. He was also very sharp in recognizing his opponent's weaknesses. He alone did not have a weakness, but he had no exceptional weapon either. He never gave any free points to his adversaries; his fundamental strokes were very well balanced. His forehand as well as backhand drop shots and his drop volleys provided for solid outcome. He made his way through to four Grand Slam quarter-finals; he beat Gonzales, Connors, Vilas, Orantes, and many others. Besides the 1973 Wimbledon singles finals he reached mixed doubles finals twice with Olga Morozova. For fourteen years he played on a Davis Cup team and finished 105 matches. Already in junior years the Soviets started sending him regularly to play in Australia, where he won many tournaments on grass.

Ilie Nastase
(*July 19, 1946, Bucharest, Romania)

One of my biggest rivals. By nature enormously talented! Phenomenal feet and reflex that only Rosewall and Okker could match but they gained it through hard labor. On the other hand, Ilie was a mischievous child, a naughty lad. He was either all jokes, or mulish annoyance which alternately gained or lost him friends and foes depending on whether the game went his way or not. Occasionally, he created big scenes, he had little respect for anyone or anything, and often he behaved improperly with older players who the rest of us respected. I did not understand why, but the players tolerated his behavior!

Ilie was a typical drama-king! He acted in any situation and with anything. On the courts he was capable to put on such a show that professional actor would be impressed. He tried to affect his opponents with his antics, unnerve them and lose concentration. I experienced it myself, and not just once...

He had a great total game but from time to time he could not control his extreme temperament. During the Davis Cup final in Bucharest even his home audience heckled him. Nobody ever knew with certainty how he would end up. He was capable to win it all and, at the same time, he was able to lose it all. It depended on – which side of bed he rose from??

He was considered the biggest talent of all times. However, his game lacked more luster.

Ilie presented an attractive game. He had quick feet, catlike movement, and fantastic reflexes that he applied particularly at the net. His natural talent showed through his amazing drop-volleys. His unstable character also evoked difficulties. Sometimes he played easy shots carelessly and made mistakes. His opponents never knew what might come next. Normally, players become nervous in crucial moments and try to concentrate and focus; Nastase did the opposite! He would totally disengage in such extreme situations, and he won, perhaps, thanks to his fecklessness.

John Newcombe
(*May 23, 1944 Sydney, New South Wales, Australia)

Besides his exceptional serve that never eluded him even in the most crucial moments it was hard to find any stroke that would be extraordinary in comparison to others. He possessed a very solid well-rounded arsenal of strokes, and to play against such an opponent is always very difficult. It was tricky to find a loophole in his close to perfect performance. He represented a typical Australian tennis school. Famous for his outstanding physical endurance and mental stability he played downright high-power tennis applying forceful pressure. This type of a game does not require much strategy and sometimes it seemed that he followed religiously his pattern - serve, quick approach to the net, and forceful put-away volley. He hardly ever attempted to improvise something else, he played stereotypically. But he did not flutter in games either. Though his game did not require much thinking he was able to get himself out of very ominous situations thanks to his natural intelligence and good tactics.

As simple as his game on the tennis court appeared he was that much smarter in his private life. Already in times of our tournament encounters he owned a tennis ranch in Texas. There were several dozen tennis courts, a hotel, a swimming pool and an indoor covered bubble, coaches, and practice ball machines. Young Americans from well-off families came here to spend vacations and simultaneously pick up tennis. Already then this was a very prosperous enterprise.

Tom Okker
(*February 22, 1944, Amsterdam, Holland)

He was the European amateur champion for many years, though Alexander Metreveli pursued him closely. His signing the professional contract did not accelerate his performance but, I believe, playing not just for trophies but also for big money increased his ambition and fighting spirit. Gradually he improved so much that he was earning close to the top among the professionals. Physically he was not in the best condition but he had three strong weapons: quick feet, excellent forehand and – a sharp mind. There were not many who were as clever on the court as he was. Each of his strokes had sense, a purpose; he never played "blindly". He was a thinker who played each point differently. He could do so because he possessed a great stroke variety with excellent technical execution. Thanks to his quick feet he was able to run down even seemingly lost points. For that he was nicknamed "Flying Dutchman". It was a treat for me to watch his game.

Manuel Orantes
(*February 6, 1949, Granada, Spain)

He was very popular in Spain, the second Manolo – after Santana. A splendid sprinter and physically so fit that he could have challenged body builders. He was a technically well equipped player but he did not use this advantage enough for his own benefit. He hit a fine volley particularly from the backhand side; however he did not find enough courage to come to the net more often. If I had been in his place I would have played a more aggressive game. Being a left-hander he had some advantage in approaching the net via the right-hander opponent's backhand but his forehand was sometimes inconsistent. He played excellent drop-shots, and he punished opponents with his precise passing shots or lobs. When the game was going his way he was hard to beat. His opponents then hoped that he would botch an easy shot and that would bring him out of his equilibrium. He then had a tendency to lose the last drop of confidence, which resulted in a significant turn-around and the match reversed and finished with his upset. I perceived such incidents as unbelievably sad achievement slumps. His decisiveness and energy converted in a flash into lethargy and loss of confidence when he was able to mess up even a series of points that would otherwise have gone his way. When he was in his comfort zone, his touch for the ball was astounding. He was always capable to sway the audience to his side.

Adriano Panatta
(*July 9. 1950, Rome, Italy)

Very talented, somewhat bohemian, in some respect similar to Nastase, with the difference in the game that was more powerful and invoked more pressure. His forehand approach shot was exceptional; however his backhand passing shot was weaker. He played lobs often and well and at very opportune times! He also managed a very good serve and volley game. His aggressive game reached success even on clay in Rome and in Paris, where he celebrated a grand victory in 1976 over a two-time Roland Garros champion Bjorn Borg and with that gained popularity of a tennis star. Similarly to Nastase he often struggled with concentration and his game suffered great ups and downs. He was able to win it all but also lose it all. Nevertheless, female fans went crazy for him win or lose.

Nicola Pietrangeli
(September 11, 1933, Tunis, Tunisia)

I played with him at the end of his career. He was a master of clay-court tennis in the nineteen-sixties. His father was French, his mother was Russian. He grew up on clay-courts in Tunisia but played Davis Cup for Italy. He holds the world record for having played the most Davis Cup matches in history – 164, winning 120! He played the most singles – 110, winning 78, and the most doubles – 54, winning 42. In all, he played 66 Davis Cup encounters. He was a darling of the Italian as well as French public. With his precise drop-shots and lobs he was able to make his opponents look like total losers. He also possessed an excellent backhand passing shot; his backswing did not show whether he was going to play a passing shot, lob or low drop-shot to his opponent's feet thus it was impossible to anticipate it. He reached the Roland Garros finals four times and won it twice. Besides that he also managed to win other most important European championships in Rome, where he defeated Laver in the finals, and also in Monte Carlo and in Hamburg. On grass he reached the semis at Wimbledon in 1960 losing to Laver in five sets. His doubles partner was tall Orlando Sirola. Together they won Roland Garros and reached Wimbledon finals. He became the non-playing Davis Cup captain after his own career came to a close and it was then that Italy triumphed in Davis Cup.

Niki Pilic
(*August 27, 1939, Split, Yugoslavia)

The best player of Yugoslavia since the World War II to the time of Goran Ivanisevic. Member of a professional team "Handsome Eight 1968." One of few players who managed to defeat Laver even during the peak of his career. A respected player on all surfaces. A left-hander with a powerful serve and forehand. He was the second oldest finalist at the French Open, where he lost to the Romanian Nastase in 1973. A semi-finalist at Wimbledon in 1967 where he defeated the second seeded Roy Emerson and later lost to Newcombe, the champion. He reached a US Open final doubles with the Frenchman Pierre Barthes. He played Davis Cup for his country eleven years before he left and became a citizen of Germany. He has been the only non-playing Davis Cup captain who brought teams of two countries to the victory – Germany with Boris Becker in the years 1988-1989, and Croatia with Ljubicic in 2005.

Tony Roche
(*May 17, 1945, Tarcutta, New South Wales, Australia)

A very unpleasant left-handed adversary; "Laverlike" type of a player who, however, put into play more spastic-like power. Perhaps that was the reason why he often suffered from back problems, shoulder and tennis elbow pains. His serve picked up an unpleasant

side-spin that was often difficult to deal with. He also possessed a splendid chopped backhand and topspin forehand. He had no visible weakness in any other strokes either. He was a fighter with enormous willpower. At one moment he was considered a successor of a departing seven-years-older Laver. Soon, however, he underwent an elbow surgery. His game was never attractive the way Rosewall's or Ashe's games were but it was highly effective and for his opponents difficult to deal with. And that is what made him one of the top world players.

Ken Rosewall
(*November 2, 1934, New South Wales, Australia)

Five foot six inches short, but all muscle, tendon and ligaments. One of the most solid tennis players ever, who managed to get in tip-top condition and readiness for every match. He was a complete player and my strong role model. He was a tennis player with unbelievable sense to foresee what would come next. He played tennis like playing a game of chess. He knew how to play a ball, and from his own play he predicted what his opponent might do. After a certain shot his opponent had only two choices how to return a ball – down the line, or with a lob. Thus Ken guarded only these two options and left the rest of the court unguarded. If his opponent attempted to return a shot cross-court it was usually so feeble and inaccurate that it became Ken's easy pray. His serve was very consistent, not a bomb but rather incredibly accurate. Only seldom he played a fault on his serve; more often he placed it in a corner, so that the opponent could not hurt him with his return. In the next contact with the ball he then applied more power and depth and thus opened up an all-court carousel.

If he decided to place a ball close to the line then it landed within 8 inches of the line! It was rather atypical for him to hit a ball a foot and a half out! He was able to counter even the hardest hits of his opponent with ease and control. He played precision tennis. Since he did not strike any "aces" one held the first impression that he did not have much of a game. With his timely backswing and fantastic footwork his game looked effortless. It is my humble opinion that Ken Rosewall along with Rod Laver and Pancho Gonzales formed the best tennis personalities of all times. They created a constellation that remained unrivalled and unmatched. Their tennis equaled a mature art-form.

Manuel "Manolo" Santana
(*May 10, 1938, Madrid, Spain)

He won the French Open twice in the years 1961 and 1964. He was the very first player who grew up on red clay but succeeded in adapting his game later to grass and winning the US Open in 1965, and triumphing in Wimbledon a year later. He became a national icon and the best athlete of Spain; General Franco presented him with a medal of the Queen Isabella!

Manolo was the first European to win the US Open on grass at Forest Hills since the era of Cochet in 1928! Rod Laver declared: "Manolo is able to play unbelievable short angles, and then he drives you crazy with incredible topspin lobs and unreachable drop-shots. He played around with me like that in Europe a couple of times and gave me quite some lesson on clay!" After the Italian Pietrangeli and Romanian Nastase he comes third in the count of matches played on a Davis Cup team – altogether he played 120 of them! His successor "Manolito," little Manolo Orantes, won the US Open in 1975, when he defeated Connors, but that was already on grey clay called "hard-thru."

Santana was later the non-playing captain of the Spanish Davis Cup team, also a television commentator and an advisor to his followers.

Stan Smith
(*December 14, 1946, Pasadena, California, USA)

A tennis court gentleman, a player with a profound sense of fair play. A tennis player – one and the same as decency and nobleness; in play and in character. Beside the fact that he earned the top rung in world tennis in his time he was also pronounced the most elegant. And it befitted him!

Stan never showed desire to be extravagant in any way, even though his stature was one of a model. I have always felt that he was not the type who hankered after that kind of attention. He was inconspicuous, decent, classic, and level-headed. He was a good tempered guy, ambitious, and never conceited. He reached the top thanks to his work ethic, honesty, and tough training. It is my opinion that he was half as talented as Nastase, Panatta or Connors, but he put forth more of his intelligence, willpower, and strategy. His tennis form was physically more demanding than of many other world class players but he was so well trained and prepared that he was able to deal with that. He played a simple game, not as technical as other players did. Stan had an outstanding serve, at that time the best in the world. Sometimes he reminded me of Newcombe, who was, however, more of a "bull." His other effective weapon was his smash and excellent net play. For that very reason he was more successful on grass and fast surfaces. On clay he did not shine far as much as on grass. If I am to return to his strokes I must mention that his weakest stroke must have been his backhand that he often tried to avoid and ran around it. He worked long and hard to reach the world top rank. It did not come to him easy. Together with Bob Lutz they produced one of the most successful doubles teams ever.

Frederick "Fred" Stolle
(October 8, 1938, Sydney, Australia)

At the beginning of his career he asserted himself as an excellent doubles player. With time, however, he also became a world-class singles player thanks to his determination and aptitude.

He was a purely aggressive player, who applied a serve-volley game-plan very effectively. His excellent play at the net, where he took advantage of his size and performed brilliant volleys, carried him all the way to Wimbledon finals three times in a row in 1963-1965! His quick approach to the net following the serve was remarkable. He compensated for his slower footwork with a superb return particularly from the backhand side. That helped him win other singles Grand Slams on grass at the US Open at Forest Hills, and even on clay at Roland Garros in Paris! He was a menace for all players in doubles as he won all Grand Slam tournaments several times and with varying partners – Hewitt, Emerson and Rosewall. At his age of forty-one and Emerson's forty-three they reached the US Open semi-finals at Flushing Meadows! He won thirteen out of sixteen Davis Cup matches and together with the British Ann Jones they won Wimbledon mixed-doubles. His son Sandon won the 1998 US Open doubles title with Cyril Suk.

Roscoe Tanner
(October 15, 1951, Chattanooga, Tennessee, USA)

A very formidable left-hander with a tremendous serve that he executed with a fast loop. On days that he was "on" he drove his opponents to sheer resignation with his bullet-like shots that they could seldom reach. His game was risky, his drives were direct and without top spin, he gained many points with his bold returns. However, sometimes his game lacked consistency as he committed too many unforced errors due to his perilous play. After a match with him I often returned to the locker-room feeling as if I had not played much; there were few rallies, points were decided with quick winners. His risky pressing game advanced him all the way to Wimbledon finals where he succumbed to superb Borg only after a five-set battle. He won the Australian Open on grass and a several other tournaments mainly on hard surface or indoors.

Roger Taylor
(*October 14, 1941, Sheffield, Great Britain)

A lefthander with a terrific serve that he put in force on fast surfaces particularly on grass and indoor courts. He was assertive at the net with a superior drop-volley. His physical stamina helped him win many difficult matches. His serve return was weaker and so was his backhand passing shot. He was an excellent doubles player in a professional group called Handsome Eight. He was a several times over Wimbledon semifinalist, a winner of many indoor tournaments and an English idol especially after he defeated the number one player of the world Rod Laver in the peak of his fame.

Ion Tiriac
(*May 9, 1939, Brasov, Romania)

A tremendous athlete, first as a member of the National Olympic Ice Hockey team and only later as a tennis player. He was a very clever tactician with solid basic strokes, very good drop-shot and lob, on clay he often drove his opponents into cramping. He brought Romania into the Davis Cup finals three times, in the years 1969, 1971, 1972 where they always lost to the USA! He proclaimed about himself "I am the best player among those who do not know how to play tennis". He guided and helped Nastase and showed him the way to go. But, he won only two tournaments in singles and 27 in doubles. Later he was a successful coach and manager of Vilas and Becker. Consequently, he became an acknowledged tournament promoter and an entrepreneur.

Guillermo Vilas
(*August 17, 1952, Buenos Aires, Argentina)

A left-hander and a great clay court player, who managed to adapt his game to all surfaces just like Borg. He alternated his very top-spun basic strokes with brilliant topspin lob. He was a menace of all aggressive players – an incredible fighter with superb physical stamina, who declared: "anybody who wants to beat me, will have to spend at least four hours on the court." He had no exceptional serve but applied a good twist to it; the only player he was afraid of was Borg.

WHAT JAN KODES´ RIVALS SAID ABOUT HIM...

He battled with them most of his career in Grand Slams, in Davis Cup, and in many other tournaments. They saw each other just about every day while they practiced together, during matches on opposite sides, and on their travels from one side of the globe to the other. They got to know each other very well. We spoke to and asked some questions of Jan Kodes' biggest rivals with whom he had fought on the court several times over.

How do you remember Jan Kodes as a player from your many mutual encounters on the world circuit; what was he like as a person? What do you think about his victories at the French Open in the years 1970 and 1971? On which surface was he more of a menace: on clay or on grass? How did you feel about his 1973 Wimbledon victory? Do you remember Jan Kodes as a Davis Cup player?

This is how some of them answered.

I believe that, in his time, Jan was one of the best players in the world. I am very glad to have had the honor to play him many times. He was a tough opponent and he was hard to beat. He was a complete player with an all-court game. He earned his place in tennis history as a great champion.

The relationship between the Czechs and the Swedes was always sincere and friendly. And the same was true about me and Jan. Our friendship has lasted till today. I have respected him, and the rest of the tennis world has too, whether it has been him as a tennis player on the court or off the court.

He won the French Open and Wimbledon, and he reached the finals of the US Open twice. He accomplished a number of other remarkable achievements as well. He was a player who could perform on any surface and who could become a menace for any player. For those reasons it did not surprise me that he won the French Open two times in a row. And Wimbledon? That title came at the peak of his career! Just about any player will tell you that winning the Wimbledon title is special; it is so special expressly for its traditions. To win Wimbledon is grand. To win any other Grand Slam tournament is amazing but a Wimbledon victory carries a special tribute that no other tournament can duplicate. Perhaps, with a bit of luck, Jan and I might have met each other in Wimbledon semifinals. I believe I had a chance to win the quarterfinal match but I lost it in five sets to Roger Taylor. I was too young then, still inexperienced and lacking confidence. On the contrary, Jan exhibited everything one needed to win Wimbledon. He earned the title. Even if I had surpassed Roger, most likely I would have succumbed to Jan. We later played a number of even-leveled matches, for instance in Boston in 1974. I was up two sets to none. Jan tied the score and led 5:1 in the fifth. But I had a comeback and won the match in a tie-break. These are matches you never forget! Another similar match took place during the Davis Cup final in Stockholm in 1975. The Czechs were then under more pressure than we were even in spite of us playing on home turf. Jan and I played the first match on the last day, a match that could have been decisive. And it was! Jan played under tremendous pressure and I knew that a defeat meant a great disappointment for him. Surely he thought that it was his last chance to clutch the Davis Cup bowl. I remember that match well, and I am sure that he does too.

Björn Borg

A fighter and a good friend. A player with a superb backhand and volleys; unyielding competitor like Connors, smart, and an excellent clay-court player. Always proper, on and off the court. He helped me a lot with my tennis. I once asked him to play doubles with me when nobody knew me yet. He met my wish and we won Munich in 1975, Barcelona in 1977, Madrid in 1978, and we even reached the Roland Garros finals in 1977!

Wojtek Fibak

Jan Kodes had a great tennis career. He was one of my most difficult opponents, especially on "his" surface, the clay-court. He was unbelievably tenacious, physically well prepared, there was not a point ever lost to him. He was capable to get the most out of himself especially in the most important tournaments. There is no wonder that he won Grand Slams at Roland Garros – in 1970 and the following year. He also made Wimbledon history and joined the line of champions there in 1973.

I remember all our exhausting and physically grueling matches at Roland Garros. In Davis Cup we met only twice. My best memories take me to Paris in 1966 when I defeated him in five sets only after he had me down 6:3, 6:1 and 3:0. Nine years later he paid me back in Prague in a similar fashion in a very important Davis Cup match when the score was tied at 2:2.

François Jauffret

When I think of Jan the first thing that comes to my mind is his character of a true fighter. Jan Kodes was one of my foremost rivals in important tournaments and championships. On the court he was a full-hearted opponent, talented strategist, and a very well prepared player technically and physically. In spite of the fact that politics played its problematic role in our relationship he was able to forget and forgive. We always found a way to communicate even after a brief pause when our friendship edged away for a period time due to the invasion of Czechoslovakia in 1968.

Jan was one of the best players on clay and his French Open victories were a natural outcome. I believe he would have accomplished still more had he been able to arrange his own schedule of tournament entries. We had tougher conditions than players in the "free" countries.

He played well on clay as well as on grass but it is my opinion that he was stronger on clay. There are some voices who think that his Wimbledon victory was not persuasive since not all players entered the championship that year. That was not his fault, however, and, incidentally, the draw was very challenging in spite of it. If I take into consideration all previous as well as following tournaments and the five set final with Newcombe at US Open a few weeks later, his Wimbledon title looks well deserved.

We met regularly in Davis Cup, once we played in Czechoslovakia, next time in the USSR. Our matches were always highly strung, full of emotions, claiming strong wills and also team spirit. We usually took the matches to five sets. I remember those moments well even today.

Alexander Metreveli

We played each other many times and since it was certainly more than ten times he also beat me several times. We met and competed already as juniors. He was a brilliant opponent, and for me that much more challenging for his unbelievably ambitious fighting spirit. When he was losing he fought with extra ferocity still. We became good friends as we were of the same age and we played the same tournaments. I remember our train ride from Moscow to Tallinn. We then played doubles together. As I think of it all I realize that I have known him for forty years!

We both started playing and learned tennis on clay. But if one wanted to be a top world player then adapting the game to all surfaces was a must. It was not easy for us but we accomplished it. Outcome of Wimbledon 1973 was better for him – he won! It was a great year for him because after Wimbledon he reached semi-finals or even finals at the US Open! I don't remember the details any more. He proved then that he was able to win on all surfaces.

We played against each other in Davis Cup only once in Romania but by then we were both thirty or thirty one. We met each other more in big tournaments like the French Open, in Italy and in Spain. We fought long grueling matches. Once it was his turn to win, next time mine. At any rate, it was always a great challenge.

Ilie Nastase

Jan was a very difficult opponent who fought for each and every point and whose game had, virtually, no weakness. He always appeared to be a friendly chap, though a bit reserved and distant. That might have been related to the fact that Central Europe was then suffering from the Russian occupation. I remember how all WCT players played in Rome, where Kodes defeated me, Stolle, and Roche only to lose to Laver in the finals. Immediately after that neither I, nor Rosewall, nor Roche, nor Laver were allowed to play at Roland Garros.

Nevertheless, Jan was superb on clay. He grew up on it and I am sure that it was his favorite surface, on which he delivered his best performances. He did not have much experience on grass, yet he surprised everybody in 1971 when he advanced all the way to the US Open finals. I was seeded as number one since I had won Wimbledon in 1970 and 1971 but Jan beat me in four sets in the first round. Two years later 84 players did not enter Wimbledon but he sealed his best career performance when he advanced all the way to the finals of the US Open where all players were present and he only lost to me in a five set final match. Unfortunately, we met in Davis Cup only once in a semifinal match in Melbourne in 1973. Australia then won 4:1...

John Newcombe

Jan is a very well educated man who I have always respected. He was one of the dominant players of his generation and has achieved excellent results in Grand Slam tournaments. In particular his two successive Roland Garros victories were unbelievable accomplishments. He was most successful on clay. The players who boycotted Wimbledon in 1973 wished only one thing and that was for Nastase or Taylor not to advance to the finals and win since they did not join the boycott. Kodes and Metreveli could not participate in the boycott for their own political struggle at home. Kodes' surprising victory was welcome. Yet, I remember that some critics tried to discredit that victory in tennis world and did not consider it for its full value. But, there were 128 players as always and they played three out of five sets as had been done before. In Davis Cup one particular match got etched into my memory - the semifinals in Prague in July of 1975. After the first day the

**Patrick Proisy reached
1972 Roland Garros
finals after beating
Kodes and Orantes,
lost to Andres Gimeno.**

Czechs were leading 2:0 and their doubles team was favored in the following day contest. But Dominguez and I won that match after an amazing five-set battle against Kodes – Hrebec. Patrick Dominguez then tied the score 2:2; but we lost 2:3 in the end.

Patrick Proisy

Jan was always a formidable opponent, he fought hard till the end. Overall he was a very good all-court player. I trust he managed his career very well. In his time he belonged to the best clay-court players in the world, and he deserved the two-time French Open title. When he won Wimbledon in 1973 I felt that only Nastase could have defeated him but he had lost sooner than they would meet each other.

We are still good friends with Jan; I always respected him as a player and as a man. In Davis Cup we never came across each other but I know how much he accomplished for the benefit of Czech tennis.

Stan Smith

And other players.

Naturally, there are many more players who I came across on the opposite side of the net and who also deserve recognition; for instance the "booming" servers: Dennis Ralston, Clark Graebner, Frank Froehling, Charles Pasarell, Victor Amaya from the US as well as Colin Dibley, Dick Crealy, Mark Edmondson, from Australia, Robert Maud from South Africa, Ove Bengtson from Sweden, Victor Pecci and other good ones as Wilhelm Bungert, Ingo Buding, and others like Karl Meiler, Jurgen Fassbender from Germany or Bernard Mitton and Andrew Pattison from South Africa.

There were outstanding doubles players – Marty Riessen, Bob Lutz, Bob Hewitt, Frew McMillan, Raul Ramirez, John Alexander, Phil Dent, Peter McNamara, Allan Stone, Colin Dowdeswell, Wojtek Fibak.

Or two-handed backhand players like Beppe Merlo, Cliff Drysdale, Paul McNamee, Eddie Dibbs and Harald Solomon.

Or lefthanders Torben Ulrich, Ismail El Shafei, Owen Davidson, Thomaz Koch, Jan Leschly, Jim McManus, Patrice Dominguez, Barry Phillips-Moore, Ray Ruffles. Then very good mid-Europeans as Toomas Lejus, Balazs Taroczy, Wojtek Fibak, Stabholcs Baranyi, Peter Szoke, Peter Pokorny and Hans Kary.

And then there were the unyielding fighters: Mal Anderson, Cliff Richey, Juan Gisbert, Jose Higueras, Brian Gottfried, Corrado Barazzutti, Nicola Spear, Brian Fairlie, Onny Parun, Istvan Gulyas, Edson Mandarino, Pato Rodriguez, Pato Cornejo and others.

What about the grass-loving Indians? – Ramanathan Krishnan, Premjit Lall, Jaidip Mukerjea, or brothers Vijay and Anand Amritraj.

THE CHAMPIONS SINCE

Mats Wilander

(August 22, 1964, Vaxjo, Sweden)

Bjorn Borg's successor and the youngest Roland Garros champion in 1982. He was seventeen and nine months! He was then the youngest Grand Slam champion but three years later Boris Becker took away that recognition when he won Wimbledon at seventeen and seven months. That record, however, was still broken and is held till this day by Michael Chang, who won Roland Garros in Paris at seventeen and three months in 1989.

Mats was an outstanding baseliner with two-handed backhand and stupendous concentration in the clutch moments. His improved play at the net, great court coverage, ability to assess situation at any given moment and, based on it, putting immediate action plan in force earned him seven Grand Slam titles! He was able to adapt his game to grass as well as hard surface. He was the only player of that era to come close to winning a Grand Slam title when he won the Australian Open in 1988, as well as Roland Garros and the US Open. However, he got unexpectedly overwhelmed in Wimbledon quarter-finals by Miloslav Mecir, who became the Olympic champion that year in Seoul. Mats won Wimbledon doubles title with Joakim Nystrom and he also assisted Swedish Davis Cup team in several Davis Cup victories.

Boris Becker
(November 22, 1967, Leimen, Germany)

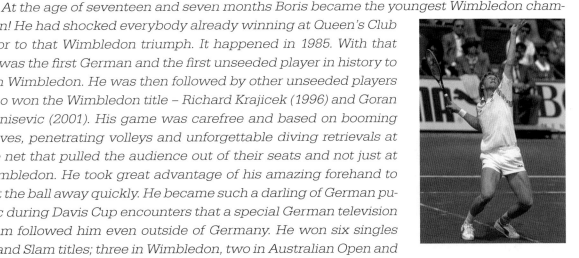

At the age of seventeen and seven months Boris became the youngest Wimbledon champion! He had shocked everybody already winning at Queen's Club prior to that Wimbledon triumph. It happened in 1985. With that he was the first German and the first unseeded player in history to win Wimbledon. He was then followed by other unseeded players who won the Wimbledon title – Richard Krajicek (1996) and Goran Ivanisevic (2001). His game was carefree and based on booming serves, penetrating volleys and unforgettable diving retrievals at the net that pulled the audience out of their seats and not just at Wimbledon. He took great advantage of his amazing forehand to put the ball away quickly. He became such a darling of German public during Davis Cup encounters that a special German television team followed him even outside of Germany. He won six singles Grand Slam titles; three in Wimbledon, two in Australian Open and one in US Open. In addition he won the ATP World Championships, Grand Slam Cup, and he reached the Davis Cup finals three times winning the event twice. In 1992 he captured the Olympic gold medal together with Michael Stich in doubles in Barcelona. He did not shine on clay-courts where his game was not as threatening for the clay-court specialists. Reaching Roland Garros semifinals twice he ought to consider as fine accomplishments.

Stefan Edberg
(January19, 1966, Vastervik, Sweden)

Bjorn Borg's successor and one of the best players of modern era who played a serve-and-volley game. He interrupted the Swedish two-handed backhand school and followed his coach Percy Rosberg's advice to switch to one-handed backhand that proved to be more effective at the net. It showed to be a good choice because Stefan soon won a junior "Grand Slam" in 1983, a feat that only Butch Buchholz had accomplished before him in 1958. Though he grew up on clay, clay was not his favorite surface. Besides a good serve, especially his second "kick" serve, he made himself excel with his purely aggressive game, superb backhand volley and quick reflex action at the net. He covered the net very well, he was a fighter and at the same time a "gentleman," his on and

off court pleasant demeanor made him well liked by his fellow players. He won six singles Grand Slam titles; he suffered the biggest disappointment in 1989 Roland Garros final that he had longed for so much but lost in five sets to the young American, Michael Chang, in spite of leading 2:1 in sets! Altogether he played Davis Cup finals seven times and he won the US and Australian Open doubles with Anders Jarryd and then the 1996 Australian Open again with Petr Korda. Edberg received the ATP Sportsmanship and also Phillipe Chatrier Awards from the ITF.

Andre Agassi
(April 29, 1970, Las Vegas, USA)

The only player of modern era who achieved winning all Grand Slam tournaments in spite of their varied surfaces. In all of history only six players accomplished that. Two of them were Grand Slam winners Don Budge in 1938 and Rod Laver in 1962 and 1969. The other four who pulled it off but not in the same year were Fred Perry, Roy Emerson, Andre Agassi and Roger Federer! The crucial match that helped Agassi achieve that distinction was his sensational Roland Garros victory in 1999, when he conquered Andrei Medvedev in the finals 1:6, 2:6, 6:4, 6:3, and 6:4! It was a memorable final match, when the American was only six points away from losing but managed to persevere, fight and believe that even on clay it pays off to drudge along till the last point is over. Agassi had already won three Grand Slam titles - Wimbledon, US Open, and the Australian Open, and one could suppose that he needed no further motivation. For as long as twenty one Grand Slam years Andre was a unique tennis "icon" that only a few other players of the "new era" could be compared to: Ken Rosewall (29 incl.11 Pro), Jimmy Connors (23), Rod Laver (22 incl. 5 Pro), Arthur Ashe (21), Ilie Nastase (20), Guillermo Vilas (20), Stan Smith (20), and John Newcombe (19). Andre Agassi also experienced conversion to new rackets and surfaces and he succeeded in adapting to all those changes and still triumphed. He captured eight singles Grand Slam titles. His superb footwork and court coverage, his anticipation and quick reaction, his calm but effective tennis strategy, his fighting will and ability to hit the baseline shots soon after the bounce and on the rise elevated him to the category of players known as "The Greatest Players of All Times!"

Pete Sampras
(August 12, 1971, Washington D.C., USA)

A player, who will always be remembered as the best player of all times for capturing fourteen Grand Slam titles. At the age of nineteen he was the youngest US Open champion in 1990! He won that title five times, Wimbledon title seven times, and the Australian Open twice. His carefree movement, perfect serve toss and weight transfer into the ball at strike point allow for his serve to be considered one of the most attractive ever seen.

He complemented his beautiful serve and uncompromising volleys with simple direct drives from the baseline that he struck with unbelievable lightness yet enormous power! Sampras led the world ATP ranking for incredible 286 weeks and the only shadow in his tennis career remains his failure at Roland Garros, where he reached only semifinals once out of thirteen attempts. A question remains whether he did all he could to overcome his shortcoming on clay, in order to be crowned an overall "king". At times, when it was not "his day", he was able to commit unforced errors from the baseline and lose to lower-level players. However, it also remains true that he managed to win the Italian Open in Rome on clay. He played doubles seldom but he played it well, for instance when the US needed an important Davis Cup point. It is difficult to compare Sampras to Laver because of the different eras when both of them dominated. The only two times Grand Slam champion from 1962 and 1969, Rod Laver, was a more technical and more agile player, who disappeared for five years to play with the professionals. With his eleven Grand Slam titles standing he would have been able to surpass, most likely, even Pete Sampras. Who knows? Pete Sampras was more penetrating and fierce, playing in more modern times. It is very clear that both, Laver as well as Sampras, are deserving of the adjective "Greatest Players of All Times!"

Roger Federer
(August 8, 1981, Basel, Switzerland)

Roger Federer from Switzerland, who took over the world tennis circuit for several years, won Wimbledon the first time in 2003. That same year he also triumphed in the ATP Masters Cup and started his reign on the top rung of the world ranking ladder. It was his craftsmanship and solving difficult situations during his matches like changing the rhythm, interchanging variety of spins in order to get his opponents out of their comfort zone as well as his court sense that elevated him quickly to the top. He applies a powerful and well placed serve and potent basic strokes very effectively, especially his devastating backhand down-the-line that he is also capable of executing effectively with under-spin – and crosscourt. His calm and collected positive demeanor on the court drew a lot of respect from his fellow players and he was seen as almost "invincible!" He won the US Open five times in succession! He matched Bjorn Borg's record of conquering Wimbledon title also five times in a row and surpassed Pete Sampras in the number of Grand Slam titles – by now fifteen in total! He did struggle to win at Roland Garros, where his road to the title was botched by Rafael Nadal. He has realized how physically demanding the matches are in that tournament. At last he won the French clay-court title in 2009. There is no doubt that he occupies a deserving place among the "Greatest Players of All Times." His journey has not finished yet and we may live to see more victories and records from him...

Rafael Nadal
(June 3, 1986, Manacor, Mallorca, Spain)

A young Spaniard, who sank his teeth quickly into the world circuit especially on clay courts, grants no peace to the other players. He started to dominate Roland Garros in Paris single-handedly, where he defeated Roger Federer already three times in the finals. Nobody expected, however, that he would reach the top even on grass at Wimbledon, where he triumphed in 2008. It was an exciting five-set drama that will be for ever filed in history as one of the best. Nadal's basic strokes are hard, confident and struck soon after they bounce; together with his tremendous fighting spirit and superb court coverage they amount to such pressure that is hard to withstand and that often results in his opponent's total morale destruction. Nadal continues to evolve and advance and his improved net approach and volley game have turned him into favored player on all surfaces. Improving his second serve helped him to his first Wimbledon title. Most likely we'll live to see many others similar to his recent great win on hard-court surface in Melbourne, Australia in 2009. He hungers for more titles ...

PRE-TENNIS BEGINNINGS...

The Prague house „At the Old Ballroom" – No: 6, Egidiy street... today the corner of Jilska and Vejvodova No: 1 - at the time of the Austria-Hungarian-Hapsburg Empire. The emblem on the fasade shows the year 1675 with three balls and tennis racket. The house was burnt-down at 1689.

Picture shows the courtyard, „ballroom-area" at that time!

1675

Czech wood was very well known already in 20-ties. Manufacturer „Thonet - Mundus" based at Bystrice pod Hostynem near Prerov in Moravia produced besides the bended furniture also a famous tennis racquets. Picture from the year 1920.

Emblem on the house fasade at Vejvodova street shows: „ANNO 1675":

All things rest on God´s blessing.
When God´s bounty is plentiful, envy means nothing, but without
His Grace not even work can succeed.

A historical poster from International tournament held at I CLTK in 1911 on Stvanice Island, formerly called Velke Benatky (Grand Venice).

STVANICE HISTORY

The roots of lawn-tennis in Bohemia lie in ball games played by knights of the Middle Ages. In the 15th and 16th centuries these games became so popular that they were played at various feudal courts all over Bohemia. Tennis is described in the accounts of the early Bohemian travellers Martin Kabátník and Krištof Harant of Polzice and Bezdruzice. It appears that Czech commoners as well as feudal lords played these games. Tennis courts were recorded in 480 places in Bohemia before 1888; they were constructed of various materials as macadam, concrete, and layers of brick and were usually set in gardens.

Two years after the first Wimbledon Championship the first Bohemian competition with prize money was held in 1879 on the grounds of Duke Kinski´s Castle at Chocen. It was, apparently, the first event in the Austro-Hungarian Empire! Another tennis championship was held that same year at Bon Repos Castle near Nove Benatky on the first grass court in Bohemia. Zbraslav Castle was the venue for the first inter-town competition between Zbraslav and Rakovnik. The court of Count Loweter at Trebenice was a real curiosity – instead of sand, Czech garnets composed the surface.

From 1880 a Prague company "Goldsmid Brothers", based in Paris, largely contributed to the spread of ten-

First tennis emblem of I. CLTK section in Pilsen.

Foundation members of I. CLTK 1893.

Předsedové I. Č. L. T. K. v Praze.

Marian Rombald z Hochinfelsen.   Řed. Adolf Solnař.

Ph. Dr. a Dr. tech. věd. Jar. Just.   JUDr. Ed. Just.   Tov. K. Robětín.

Předsedové I. Č. L. T. K. v Praze.

Karel Cífka † 22. V. 1929.   Rössler-Orovský.

Prof. L. Šimek.   Mg. Fh. Toman.   JUDr. V. Dúras.

Chairmen history of I. CLTK at Prague, Czech Republic –
see page 538.

nis by importing rackets and balls. Tennis became more and more popular and from 1890 it was played not only as a social game but also as a competitive sport. A number of clubs with their own sand courts but without any "common status" were founded in Bohemia, while a sort of organization came into existence in Prague and also outside the capital, in Chrudim, Chocen, Plzen, Brandys nad Orlicí, Hluboka, Prelouc, Prostejov, Orlik, Hermanuv Mestec and other places. At that same time Czech Lawn Tennis Circle, the German Tennis Circle, the Nostic and Lobkowitz Circle at Stvanice, Skating club at Letná, the Prague Regatta and Tennis at Zbrojnice were formed.

Surprisingly, the history of the I. Czech Lawn Tennis Club did not start at Stvanice, but rather in Brandys nad Orlici.

Mrs.Tylda Rössler had a tennis court built there at her own expense sometime around 1890. The court was used exclusively by Czech society until 1896, when the Rössler family moved to Prague. In 1892 Dr. Josef Rössler-Orovsky rented three courts from a German club located on Zidovsky Ostrov (Jewish Island). Tennis activities there held no formal status until J. Klenka produced a translation of an English-written rule book, opening up the way towards establishing the first official tennis club.

In March 1893 Josef Cifka, an Austrian Army lieutenant and an enthusiastic promoter of Czech tennis, was transferred to Prague. His initial activities took place in Pilsen rather than Prague. In June of the same year he demonstrated a previously unseen spectacle called "lawn-tennis" in the Municipal Park Obcizna in Pilsen. His exhibition partner was a local multiple cycling champion and an employee of Skoda Works, Rudolf Provaznik. The exhibition was so successful that it gave rise to formation of a Tennis Section of the Czech Cyclists' Club in Pilsen. Cifka then realized his dream by establishing the I. Czech Lawn Tennis Club (I.CLTK) later that year on Strelecky Ostrov (Island) in Prague. Cifka's brother Karel became the first President of the club as Josef Cifka himself, being a military officer, was not allowed to accept any such position.

About forty more members joined the club in no time. By the Fall of 1893 the first club regulations were drawn up and indorsed. The Club was further strengthened by family and players of Dr. Rössler-Orovsky's group.

By spring 1895 the membership rose to over eighty members; the Club prospered and it even organized its first International tournament called the Championship of the Czech Crown. They also held

Historical emblems from 1898.

their first club tournament that was won by Josef Cifka. Their membership continued to grow, more international tournaments took place, and the I. Czech Tennis Club became a meeting point of high society. In 1900, when Davis Cup was played for the first time, the Club was offered an opportunity to establish itself at "Velke Benatky" Island," today's "Stvanice Island". The I. CLTK relocated there in 1901.

New, very modern and accommodating clubhouse at that time was erected, and five courts were built, all that in a beautiful old garden in the very center of Prague. New facilities attracted still more members, and the I. Czech Lawn Tennis Club gained great reputation even outside the Austrian borders.

I. CLTK was one of the club foundation members of Czech Lawn Tennis Association in 1906.

Some of the participants from the doubles tournament. The Zemla brothers (not pictured) won the Austrian title.

Zdenek Zemla-Jansky and Ladislav Zemla-Razny.

Josef Cifka, an Austrian Army Colonel and promoter of Paris Czech tennis.

Czechoslovakia vs. New Zealand in 1926. From left: Rodzianko, Soyka, Hyks, Jan Kozeluh, Prof. Dr. Jaroslav Just, Fisher, Stejskal, Zemla and Gerke.

Original clubhouse was built in 1928.

This was the time of the beginning of the Zemla brothers' career. In 1909 the Club contracted its first professional coach, Frantisek Burianek. The Zemla brothers won the 1906 Austrian Championships in doubles, and remained among the best European teams until 1911. While Zdenek Zemla was forced to end his athletic career that year due to illness, his brother Ladislav went on to become a tennis legend. He was able to keep in top form for 17 years, till 1926, when he advanced to the third round of Wimbledon and was eliminated only by Jacques Brugnon from France. He also won the Olympic bronze medal at the 1920 games in Antwerp in mixed doubles with Milada Skrbkova, his future wife. During his career, Ladislav Zemla, who had returned from the World War I as a captain of the French Legion, became the Czechoslovak International Champion in singles.

Czechoslovakia participated in Davis Cup for the first time in 1921. The first round matches were played at Stvanice, with the local team losing 2:3 to Belgium. Zemla, however, succeeded in beating Jean Washer – the fourth best player in the world rankings. All players representing Czechoslovakia – Ladislav Zemla, Karel Ardelt and Jaroslav Just – came from the I. Czech Lawn Tennis Club. In the same year, the Club at Stvanice was joined by Pavel Macenauer, who later formed a strong duo with Jan Kozeluh, staring in 1924 to 1926 Davis Cup matches. Jan Kozeluh reached as far as the quarter-finals in Wimbledon twice in a row, in 1926 and 1927, both times getting eliminated by French players – Jean Borotra the first time, and then René Lacoste.

Davis Cup: CSR-France in Prague, 1926 Jan Kozeluh lost opening match to Rene Lacoste (right) in five sets: 5:7, 7:5, 3:6, 8:6, 3:6. Kozeluh reached two Wimbledon quarter-finals in 1926 and 1927 (lost to Borotra and Lacoste).

Stvanice 1929: exhibition between Jan Kozeluh and Bill Tilden.

In 1926, the Club commissioned three new courts and, a year later, also a centre court, capable of accommodating almost five thousand spectators, although one of the stands located along the length of the court only allowed standing visitors. A new clubhouse was built shortly thereafter, with an investment of 750 thousand Korunas. It remained in use until 1983.

Picture from 1900 showing a tennis game at Vysoke Myto.

Karel Ardelt with Count
Ludi Salm (left).

Ladislav Zemla was eight times singles and eleven times doubles champion of Bohemia and Moravia. He won the Nationals again four times after WWI and represented CSR in DC in 1921-1927. He reached the forth place in 1906 Athens Olympics (singles) and bronze medal in 1920 at Antwerp with Milada Skrbkova (mixed doubles).

Josef Rössler-Orovsky (sitting 2nd from the right) in 1908.

One of the first Czech indoor courts in Prague-Smichov, 1910.

During all those successful years, the Club's committee was presided over by Prof. Dr. Jaroslav Just, who had already served as the President of Czech Tennis Association (founded May 15, 1906) from 1912 and then served as President of **C**zechoslovak **T**ennis **A**ssociation (1919–1928). CTA was established at the exceptional board meeting held on December 13, 1918; it was renamed "federation" or "union" during the communist era. Under his supervision, the unimportant local club evolved into one of great international significance! His post was taken over by his brother Eduard Just for a short term, later replaced by Karel Robetin.

During the era between the two world wars the club acquired more than just tennis trophies, as many top players also revelled in playing ice hockey in winter time. From 1938 the club found itself under the supervision of Jaromir Becka, replacing Karel Roubetin, who was forced to leave for England. Becka remained in the top post until 1948. At that time, a new name appeared among those visiting Stvanice - Jaroslav Drobny, aged three. He was brought in by his father, who had become the new club custodian. Ladislav Hecht, who moved to Stvanice from Zilina in 1931, exercised profound influence on Drobny's development.

Hecht, the best Slovak tennis player, represented the country in Davis Cup competition for eight years in a row. He played a total of thirty seven matches in eighteen encounters. In 1938 Wimbledon he fought his way into the quarter-finals where he was defe-

Ladislav Hecht (left) with Donald Budge – I. CLTK 1938. In that year Budge won the „Grand Slam" and Hecht reached the quarter-finals at Wimbledon, lost to Henner Henkel.

Roderich Menzel played the Roland Garros final in1938 opposite the American, Donald Budge, and lost 3:6, 2:6, 4:6. At Wimbledon he was beaten twice in quarter-finals in 1933 by Ellsworth Vines and in 1935 by Fred Perry. Was ranked among the World's top 10 in 1934-35 and 1937-38.

ated by Henner Henkel from Germany. A year earlier he and his doubles partner Roderich Menzel won third place on the grass courts of the All England Lawn Tennis Club. Menzel himself made it to the Wimbledon quarter-finals twice – in 1933 (lost to the American Ellsworth Vines), and in 1935 (lost to Fred Perry from England).

1938 was the first year when a Grand Slam champion, Donald Budge, played at Stvanice and defeated Hecht in the finals of the Czechoslovak International Championship. Hecht left for the United States shortly after that.

Not even during the years of German Protectorate did Stvanice stay idle. With the exception of 1939, when Frantisek Cejnar reached the Championship title, the World War II era was dominated by Jaroslav Drobny. Although the German occupation slowed down the athletic as well as the social boom of the club, it was possible to resume the prosperous pre-war activities in 1945. Club rankings were still dominated by the same name – Jaroslav Drobny. He succeeded in defending his National title four times and he was the top player of the Davis Cup team that won the European Zone in 1947 and 1948.

Drobny advanced to Wimbledon semi-finals in 1946 and a year later, teamed up with Lenart Bergelin from Sweden (who later became Björn Borg's coach) they won Roland Garros doubles defeating the Australian duo Harry Hopman – Frank Sedgman in the finals. His greatest achievements did not come until the early 1950s when he won at Roland Garros twice, in 1951 defeating Eric Sturgess and 1952 overcoming Frank Sedgman. In 1954 he won Wimbledon over young Ken Rosewall, however, he was no longer representing Czechoslovakia; instead, he was in possession of an Egyptian passport as he had decided to emigrate shortly after the February communist coup in 1948,.

The socialist concept of sport severely impacted the I. CLTK's activities. Tennis was considered a bourgeois sport, far from suitable for the new social-conscious mind and frame. People had to hide their tennis rackets but the love of the sport remained. During the process of centralization and merging various athletic clubs and associations, the club came under the patronage of Jan Sverma Jinonice Plant, and was named DSO Spartak. It was later renamed to Sokol Sverma Jinonice. In 1952 they won the Czechoslovak National team title. The period of the greatest success came between 1956 and 1965 under the name of Spartak Praha Motorlet, when the tennis section won ten National titles back to back.

Exhibition: Motorlet vs. Sydney on May 30-31,1961 at Stvanice. Laver beat Javorsky 5:7, 6:3, 6:1. Jiri Javorsky with 9 singles and 11 doubles national titles was a dominant player of the late 50s and early 60s. In 1957 he was a mixed-doubles title winner with Vera Puzejova in Paris.

The backbone of winning teams was formed by core players: Jiri Javorsky, Jan Krajcik, Pavel Benda, Pavel Korda, Milan Necas, Milan Siroky, Petr Strobl, Vera Puzejova, Jirina Elgrova and Olga Miskova-Gazdikova.

In 1957 Vera Puzejova reached the singles' semi-finals at Roland Garros and won the mixed doubles together with Jiri Javorsky. Five years later she became the first Czechoslovak woman to advance to the finals of the most prestigious tournament in the world – Wimbledon!

Many world-class players visited and played exhibition matches at Stvanice during the 1950s and 60s: Art Larsen, Budge Patty, Herbie Flam, Lewis Hoad, Rod Laver, Roy Emerson, and Neale Fraser. International tournaments were attended by Fred Stolle and Tony Roche, and the fans witnessed Davis Cup battles staged by Kurt Nielsen, Nicola Pietrangeli, and Manuel Santana.

The club also initiated a youth program that soon caused for more a scarcity of open and available courts. That was why the construction of additional courts, training walls and a separate youth clubhouse commenced in 1960. At that time Jan Kodes started appearing in the club rankings as a young player with potential. The I. Czech Lawn Tennis Club, playing under the name of Motorlet Praha, won yet another team National League title in 1966, represented by Javorsky, Strobl, Kodes, Medonos, Vopickova-Kodesova, and Neumannova. Kodes himself transferred to Sparta Praha shortly thereafter, and Pavel Benda left for Austria to coach; still, Motorlet Praha was able to clinch another title in 1968.

In 1970, the whole tennis section representing the I. CLTK moved under the patronage of Prague's Public Transport Company. With the old centre court in dilapidated condition, the new sponsor made it possible for Stvanice facility to return, once again, to its glory.

The following spring, Davis Cup rounds against Portugal, and subsequently against USSR

Motorlet won Nationals teams in 1966: Jiri Javorsky, Jiri Medonos, Marie Neumannova, Vlasta Vopickova, Jan Kodes and Petr Strobl (from left).

President Edvard Benes – Stvanice Island in 1947.

UDA, the Army Club in 1928 Demolished in 2009 due to Blanka tunnel construction.

Jan Masaryk, Czechoslovak Minister of Foreign Affairs at Stvanice - Davis Cup vs. France in 1947.

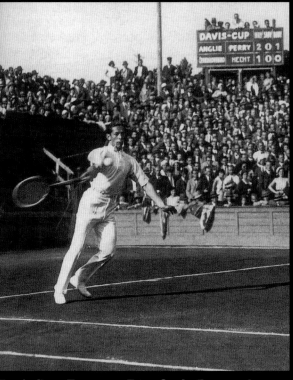

Davis Cup - European Zone finals: Prague, Aug 8-10,1931. Ladislav Hecht beat Henry „Bunny" Austin, but he lost to Fred Perry. Great Britain won 4:1.

Czech Ladislav Hecht with Jean Borotra (right).

Jaroslav Drobny (center) with Milan Vopicka (Jan´s brother-in-law) and Jan Kodes. They both scored a great many goals under I. CLTK ice-hockey teams in their times (pic. from 1993).

and Spain, were already played on the modernized centre-court. The capacity for seated spectators increased to 2453 at the expense of the number of standing spectators. The total capacity of the grandstands – 4500 visitors – remained unchanged.

In 1972 the team of the I. CLTK dropped out of the top league for the first time in its history. Obviously, this was not accepted easily by the management of the Public Transport Company that vehemently interfered in the affairs of the tennis club. Situation changed after Milos Konrad, an experienced coach, was recruited. The team responded by winning the title again in 1975 after beating Slavia LTC Praha in the deciding match.

Once the complete reconstruction (1983-1986) of the new tennis facility at Stvanice was finished, the club resumed playing and was able to win the National title one more and the last time in 1990. Entering the league again under the name of I. CLTK, the title was reached with a new generation team formed by Milan Srejber, Martin Strelba, David Rikl, Daniel Vacek, Lukas Hovorka, Jan Kodes Jr., Andrea Strnadova, Leona Laskova and Iva Budarova.

At this point we need to go seven years back into the past. June 6, 1983 was an emotional occasion for all. On that day, the "Farewell to Old Stvanice" event was held on the dilapidated Centre Court. Demolition started immediately afterwards. The club was still able to operate provisionally on three courts, with one air bubble available during winter season, and the clubhouse being replaced by portables.

Recreational amateur members stopped coming altogether and most of the league players left to compete for other Prague clubs. Although many of them later returned, the club-life revived slowly after the construction was completed. That was also one of the shortcomings that Jan Kodes was deemed responsible and later criticized for.

The social life of the club came to a halt and remained so for four years. It was hardly possible to keep the club alive with only three courts and members having to queue for two makeshift showers in the portables!

Extra-league players, however, were allowed to continue their activities thanks to an agreement with the construction company...

More than three years passed and the new Tennis Centre Court with the capacity of seven thousand spectators was inaugurated in 1986 on the occasion of the Federation Cup. That, however, opens a new chapter.

SAFE STVANICE!

It has all been inspired by Arne Polednak, the vice-president of the club, and an employee of Prague's Public Transport Company. Sometimes in early 1982, he said to Jan Kodes: *"Look, Jan, I'll be frank with you. The only person, who can do something about salvaging tennis at Stvanice, is you."*

American Karen Susman with famous Wimbledon „plate" in 1962. The finalist
Vera Sukova worked as national coach and Fed Cup captain later. Vera was not
able to see the „new" Stvanice opening in1986, passed away on May 13, 1982.

The club was threatened with abolition and relocation. Parts of Stvanice Island were being occupied by Metrostav, constructing the "C" Line of the Underground, a segment located under the Vltava River, connecting Florenc and Vltavska Stations. Prague Chief Municipal Architect's office received studies of everything but Stvanice tennis facility...

I wondered: "Why me?"

"Because you won Roland Garros and Wimbledon! You are the only person they will listen to; you can persuade them to preserve Stvanice for tennis!"

Given Kodes's purposeful approach and determination it was easy to anticipate what he was going to consider next. Initially, Kodes' brother-in-law, Milan Vopicka, a design engineer with the Prague Planning Institute, delivered the dire news: "Tennis is bound to be taken away from Stvanice! There will be an underground ventilation shaft built in the exact place of one of the courts. They have already decided where tennis will be relocated in Kobylisy district. There will be maximum three to four courts, a clubhouse and that will be it!"

Discussions about unfavourable conditions at Stvanice took no end for a long time. The issue popped up every time the Czech team won another Davis Cup round. The Davis Cup triumph in 1980 opened the can of worms yet again when Lubomir Strougal, the Prime Minister, received the team in Hrzansky Palace after the final victory against the team of Italy.

Once I decided to stand up for tennis at Stvanice, my main insightful argument was: "Mr. Prime Minister, tennis players give a huge portion of their prize money over to Pragosport and from there the money goes into the State Treasury. I think that tennis deserves something in return; a new stadium, for instance."

Under the former regime, every World or European Championship organized in the country had to be approved by the Secretariat of the Central Committee of the Communist Party of Czechoslovakia. The Central Committee of CUPES (Czechoslovak Union of Physical Educati-

This is the last picture of Centre Court before the reconstruction...

on and Sports) always proposed a four-year plan. In 1982 its Chairman, Antonin Himl, presented a plan proposing, besides the 1985 Ice Hockey World Championship or the 1986 Women's Volleyball World or European Championships, also Tennis Federation Cup. Comrades from the Central Committee approved the plan without realizing that there was no facility within the Czechoslovak Republic that would meet the ITF (International Tennis Federation) standards for such a major world team competition.

The President of the Czechoslovak Tennis Federation, Cyril Suk, and I negotiated this issue with Mr. Philippe Chatrier, the ITF President. Once we were able to promise that Prague would have a suitable tennis facility by 1986, the ITF awarded the Federation Cup to us.

There were four years left, which was rather a tough call.

There had been many discussions about the future of the old Stvanice. And, there were many different options under consideration – a reconstructed tennis stadium, a public park,

Otakar Ferfecky

Even the old club-house built at 1928 had to go ... The historical Negrelli railway bridge from 1850, which had to span both shoulders of the Vltava (Moldav) river over the Stvanice Island (formerly called New or Grand Venice) can be seen in the background.

public baths, and other ideas for public recreation. Some of them emerged as design studies from the studios of Sportprojekt, a company that actually brought the design of the new centre court to its realisation.

Even in the early phase of the project there was opposition. The loudest of the opponents was Prague Municipality; many of its representatives argued that no compact building befitted Stvanice. "If anything at all, it must be light and airy to fit well with the greenery and its surroundings." Once it was clear that tennis would prevail at Stvanice several design studies were produced. The zoning decision on locating the Tennis Centre Court at Stvanice was issued by the Chief Architect's Office on 15 April 1982. Finally, it was Sportprojekt that came up with a revolutionary design. Galleries and a lot of free transparent space – that was what the Prague Municipality was looking for.

By the way – at that point, Kodes had already led the Czech Davis Cup team through its first round match as a captain against Germany, and he was still under a contract playing actively for TC Amberg...

Some preliminary work was done in 1982, namely the construction of a sewer tunnel built under the bed of the river along with the subway line. This allowed Stvanice to connect to the city sewer system.

On Monday, June 6, 1983, it was time to say farewell to the old Stvanice. Spectators and fans had a great time, as they were also celebrating the I. CLTK's 90th anniversary. There were tennis exhibitions in old-time costumes from the previous century; Kodes and Smid played doubles against Hrebec and Slozil. Popular singers staged a concert on that occasion and everybody had a good time.

We had a lot of fun and, simultaneously, shed a few emotional tears. A train went by for the last time; the engineer stopped, blew the horn, and sounded the whistle. And that was it! As soon as the event ended, they started to tear down the Centre Court grandstands.

Jan Kodes was not present at the issue of Stvanice's preliminary project documentation, since he did not yet hold the position of the construction coordinator.

Time is short! - Federation Cup dates are coming up soon...

Nevertheless, I remember one of the earliest Sportprojekt meetings held on April 11, 1983 on the premises of the Swimming Stadium in Podoli. I was there along with the I. CLTK representatives of the Public Transport Company, Frantisek Stejskal and Arne Polednak. We discussed requirements regarding the Centre Court layout.

This was Kodes' first opportunity to pass his opinion on the project that had been worked out by a husband-wife team of architects, Ladislav Novotny and Jana Novotna, and supervised by Sportprojekt Manager-architect, Josef Kales.

There were requirements expressed by the ITF that concerned not only the Federation Cup or ATP Tour tournaments but also Davis Cup matches: the number of surrounding courts, height of the fences, court-dimensions outside the lines – the running space, drainage, score boards, clay quality. The ITF also dictated the number and size of lockers in the changing rooms, number of showers, size and equipment of the head umpire's office, and many other specifications.

Proposals did not come solely from Kodes but also from the Construction Commission of the PPTC. Since authors of the design had their reservations some of the proposals were not carried out. There were instances in which Sportprojekt was not totally familiar with the details of ITF regulations. And since Kodes was particularly detail-oriented, he frequently consulted with his brother-in-law Milan Vopicka, a designer with the Prague Project Institute.

I approached him often to pick his brains, "You've seen it abroad. Now tell me, how it is supposed to be done!"

He thought of cedar shrubs between the courts, skewed corners, wedged rear court areas. He produced drawings and gave them to me to present to Sportprojekt. I was then able to go to the Sportprojekt team and say: "Take a look at this – this is what it should look like."

And they did. - One day Milan and I went up to the old Maternity Clinic, which had been vacant and unused for several years and we took another look down at the site. We stood on the original path and projected: "Centre Court should be here, five courts up there. Couldn't we fit three more courts down below?"

It caught my brother-in-law's attention immediately: "Imagine if we set them several yards below the level of the surrounding terrain? That would be fantastic! People could be walking up and down the walk-way but the players below would never hear them and would not be disturbed by the noise!"

"Draw it out and I'll take it to them to see what their reaction is like" – I encouraged him.

However, there was a friction – finding a new location for the old Maternity Clinic. A large structure of the clinic right beside a Centre Court for seven thousand spectators was unthinkable! Otakar Ferfecky, a special government envoy for the construction of Prague's Underground, who was also supervising the reconstruction of Stvanice, dryly stated: "Medical community has pleaded for free prosthetics clinic and that's what I promised. Give me a few days to think everything over."

In the end, the problem was solved. Otakar Ferfecky told me that he was going to find another location for the Prosthetic Clinic. He was able to use his influence to push forth the idea of new Stvanice: "Once the decision to rebuild Stvanice was made the site must be reconstructed and we must give tennis enough space and air!" His suggestion made the best sense, as both ATP and ITF rules were clear: "Unless there are at least eight courts within the facility, it would be impossible to host either a tournament or any other world-class tennis event!

Jan Kodes was able to offer some suggestions and a few of his ideas were carried out, such as an indoor training hall with two courts located under the main grandstand. There were still other aspects that he could no longer change, namely the decision to use electric accumulation boilers for heating across the whole stadium. In those days it was believed that there was no way to connect Stvanice to gas supply. However, it was altered during the most recent reconstruction following the destructive floods of 2002.

It would have been a miracle if such a large project ran totally smoothly. Many problems popped up even before the construction began and some of them were rather difficult to resolve. New glitches kept creeping in throughout the construction process.

There was nothing more but a deep hole in the ground at Stvanice, the project still existed mostly on paper, and the tennis community was already wondering about: Who would manage the new Stvanice Tennis Center after the Federation Cup was over?

My thoughts were elsewhere at that point. My vision was clear and simple: a single-purpose Czechoslovak tennis facility like Roland Garros in Paris. My priority was dedicating the stadium solely to tennis once the Federation Cup ended. It made no difference to me who was going to manage it - the Public Transport Company, the Tennis Federation, or the I. CLTK? It did not concern me then.

However, there was growing pressure to make Stvanice a multi-purpose facility, not just a tennis facility. These suggestions were heavily backed by other sports under the patronage of the PPTC.

Gymnasts needed a new gymnasium, the bowling team did not have their own skittle alley, and volleyball players needed a new court and even raised an idea of removable net posts and alternating usage of the courts! And what about, say – shooting range or archery targets? I was under enormous pressure, having to fight off the weirdest ideas and still trying to stick to my vision of a single-purpose tennis facility.

Besides that, the I. CLTK members were often heard voicing their notions of entitlement to the new stadium. Their primary argument was: "We have established ourselves here since long ago!"

It did not occur to me then, that this was the origin of my problems that would finally peak many years later, after 1989. Granted, the I. CLTK and year 1893 marked the beginning of Czech tennis; nobody can take away its historical role. It is unfortunate that in early 1980s Stvanice was in such dreadful condition that the very existence of the club was threatened, primarily because the land it occupied was owned by the State. Technical inspection headed by J. Ungr, an appointed expert, assessed the value of the club facilities – the clubhouse, changing rooms, courts, and fences – at CZK 647,841 (USD approx. 30,000 in those days), which was a negligible amount compared to the future value of the new tennis stadium.

And so it went that the original question "Who will manage Stvanice?" gradually transformed into a significantly trickier one "Who will own Stvanice?"

That would have to be resolved in due course; let us not get ahead of ourselves. We are still in early 1980s, Stvanice is undergoing initial preconstruction work mostly required by the construction of an extension of an Underground line under the Vltava (Moldaw) river and Stvanice Island connecting the Prague center and Florenc and Vltavska stations with Prague 7-Holesovice. The hoisting gear was erected at Stvanice over an enormous construction pit. Tunnels were driven from the pit under the river in both directions, towards the opposing banks of Vltava River. A sewer duct had been drilled shortly before that, connecting Stvanice to the city sewer line under the Vltavska Underground station. This made Stvanice the first island in Prague with sewer pipes.

Jan Kodes must have felt like between rock and hard place. On one hand, he constantly defended the exclusive right of the "white sport" and the potential benefit that the Center at Stvanice could bring for Czech tennis in the future. On the other hand, he was periodically challenged by other athletic departments of Public Transport Company. He did all the work out of his own volition, speaking primarily from the position of the Czechoslovak Davis Cup team captain and a member of the Tennis Federation's Executive Committee!

Arguments over the future ownership of the stadium had no end. Its development was included as part of the Underground construction project, funded by the Public Transport Company and the question who would eventually own it remained unanswered. Should the Company use the facilities as it deemed fit? Or should the whole facility be handed over to the local tennis club? But why should only the tennis club benefit from it? Finally, Prague Public

The old Maternity Hospital was knocked down on September 30, 1984 making way for three additional tennis courts with space for spectator seating.

Transport Company decided to enter in an agreement with CUPES - Czechoslovak Sports Union of Physical Education and Sports, making Stvanice a joint venture.

The designers warned me that a joint venture was the worst option anyone could have chosen; that it was going to lead to endless squabbles over who owned which piece of furniture. I let it hang. There was only one thing on my mind - the end product: the tennis stadium! I kept asking about the capacity of the spectator stands, both the larger one and the smaller one. I enquired about the indoor training hall, where the entrance was going to be and how much space there would be between the baseline and the fence? Those were the issues I was preoccupied with.

Originally, it was projected that the Centre Court would be used only during summer seasons. The doors would be locked by the end of September, and opened again in April, at the beginning of the following season. This concept was accepted even by Otakar Ferfecky, who was the key man over the State money invested in the enormous Underground project.

Yet, I kept telling him that tennis needed something more. Something we could use all year round. I wanted a hall with two courts, a fitness gym, offices, changing rooms, a physiotherapy ward, even a restaurant. We needed a tennis center. His answer was loud and clear: "We can't afford that. The CUPES would have to pitch in!"

What choice did I have? I hurried over to see Antonin Himl, the CUPES Chairman and spilled out to him, "Mr. Chairman, you need to make a contribution to Stvanice on behalf of CUPES. Otherwise, the end result will not satisfy our specifications, and we may well miss our only chance of having a tennis facility of international status in Prague."

In the end, Kodes had his way. A meeting with the Mayor of Prague, Frantisek Stafa, held on March 5, 1984, resulted in a decision to tear down the old Maternity Clinic at Stvanice. Sportprojekt then worked out plans to add three more tennis courts. The actual demolition order of the former Maternity Clinic was issued by the Public Transport Company office on

A breakthrough for the sport! Who would have ever thought , that in 1985 children playing with tennis rackets would feature in the communist Spartakiade?

June 2, 1984. The large building was knocked down on September 30, 1984, making way for three additional tennis courts with space for spectator bleachers. A hall located under the main grandstand, containing two indoor training courts, was drawn into the plans of the project! The question of future management and ownership of the stadium was still unanswered but the most important matters have, finally, been settled. CUPES agreed to provide the additional necessary funding!

Kodes did not interfere in the selection of the future manager, or the owner. Those negotiations started when the construction was already fully under way. About half-a-year later, at one of his regular meetings with Mikulas Lacek, the General Director of Prague's Public Transport Company, Kodes received a surprising piece of news: "Since the PPTC provides the largest share of money, we have decided to keep Stvanice Sport Center as our asset. And since we don't have anyone else to manage it, we will have you do it! As soon as the construction finishes, you will be appointed the Director of the new stadium. So, get yourself ready for it!"

Lacek's decision generated numerous enemies across the Company. Some of his deputies criticised him; times were not easy for him.

What good will come of all that? And who is going to cover the operating expenses?

I explained to them patiently that the stadium was constructed for the needs of the 1986 World Women's Team competition - the Federation Cup. I further explained that

Even a stamp with a tennis motive were printed.

it would be my call to attract more international tournaments and Davis Cup matches in the years to come. We needed three or four major events a year, plus a few more minor ones, to stay afloat. And that was, more or less, what we achieved.

The fact that Kodes became a "director" of the newly established facility irritated his opponents among the members of the tennis club. Soon, there were claims that he was hurting the club, even though it was the exact opposite – he defended I. CLTK's interests. It was he, who said that tennis must stay at Stvanice considering its history that dated back to 1893! The I. CLTK, however, failed to realize that it never owned the estate at Stvanice. The land has always belonged to the State and the City of Prague, which was, therefore, entitled to decide what to do with it.

The deep tradition was my only, albeit the strongest, argument. Members of the club thought the State had robbed them of their land and demanded it to be returned to them. That was, obviously, completely unrealistic. The State could not simply give away gratis a Stadium valued at CZK 120 million (USD approx. 6 million) while it stood on State-owned land!

MARTINA HOME AGAIN

The construction could not be delayed; all was planned exactly for the "D' day. The Stvanice complex was opened on May 9, 1986. The fact that the date coincided with the liberation of Prague by the Russian Army in May 1945 was a result of a socialist resolution thought out by Otakar Ferfecky. It was still during the years when only one party ruled the country. It is to be mentioned that the timely completion about two months before the Federation Cup opening ceremonies was due to that resolution. Hundreds of people took part in the process; all those individuals who dug the soil, drilled, set up carpentry, installed glass windows, poured concrete, welded metal, assembled interiors as well as seats in the stands, and above all those who had worked out the idea and design, created the blue prints, and those who directed the entire project.

The main construction manager in the field was Ing. Josef Martinovsky, who directed his staff and many other individual "teams" like carpenters, railroad workers, operatives, machine industry, a team from Prague's Metrostav, from Mostarna Liskovec, Prefa Hyskov, Stavebni strojirenstvi Brno. There were endless numbers of diligent, complaisant, and often nameless people. More than two hundred swarmed around daily on the construction sight of the future tennis arena. A group of Stanislav Hanzelka from Ostrava's Hutni montaze carried out assembling the steal framework weighing 570 tons; then came Water and Sewer Co. to install water and sewer systems, and finally prefabricated parts of the individual levels of stands came in to be installed. And that is how it went day after day, hour after hour. Rain, shine or snow the centre court and the adjacent court number 1 were growing in front of one's eyes.

Yet, not all was perfectly finished by that day of May 9, 1986. During the month of May the finishing touches were in progress to complete the interiors, acoustics, the landscapes, the entrance walkways, the surrounding greenery and the Information Center in order to have everything in tip-top shape for the Federation Cup. Shortly after the opening of the Center a quality "stress test" was conducted that had been prepared by Jan Kodes, who was the director of the Center at that point, together with Borivoj Kacena.

A number of exhibition matches took place on the clay of the Centre Court (prepared for the entire Stvanice complex by no other but experienced clay court builder Jaromir Sibera) at the beginning of June. Some seven thousand spectators sat in the stands – all builders of Stvanice.

And we watched the court's reaction to stresses of the structure, we watched what happened when the audience applauded, cheered and roared. It was all evaluated by professio-

Martina Navratilova
waited for eleven years to come
back...

Her extraordinary record!
Total Grand Slam titles: 18 in
singles, 31 in doubles and 9 in
mixed doubles with her total 167
singles and 175 doubles career
tournament titles make her the
most successful tennis player of
all time, male or female!

Cyril Suk, Jan Kodes and Barbara Wancke, the acting ITF Executive Director for the Federation Cup.

Jan Kodes returned to Prague less than twenty-four hours before the Federation Cup Opening Ceremonies began.

A steering committee was formed the moment the ITF awarded Prague with 1986 Federation Cup organization and Cyril Suk heading it as the Tennis Federation Chairman. Naturally, Jan Kodes took part in it as well but due to his other engagement as a Davis Cup team captain he sometimes missed meetings. And he was away from Prague even in July 1986, shortly before the opening ceremonies, when last minute finishing touch ups were taking place. He was in Yugoslavia with the Davis Cup team; Mecir, Srejber and Smid played a very tough match in Sarajevo. The home team was favored since their top player, Slobodan Zivojinovic, had reached Wimbledon semifinals only a week before, succumbing to Ivan Lendl in five sets. Kodes gave Srejber his first opportunity in singles and Milan seized the chance to deliver. Though individual matches were close the final score was 5:0 in favor of Czechoslovakia!

As soon as the encounter concluded Kodes briskly packed his bags and left for Prague. The Federation Cup Opening Ceremonies were going to take place at Stvanice the following day. It was lucky that the matches were played indoors in Zetra Hall. Should they have taken place outdoors all kinds of complications could have arisen leading to match suspension for darkness or for rain till the next day. It is unfathomable to think that the person most responsible for the construction of the new tennis facility at Stvanice would miss the festive Federation Cup Opening Ceremony!

U.S. Fed Cup team: captain Marty Riessen, Martina Navratilova, Chris Evert-Lloyd and Zina Garrison (Pam Shriver arrived later).

nals and specialists. For instance, we found out that it was impossible to hear the announcer; we also realized that there were not enough toilets for the full capacity of spectators. All that needed to be adjusted, changed or transformed during the month of June and July in order to pass the inspection and have the official approval by July 20, 1986.

On that day, the filled to capacity Centre Court welcomed the members of thirty two teams of the 24th Federation Cup – the unofficial world women's team championship. Prague could be proud of three superlatives. The most countries ever were represented by their teams, many of which had to pass through qualifying rounds in order to earn a coveted spot in the Czechoslovak Capital. It was the first time that such an important event took place in Eastern Europe. Finally, after eleven years, Martina Navratilova returned home!

No wonder that the interest of the public surpassed the expectations! And nobody knew yet that in the course of that week Hana Mandlikova would be secretly wedded to an Australian Czech Jan Sedlak at the Staromestska Radnice (the Old Town Hall)!

And it was exactly Hana Mandlikova who welcomed "our friend Martina Navratilova" in her opening ceremony speech and in the name of all players! The filled up Stvanice rose as one man and gave a deafening standing ovation, including the members of the presidential box who got swallowed up by the viscera of the stadium.

Martina shed an emotional tear and during the Czechoslovak anthem she could not hold back a flood of emotion. Chris Evert held her hand for she understood well the meaning of that moment for Martina.

In 1982, the ITF assigned to us the organization of the 1986 Federation Cup on one condition: "if you want to organize this event you must issue entry visas to all nominated players". This meant that Martina Navratilova would also receive one. There was a simple reason – this was, practically, an event equal to the World Team Championships.

Popular Teddy Tinling made the opening speech.

Most likely nobody thought of this likelihood then, in spring 1982. But in spring 1986 the United States announced its team roster in which Martina Navratilova was included beside Chris Evert-Lloyd, Zina Garrison and Pam Shriver.

That caused a pretty razzle-dazzle; suddenly, people woke up to the reality and what that meant. A player, who had not been allowed to be mentioned in our media, who had been erased from the public's memory, was going to show up at home!

I was in Paris then, at Roland Garros, when all of a sudden Nancy Jeffett from the U.S. Tennis Association ran up to me. As a person in charge of the Federation Cup Team she articulated her concern: "Jan, we are worried that something might happen to Martina in your country. We received reports that they might put her in jail there. Do you have security in place?"

I dismissed her assuring her that it was all nonsense and, without delay, I approached Martina. "Listen, what's wrong with the Americans? Is something going on? Are you really worried about coming to Prague?"

"Well, you know, I hear that many do not want me to come or they feel strongly against my participation there".

"But that is total nonsense! Most don't even know that you have been nominated!"

Czechoslovak Fed Cup team: coach Vladimir Krch, Helena Sukova, Regina Marsikova, Hana Mandlikova, Andrea Holikova and captain Jiri Medonos.

I also approached Marty Riessen, the American Federation Cup team captain, in order to calm him down. "Marty, please, stay cool and assure everybody at the USTA that no harm will come in Martina's way; there is no reason to worry."

Nevertheless, after his return to Prague, Jan Kodes wanted to find out for himself how the question surrounding Martina's security would play out. He headed to the Central Committee of CUPES and to Antonin Himl. "Comrade Chairman, I have overheard ru-

International Olympic Committee Chairman Juan Antonio Samaranch with the ITF President Philippe Chatrier.

mors that something should happen to Martina Navratilova during the Federation Cup competition here.

She told me about it personally, just now, in Paris; even representatives of the USTA approached me expressing concern regarding her safety here."

"Jan, don't listen to that; elements on our side are just talking. You must know the origin of this."

I realized that those, who had caused her emigration in the first place, were now worried about her popularity. They were worried that now the several-times-over Wimbledon champion could become an idol and a symbol of resistance against the regime. For that reason they started spreading these rumors having a focal intent in mind - they wanted the Americans to take her off the roster and thus prevent her from coming to Czechoslovakia; yet, simultaneously, Martina was ecstatic about returning home after those eleven years.

The hostility and hatred of some of the comrades towards Martina reached such proportions that a publication, and a rather expensive publication at that, of the "Cup Queen and the Princess" was canceled. In the original color publication there was a chapter dedicated to Martina Navratilova. It listed not only her accomplishments under the Czechoslovak flag but also her achievements worldwide that she reached as a citizen of the United States. That publication was intended to be sold during the Federation Cup competition but it got destroyed and quickly reprinted in black and white and without much mention about Martina to whom they spared only a few lines.

Some, the naive ones, thought that the publishers forgot the best player of the world. Fortunately, a few original copies were saved and were distributed among the tennis fans; one copy found its way even into Martina's hands. However, neither she nor anyone else ever found out who, specifically, was behind the liquidation of the original outlay.

The Queen and the Princess around the Cup was not the only publication that succumbed to censorship. The printed program did too! It was prepared by Pavel Vitous, a reputable journalist from Mlada fronta, who was selected by the Tennis Federation. This journalist and home fan had a wonderful opportunity to find out all about her triumphs that the native Czech and later emigrant achieved. The opportunity came after many years when top women's tennis was a "taboo" subject to write about due to Martina's emigration.

Regrettably, even the printed program was subjected to the approval of the Communist Party, and not only the text but also the photos. Though the authorities were obliged to grant Martina an entry visa they still had the power to "omit" any mention of her from the program and thus prevent the Czech fans to find out anything about the seven times Wimbledon champion.

The program was returned to the author from the ill-fated communist edifice by the river Vltava (Moldav) with an accompanying letter from Jaroslav Stanek. This ex-table tennis champion and once top European player became the head sports-page columnist for Rude pravo and, in 1986, a trainee at the Central Committee of the Communist Party. He wrote that names of "problematic" individuals could not be printed in the program and that the name Navratilova could be left only in Chatrier's foreword and in world ranking charts.

"Only in Chatrier" referred to leaving Navratilova's name in the introductory words of ITF President Philippe Chatrier; however, that was permitted only in the English edition! In the Czech translation the American team line-up including Navratilova was omitted! Similarly omitted was the Czechoslovak team line-up from the year 1975 when the team won the Federation Cup in Aix en Provence largely thanks to Martina Navratilova's accomplishment there.

This absurd action of "omission" included Navratilova's photographs and it reached such proportions that the Central Committee of the Communist Party deleted photos of players from all "problematic" countries such as Israel, Chile, Korea, and Taiwan. They accomplished that even in spite of ITF's demand that photos of all teams should be printed in the program and the negatives of the teams' photos had been supplied by the ITF. The volume of the program diminished; only the motto was left "With Sport for Peace and Friendship Among Nations".

The Czechoslovak players were defending their title from 1985 championship in Nagoya, Japan. The team made up of Hana Mandlikova, Helena Sukova, Regina Marsikova and Andrea Holikova and led by their captain Jiri Medonos knew that they had a profoundly difficult task ahead of them. The mood was overly optimistic, perhaps too much so: "host team is able to beat the Americans, the favorites of the Cup." The journalists got into this positive frame of mind along with tennis experts and fans due to Mandlikova's achievement in the "match of her life" the previous year's US Open. In the finals she beat Martina Navratilova 7:6, 1:6, 7:6, and in the semi-finals she defeated Chris Evert-Lloyd!

I saw that final match and it was an amazing one. I can't describe it in any other fashion only that it was a real "meat-grinder"!

Considering the fact that Helena Sukova was an exceptional doubles player the calculations pointed clearly in one direction: Mandlikova would make points in singles and the doubles would decide the final match score. There was a possibility that under favorable conditions the doubles could be won. Some also calculated that Martina might be nervous after eleven years away and playing in front of her home crowd for the first time. However, things turned out differently in the end, and though it sounds paradoxical the home audience helped the outcome.

The home team advanced masterfully to the finals just as the American team did. But, in the finals, they were met by the star "constellation" made up of Chris Evert –Lloyd and Martina Navratilova in singles, and Martina with Shriver in doubles.

The Czech players slumped a bit in the tense atmosphere. Helena Sukova lost 5:7, 6:7 to Chris Evert in a very edgy match when Chris was ahead 4:0, and 5:2 but Helena fought her way back into the match and turned it around to lead 6:5. And the tie-break in the second set was similar. The American was ahead 4:0, Sukova tied the score at 5:5 but the last two points were taken by the American.

The second singles was between Hana Mandlikova and Martina Navratilova. Till then they played altogether twenty five times and Martina won nineteen of those encounters. She won in Prague too: 7:5, 6:1.

I see that match as if it were played today. The Centre Court was filled till the last seat and people cheered spontaneously for Martina. It must have been an awful match for Hana Mandlikova. After the match she sobbed inconsolably. I tried to calm her down: "Hana, it is not that people here do not like you. They just wanted to show Martina that they still stand

Hana Mandlikova after winning a U.S Open
matchpoint in 1985, where she reached the victory
of her life. She accomplished great wins over Chris
Evert-Lloyd 4:6, 6:2, 6:3 in the semifinals and Martina
Navratilova 7:6, 1:6, 7:6 in the finals. In the years 1980
and 1987 she won the Australian Open and in 1981
the French Open. She also played two Wimbledon
finals in 1981 and 1986 but lost to Evert-Lloyd
and Navratilova.

Steffi Graff was injured and could not play, but she was one of the coaches for the German team.

Steffi Graff won the Grand Slam and Olympic Games two years later. She reached an incredible total of twenty two Grand Slam singles titles

The German team held considerable prospect of reaching the Federation Cup finals. Tennis experts valued Kohde – Graf squad very high. Their hopes were marred only by an unbelievable coincidence, when young Steffi suffered an injury during lunch by a fallen table-umbrella that broke her big toe! Thankfully, her father did not take offense against the Center and at the next dinner opportunity he closed a coaching agreement and cooperation with Pavel Slozil.

The following year Steffi became the world number one player and remained under Slozil's guidance for five years. Her achievement outcome? – Fifty five championship titles, ten of them Grand Slam: three Australian Open titles, two Roland Garros, three Wimbledon and two US Open titles. At the press conference in Brühl, where she announced termination (1992) of her contract with Pavel Slozil, she said about him: "From the beginning to the end I valued Pavel's whole-hearted involvement with us."

It was not an uncomplicated post for Pavel Slozil and it was admirable for him to have worked with a player of such caliber for that many years.

behind even though she had emigrated."

"But I am the one representing Czechoslovakia, I am playing at home and my home audience cheers against me. Jan, how can you stand living here? I simply don't understand that!" At that point Hana already lived in the United States for most part of the year.

At the final press conference neither of the Czech players had very complimentary comments on behalf of the audience. Both, Hana Mandlikova as well as Helena Sukova had the impression that the audience did not support them, or they cheered down right against them. That was, without a doubt, true, especially in the match between Mandlikova – Navratilova throughout which the spectators showed visibly with whom they sided. Evidently, the players did not realize that more than tennis was being contested that afternoon.

Hana Mandlikova's comment made me remember again the question: "Live at home, or emigrate?" Some emigrants, who came back after the year 1989, were often excessively celebrated in my opinion. What

Chris Evert and Martina Navratilova were the „star attractions" for the opening of the Czechoslovak tennis centre. They are both among the greatest players of all time together with Margaret Smith-Court and Billie Jean King!

for? That they fled? Working here, at home, for the Czech Tennis was often more difficult than emigrating, and then living and playing in Florida.

When Jaroslav Drobny told me years ago that it was I, who would have to concern himself with Czech tennis one day, I felt great sense of responsibility for tennis and people around it. Truly, the United States did not entice me. Martina Navratilova and Ivan Lendl chose it but I was not enchanted by it. Life there seemed too simple and without flavor. Europe boasts its history and culture. I liked the United States but after two months I was ready to hurry home!

What she said about Jan Kodes
Hana Mandlikova

Jan was already a world star when I was starting my tennis career as a little girl in Sparta. I was only about eight but I remember it exactly. There was a weeping willow next to the courts and I sat there watching him practice or play league club matches.

I remember that till today each time we meet. The name Jan Kodes equaled "gentleman" in my book for his behavior on the court and off the court. He has treated me well ever since we got to know each other.

I remember him as a colossal fighter, especially in Davis Cup matches that I always watched. I hardly registered his Roland Garros victories but I rejoiced when he won the Wimbledon title. It was close to unbelievable, and I myself shared immensely the emotions of that achievement. At home, above my bed, I had a poster of Jan with the cup. Whenever I laid my eyes on the poster I said to myself: "One day I'll win there too!" Jan was my huge role model.

When Jan finished his active tennis career he put his energy into the creation of a tennis stadium; if it weren't for him Stvanice would not exist today and there would have been no Federation Cup in Prague in 1986. Though, admittedly, it was not a pleasant experience for me, especially my match opposite to Martina Navratilova in the finals against the USA, when the audience rooted more for her than for me. I was the one representing Czechoslovakia, a country of my birth and tennis upbringing! At that moment I did not understand the emotions of the circumstances. She had not lived here for a longer period of time so why did people stand behind her? I was naive and did not realize that something totally different played out its role that had nothing to do with tennis or me. The spectators were not against me! When I looked back years later I saw it clearly! It was politics that concerned people! Martina was a symbol of resistance against the regime, which was why they stood behind her! For many she was a model. She wanted to achieve the greatness and that prompted her to emigrate.

I appreciate another thing about Jan. He, too, could have emigrated many times over and live and play abroad but – he did not do it! I realized how much of a patriot he was. I also feel patriotic, in spite of having lived abroad for many years; but I never voiced it the way he has.

When I finished my competitive tennis career and traveled to tournaments with Jana Novotna I did not see Jan much any more. At the time when he was the Tennis Association President I was a captain of the Federation Cup team. It was Jan who was behind putting Jana and Helena together, and thanks to that move the team returned to the top division. We have strengthened our friendship since that time. Jan is goal driven and confident. He is straight with people and says things squarely, which some people in our country do not appreciate. I would confide in him just about anything because I trust him one hundred percent!

Hana Mandlikova

Jan Kodes saw Martina Navratilova at the Stvanice Center several times during the Federation Cup week but their personal encounter took place at the American Embassy during a reception for the team players and some guests.

As usual, we embraced; meeting Martina was nothing special or extraordinary for me. We had seen each other in Wimbledon and Paris. The point that was special was the exact fact that I was actually there, at the reception. I believe it took place in the middle of the week, on Wednesday or Thursday, and the secretary Sandra Klimova summoned me to the restaurant of the Snack Bar on the other side of the stadium, where I should meet the Tennis Federation Chairman Cyril Suk. By the time I got there I found not only Suk and Polak there but also Jaroslav Stanek, the Communist Party Committee member. They informed me about the reception at the American Ambassador's residence in Prague 6, hosted by the Ambassador Shirley Temple.

"We have just decided not to go," announced Stanek. However, in order to fulfill the Federation Cup regulations Medonos and Marsikova will go and will represent our team. The girls are tired anyway – meaning Mandlikova and Sukova - "and we don't think you should go either".

The new center was sold out during the Federation Cup for the first time.

They made a point of telling me that I could suffer repercussions in the future if I attend the reception; I could then be sorry. And they waited for my reaction.

"You must excuse me but I can't do that. I'll go there just for Martina."

Upon that they warned me again to think it over....

At the reception, to my great surprise, I met besides Martina our ex-Davis Cup player and Martina's coach Jiri Parma.

The Federation Cup came to a close. The attendance surpassed expectations, but in its nakedness a problem cropped up that Jan Kodes had drawn attention to already during the earlier phase of the construction of the new Centre Court.

When the Subway line between the stations Florence and Vltavska was under constructi-on the bus stop at Stvanice was not in service. I suggested that subway exits should be constructed at Stvanice – some simple station that would be activated only during functions at Stvanice's Centre Court.

Unfortunately, the suggestion was never acted upon. The expense was financially objectionable, and there was not enough time to bring the construction to completion in time. In the end, an agreement was reached that a station could be built simultaneously with the demolition of the Ice Ring across the street of the bridge. Everything was postponed to the second phase, which should have started soon after the completion of the Centre Court. However, till today in 20 years later has not commenced.

And so, the decrepit Ice Ring wastes away and it repels rather than invites spectators to the tennis center Stvanice. If people come by car they'll find it difficult to locate a parking spot since the number of parking spaces is limited. And when they choose to walk from the subway of either Florenc or Vltavska station they'll hardly think it enjoyable due to the noise of the traffic and the exhaust from the cars along the expressway, notwithstanding the dangers of the busy traffic. Jaywalking from one side of the expressway to the other would be unwise.

Several serious accidents happened there already, one of them, a deadly one, in the first half of the nineties during an ATP Tour....

The Federation Cup competition was the first grand event that took place at the new Stvanice Center. Within a year Jan Kodes fulfilled his promise and achieved that Prague made the Grand Prix roster. In August 1987 Stvanice organized the first men's Cedok Open that began the twelve tournament ATP Tour Series. Jan Kodes was the tournament director.

While the tournament ran only a week the preparations took close to a year. When the final of one tournament was over the tournament director engaged at once in preparation for the next year event.

Jan Kodes' daily routine at Stvanice started out with no less engagement than: tennis club chairman from 1987, Stvanice Center director, ATP Tour tournament director, board member of the tennis association executive committee, and the non-playing captain of the Davis Cup team. There was abundance of work and responsibility but his own dominant priority was preservation of the Stvanice Center's function purely for tennis, as had been originally agreed upon.

I wanted to achieve a situation that was well established in many places in the world, and, also domestically, in ice hockey. The Hockey Association resided in the Sports Hall, where hockey league took place, and so did the international encounters, and, from time to time, World Championships. I had a similar image in my mind for the function of Stvanice.

As a director Jan Kodes was in charge of the I. CLTK (First Czech Lawn-Tennis Club) club committee and had to establish the Center's rules of operation, as well as safety and evacuation rules, and rules of play according to which the club would function.

However, further problems arose at the Czechoslovak Union of Physical Education and Sports; they did not want the tennis association to move from the common building Na Porici to Stvanice Center. They argued that: tennis was growing way too independent, and the tennis association would not be under their close supervision. At that time all of the office supplies were already at Stvanice.

I overheard: "Kodes has his own copy and fax machines! How is that possible? This takes tennis from under our control. We no longer know who they communicate with."

I had arranged all this at Stvanice through the main Federation Cup sponsor, the Japanese firm NEC. Thus, from that point on, ITF started sending faxes directly to me or to the secretary of the Tennis Association instead of via the International Department of the Czechoslovak Union of Physical Education and Sports, as was customary before. The CUPES sensed that they were losing their grip on tennis.

At the same time, there were constant battles for space at the CUPES building. Tennis occupied two or three rooms and voices could be heard: "Let them go to Stvanice! They'll vacate some space that we can take over!" Some CUPES officers approved the transfer of tennis to Stvanice.

Personally, I was surprised that Michal Polak, the Tennis Association secretary did not even want to entertain the idea of transfer! When I asked him why, he claimed that he would have to commute far! "And who is going to be the "gopher" between Stvanice and CUPES?"

"Why should you be a "gopher" running back and forth? Once you are with the Tennis Association you will deal with the international tennis authorities directly. Why would you have to go via CUPES? You'll go there once a week to a meeting with the other secretaries and that's it! End of story!"

This was a classical example of our politically tight centralized democratic system and how it operated. Again, the Chairman of CUPES's Central Committee, Antonin Himl stepped in: "Since tennis has its stadium let them move there in peace!"

I got into conflicts with Polak several times because I had a function of the International Secretary as well as of a Davis Cup team captain at the time of heightened friction around Ivan Lendl. I remember the time when Ivan wished for his parents to come to the

Master's tournament in New York. The Chairman of CC of CUPES agreed to it and I was put in charge of arranging all necessary formalities with the help of the Tennis Federation manager. At that time the secretary, Michal Polak, filled out the necessary forms for Ivan's parents' exit permits and he assured me that all would be ready on time. But the Master's tournament was approaching and I still had nothing from him! In the end it was discovered

Jan Kodes with Juan Mario Samaranch (center) and Antonin Himl. Cyril Suk (behind).

that the forms were left in the secretary's drawer at the tennis association and never made it to the Ministry of Interior. Only after several interventions by Antonin Himl the issue was resolved and Ivan's parents flew to New York. However, my squabbles with Michal Polak continued on. He left the Association only under the chairmanship of Jiri Lendl, when it transpired that Polak was a Secret Police Agent (StB) with two code names: "Tenista" (tennis player) and "Sekretar" (secretary).

At this point I can't help but elevate again the Chairman of the Central Committee of CUPES. If it were not for him and the Prime Minister Lubomir Strougal tennis would have been defeated in a lopsided battle by the "normalizers" like Husak, Bilak, Fojtik, and others. It was fortunate that there was a man at the head of our athletics who understood sports, liked sports, rooted for sports, and was well aware that athletic achievements of our athletes, not just of tennis players, on foreign soil were the best advertisement for our country.

There is nobody who could even start to imagine how many times Antonin Himl cringed because he had to smooth out problems or resolve incidents; how many times he stood up for a number of our athletes. He could have been liquidated since the communist "apparatus" had limitless power. One word and he would have been gone! Yet, they did not take him out. Why? Because he drew respect. Albeit a communist he did not permit to be blinded by Bolshevik slogans and he always intended to help the right cause. He was a personality with an amazingly strong character, who managed to observe things with an objective attitude and open mind. At the same time, as I myself found out, he was also a visionary.

Some time in the middle of the Stvanice construction, quasi in 1985, when the Centre Court was deployed and the steel structure of the future stands was up, the entire Center had a run-through test day. Himl called me the day before to let me know that he would be coming with the vice-chairman Eliasek. He wanted to have an idea of how far the construction has progressed, and judge from it whether it was realistic to expect it to be finished by the Federation Cup date.

We climbed the skeletons of the stands all the way up to the top of the Centre Court. Himl looked in all directions and after a while he turned to me and said: "Well, Jan, this is truly fine! What a stadium! Many tennis countries around us would die for it! But I must mention one thing to you."

"And what is that Mr. Chairman?"

"You'll remember me one day. Time will come and, you'll see, they won't even let you play here!"

Jan Kodes will return to Prague not even twenty four hours before the Federation Cup Opening Ceremonies. When ITF delegated the 1986 Federation Cup Championship to Prague a Steering Committee was formed led by the Tennis Association Chairman Cyril Suk. Naturally, Jan Kodes had a seat on that committee. However, considering his involvement with and duties to the Davis Cup team he missed several meetings. He was also absent in July 1986, shortly before the opening ceremonies, when the Steering Committee's responsibilities were culminating; he was in Yugoslavia with his Davis Cup team. The match took place in Sarajevo; Mecir, Srejber and Smid endured a very tough challenge there. The home team felt strongly superior; their number one player was Slobodan Zivojinovic, who had reached Wimbledon semifinals only a week before, surrendering to Ivan Lendl in five sets. Jan Kodes gave a chance to Milan Srejber for the first time and Srejber grabbed the opportunity. Though the individual matches were not easy the final score was 5:0 for Czechoslovakia!

After the Davis Cup encounter conclusion Kodes packed up his bags in a flash and flew to Prague. The very next day was the Federation Cup opening day! Thank God the matches in Sarajevo were played in the indoor stadium Zetra. Who knows what would have happened had it been played outdoors?! It could have been delayed for darkness or rain, and games would have been postponed to the next day. Can anyone imagine that the man, who was so responsible for the success of the entire Stvanice Tennis Center project, would miss the Opening Ceremonies of the Federation Cup?

WHO OWNS STVANICE?

The construction of new Stvanice Stadium that opened in 1986 for the Federation Cup finals, was funded by the government through Prague Public Transport Company. That was why, at the time, nobody found it surprising that the modern tennis facility, the envy of many other countries with far-reaching tennis traditions, was also owned by the state. After all, it was located on state-owned land, and the organization that had built it was also responsible for its maintenance. There was just one entity unable to come to terms with that provision – the I. Czech Lawn Tennis Club.

Once the Federation Cup ended in July 1986, the stadium entered normal operations. Jan Kodes was, indeed, able to stand up to his promise to hold several major tennis events throughout the year; the first of them was a Davis Cup match on October 3, in which Czechoslovakia suffered a defeat against Sweden. The next took place in August of the following year; it was the first round of the Grand Prix Tour – the Cedok Open with USD 176,000 purse. Marian Vajda from Slovakia grabbed the title.

At that point Jan Kodes wore two hats. First and foremost he was elected Chairman of the I. Czech Lawn Tennis Club, while also being employed by the Prague Public Transport Company as a director of the facility. He had no idea what kind of hell would break loose in just a few months.

Still before the 1989 Velvet Revolution, the Czechoslovak government decided to transfer the ownership of Stvanice Stadium from the Prague Public Transport Company to CUPES (the Czechoslovak Union of Physical Education and Sports). Shortly after the Revolution, however, the original CUPES was replaced by the new CCSPA (Czechoslovak Confederation of Sports and Physical Associations) that made quite a logical decision: since Stvanice was a tennis facility, let the Czechoslovak Tennis Association handle it. At that time, the Tennis Association was presided over by Jiri Lendl (father of Ivan Lendl), who succeeded Cyril Suk. Nobody properly thought through the possible consequences of this decision. Above all it was condemned by numerous members of the I. Czech Lawn Tennis Club who promoted tradition and attempted to protect their alleged "rights". Their reasoning thus went: "The new Stvanice

Stadium belongs to us because our Club has resided here from its very inception! We can manage the facility ourselves! At the same time we can allow the Tennis Federation to hold its own events, such as Davis Cup, the way they always have!"

They attracted an influential supporter to side with them who, despite living mostly in Luxembourg between 1984 and 1988, visited Prague quite frequently and knew what was going on there. It was a very clever move, since the person they recruited was Frantisek Stejskal Jr., a member of a family with strong ties to the I. CLTK. His father, Frantisek Stejskal Sr., who became a member of the club in 1921, spent great many years at Stvanice. In 1983 he took part in the "Good Bye to Old Stvanice" Event. The slogan of that day was: "I. CLTK - the oldest Czech tennis club. Let's cling to tradition!"

Posters were hung all around the stadium and Kodes received anonymous threats of physical riddance. They called him a Communist, even though he had never joined the Party. He remembered all too well what the communists did to his father in 1951! Admittedly, he was received twice by Lubomir Strougal, the Prime Minister of the communist government, upon victories at Wimbledon and in Davis Cup. It is also true that the work he did on behalf of tennis after he had ended his active tennis career required him to deal with representatives of the regime. After all, he spent most of his life under the single-party rule; he did not have much of a choice. He lived doing the same thing as those who later publicly criticized him.

The annual club conference, held in spring 1990, decided everything. The opposition blamed Kodes for all kinds of things and went as far as rigging the vote. In spite of it, Jan managed to get through by a few votes but his enemies celebrated crucial victory, since the club also voted in a new president, Frantisek Stejskal Jr. At this point Jan Kodes did not have a single ally. They still offered to make him a committee member, but he refused. The coup succeeded!

Nevertheless, the cardinal question as to "Who owns Stvanice" was not yet answered. Individual sport associations took advantage of newly acquired freedom and desired managing their own affairs. In 1991, when it became obvious that future of the Federation of Czech Lands and Slovakia was in jeopardy, they started splitting assets. Those located in Slovakia fell to the Slovaks, while Czechs got assets located in the Czech territory, including the Stvanice tennis stadium, presently owned by the sports associations' confederation. Its subsequent transfer to the Czech Tennis Association meant one thing for Jan Kodes, still its director: the Stvanice Stadium would serve no other purpose but tennis events!

Instead, however, other conflicts came up. On the Eve of 1993 the Czech and Slovak Federation ceased to exist. As a consequence, so did the Czechoslovak Tennis Association, taking with it all its legal obligations. Its assets and legal identity were taken over by the Czech Tennis Association, headed by Jindrich Kincl from Brno, the Capital of Moravia. In reaction, some members of the I. CLTK started calling for the abolition of Kodes' position, saying that the operation of the stadium could be safely delegated to the Club.

Chairman Kincl had a different suggestion; he proposed a motion to replace Kodes' position with a new contract signed by the Czech Tennis Association and Kodes' own Pro Tennis JK Agency to organize ATP Tour and WTA Series tournaments at Stvanice. This contract remained in place till December 31, 1998, when it was discontinued by the new president of the Czech Tennis Association, Ivo Kaderka, reasoning that Czech Tennis did not need major tournaments, such as those brought about by the ATP Tour. Simultaneously, Kaderka surrendered the Prague Tournament's time slot that Jan Kodes had secured and included among the Tennis Association's assets totally "gratis" in 1987 after much effort, making Czechoslovakia the first post-communist country ever to achieve that.

What I resented most of all was the attitude of Frantisek Stejskal, the new president of the I. CLTK, my peer and the very same person, who sat with me in the Sportprojekt office ten years earlier, discussing enthusiastically the Tennis Centre Court Project. The transfer of ownership to the Czech Tennis Federation had no impact on the I. CLTK's ability to use the

The three most important founding dates: 1893 – I. Czech Lawn Tennis Club, 1906 – Czech Tennis Association, 1918 – Czechoslovak Tennis Association.

facilities, albeit on state-owned land. The new president of the club claimed, however, that the state stole what belonged to the club and that I signed my name under it! The contrary was true! I have always honoured historical arrangements and always defended the interests of the club! The original value of the dilapidated club facilities at Stvanice, according to an expert study published on 19 August 1983 amounted to mere 647,841 Korunas (approx. USD 30,000) at that time. The new facility, valued now at some 120 million Korunas (approx.USD 6 million) was handed back to the Tennis Association! Was all that my fault? What if the new stadium was never constructed? Would tennis still exist at Stvanice today?

While still in a position of the director of the tennis stadium at Stvanice, Kodes reasoned that "the I. Czech Lawn Tennis Club should be allowed to reside at Stvanice, as it belonged there historically." He went on to close a contract with Stejskal – the president of the I. CLTK – allowing the Club to stay at Stvanice for 25 years with an option of possible indefinite use. However, the club will never boast absolute guarantee to using the land since it is state-owned, unless it decides to buy the expensive estate, and the state is willing to sell it!

The Centre Tennis Court has been around for 25 years now. Throughout the years it has witnessed thirteen ATP Tour Tournaments, Davis Cup and Fed Cup matches, WTA, Challenger, and ATP veteran tournaments, international and local youth and junior events, exhibitions, league matches, VIP tournaments for politicians and businessmen, beach volleyball and also commercials shooting and concert events.

Ivo Kaderka, the new Czech Tennis Association president, entered into an agreement with the I. CLTK, splitting the facility and managerial duties in two. At the same time this contract worked to the effect of a ceasefire arrangement, giving the Club an illusion of being their own masters, managing their own affairs under their own bank account. Yet, the land under the facilities has never belonged to the Club. The whole "Kodes saga" looks like a revenge against a man, who was a visionary; he did what he did for the sake of tennis in the name of progress!

Following the destructive floods of 2002, Stvanice used the insurance funding to renovate its interiors. However, the attractive Stadium has not held a major event it so clearly merits... New plans for a reconstruction of the tennis stadium are being drawn, inspired by Kodes' successor Ivo Kaderka. There was even speculation saying that, should Prague decide to apply for the organization of the Olympic Games in 2020 or 2024, the Stvanice Centre Court could be transformed into a multi-purpose sports hall.

Suddenly, nobody is voicing concern about the future of tennis at Stvanice...

Stvanice Island on Vltava (Moldav) river – great view from the air, formerly called: Grand or New Venice!

GRAND PRIX – ATP TOUR

1973 was the first year in Prague's history to host one of the Grand Prix series tournaments played for prize money – something unheard of until then. The home team triumphed when Jiri Hrebec beat Jan Kodes in the Czechoslovaks-only final. Held in Prague's Ice-Hockey Arena, the tournament was featured upcoming stars such as Björn Borg and Guillermo Vilas, and numerous seasoned players previously known to Czechoslovak tennis fans only from rare TV appearances – Roger Taylor, Roscoe Tanner, Nikki Pilic, Ove Bengtson, and Balazs Taroczy. It seemed that the tournament might become a regular event; however, it took fourteen long years before Prague hosted another event of such calibre.

In 1987, a series of thirteen tournaments commenced at Stvanice Island, during which three Roland Garros winners introduced themselves to the Czech public - Sergi Bruguera, Yevgeny Kafelnikov, and Thomas Muster, as well as Barcelona Olympics winner Marc Rosset, and many other excellent players – mostly clay-court specialists. Jan Kodes directed twelve of those thirteen events, known through the years as Cedok Open, Czechoslovak Open, Skoda Czech Open, Paegas Czech Open and Tento Czech Open.

It is hard to imagine how difficult it was in 1987 to obtain dollar funding for a tournament to be included in the Nabisco Grand Prix Series. Pulling this off during the communist era was a small miracle in itself. The tournament had to be approved by the Ministry of Finance and the CUPES' committee. It was financed mostly by Cedok, then the country's largest travel agency that, thanks to Kodes' contacts, entered in an agreement with the Czech Tennis Association in January 1987 to organize jointly the International Grand Prix Cedok Open events from 1987 to 1990. Cedok also coordinated a five-day stay for foreign visitors, combining entries to the most important tennis matches with tours of Prague's historic landmarks. In addition they also offered tennis clinics!

Kodes secured a time window for the tournament in mid-August. The first event attracted a total of 15,000 spectators; nine of the world's top 100 players entered the tournament, including legendary Guillermo Vilas from Argentina. His participation held almost a symbolic value. Fourteen years earlier he played in Prague's Sports Ice-Hockey Arena as hardly known novice; this time he arrived at Stvanice as a winner of four Grand Slams titles.

On the first three occasions, in years 1987 to 1989, Cedok provided USD 176,000 in prize money; however, following the third tournament, they announced that they would not be able to sponsor the event anymore!

Political tension was high across the country.

Through Kodes' efforts a Monte Carlo-based Telemundi Group was brought in. The owner of the company, Wolfgang Stein, provided the USD 176,000 worth of prize money. Jan Kodes then secured more funding from local sponsors to cover the tournament's operating expenses.

The early years of the tournament demanded enormous efforts from its Director. He had to use his foreign connections in order to bring the Nabisco Grand Prix to Prague. It was not easy; it involved negotiating with players or their managers, persuading them to come to Prague, arranging contracts, providing transport and accommodations, making Stvanice ready and compliant with ATP regulations, contracting TV coverage, and presiding over the organizing committee. That, in turn, had to cope with ever growing number of additional tasks – promotions, advertising, building of VIP facilities, press core operation, programme and tickets printing, registration, player and umpire catering, and staffing. Considering the number of contracts with all sponsors and business partners, there was an overwhelming responsibility put on a single person.

The third Roland Garros title for Jan Kodes was in the Senior Doubles 1988. With Jaime Fillol, they won over Bob Hewitt and Frew Mc Millan in the finals 6:2,7:6. From left: Mc Millan, Hewitt, Kodes, Fillol. The trophy was given by Marcel Bernard, Roland Garros winner from 1946.

Peter Kovarcik, then a Telemundi Group representative for Eastern Europe, introduced Jan Kodes to Wolfgang Stein. The sponsoring company was a sister company of Telemundi firm that resided in Bratislava, Slovakia, and sponsored numerous other events.

Thus, in March 1990, the Czech Tennis Federation and Telemundi entered a five-year contract for tournament sponsorship, with Telemundi Holding exclusive marketing rights. The contract also included a condition that Kodes would remain in the post of the tournament Director.

In 1990, the deceptiveness of the summer date appeared for the first time, since it was also perceived as part of the ATP Tour series. Due to the upcoming US Open and strong hard court competition held in the US, many top players were lured away from Europe during August, making Kodes rethink the date of the tournament. Despite of it all he managed to obtain higher prize money (USD 365,000), raising the tournament appeal and with that attracting players' interest again.

A major change came in 1992. In May, the Czechoslovak Tennis Federation closed a new contract with Teleaxis Holding Company.

Disagreements between Mr. Stein and Mr. Kovarcik started to show in the course of the previous year. This may have been caused by Peter Kovarcik's growing involvement. His goal was transparent – to infiltrate Czech tennis, unscrupulously taking advantage of the Czech media to promote that objective. New contract was signed after Kovarcik and Stein parted for good. Telemundi Eastern Europe transformed into Teleaxis Holding A.G. that no longer had anything to do with the original Telemundi Group Company and Wolfgang Stein. Kovarcik was left only with his contacts and "know-how" aspirations and he managed his new company single-handed, aided by his business partner Helmut Amhof from Vienna.

The above mentioned new contract was signed by Jiri Lendl, the new President of Czechoslovak Tennis Federation, and Helmut Amhof representing Teleaxis. That year the Czechoslovak Tennis Federation held five major events: men's ATP Prague Challenger, Davis Cup, WTA women's tournament, men's ATP Tour Czechoslovak Open, and a Junior satellite tour. All marketing aspects of those five events were sold to Teleaxis for CZK 25 million (USD approx. 800,000); however the Tennis Federation still acted as the owner and organizer! Teleaxis was only responsible for financing, being entitled to re-sell the events, use them for marketing purposes, and sell TV as well as advertising rights...

Grand Prix Prague1987 - Official draw was made on centercourt. From left: Jan Kodes, ATP Tour Manager Vittorio Selmi, referee Knut Gräbner and ATP Supervisor Thomas Karlberg.

Unfortunately, Teleaxis Holding did not perform as contracted. Funds should have been sent to the Czechoslovak Tennis Association according to a schedule specified by the contract. Most payments, however, were delivered late. In addition, Peter Kovarcik started interfering in organizational issues, which were the responsibility of the tournament Director.

He must have thought that since he represented the marketing company bringing in all the money, he had the right to do as he pleased.

The trouble culminated in 1993 on the I. Czech Lawn Tennis Club's 100th anniversary. Marketing related to the celebrations of this momentous event was, once again, delegated to Teleaxis; however, Peter Kovarcik declared that the occasion did not merit the presence of either Ivan Lendl nor Martina Navratilova!

Our relationship was deeply disturbed. Telemundi alias Teleaxis no longer represented our true interests the way it had in the past; the present-day Teleaxis and the Association were not following common goals anymore. I suddenly realized that Peter Kovarcik was not a respectable partner.

Gradually, Jan Kodes found himself again in a difficult spot. In 1987, he became a Director of an ITF Grand Prix tournament while retaining his other position with the Executive Committee of the Czechoslovak Tennis Federation. Suddenly, he began to realize that even though he was not acting as the President of the I. Czech Lawn Tennis Club anymore, certain people still viewed his two positions – a Director of Stvanice stadium and of the tournament – with apprehension. He sensed that the Tennis Federation looked at him as an individual with too much power. He also felt that the ranks of his opponents were being strengthened by some members of the I. CLTK – namely those who inspired his departure from the position of the Club's President. Obviously, they were still unable to come to terms with the fact that the Stvanice facility neither belonged to, nor was run by the Club.

It did not come as a surprise to me to hear that some members of the Tennis Federation management started to proclaim that should the Stvanice stadium be handed over to the Tennis Federation, the position of the stadium's director would become redundant.

The position of the Director of the Tennis Center was abolished on 27 February 1992, while the Czechoslovak Tennis Federation President, Jiri Lendl, was still in office. His own post ceased when the former Czechoslovak Federal Republic split into Czech and Slovak Republics as of January 1993. From the beginning of 1993, his responsibilities were taken over by Jindrich Kincl, the President of CTA (Czech Tennis Association). After Jan Kodes left his post and handed over the tennis stadium officially to the CTA, the Association still expected him to continue organizing the ATP Tour event.

The new Tennis Association President decided to hire me as a contractor to organize and manage the ATP Tour event, which meant that I actually directed the tournament as a private entrepreneur. We entered a three-year contract with an option for three more years. I signed it on April 13, 1993 with an expiration date of December 31, 1995. On December 18, 1995, the contract was extended until December 31, 1998.

The actual wording of the contract was also influenced by Jiri Lendl, the President of the Federal (Czechoslovak) Tennis Federation (since 1993 Association), since the negotiations had begun in late 1992. From my point of view, the key issue of the contract was to include my own fee in the budget. In other words: the Czech Tennis Association did not pay me a penny; on the contrary, it was my responsibility to get sponsors to provide prize money, cover tournament costs, starting fees for certain players, and my own salary. The association only had to bear the operating costs of the facilities, mostly maintenance and necessary modifications. I was also allowed to use the administrative equipment of the tennis association, and the tennis stadium.

During the twelve years that Jan Kodes acted as the Tournament Director, Prague saw a number of world-class players and witnessed numerous thrilling matches. Sergi Bruguera, a double Roland Garros champion, won the tournament twice, beating Andrei Chesnokov from Russia in the 1993 finals, and Andrei Medvedev from the Ukraine in the finals of 1994. Yevgeny Kafelnikov – another winner of the French Open – overcame our local Czech player, Bohdan Ulihrach, in the 1996 final.

The very first event held in 1987 was won by Slovak Marian Vajda, followed by Thomas Muster (1988), Marcelo Filippini (1989), Jordi Arrese (1990), and Karel Novacek (two consecutive wins in 1991 and 1992). Bohdan Ulihrach triumphed in 1995. Following Kafelnikov's win of 1996, there were three more winners – Cedric Pioline (1997), Fernando Meligeni (1998), and – the last symbolic winner, again another Slovak, Dominik Hrbaty (1999). In 1999, however, Jan Kodes did not act as the head of the tournament anymore...

We must be reminded that it was Kodes who pushed through the idea of holding minor tournaments just before the main ATP Tour Czech Open event. Inspired by the tournaments in Cincinnati and Miami, the ATP Prague Challenger with prize money totalling USD 25,000 began in 1991, offering an opportunity mostly to young Czech players. They were given two occasions to gather points in two qualifying and two main tournaments. The Tennis Association was allowed to assign double the number of wild cards, even to players who had not gained enough points. There were mostly sporting rewards for the organizers. The ATP Prague Challenger was won by Jan Kodes Jr. (1991), Karol Kucera (1992), Gilbert Schaller (1993), Jiri Novak (1994), Albert Portas (1995, 1997), Galo Blanco (1996), and Michal Tabara (1998). Additional players reached the finals, among them Hicham Arazi (1995), Gustavo Kuerten (1996), and Radek Stepanek (1998).

It was immensely motivating for them because each winner was awarded a wild card for the upcoming "major" tournament. That was the case – for example – with Jiri Novak. Challenger finals were broadcast on TV and young players had a chance to get a whiff of world-class tennis and all that it entailed.

The Prague Challenger Tournament continues to be held till today. The following players celebrated victories between 1999 and 2008: Michal Tabara (1999), Albert Montanes (2000), Ctislav Dosedel (2001), Olivier Patience (2002), Sjeng Schalken (2003), Jan Hernych (2004 and 2005), Robin Vik (2006), Dusan Lojda (2007), and Jan Hernych (2008). Prize money has fluctuated between USD 50,000 and 125,000. In 2001 and 2002, the tournament was titled ATP Challenger – ECM Cup, and it has been known as the ECM Prague Open since 2003. Sadly, it is seldom mentioned that the tournament was founded in early 1990s.

**Marian Vajda become the first Grand Prix winner at Stvanice in 1987.
Surprisingly beat Tomas Smid 6:1, 6:3 in the finals.**

Let us commemorate individual years of the ATP Tour tournament held in Prague in more details.

There were always 32 players in the main draw event but the draw-sheets enclosed show only matches starting from the quarter-finals.

Year 1: Cedok Open 1987

Organization of the tournament was possible thanks to Cedok that provided the necessary funding. However, there were fears that foreign players would not readily find their way to Prague, since it was a new addition to the Grand Prix Series schedule. As much as a half of the 32 starting positions was reserved for foreigners! Nine players came from the World Top 100, the best among them was Miloslav Mecir, ranked as No. 5 in the world. A world-class tennis star, Guillermo Vilas, also entered but got defeated in the semi-finals. That made it possible for the finals to become a purely home players' affair. Nineteen-year-old Petr Korda staged the biggest surprise of the tournament when he advanced as far as the quarter-finals after beating Jordi Arrese from Spain and compatriot Milan Srejber. Those conquests improved his world ranking position from the 500s to 280. Tomas Smid's defeat in the finals astonished many.

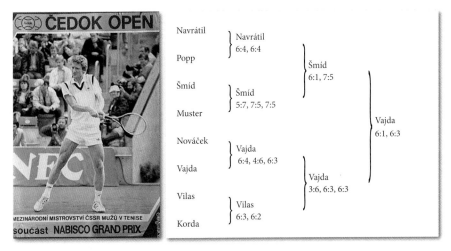

Navrátil	Navrátil 6:4, 6:4		
Popp		Šmíd 6:1, 7:5	
Šmíd	Šmíd 5:7, 7:5, 7:5		
Muster			Vajda 6:1, 6:3
Nováček	Vajda 6:4, 4:6, 6:3		
Vajda		Vajda 3:6, 6:3, 6:3	
Vilas	Vilas 6:3, 6:2		
Korda			

Finals: Vajda – Smid 6:1, 6:3

Year 2: Cedok Open 1988

Prague welcomed presence of Guillermo Perez-Roldan from Argentina, who had collected several trophies on European clay courts, and Thomas Muster; who seemed to want to alert other world-class players to the existence of the Prague tournament. Once again,

Mečíř	Luna 6:2, 6:4		
Luna		Muster 6:3, 6:1	
Muster	Muster 6:2, 6:1		
Duncan			Muster 6:4, 5:7, 6:2
Šrejber	Střelba 6:4, 6:1		
Střelba		Perez-Roldan 6:1, 6:1	
Nováček	Perez-Roldan 6:4, 6:4		
Perez-Roldan			

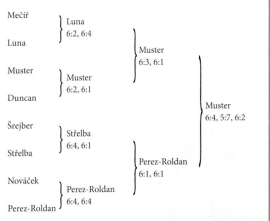

top players did not prosper. Mecir was eliminated by Spanish veteran Fernando Luna, other players were dispatched from the draw by local junior Martin Strelba. Occupying the 240 position in the world rankings, he only made it to the main tournament on a wild card. Then, in sequence, he beat previous year finalists Vajda and Smid, and went on to eliminate Srejber! His "wild ride" was stopped by Perez-Roldan in the semi-finals. Muster also showed his qualities and much fighting spirit, and earned a well-deserved victory.

Finals: Muster – Perez-Roldan 6:4, 5:7, 6:2

Year 3: Cedok Open 1989

While nobody was sure if foreign players would arrive in Prague for the first two Cedok Opens, this time the situation was exactly the opposite. Only two locals, Strelba and Korda, advanced to the final stages of the tournament, though only to the quarter-finals. The

Martin Strelba reached the semis in 1988, but his best ever wins over Edberg were in Munich. He beat him there twice: in 1989 and 1990.

Marcelo Filippini

highest-ranked player, Arrese from Spain, was eliminated by Petr Korda in the second round. The Austrian Horst Skoff promised to emulate Thomas Muster's success from the year before, however Uruguay's Marcelo Filippini from Montevideo proved to be too much of a match for him. At the press conference Skoff, a likeable and funny character himself, blamed the lack of success in the finals on his chasing after Prague's girls, not saving enough energy for the match.

Finals: Filippini – Skoff 7:5, 7:6

Year 4: Czechoslovak Open 1990

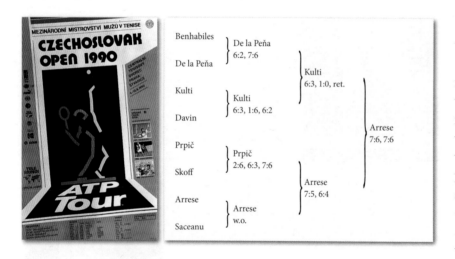

In 1990, the friction due to holding the event in summer began to manifest itself for the first time, as a result of simultaneous hard court tournaments played in the US. Cedok was replaced by a new sponsor, the Telemundi Group (later Teleaxis), and the tournament was renamed to Czechoslovak Open. Top Czechoslovak players headed by Mecir, Srejber, Korda and Novacek did not include Prague in their schedules that year. When Magnus Gustafsson from Sweden turned down the entry, and after Muster, Perez-Roldan, and De la Pena defaulted from their matches prematurely, it was Spaniard Jordi Arrese's chance to rehabilitate himself and compensate for previous year's failure. He went on and overwhelmed Swedish Nicklas Kulti in extremely hot conditions.

Finals: Arrese – Kulti 7:6, 7:6

Year 5: Czechoslovak Open 1991

With more points and total prize money of USD 365,000) being offered, local players as well as world top clay-court specialists returned to fight for the title. Spectators witnessed two outstan-

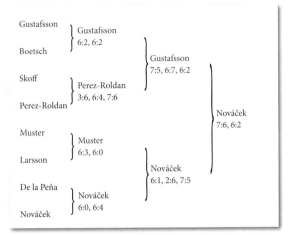

Gustafsson	Gustafsson 6:2, 6:2		
Boetsch		Gustafsson 7:5, 6:7, 6:2	
Skoff	Perez-Roldan 3:6, 6:4, 7:6		
Perez-Roldan			Nováček 7:6, 6:2
Muster	Muster 6:3, 6:0		
Larsson		Nováček 6:1, 2:6, 7:5	
De la Peña	Nováček 6:0, 6:4		
Nováček			

Magnus Gustafsson reached the 1991 Prague finals. In 1989 has became famous by victories over Andre Agassi and Mats Wilander at Stockholm.

ding semi-final matches with Gustafsson overcoming Perez-Roldan in a formidable battle. Karel Novacek, a fresh winner of the Kitzbühel tournament, and having also won the titles in Auckland and, most importantly, in Hamburg was going through the best season of his life. He played three difficult sets against Thomas Muster in the semis and overwhelmed Magnus Gustafsson in the finals, as he had earlier in Kitzbühel. His win elevated him to the eighth ATP position, the best rank of his career.

Finals: Novacek – Gustafsson 7:6, 6:2

Year 6: Skoda Czechoslovak Open 1992

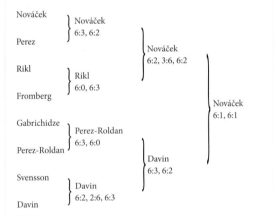

Nováček	Nováček 6:3, 6:2		
Perez		Nováček 6:2, 3:6, 6:2	
Rikl	Rikl 6:0, 6:3		
Fromberg			Nováček 6:1, 6:1
Gabrichidze	Perez-Roldan 6:3, 6:0		
Perez-Roldan		Davin 6:3, 6:2	
Svensson	Davin 6:2, 2:6, 6:3		
Davin			

Karel Novacek took the Prague Open titles in 1991 and 1992.

This year the tournament was named after the Skoda Auto car maker, part of the VW Group. Karel Novacek was suffering from back problems and hesitated whether he should enter at all. In the end, he decided to come and try to defend the title and it proved to be the right decision. Similarly, Jordi Arrese's appearance was in jeopardy. The silver medallist from the Barcelona Olympics was also uncertain; Arrese's agent announced that the Spanish player was immensely exhausted and would not be coming to Prague. However, Arrese got himself in gear and, living up to his promise, he arrived and played. However, the exhaustion from the Olympics took its toll and, in the end, Arrese lost in the second round to the soon-to-be finalist. Surprisingly, Franco Davin went on to win over his compatriot Perez-Roldan. In the finals, Karel Novacek demolished the Argentine in 54 minutes.

Finals: Novacek – Davin 6:1, 6:1

Sergi Bruguera arrived in Prague as a two times Roland Garros winner in 1993 and 1994 . He beat two Andrei´s - Chesnokov and Medvedev. Picture: Trophy given by Jan Kodes.

Year 7: Skoda Czech Open 1993

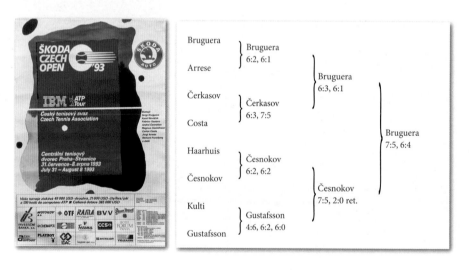

Sergi Bruguera, a Roland Garros champion and the world's top clay-court player, arrived! He was chaperoned by his father, who wanted to see Prague and also claimed better influence over his son than the player's agents. It was to Kodes' credit that the Prague tennis fans had the opportunity to watch the "clay-court king" in action. Jan had known Bruguera senior from his own days around tennis establishments. Six more players ranked in the world top 50 appeared at Stvanice, as did the newcomers Carlos Costa and Paul Haarhuis. Several players were attracted away by the Kitzbühel tournament, held at the same time and offering USD 400,000 in prize money. Not even one Czech player reached the quarter-finals in the talent-packed Prague event.

Finals: Bruguera – Chesnokov 7:5, 6:4

The doubles Skoda Czech Open winners in 1994. Karel Novacek (left) and Mats Wilander.

Year 8: Skoda Czech Open 1994

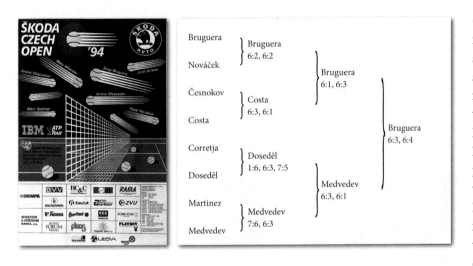

Bruguera
Nováček
} Bruguera 6:2, 6:2

Česnokov
Costa
} Costa 6:3, 6:1

} Bruguera 6:1, 6:3

Corretja
Doseděl
} Doseděl 1:6, 6:3, 7:5

Martinez
Medvedev
} Medvedev 7:6, 6:3

} Medvedev 6:3, 6:1

} Bruguera 6:3, 6:4

Only the Czech junior, Jiri Novak, showed some resistance to the Spanish title-defender in the first round, when he stole a set from him. This aside, both players from the world top 10, Sergi Bruguera and Ukrainian Andrei Medvedev, proved their dominance. Both advanced easily into the finals. In the end, even Medvedev, who had not lost a set before the finals, succumbed to Bruguera. Karel Novacek, a fresh winner of the Dutch Championship in Hilversum, was stricken by bad luck throughout the tournament. First, his luxury Mercedes was stolen, including all his tennis gear making him play against Mats Wilander with an old racket he found in his cellar. The following night, he had to stay up with his sick daughter, and an unfavourable draw made him face Bruguera as early as in the quarter-finals. - After the tournament ended, the Czech Tennis Association withdrew from its contract with Teleaxis, and marketing services for the following events held between 1995 and 1998 were provided by a newly established CTA Marketing Company.

Finals: Bruguera – Medvedev 6:3, 6:4

Year 9: Skoda Czech Open 1995

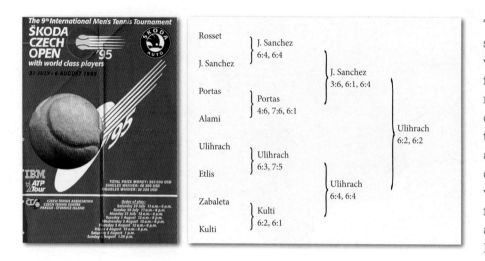

```
Rosset
              J. Sanchez
              6:4, 6:4
J. Sanchez
                              J. Sanchez
                              3:6, 6:1, 6:4
Portas
              Portas
              4:6, 7:6, 6:1
Alami
                                              Ulihrach
                                              6:2, 6:2
Ulihrach
              Ulihrach
              6:3, 7:5
Etlis
                              Ulihrach
                              6:4, 6:4
Zabaleta
              Kulti
              6:2, 6:1
Kulti
```

Two of the three seeded players withdrew early from the tournament. The first one of them was the tournament star and attraction, Andrei Medvedev, who started his first round match against Nicklas Kulti from Sweden, but defaulted due to upset stomach and fever. Karel Novacek defaulted because of a back injury, and the top-seeded Marc Rosset from Switzerland followed suit soon after, failing to earn much sympathy from spectators or journalists due to his arrogant demeanour.

After a three-year pause, the tournament celebrated, once again, a victory of a local player. Bohdan Ulihrach, at only 18 years of age, won his first ATP Tour event after defeating the world's best junior player, Nicklas Kulti of Sweden in the semi-finals, and overwhelming the unforced error stricken Spaniard, Javier Sanchez, in the finals. This success elevated him to the world's top 50 players.

Finals: Ulihrach – J. Sanchez 6:2, 6:2

Czech Bohdan Ulihrach played three consecutive finals but won only one in 1995. Trophies were given by Jan Kodes and Prime Minister Vaclav Klaus (from 1998 till 2002 Chairman of the Congress and since 2003 President of the Czech Republic).

472

WITHOUT A RACKET

Year 10: Skoda Czech Open 1996

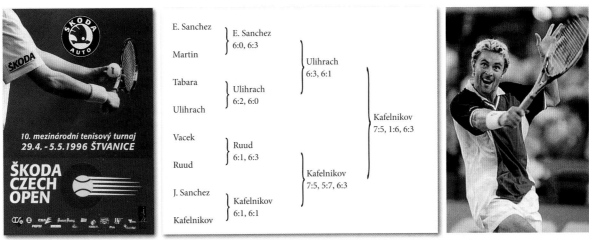

E. Sanchez
Martin } E. Sanchez 6:0, 6:3 } Ulihrach 6:3, 6:1 }

Tabara
Ulihrach } Ulihrach 6:2, 6:0

Vacek
Ruud } Ruud 6:1, 6:3 }

J. Sanchez
Kafelnikov } Kafelnikov 6:1, 6:1 } Kafelnikov 7:5, 5:7, 6:3 } Kafelnikov 7:5, 1:6, 6:3

Spaniard Felix Mantilla arrived to Prague as a quaterfinalist from Monte Carlo and eliminated the number one seed Thomas Enqvist in the first round!

The 10th year was held in spring, immediately following the Monte Carlo tournament. The second seeded player Thomas Enqvist from Sweden lost surprisingly to Felix Mantilla from Spain.

Even the biggest star, Yevgeny Kafelnikov from Russia, was seriously threatened in the semi-finals, defeating the Norwegian Christian Ruud only after a tough battle. The likeable Norwegian then explained that even in a country such as Norway that has no major tennis tradition they hold National Championships that he had won already four times. Marcelo Rios of Chile, a rising star of the ATP Tour, stirred quite some excitement when he asked to be examined by the tournament's official physician, picked up a report of an injured ankle, and then quickly and quietly left.

After the elimination of Enqvist and the French Arnaud Boetsch, the only one left to confront Kafelnikov was a local player Bohdan Ulihrach, who showed great fitness level, beating Emilio Sanchez from Spain in the semi-finals. Kafelnikov, however, proved to be too much for him but Stvanice witnessed an amazing match develop throughout. The crowd hardly ever saw such a relentless fight before!

Finals: Kafelnikov – Ulihrach 7:5, 1:6, 6:3

Yevgeny Kafelnikov won Roland Garros in 1996, just two weeks after his Prague victory. During 90's he was ranked in the Top 5 in the world and also took the Australian title in 1999 and helped Russia to win the Davis Cup in 2002.

Year 11: Paegas Czech Open 1997

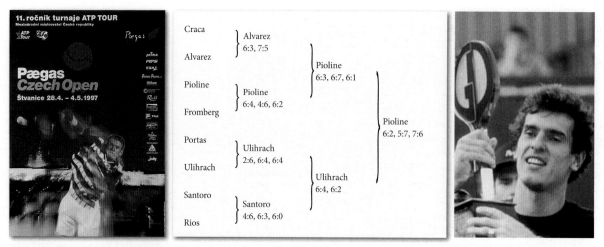

Craca				
	Alvarez 6:3, 7:5			
Alvarez				
		Pioline 6:3, 6:7, 6:1		
Pioline				
	Pioline 6:4, 4:6, 6:2			
Fromberg				
			Pioline 6:2, 5:7, 7:6	
Portas				
	Ulihrach 2:6, 6:4, 6:4			
Ulihrach				
		Ulihrach 6:4, 6:2		
Santoro				
	Santoro 4:6, 6:3, 6:0			
Rios				

Frenchman Cedric Pioline played one of the best finals in the Paegas Czech Open in 1997. He overcame Bohdan Ulihrach in three sets – the third in the tie-breaker!

In the eleventh year the tournament once again changed its title. The draw included four players rated among the world's top 30 with Kafelnikov and Rios rating among the top 10. Both were, however, eliminated in early rounds. Kafelnikov lost to Germany's Marcello Craca, a player rated in the two hundreds! Ulihrach fought his way into the finals for the third time in a row, only to lose for the second consecutive time. Though he defeated Rios' conqueror Fabrice Santoro from France in the semi-finals he came across another French player, Cedric Pioline, in the finals. He staged an exciting performance similar to the preceding year and a dramatic feat in the final tie-breaker.

There were only two more Czech players besides Ulihrach in the main draw – Daniel Vacek and Michal Tabara; both got in on a wild card. Tabara was eliminated in the first and Vacek in the second round. The tournament was made all the more interesting by the participation of Indian players specializing in doubles – Mahesh Bhupathi and Leander Paes. The Indian players gave a great performance and won easily.

Finals: Pioline – Ulihrach 6:2, 5:7, 7:6

Year 12: Paegas Czech Open 1998

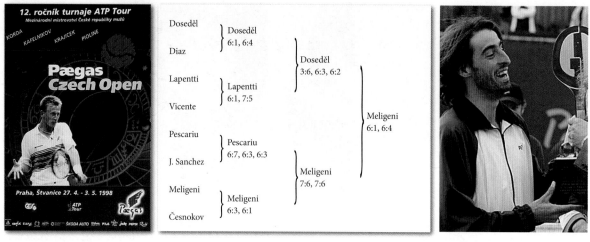

Doseděl				
	Doseděl 6:1, 6:4			
Diaz				
		Doseděl 3:6, 6:3, 6:2		
Lapentti				
	Lapentti 6:1, 7:5			
Vicente				
			Meligeni 6:1, 6:4	
Pescariu				
	Pescariu 6:7, 6:3, 6:3			
J. Sanchez				
		Meligeni 7:6, 7:6		
Meligeni				
	Meligeni 6:3, 6:1			
Česnokov				

Fernando Meligeni from Brazil was happy to win in Prague.

It took several years before the best Czech tennis player, Petr Korda, entered the tournament at Stvanice again. However, the top seeded player was eliminated in the second round by another Czech Ctislav Dosedel. The previous year's finalists, Pioline and Ulihrach, lost their first round matches; the first was defeated by Renzo Furlan from Italy, the latter by the Ecuadorian Nicolas Lapentti. Fernando Meligeni, a left-hander from Brazil, eliminated Kafelnikov, who had beaten Jiri Novak. There were also some new faces, one of them Marat Safin, who staged a major excitement a few weeks later at Roland Garros when he defeated Andre Agassi in the first round!

Although Prague clay courts suited Dosedel well, he lost surprisingly easy to Fernando Meligeni in the finals. Dosedel, who suffered from flu all that week, had his share of bad luck in the finals. The combination of rain, cold, and high fever all worked against him; Meligeni needed only two sets to beat him in the only final that was played on court two due to heavy rain. For the second and also the last time, the tournament was titled the Paegas Czech Open, and for the twelfth and the last time, it was directed by Jan Kodes.

Finals: Meligeni – Dosedel 6:1, 6:4

Year 13: Tento Czech Open 1999

Tomas Smid accepted the offer to become the new tournament Director, and Teleaxis marketing company was back in action, with Tento, a manufacturer of hygienic paper products, acting as the main sponsor. Prize money was raised to USD 457,000. The official entry form offered a list of attractive names: 1. Yevgeny Kafelnikov, 2. Andre Agassi, 3. Goran Ivanisevic, 4. Marat Safin, followed by Ulihrach, Hicham Arazi from Morocco, defending champion Meligeni from Brazil, locals Ctislav Dosedel and Jiri Novak. Merely two of the four players listed first actually arrived. Agassi drew crowds from the poster but nobody got to see him play. Kafelnikov was eliminated in the first round... Destiny may have had its say, as the finals saw a battle of the very same two nations that played for the first title 13 years earlier. There was just one minor difference – it was no longer a Czechoslovak duel but rather Czech vs. Slovak. Dominik Hrbaty won, thus becoming the last winner and the swan song of the dwindling ATP Tour Prague Tournament...

Finals: Hrbaty – Dosedel 6:2, 6:2

T- Mobile, Paegas General Director Klaus Tebbe (center) with Peter Korda and Gustav Hraska.

MUSTER MATTER

During the thirteen years in which Prague hosted an ATP Tour Tournament, Tennis Association presidents came and went and so did their secretaries. During Jiri Lendl's term the position of his secretary was held by Michal Polak. Under Jindrich Kincl, this post was taken by

Thomas Muster won in 1988 over Guillermo Perez-Roldan from Argentina. Tournament Director Jan Kodes (center).

Jan Pospichal, who was later replaced by Karel Papousek.

This is mentioned for one simple reason. Secretaries were charged with running the tennis stadium at Stvanice and that was causing all sorts of trouble. They did not know how things worked and, all of a sudden, officials from outside of Prague wanted their say in what was going on. They did not understand that the tournament was established to promote and help Czech Tennis above all other reasons. For them it represented a "gold-mine!" They tended to see it as a kind of showing off. There were VIP facilities with free food, TV crews all around, and it all looked a little bombastic and overwhelming. Many officials from around the country felt like the ATP Tour was digging into their shares of money.

This evolved into a huge problem. I was bound to what the ATP and our sponsors demanded. All contracts that we entered in with companies contributing to the tournament had provisions stating what the companies wanted in return in terms of promotion, services, or space reserved within the facility. It was up to me to produce a budget and oversee the costs.

As a Director of Prague's ATP Tour tournament Jan Kodes faced two major responsibilities. Above all he headed the whole organizing committee; secondly, he was accountable to the ATP. This meant, among other things, negotiating contracts with some of the participating players or their managers. And this was an area where Peter Kovarcik wanted to have his say.

As years went, there was always someone to suggest that the tournament was attended by second-class players only; that Prague was not going to attract spectators without the likes of Becker or Agassi.

I managed the tournament for twelve years and it kept improving all the time. How? People became used to it as a natural part of the Tour. Starting with 1987, nine consecutive tournaments were held in August. Unfortunately, the Tour schedules at the time were split between two continents. The US enticed players with bigger money and hard surfaces that suited players preparing for the US Open. Later, following a recommendation by the ATP Management and approval of the ATP Tournament Directors, our tournament was moved to spring-time, the peak of the clay-court season.

"A clay-court tournament held three weeks before Roland Garros; that should help you." That was what the director from Prague heard from the ATP Management. In August, the world's best players were playing in Toronto, New Haven, or other American tournaments preceding the US Open. Only those specializing in clay court play remained in Europe. It was hard for Kodes to attract any of the world's Top 10 players to Prague.

Both Skoda and Paegas (T-Mobile), being the main sponsors, had a condition: "We will provide prize money and pay for the players, but our name must be included in the title of the tournament, and the Director needs to guarantee that at least one player form the Top 10, and two from the Top 20 will attend." Paegas, sponsoring the tournament in 1997 and 1998, went even fur-

Skoda Auto Marketing Director Frank Farsky with NHL Hockey star Jaromir Jagr and Jan Kodes at the players party.

ther, and demanded one top 5 player and two more in top 20 players, thus Kodes had to attract 3 players ranked among the world's top 20. A tough task indeed!

Contracting any of the world's top 20 players is not simple. You need to contact the top 10 players' managers at least a year in advance, or even two years. To get Kafelnikov, who won in Prague in 1996, Kodes had to contact the IMG two years in advance and tell them he wanted Kafelnikov to play "two years from now!"

We had to overcome some difficulties and accept IMG's conditions; in the end Kafelnikov signed. I remember that he lost in the first rounds of a few tournaments preceding ours. Was he injured? Was he losing his form? When the same thing happened in Monte Carlo shortly before our tournament I was perturbed and immediately called the ATP headquarters.

However, Vittorio Selmi, an ATP Tour Manager who had seen the Monte Carlo tournament, reassured me: "Be glad that he keeps being eliminated in the first round. He will need to score a few wins once he arrives in Prague. You will see that he is going to win your tournament. If he were winning now, he would go to Prague only to get some rest, and then he might lose in the first round."

That was exactly what happened. Kafelnikov won in Prague, and went on to triumph at Roland Garros fourteen days later!

Next year, the situation was similar. In order to meet the sponsor's requirement of one of the world's top 5 players, he invited Kafelnikov once again since he was the only top player available; otherwise Jan would not have been able to observe the contract condition. This time, however, Kafelnikov lost in the second round...

This brought a storm of accusations on Kodes. Why did he invite Kafelnikov again if his play was so weak? There must have been something in it for him; otherwise, he would have contracted someone else. Why did he not ask for another player? Strangely, there were no such comments by the Czech media in 1999, when the marketing services for the tournament were being provided once again by the Teleaxis Company, and Kafelnikov made his third appearance in Prague...

It was impossible to contract another player from the Top 5 – just Kafelnikov! Getting two more Top 20 players was even more difficult. We had Thomas Enqvist in 1996. He held the 13th position in ATP rankings but had some tough luck in Prague, because the first round draw made him face previous week's finalist from the Monte Carlo tournament, Felix Mantilla from Spain, who proved to be very menacing. Enqvist did his best, he even had a 5:3 lead in the first set, but he lost!

New allegations did not take long to arrive! "Enqvist lost in the first round. He must have had a disagreement with Kodes! I bet Kodes owes him money!"

It felt like I was held responsible for everything that went wrong at any moment. I was trying to disregard the nasty gossip because once you have to supervise such an event, you are unable to sleep anyway, and there is no point in fussing over unfounded allegations! It is hard to imagine how much there was to worry about. I kept waking up at night, knowing that until I saw Kafelnikov, Enqvist, Rios, and Novacek getting off a plane in Prague, I could not be sure I would actually see them on the court.

Anything could go wrong at any time. Should a player become ill or injured shortly before a tournament, the down payment is returned to the organizers. Certain journalists, however, were able to make a story out of such occurrences, speculating that the given player simply threw-in the towel. Cases like that are usually difficult to judge, but there are exceptions to that rule; one of those was the appearance of Thomas Muster in 1990, which stirred up a huge campaign in the media. A winner of the 1988 Prague tournament, who also won the French Open later in 1995, only played a single match in the first round in 1990 and withdrew from the match "due to injury."

Thomas Muster appeared at Stvanice a year later, in 1991, making it into the semi-finals, where he lost to Novacek in a dramatic duel.

In 1990 Thomas's appearance in the tournament was arranged by Peter Kovarcik from Teleaxis Holding.

Even though the Austrian player was enrolled in the event by his managing company, he announced quite unexpectedly that he did not intend to enter. His manager was Ronald Leitgeb from Austria. Allegedly, Muster was scheduled to play an exhibition match against Becker in Germany before the end of the Prague tournament, and he was not at all happy about having to go to Prague. The ATP, however, let him know quite clearly that once he was entered, he either had to play or face the risk of being put in front of a disciplinary committee and be fined. Potential injuries had to be confirmed by a physician's statement.

To fulfil the ATP requirements, Muster arrived in Prague, went to the centre court and finished one game by shooting all the balls out of the court. It was a gesture of defiance; not towards me, but rather towards the ATP.

As expected, there was sharp reaction that radiated from the media and I was not mistaken: "Kodes did not pay Muster's appearance money!" - I did not even negotiate the terms of the contract! Muster severely injured the tournament's reputation. I found out later, that this was not the only such exploit of his. The ATP has strict rules in place to tackle this kind of behaviour. Once entered, the player is bound to attend. Muster was later sued by the ATP, having to appear before a court in New York, and was fined quite heavily, because the ATP Supervisor included his case in the "Official Tournament Report". As a Director of the tournament, I also had to sign that report; Thomas Muster alone caused the whole sting and not even his manager was able to help him.

ITF General Meeting at Vancouver in 1993. From left: Thomas Hallberg, Jan Kodes, Josef Brabenec, President Philippe Chatrier and ITF Head coach Doug MacCurdy.

CZECH TENNIS PRESIDENT

Jindrich Kincl's term in the office of a President of the Czech Tennis Association was coming to an end. He initiated new elections that were going to be held in April 1994 in Brno, with Jan Kodes invited as a guest.

"Don't let anybody talk you into anything," cautioned his wife Martina and daughter Tereza shortly before he left. "You have had enough work and anxiety with the ATP Tour tournament!"

His reaction was: "Don't worry. Do you think I am crazy to force my way into additional commitments?"

The conference hall was packed, tension running high. The three candidates, Milan Matzenauer, Milan Srejber, and Jiri Lendl took turns introducing their plans for the future of Czech Tennis.

Subsequently, delegates representing individual regions came forward with their attitudes and points of view about the candidates, systematically attacking all of them. No decision was made, not even in the second round. In case of such stalemate in voting for president, the rules of the Czech Tennis Association allow for any of the delegates to suggest a new candidate. A few names were offered and then, Milos Vipler, an umpire from Jicin, took the floor and said: "I think Kodes is the right guy. He is a former player, understands the business, he participated in Davis Cup as a player and captain, he knows how to organize tournaments, and he has been a member of the committee for twelve years. "

There was a half-hour break to think this suggestion over.

A few officials pounced on me: "Take it! Do it for tennis, if not for us."

All of a sudden I thought - why not, if that is what they want! I felt that people stood behind me and were going to support me. I later realized that I must have been struck by some illusion since there were actually only a few individuals in my support there. Nevertheless, I came forth and declared that I was ready to accept.

It took five rounds to elect the new president. Jan Kodes was voted in by 96 out of the 113 votes. He came back to Prague, pondering what to do next and whether he made the right decision.

Characteristically for Kodes, the beginning of his new career was marked with complications; as if he attracted trouble. There were problems with subordinates, regions, partners, journalists. Why were they attacking him personally? He had been under fire already for issues related to Stvanice construction, for his performance in the position of Davis Cup team captain, and for insignificant shortcomings in connection to Prague's ATP Tour tournaments.

During the 80's and 90's, the National Bank minted only seven commemorative 500 CZK (Czech Crown) silver coins! On Jan Kodes' initiative, in 1993, tennis was the only sport to be included amongst luminaries such as Jan Amos Komensky, National Theater, Ludovit Stur, Josef Lada, Matica Slovenska and Czechoslovak State Federation.

Why? Was it his demeanour that provoked them? Was he doing things incorrectly? Perhaps, sometimes, he could have acted differently. Everybody makes mistakes sometimes but it does not mean that those occasional errors are made intentionally! On the contrary! All his decisions were motivated by his desire to generate the best returns for Czech tennis.

In no time he experienced the first shock. Going over the financial affairs of the Association he found out that there was a debt of 10 million Korunas (over USD 300,000)! It was a direct result of a failed 1993 HIT TENNIS lottery held on the 100th anniversary of Czech tennis. The initial estimates said that the lottery might earn as much as 300 million Korunas (USD approx. 10,000,000). Unfortunately, only a fraction of the tickets was sold, with earnings barely covering the cost of distribution provided by the Sazka Company. The LTC Agency Group, contracted organizer of the lottery, failed to pay the 10-million fee to the Czech State, went bankrupt, and now the Ministry of Finance levied the fee from the Tennis Association.

The former management simply let the matter sleep, knowing that they still owed the money! And now I inherited it as my liability. We initiated talks with the ministry, requesting of them to forego the regulation charge; it was to no avail.

Jan Kodes waited for the Minister's reply in vain. This should have been the first warning for the newly elected Tennis Association President that there was, indeed, something rotten in the making. However, he paid little attention to it since his focus was, primarily, on Czech tennis. Not much time passed and more problems surfaced. After less than four months in office, the executive committee voted to withdraw from contract with Teleaxis. From the standpoint of the Czech Tennis Association, even the earlier contract with Telemundi was highly unprofitable. Since 1992, there were several conflicts that may have been perceived as failing to perform according to the contract. In 1993, there was a growing dissatisfaction with how much money Teleaxis paid to the Association, compared to how much they kept for themselves. Withdrawing from the agreement was a logical conclusion, which came about in late August 1994. The Teleaxis Holding's executive Peter Kovarcik reacted by suing the Czech Tennis Association thinking that offence would be his best defence. In 1996, when he was confronted by defeat, he dropped the charges, declaring that he did not want to stir up any conflict in tennis...

MARTINA'S EXHIBITION

One of the most prestigious events that also brought significant financial profit into the Association's coffer was Martina Navratilova's Exhibition. After many years I witnessed Stvanice utterly sold out again on June 17, 1995. That happened only three times in the Centre's history; during the Federation Cup finals in 1986, at the point of Davis Cup round against Sweden in October of the same year, and at Martina's Exhibition almost ten years later. Jana Novotna, Mary Pierce and Magdalena Maleeva joined Martina.

The first step I had to take was discussing the issue with Martina. I met her in Florida during Lipton Open in Key Biscayne, and extended her my offer, which she accepted. She was great and agreed to a lower purse than was customary, additionally requesting that a half of the proceeds be used for reconstruction of the clubhouse facilities and courts in Revnice outside of Prague, where she had first started playing tennis.

The Exhibition of four world-class women players attracted many cash-paying sponsors. Harvard Investment Funds contributed the highest sum. Bringing in Jana Novotna was not a problem at all; she represented us in Fed Cup and we closed a contract with Advantage, her managing company. Arrangements with Pierce and Maleeva were done at Roland Garros; they were both represented by IMG's Patrick Proisy.

President Vaclav Havel enjoyed with Martina my office before the exhibition.

This shows that I mostly dealt with people I knew from before. Naturally, that was advantageous.

And then, something happened that bestowed even more glimmer to the exhibition. A phone call came from the Castle, from the President's office, saying that Vaclav Havel, the President of the Czech Republic, was going to come to Stvanice. It occurred to me immediately that the two of them would be happy to meet. I remembered the TV coverage of our President Havel's speech before the US Congress in early 1990. There was teary Martina saying proudly that after many decades our country finally had a real President.

Shortly before the exhibition started a limousine pulled up in front of my office and Vaclav Havel stepped out. I invited him in, and the three of us – Mr. President, Martina, and I had a chance to chat frankly undisturbed. I then ushered Mr. President to his box in the grandstands and left him alone with Martina. Though he stayed only for a few games Martina enlightened him to tennis fundamentals. It did not matter that he did not know much about tennis and obviously came to Stvanice to meet Martina, the gesture was, undoubtedly, a great honour for tennis. It was also a great experience for me, as it was the first time I met a president in tennis setting.

It is desirable to conduct events like that from time to time. The Exhibition turned a profit - the Tennis Association received funding from sponsors and Martina's matches got great TV coverage. Most importantly, Martina was awarded well deserved honours.

However, problems did not cease. On the contrary! A contract with TV Prima, which was obviously advantageous for the Association as it allowed the private TV to broadcast all Davis Cup matches, ATP Tour Czech Open finals and semi-finals, Fed Cup, Challenger cups, junior Nationals in Pardubice, and even spots from the tennis extra-league, was still viewed with a grudge by many officials. And criticism focused on Jan Kodes – the new President.

Jan Kodes – Wimbledon Singles Winner 1973 introduced to Her Majesty Queen Elizabeth II by Czech President Vaclav Havel in Prague Castle, March 1996.

How did I dare sell rights for the Junior Nationals in Pardubice! I argued that it was organized by the Czech Tennis Association but they were not ready to accept such answers, however logical.

The press began to publish articles slandering Kodes. They were inspired by Peter Kovarcik, who was heard to say that Kodes "did not know how to deal with people, was bad at diplomacy, and did not understand business." It was obvious he was still trying to claim power in Czech tennis.

Kodes was not criticised only for his activities as the President of the Tennis Association but also as the Director of the Czech Open ATP tournament. His critics declared that "the tournament had no direction and it needed a manager capable of attracting the most magnetic players, including domestic players that would draw spectators and fill the Stadium." Kodes responded with names of players who had already played in Prague – Bruguera, Kafelnikov, Muster, Rios, Enqvist, Safin, Medvedev, Novacek, Corretja, Kucera, Kuerten, Arrese, and others. But no answer held up against the criticism, not even the fact that besides the deal with TV Prima there was also an agreement with Eurosport – negotiated through the ATP – to broadcast the ATP Czech Open, a deal which covered the full cost of organizing and running the tournament. His opponents still viewed Kodes as someone, who held the ATP tournament out of his own personal interest and spent a lot of money on it that took funds away from other regions...

I found out quickly that accepting the position of the President of the Tennis Association had been absolutely foolish of me.

More incidents followed. Money was embezzled by one of the Association's employees, and then, the illegal entry of Martina Hingis in the Czech extra-league, based on a fake ID.

HINGIS: FAKE CITIZENSHIP

I no longer remember that Milan Matzenauer, the Chairman of the Tennis Association's Executive Committee, supposedly told me: "See? You won't be able to run for another term. You were harmed too much by the Hingis affair. Nobody in Prostejov will ever forget that."

That ambitious Prostejov club! They had won the extra-league before. In mid-1990s they carried a proposal to allow each of the extra-league clubs take on one foreign player, to make the league more interesting. Nobody took into consideration the prospect that foreign players might replace young local players.

In 1996, they contracted Emilio Sanchez from Spain, and by naturalizing their previously foreign player, Martina Hingis, they entered her into their roster as a Czech player!

About a week before the league started, I asked Milan Matzenauer, how was the extra-league coming along?

"We are going to win, no doubt. We have got Sanchez and Hingis. Mirek Cernosek keeps everything under control. "

"Wait! You kept Martina? That would make her your second foreign player!" I objected.

"No, she is ok. She's got her citizenship squared away long ago!"

I shrugged, giving no reply. It all seemed weird but I thought that it simply slipped my attention and I was not aware of those developments.

Then, the extra-league finals played between Prostejov and Prerov were over; Prostejov won, as Milan Matzenauer had predicted.

About two weeks later, I received a letter from Petr Hutka, Prerov's Executive Manager: "We object to the extra-league results! We demand all matches played by Martina Hingis to be nullified! She does not have a Czech citizenship, she played illegally!"

**Martina Hingis won Wimbledon, U.S.Open and Australian Open
at following year naturally - of course as Swiss citizen.**

I contacted the Ministry of the Interior. Three days later, they replied with a letter dated July 17, 1996, saying that "Martina Hingis has never been a citizen of Czechoslovakia or the Czech Republic. She was born in Kosice, Slovakia, but she has never been issued either a Czechoslovak or a Czech passport!"

That made all her matches illegitimate.

It was up to the Executive Committee to resolve the situation. The meeting was held in Prostejov, and it is merely an understatement to say that it was tempestuous. Prerov was represented by Petr Hutka, accompanied by an attorney. Prostejov hired JUDr. Tomas Sokol, who was the first to speak. He came up with a long passionate and sometimes sentimental speech, saying that Martina's grandmother lived in Roznov pod Radhostem, where Martina visited her regularly and, sometimes, she came to Prostejov to practice. He scolded the appeal as invalid since Martina had a Czech ID and thus all her matches were legal.

Then, the lawyer brought in by Prerov made his speech, saying only three sentences: "Dear colleague, you know very well that what you are saying here is not true. The fact that Martina's grandmother lives in Roznov is nice but you may only acquire citizenship by proving it with your birth-place shown on the "Birth Certificate"; Martina's Birth Certificate says that she was born in Kosice (he produced the copy). That makes her Slovak in addition to her Swiss citizenship; she has never been a Czech citizen."

It was all clear. Nevertheless, what followed was a flaming debate of whether Martina could or could not be a Czech citizen. The Prostejov supporters were frantically searching for any argument that would make their case.

I joined the discussion but I would have done better just staying on the sidelines. "This year, I was at Roland Garros, at Wimbledon, even at the US Open. Everywhere it said: Martina Hingis – SUI, Switzerland. There was no mention of the Czech Republic! How can you attend the largest tournaments in the world as a Swiss, and then come to Prostejov and play as a Czech? That can't work!"

"She can have a double citizenship," they argued.

Yes, she can, but that would be Slovak citizenship, as she was born there; in addition, of course, to the Swiss.

Finally, the Executive Committee voted and decided by six votes to three that Martina Hingis' matches were to be nullified and proclaimed Prerov the winners of the extra-league. The fact that the General Secretary abstained from voting and the Executive Committee Chairman, Milan Matzenauer, voted in Hingis' favour appeared paradoxical!

A few weeks later I heard from members of the Association that "Kodes did not allow Hingis to play for Prostejov and had all her matches nullified, depriving them of the title." They did not hesitate to circulate such nonsense and totally ignored the existence of a Compliance Commission that annulled her matches based on their findings.

Among others, even Milan Matzenauer came to me, saying, "Jan, you should not have done that. You struck a nail in your own coffin."

That was beyond my comprehension! They had false ID papers made out! I still do not have any idea how they managed to manipulate the Police. I do not know if, or where, Martina signed receipt of the ID. I am still baffled. They must have known they were never going to get away with it! Were they so blind or arrogant? Was it worth the risk? They would have probably won even without Martina.

At any rate, there were no other repercussions, though I think that the Czech criminal code has some penalty for it but none was ever enforced.

The activities of the Marketing Department of CTA, established after Tennis Association broke ties with Teleaxis Holding, worked like thorns in the backside of many. There was criticism of alleged lack of transparency in its management despite the fact that CTA Marketing kept bringing in the largest sums of money since 1989! Could it have been the traditional Czech vanity, perhaps supported by a media campaign inspired by a certain person from whom the Tennis Association parted itself in 1994? Same as every year, the CTA Marketing finished the year 1997 with a minor loss.

That was quite normal. The loss was covered by marketing income guaranteed by next year's contracts.

Unfortunately, this issue was turned against Kodes in the 1998 general assembly of the Czech Tennis Association. He was not elected for another four-year term. The two-round election circus was even joined, on the side of Kodes' opponents, by Vaclav Klaus, the former Prime Minister and the current President of the country. As was the habit with Kodes, he fought until the end, rejecting the well-meant advice not to run for the office at all, and knowing that he did not stand a chance.

The speech Kodes gave at the general assembly of the Czech Tennis Association was pointed, confident, sharp, yet polite, as was customary with Kodes.

I criticised the Tennis Association's secretariat and some of its employees because they had conspired against the Association's President in an attempt of bringing him down at all cost. In the discussion that followed, nobody supported me. Should I have been miraculously elected, I would probably have refused the post anyway.

The first round ended up in a tie, leaving Vaclav Klaus annoyed with the way the Tennis Association was divided. He expected greater support. The election was delayed by a month and a special as-

Helena Sukova played two Australian Open (1984, 1989) and two U.S.Open (1986,1993) finals. The singles crown eluded her, but she did win nine doubles and five mixed doubles titles. Seven of them at Wimbledon.

sembly was then held. There were two candidates only; Jan Kodes, the current President, and Ivo Kaderka, the Deputy Minister for regional development. Vaclav Klaus excused himself for illness and since he did not attend the assembly he lost his vote. That year he became the Chairman of the Czech Congress!

120 delegates from around the country were, once again, supposed to elect the new president. Well-informed sources predicted that the second round was going to run smoothly because most delegates were ready to vote for Ivo Kaderka, a person almost unknown to the world of tennis.

I went there, even though I knew I did not stand a chance. I was reconciled with what was going on but I wanted to have my conscience clean. I wanted the tennis representatives decide that they did not want me any more. Once again, I said in my speech that I was ready to stay in the office for four more years. Then Ivo Kaderka spoke and I noticed that nobody was listening much. - I got 12 votes, he got 80. I stood up and addressed him: "Mr. President, my congratulations on the vote. I wish you good luck!"

Upon that I left.

Even though he was not the Association's President anymore, he thought he would go on as the ATP Tour Director. The twelfth year was held at the turn of April and May 1998. Less than two months later, Kodes received a letter from Ivo Kaderka. It said: "The Executive Committee of the Tennis Association agreed unanimously that you are not desired to hold the position of the Director of the Paegas Czech Open tournament anymore."

I was supposed to hand over my office, documentation, and keys, and the company car to Tomas Smid, the new Director. At that point I did not feel like arguing. I was terribly worn out and disgusted by people's intrigues, their plotting, and all the dirt. The tremendous responsibility I had to carry all those years wore me down.

I set up all the documents in the office; there was a heap of file folders on the desk.

Tomas came in and wondered, "Why are you giving me all this?"

"This is everything concerning the Tournaments – assessment, organizing committees, budgeting, contracts, trophies, everything."

He stared at me in disbelief. "I am not going to do all that. As a Director I am only going to make contracts with players." I spent a while trying to explain everything that was inherent to that position. He did not want to hear any of it so I finally gave up. "Do you know what, Tomas? Sign here that you received all this, and then do whatever you wish with it."

He signed it and put the whole lot in a filing cabinet. This was witnessed by a member of the committee of the I. Czech Lawn Tennis Club, Vladislav Savrda, a newly elected member of the Executive Committee of CTA. We signed the hand-over report; I stepped out and closed the door. That was the end of all of it.

While Jiri Lendl was still in his office, Jan Kodes participated in founding an International Women's Tournament, included in the WTA Kraft Tour with the prize money minimum of USD 100,000, later renamed to WTA Corel Tour. The first year was directed by a secretary Michal Polak; once he left, Vladimir Safarik became the next Director. During 1996 to 1998, the post was held by Katerina Bohmova, a former player. The 1992 round was held under the HTC Prague Open title (won by Radka Zrubakova, CSFR), the next two were played under a new sponsor as BVV Prague Open (won by Natalia Medvedeva from Ukraine in 1993 and Amanda Coetzer from the RSA in 1994).

Due to a contract between the Tennis Association and Teleaxis Company, marketing for all those years was done by Teleaxis, while technical aspects were managed by Jan Kodes, then the Director of new Stvanice Tennis Center.

Upon cancelling the Teleaxis contract, Kodes, as the newly elected President of the Association, used the association's money to fund the needs of the tournament and contracted the Porcela Plus Glass Company to back the event in the future. Unexpectedly, Porcela managers withdrew from the three-year contract prematurely but Kodes managed to extend the scope of cooperation with Skoda Auto, then one of the largest commercial partners of Czech Tennis Association. The minimum prize money required was the same USD 160,000. Tournaments held in the following years were won by French Julie Halard (Prague Open, 1995), Romanian Ruxandra Dragomir (Pupp Karlovy Vary, 1996), South-African Joanette Kruger (Skoda Prague Open, 1997), and Jana Novotna (Skoda Prague Open, 1998). After Jan Kodes left the post of the Association's President, the tournament ceased to exist, even though it was at its peak at the time, with WTA rules allowing Jana Novotna, the 1998 Wimbledon winner, to participate.

Between years 1999 – 2004 the tournament did not take place at all. Then, thanks to the initiative of tennis coach Vladimir Houdek, who negotiated ECM sponsorship for the Men's Prague Challenger in 2001, a WTA tournament was held in Prague again, following a six-year pause. The last five ECM Prague Opens were won by the Russian Dinara Safina (2005), Israel's Shahar Peer (2006), Japan's Akiko Morigami (2007), another Russian, Vera Zvonareva (2008) and Austrian Sybille Bammer (2009).

WTA Prague Open Trophy.

While there was a women's tournament held again at Stvanice, the case was different with men's tennis. It did not take long for the ATP tournament that had been built up by Jan Kodes for twelve years to disappear from the world's tennis schedule.

In 1999, I was surprised to hear that the ATP Tour Tento Czech Open, directed by Tomas Smid, was once again being marketed by Peter Kovarcik, who had struck an agreement with Ivo Ka-

Jana Novotna – happiest time at Wimbledon.

derka, the new President. The tournament was won by Dominik Hrbaty from Slovakia, but he did not receive the $50,000 purse! The same thing was happening all over again! In the end, he got paid by the ATP Inc., that resided in Florida and Mr. Kovarcik was rid of his winter tournament, the Czech Indoor held in Ostrava, and the Czech Tennis Association received a strict warning.

The new and short-lived Kaderka – Kovarcik collaboration ended with a fiasco, when Kodes' old sponsors, such as T-Mobile (Paegas), Skoda Auto, and Czech Airlines declined sharing responsibilities with the new presidency. CSOB, one of the largest Czech banks, withdrew its support they provided to junior tennis programme but later extended backing of the Czech edition of this book dedicated to Jan Kodes and Czech tennis. Czech Tennis Association had a year to decide what to do next. They could have rented or sold the prestigious tournament time slot but they did nothing. In the end, the ATP Inc. stripped them of the slot. They wasted something that Jan Kodes acquired gratis many years ago and that was worth hundreds of thousands of dollars these days! Unfortunately, we'll never know whether it was the Association's incompetence or malicious intent to lose the ATP tournament …

The newly elected president, Ivo Kaderka, was heard saying shortly thereafter that Czech Tennis did not need a tournament of such calibre; that he would prefer turning focus onto junior tennis. Nevertheless, junior tennis failed to gain much visibility throughout the entire decade. A few months later, surprisingly, the "Czech Open" title was assigned to a less significant ATP Challenger tournament held in Prostejov…

A few weeks after the new President took office, the press began printing stories alleging that the former President not only put the Czech Tennis Association in debt but also embezzled its funds! These allegations have never been proven by police investigations…

It was horror of horrors what was written about me in the press. Nobody took any interest in the sixteen years of service (1982 – 1998) that I dedicated to Czechoslovak, later Czech, tennis, or to the construction of Prague Tennis Stadium, or to establishing the three major tennis tournaments. Though I did not expect it, I hoped for a word of thanks; it never came. Nobody remembered the funding we had received from our sponsors; nobody valued the fact that I showed them how to organize big tournaments. I did all that for compensation that was ridiculously low compared to Western standards!

What was even more disturbing was the new management's attitude towards all former national tennis stars; they refused to cooperate with them and that stands till this day. Such attitude may soon backfire against the Czech tennis…

What he said about Jan Kodes
Jiri Lendl (Ivan Lendl´s father)

President of the Czechoslovak Tennis Association, 1990–1992

I hold high regard for Jan Kodes especially for his contribution to Czech tennis. Besides his competitive achievements I recognize his effective role in producing great accomplishments in the dark times of our history when tennis was considered a bourgeois sport and played only a second fiddle to sports like ice-hockey, soccer and other sports on the Olympic roster. Jan made tennis popular in spite of the fact that it was perceived with scorn as a capitalist sport. With each title that he conquered Jan raised the reputation of Czech tennis. He was a great player who inspired many followers and successors and with that overall popularity of tennis boomed. Politicians began to view it differently and made conditions for the younger generations more attractive. His diligence, tenacity, spirit, and responsible approach to training made him a great role model for the juniors, which in turn helped strengthen the tennis foundation. It is my opinion that he rightfully occupies one of the top spots among the best players in our tennis history.

It is not only a matter of individual achievements, but also his contribution to Davis Cup success. He cherished and gave priority to representing his country; he was the Davis Cup team pillar. He was a great fighter, world-renowned for his resilience.

I consider his contribution to the construction of the new stadium at Stvanice to be his greatest political success. Thanks to his tough nature, he was able to see the construction process all the way to its completion through difficult conditions and circumstances. He dodged great many obstacles; construction in Czechoslovakia then was not as easy an endeavour as it is today.

While working as the Association's official, he enjoyed certain advantage due to his immense popularity both, at home and abroad, as well as the contacts he had gathered during his active years. It came handy to him while directing the ATP Tour tournament in Prague. I was a President of the Association then, and I know that he accepted responsibility for just about everything, even for the tournament entries. And I certainly cannot agree with what the press sometimes said in those days – that the players he invited were not good enough. Just review the names – all of them previous or later winners of the French Open – Bruguera, Kafelnikov, Muster, Kuerten as well as others like Rios, Safin; remember their ATP rankings!

But it was not all about the stars. There were other great players who played on clay courts and were coming to us. ATP Tour Czech Open has definitely been the best tournament ever held here.

Jan did a lot of good work. He worked for the Executive Committee, maintained international relations, directed the stadium, directed the tournament, and later he even presided over the Association. There is much to thank him for and one thing is for certain - he is a great tennis icon.

Jiri Lendl

Jana Novotna become first since Doris Hart (1951) to win
Wimbledon after losing finals twice. She lost finals 1993 to Steffi
Graf (from 4:1, 40:30 lead) and to Martina Hingis in 1997 (6:3
in the 3rd set). Her historical triumph come in 1998. Jana beat on
the way Venus Williams 7:5, 7:6, Martina Hingis 6:4, 6:4
and Nathalie Tauziat 6:4, 7:6.

Karel Koželuh
8.iv.46.

LAWN TENNIS CERCLE

During the course of his career Jan Kodes was a member of two clubs in Prague – I. CLTK at Stvanice Island and Sparta in Stromovka Park. In view of the fact that he was "baptized" by the Moldav River, we mustn't overlook another club – LTC Prague, that was the counterpart of I.CLTK and Sparta all throughout Kodes' tennis career.

I remember this club with fondness since I worked out with their players, Frantisek Pala and Vladimir Zednik, as a visitor during a certain period of time. Many "true blue" members watched me from the clubhouse veranda, for instance Vilem Chadima, Karel Cefelin, Vlada Kalous, Jaromir Blabol, Milos Konrad and Petr Korda. They always made me feel welcome even though I was not a member there.

On September 7, 1903 a law student B. Klima wrote a letter to his friend Jechenthal and in the letter he talked about the need to organize a tennis society at Letna. The student Klima wrote: "We are now all obsessed with the idea of a tennis club and we have taken the matter into our hands; it seems that the suggestion inspired much enthusiasm also among the ladies." Preparatory committee was set up within the next two weeks; it was made up primarily of future jurists and lawyers to found the Academic Lawn Tennis Cercle Prague. The word "academic" was left out of the club charter and on February 7, 1904 the new athletic association was registered at Prague Land Register Office as a legal subject Lawn-Tennis Cercle. On the very same day a general assembly met in Pilsen Pub "U Pinkasů" and elected the first board of directors headed by JUDr. Frana.

They rented a large sandy recreational ground from SK Slavia, and in the adjacent soccer stadium they rented locker rooms. In a very short time – by mid-March – the first five tennis courts sprung up and tennis lessons were offered under the leadership of an experienced tennis player, Ing. Karl Hammer. In one month, by April 24, 1904, LTC played its first inter-club match against I. CLTK and, naturally, lost 2:18. At Stvanice Island they had been playing for ten years then and they had the first Czech champion Cistecky on their team; it was considered a great achievement that LTC won two points.

Still in spring of that year new members joined the club, among others Jan Masaryk, the future minister of exterior, and Joe Gruss, future chairman of the Olympic Committee, and several other prominent Prague citizens like prince Karel Schwarzenberg.

Activities of the LTC flourished. In 1905 they issued club and play set of rules, and courts' custodial operations. The club had a membership of 113 and the first paid custodian, by the name of Vaclav Kozeluh, was hired in 1906. That marked the start of Kozeluh family's role in LTC Prague. That summer the club became the founding member of Czech Lawn Tennis Association and they organized their first tournament.

Davis cup played at LTC: CSR vs.Belgium in 1929
P. Macenauer - J. Kozeluh won the doubles over
A. Ewbank - A.La Croix (from left) 6:2, 6:3, 6:4.

Jan Kozeluh represented Czechoslovakia in Davis Cup from 1924 till 1930!

In 1908 O. Husak joined the club. He became a brilliant tennis theoretician and after the 1st World War he published the first Czech tennis textbook "Syllabus of How to Play Lawn Tennis". In the same year Olga Masarykova, the daughter of President Tomas Garrigue Masaryk, achieved remarkable success when she won the International Championship of the lands of the Czech Crown. She sealed that accomplishment when she repeated this triumph the following year.

Soon organized ball-boy service was established. It had been uncontrolled but, at this point, unified reimbursement per number of games was set up for the ball-boys. The Kozeluh lads, who lived around the corner of Letna, worked regularly among the ball-boys – Antonin, Karel, Jan and Alois.

After the 1st World War the name of the club was slightly re-arranged to Lawn Tennis Club Prague in order to preserve the abbreviation LTC. The club expanded its grounds by four more courts and that attracted another influx of new members. The elite of Czech tennis formed the core of LTC – Frantisek Burianek, the later coach and legendary tennis teacher, Jan Kozeluh, four times the winner of the Czechoslovak International championships from 1925 – 1928, and a tennis-gentleman Pavel Macenauer. The two players, together with Ladislav Zemla, formed the I. CLTK selection that represented Czechoslovakia for many years.

In 1924 the first Centre Court was constructed at Letna for two thousand spectators based on a project designed by a Davis Cup player and an architect Ing. Karel Ardelt. Many world greats later played on that court – the legendary Frenchwoman Suzanne Lenglen, the tennis musketeers Borotra, Cochet, Brugnon and others.

In 1926 construction of a new modern garden clubhouse began according to the design of an architect B. Kozak. It was beautifully furnished in the living as well locker room areas.

Father and son Malecek joined the club in 1926; the older Malecek was responsible for initiating the foundation of an Ice Hockey section of the club. In conjunction with other tennis players Jiri Tozicka, Oldrich Kucera and Frantisek Pergl, ice hockey brought fame to LTC internationally. The LTC hockey players won the Spengler's Cup in Davos, Switzerland, three times in succession between 1931 and 1933. Malecek became the International Singles Champion of Czechoslovakia in 1930, Marie Kozeluhova accomplished the same the year before.

For twenty years in between the wars LTC Prague and I. CLTK battled for dominance in Czech tennis. The LTC's domain was in doubles, where they captured 27 Czech championship titles as opposed to "only" nine in singles. At that time Josef Siba, Jiri Krasny, Josef Caska, and Frantisek Cejnar were at the top of their tennis careers. Others like Jan Kozeluh, Jaromir Blabol, Vilem Chadima, and coaches Robert Ramillon from France and Frantisek Burianek, who had played against Bill Tilden of the USA, were also active members of the club.

During the hard times of German protectorate tennis was seldom played. The main cause was the lack of tennis balls; however it gave rise to soccer playing on the courts and in winter the courts were transformed into a skating and hockey site. Soccer players like Vlasta Kopecky,

Prague's Letna between the two World Wars.

This is what the SK Slavia LTC Clubhouse looked like in 1928.

Legendary Suzanne Lenglen travelled to Prague and played in LTC on October 16, 1925 with Kozeluh brothers. From left: Antonin, Jan, Suzanne and Karel.

Josef Caska at Stvanice during a Davis Cup match.

In 1948 a textile factory in Nachod was nationalized; it had belonged to three Caska brothers. Only one of them was fluent in three languages which necessitated his presence in managing the factory and limited his time he wanted to spend playing tennis. After the "comrades" took over their plant and offered the brothers inferior jobs they decided to leave the country along with their father. In 1950 they rented a villa in Marianske Lazne (Marienbad) and together with a hired "smuggler" they planned their escape in two stages. The first one to leave was the father who reached Paris successfully. The three sons followed him three months later in their quest of reaching the dreamed up freedom, however, supposedly due to the smuggler's error who led them on a different path, they fell into the hands of the Czech boarder guards. Illegal border-crossing was then considered high treason; in 1951 Josef Caska was sentenced to eight years in prison for treason and complicity in aiding his father's escape. He served four years and after his release he left for Hradec Kralove where he worked as a day-laborer. Thanks to his previous tennis contacts he succeeded in transferring to Ostrava at the turn of 1961-62, where he coached tennis till 1964. He then left for Sparta Prague and for a short period of time he also became the Davis Cup team coach from 1965 till 1966.

Centre Court on Stvanice Island in 1942.
Josef Caska, Frantisek Cejnar, Josef Siba and Milos Solc (from left).

Training at Klamovka in 1966.
From the left: Josef Caska, Jan Kodes, Milan Holecek, Stepan Koudelka.

Joseph (Pepi) Bican and other athletes like Jaroslav Drobny and a table tennis player Ivan Andreadis also frequented the club. The one condition was that they all played tennis actively. After the war the soccer scrimmages became traditional and remained so till the 80s of the last century. The best tennis players from all over Prague participated in these "battles", including Javorsky and Kodes.

Many outstanding tennis players played for LTC after the World War II: Vladimir Cernik, Josef Caska, Vladimir Zabrodsky, Jan Smolinsky, Jaromir, Blabol, Vilem Chadima

LTC in 1945. Jaromir Blabol, Jaroslav Drobny, Vojtech Vodicka and Jaromir Becka.(from left).

as well as the hockey giants Gustav Bubnik, Oldrich Zabrodsky, Stanislav Nepomucky – almost all members of the Czechoslovak National Ice Hockey team. Furthermore membership included the ladies Lola Vseteckova, Vratislava Karmazinova-Zdvihalova, Zdenka Dalecka a Zdenka Czechmannova, all junior champions between 1943 and 1949. With that, however, the glorious era of LTC, the most famous Czech tennis and ice hockey club, came to an end.

In between the wars the following members directed the club: Chairman - Ing. Kvet, Ing. Pilman, J. Blabol, V Chadima, Dr. Slavik, O. Zabrodsky, A. Vasak, Ing. Arch. V. Krasny, I. Andreadis.

After the 1948 communist coup d'etat LTC was integrated with Sokol Prague 7. All the club's effects, belongings and gear were transferred into "bolshevized" Czech Sokol community and in June 1950 Prague LTC was dissolved as a legal entity. The comrades stole away everything from the Letna clubhouse and they burned the archives. Within the next two years all LTC members were dissipated. In the converted club, now called DSO Dynamo, only those original members were allowed to stay who worked in power engineering or who lived in Prague's District 7. In 1956 the entire inventory of the tennis club was moved over to the Czechoslovak Union of Physical Education and Sport (CUPES) as common property. During the construction of Letna tunnel the club lost two tennis courts that fell victim to tunnel ventilators, to the Ministry of Interior's jamming devise pole, and to the entrance into an antiatomic shelter.

In 1968 the name changed again upon agreement with Slavia Club to Slavia Prague LTC and, gradually, a revival of the athletic and social activities took place. Tennis players of resonant names began to appear on Letna courts: Milan Holecek, Vladimir Zednik, Frantisek Pala, Tomas Smid, Pavel Slozil, Jiri Granat, Jiri Prucha, Ivan Hora, Mirka Kozeluhova, Marie Neumannova, Iva Budarova, Lea Plchova, Michaela Pazderova – almost entirely national champions. In the first half of the nineties club's "disciple" Petr Korda brought fame to LTC. Coaches of that time period were: Jiri Dobes, Milos Konrad, Vlada Kalous and Petr Korda senior. In 1970-1975 Karel Cefelin was the club Chairman after Karel Dusek, and in 1976-1981 it was Ing, Rene Marik. Vilem Chadima was the soul of the club.

However, the process of normalization in 1970 affected even the tennis club via Slavia's new patron – the construction company IPS. The LTC officials were gradually pushed out of the committee, the club changed its name again to TJ Slavia Prague IPS, and the new leadership turned considerably red and pro-communist.

In 1987 the club leadership carried out unreasonable reconstruction of the beautiful garden courts to gray concrete semi-stadium, till this day left unfinished. The active athletic as well as social life was interrupted for two years. During the reconstruction part of the park around the courts was destroyed to such extent that members of the club who lived abroad during that time and returned after 1989 no longer recognized their beloved club.

At 1991 annual meeting the prominent officials of Slavia club announced that only the club that recovers on his own will be able to survive and go on. A representative of the Czech Tennis Federation, Rene Marik, suggested to all to consider recovery of legal identity and thus free the club of undemocratic obligatory governing. For that it was necessary to draw up a new code of rules because presently the club SK Slavia had none. On May 27, 1991 members voted by a landslide to revive the original legal subject under the historical name LTC Prague. With that the 1950 forced dissolution was legally canceled.

It was assumed that LTC would become a corporate member of Slavia and the two subjects would negotiate their latest legal relationship. However, a new and dramatic twist took place that September. Without the tennis players' prior knowledge Slavia's Chairman Komarek treacherously violated the agreement and rented the tennis property at Letna for twenty years to a C & C Company of Vratislav Cekan for purpose of a business enterprise. Furthermore, he did it for a suspiciously low amount of money! The LTC Prague committee reacted in the only possible way – they requested from SK Slavia Prague outright return of rights in property according to the valid restitution laws. Slavia refused to do so and they pulled down the built-in interior installations of the clubhouse. Where it all disappeared is unknown. The club life was thus destroyed. Shortly before, the LTC approached the Regional Commercial Court in Prague with a request of restitution ordinance. In 1992 the official authority of the Czech Ministry of Finance annulled the C & C's occupational lease...

Petr Korda kissing the Australian trophy winning his Grand Slam title over Chilean Marcelo Rios 6:2, 6:2, 6:2 in 1998.

The court restitution proceedings dragged on thanks to the filibuster of SK Slavia's defense counsel. Slavia's officials admitted that they recognized the Letna tennis courts and clubhouse to be property of LTC Prague but they wanted LTC to establish that right in court... Causation LTC versus Slavia lingers on; each club has its own courts and surrounding territory. It is paradoxical that the original historical clubhouse that belongs to LTC is of service to all, even for general-public refreshments...

Let us hope that it does not remain like this for ever!

Petr Korda won the 1993 ITF Grand Slam Cup in a five-set battle with Michael Stich 2:6, 6:4, 7:6, 2:6, 11:9 in Munich. On the way to the finals he overwhelmed the world's number one player Pete Sampras 3:6, 7:6, 3:6, 7:6, 13:11.

HALL OF FAME

It is the same euphoric moment as when an actor is awarded the Oscar and with that is admitted into the society of the most famous and reputable personalities of the film screen. Jan Kodes was inscribed into the list of the most celebrated and accomplished names of tennis when inducted into the International Tennis Hall of Fame in 1990. He was only the second Czech at the time to receive the distinction, joining Jaroslav Drobny, who was inducted in 1983. As a two-time Roland Garros Champion and a 1954 Wimbledon winner, Drobny entered the Tennis Hall of Fame as a British citizen. However, he reached many extraordinary results on tennis courts all over the world still representing Czechoslovakia.

Jan Kodes joined him as the second inductee seven years later. Admission into the Tennis Hall of Fame honored his life's achievements and success. It was not only his triumphs at Roland Garros in 1970 and 1971 and his Wimbledon victory in 1973 but also the number of Davis Cup matches in which he represented his country, as well as his tireless work on behalf of the Czechoslovak tennis that earned him the nomination. A member of the Tennis Hall of Fame and the US Open Director Bill Talbert, who had been a great American Davis Cup player himself, designated Jan Kodes for the honor.

The third Czech inductee in the "Hall" was Hana Mandlikova in 1994, predominantly based on her wins at the Australian Open in 1980 and 1987, the French Open in 1981 and the US Open in 1985. Shorlty after came the inductions for Martina Navratilova in 2000, Ivan Lendl in 2001, and Jana Novotna in 2005. All three are U.S. citizens now but they achieved most of their accomplishments still connected to their birth country.

International Tennis Hall of Fame insignia awarded to each recipient.

Ted Tinling's 80th Birthday celebration in Philadelphia in 1989.
From the left: Frank Sedgman, Tony Trabert, Vic Seixas, Fred Perry, Marilyn Fernberger, Don Budge, Ted Tinling, Lucy Hopman, Fred Stolle and Ed Fernberger.

The seventh and, so far, the last Czech recognized for the Newport's Hall of Fame honor on July 15, 2006 in memoriam, was Karel Kozeluh. A tennis genius of his time, he received this warranted recognition more than fifty five years after his death.

The International Hall of Fame is a very conservative American institution that watches over the history of the American and world tennis. It resides in Newport, Rhode Island, south of Boston, in a historical quarter called the Newport Casino. The first US Championship in 1881 took place on these original grass courts and till this day a traditional men's tournament takes place there annually immediately after Wimbledon. The US Championships, the modern-day US Open, was held in Newport till 1914, when it transferred to the West Side Tennis Club at Forest Hills, NY.

In 1954 a tennis innovator James van Alen founded the Tennis Hall of Fame in order to provide a sanctuary for tennis idols. The USTA officially endorsed the Hall of Fame in that same year and the International Tennis Federation (ITF) recognized it in 1986. There is a museum on the premises that showcases artifacts and videos of tennis history. It gathers historical articles of tennis champions of the past, some of which have been donated to the museum by contemporary tennis personalities and superstars. The entire complex was erected in 1880 and it underwent an extensive 5-year reconstruction in 1997. The reconstruction brought the complex to its original resemblance and it cost $ 7.5 million. Originally, the Newport Casino was built as a recreational social club, not as a site for gambling as the name might suggest. "Casino" derives from the Italian word "casina" meaning estate or lodge. The architectural concept envisaged the first floor to be used by merchants, and the second floor as a club. This was a unique idea for that time period. Besides the Hall of Fame and its museum the Casino of today offers its visitors assorted types of activitiest: archery, billiards, bowling, concerts, dance, restaurant, horse shows, bow-

Jan Kodes and Joseph F. Cullman in 1990.

FRI./SAT./SUN., JULY 13-15, 1990

TENNIS

Czechoslovakia's Kodes earns spot in Hall of Fame

By Doug Smith
USA TODAY

NEWPORT, R.I. — Jan Kodes received $10,000 for winning the Wimbledon men's singles title in 1973.

He chuckled when reminded that Stefan Edberg got $404,800 last week for the same title.

"The money is very nice these days," said Kodes. "I wish to be young again."

Because he was among the best of his era, Kodes, 44, of Czechoslovakia will be inducted Saturday into the International Tennis Hall of Fame.

Joseph Cullman III, chairman emeritus of Philip Morris, also will be inducted. Cullman provided the financial support that helped launch the women's pro tour in 1970. He also provided money to help restore and preserve the Newport Casino, home of the International Tennis Hall of Fame.

Noted primarily for his play on clay courts, Kodes also won the French Open (1970-71), the Italian Open (1970-72) and was a U.S. Open finalist in 1971 and 1973.

"I played against him on clay at some event in North Carolina," said former pro Barry MacKay. "He jerked me around something fierce. His forehand was a real weapon ... He was something like (Ken) Rosewall, a heck of a competitor who gave 110 percent. He deserves the honor."

Kodes was on the Czechoslovakian Davis Cup team from 1964-80. He led the team to the final in 1975 and was a member of Czechoslovakia's championship team in 1980. He was captain from 1982-87.

Kodes says it is difficult to compare the top players of his era with today's top pros, but the competition is generally tougher.

"Ken Rosewall didn't have to worry about losing in the first or second rounds," said Kodes. "Today, it's a lot tougher for the top players to get by the first few rounds."

Kodes graduated from the University of Prague in 1973 as an economics major. He is director of the Czechoslovakian Tennis Center, tournament director of the Czechoslovakian Open and a board member of the Czechoslovak Tennis Association.

ling on grass, reading room, tea room, theatre performances and, naturally, grass-court tennis. The Casino courts are the oldest grass-courts in the world used regularly for a tennis tournament and, at the same time, they are accessible to the public. James van Alen, who inspired the idea of the Hall of Fame and was its first president, twenty years later thought out and implemented the "tie-break" in tennis scoring, that is now accepted around the world. It is also worth mentioning that annually the Tennis Hall of Fame serves as the location for the opening concert of Newport's Jazz Festival. The first such concert took place in 1954.

To be a member of the International Tennis Hall of Fame is one of the highest honors for the ex-tennis stars. It is governed by its President (presently by Tony Trabert), several Vice-Presidents and the executive council. Two-thirds of the inductees are already deceased, but inductees include the following; William T. Tilden, Suzanne Lenglen, Althea Gibson, Jean Borotra, Maureen Connolly, Donald Budge, Jacques Brugnon, Dwight F. Davis, Jaroslav Drobny, Rene Lacoste, Lewis Hoad, Frank Sedgman, Alex Olmedo, Roy Emerson, Rod Laver, Ken Rosewall, Manuel Santana, John Newcombe, Bjorn Borg, Billie-Jean King, Stan Smith, Yvonne Goolagong, Virginia Wade, Ilie Nastase, Chris Evert, Jimmy Connors, John McEnroe, Boris Becker, Stefan Edberg, Steffi Graf, Jim Courier, Yannick Noah and others... In 1990 the founder of the Virginia Slims Circuit and later the director of the US Open Joseph F. Cullman and Jan Kodes were added.

It was a huge achievement, and not just my own. In the United States they celebrate this accomplishment to honor

JAMES H. VAN ALEN
1902-1991
FOUNDER OF THE INTERNATIONAL TENNIS HALL OF FAME

Generations of tennis players will remember Jimmy for his innovative contributions to the sport. A version of his tie-breaker, which he championed for 19 years before it was adopted, is now accepted worldwide. VASSS (the Van Alen Simplified Scoring System) is used at all intercollegiate competitions. Night tennis and the electric scoreboard were also his creations.

A poet of note, an accomplished musician, a publisher, a raconteur, a Hall of Fame enshrinee, a civic leader, and a man with a sparkle in his eye, Jimmy Van Alen was truly one of a kind.

INTERNATIONAL TENNIS HALL OF FAME ENSHRINEES

• **1955** Richard Sears James Dwight Henry Slocum Oliver Campbell Robert Wrenn Malcolm Whitman Joseph Clark • **1956** William Clothier Dwight Davis May Sutton Bundy William Larned Holcombe Ward Beals Wright • **1957** Mary K. Browne Maurice McLoughlin Hazel Hotchkiss Wightman Richard Williams, 2nd • **1958** Bill Johnston Molla Bjurstedt Mallory R. Lindley Murray Maud Barger-Wallach • **1959** Bill Tilden Helen Wills Moody Roark • **1961** Vincent Richards Frank Hunter Malcolm Chace Fred Alexander Harold Hackett • **1962** John Doeg Ellsworth Vines Helen Hull Jacobs • **1963** Wilmer Allison Sarah Palfrey Danzig John Van Ryn Julian Myrick • **1964** Alice Marble Don Budge George Lott Frank Shields George Adee Sidney Wood • **1965** Pauline Betz Addie Don McNeill James Van Alen • Theodore Pell Ted Schroeder • Margaret Osborne duPont Allison Danzig Jack Kramer Pancho Gonzales Eleonora Marie Wagner Karl Behr Doris Trabert Perry Jones Shirley Althea Gibson Elisabeth Moore Bryan "Bitsy" Grant Gardnar Alastair Martin Darlene Hard Townsend Toulmin Fred Hovey Falkenburg • **1975** Lawrence Roosevelt • **1976** Rene Lacoste Jacques Brugnon Mabel Cahill Norman Brookes Budge Patty Gottfried von Cramm • **1978**

1990
Joseph F. Cullman 3rd
Jan Kodes

Ellen Hansell Watson Washburn **1966** Joe Hunt Frank Parker **1967** Bobby Riggs Bill Talbert Louise Brough Clapp • **1968** Maureen Connolly Brinker Sears • **1969** Chuck Garland Hart Art Larsen • **1970** Tony Fry-Irvin Clarence Griffin • **1971** Vic Seixas Arthur Nielsen • **1972** Mulloy Elizabeth Ryan • **1973** Gene Mako • **1974** Bertha Juliette Atkinson Bob Baker, Sr. Fred Perry Ellen Jean Borotra Henri Cochet Dick Savitt • **1977** Manuel Alonso Betty Nuthall Shoemaker Maria Bueno Pierre Etchebaster

Kathleen McKane Godfree Harry Hopman Suzanne Lenglen Anthony Wilding • **1979** Margaret Smith Court Jack Crawford Gladys Heldman Al Laney Rafael Osuna Frank Sedgman • **1980** Ken Rosewall Lew Hoad Reginald Doherty Lawrence Doherty Gustaf V, King of Sweden • **1981** Rod Laver W.E. "Slew" Hester Mary Outerbridge Dorothea Douglass Chambers • **1982** Roy Emerson William McChesney Martin Tom Pettitt Lance Tingay • **1983** Clarence Clark Lottie Dod Jaroslav Drobny Ernest Renshaw William Renshaw • **1984** John Bromwich Adrian Quist Neale Fraser Manuel Santana Pancho Segura • **1985** Arthur Ashe David Gray Ann Haydon Jones Fred Stolle • **1986** Dorothy Round Little Chuck McKinley John Newcombe Nicola Pietrangeli Tony Roche Ted Tinling • **1987** Bjorn Borg Billie Jean Moffitt King Dennis Ralston Alex Olmedo Stan Smith • **1988** Evonne Goolagong Cawley • **1989** Gerald Patterson Virginia Wade

1990 souvenir tile with names of all members of ITHF up to that date.

1994: Arthur "Bud" Collins Jr. and Hana Mandlikova.

2000: Martina Navratilova, Robert Kelleher and Malcolm Anderson.

2001: Ivan Lendl and 1958 Roland Garros Champion Mervyn Rose, Australia.

2005: Hall of Fame President Tony Trabert and Jana Novotna.

**Martina Navratilova's induction into the Tennis Hall of Fame.
From the left: Jan Kodes, Martina, Bud Collins and Martina's mother Jana.**

each country that was represented by an individual in an outstanding manner. It was a tennis accomplishment of all of Czechoslovakia! The main criteria for the nomination have been Grand Slam titles. However, not only players get nominated. There have been many tennis celebrities admitted into the Hall of Fame like Lamar Hunt or Judge Robert J. Kelleher, who opened up a 1967-1968 campaign that resulted in opening tennis to professionals. Every year three to four tennis greats are admitted based on the nomination by a committee of twenty one member, headed by Trabert, who meet throughout the year.. After the US Open ballots are sent all over the world to tennis personalities – experts, journalists, and also the existent Hall of Famers. The votes are counted in a few months time and the final selection is made.

I was rather surprised that I was admitted to the International Tennis Hall of Fame already in 1990. Even though my generation was coming up I still thought I would wait another five years before I was to be considered. Laver and Rosewall were inducted in 1988 and 1989. Next came Smith and Nastase's turn. I knew I was among fifteen nominated candidates but did not expect to be chosen so soon.

When Jan Kodes entered the Hall of Fame it was, as always, a huge gala. The entire ceremony had a festive opening with soldiers in showy uniforms; the Czechoslovak flag flew in Newport for the first time. A celebratory dinner followed, and the next day the patrons treated us to lunch with another ceremony to follow on the main court. Jan Kodes was the first tennis player from behind the Iron Curtain to be inducted into the Hall of Fame.

It was an extraordinary experience for me; unforgettable.

According to the tradition he sat at the best table during dinner with Bill Talbert, Donald Budge, Jack Kramer and others...

Kodes All Smiles

JAN KODES of Czechoslovakia, who was inducted into the International Tennis Hall of Fame at the Newport (R.I.) Casino on Saturday, has had other things to smile about recently.

Besides being pleased to gain recognition at the age of 44 for steady court talents that won him the spot with 150 others in the Hall, Kodes is also delighted about significant political changes taking place in his country.

Kodes, who was his nation's top-ranked men's singles player from 1966 to 1977, was at the top of his game from 1970 to 1973. In that period, he twice won the French Open on clay, his best surface, won Wimbledon in 1973, and was a two-time finalist in the United States Open.

Like most of his countrymen, Kodes is an enthusiastic supporter of Vaclav Havel, the new president of Czechoslovakia.

"Havel is a man of whom we are proud because of the democratic changes he is bringing," Kodes said last week, "and because of his stature as an international spokesman."

Unlike some other native Czechoslovaks like Martina Navratilova and Ivan Lendl, who chose to leave the restrictions of their country's tennis federation to pursue independent careers, Kodes remained in Prague. "I rejected offers and opportunities to stay with my family and my parents," he said.

Kodes is now the director of the Czechoslovakian Tennis Center, the tournament director of the $176,000 Czechoslovakian Open tournament and is in charge of international affairs for the Czechoslovak Tennis Association.

"Our national association, which used to be under the ministry of sports, has now gained independence and we are looking forward to better things," he said. "We have plenty of youngsters from 14 to 18 who are gaining European and international recognition. The Open tournament at Prague will soon increase its purse money to $300,000."

One other tennis development pleases Kodes, too. The Czechoslovak national champion for boys 18 and under is Jan Kodes Jr., who is rated in the top 10 internationally.

THOMAS ROGERS

With Jack Kramer at Champion's dinner in Paris in 2001.

The conversation included all kinds of topics including the Czech tennis. How is it possible that so many amazing players came out of your country?

I explained to them that Czechoslovakia might be a small country but tennis has been popular for many years.. "Right" said Kramer; "We remember Drobny".

"Yes, but there was another splendid player before him – Karel Kozeluh" I added. Don Budge jerked: "Karel? That was my coach when I first started playing Davis Cup!"

It was at that moment that Jan Kodes began to wonder how good Karel Kozeluh really was, and he started researching Kozeluh's tennis past.

KOZELUH DYNASTY

Karel Kozeluh was born in Prague in 1886. In his youth he earned some money as a ballboy at Letna. From their small apartment in Skroupova Street the club was only a short distance

Rodin's oil painting of Karel Kozeluh (Czech National Museum).

for him and his brothers Frantisek, Josef, Karel, Antonin, Alois, Jan, Marie; all of them played tennis. Only the second sister, Anastazie, became a wonderful cook and with time her culinary art led her to President Masaryk's home. It may sound unbelievable but at the age of twelve Karel played so much by the book that he became a tennis teacher! At fourteen he received an invitation from Tennis Club Iphitos in Munich to become a tennis teacher that season for a monthly salary of 80 marks. His parents hesitated to let him go out into the world but his brothers interceded for him. Since even Professor Masaryk put in a word for him after Karel improved Miss Olga Masarykova's backhand, the family council agreed to let him go.

His athletic versatility was remarkable. He represented Czechoslovakia as an ice-hockey player, soccer player and a tennis player. During the World War I he was Sparta's offensive soccer forward along with his brother Frantisek; Vlasta Burian was the goalie. Afterward, Kozeluh transferred to DFC Prag,

This oil painting is exhibited in Newport as a testimonial to the beginning of ladies' tennis.

a team of Prague's Germans, and from there he headed to Northern Bohemia. He took part in the first soccer trip ever to South America with Teplitzer FC. In time he returned to Sparta and in May 1923 he played two international games as a Czechoslovak center forward. He concluded his soccer career in Sport Club Vienna.

Simultaneously, he excelled in field and ice-hockey. He played for the league title-holder Sparta as a forward along with brothers Frantisek and Josef, and he represented Czechoslovakia in 1923 and 1925 European Championships, capturing the gold medal at Strbske Pleso in 1925.

Nevertheless, his number one sport became tennis. He chose tennis over the other sports with definite resolve during a Vienna tournament in 1925, when he defeated the French player Feret. Feret's compatriot, Rene Lacoste, the Wimbledon champion that year, drew in his notebook Kozeluh's strokes. Another of the French tennis musketeer's, Jean Borotra, invited him to play a professional tournament on the French Riviera. At thirty years old Karel became the Professional World Champion in Deauville, France. His most significant results came between 1925 and 1932, when he practically, he did not lose

Gallic Rooster - Championship trophy from Chicago (Czech National Museum).

any important matches and his results brought him the fame of being unbeatable. Six times in succession he won the Bristol Cup, while also winning the French-European Professional Championships, and winning three titles in 1929, 1932 and 1937 at the U.S. Pro Championships. From 1931 through 1937 he was a member of a professional traveling group that included Bill Tilden. Even though he never played Wimbledon he was considered the world's best tennis player. Since he was a professional he was not allowed to enter Grand Slam tournaments.

In the first two decades of the 20th century the expression "tennis coach" did not exist but tennis professor did. The achievement of being the "World Champion" in pro tennis opened up clientele in the highest circles for Karel Kozeluh. He taught in Berlin, London and, most of all, in the United States. He lived in Florida but he constantly traveled. His customers included government officials, diplomats, members of the House of Commons and the House of Lords, members of the US Navy, and also Henry Ford. He even taught tennis fundamentals to a boy with a name not yet well known then – George Herbert Walker Bush. In addition he formed a wonderful mixed doubles team with the French star Suzanne Lenglen. They played in many exhibitions in Czechoslovakia and around the world. Suzanne Lenglen said of him, "He was pensive in private but once he gripped the racket it was as if elixir of life bespattered him."

In 1926 Karel Kozeluh defeated the two-time Bristol Cup winner from years 1924-25, the Irish Albert Burke in Beaulieu-sur-Mer 2:6, 6:1, 6:2, 6:0.

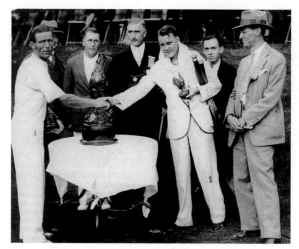

Karel Kozeluh won the US Pro-title for the first time in 1929. He beat the American Vincent Richards 6:4, 6:4, 4:6, 4:6, and 7:5.

Chicago Mayor Antony Joseph Cermak presented a gift of the Czech Athletes in USA - a Silver Tennis Racket (Czech National Museum).

Karel Kozeluh won his first Bristol Cup (the cup without a top) in 1926-1929, and the second cup variety with a top in 1930-1932 (Czech National Museum).

His greatest rival was the three times Wimbledon Champion Bill Tilden, who turned professional toward the end of 1930. He defeated Kozeluh in their first encounter 6:4, 6:2, and 6:4 in front of 14 000 spectators in Madison Square Garden. Their mutual game score was pretty even though it almost became a rule that they each lost when they wanted to win the most. Kozeluh lost in front of his compatriots in Chicago, Tilden got overpowered in Hollywood in front of Charlie Chaplin, Buster Keaton, Greta Garbo, Mae West and others. Karel Kozeluh's match in Prague in 1932 ended similarly. Fifteen thousand people came to watch the match that took place at Sparta soccer stadium; they saw a beautiful game but also Karel's defeat in four sets 6:4, 2:6, 2:6, and 3:6.

Kozeluh's game possessed three basic elements: fighting spirit, speed and confidence. Based on that he developed a game that was not so appealing but it was controlled, more defensive than offensive, and highly strategic. Kozeluh mastered all kinds of strokes. He

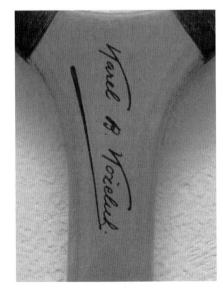
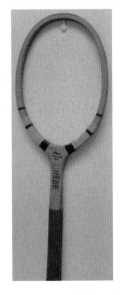
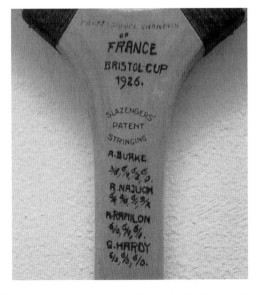

The original tennis racket from 1926 with Karel Kozeluh's authentic signature (Private Collection).

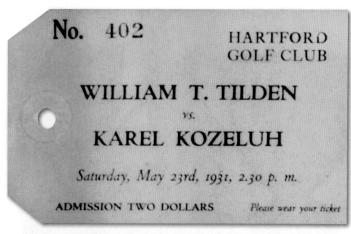

Tilden vs. Kozeluh entrance ticket - ITHF Museum.

was able to play bullet like serves and in no time switched to a highly bouncing American twist. His drop shots sometimes bounced back over the net; and he was able to lob his opponents precisely so that they could not reach up to it yet the ball bounced very close to the baseline. His forehand brought confidence into his game but his backhand was the best, and he was able to play it in a variety of ways. He did not approach the net often, he was more of a baseliner; he held his opponent away from the net with his baseline strokes. If his opponent chose to attack and approach the net right after the serve Karel passed him with precision shots most of the time. That made his opponents nervous and, commonly, he would give up trying it again.

Kozeluh's strokes were unbelievably precise. He was able to place the ball anywhere and everywhere from any position on a court. He hit a ball box or a handkerchief placed in a corner of a court even while running – in flight, four out of five times. Stories about his precision circulate around even today. Americans nicknamed him "Legs" and with that they uncovered the foundation of his success. He ran down just about everything and was able to play a point even from the most difficult of positions and still hit the next ball at impossible angles targeting the lines unswervingly.

Kozeluh's fighting spirit must be discussed separately. There was not even one match that he won without thorough preparation in order to deliver the best possible performance, and there was not one defeat in which he did not expend all he had in him. He was a quiet man, restrained, not theatrical. He had an iron will and muscles made of steel. And he fought until the last point was over, never underestimating his opponent.

During the World War II Karel Kozeluh wanted to join the Czech forces overseas, however, his longtime friend and Foreign Minister Jan Masaryk tal-

Karel Kozeluh

Bill Tilden and Karel Kozeluh competed in several exhibitions all over United States.

Paris 1930 before the Inter-Zonal final between USA – Italy. Karel Kozeluh was the American team's coach. From the left: captain J.E. Ditton, John Doeg, George Martin Lott, John van Ryn, Wilmer Allison, Gregory Maugin and Karel Kozeluh.
In the finals the US succumbed to France 1:4, in spite of Bill Tilden reinforcing the team.

ked him out of it. He returned to Prague soon after the liberation but he did not settle there permanently until after 1946. He opened up a sport equipment shop between Opletalova and Jindrisska Streets and he also continued to teach tennis; he even became the Davis Cup team coach. He also became an avid golfer. For that reason he built a villa on a piece of land in Klanovice close to a golf course.

Everything changed after the communist coup d'etat in February 1948. Karel refused to incorporate his shop in the National Company and chose to close it altogether. Friends helped him get a position of a sport agent with a Stavobet Firm. He did not believe that communists would hold power for long...

His life and tennis story came to an end sooner than anybody expected. It happened on April 27, 1950 when he was returning from a Stavobet Firm celebration; he missed his train and a colleague offered to give him a ride in the company truck. Karel, who was an excellent driver, was not driving that time. There are several versions to the story; according to one they had an accident in a dangerous curve in Klanovice. Others claim that the accident took place in Bechovice. Lately, however, the third version of the tragic end of Kozeluh's life popped up. Today a seventy-five year old Stanislav Dlouhy from Chvalkovice contradicts the version of an accident in Klanovice and affirms that it happened on a perfectly straight stretch in Ujezd nad Lesy in front of a family home number 220, where he then lived with his parents. "It must have happened around mid-night when I awoke with a bang. There were no municipal lights so it was dark outside and I only saw a silhouette of a truck and a passenger car crashed into it from behind. I began to dress to go and see what has happened but my father was just returning and talked me out of going out. I was not even seventeen and had to grant my father's wish. The next day I found out that Karel Kozeluh was killed in that passenger car."

No matter what happened that day one thing is for sure; very soon after that tragedy, members of StB entered the villa and accused Karel's wife Miroslava of not registering Karel's gold medals with their office. She then spent a year in prison; upon her return she lived in a garden cottage for a while before she was allowed to come into her home. After the StB swoop she found the villa short of valuable furniture pieces, carpets, tapestries, eight oil canvases from Vaclav Brozik....

Karel Kozeluh was one of the non-American players, who reached their best accomplishments before 1954. Even though the Hall of Fame was not founded before then, it is the kind of an institution that cannot afford omitting players of such caliber like, for instance, the French "musketeers" Cochet, Lacoste, Borotra, and Brugnon. For that reason even those players have been added gradually regardless that some of them have passed away. When Jan Kodes realized that Spencer W. Gore, the first Wimbledon Champion from 1877, and several Grand Slam winner Anthony Wilding have been entered in the Hall of Fame an idea struck him: "Shouldn't Karel Kozeluh be here as well?

I discovered that several Hall of Famers did not advance past Karel Kozeluh in Grand Slams. I acknowledged that the issue of Hall of Fame membership was a complicated one since Karel Kozeluh was a professional; however, why should we not attempt to have him still inducted even if post mortem?

I approached his niece, Mrs. Sladkova-Kozeluhova, and encouraged her to send a letter to Newport asking the committee why her uncle has not been yet nominated for the Hall of Fame honor.

It took close to two years during which the nominating committee examined Karel Kozeluh's accomplishments under Jan Kodes's persistence and they evaluated his tremendous significance for the development of tennis in the United Stated and elsewhere in the world. They further acknowledged that there were more players of similar caliber and, without the usual voting, they nominated six more players in addition to Karel Kozeluh into the Hall of Fame: Nancy Bolton (Australia), Marion Farquhar (USA), Arthur Gore, Herbert Lawford (both Great Britain), Simone Mathieu (France) and Hans Nüsslein (Germany).

ITHF Certificate - im memoriam!

Hana Kozeluh – Sladek with Jan Kodes on July 15, 2006. Behind them is set up a new plate to present Karel Kozeluh.

In context of celebration of the previous generation of outstanding players Tony Trabert revealed: "Each one of these players had a very special influence on the development of tennis. Their careers were impressive and it is our duty to commemorate them by inducting them into the Hall of Fame."

It took yet two more years before Hana Sladkova-Kozeluhova received an official letter informing her that her uncle, Karel Kozeluh, would be inducted into the International Tennis Hall of Fame on July 15, 2006! He was thus the seventh Czech who received this celebratory honor after Jaroslav Drobny, Jan Kodes, Hana Mandlikova, Martina Navratilova, Ivan Lendl and Jana Novotna. Karel Kozeluh's niece Hana Sladkova-Kozeluhova avowed: "I am truly happy to have worked with Jan Kodes and succeeded in having my uncle inducted into the Hall of Fame. I do not believe we could have asked for higher honor on his behalf!"

SOTHEBY'S, JULY 11, 2002

Jaroslav Drobny passed away on September 13, 2001. He emerged at Wimbledon in 1938 for the first time, when he was only sixteen. In 1946 he staged a big upset when he defeated the second seeded American Jack Kramer and advanced all the way to the semi-finals, where he lost to the Australian Geoff Brown. While representing still Czechoslovakia he fought his way into the Wimbledon finals in 1949 but got overpowered by the American Ted Schroeder. In 1952, this time already with an Egyptian passport, the Australian Frank Sedgman sealed Drobny's finals loosing fate. It took three Wimbledon finals before he became the Champion at last. In 1954 he defeated the Australian Ken Rosewall. He was an amazing player who won unbelievable 133 tournaments and who was inducted into the International Hall of Fame in 1983 with many distinctions.

When I learned the sad news of his passing and simultaneously found out that his daughter decided to auction out all her father's trophies at a London auction house I called on his close friend and magnificent golf player Lady Louisa Abrahams. I tried to convince her to contact the Czech Tennis Federation as well as the I. CLTK. She assured me that she had already spoken with the leadership of the club and that everybody at Stvanice knows that something must be done in order to secure at least some of Jaroslav's trophies "at home." After a few days she informed me that there was no need to worry for everything was on the right track. She discussed with me the tennis sponsorship or collection that was already undertaken. Her companion and Jaroslav Drobny's close friend, Milos Vainer, a British citizen since 1948, was one of the individuals who were to be personally present at the auction with monies collected from the Czech tennis circles.

Jaroslav Drobny - Official ITHF certificate.

Almost a year passed. I was just getting up one summer morning around nine and sitting down to my hot cup of tea, when my eyes lay on a calendar; there was a red circle around the date 7. 11. 2002 and a scribble said: Drobny - Auction at Sotheby's!

I picked up the receiver at once and rang up Milos Vainer in London. "Hello Milos! I hope I didn't wake you up! I have just gotten up and see that Jarolav's auction takes place today. How does it look?"

On the other end of the line Milos said: "I have no funds; everybody made promises but nothing came out of anything!"

I could not believe it. Is that at all possible? I called at once one of my contacts, Jiri Jonas, the owner of a restaurant "At Seven Angels" in Prague. "Jiri, imagine, everybody abandoned the Drobny auction!"

He responded: "Hey, how much would it cost? I'll buy it."

"Jiri, are you seriously considering it?"

"Yeah; just tell me what it involves?"

Prices are in British Pounds and they are pretty high. I believe that the most important piece to insist on getting would be the trophy he received on Centre Court after his Wimbledon victory over Rosewall. It is not the golden one that you might be familiar with. In those times the Champions received a silver one called the President's Cup. Naturally, it is only a smaller copy of the original that each winner keeps with his name engraved in it. But, it is a rarity because after 1988 that cup was no longer presented to the champions!"

"Ok; call Vainer and ask him to secure it for me in the auction. I'll pay him by return of post!"

I caught Milos less than ten minutes before his departure to Sotheby's. Two hours later he called me back that he got the trophy!

The next morning I read in Lidove noviny (Popular Newspaper): "Articles of the Czech ice hockey and tennis star Jaroslav Drobny were auctioned off for 40, 384, which is a sum two and a half times bigger than what the famous Czech had earned for all his victories. Trophies, medals, rackets, glasses, tennis shoes, tennis clothes, certificates, and other pieces of Jaroslav Drobny's possessions were auctioned off. According to the London Auction House Sotheby's there are no Czechs among the new owners of Jaroslav's possessions! Not even one article would travel to the Czech Republic..."

I was very pleased and had a good feeling about securing the trophy. At least one valuable part of Drobny's collection with an official certificate would return home, where Jaroslav was born and where he learned how to play tennis.

Drobny represented our country in ice hockey and tennis, and he represented it well – in world championships, in the Olympics, in prestigious tennis tournaments. I gave myself a question then: Is there no organization in this country that would not only remember him but would also try to retain something of his personal belongings for immortality? What about ice-hockey and tennis federations, or the Czech Olympic Committee? This should shake up our young generation...

Mr. Jiri Jonas made it happen. We thank him profusely! It cost him about $10,000... Later he sold the trophy to my tennis friend Josef Vlasek.

Jaroslav Drobny with his Wimbledon trophy.

FAMILY

Nobody doubted that he would follow his famous father's route.

He took his first tennis steps in Sparta Club in Stromovka but he further developed at Stvanice Center. He trained and played in such style that he was soon perceived as a talent and, potentially, the next "great" in Czech tennis. He became the National Champion of Junior Under 16 and Junior Under 18 categories.

His victory in Perth, Australia, a year later marked huge success for him. Together with teammates Martin Damn and Lukas Hovorka the trio returned from the 4th Youth Cup Competition, a junior competition similar to Davis Cup, as World Champions! Successively they defeated Japan, New Zealand, Yugoslavia and they took the United States by surprise in the finals.

In 1989, at the age of seventeen, he won the Junior Nationals in Pardubice, upsetting players like Karol Kucera, David Rikl, Radomir Vasek along the way to the finals where he overwhelmed Daniel Vacek. Thus the name Jan Kodes appeared after twenty five years for the second time among the Junior Champions. The only father and later son champions of Pardubice Nationals in the history of Czech tennis!

In January 1990 Jan junior occupied the 4th place in the ITF junior ranking. He received a wild card to the ATP Tour Czechoslovak Open and surprisingly defeated seeded Cedric Pioline from France in the first round and lost to the winner, Jordi Arrese from Spain in three sets. Journalists were delighted with young Kodes' play.

Young Kodes puts Czechs top of world

CZECHOSLOVAKIA atoned for two disappointing years in boys' junior tennis by winning the World Youth Cup in Perth yesterday.

Its team of Martin Damm and Jan Kodes clinched the final 2-1 downing the third-ranked Americans, Brian MacPhie and Jonathan Leach, in the singles at Royal Kings Park.

Key to the Czech victory was the slightly built Kodes, son of 1973 Wimbledon winner Jan Kodes. He opened up nervously against America's No.2 player Leach before winning 7-6 6-2.

Damm defeated MacPhie 6-2 6-7 6-4.

The Americans won the doubles 6-4 6-4.

A year later he won the first ATP Prague Challenger against Thomas Enqvist from Sweden in the finals. However, Kodes' further tennis development then started to stagnate. Instead of treading on the heels of Mecir, Novacek and Korda in 1992 he dropped to the fivehundreds in ranking. He suddenly and personally recognized that pro tennis worldwide was pretty evenly balanced and very difficult to break through.

His parents' divorce might have also had its affect

Jan Kodes Jr. in Prague during ATP Tour event...

on his performance; he was sixteen and had a difficult time dealing with it.

I am sure it marked him profoundly. People often asked me why he did not turn out to be a world top player the way I had been. He played well technically; he had no weakness but he had no real unique weapon either and that was crucial to making it onto the world platform. In addition, he was not strong enough physically or mentally. It remains true that he did not succeed in making competitive tennis his career....

Presently he runs JK Tennis Academy, which is based in the Head Tennis Centre in Vestec near Prague, where some 120 players of all levels and ages take advantage of his teaching experience. Several good players, who entered the national league and tournaments, have come out of his group.

I helped Jan at the beginning. He is now the head coach of the academy and he runs the tennis school under my patronage.

His daughter Tereza also learned how to

University of Durham, England. Martina and I arrived for Tereza's graduation ceremony on July 2, 1997, directly from Wimbledon. Here we are discussing her feelings just after the ceremony, in which she was decorated by the famous actor, Sir Peter Ustinov.

Anna enjoyed the Kooyong Lawn Tennis Club. Her father re-visited Melbourne, Australia after 35 years, where he played the Davis Cup tie in 1973.

play tennis but she enjoys it just recreationally. After finishing high school she studied in England for five years and earned her Bachelor's degree in Psychology at the University of Durham and Master's degree at the University of Manchester in International Trade. She is single and works as a marketing director of a British International Law Firm.

Two years after his divorce, Jan met Martina Schlonzova. Together they have a daughter Anna, who was born on May 21, 1996, at the time when her father was the President of Czech Tennis Association.

TENNIS CONSULTING

At the end of 1994 Jan Kodes received an offer to represent the Hugo Boss firm. Jan agreed to go into that venture with friends Ivan Chadima and Ranko Pecic and together they opened a luxury store in Jungmannovo Square in Prague. Boss expanded his collection by ladies fashions over the next few years and opened another store in famous Parizska Street.

As one of the agents I engaged mainly in observation of Hugo Boss firm requisition, including planning permissions, reconstruction of both stores, budget, supply operations, inspections, opening dates and later selection of goods in Metzingen, Germany, and then sales. The company was in operation for close to ten years. In September 2003 we decided to sell it.

Restaurant La Provence in Prague. Jan and Martina with Carmen and Muki Bolton (on right).

In spite of these business ventures tennis was still his main point of interest. In 2000 he took part in a Centre Court ceremony dedicated to all Wimbledon champions and some runner-ups selected by AELTC. He was also present to Martina Navratilova's induction into the Tennis Hall of Fame in Newport. A year later, after the US Open, he witnessed the tragic events of 9.11., the terrorist attack on the World Trade Center in New York, the catastrophe that affected all of the United States and the world.

The following year, in 2002, Prague experienced a horrific flood calamity. In spite of assurances that our building was safe the family apartment and office edifice located in Karlin was submerged nine feet in water. It took a year to restore things back to normal.

There was a great view of Manhattan from the Tenisport Tennis Club (canceled in 2009), where I played a game of doubles with M.D. Joseph G. McCarthy´s son Stephen (right) against his father and his father-in-law Walter Schneider (left). I do not remember who won, but I will always remember the time I spent from September 8 till October 26, 2001 in New York with my family!

At the beginning of 2004 Jan received a heart-warming invitation to Newport; he was requested to take part in celebrations on the occasion of a fifty-year anniversary of the International Tennis Hall of Fame's existence. It was a very enjoyable weekend until the moment when a moderator approached him and said: "Jan, you will speak on behalf of Europe!"

My throat dried up quickly and I was unable to do anything for the rest of that day. I kept in mind that over five hundred guests remembered me from a similar evening in 2000!

The colorful journalist Bud Collins opened the "tuxedo" dinner event. He welcomed everybody and briefly informed us that selected players would speak on behalf of individual continents in just a few minutes. The first on the program he introduced a player who he first saw in Prague in 1971 during Davis Cup against USSR. He witnessed an incredible atmosphere that is difficult to ever forget. He then listed a few of Jan Kodes' achievements and then called him out!

Only then I noticed that there was a raised platform in the middle of the room with spiral staircase leading up to it. I walked up there to give my speech but, suddenly, the lights went out. Naturally, I did not expect that. Only one spotlight was shining right at me! I do not know how it happened but my nervousness disappeared and I delivered the best speech I have ever given in my life! I realized it only after I had finished and the lights came back on; gradually, participants stood up and clapped and soon it turned into a standing ovation...

I was followed by Frew McMillan, then John Newcombe, Chris Evert and Stan Smith in the end. They did not enjoy as much applause as I did. When I returned to my table everybody congratulated me. Soon John McEnroe approached me and said: "Jan, you were great! You could not have said it any better!" I was tickled to death!

At breakfast the next day Bud Collins admitted: "Jan, I was a bit worried but you gave me a nice surprise. I truly did not anticipate that!"

I recognized what great appreciation I received from everybody, even from those, who did not know me. That moment gave me high hope for possible induction of Karel Kozeluh into the Hall of Fame; I felt we were on the right track.

My presence at Karel Kozeluh's induction into the Tennis Hall of Fame in 2006 was coupled

Wimbledon 2005. Jan with Jimmy Connors in the Members Enclosure.

with one set doubles exhibition with Patrick Rafter against Stan Smith and Nicolas Pereira on the Newport historical grass court. The following day I took part in another event organized by the Gullikson Foundation. The founder of that endowment was Rosemary L. Gullikson after Tim's untimely death. There were other participants there beside us – Rod Laver, Martina Navratilova, Malivai Washington, Stan Smith, Todd Martin, Richey Reneberg, Tim Mayotte, guests and sponsors. These were fun days when tennis rackets, paintings, tennis shoes, T-shirts, and other items were auctioned off and the profit was going to be used to educate enable them to engage in everyday life.

Since January 2006 Jan Kodes has been a member of the selection committee that nominates players for the "International Golden Achievement Award", one of the most important awards in tennis worldwide. The award is jointly presented by the International Tennis Hall of Fame and International Tennis Federation and is given annually to a person who has made important contributions to tennis in the fields of administration, promotion or education and has devoted long and outstanding service to the sport. The selection committee has seven members: Chairman James Harvie-Watt, Jane Brown-Grimes of the USTA, Jan Kodes, President of Tennis Australia Geoff Pollard representing ITHF, ITF President Francesco Ricci-Bitti, ETA Chairman John James and Barbara Travers representing the International Tennis Federation.

In 2008 Jan has also become a member of the Enshrinee Nominating Committee, Chaired by Tony Trabert, that nominate a new eligible candidates to the international voting ballot for induction into the International Tennis Hall of Fame.. This group meets regularly during Wimbledon. There he also takes part in the Annual International Tennis Clubs conference in the role of a Czech IC Vice-president.

Together with Helena Sukova, the Czech Republic IC President, he maintains contacts with other tennis countries. Czechoslovak IC was founded already in 1933 as fifth in the world! During the communist era Czech membership was lost but again renewed in London on June 29, 1999. Helena Sukova was appointed into the executive committee of all 34 IC member countries in January 2001.

Jan also visits the place of his two Roland Garros victories, the traditional ITF Champions' Dinner in Paris, as well as the Annual Newport Gala in New York during the US Open with pride and satisfaction. Those are the moments one never forgets regardless how many other experiences came his way, good or bad. After all, he practically dedicated his life to tennis.

U.S.Embassy Residence in Prague 2002. Farewell Doubles tennis event for the 1st U.S.Secretary Steve Coffey. From left: Jiri Miles, Zdenek Klezl, M.D., U.S.Ambassador Craig Stapleton, Jan Kodes, Steve Coffey, Croatia Amb. Zoran Piculjan, European Union Representative Andreas Nicklisch, Greece Am. Eleftherios Karayannis and Chilean Richardo Concha. Coffey and Kodes won the tournament.

AWARD FOR SERVICES IN THE GAME

Presented to

Jan Kodes

1988

President
International Tennis Federation

EPILOGUE

The idea of writing a book about Jan Kodes, the only Czechoslovak Wimbledon Champion, was first suggested to me by the Czech Tennis Association's spokeswoman, Mrs. Blanka Rokosova. "He turned sixty and it would be nice to remind the sport-fans about his tennis feats," she told me when we met at a press conference. "Would you help me make it happen?" - I did not hesitate!

The first attempt did not work out due to inadequate funding. Then, about a year later, my phone rang and the caller said, "This is Jan Kodes. Are you still interested in writing my book?" My answer was affirmative. "I do not know how Mrs. Rokosova feels about it but you can count on me!"

As a former sports journalist I was naturally attracted by the offer. It was a chance to get back to sports after years spent among actors, singers, and other performers, artists, scientists and politicians! On the other hand, there were the words of warning I heard from other journalists through the years: "It is difficult to work with Kodes. He's hard to get along with! He does not know how to deal with people properly. He always has his way. He treats everyone with arrogance! Working with him is extremely exhausting!" This made me even more interested. A real personality; a Wimbledon and Roland Garros Champion, the one who built new Stvanice Stadium, who did so much for Czech tennis and managed to turn so many people against him! Wow? Was it just his natural character? Was he a pompous buffoon?

Even after I started working on this book I kept hearing more. "A Wimbledon champion does not have to sweep the court after play," was what he was supposed to have said after a match at Stvanice. "He treated everyone else with disdain," I was told by a movie director who filmed a documentary with Kodes twenty five years earlier.

Everyone had their own opinion. Players did not like him much for his doggedness and fighting spirit with which he fought for every point. Colleagues and subordinates were often unable to come to terms with his devotion to diligence. On the other hand, there were those who were hugely impressed by his approach to both, tennis and work.

I spent almost two years working close to him. I visited his family, and he introduced me to many important individuals among Czech and world-class players: Martina Navratilova, Hana Mandlikova, Ivan Lendl... I admit I had never seen him play live! I had watched his Davis Cup matches on TV. I was out of luck in 1975 when, upon arriving in Prague with our teacher and classmates from Kutna Hora Grammar School, two of us deserted the class and went to Stvanice, rather than going on an educational tour of historical sites before that evening's National Theatre performance. Czechoslovakia played the Davis Cup semi-finals that weekend against Australia! I saw Tony Roche; I heard the strong words that Jiri Hrebec used when commenting on his backhand in a training session, but I did not get to see Jan Kodes.

I met him personally more than twenty years later, in autumn 1997, at a meeting he held with the press as a President of Czech Tennis Association. Six months later, everything turned against him and he was forced to leave the Czech tennis scene altogether. Five years after that I phoned him to enquire about an article I wanted to write about him for a magazine I was working for. It was the 30th anniversary of his victory at Wimbledon. Only then I realized what level of attention he paid to every detail. He kept checking facts and polishing the text until the very last moment. The magazine was ready to print and he called in to say that he wanted to make yet another change, having found a new and very important piece of information in his archives.

As we were working on this book, there were hundreds of moments like that. I visited Jan for the first time in February 2005. Recording the first cassette I had no idea that we were going to produce fifteen of them. It was 45 hours worth of stories, not all of them tennis-related, some of them funny and some of them serious. There were memories of people that Kodes met: team mates from the Davis Cup team, coaches, officials, designers, builders... More cassettes – and then, his archives. Thorough, precise, well categorized, kept originally by Kodes' father right up until his death. Photographs, newspaper clippings, articles, statistics, results, rankings. Everything meticulously arranged year-by-year, month-by-month, day-by-day. There was more "paperwork" in the cabinet. Contracts, letters, reports, applications, photographs, assessments, heaps of table sheets, results and Czechoslovak, Czech and foreign magazines. Virtually any fact stated by the book can be supported by a document from Jan Kodes' archives...

It was with awe that I accepted the high pile of facts: "God, how am I going to sift through all that?" It is up to others to judge whether I have succeeded. I can only hope I have fulfilled Kodes' wish, the one he kept repeating almost every time we met: "What I want is that every tennis fan looking for a piece of information concerning the history of our tennis can enlighten himself with: well, it must be in Kodes' book!"

We spent almost two years together. During that time, I have come to understand how much he loved his parents, especially his father, and how much he missed them both. Stepping through the door of his study, located on the ground floor of the family villa, was like being launched back 80 years. Contracts, invoices, letters arranged neatly on the table and a small sculpture of Kodes' father standing in the corner. He started browsing through one of the earliest albums compiled by his dad, and his eyes got teary...

Later, I met him once more. It was Spring 2006, and he was happily showing me a thirty years-old article cut out of the Czechoslovak Sport newspaper, saying that JUDr. Jan Kodes, the former secretary of the Czech Olympic committee, was awarded an "3rd level of Honourable Recognition, for his contribution to the development of Czech sports." The certificate was dated November 11, 1963, and was bestowed on June 16, 1966! He read the whole article to me again, and his eyes, once again, clouded over with tears...

He knew tennis under two political regimes. He did his best under the first one by winning Roland Garros, Wimbledon, Davis Cup. Thanks to him, the comrades could not put tennis on any side track, which

The plate on Davis Cup trophy from the finals played at Stockholm in 1975. Sweden beat Czechoslovakia 3:2.

The plate on Davis Cup trophy from the finals played at Prague in 1980. Czechoslovakia beat Italy 4:1.

was exactly what happened in neighboring Poland and East Germany. It was he who opened the doors for the next generation of players: Lendl, Smid, Slozil, Mecir, Korda, Navratilova, Mandlikova, Novotna, Sukova...

Under the latter regime he tried to do his best once again as an official, Tournament Director, and a President of the Tennis Association. His effort was not always appreciated. Even that is explained in this book. Whoever he was, whatever he may have been accused of - his relations with the former regime officials, his demeanor, or false accusations of embezzlement - his contribution to Czech tennis is undeniable. If nothing else, he saved tennis in Prague's very centre and defended the tradition of tennis at Stvanice Island during the difficult totalitarian era; that was an admirable achievement. The I. Czech Lawn Tennis Club came only so close to be removed from the heart of Prague, or, possibly, even from the whole Czech tennis scene.

While I was working on this book I came to realize two things. First, tennis is a strange game, especially at the top level. I finally understood that the game itself was not as important as politics and money that surrounded it. A lot of money. Money that could affect various people in various ways... I do not actually know if this is also the case in the West but it is definitely so in our country. There are always some individuals who cannot resist unfair practices in order to safe-guard the best results possible for themselves.

During his life-time, Jan Kodes met many characters living in the complex world of tennis. Friendly ones, as well as mean ones, both friends and enemies. He keeps meeting his greatest opponents till these days; they still pay each other the same respect, and when they meet in Wimbledon or at the US Open they reminisce about the good old times. Stan Smith, John Newcombe, Alexander Metreveli, Björn Borg... Dialing the phone number of Ilie Nastase, Jan expects nothing else than the usual line: "Hello, Russian!"

Not all of his friends are former tennis players. Ivan Chadima, the Bolton family residing in the US, Joseph McCarthy, a top physician with New York University Medical Centre. Sometimes, friendship can be complicated, as it is often difficult to recognize how earnest it is. In recent years, Kodes has encountered additional genuine people who helped him take care of his daughter Anna's health issues. He holds all of them in high esteem and considers them his friends: Prof. Jarmila Boguszakova, M.D., Boris Zivny M.D..

Who, then, was Jan Kodes? Who has he become?

A tough guy? - He had to be! On and off the court he had to be very demanding of himself, and also of his wife and children. Living with him was not easy, that is for sure. Tennis has always been number one, and the family suffered for that. Nevertheless, divorce was a truly shattering experience...

He was a great tennis player. While he excelled on clay courts, he once said in 1971, that "playing on grass was a joke." Yet, at the US Championships held at Forest Hills later that year he demonstrated that it was not Kodes who the joke was on. His victory over John Newcombe, the Wimbledon conqueror, and the way he progressed into the finals, became the feat of the year. He enjoyed his joke. He then won at Wimbledon, even though he had been avoiding the tournament previously. And he went on to prove that his Wimbledon title was not a chance victory. At the 1973 US Open, he came a breath short of occupying the top post in the world rankings. Despite that, his rightful place among the world class will probably be always disputed. And he will always feel a bit hurt even though, personally, he should be satisfied. He faced the grass court challenge and he triumphed!

Kodes is a patriot. He has never emigrated, in spite of many offers and opportunities; he has always placed Czech tennis first. Occasionally, you would hear him say that it was a mistake. He could have been coaching Ivan Lendl and travelling the world with him. I heard him say that so many times, especially as we were working on the finishing parts of the book and he was suddenly recalling the unpleasant memories of his tennis-official days. I have often heard him reflect on Ivan's opinion on Czech tennis, which shocked him at first, and which took him a long time to accept as accurate.

He brought his temper and fighting spirit with him from the courts to his civil life. That has not always been a good thing either. He used to occupy management posts that sometimes required the ability to compromise; he was not always capable of that. It is impossible to change someone's personality. It was in his nature to follow that single goal of his – serving and benefiting Czech tennis!

It is forever on his mind, even though he does not hold any official position anymore. Could anyone else have made such an effort to promote Karel Kozeluh to the International Tennis Hall of Fame? That is unlikely!

Kodes is happy to see Tomas Berdych, Radek Stepanek and some women players on the scene, making Czech tennis visible once again. The present does not compare to those successful 1970s and 1980s but the future could still prove Kodes wrong, when he declared at the 30th anniversary of his triumph at Wimbledon: "I wish for our tennis, especially men's tennis, to have another Wimbledon winner. But I doubt I'm going to live to see it!"

I am glad I crossed paths with Jan Kodes. I am thankful for all those days, weeks and months I spent in his presence and I am happy for the opportunity to get to know him – however controversial he was – a person who did more for the popularity of our country than all of the former and present regime politicians combined. It cost me dearly – so much energy, so many problems, so much anxiety, those sleepless nights, even whole weekends in front of a computer. I came to know someone who has, personally, proven the saying that the Czech nation does not honor its heroes, however sad it may be. To describe him in one word, I would repeat an answer I received from one of Kodes's former opponents and also his former doubles partner. In reply to my question: "How do you perceive Jan Kodes, both as a player and as a person?" Wojtek Fibak responded: "What a Fighter!"

Petr Kolar
Prague, March 26, 2010

The Millennium Champions Parade, Saturday July 1, 2000 on the most famous grass in the world.

...LATER AND PRESENT

Tennis, often called the "white sport" here, has always been a favorite in the Czech lands. Knowing how to play the game was an inherent part of one's education in the upper classes not only in the days of the Austro-Hungarian Empire but above all during the First Czechoslovak Republic established at 1918.

In every era we had players who dominated not only on their own country's courts but who were also able to make their presence felt in European and thereafter world arenas. We could name tens of such players but we will rather name none. We might possibly forget someone...

A separate and very specific chapter is made up of the four decades of Communist rule, which after their takeover in 1948, sent Czech tennis onto a side-track. The regime tagged it a 'bourgeois' sport, which due to its individualistic character was completely out of keeping with the official ideology of the time. The paradox is that this period produced the best tennis players, men and women, that this country ever had. There were winners of Grand Slam tournaments, winners of the Davis Cup, Federation Cup and many other significant tennis events. Again, we shall not name anyone in particular but the list of their names and the Grand Slam titles which they won in their careers would take up a lot of space in this book...

"How is it possible that you have so many exceptional tennis players?" was the question that foreign tennis players and tennis experts and writers kept asking at that time, especially those from beyond the Iron Curtain, the Americans, English, French and Australians...... Apart from the abovementioned popularity of tennis here, there was one huge motivating factor. Tennis and any other top level performance sport in general, offered one of the few opportunities of travel to the Western countries in that time of totalitarian darkness and in the case of tennis even presented the possibility of making some decent money in "hard currency."

It was a strange time, full of paradoxes and perversions. The "Velvet Revolution" of 1989 returned our homeland to its place among "normal" countries. The doors to the world were re-opened and if one of the young up and coming players wanted to enroll in Nick Bollettieri's Tennis Academy in Florida, he no longer had to emigrate to do so. Many people believed that the evolution of a normal democratic society would bring with it a huge tennis boom and Czechs would once again conquer the tennis world in even greater numbers than before. Unfortunately, the opposite was true...

Our last two players to win Grand Slam tournament titles did so in 1998 in Melbourne and Wimbledon. They were both still products of the pre-revolution tennis development program...We have waited in vain for more than ten years. Even though in 2009, our women were one point away from advancing to the finals of the Fed Cup and after a break of 29 years our men's team fought their way to the finals of the Davis Cup and lost to Spain 0:5! Czech tennis has fallen into the doldrums. Why? Is it the motivation, the will or the effort to break through that is missing? Has the enthusiasm of the parents, who in the past drove their children from tournament to tournament and were willing the spend nights sleeping in tents in order to save money to pay for coaches and courts, fallen off? Or is the problem in the fact that the gates to the world have opened for the young and they can now travel wherever and whenever they want in order to study or work abroad?

Is it that today they have computers, mobile telephones, the internet with Facebook and Skype, MP3's and many other possibilities so that little time or interest remains for general sport and tennis in particular? Is the Czech Tennis Association playing its role properly in the education of young tennis players? The truth will probably lie somewhere in between. Unfortunately, there is practically no-one waiting in the wings of whom it could be said that they could lift the level of Czech tennis back to the highest stage of Grand Slam tournaments, to which we were accustomed up till the recent past, after the name bearers of today's at least partial successes of Czech tennis pass.This is truly a sad thought...

Let's hope it will change again in time...

Jiri Novak won seven ATP Tour singles events, played DC for eleven years, reached two GS doubles finals at Wimbledon 2001 and US Open 2002 (with Rikl and Stepanek). Best ranked No:7, defeated Andre Agassi in the ATP Masters 2002.

Lucie Safarova chaptured four titles so far, two in 2005 at Estoril and Forest Hills, Gold Coast 2006 and Forest Hills again in 2008. She had few great wins during 2007 season. She beat Amélie Mauresmo twice at Australian Open and Roland Garros. Later in the year won at Paris Indoor over Svetlana Kuznecova and Justine Henin to reach the finals, lost to Nadia Petrova.

Radek Stepanek advanced into Wimbledon quarter-finals in 2006 and won four ATP singles events: Rotterdam in 2006, L.A. in 2007, Brisbane and San Jose in 2009. Helped Czechs to reach the 2009 Davis Cup final.

Lukas Dlouhy achieved several good results in doubles only. With different partners reached the ATP World Tour Masters (Finals). His best wins so far are 2009 Roland Garros and US Open titles, teamed with Leander Paes.

Iveta Benesova, still promising player won 2004 WTA Tour in Acapulco and from 2002 till 2009 reached six finals: Bratislava, Forest Hills and twice in each: Estoril and Hobart.

Tomas Berdych, the future hope of Czech tennis, won 2005 Paris Indoor at Bercy, 2008 Tokyo and reached the quarter-finals at Wimbledon in 2007 losing to Rafael Nadal.

Nicole Vaidisova played two quarter-finals at Wimbledon 2007 and 2008, lost to Anna Ivanovic and Jie Zheng.

Jan Kodes – 50 Best Tournament Singles Matches

1969	US Indoor, Philadelphia 2nd R:	Arthur Ashe (USA)	6:4, 4:6, 6:2
1969	US Indoor, Philadelphia QF:	Stan Smith (USA)	6:2, 2:6, 6:2
1970	Italian Open, Roma, QF:	Mark Cox (GBR)	5:7, 6:3, 6:2, 6:2
1970	Italian Open, Roma, SF:	Alex Metreveli (URS)	6:3, 8:6, 6:4
1970	Roland Garros, Paris, 4th R:	Ion Tiriac (ROM)	4:6, 7:5, 4:6, 6:2, 6:2
1970	Roland Garros, Paris, QF:	Martin Mulligan (ITA)	6:1, 6:3, 7:5
1970	Roland Garros, Paris, SF:	Georges Goven (FRA)	2:6, 6:2, 5:7, 6:2, 6:3
1970	**Roland Garros, Paris, Finals:****	**Zeljko Franulovic (YUG)**	**6:2, 6:4, 6:0**
1970	Grand Prix, Cincinnati, QF:	Stan Smith (USA)	6:3, 1:6, 6:2
1970	PSW-Los Angeles, 2nd R.	Dennis Ralston (USA)	7:6, 6:3
1971	Italian Open, Roma, 3rd R:	Tony Roche (AUS)	6:4, 5:7, 7:6
1971	Italian Open, Roma, QF:	John Newcombe (AUS)	2:6, 6:1, 7:5
1971	Italian Open, Roma, SF:	Tom Okker (NED)	4:6, 6:3,7:5, 6:4
1971	Roland Garros, Paris, 4th R:	Francois Jauffret (FRA)	4:6, 6:2, 5:7, 6:0, 6:4
1971	Roland Garros, Paris, QF:	Patrick Proisy (FRA)	6:4, 8:6, 1:6, 6:1
1971	Roland Garros, Paris, SF:	Zeljko Franulovic (YUG)	6:4, 6:2, 7:5
1971	**Roland Garros, Paris, Finals:****	**Ilie Nastase (ROM)**	**8:6, 6:2, 2:6, 7:5**
1971	US Open, NY, 1st R:	John Newcombe (AUS)	2:6, 7:6, 7:6, 6:3
1971	US Open, 2nd R:	Pierre Barthes (FRA)	2:6, 5:7, 6:4, 6:4, 6:3
1971	US Open, NY, 4th R:	Bob Lutz (USA)	6:4, 6:2, 6:4
1971	US Open, NY, QF:	Frank Froehling (USA)	6:0, 7:6, 6:3
1971	**US Open, NY, SF:****	**Arthur Ashe (USA)**	**7:6, 3:6, 4:6, 6:3, 6:4**
1971	Stockholm Open, QF:	Rod Laver (AUS)	4:6, 6:4, 7:6
1971	Stockholm Open, SF:	Cliff Drysdale (JAR)	2:6, 6:2, 6:4
1971	Grand Prix Masters, Paris:	Stan Smith (USA)	6:4, 3:6, 6:4
1971	Grand Prix Masters, Paris:	Clark Graebner (USA)	7:6, 6:4
1972	Italian Open, Roma, SF:	Ilie Nastase (ROM)	6:4, 1:6, 6:3, 6:3
1972	Spanish Open, Barcelona,QF:	Andres Gimeno (ESP)	6:4, 6:3
1972	Spanish Open, Barcelona, SF:	Ilie Nastase (ROM)	9:7, 6:4, 6:1
1972	**Spanish Open, Barcelona, Finals:**	**Manuel Orantes (ESP)**	**6:3, 6:2, 6:3**
1973	WCT Cologne, 2nd R:	Tom Okker (NED)	6:4, 6:3
1973	WCT Cologne, QF:	Marty Riessen (USA)	6:1, 7:5
1973	WCT Cologne, SF:	Mark Cox (GBR)	6:3, 6:7, 6:1
1973	WCT Cologne, Finals:	Brian Fairlie (NZL)	6:1, 6:3, 6:1
1973	WCT Vancouver, QF:	Alex Metreveli (URS)	6:4, 6:2
1973	WCT Vancouver, SF:	Ken Rosewall (AUS)	7:6, 2:6, 6:3
1973	WCT Cleveland, 2nd R:	Alex Metreveli (URS)	6:4, 5:7, 6:3
1973	**Wimbledon,London, SF:**	**Roger Taylor (GBR)**	**8:9*, 9:7, 5:7, 6:4, 7:5**
1973	**Wimbledon,London, Finals:****	**Alex Metreveli (URS)**	**6:1, 9:8*6:3**
1973	**US Open, NY, SF:****	**Stan Smith (USA)**	**7:5, 6:7, 1:6, 6:1, 7:5**
1974	**WCT Denver, QF:**	**Rod Laver (AUS)**	**6:2, 6:4**
1974	**WCT Dallas, Masters:****	**Ilie Nastase (ROM)**	**7:6, 6:1,7:5**
1974	Wimbledon, London, 4th R:	Tom Gorman (USA)	6:8, 2:6, 6:3, 9:7, 6:4
1975	Grand Prix, Madrid, QF:	Ilie Nastase (ROM)	6:4, 6:4
1975	Grand Prix, Madrid, SF:	Jaime Fillol (CHI)	5:7, 2:6, 7:6, 6:2, 6:3
1975	**Grand Prix, Madrid, Finals:**	**Adriano Panatta (ITA)**	**6:2, 3:6, 7:6, 6:2**
1975	German Open, Hamburg, QF:	Guillermo Vilas (ARG)	6:3, 6:2
1976	Grand Prix, Madrid, 3rd R:	Vitas Gerulaitis (USA)	6:2, 4:6, 6:1
1977	WCT Monte Carlo, 2nd R:	Manuel Orantes (ESP)	6:4, 6:3
1977	WCT Monte Carlo, QF:	Wojtek Fibak (POL)	6:4, 6:4

* tie-breaker at 8:8   ** most important matches

Jan Kodes – Best International Tournaments

Singles Titles (25)

1965	Varna	Jozef Orlikowski (POL)	2:6, 6:0, 6:1	Clay
	Plovdiv	Jozef Orlikowski (POL)	4:6, 6:3, 9:7	Clay
1967	Lyon - Cozon Cup	Jan Kukal	4:6, 6:1, 8:6	Indoor-wood
	Cannes	Ilie Nastase (ROM)	6:0, 6:1	Clay
	Bratislava	Ion Tiriac (ROM)	1:6, 13:11, 6:1, 6:2	Clay
	Luxembourg	Patrick Hombergen (BEL)	6:1, 6:2	Clay
1968	Paris - Cup Poreé	Milan Holecek	8:6, 6:3, 6:2	Clay
	Viňa del Mar	Pato Cornejo (CHI)	7:5, 7:5, 6:1	Clay
1969	Pittsburgh	Herb Fitzgibbon (USA)	8:6, 6:1	Indoor-Clay
	Santiago	Milan Holecek	4:6, 6:3, 1:6, 6:1, 6:2	Clay
	Sao Paolo	Milan Holecek	4:6, 6:3, 1:6, 6:4, 6:3	Indoor-Clay
1970	St. Petersburg (USA)	Joaquin Loyo-Mayo (MEX)	6:3, 6:3, 6:2	Clay
	Roland Garros - French Open	Zeljko Franulovic (YUG)	6:2, 6:4, 6:0	Clay
	Bratislava	Milan Holecek	3:6, 6:3, 6:2, 7:5	Clay
1971	Catania	Georges Goven (FRA)	6:3, 6:0, 6:2	Clay
	Roland Garros - French Open	Ilie Nastase (ROM)	8:6, 6:2, 2:6, 7:5	Clay
	Bratislava	Szabolcs Baranyi (HUN)	4:6, 6:3, 5:7, 6:4, 6:3	Clay
1972	Zaragoza	Barry Phillips-Moore (AUS)	4:6, 9:7, 9:7, 6:3	Clay
	Barcelona - Trofeo de Godo	Manuel Orantes (ESP)	6:3, 6:2, 6:3	Clay
	Split	Nicky Kalogeropoulos (GRE)	8:6, 6:4, 6:8, 2:6, 9:7	Clay
1973	Cologne - WCT	Brian Fairlie (NZL)	6:1, 6:3, 6:1	Ind-supreme
	Wimbledon	Alex Metreveli (URS)	6:1, 9:8*, 6:3	Grass
	Bayrút - Brumanna	Juan Gisbert (ESP)	6:3, 10:8, 4:6, 6:1	Clay
1975	Madrid	Adriano Panatta (ITA)	6:2, 3:6, 7:6, 6:2	Clay
1976	Basel	Jiri Hrebec	6:4, 6:2, 6:3	Ind-mateflex

Singles Runner-up Finishes (27)

1965	Sofia	Jozef Orlikowski (POL)	4:6, 1:6, 6:8	Clay
1966	Bratislava	Ion Tiriac (ROM)	1:6, 2:6, 6:0, 4:6	Clay
1967	Aix en Provence	Alex Metreveli (URS)	6:4, 4:6, 2:6, 2:6	Clay
	Paris - Coubertin	Tom Okker (NED)	2:6, 6:3, 3:6, 4:6	Indoor-wood
	Paris - Cup Poreé	Pierre Darmon (FRA)	1:6, 2:6, 2:6	Clay
1968	Santiago	Pato Cornejo (CHI)	10:8, 1:6, 4:6, 1:6	Clay
1969	Baranquilla	Ilie Nastase (ROM)	4:6, 4:6, 10:8, 6:2, 3:6	Clay
	Charlotte	Mark Cox (GBR)	11:13, 2:6	Clay
1970	Roma - Italian Open	Ilie Nastase (ROM)	3:6, 6:1, 3:6, 6:8	Clay
1971	Nice	Ilie Nastase (ROM)	8:10, 9:11, 1:6	Clay
	Roma - Italian Open	Rod Laver (AUS)	5:7, 3:6, 3:6	Clay
	Forest Hills - US Open	Stan Smith (USA)	6:3, 3:6, 2:6, 6:7	Grass
	Stockholm - WCT	Arthur Ashe (USA)	1:6, 6:3, 2:6, 6:1, 4:6	Indoor-rubber
1972	Nice	Ilie Nastase (ROM)	0:6, 4:6, 3:6	Clay
	Roma - Italian Open	Manuel Orantes (ESP)	6:4, 1:6, 5:7, 2:6	Clay

* tie-breaker at 8:8

1973	Vancouver - WCT	Tom Gorman (USA)	6:3, 2:6, 5:7	Ind-supreme
	Forest Hills - US Open	John Newcombe (AUS)	4:6, 6:1, 6:4, 2:6, 3:6	Grass
	Prague	Jiri Hrebec	6:4, 1:6, 6:3, 0:6, 5:7	Indoor-nisaplast
1974	Acapulco	Tom Okker (NED)	2:6, 6:7	Indoor-hard
1975	Hampton	Jimmy Connors (USA)	6:3, 3:6, 0:6	Ind-supreme
	Hamburg	Manuel Orantes (ESP)	6:3, 2:6, 2:6, 6:4, 1:6	Clay
	Düsseldorf	Jaime Fillol (CHI)	4:6, 6:1, 0:6, 5:7	Clay
	Kitzbühel	Adriano Panatta (ITA)	6:2, 2:6, 5:7, 4:6	Clay
1976	Nice	Corrado Barazzutti (ITA)	2:6, 6:2, 7:5, 6:7, 6:8	Clay
	Kitzbühel	Manuel Orantes (ESP)	6:7, 2:6, 6:7	Clay
1977	Kitzbühel	Guillermo Vilas (ARG)	7:5, 2:6, 6:4, 3:6, 2:6	Clay
1978	Bregenz	Jiri Hrebec	3:6, 7:6, 4:6, 6:3, 2:6	Clay

Doubles Titles (31)

1966	Bratislava	J. Kodes J. Javorsky	R. Howe (AUS) M. Sangster (GBR)	6:3, 2:6, 2:6, 7:5, 6:4	Clay
1967	Lyon	J. Kodes J. Kukal	R. Suominen (FIN) M. Werren (SUI)	6:8, 8:6, 6:2	Indoor-wood
	Luxembourg	J. Kodes F. Pala	I. Mikysa P. Mls	6:1, 6:4	Clay
1968	Viña del Mar	J. Kodes P. Rodriguez (CHI)	J. Pinto-Bravo (CHI) P. Cornejo (CHI)	6:2, 6:3, 7:5	Clay
	Hilversum	J. Kodes J. Kukal	I. Buding(GER) H. Elschenbroich(GER)	6:3, 6:1	Clay
1969	Macon	J. Kodes J. Kukal	M. Cox (GBR) P. Curtis (GBR)	13:11, 10:8	Indoor supreme
	Pittsburgh	J. Kodes J. Kukal	Z. Franulovic (YUG) R. Holmberg (USA)	4:6, 6:3, 6:4	Clay
	Caracas	J. Kodes J. Kukal	M. Orantes (ESP) J. McManus (USA)	2:6, 10:8, 6:3, 8:6	Clay
	Istanbul	J. Kodes J. Kukal	B. Hewitt (RSA) R. Maud (RSA)	8:10, 6:4, 5:7, 7:5, 9:7	Clay
	Santiago	J. Kodes M. Holecek	J. Fillol (CHI) P. Cornejo (CHI)	4:6, 6:2, 6:4, 6:2	Clay
1970	Baastad	J. Kodes Z. Franulovic (YUG)	D. Crealy (AUS) A. Stone (AUS)	2:6, 6:2, 11:11, unfinished	Clay
1971	Bratislava	J. Kodes J. Kukal	J. Hrebec P. Huťka	6:2, 1:6, 6:3	Clay
	Indianapolis	J. Kodes Z. Franulovic (YUG)	C. Graebner (USA) E. Van Dillen (USA)	6:7, 7:5, 6:3	Clay
1972	Nice	J. Kodes S. Smith (USA)	I. Nastase (ROM) F. McMillan (RSA)	6:3, 3:6, 7:5	Clay
	Hamburg	J. Kodes I. Nastase (ROM)	I. Tiriac (ROM) B. Hewitt (RSA)	4:6, 6:0, 3:6, 6:2, 6:2	Clay
	Zaragoza	J. Kodes F. Pala	S. Baranyi (HUN) P. Szőke (HUN)	6:8, 6:4, 6:4	Clay
	Split	J. Kodes J. Kukal	N. Kalogeropoulos (GRE) B. Jovanovic (YUG)	w.o.	Clay
1973	Bayrút - Brumanna	J. Kodes J. Kukal	A. Mayer (USA) I. Gulyas (HUN)	2:6, 3:6, 6:4, 7:5, 7:5	Clay
	Los Angeles	J. Kodes V. Zednik	J. Connors (USA) I. Nastase (ROM)	6:2, 6:4	Clay
	Prague	J. Kodes V. Zednik	B. Taróczy (HUN) R. Machan (HUN)	7:6, 7:6	Ind-mateflex
1974	Palm Dessert	J. Kodes V. Zednik	R. Moore (RSA) O. Parun (NZL)	6:4, 6:4	Hard

1975	Munich	J. Kodes W. Fibak (POL)	M. Holecek (TCH) K. Meiler (GER)	7:5, 6:3	Clay
	Düsseldorf	J. Kodes F. Jauffret (FRA)	H. Elschenbroich(GER); H. Kary (AUT)	6:2, 6:3	Clay
	Madrid	J. Kodes I. Nastase (ROM)	M. Orantes (ESP) J. Gisbert (ESP)	6:4, 3:6, 9:7	Clay
1976	Kitzbühel	J. Kodes J. Hrebec	H. J. Pohmann (GER) J. Fassbender (GER)	6:7, 6:2, 6:4	Clay
1977	Monte Carlo	J. Kodes F. Jauffret (FRA)	T. Okker (HOL) W. Fibak (POL)	2:6, 6:3, 6:2	Clay
	Barcelona	J. Kodes W. Fibak (POL)	B. Hewitt (RSA) F. McMillan (RSA)	6:0, 6:4	Clay
1978	Stuttgart	J. Kodes T. Smid	C. Kirmayr (BRA) B. Prajoux (CHI)	6:3, 7:6	Clay
	Madrid	J. Kodes W. Fibak (POL)	T. Smid P. Složil	6:7, 6:1, 6:2	Clay
1979	Hamburg	J. Kodes T. Smid	M. Edmondson (AUS) J. Marks (AUS)	6:3, 6:1, 7:6	Clay
1982	Hilversum	J. Kodes T. Smid	B. Taróczy (HUN) H. Günthardt (SUI)	7:6, 6:4	Clay
	Nairobi	J. Kodes D. Gitlin (USA)	B. Pils (AUT) H. Stiegler (AUT)	6:4, 3:6, 6:3	Clay

Doubles Runner-up Finishes (29)

1967	Paris Cup Poreé	Jan Kodes Frantisek Pala	Nicky Kalogeropoulos (GRE) Frew McMillan (RSA)	5:7, 1:6	Clay
1968	Curaçao	Jan Kodes Jan Kukal	Tom Okker (NED) Marty Riessen (USA)	3:6, 8:10	Hard
	Munich	Jan Kodes Milan Holecek	Robert Maud (RSA) Frew McMillan (RSA)	4:6, 4:6, 4:6	Clay
1968	Paris Cup Poreé	Jan Kodes Milan Holecek	Bob Carmichael (AUS) Ismail El Shafei (EGY)	4:6, 6:8	Clay
1969	Hilversum	Jan Kodes Jan Kukal	Tom Okker (NED) Roger Taylor (GBR)	3:6, 2:6, 4:6	Clay
1970	Baastad	Jan Kodes Zeljko Franulovic (YUG)	Dick Crealy (AUS) Allan Stone (AUS)	2:6, 6:2, 11:11 unfinished	Clay
	Kitzbühel	Jan Kodes Zeljko Franulovic (YUG)	John Alexander (AUS) Phil Dent (AUS)	8:10, 2:6, 4:6	Clay
	Bratislava	Jan Kodes Jan Kukal	Peter Szőke (HUN) Robert Machan (HUN)	5:7, 6:8	Clay
	Phoenix	Jan Kodes Charlie Pasarell (USA)	Dick Crealy (AUS) Ray Ruffels (AUS)	6:7, 3:6	Hard
	Buenos Aires	Jan Kodes Zeljko Franulovic (YUG)	Bob Carmichael (AUS) Ray Ruffels (AUS)	5:7, 2:6, 7:5, 7:6, 3:6	Clay
1971	Macon	Jan Kodes Zeljko Franulovic (YUG)	Clark Graebner (USA) Tomas Koch (BRA)	3:6, 6:7	Indoor supreme
	Catania	Jan Kodes Jan Kukal	François Jauffret (FRA) Pierre Barthes (FRA)	6:7, 6:2, 3:6	Clay
1972	Montreal	Jan Kodes Jan Kukal	Ilie Nastase (ROM) Ion Tiriac (ROM)	6:7, 3:6	Clay
1975	Salisbury	Jan Kodes Roger Taylor (GBR)	Ilie Nastase (ROM) Jimmy Connors (USA)	6:4, 3:6, 3:6	Indoor canvas
	Hamburg	Jan Kodes Wojtek Fibak (POL)	Manuel Orantes (ESP) Juan Gisbert (ESP)	3:6, 6:7	Clay
	Toronto	Jan Kodes Ilie Nastase (ROM)	Cliff Drysdale (RSA) Ray Moore (RSA)	4:6, 7:5, 6:7	Clay

1977	Baltimore	Jan Kodes / Ross Case (AUS)	Ion Tiriac (ROM) / Guillermo Vilas (ARG)	3:6, 7:6, 4:6	Indoor supreme
	Roland Garros	Jan Kodes / Wojtek Fibak (POL)	Brian Gottfried (USA) / Raul Ramirez (MEX)	6:7, 6:4, 3:6, 4:6	Clay
	Oviedo	Jan Kodes / Raul Ramirez (MEX)	Sherwood Stewart (USA) / Fred McNair (USA)	3:6, 1:6	Clay
	Videň	Jan Kodes / Wojtek Fibak (POL)	Bob Hewitt (RSA) / Frew McMillan (RSA)	4:6, 3:6	Indoor greenset
1978	Springfield	Jan Kodes / Marty Riessen (USA)	Stan Smith (USA) / Bob Lutz (USA)	3:6, 3:6	Indoor supreme
	Nice	Jan Kodes / TomaS Smid	François Jauffret (FRA) / Patrice Dominguez (FRA)	4:6, 0:6	Clay
	Aix en Provence	Jan Kodes / TomaS Smid	Guillermo Vilas (ARG) / Ion Tiriac (ROM)	6:7, 1:6	Clay
	Roma	Jan Kodes / TomaS Smid	Victor Pecci (PAR) / Belus Prajoux (CHI)	7:6, 6:7, 1:6	Clay
1979	Hilversum	Jan Kodes / TomaS Smid	Tom Okker (NED) / Balazs Tarózcy (HUN)	1:6, 3:6	Clay
	Indianapolis	Jan Kodes / TomaS Smid	John McEnroe (USA) / Gene Mayer (USA)	4:6, 6:7	Clay
1980	Madrid	Jan Kodes / Balazs Tarózcy (HUN)	Hans Gildemeister (CHI) / Andres Gomez (ECU)	6:3, 4:6, 8:10	Clay
	Cologne	Jan Kodes / TomaS Smid	Bernie Mitton (RSA) / Andrew Pattison (RSA)	4:6, 1:6	Indoor greenset
1983	Hilversum	Jan Kodes / TomaS Smid	Balazs Tarózcy (HUN) / Heinz Günthardt (SUI)	6:3, 2:6, 3:6	Clay

Jana Kodes – Five Set Matches Played

Total (79) Won (43) Lost (36) – Winning matches in bold letters

1964	**Vichy**	**Z-4**	**Alex Ivanov (URS)** 3h 30 min	**5:7, 4:6, 10:8, 8:6, 6:3**	**Clay**	**GP**
1965	Vichy	Z-2	Alex Ivanov (URS)	5:7, 6:3, 6:3, 2:6, 1:6	Clay	GP
	Paris (do 20 let)	**SF**	**Patrick Hombergen (BEL)**	**6:4, 8:6, 16:18, 3:6, 10:8**	**Indoor wood**	
1966	**Prague-Klamovka**	**F**	**Frantisek Pala**	**6:3, 6:4, 3:6, 3:6, 6:3**	**Indoor clay**	
	Monte Carlo (do 20 let)	**F**	**Giordano Maioli (ITA)**	**2:6, 5:7, 7:5, 6:3, 6:0**	**Clay**	
	Bratislava (Davis Cup)	**Z-1**	**Ernst Blanke (AUT)**	**4:6, 3:6, 6:4, 6:4, 6:2**	**Clay**	**DC**
	Prague - MM	**1/32**	**Jaroslav Vrba**	**6:2, 6:2, 3:6, 4:6, 6:3**	**Clay**	
	Paris (Roland Garros)	**1/128**	**Zeljko Franulovic (YUG)**	**1:6, 4:6, 6:3, 6:2, 6:1**	**Clay**	
	Paris (Roland Garros)	1/64	Ilie Nastase (ROM)	3:6, 7:5, 7:5, 4:6, 1:6	Clay	
	Paris (Davis Cup)	Z-4	François Jauffret (FRA)	6:3, 6:1, 3:6, 4:6, 4:6	Clay	DC
	Ostrava MR	**1/8**	**Jan Kukal**	**5:7, 6:2, 6:2, 7:9, 6:2**	**Clay**	
	Moscow	**1/8**	**Toomas Lejus (URS)**	**5:7, 3:6, 6:1, 6:4, 6:4**	**Clay**	
1967	Prague (Davis Cup)	Z-2	Pato Rodriguez (CHI)	6:3, 1:6, 3:6, 6:4, 0:6	Clay	DC
	Paris (Roland Garros)	1/16	Tony Roche (AUS)	4:6, 2:6, 10:8, 6:2, 4:6	Clay	

1968	Bangalore	1/8	**Premjit Lall (IND)**	**3:6, 6:1, 8:6, 2:6, 6:3**	**Clay**	
	Bangalore	SF	Ion Tiriac (ROM)	6:3, 4:6, 0:6, 6:4, 1:6	Clay	
	Roma	**1/32**	**Pato Rodriguez (CHI)**	**6:3, 4:6, 3:6, 7:5, 6:0**	**Clay**	
	Roma	1/16	Bob Hewitt (RSA)	6:3, 1:6, 6:8, 6:2, 2:6	Clay	
	Brussels (Davis Cup)	**Z-1**	**Eric Drossart (BEL)**	**4:6, 6:3, 4:6, 6:2, 6:1**	**Clay**	**DC**
	Brussels (Davis Cup)	Z-4	Patrick Hombergen (BEL)	6:3, 6:2, 3:6, 2:6, 4:6	Clay	DC
	Hilversum	SF	Robert Maud (RSA)	7:5, 6:8, 4:6, 6:2, 5:7	Clay	
	Hamburg	1/16	Harald Elschenbroich (GER)	4:6, 6:3, 3:6, 6:2, 4:6	Clay	
1969	Barranquilla	F	Ilie Nastase (ROM) 4 h 12 min	4:6, 4:6, 10:8, 6:2, 3:6	Clay	
	Roma	1/32	Nicola Pierangeli (ITA)	4:6, 4:6, 6:3, 7:5, 6:2	Clay	
	Roma	SF	John Newcombe (AUS) 3 h 30 min	3:6, 6:4, 1:6, 9:7, 3:6	Clay	
	Paris (Roland Garros)	1/16	John Newcombe (AUS) 4 h 15 min	1:6, 4:6, 6:0, 10:8, 9:11	Clay	
	Wimbledon	**1/128**	**Pato Cornejo (CHI)**	**6:3, 3:6, 5:7, 6:3, 6:1**	**Grass**	
	Wimbledon	1/64	Bob Lutz (USA)	6:2, 6:4, 1:6, 2:6, 5:7	Grass	
	Baastad	SF	Manolo Santana (ESP)	4:6, 6:1, 5:7, 6:4, 2:6	Clay	
	Hamburg	**1/64**	**Alex Kurutz (FRG)**	**7:5, 9:7, 6:8, 6:8, 6:1**	**Clay**	
	US Open (Forest Hills)	1/64	Butch Buchholz (USA)	2:6, 6:3, 3:6, 6:4, 2:6	Grass	
	Santiago	**F**	**Milan Holecek**	**4:6, 6:3, 1:6, 6:1, 6:2**	**Clay**	
	Sao Paolo	**F**	**Milan Holecek**	**4:6, 6:3, 1:6, 6:4, 6:3**	**Indoor clay**	
1970	Barranquilla	SF	Nikola Spear (YUG) 4 h 45 min	6:4, 8:10, 6:3, 3:6, 5:5 w.o.	Clay	
	Turin (Davis Cup)	**Z-1**	**Massimo di Domenico (ITA)**	**6:3, 1:6, 3:6, 6:4, 6:4**	**Clay**	**DC**
	Paris (Roland Garros)	**1/16**	**Ion Tiriac (ROM)**	**4:6, 7:5, 4:6, 6:2, 6:2**	**Clay**	
	Paris (Roland Garros)	**SF**	**Georges Goven (FRA)**	**2:6, 6:2, 5:7, 6:2, 6:3**	**Clay**	
	Wimbledon	1/128	Alex Metreveli (URS)	2:6, 5:7, 6:3, 6:2, 5:7	Grass	
	Hamburg	**1/16**	**Owen Davidson (AUS)**	**2:6, 6:4, 6:0, 2:6, 6:3**	**Clay**	
1971	**Hamburg**	**1/32**	**Hans Plötz (FRG)**	**5:7, 4:6, 6:4, 6:0, 6:0**	**Clay**	
	Paris (Roland Garros)	**1/16**	**François Jauffret (FRA)**	**4:6, 6:2, 5:7, 6:0, 6:4**	**Clay**	
	Prague (Davis Cup)	Z-2	Alex Metreveli (URS)	5:7, 6:3, 6:4, 5:7, 3:6	Clay	DC
	Bratislava MM	**F**	**Stabholcs Baranyi (HUN)**	**4:6, 6:3, 5:7, 6:4, 6:3**	**Clay**	
	US Open (Forest Hills)	**1/64**	**Pierre Barthés (FRA)**	**2:6, 5:7, 6:4, 6:4, 6:3**	**Grass**	
	US Open (Forest Hills)	**SF**	**Arthur Ashe (USA)**	**7:6, 3:6, 4:6, 6:3, 6:4**	**Grass**	
	Stockholm Open	F	Arthur Ashe (USA)	1:6, 6:3, 2:6, 6:1, 4:6	Indoor rubber	

1972	Madrid	SF	Ilie Nastase (ROM)	6:3, 7:6, 6:7, 6:7, 3:6 3. set led 5:2!–2 matchpoints	Clay	
	Paris (Roland Garros)	1/8	Patrick Proisy (FRA)	3:6, 8:6, 6:2, 2:6, 1:6	Clay	
	Düsseldorf (Davis Cup)	**Z-4**	**Harald Elschenbroich (GER)**	**6:4, 4:6, 6:2, 1:6, 8:6**	**Clay**	**DC**
	Barcelona (Davis Cup)	Z-1	Juan Gisbert (ESP) 3 h 45 min	8:6, 6:4, 5:7, 0:6, 4:6	Clay	DC
	US Open (Forest Hills)	1/64	Alex Mayer (USA)	7:6, 6:3, 6:7, 3:6, 1:6 in 3. set had 2 matchpoints	Grass	
	Split	**F**	**Nicky Kalogeropoulos (GRE)**	**8:6, 6:4, 6:8, 2:6, 9:7**	**Clay**	
1973	**Paris (Roland Garros)**	**1/16**	**Boro Jovanovic (YUG)**	**4:6, 6:3, 4:6, 6:0, 7:5**	**Clay**	
	Wimbledon	**1/8**	**Vijay Armitraj (IND) 2 h 45 min**	**6:4, 3:6, 4:6, 6:3, 7:5**	**Grass**	
	Wimbledon	**SF**	**Roger Taylor (GBR) 3 h 36 min**	**8:9, 9:7, 5:7, 6:4, 7:5**	**Grass**	
	Prague (Davis Cup)	Z-1	Corrado Barazzutti (ITA)	5:7, 6:3, 4:6, 6:2, 1:6	Clay	DC
	US Open (Forest Hills)	**1/8**	**Niki Pilic (YUG)**	**6:2, 4:6, 6:1, 3:6, 7:5**	**Grass**	
	US Open (Forest Hills)	**SF**	**Stan Smith (USA) 2 h 56 min**	**7:5, 6:7, 1:6, 6:1, 7:5**	**Grass**	
	US Open (Forest Hills)	F	John Newcombe (AUS) 2 h 50 min	4:6, 6:1, 6:4, 2:6, 3:6	Grass	
	Prague (Grand Prix)	F	Jiri Hrebec	6:4, 1:6, 6:3, 0:6, 5:7	Indoor mateflex	
1974	**Wimbledon**	**1/64**	**Leif Johansson (SWE)**	**3:6, 7:5, 6:3, 4:6, 6:4**	**Grass**	
	Wimbledon	**1/32**	**Dick Crealy (AUS)**	**4:6, 6:4, 6:3, 2:6, 7:5**	**Grass**	
	Wimbledon	**1/16**	**Tom Gorman (USA)**	**6:8, 2:6, 6:3, 9:7, 6:4**	**Grass**	
	Wimbledon	1/8	Jimmy Connors (USA)	6:3, 3:6, 3:6, 8:6, 3:6	Grass	
	Doneck (Davis Cup)	Z-4	Alex Metreveli (URS)	6:4, 3:6, 6:4, 3:6, 5:7	Clay	DC
	US PRO Boston	SF	Björn Borg (SWE)	6:7, 0:6, 6:1, 6:2, 6:7 in 5. set led 5:1!!	Clay	
	US Open (Forest Hills)	**1/32**	**Balazs Taróczy (HUN)**	**5:7, 4:6, 7:6, 7:6, 6:3**	**Grass**	
1975	**Hamburg**	**SF**	**Paolo Bertolucci (ITA)**	**4:6, 6:3, 2:6, 7:5, 6:3**	**Clay**	
	Hamburg	F	Manolo Orantes (ESP)	6:3, 2:6, 2:6, 6:3, 1:6	Clay	
	Wimbledon	1/64	Geoff Masters (AUS)	6:2, 6:2, 4:6, 6:8, 4:6	Grass	
	Prague (Davis Cup)	**Z-1**	**Balazs Taróczy (HUN)**	**6:3, 4:6, 6:8, 7:5, 8:6**	**Clay**	**DC**
	Prague (Davis Cup)	**Z-5**	**Stabholcs Baranyi (HUN)**	**8:6, 4:6, 3:6, 7:5, 6:4**	**Clay**	**DC**
	Madrid	**SF**	**Jaime Fillol (CHI)**	**5:7, 2:6, 7:6, 6:2, 6:3**	**Clay**	
1976	Nice Open	F	Corrado Barazzutti (ITA)	2:6, 6:2, 7:5, 6:7, 6:8	Clay	
	Paris (Roland Garros)	**1/128**	**Patrice Dominguez (FRA)**	**4:6, 7:6, 6:7, 6:0, 6:0**	**Clay**	
	Kitzbuhel	F	Guillermo Vilas (ARG)	7:5, 2:6, 6:4, 3:6, 2:6	Clay	
1979	**Paris (Roland Garros)**	**1/128**	**Dick Crealy (AUS)**	**7:6, 6:7, 3:6, 6:4, 8:6**	**Clay**	
	Hilversum	SF	Balazs Taróczy (HUN)	6:4, 3:6, 5:7, 7:6, 3:6	Clay	
	US Open (Flushing)	**1/128**	**David Schneider (RSA)**	**4:6, 5:7, 6:4, 6:3, 6:1**	**Hard**	

Davis Cup Best Singles Matches

1966	Bratislava, CZE-AUT	5:0	(1st match)	E. Blanke	4:6, 3:6, 6:4, 6:4, 6:2
1968	Prague, CZE-BRA	3:2	(1st match)	T. Koch	6:2, 6:3, 3:6, 7:5
1968	Prague, CZE-BRA	3:2	(at-2:2)	E. Mandarino	8:6, 6:4, 8:6
1969	Copenhagen, DEN-CZE	2:3	(1st match)	J. Leschly	6:2, 6:2, 6:3
1969	Copenhagen, DEN-CZE	2:3	(at-2:2)	J. Ulrich	6:2, 6:2, 6:4
1970	Turin, ITA-CZE	2:3	(at-2:2)	A. Panatta	6:3, 6:2, 6:2
1971	Prague, CZE-ESP	3:2	(at-2:2)	M.Orantes	7:5, 4:6, 7:5, 6:4
1971	Prague, CZE-ESP	3:2	(at-0:1)	J. Gisbert	6:3, 4:6, 9:7, 7:5
1972	Dusseldorf, GER-CZE	2:3	(at-2:2)	H.Elschenbroich	6:4, 4:6, 6:2, 1:6, 8:6
1974	Munich, GER-CZE	2:3	(3rd-point)	K.Meiler	6:1, 7:5, 6:0
1975	Prague, CZE-HUN	4:1	(2nd-match)	B. Taroczy	6:3, 4:6, 6:8, 7:5, 8:6
1975	Prague, CZE-FRA	3:2	(at-2:2)	F. Jauffret	6:1, 7:5, 6:1
1975	Prague, CZE-AUS	3:1	(1st match)	J. Alexander	6:4, 2:6,7:5, 6:4
1975	Prague, CZE-AUS	3:1	(3rd-point)	T. Roche	6:3, 6:1, 6:4
1975	Stockholm, SWE-CZE	3:2	(1st match)	O. Bengtson	4:6, 6:2, 7:5, 6:4

Davis Cup Best Doubles Matches

1966	Paris, FRA-CZE	4:1	(at0:2)	w. Javorsky-Contet-Beust	8:10, 5:7, 6:3, 6:4, 6:2
1968	Prague, CZE-BRA	3:2	(1:1)	w. Holecek-Koch-Mandarino	6:4, 6:4, 4:6, 7:5
1969	Copenhagen, DEN-CZE	2:3	(1:1)	w. Kukal-Leschly-Ulrich	8:6, 9:11, 6:2, 6:4
1971	Prague, CZE-URS	3:2	(1:1)	w. Kukal-Metreveli-Lichacev	3:6, 6:4, 2:6, 7:5, 6:3
1972	Dussel., GER-CZE	2:3	(1:1)	w. Kukal-Fasbender-Pohmann	4:6, 6:3, 3:6, 6:2,19:17
1974	Doneck, URS-CZE	3:2	(1:1)	w. Zednik-Metreveli-Korotkov	6:4, 6:1, 6:3
1978	Prague, CZE-NED	3:1	(1:1)	w. Smid-Okker-Sanders	9:7, 6:2, 6:2
1979	Paris, FRA-CZE	1:4	(1:1)	w. Smid-Noah-Moretton	7:5, 6:4, 5:7, 6:2
1979	Prague, CZE-SWE	3:2	(1:1)	w. Smid-Borg-Bengtson	2:6, 6:3, 6:4, 6:0
1980	Bucharest, ROM-CZE	1:4	(2:0)	w. Lendl-Haradau-Segarceanu	6:3, 6:2, 6:4

Jan Kodes – Czechoslovak Nationals (12)

Finals Results

SINGLES (4)			
1966	Ostrava	Jan Kodes – Milan Necas	0:6, 6:3, 6:3, 6:2
1967	Pilsen	Jan Kodes – Milan Holecek	9:7, 6:2, 6:3
1969	Ostrava	Jan Kodes – Jan Kukal	6:2, 6:3, 6:3
1972	Ostrava	Jan Kodes – Frantisek Pala	6:4, 6:0, 6:1
DOUBLES (5)			
1966	Ostrava	Jan Kodes, Frantisek Pala – Milan Necas, Jan Kukal	6:8, 6:2, 7:5, 4:6, 6:2
1969	Ostrava	Jan Kodes, Jan Kukal – Milan Holecek, Vladimir Zednik	2:6, 6:1, 8:6, 8:10, 8:6
1970	Ostrava	Jan Kodes, Frantisek Pala – Milan Holecek, Vladimir Zednik	6:3, 6:0, 6:1
1972	Ostrava	Jan Kodes, Frantisek Pala – Jan Pisecky, Vladimir Zednik	6:3, 6:1
1979	Bratislava	Jan Kodes, Tomas Smid – Jiri Hrebec, Pavel Slozil	6:0, 6:0, 6:4
MIXED DOUBLES (3)			
1967	Pilsen	Jan Kodes, Vlasta Vopickova – Milan Necas, Olga Lendlova	4:6, 8:6, 6:3
1969	Ostrava	Jan and Lenka Kodes – Frantisek Pala, Vlasta Vopickova	6:2, 7:5
1972	Ostrava	Jan and Lenka Kodes – Petr Hutka, Alena Lerchova-Pavliskova	6:3, 6:1
CLUB LEAGUE (10)			
1963, 1964, 1965 – Spartak Prague Motorlet			
1966 – Motorlet Prague			
1970, 1971, 1972, 1973, 1974 a 1976 – Sparta CKD Prague			

1969 a 1972 won all 3 titles (S–D–M) 1971, 1973, 1982, 1983 – not played; 1974, 1976, 1977, 1978 – played in singles only; 1979 – played in doubles only

Davis Cup – Czechoslovak/Czech All-Time Records

Most Total Wins (total matches won and lost)	Jan Kodes (60–34) singles (39–19) doubles (21–15)
Most Singles Wins (matches won and lost)	Roderich Menzel (40–12)
Most Doubles Wins (matches won and lost)	Jan Kodes (21–15)
Best Doubles Team (matches won)	Jaroslav Drobny – Vladimir Cernik (11)
Most ties played (number of ties)	Jan Kodes (39)
Most matches played (singles and doubles)	Jan Kodes (96)* singles (58) doubles (36)
Most years played (number of years)	Jan Kodes (15)

* two unfinished singles matches - 1972 (SWE) a 1976 (HUN) included

The results from all Jan Kodes Davis Cup ties - matches with more informations about Czechoslovak and Czech players available on official ITF website:

www.daviscup.com/teams/playerwinloss. asp

Wimbledon – Czechoslovak/Czech Players Best Results

1926	Q	Jan Kozeluh	Jean Borotra (FRA)	4:6, 6:4, 7:9, 1:6
1927	Q	Jan Kozeluh	Rene Lacoste (FRA)	4:6, 3:6, 4:6
1933	Q	Roderich Menzel	Ellsworth Vines (USA)	2:6, 4:6, 6:3, 3:6
1935	Q	Roderich Menzel	Fred Perry (GBR)	7:9, 1:6, 1:6
1938	Q	Frantisek Cejnar	Don Budge (USA)	3:6, 0:6, 5:7
1938	Q	Ladislav Hecht	Henner Henkel (GER)	5:7, 1:6, 2:6
1946	SF	Jaroslav Drobny	Geoff Brown (USA)	4:6, 5:7, 2:6
1947	Q	Jaroslav Drobny	Budge Patty (USA)	6:3, 4:6, 9:7, 2:6, 3:6
1949	F	Jaroslav Drobny	Ted Schroeder (USA)	6:3, 0:6, 3:6, 6:4, 4:6
1950	SF	Jaroslav Drobny (EGY)	Frank Sedgman (AUS)	6:3, 6:3, 3:6, 5:7, 2:6
1952	F	Jaroslav Drobny (EGY)	Frank Sedgman (AUS)	6:4, 2:6, 3:6, 2:6
1953	SF	Jaroslav Drobny (EGY)	Kurt Nielsen (DEN)	4:6, 3:6, 2:6
1954	W	Jaroslav Drobny (EGY)	Ken Rosewall (AUS)	13:11, 4:6, 6:2, 9:7
1955	Q	Jaroslav Drobny (EGY)	Tony Trabert (USA)	6:8, 1:6, 4:6
1972	SF	Jan Kodes	Stan Smith (USA)	6:3, 4:6, 1:6, 5:7
1973	**W**	**Jan Kodes**	**Alex Metreveli (URS)**	**6:1, 9:8*, 6:3**
1974	Q	Jan Kodes	Jimmy Connors (USA)	6:3, 3:6, 3:6, 8:6, 3:6
1983	SF	Ivan Lendl	John McEnroe (USA)	6:7, 4:6, 4:6
1984	SF	Ivan Lendl	Jimmy Connors (USA)	7:6, 3:6, 5:7, 1:6
1984	Q	TomaS Smid	Ivan Lendl	1:6, 6:7, 3:6
1986	F	Ivan Lendl	Boris Becker (GER)	4:6, 3:6, 5:7
1987	F	Ivan Lendl	Pat Cash (AUS)	6:7, 2:6, 5:7
1988	SF	Ivan Lendl	Boris Becker (GER)	4:6, 3:6, 7:6, 4:6
1988	SF	Miloslav Mecir	Stefan Edberg (SWE)	6:4, 6:2, 4:6, 3:6, 4:6
1989	SF	Ivan Lendl	Boris Becker (GER)	5:7, 7:6, 6:2, 4:6, 3:6
1990	SF	Ivan Lendl	Stefan Edberg (SWE)	1:6, 6:7, 3:6
1998	Q	Petr Korda	Tim Henman (GBR)	3:6, 4:6, 2:6
2006	Q	Radek Stepanek	Jonas Björkman (SWE)	6:7, 6:4, 7:6, 6:7, 4:6
2007	Q	Tomas Berdych	Rafael Nadal (ESP)	6:7, 4:6, 2:6

Q – quarter-finals SF – semifinals F – finals W – winner

* tie-breaker at 8:8